GOVERNING TEXAS

FOURTH EDITION

CHAMPAGNE · HARPHAM · CASELLAS

BLINN COLLEGE

**NORTON
CUSTOM**

W. W. NORTON & COMPANY, INC.

NEW YORK · LONDON

W. W. Norton & Company has been independent since its founding in 1923, when William Warder Norton and Mary D. Herter Norton first published lectures delivered at the People's Institute, the adult education division of New York City's Cooper Union. The Nortons soon expanded their program beyond the Institute, publishing books by celebrated academics from America and abroad. By mid-century, the two major pillars of Norton's publishing program—trade books and college texts—were firmly established. In the 1950s, the Norton family transferred control of the company to its employees, and today—with a staff of four hundred and a comparable number of trade, college, and professional titles published each year—W. W. Norton & Company stands as the largest and oldest publishing house owned wholly by its employees.

Editor: Katie Hannah
Director of custom strategy: Susan Brennan
Managing editor, College: Marian Johnson
Project editor: Hannah Bachman
Assistant editor: Alexandra Gakos
Editorial assistant: Kaushika Suresh
Associate production manager: Jeremy Burton
Production associate: Lindsay Fischer
Design director: Rubina Yeh
Custom cover designer: Michael Wood
Text permissions manager: Megan Schindel
Photo permissions manager: Aga Millhouse

ISBN: 978-0-393-43130-8

W. W. Norton & Company, Inc., 500 Fifth Avenue, New York, NY 10110
www.wwnorton.com
W. W. Norton & Company, Ltd., 15 Carlisle St., London W1D 3BS

1 2 3 4 5 6 7 8 9 0

Government at Blinn College

Texas Education Code, Subchapter F, Section 51.301 requires students graduating with a baccalaureate or lesser degree from a public institution in Texas to have credit for six semester credit hours (SCH) in government or political science, including the Constitution of the United States and the constitutions of the states, with special emphasis on Texas. At Blinn College, the instructional pattern represented by the TCCN course sequence GOVT 2305 and 2306 satisfies this requirement.

GOVT 2306 TEXAS GOVERNMENT (TEXAS CONSTITUTION AND TOPICS)

Origin and development of the Texas constitution, structure and powers of state and local government, federalism and inter-governmental relations, political participation, the election process, public policy, and the political culture of Texas.

Three credit hours

LEARNING OUTCOMES

Upon successful completion of this course, students will:

1. Explain the origin and development of the Texas constitution.
2. Describe state and local political systems and their relationship with the federal government.
3. Describe separation of powers and checks and balances in both theory and practice in Texas.
4. Demonstrate knowledge of the legislative, executive, and judicial branches of Texas government.
5. Evaluate the role of public opinion, interest groups, and political parties in Texas.
6. Analyze the state and local election process.
7. Identify the rights and responsibilities of citizens.
8. Analyze issues, policies, and political culture of Texas.

Student learning outcomes from Lower-Division Academic Course Guide Manual, Spring 2019, Texas Higher Education Coordinating Board.

Tools for Success in Government 2306

Your textbook comes with a wealth of study tools to help you prepare for tests and assignments and meet the Texas Learning Outcomes for this course.

EBOOK

Your Norton Ebook version of *Governing Texas*, Fourth Edition, is the same as the paper book. Page for page, you'll have everything you have in your print book, plus

- **Pop-up Key Term Definitions** give you useful context for new terms as you read.
- **Sticky Notes** Sticky Notes help you remember important course information. Your notes are saved in the Norton ebook and can be accessed from any Internet-connected computer.
- **Highlighting** Highlight your ebook just as you would a paper book. Your highlights are saved in the Norton ebook and can be accessed from any Internet-connected computer.
- **Accessibility** Read your book anywhere there's an Internet connection. You can also download sections of the book for offline reading.

INQUIZITIVE

Norton's adaptive learning tool—compatible with any mobile device—preserves valuable lecture and lab time by personalizing quiz questions for each student and building knowledge outside of class. A variety of question types—that include images, maps, primary sources, and more—test your knowledge with engaging, game-like elements. You set your confidence level on each question to reflect your knowledge, track your own progress easily, earn point bonuses for high performance, and review learning objectives you might not have mastered. Quizzes are structured in sections that build knowledge through levels of Bloom's Taxonomy and across all learning objectives of each chapter, while links to our ebook make it easy for you to reference your textbook as you work.

Governing Texas

4TH EDITION

TH EDITION

Governing Texas

★★★★★★★★★★★★★★★★★★★★★★★★★★★★★★★★★★★★★★★

Anthony Champagne
UNIVERSITY OF TEXAS AT DALLAS

Edward J. Harpham
UNIVERSITY OF TEXAS AT DALLAS

Jason P. Casellas
UNIVERSITY OF HOUSTON

W. W. NORTON & COMPANY
NEW YORK · LONDON

W. W. NORTON & COMPANY has been independent since its founding in 1923, when William Warder Norton and Mary D. Herter Norton first published lectures delivered at the People's Institute, the adult education division of New York City's Cooper Union. The firm soon expanded its program beyond the Institute, publishing books by celebrated academics from America and abroad. By mid-century, the two major pillars of Norton's publishing program—trade books and college texts—were firmly established. In the 1950s, the Norton family transferred control of the company to its employees, and today—with a staff of four hundred and a comparable number of trade, college, and professional titles published each year—W. W. Norton & Company stands as the largest and oldest publishing house owned wholly by its employees.

Editor: Peter Lesser

Assistant Editor: Anna Olcott

Project Editors: Christine D'Antonio and Laura Dragonette

Manuscript Editor: Roger Mensink

Managing Editor, College: Marian Johnson

Managing Editor, College Digital Media: Kim Yi

Production Managers: Ashley Horna and Stephen Sajdak

Media Editor: Spencer Richardson-Jones

Associate Media Editor: Michael Jaoui

Media Editorial Assistant: Tricia Vuong

Media Project Editor: Marcus Van Harpen

Marketing Manager, Political Science: Erin Brown

Art Director: Rubina Yeh

Director of College Permissions: Megan Schindel

Permissions Assistant: Patricia Wong

Text Design: Tamaye Perry

Photo Editor: Travis Carr

Information Graphics: Kiss Me I'm Polish LLC, New York

Composition: Achorn International, Inc.

Manufacturing: LSC Kendallville

Permission to use copyrighted material is included in the credits section of this book, which begins on page A49.

Library of Congress Cataloging-in-Publication Data

Names: Champagne, Anthony, author. | Harpham, Edward J., author. |
    Casellas, Jason Paul, 1977- author.
Title: Governing Texas / Anthony Champagne, Edward J. Harpham, Jason P. Casellas.
Description: 4th edition. | New York : W.W. Norton & Company, 2019. |
    Includes bibliographical references and index.
Identifiers: LCCN 2018046031 | **ISBN 9780393644302** (pbk.)
Subjects: LCSH: Texas—Politics and government.
Classification: LCC JK4816 .C48 2019 | DDC 320.4764—dc23 LC record available at
https://lccn.loc.gov/2018046031

W. W. Norton & Company, Inc., 500 Fifth Avenue, New York, NY 10110
wwnorton.com

W. W. Norton & Company Ltd., 15 Carlisle Street, London W1D 3BS

1 2 3 4 5 6 7 8 9 0

Contents in Brief

Contents

2 • The Texas Constitution   45

5 • Campaigns and Elections   149

6 • Interest Groups and Lobbying   183

7 • The Legislature 213

8 • The Executive Branch   251

9 • The Judiciary 293

10 • Local Government 327

13 • Crime, Corrections, and Public Safety   441

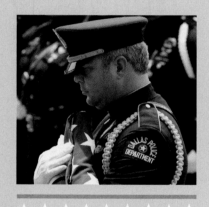

14 • Building the Future: Public Policies for a Changing Texas   479

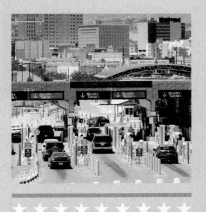

O UR GOAL in this text is to offer readers a broad understanding of the factors that are reshaping political processes and institutions in the Lone Star State in the first two decades of the twenty-first century. We are particularly concerned with explaining how the principles underlying constitutional government in Texas are being reworked in the face of new political, economic, and demographic changes. By supplementing our institutional analysis with concrete examples from everyday political life in Texas, we hope to show the reader that politics and government in Texas are not only important to their lives but endlessly fascinating as well.

Features of the Fourth Edition

Another, related goal of the book is to provide students with extensive pedagogical support throughout each chapter. In every chapter, several features engage students' interest and help them master the learning objectives for the topic.

- **NEW Chapter 14: Building the Future: Public Policies for a Changing Texas** presents more coverage of critical policies: immigration, transportation, higher education, and water supply. As Texas continues to grow, these issues will no doubt take center stage. The authors unpack the controversies around these policies and ask students to think critically about what Texas will look like in the future.
- **NEW "What Do Texans Think?" features in every chapter** highlight fascinating public opinion data in Texas. The features allow students to compare their opinions on major issues to people across the state and the nation. Accompanying PowerPoint slides make it easy for instructors to poll their own classrooms on hot button topics in Texas government and politics.
- **Updated "What Government Does and Why It Matters" chapter introductions** draw students into the chapter by showing them why they should care about the chapter's topic.
- **Chapter Goals** appear at the start of the chapter and then recur at the start of the relevant sections throughout the chapter to create a more focused, active reading experience.
- **Core Objectives are woven into every chapter**, helping students gain proficiency with critical thinking, effective communication, personal and social responsibility, and quantitative reasoning.
- **Updated "Who Are Texans?" infographics** engage visually oriented students with a "statistical snapshot" of the state related to each chapter's topic. Through accompanying quantitative reasoning questions, these features help students grasp the political implications of demographic, political, economic, and regional diversity in Texas. Related exercises in the online coursepacks and slides in the instructor PowerPoints make it easy for instructors to bring these graphics into their online or face-to-face classrooms.

- **Updated "Texas and the Nation" infographics** enable students to compare Texas's government and politics to other states'. Critical thinking questions accompany each "Texas and the Nation" graphic and encourage students to engage deeply with the graphics and draw their own conclusions. Related exercises in the online coursepacks and slides in the PowerPoints make it easy for instructors to bring these graphics into their online or face-to-face classrooms.
- **Revised "You Decide: Voices of Texas" boxes in every chapter** address controversial issues in Texas politics that students care about. These boxes encourage students to think beyond their knee-jerk reactions, consider all sides of the debate, and think about communicating their own effective arguments.
- **"Future of Texas" sections at the end of every chapter** examine how Texas government and politics are likely to change in light of Texas's shifting demographics and economy.
- **Extensive end-of-chapter review sections organized around Chapter Goals** include section outlines, practice quiz questions, and key terms. Students have everything they need to master the material in each section of the chapter.

Revisions to the Fourth Edition

In the fourth edition of *Governing Texas,* we have tried to provide students with the most up-to-date account of Texas government and politics. Every chapter was scrutinized with help from dozens of outside reviewers, and we have tried to provide the most current examples and data throughout the text. Highlights of the new edition include:

- Chapter 1 (The Political Culture, People, and Economy of Texas) has been fully updated with the most recent available economic and demographic data. Material has also been added to help students understand the complexity of political culture in Texas and the impact of changing demographics in the state.
- Chapter 2 (The Texas Constitution) has been updated and refined to include more material on the Texas Founding and the transformation of the Texas Constitution.
- Chapter 3 (Texas in the Federal System) has been rewritten to discuss how federalism in Texas has evolved over time, including recent decisions in the Texas legislature.
- Chapter 4 (Political Parties) has been updated throughout with particular attention to the influence of the Tea Party in state Republican Party politics. The chapter also highlights the role of the Latino community in changing Texas and Democratic Party competition.
- Chapter 5 (Campaigns and Elections) includes a new opener highlighting the gubernatorial and senatorial races in 2018, emphasizing why students should care about what happens in elections. This chapter also includes a revamped and updated section on recent changes to electoral practices, including redistricting, voter ID litigation, and straight-ticket voting.
- Chapter 6 (Interest Groups and Lobbying) includes many updated examples and stories to highlight the changing role of interest groups in state politics, and devotes considerable attention to recent attempts at ethics reform.

- Chapter 7 (The Legislature) begins with a new opener highlighting the escalating tension among legislators during the recent session of the Texas legislature. It includes updated data to reflect the changed composition of the legislature and Joe Straus's speakership.
- Chapter 8 (The Executive Branch) has been significantly rewritten to take into account all the officials in the Executive Branch and recent executive actions during the 2017 legislative session. Comparisons are also made between the actions of current officials and those of previous ones—for example, between Governor Perry and Governor Abbott.
- Chapter 9 (The Judiciary) has been updated throughout, with new content added regarding judicial ethics and misconduct. It also discusses specialty courts, county courts, and how straight-ticket voting affects judicial elections.
- Chapter 10 (Local Government) has been significantly updated to account for changes in local governments and local officials. A new discussion of home-rule cities and preemption is now included.
- Chapter 11 (Public Finance) has been fully updated with the data made available to political leaders for the 2017 legislative session. An enhanced discussion of the challenges of both budgetary surpluses and deficits is also included.
- Chapter 12 (Public Policy) has been fully updated. New discussions of the problems facing policy makers in education and health care have been added focusing on the importance of recent court decisions. Explicit linkages have also been made between theories of the policy-making process and the substantive policy areas. A new graphic has been added investigating de facto segregation at the local level in the state.
- Chapter 13 (Crime, Corrections, and Public Safety) has been extensively revised to include more on policing in Texas—including controversies around alleged racial profiling and police brutality—and open carry laws. The chapter opens with the story of the tragic Dallas police shooting.
- NEW Chapter 14 (Building the Future: Public Policies for a Changing Texas) includes new content on policy areas like transportation, higher education, immigration, and water resources in Texas.

We believe that these changes will assist professors in teaching students the nuts and bolts of Texas government and politics, as well as the broad themes and issues that will shape the Lone Star State in the coming decades.

A Cohesive, Flexible Set of Teaching and Learning Resources

Norton's study tools, featuring InQuizitive, help students understand the reading, master key concepts from each chapter, and apply what they've learned. This ensures they arrive better prepared for lecture. Assessing students on the Texas Student Learning Objectives (SLOs) is easy with the Texas SLO test bank, InQuizitive (with questions tagged to SLOs), and variety of activities built specifically to complement the book. And creating dynamic classroom and online presentations is easy with the variety of instructor resources written by instructors who teach this course.

- InQuizitive is Norton's award-winning, easy-to-use adaptive learning tool that personalizes the learning experience for students and helps them master—and retain—key learning objectives. It helps students think critically about recent political events and controversies.

- InQuizitive is proven to increase students' scores on exams. Norton recently conducted a within-subjects efficacy study (designed by Dustin Tingley, *Harvard University)* of InQuizitive for American government, and among the students who did not earn a perfect score on the pre-test, we saw an average InQuizitive Effect of +17 points on the post-test.
- InQuizitive personalizes student learning paths based on their success in answering questions linked to learning objectives.
- Answer-specific feedback and the opportunity for students to keep working until they reach their desired mastery level makes InQuizitive a fun, efficient, low-stakes learning environment.
- Each question in InQuizitive is tied to one of the Texas SLOs, and instructors can run a report that measures class performance on the SLOs.
- The InQuizitive course for *Governing Texas*, Fourth Edition, expands upon the Third Edition's by offering more questions that focus on the following:
  - Concepts and term comprehension
  - Concept application
  - Critical thinking (linked to text features)
- The convenience of Learning Management System (LMS) integration saves you time by allowing InQuizitive scores to report right to your LMS gradebook. (LMS integration with InQuizitive is provided by a Norton specialist for qualified adoptions.)

- After students complete a chapter's **InQuizitive** assignment (Cory Colby, *Lone Star College*), instructors can further assess and enhance their learning by assigning fully editable, **book-specific activities right from their LMS**. Each activity is aligned with at least one Texas SLO and Core Objective. A chart of these alignments is provided for instructors. Activities include:
  - NEW simulations, with related assessments, explore the perspectives of political actors and participants in Texas politics.
  - Animated "Who Are Texans?" and "Texas and the Nation" infographics—with related assessments—examine Texas demographics and how Texas politics compare with the politics of other states.
  - NEW "What Do Texans Think?" features allow students to answer polling questions via Learning Management System survey tools.
  - News video exercises and quizzes provide current, real-world examples of concepts and issues in Texas politics.

- The **test bank** (Rachel Bzostek, *University of Texas, Tyler*), available within a Learning Management System in addition to traditional formats, is sorted by Texas SLOs and Bloom's taxonomy. It was thoroughly revised for the Fourth Edition and includes more conceptual questions.

- To round out students' experience in lecture, Norton provides high-quality teaching resources for instructors. A new **Interactive Instructor's Guide** (Emily Erdmann, *Blinn College*) offers a wealth of teaching materials, including discussion questions, suggested multimedia lecture launchers, and tips for teaching with InQuizitive or other student assessment tools. **Lecture PowerPoints** ease lecture prep by providing all of the photos, graphs, tables, and infographics from the text, as well as new "What Do Texans Think?" clicker questions.

About the Authors

Over the past 25 years, we have worked together on a number of books that have studied various aspects of government and political life in Texas. We come to the study of Texas politics and government from very different backgrounds.

Anthony Champagne was born in Louisiana as the French surname suggests. His mother's family, however, were pioneer farmers and ranchers in Hopkins County, Texas. It was growing up with Louisiana and Texas connections that gave him a life-long interest in politics. When he moved to the University of Texas at Dallas in 1979, he immediately visited the Sam Rayburn Library in Bonham. Sam Rayburn was one of the Texas's most influential political figures. He was elected to the U.S. House of Representatives in 1912 and served until his death in 1961. During that time, he was chairman of one of the most influential committees of the House, was Majority Leader, Speaker, and Minority Leader of the House. He is responsible for much of the major legislation in the New Deal and for his key role in the politics of the Truman, Eisenhower, and early Kennedy Administrations. A chance meeting at the Sam Rayburn Library with H. G. Dulaney, Sam Rayburn's secretary for 10 years, led to the opportunity to do over 130 oral histories with persons associated with Sam Rayburn. As a result, Champagne was completely hooked on studying Texas politics. He was particularly interested in the transformation of the state from an overwhelmingly Democratic state to a Republican bulwark. And, he was interested in how Texas changed from being a key partner with the national government in the cooperative federalism of the New Deal period to a state whose leaders are frequent critics of national power today. Political change in the state from the Sam Rayburn era to today is a key research focus of his.

Edward Harpham, in contrast, was born in Montreal to second generation Canadian parents who immigrated to the United States soon after his birth. His family's migration over the last 100 years from Sheffield to Toronto (1919) to Delaware (1952) to Texas (1978) and the industries that employed the family (auto service industry, chemical industry, and academia) mirror the demographic changes that have reshaped much of the population movement in the United States and Texas throughout the twentieth century. Trained as a political theorist with a deep interest in political economy, Harpham's move to Texas sparked an interest in how economic changes in the late twentieth century were changing the contours of the state's traditional political life in new and unexpected ways. At the heart of his work lies an abiding interest on the role that ideas play in shaping the growth and development of political institutions and public policies in the modern information age.

Jason Casellas was born in New Orleans and has always had an interest in state and local politics. His grandfather was a professor of Spanish literature at Our Lady of the Lake University in San Antonio. He inspired him to pursue a career as a professor. After graduating from Loyola University in New Orleans, he attended graduate school at Princeton University where he earned a Ph.D. in Politics. His dissertation and book examined Latino representation in state legislatures and Congress, with Texas as one of the key states in his study. Even though he was not born in Texas, he got there as fast as he could. He moved to Texas in 2005 to take an assistant professorship at the University of Texas at Austin, where he continued his immersion in all things Texas. In 2013, he moved not very far to the University of Houston, where he is now an associate professor. Most of his extended family fortuitously reside in all parts of the Houston area. He has continued to teach, research, and comment on Texas politics with a specific expertise in the growing Latino population, and how it might transform the state in the future.

Acknowledgments

WE ARE GRATEFUL for the suggestions that we have received from many thoughtful and experienced government instructors across the state. For their input on the plan and execution of this book, we thank:

Jason Abbott, *Hill College*

Lee Almaguer, *Midland College*

Natasha Altema McNeely, *University of Texas–Rio Grande*

Marcos Arandia, *North Lake College*

Ellen Baik, *University of Texas–Pan American*

Robert Ballinger, *South Texas College*

Annie Johnson Benifield, *Lone Star College–Tomball*

David E. Birch, *Lone Star College–Tomball*

Robin Marshall Bittick, *Sam Houston State University*

Walt Borges, *University of North Texas at Dallas*

Patrick Brandt, *University of Texas at Dallas*

Gary Brown, *Lone Star College–Montgomery*

Lee Brown, *Blinn College*

Jonathan Buckstead, *Austin Community College*

Daniel Bunye, *South Plains College*

James V. Calvi, *West Texas A&M University*

Michael Campenni, *Austin Community College*

Larry Carter, *University of Texas at Arlington*

Dina Castillo, *San Jacinto College*

Max Choudary, *Northeast Lakeview College*

Mark Cichock, *University of Texas at Arlington*

Adrian Clark, *Del Mar College*

Andrew Clayton, *McLennan Community College*

Cory Colby, *Lone Star College*

Tracy Cook, *Central Texas College*

Cassandra Cookson, *Lee College*

Leland M. Coxe, *University of Texas at Brownsville*

Rosalyn Crain, *Houston Community College–Northwest*

Sandra K. Creech, *Temple College*

Philip Crosby, *Central Texas College*

Kevin Davis, *North Central Texas College*

Steve Davis, *Lone Star College–Kingwood*

Henry Dietz, *University of Texas at Austin*

Brian K. Dille, *Odessa College*

Douglas Dow, *University of Texas at Dallas*

Jeremy Duff, *Midwestern State University*

David Edwards, *University of Texas at Austin*

Matthew Eshbaugh-Soha, *University of North Texas*

Lou Ann Everett, *Trinity Valley Community College*

Victoria Farrar-Myers, *University of Texas at Arlington*

John P. Flanagan, *Weatherford College*

Ben Fraser, *San Jacinto College*

Joey Fults, *Kilgore College*

Frank J. Garrahan, *Austin Community College*

Will Geisler, *Collin College*

David Garrison, *Collin College*

Patrick Gilbert, *Lone Star College—Tomball*

Mandi Gilligan, *El Centro College*

Shaun M. Gilligan, *Cedar Valley College*

Terry Gilmour, *Midland College*

Randy Givens, *Blinn College*

Donna Godwin, *Trinity Valley Community College*

Elsa Gonzalez, *Texas State Technical College–Harlingen*

Larry Gonzalez, *Houston Community College–Southwest*

Christine Gottemoller, *Del Mar College*

Paul Gottemoller, *Del Mar College*

Kenneth L. Grasso, *Texas State University*

Heidi Jo Green, *Lone Star College–CyFair*

Sara Gubala, *Lamar University*

Yolanda Hake, *South Texas College*

Sabrina Hammel, *Northeast Lakeview College*

Jeff Harmon, *University of Texas at San Antonio*

Tiffany Harper, *Collin College*

Billy Hathorn, *Laredo Community College*

Ahad Hayaud-Din, *Brookhaven College*

Virginia Haysley, *Lone Star College–Tomball*

Tom Heiting, *Odessa College*

John Hitt, *North Lake College*

Kevin Holton, *South Texas College*

Nathan Hosey, *Mountain View College*

Taofang Huang, *University of Texas at Austin*

Casey Hubble, *McLennan Community College*

Gregory Hudspeth, *St. Philip's College*

Glen Hunt, *Austin Community College*

Tammy Johannessen, *Austin Community College*

Catherine Johnson, *Weatherford College*

Doris J. Jones, *Tarrant County College*

Joseph Jozwiak, *Texas A&M Corpus Christi*

Christy Woodward Kaupert, *San Antonio College*

Michael Kelley, *Central Texas College*

David Kennedy, *Lone Star College–Montgomery*

Edward Korzetz, *Lee College*

Melinda Kovacs, *Sam Houston State University*

Heidi Lange, *Houston Community College–Southwest*

Boyd Lanier, *Lamar University*

James Lantrip, *South Texas College*

Kalan Laws, *Texas Southern University*

David Lektzian, *Texas Tech University*

Raymond Lew, *Houston Community College–Central*
Frank Lewis, *Texas State Technical College–Harlingen*
Bob Little, *Brookhaven College*
Robert Locander, *Lone Star College–North Harris*
Nicholas Long, *St. Edward's University*
George Lyon, *El Paso Community College*
Mitzi Mahoney, *Sam Houston State University*
Lynne Manganaro, *Texas A&M International University*
Sharon Manna, *North Lake College*
Bobby J. Martinez, *Northwest Vista College*
David McClendon, *Tyler Junior College*
Mike McConachie, *Collin College*
Elizabeth McLane, *Alvin College*
Lindsey McLennan, *Kilgore College*
Phil McMahan, *Collin College*
Eddie Meaders, *University of North Texas*
Gay Michele, *El Centro College*
Tom Miles, *Texas Woman's University; University of North Texas*
Banks Miller, *University of Texas at Dallas*
Eric Miller, *Blinn College–Bryan*
Patrick Moore, *Richland College*
Sherri Mora, *Texas State University–San Marcos*
Dana Morales, *Lone Star College–Montgomery*
Amy Moreland, *Sul Ross State University*
Rick Moser, *Kilgore College*
Mark R. Murray, *South Texas College*
James Myers, *Odessa College*
Sugumaran Narayanan, *Midwestern State University*
Sharon Navarro, *University of Texas at San Antonio*
Jalal Nejad, *Northwest Vista College*
Glynn Newman, *Eastfield College*
Matthew Newton, *Lone Star College—Kirkwood*
Timothy Nokken, *Texas Tech University*
James Norris, *Texas A &M International University*
John Osterman, *San Jacinto College*
Cissie Owen, *Lamar University*
William Parent, *San Jacinto College*
Hyung Park, *El Paso Community College*
David Putz, *Lone Star College Kingwood*
Himanshin Raizada, *Lamar University*
Prudencio E. Ramirez, *San Jacinto College*
John Raulston, *Kilgore College*

Daniel Regalado, *Odessa College*
Darrial Reynolds, *South Texas College*
Donna Rhea, *Houston Community College–Northwest*
Laurie Robertstad, *Navarro College*
Mario Salas, *University of Texas at San Antonio*
Larry Salazar, *McLennan Community College*
Michael Sanchez, *San Antonio College*
Raymond Sandoval, *Richland College*
Gilbert Schorlemmer, *Blinn College*
Mark Shomaker, *Blinn College*
Dennis Simon, *Southern Methodist University*
Shannon Sinegal, *Temple College*
Steve Slagle, *Texas State Technical College–Harlingen*
Brian William Smith, *St. Edward's University*
Michael Smith, *South Plains College*
Thomas E. Sowers II, *Lamar University*
John Speer, *Houston Community College*
Debra St. John, *Collin College*
Jeff Stanglin, *Kilgore College*
Jim Startin, *University of Texas at San Antonio*
Andrew Teas, *Houston Community College–Northwest*
Erica C. Terrell, *Richland College*
John Theis, *Lone Star College Kingwood*
Sean Theriault, *University of Texas at Austin*
James Thurmond, *University of Houston*
John Todd, *University of North Texas*
Delaina Toothman, *Texas State University*
Steven Tran, *Houston Community College*
Homer D. Trevino, *McLennan Community College*
Christopher Turner, *Laredo Community College*
Ronald W. Vardy, *University of Houston*
Linda Veazey, *Midwestern State University*
Albert Waite, *Central Texas College*
David Watson, *Sul Ross State University*
Reed Welch, *West Texas A&M University*
Clay Wiegand, *Cisco College*
Geoffrey Willbanks, *University of Texas at Tyler*
Neal Wise, *St. Edward's University*
Kathryn Yates, *Richland College*
Michael Young, *Trinity Valley Community College*
Tyler Young, *Collin College*
Rogerio J. Zapata, *South Texas College*

We thank the following University of Texas at Dallas students for their assistance: Lisa Holmes, Josh Payne, Ali Charania, Alan Roderick, Basel Musharbash, Liza Miadzvedskaya, and Sachi Dave.

At W. W. Norton, Peter Lesser provided editorial guidance throughout the process of developing and publishing the book. Project editors Laura Dragonette and Christine D'Antonio and assistant editor Anna Olcott kept everything organized. Copy editor Roger Mensink helped polish the text. Production managers Stephen Sajdak and Ashley Horna made sure we ended up with a high-quality book, right on schedule. Media editor Spencer Richardson-Jones, associate media editor Michael Jaoui, and media editorial assistant Tricia Vuong worked with the authors of accompanying resources to develop useful tools for students and instructors. Our sincere thanks to all of them.

Anthony Champagne
Edward J. Harpham
Jason Casellas
December 2018

Governing Texas

4TH EDITION

★ ★

In some ways, state-level politics in Texas resembles national politics, but in other ways Texas's political culture is quite distinctive. Here, protesters at the state capitol in Austin rally against a controversial bill being considered by the legislature.

The Political Culture, People, and Economy of Texas

WHY TEXAS'S POLITICAL CULTURE MATTERS In his *Travels with Charley*, John Steinbeck once described Texas as "a state of mind . . . a mystique closely approximating a religion." Steinbeck believed that Texas, despite its vast space, its varying topography, its many cultures and ways of life, had a cohesiveness that may be stronger than in any other part of America. He wrote, "Rich, poor, Panhandle, Gulf, city, country, Texas is the obsession, the proper study and the passionate possession of all Texans."

Certain myths define the obsession that is Texas—and Texans—in the popular imagination. The cowboy who challenges both Native American resistance and Mexican rule, the rancher who exerts an almost feudal sway over a vast domain, the wildcatter who risks everything to drill just one more oil well in a desperate quest for wealth and fortune, the independent entrepreneur who fiercely opposes the intrusion of government into his life—such are the myths about Texans from the past. Other more recent myths are equally powerful. The poor Latino peasant who slips across the border in search of economic opportunity and builds a thriving business, the smooth-talking preacher who promotes a gospel of prosperity to all who will listen, the poor woman who helps establish the right to abortion in the United States and then changes her position on the issue—such are the stories about Texans today that will generate their own myths.

These myths surround various politicians who have led the state since its founding: the visionary Stephen F. Austin, who was locked in a Mexican jail after presenting Texans' grievances to the authorities; the heroic Sam Houston, who won the key Battle of San Jacinto in the Texas Revolution against Mexican rule but was thrown out of office when he rejected the state's secession from the Union; the irrepressible Pa and Ma Ferguson, who served as back-to-back husband-and-wife governors; and the larger-than-life Lyndon Baines Johnson, who began his career as a schoolteacher in Cotulla, Texas, and completed it as a president championing civil rights and the poor.

The underlying reality of Texas today is much more complicated than these popular myths about its people and leaders. Yes, Texas is big. The second-largest state in the Union, comprising more than 261,000 square miles, it is also the second most populous. But Texas is much more diverse than commonly thought. In 2017, Texas was estimated to have a population of over 28 million people, and that population is rapidly growing and becoming composed more and more of ethnic minorities. Non-Hispanic whites, often called Anglos, constitute 42 percent of the population, while Latinos constitute more than 39.4 percent. Approximately 12.7 percent of the population are African American, and 5 percent are Asian. Eighty-five percent of Texans live in urban areas, with many involved in an economy driven by high-tech industry and globalization. More than 28 percent of the population have a bachelor's degree. On the whole, Texans are young, with 26 percent under the age of 18 and 12.3 percent over the age of 65.

Throughout this text, we will examine how Texas is undergoing rapid economic, demographic, and political change. In the process, new myths are being created about the people, politics, and politicians found in the state. As in the past, however, the reality of Texas—its people and its politics—is much more complex than the myths we spin about it. Conservative Republicans may control today's political agenda, but their long-term dominance is not certain. Increasing racial and ethnic diversity points to a new Texas, one that looks sharply different from the one in the history books and one that appears to favor Democrats (the party preferred today by most Latinos, African Americans, and recent immigrants). The future of the state will be determined in large part by the struggle between an assertive Republican majority and a Democratic minority trying to regain power as both parties try to address the various political, economic, and demographic challenges facing its people. Moving our understanding of governance and politics beyond the myths about Texas is the goal of this chapter and the book.

CHAPTER GOALS

- Describe the defining characteristics of political culture in Texas (pp. 5–7)
- Explain how Texas's geography has influenced its political culture (pp. 7–10)
- Trace the evolution of Texas's economy (pp. 11–22)
- Explain how the population of Texas has changed over time (pp. 22–31)
- Describe Texas's shift from a rural society to an urban one (pp. 31–39)

Texas Political Culture

Political scientists have long recognized the importance of **political culture**, that is, the broadly shared values, beliefs, and attitudes about how the government should function and politics should operate. American political culture is traditionally viewed as emphasizing the values of liberty, equality, and democracy. These terms have meant a variety of things to Americans in different times and places.

States often exhibit a distinctive political culture that is the "product of their entire history."[1] Presumably the political culture of a state has an effect on how people participate in politics and how individuals and institutions interact.[2] Often, Texas is categorized as having a **"traditionalistic individualistic" political culture** in which deference is shown to political elites by the masses and hard work and self-interest are valued as core virtues in the economic life of the state.[3] Taxes are kept low, and social services are minimized. Political elites, such as business leaders, have a major voice in how the state is run. In spite of the difficulty in measuring this concept of "traditionalistic individualistic" political culture in any empirical way, it is widely regarded as useful in explaining fundamental beliefs about the state and the role of state government.

When considering the political culture of Texas, one must recognize that it can change over time. It is also difficult to classify the political culture of a state as large and as diverse as Texas in any one category. The liberal cultural norms of urban areas such as Houston, Dallas, and Austin often stand in sharp contrast to those found in the conservative suburban (places outside a city) and exurban (prosperous places beyond the suburbs) areas of these cities. These, too, differ from the political cultures found in south Texas along the border or in the rural Panhandle of west Texas. In fact, Texas has many different political cultures or subcultures within its borders.[4]

To understand the complexity of political culture in Texas today, it is useful to consider three long-lasting patterns in Texas politics and the changes that they are undergoing: the one-party state, the idea of provincialism, and business dominance.

The One-Party State Persists

For over 100 years, Texas was dominated by the Democratic Party. Winning the Democratic primary was tantamount to winning the general election. The pattern was broken in 1978 when Republican William Clements first won the governorship to the surprise of many, and again in 1986 when he won his second term. During the 1990s, substantial competition also emerged between the parties for control of the state legislature. Following redistricting in 2002 the Republicans secured a 7-vote majority in the state senate and a 24-vote majority in the state House. They continued to expand these majorities for the next 15 years. Between 2002 and 2016 all major statewide elected offices were controlled by Republicans. (One Court of Criminal Appeals justice switched to the Democratic Party in December 2013 after being elected as a Republican, but was defeated in

political culture broadly shared values, beliefs, and attitudes about how the government should function and politics should operate; American political culture emphasizes the values of liberty, equality, and democracy

"traditionalistic individualistic" political culture the belief that government should be dominated by political elites and guided by tradition, influenced by the culture of the South, combined with the belief that government should limit its role in providing order in society so that citizens can pursue their economic self-interest, influenced by the culture of the mid-Atlantic states

The seal of Texas reflects the state's individualistic political culture.

provincialism a narrow, limited, and self-interested view of the world often associated with rural values and notions of limited government

the November 2016 general elections.) Few observers doubt that Republicans and conservative values will continue to dominate state politics in the near future. But changes are in the wind. A powerful Republican Party controls most suburban, exurban, and rural areas and has grown increasingly conservative and divided. Moderate pro-business Republicans have begun to clash with a strident group of cultural conservatives championing such issues as traditional marriage, border security, and school choice. The Democratic Party that controls Texas cities has become a party of liberal whites and minorities seeking to promote a progressive agenda emphasizing pro-choice, LGBT rights, and public education. Democrats see in the expanding young Latino population a route back into political prominence. It may be difficult to predict the full impact of these changes on the "traditionalistic individualistic" political culture in Texas. But impact it they will.

Provincialism

A second pattern that once defined Texas political culture is **provincialism**, a narrow view of the world that is often associated with rural values and belief in limited government. The result often was an intolerance of diversity and a concept of the public interest that dismissed social services and expenditures for education. Some of the more popular politicians in Texas in the past have espoused such attitudes, along with corn pone—a rural rejection of the cosmopolitanism found in large urban areas. Racism and intolerance of other cultures played important roles in defining provincialism in the traditional Texas political culture. Increasing urbanization, the growing influence of minorities, women, and LGBT people in politics, and the state's rising importance in the global economy has undercut some of Texas's traditional provincialism. But recent episodes of intolerance toward transsexuals, minority religious groups, and new immigrants from Asia, the Middle East, and Latin America show a resurgence in some of the values associated with provincialism in Texas, at least in important parts of the population.

PERSONAL RESPONSIBILITY: WHAT WOULD YOU DO?

- Do you agree with the popular myth that Texas is overly provincial—that is, intolerant, narrow minded, and overly critical of government? Do you think that there has been a resurgence of provincialism in recent years?

- What are the economic and political consequences of provincialism in modern America? What do you think government and the people should do to foster more open-mindedness in Texas?

Business Dominance

A third, continuing pattern that has helped define Texas's political culture is its longtime dominance by business. Labor unions are rare in Texas except in the oil-refinery areas around Beaumont–Port Arthur. Other groups that might offer an alternative to a business perspective, such as consumer interest groups, are poorly organized and poorly funded. Business groups are the major players in Texas politics, in terms of campaign contributions, organized interest groups, and lobbyists. The concerns and values of business groups continue to shape political culture in Texas today. But this business influence is being challenged by a powerful social conservative wing in the

Ties between business and politics have always been close in Texas. Here, Governor Greg Abbott signs a bill prohibiting local government attempts to ban fracking as a way to continue to get oil and natural gas out of the ground.

Republican Party that is less concerned with business interests than bathroom regulation, border control, and traditional marriage.

This chapter will investigate the economic, social, and demographic changes that transformed Texas's political culture during the twentieth century and have continued to shape it in the second decade of the twenty-first century.

The Land

 Explain how Texas's geography has influenced its political culture

Much of Texas's history and political life has been shaped by the relationship forged between its people and the land. When Texas became a republic in 1836, it claimed 216,000,000 acres (approximately 350,000 square miles) of unappropriated land as its own. At its founding, Texas was land rich but money poor, having only $55.68 in its treasury. Texas was the only state other than the original 13 colonies to keep control of its public lands when it entered the Union, in 1845. Privatizing these public lands was probably the most important ongoing public policy pursued by the state in the nineteenth century. Although Texas turned a large portion of its public lands over to private ownership, it retained ownership of the minerals under some of this land, including land containing oil and natural gas. **Privatization of public property** established the property rules and regulations under which economic development would take place in the state. It also gave the state an ownership of mineral rights that would provide funding for elementary and secondary education as well as higher education for the next 160 years.

privatization of public property the act(s) by which Texas gave public land owned by the state over to private individuals for cultivation and development

Privatization was not the only political issue surrounding land in Texas in the nineteenth century. The exact boundaries of Texas were contentious throughout the 1840s and 1850s. Following the Mexican-American War, the Treaty of Guadalupe Hidalgo in 1848 established the Rio Grande as the southern border of the state. After Texas threatened to use military force to reassert its land claims in the west, the Compromise of 1850 established Texas's current western borders. In exchange for $10 million in federal bonds, Texas gave up claims to 67,000,000 acres of land in what are now New Mexico, Wyoming, Colorado, Kansas, and Oklahoma. The Compromise of 1850 enabled Texas to pay off the public debts incurred during the Republic and to retain 98,000,000 acres in public lands.[5]

Today, Texas is the second-largest state, next to Alaska, and its size is perhaps the most distinctive characteristic of its geography. To understand the dynamics of political life and governance in Texas demands an appreciation of the vast spaces and topography that define the state. The longest straight-line distance across the state from north to south is 801 miles; the longest east–west distance is 773 miles. To put this into perspective, the north–south distance between New York City and Charleston, South Carolina, is 763 miles, cutting across seven different states. The east–west distance between New York City and Chicago is 821 miles, cutting across six different states.

Distances alone, though, do not tell the whole story of the state's diverse geography. There are four distinct physical regions in Texas (Figure 1.1)[6] whose distinctive features have shaped its politics in a number of important ways.

The Gulf Coastal Plains

The Gulf Coastal Plains extend from the Louisiana border and the Gulf of Mexico, along the Rio Grande up to Del Rio, and northward to the line of the Balcones Fault and Escarpment. As one moves westward, the climate becomes increasingly dry. Forests become less frequent as post oak trees dominate the landscape until they too are replaced by the prairies and brushlands of central Texas.

The eastern portion of the Gulf Coastal Plains—so-called east Texas—is hilly and covered by forests of pine and hardwoods. Almost all of Texas's timber production takes place here, which is also the home of some of the state's most famous oilfields. To the west is the Blackland Belt. Rolling prairie soil made the Blackland Belt a prime farming area, especially for cotton, during the late nineteenth and early twentieth centuries. Today, it is the most densely populated area of the state and has a diversified manufacturing base.

The Coastal Prairies around Houston and Beaumont were the center for the state's post–World War II industrial boom, particularly in the petrochemical industry. Winter vegetable and fruit production plays a major role in the Lower Rio Grande Valley, while livestock is important in the Rio Grande Plain, an area that receives less than 24 inches of rainfall on average every year and loses much of that to evaporation during its very hot summers.

Texas's political life grew out of the Gulf Coastal Plains. The land grants offered to Americans willing to come to Texas in the first half of the nineteenth century were located in this region, which was the birthplace of plantation slavery and, after the Civil War and Reconstruction, of Jim Crow segregation in the state. East Texas also saw the first oil booms in Texas in the early decades of the twentieth century. The Dallas–Fort

FIGURE 1.1

The Physical Regions of Texas

SOURCE: Dallas Morning News, *Texas Almanac 2000–2001* (Dallas: Dallas Morning News, 1999), p. 55.

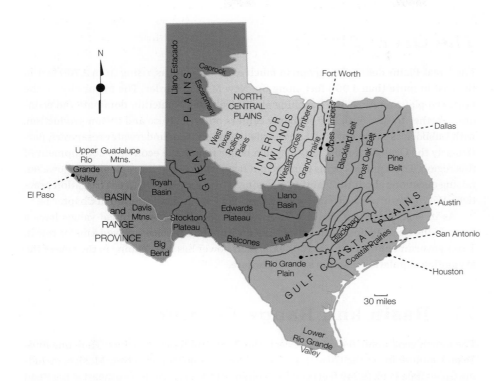

Worth area in the northwestern part of this region was once a bastion of a small Republican Party. A union movement grew out of the industrialized areas along the coast, providing support to a liberal wing of the Democratic Party. For the most part, though, the Gulf Coastal Plains were dominated by rural conservative values, whether in the Democratic Party (from the end of Reconstruction in 1876 to the early 1990s) or the Republican Party (from the 1990s to today). Urbanization and suburbanization in Houston and Dallas–Fort Worth have added new dimensions to the political life of this region. In the twenty-first century, urban areas have become increasingly Democratic, while suburban areas have become more Republican.

The Interior Lowlands

The Interior Lowlands are an extension of the lowlands that run south from Canada through the Midwest. They are bordered by the Balcones Escarpment (the surface expression of the Balcones Fault) on the east and south and the Caprock Escarpment on the west. Extending west from Fort Worth, the Interior Lowlands have a predominantly agricultural economy and rural population. In the western portion, which rises from 750 to 2,000 feet in elevation, the West Texas Rolling Plains contain much level, cultivable land, along with a large cattle-raising industry. Many of the state's largest ranches are located here. Like other rural areas of Texas today, this region is dominated by conservative politics and the Republican Party.

The Great Plains

The Great Plains define the terrain in much of western Texas, rising from 2,700 feet in the east to more than 4,000 feet along the New Mexico border. The major city on the northern plains is Amarillo. Ranching and petroleum production dominate the economy. Farther to the south, the economy centers on agriculture and cotton production, with Lubbock as the major city. Large-scale irrigation from underwater reservoirs, particularly the Ogallala Aquifer, has played a major role in the economic development of this region. The aquifer is being pumped out faster than it is being replenished, however, raising questions about the viability of basing future growth on current irrigation practices. We will return to a discussion of the problem of aquifer depletion in Chapter 14.

As in east Texas and the Interior Lowlands, conservative political values have a home in the Great Plains. Although politicians from this area have played a major role in Texas government over the last 100 years, their power has been ebbing in the face of the expanding population of urban areas elsewhere.

The Basin and Range Province

The fourth geographic region in Texas is the Basin and Range Province. Here one finds Texas's mountains in the Guadalupe Range along the border with New Mexico, including Guadalupe Peak (8,749 feet) and El Capitán (8,085 feet). To the southeast is Big Bend country, so named because the Rio Grande surrounds it on three sides as the river makes its southward swing. Rainfall and population are sparse in this region.

The area along the Mexican border, running from the Basin and Range Province through the southern Great Plains and Gulf Coastal Plains to the Lower Rio Grande Valley and the Gulf of Mexico, has always had a distinctive political culture, dominated by the fact that Texas and Mexico have been connected economically and demographically. The population in this region is overwhelmingly Latino. In the twenty-first century, the Border region, including the cities of El Paso, McAllen, and Brownsville, has remained a Democratic Party bastion.

Economic Change in Texas

 Trace the evolution of Texas's economy

The famous twentieth-century economist Joseph Schumpeter characterized the capitalist economic system as being a process of "creative destruction."[7] By this he meant that capitalism underwent periodic waves of disruptive transformation fueled by technological innovations in production and distribution. These waves were created by entrepreneurs who had visions of new ways to produce and distribute goods and services and then made those visions a reality. But the capitalist process of creative destruction not only creates a new economic and social world; it destroys old ones. During the late nineteenth century, the world of railroads, steam power, and steel transformed American economic and social life by nationalizing the market—creating ways to buy and sell the same goods and services nationwide—and making new opportunities available to businesses and individuals. Farmers no longer grew their crops simply for local or regional markets in Texas but for national markets in such widely dispersed cities as New York, Philadelphia, Chicago, Kansas City, and San Francisco. Their economic livelihoods were no longer controlled just by the rhythms of the weather in Texas but by vagaries of supply and demand in far-off cities and states. The technological innovations tied to gasoline combustion engines, electricity, and radio radically restructured the American economy again in the 1920s, leaving in their wake a society that would never be the same. The last great wave of creative destruction, one that Schumpeter himself never saw, began in the 1980s and carried through into the early decades of the twenty-first century as digital technology tied to the information age and the internet restructured yet again how business was conducted and people interacted.

Over the last 150 years, three great waves of technological change have helped define and redefine the state's economy. The first centered on the production of cotton and cattle and their distribution by an extensive railroad system. The second grew out of the oil industry. The third and most recent is tied to the development of the high-tech digital economy.

Cotton

Cotton is one of the oldest crops grown in Texas.[8] Missions in San Antonio in the eighteenth century are reported to have produced several thousand pounds of cotton annually, which were spun and woven by local artisans. Large-scale cultivation began in 1821 with the arrival of white Americans. Political independence, statehood, and the ongoing removal of the Native American "threat" in the years before the Civil War promoted the development of the cotton industry. By the mid-nineteenth century, production had soared, placing Texas eighth among the cotton-producing states in the Union. By 1880, Texas led all states in the production of cotton in most years.

A number of technological breakthroughs further stimulated the cotton industry in Texas. First, in the 1870s barbed wire was introduced, enabling farmers to cordon off their lands and protect their crop from grazing cattle. Second, the building of railroads

During the late nineteenth century, in most years Texas produced more cotton than any other state. But although one-quarter of the cotton produced in the United States still comes from Texas, the importance of the cotton industry to the state's economy has declined since the 1920s. This photo shows land and machinery used to farm cotton.

brought Texas farmers into a national market. Finally, a newly designed plow made it easier to dig up the prairie soil and significantly increased farm productivity.

Throughout the 1870s immigrants from the Deep South and Europe flooded the prairies of Texas to farm cotton. Most of these newly arrived Texans became tenant farmers or sharecroppers. Tenants lived on farms owned by others, providing their own animals, tools, and seed. They generally received two-thirds of the final value of the cotton grown on the farm, while their landlord received the other third. Sharecroppers, a subset of tenant farmers, furnished only their labor and received only half the value of the final product. By the turn of the century, almost half of the state's farmers were tenants.[9]

Two important consequences resulted from the tenant and sharecropping system. First, it condemned many rural Texans to lives of social and economic dependency. Under the notorious "crop lien" system, developed by landlords and merchants to extend credit to farmers who did not own their land, farmers profited from their work only after their debts had been paid or new loans had been made to pay off old debts. The result often was to trap farmers in a debt cycle from which they could not escape. Second, the tenant and sharecropping system helped fuel radical political discontent in rural areas, sparking both the Grange and Populist movements. These movements played a major role in defining the style of Texas politics throughout much of the late nineteenth and early twentieth centuries.

Cotton production cycled up and down during this period as farmers experienced a series of crises and opportunities, ranging from destructive boll weevils to an increased demand brought on by World War I to a collapse in prices following the war. Overall, however, the cotton culture began a decline that continued after World War II. The 1930 Census reported that 61 percent of all farmers in Texas were tenant farmers and that one-third of these were sharecroppers. These numbers fell throughout the Great Depression and beyond. By 1987 only 12 percent of all farmers were tenants.[10]

Cattle

The history of ranching and the cattle industry parallels that of cotton in many ways.[11] Their origins extend back to the late seventeenth century, when the Spanish colonial authorities brought livestock to the region to feed their missionaries, soldiers, and civilians. During the periods of Mexican rule and independence, ranching offered immigrants an attractive alternative to farming. In the 1830s traffic in cattle was limited to local areas, but over the next two decades cattle drives and railroads began opening up new markets in the east.

Following the Civil War, the cattle industry took off, expanding throughout the state. As with cotton, the invention of barbed wire helped, closing off ranch lands used for grazing. By the end of the century, open range had given way to fenced pasturing. As a result, conflicts over land often broke out between large and small ranchers as well as between ranchers and farmers. As cattle raising became a more specialized and efficient

Cattle ranching is another of Texas's important industries. The most famous ranch in Texas is the King Ranch, shown here in 1950. Currently covering almost 1,300 square miles, it is larger than the state of Rhode Island.

business, conflicts also arose between ranchers and their employees. Throughout the twentieth century, ranching remained a cyclical industry, struggling when national and international prices collapsed and thriving during upturns in the economy.

Ranching and cotton production remain important industries in the state, although increasingly dominated by big agribusiness companies. Today, Texas normally leads the nation in both livestock and cotton production. About 40 percent of the cotton produced in the United States comes from Texas. In 2014 the cotton crop was over 6.2 million bales valued at over $2.1 billion, most of which was exported to China, Turkey, and Mexico. Production has fluctuated over the last decade because of the severe drought that plagued parts of the state.[12]

Today, however, neither cotton production nor ranching drives the Texas economy. The number of people making a living from agriculture has dropped significantly over the last 50 years as agribusiness has pushed out the family farm and ranch. In 1940, 23 percent of the population lived on farms and ranches. Another 17 percent were suppliers to farms and ranches or helped assemble, process, or distribute agricultural products. Currently, less than 2 percent of the population lives on farms and ranches, with an additional 15 percent providing support, processing, or distribution services to agriculture.[13]

In the early twentieth century, a new set of technological breakthroughs challenged the nineteenth-century dominance of cotton and cattle. These breakthroughs focused not on what grew on the land, but on what lay beneath it.

Oil

Spanish explorers first sighted oil oozing out of the ground in the mid-seventeenth century.[14] Because there was then no market or demand for it, however, nothing was done to develop this natural resource. Over a century later, encouraged by a growing demand for petroleum products following the Civil War, a scattering of entrepreneurs dug wells, but they proved not commercially viable. The first economically significant oil discovery in Texas was in 1894 in Navarro County near Corsicana. By 1898 the state's first oil refinery was operating at the site.

What catapulted Texas into the era of oil and gas was the discovery at Spindletop on January 10, 1901. Located three miles south of Beaumont along the Gulf Coast, the Spindletop discovery produced the state's first oil boom and encouraged large numbers of speculators and entrepreneurs to try their luck in the new business. Within three years, three major oilfields had been discovered within 150 miles of Spindletop. As a result, oil fever spread throughout Texas in the early twentieth century with major oilfields developed all across the state.

The oil and gas industry transformed the social and economic fabric of Texas. A cheap new source of energy helped factories and farms operate more efficiently, reducing the need for farm workers and stimulating manufacturing. This encouraged people to escape rural unemployment by moving to cities with growing numbers of industrial jobs. In addition, cheap oil encouraged automobile production and the building of roads. The Interstate Highway System built during the 1950s and 1960s changed fundamentally the transportation patterns that had shaped the movements of people and goods in Texas. The triangle formed by I-35 from San Antonio to Dallas–Fort Worth, I-45 from Dallas–Fort Worth to Houston, and I-10 from Houston to San Antonio became the heartland of the Texas economy and the location of an increasing percentage of the state's population.

The oil and gas industry also sparked a rapid industrialization of the Gulf Coast region. Among the companies developing the region's oilfields were Gulf Oil, Sun Oil, Magnolia Petroleum, the Texas Company, and Humble Oil. Their refineries, pipelines, and export facilities laid the foundations for the large-scale industrialization in the Houston–Beaumont–Port Arthur region. By 1929 in Harris County, for example, 27 percent of all manufacturing employees worked in refineries. By 1940 the capacity of all the refineries had increased fourfold from 1929.[15] The petrochemical industry continued to flourish throughout the 1960s, when demand for its products grew at the rate of 10 percent a year.

Another important effect of the oil and gas boom was a new rhythm to economic life in the state. When the economy was tied to cotton and cattle, prices of products could rise and fall, bringing prosperity or gloom to local economies. But there were natural seasonal and annual cycles in these agricultural activities, and a bond existed between the land and the people and the communities that formed around them. Oil and gas, on the other hand, introduced a boom-and-bust mentality that carried over into the communities that sprang up around oil and gas discoveries. Rural areas were often unprepared for the population explosion that followed such discoveries: housing was often inadequate or nonexistent, schools quickly became overcrowded, and general living conditions were poor as people sought to "make it big." Ironically, a major discovery that brought large amounts of new oil and gas to market could lead to a sudden collapse in prices. Local prosperity could then quickly turn into depression. And when particular fields were tapped out, boomtowns could quickly become ghost towns.

The oil and gas industry also transformed Texas government and the role that it played in the state's economy. Following the Civil War, a series of political attempts to regulate the railroads had largely failed. In 1890, however, after considerable controversy fueled by Populist hostility to railroad companies, a constitutional amendment was passed to create a regulatory agency, the Texas Railroad Commission. In 1917 the commission's powers were extended to regulation of energy, to ensure that petroleum pipelines were "common carriers" (that they transported all producers' oil and gas on equal terms) and to promote well-spacing rules (which controlled production by limiting how closely packed together oil wells could be in a particular field). In the 1930s, in an attempt to limit price fluctuations brought on by the glut of oil on world markets and to avoid wasteful production, the commission won the authority to prorate oil, that is to determine how much every well in Texas was allowed to produce. Through the late 1960s the Texas Railroad Commission was one of the most important, as well as one of the few democratically elected, regulatory bodies in the nation.

Expanding the power of state government in the economy through the Railroad Commission was only one political effect of the oil and gas industry in Texas. The industry also had an important fiscal effect. Beginning in 1905 the state collected oil production taxes, which rose from $101,403 in 1906 to over $1 million in 1919 and almost $6 million in 1929. For the 2018–19 biennium, it was estimated that such taxes, known as severance taxes, would contribute $4.9 billion to the state budget, up 29.7 percent from $3.81 billion in 2016–17. Natural gas production taxes in 2018–19 added another $1.8 billion to the state budget, up 16.4 percent from $1.6 billion in 2016–17.[16] These revenue numbers have fluctuated wildly in recent years as the price of oil and gasoline has collapsed and then recovered. As we will see in Chapter 11 on public finance in Texas, oil and natural gas production plays an important role in the state's finances through the severance tax.

Much like the state government coffers, those of higher education in Texas have benefited from the oil and gas industry. What many thought was worthless land at the time had been set aside by the state constitution of 1876 and the state legislature in 1883 as the Permanent University Fund to support higher education. As luck would have it, oil was discovered in the West Texas Permian Basin in 1923 on university land. Soon, 17 wells were producing oil there, sparking a building boom at the University of Texas. In 1931 the income of the Permanent University Fund was split between the University of Texas at Austin and Texas A&M University, with the former receiving two-thirds and the latter one-third. In 1984 the income was opened up to all University of Texas and Texas A&M schools. Along with the royalties from other natural resources on university land, oil and gas royalties created one of the largest university endowments in the world. In June 2017 the Permanent University Fund held title to 2.1 million acres in 24 counties, primarily in west Texas, and the market value of the fund was calculated to be $19.5 billion.[17]

The movement of the Texas economy out of the era dominated by oil and gas was not easy. From 1971 to 1981 the annual rate of economic growth averaged 4.4 percent. World oil prices rose to almost $35 per barrel in 1981, by which time oil-related businesses accounted for 26 percent of the state's total economic production. Fueled by a booming oil-based economy and a rapidly increasing population, real estate prices shot up in urban areas such as Houston and Dallas. Projections were made that as oil prices rose, perhaps to $70 or even $80 per barrel, future prosperity was inevitable. Indeed, there was some talk that Texas's oil-driven economy had become recession-proof. Such talk proved premature, to say the least.

World oil prices began to collapse in 1982, bottoming out early in 1986 at $10 per barrel. Other sectors of the economy began to suffer as the price of oil fell. The state went through two major recessions—one in 1982 and another in 1986–87. Real estate deals fell through, and construction projects slowed and then shut down. Speculators defaulted on their loans, and banks began to fail. Throughout the 1980s, 370 banks went under in Texas. Texas emerged from the economic malaise of the 1980s with a transformed

FIGURE 1.2

Oil Production in Texas

Note that these data refer to onshore production in Texas.

SOURCE: Texas Railroad Commission and "Historical Crude Oil Prices," InflationData.com.

■ Annual production (millions of barrels, left axis)
■ Average price per barrel ($, right axis)

economy. Though remaining an important sector, the oil and gas business was no longer the primary driving force.

One can trace the rise and decline and rise again of the oil and gas industry in Texas through production figures (see Figure 1.2). The state's oil production peaked around 1972, and decades of decline followed. But beginning in 2008, new technologies such as horizontal drilling and fracking led to a new boom era of oil and gas production in Texas. Through 2017 a large share of the new production came from the Permian Basin region in west Texas, which may be the second-largest oilfield in the world. The result of this most recent boom is that oil (and gas) has emerged again as a mainstay of the Texas economy, although it is an economy that is far more diversified than in any earlier era. With the boom came greater resources for the state's budget. But the boom also brought new demands for vast water supplies—an essential component of the new drilling and fracking technologies—and new concerns about the effects of this technology on the environment.[18]

By 2015 there were other clouds on the horizon of the oil industry. After hovering around $100 per barrel through mid-2014, the price of oil began a steady decline, fluctuating between $30 and $50 a barrel through late 2017. Not surprisingly, as the price fell, production of oil in Texas went into decline.[19]

High-Tech Industry

By the last decade of the twentieth century, new industries and technologies not based in extracting resources from the land were assuming significant roles in the state's economy. Among the most important of these was the burgeoning high-tech industry. In contrast to the 1980s, the 1990s were a period of rapid growth in the Texas economy. And, unlike in earlier periods of speculative booms such as the 1970s, the growth was grounded in a rapidly diversifying economic base. At the heart of this boom was a fast-growing manufacturing sector tied to high tech. In the 1990s, Texas went from seventh in the nation in total manufacturing employment to second. In 2017, 13 percent of the total output in the state came from manufacturing, and 7 percent of the workforce was employed in manufacturing.[20]

Today two Texas metropolitan areas stand out as national centers of the rapidly evolving high-tech industry. The Austin–San Marcos area is the home of the computer giant Dell and has become a production center for computer chips, personal computers, and related computer hardware with such companies as Google, Facebook, Flextronics, Apple, Oracle, and IBM. Seven of the area's largest employers are part of the computer or semiconductor industry. The Dallas metropolitan area, particularly north of the city, is the home of a number of important electronic and electronic-equipment companies, including Texas Instruments. Houston also has become known worldwide for its medical center and expanding research facilities in the medical field. In 2016 manufacturers exported $210 billion in manufactured goods. A 2014 study released by the Tech-America Foundation found that Texas was the leading state exporter of technology goods with $45 billion in exports in 2012. Approximately 331,000 jobs in Texas were supported by these exports.[21]

Houston has become an important center of medical research. Here Dr. C. Huie Lin of Houston Methodist Research Institute displays a 3-D printed medical model of a patient's heart, which is used to test surgical techniques.

NAFTA, USMCA, and the International Economy

Texas's place in national and international markets has been shaped by its central location within the United States, its border with Mexico, and its sophisticated transportation infrastructure.

One defining feature of the Texas economy from the 1990s on was the **North American Free Trade Agreement (NAFTA)**. Signed on December 17, 1992, by Prime Minister Brian Mulroney of Canada, President Carlos Salinas de Gortari of Mexico, and President George H. W. Bush of the United States, NAFTA sought to create a free-trade zone—an area free of customs duties—in North America that was the largest of its kind in the world. Considerable controversy surrounded its passage, with many groups arguing that free trade would hurt U.S. workers and companies because of the cheaper labor available in Mexico.

Today, NAFTA links approximately 494 million consumers in the United States, Canada, and Mexico. According to a recent Standard and Poor's study, Mexico has benefited the most from the agreement, but Texas has benefited enormously as well. NAFTA has accelerated the diversification of the Texas economy. Along the border, NAFTA has clearly stimulated trade and transport and created jobs. For example, a study found in 2015 that 56.4 percent of Texas's total international trade ($356 billion) traveled across the border

North American Free Trade Agreement (NAFTA) trade treaty among the United States, Canada, and Mexico to lower and eliminate tariffs among the three countries

The signing of NAFTA in 1992 created a free-trade zone in North America. Although many Texas workers were adversely affected by the availability of cheaper labor in Mexico, NAFTA appears to have had a beneficial effect on the state's economy as a whole. Here, President George H. W. Bush stands between President Carlos Salinas de Gortari of Mexico and Prime Minister Brian Mulroney of Canada at the signing ceremony.

with Mexico. Almost 58 percent of this cross-border trade ($204 billion) was through the port of entry at Laredo. International toll bridges alone accounted for 23 percent of Laredo's general fund revenue in 2012.[22]

The trade agreement has had some negative impact on Texas as well. A 2011 study by the Economic Policy Institute estimated that almost 683,000 jobs had been lost in the United States because of NAFTA. The study estimated that three-fifths of these jobs were in the manufacturing sector. Over 55,000 of these displaced jobs came from Texas.[23] U.S. workers generally lost their jobs because of competition from lower-wage businesses in Mexico or relocation of plants to Mexico. (Under federal law such workers are entitled to additional unemployment compensation.)

Although there were some losers in the movement toward free trade with Mexico and Canada, there were also big winners. The following statistics from 2017 put the importance of Texas's international trade, particularly with Mexico and Canada, into perspective:[24]

- Texas exports totaled $264 billion, up from $207 billion in 2012. Texas exports were 17 percent of all U.S. exports.
- The North American market (Mexico and Canada) was the destination for 45 percent of these exports.
- Mexico was the top importer of Texas exports at almost $97 billion in 2017, up from almost $73 billion in 2012.
- Canada's imports from Texas totaled $23 billion in 2013, up from $19 billion in 2010.

The Trump administration's concerns over undocumented workers in the United States and terrorism have added a new dimension to the debate over NAFTA and global trade in Texas. Most Texas political and business leaders continue to believe that expanding trade with Mexico and other countries is a good thing. A free flow of people across the border, however, is another issue. An increasing number of people, particularly conservative Republicans, now question the benefits to Texas of a porous border. During the 2016 election campaign, Donald Trump, as well as leading Texas Republicans, portrayed the large numbers of undocumented workers in Texas as a burden upon the state's social services. Moreover, fears of Islamic terrorists accompanying Mexicans and other Latin Americans seeking work in the United States have led to calls for building walls and fences that will make illegal immigration a thing of the past. Conceding that immigration is a national issue, numerous Texas politicians have called for a stricter policing of the border by state authorities. It is hard to imagine a new stricter border policy not having negative effects on the trade that has followed from NAFTA and expanding global trade (see the "What Do Texans Think?" feature on the next page).

NAFTA was replaced by a new trade agreement among the United States, Mexico, and Canada (USMCA) in the fall of 2018. Among the changes demanded by the Trump administration were provisions to protect American workers in the car industry from low wages, increased intellectual property protections, and an opening up of the Canadian milk market. Initial fears that free trade among the three nations might be a thing of the past were set aside as they agreed that increased trade under the proper conditions benefited all parties and that tariffs served no one.

NAFTA and International Trade

The North American Free Trade Agreement was an important part of national economic policy from when it was signed in the early 1990s. At both the state and national levels, Democrats and ideological liberals generally supported the agreement. But Republicans and conservatives, once strongly in favor of free-trade agreements like NAFTA, grew to oppose the agreement. In the fall of 2018 the Trump administration negotiated a new trade agreement, the United States-Mexico-Canada Agreement (USMCA) with Mexico and Canada, which mostly addressed the concerns of conservatives.

NAFTA: Mostly Good or Bad for Economy?

TEXANS	LIBERAL (%)	MODERATE (%)	CONSERVATIVE (%)	DON'T KNOW/REFUSED (%)
Good	57%	52%	29%	36%
Bad	13	19	38	10
Don't know/refused	30	29	33	54
TOTAL	21	34	36	8

NATIONWIDE	BAD (%)	GOOD (%)	DON'T KNOW/NO RESPONSE (%)
All	33%	56%	11%
Republican/Leaning Republican	54	35	11
Democrat/Leaning Democrat	18	72	10

SOURCES: (top) 2017 Texas Statewide Survey, the Texas Lyceum, April 18, 2017, 1,000 respondents; (bottom) Pew Research Center Survey, October 25–30, 2017; 1,504 respondents.

The Military in Texas

Since Texas's annexation by the United States, its economic development has been closely tied to the establishment of military bases. As population pressures pushed westward, a series of federal forts were built to protect Texans from Native Americans, who were perceived to be alien threats to the expanding Anglo-American culture. Seizing federal forts for the Confederacy was one of the first and most important acts of the Texas government following secession. And Texas provided a major military training center during both world wars. Strong leadership in Congress from Texas politicians such as Sam Rayburn and Lyndon Johnson during the New Deal and the post–World War II years brought much-needed jobs and money into the state through the building of one military installation after another (see Figure 1.3).

It is hard to overestimate the importance of these military bases to local communities. For example, Fort Bliss, which opened in 1849, is today the U.S. Army's second-largest

FIGURE 1.3

Major U.S. Military Bases in Texas

* In October 2010, Fort Sam Houston, Lackland Air Force Base, and Randolph Air Force Base were merged into Joint Base San Antonio under the jurisdiction of the U.S. Air Force 502nd Air Base Wing, Air Education and Training Command, in accordance with the recommendations of the federal Base Realignment and Closure Commission.

SOURCE: *Texas Almanac* online (texasalmanac.com), Major Military Installations. Taken from U.S. Department of Defense "Base Structure Report 2015."

base in size, covering over 1.1 million acres in Texas and New Mexico. In partnership with the city of El Paso, Fort Bliss created the world's largest inland desalination plant, providing fresh water to the base and city. Fort Hood is today the army's largest active-duty armored post. Taking up more than 217,000 acres, Fort Hood has been responsible for deploying and redeploying over 852,000 soldiers since 2003. Fort Hood is the home to over 60,000 military and civilian personnel, making it the largest single-site employer in the state. According to a study conducted by the Texas Comptroller's office, the base generated $21 billion for the state's economy.[25]

Today, military installations continue to be important to the economic well-being of certain parts of the state. In 2015 over 163,000 active-duty, reserve, and civilian personnel employed by the U.S. military were living in Texas. The military, along with the many businesses that provide consumer services to its members, is big business in Texas. Therefore, an expanding military stimulates economic growth and employment in Texas. A contracting military does not.

The Great Recession and the "Texas Miracle"

In December 2007 the nation entered what some have called the Great Recession, a time of deep, prolonged economic problems that drew analogies to the Great Depression of the 1930s. A speculative bubble in the housing market fueled by cheap credit and poor business practices culminated in a credit crisis that brought some of America's largest banks and investment houses to their knees. Only the massive intrusion of the Federal Reserve System into credit markets in the fall of 2008 prevented the banking system from melting down. The Federal Reserve reported that between November 2007 and March 2009, 86 percent of American industries cut back production. During this time, the GNP (gross national product, the total amount of all goods and services produced in the United States) dropped 1.7 percent, and household net worth fell $11 trillion, or 18 percent.[26]

Texas was one of the last states to enter the Great Recession and one of the first to exit. Prior to the recession, Texas employment had peaked at 10.6 million in August 2008. From late 2008 through 2009, 427,600 jobs were lost, but by November 2011 employment had recovered to prerecession levels. By April 2014 another 829,000 jobs had been added to the Texas economy. The story at the national level was not so rosy. By the summer of 2014 job numbers were only beginning to approach pre-Great Recession levels. Meanwhile the unemployment rate in Texas rose to 8.2 percent and hovered there throughout most of 2010. It began falling in early 2011 and continued to fall for the next two years, dropping from 6.4 percent in March 2013 to 4 percent in mid-2018.[27]

Business interests are powerful in Texas. Here, Jeff Moseley of the Texas Association of Business joins other Texas business and tourism representatives to speak out against the transgender bathroom bill, which they felt would reduce tourism and commerce in the state. Ultimately, the bill failed.

Many Texas politicians sought to take credit for the state's performance during and after the Great Recession, which some referred to as the "Texas economic miracle." Comparisons were made with big-government, high-tax states like California that suffered severely. Low taxes and low public services, pro-business government, an entrepreneurial spirit—all were given credit.[28] But the factors that may have helped Texas get by relatively unscathed were likely more economic than political. The housing market declined much less severely in Texas than in the rest of the nation. Prior to the Great Recession, Texas had not experienced the surge in real estate values found in other states like California, Nevada, Florida, and Arizona. While foreclosure rates throughout the country increased sixfold between 2005 and 2009, in Texas they rose only marginally. Texas's banking industry also appeared to have weathered the storm better than its counterparts in other states. Article 16 of the Texas Constitution, as amended in 1997, forbids consumers from using home-equity loans for credit that exceeds 80 percent of the mortgage, and this restriction probably provided a cushion against the credit crunch. Two other important factors that may have helped Texas escape the worst of the Great Recession were discussed above: an increasingly diversified economy lubricated by international trade and a resurgent oil and gas industry.[29]

Following the special session of the state legislature in 2017, some pundits began to question the rhetoric lying behind the Texas economic miracle. Economic growth in Texas no longer appeared to be outperforming that of other states as the malaise of the Great Recession faded into the past. In addition, an aggressive conservative social agenda focused on such issues as abortion, transgender bathrooms, and private vouchers in school threatened to divide the pro-business consensus in the state.

During the contentious debate over transgender bathrooms during the summer of 2017, major corporate leaders cautioned political leaders like Speaker Joe Straus to tone down the social agenda rhetoric or risk losing new businesses coming to the state. One commentator, Richard Parker, the author of *Lone Star Nation: How Texas will Transform America*, concluded that the retirement of Speaker Joe Straus in October of 2017 marked "the grisly death of the GOP" and the doom of the political center in Texas. For Parker, the end of moderate Republicans in state leadership likely spelled the end of the Texas economic miracle and the beginning of a time of political chaos in the state. Whether or not such prognostications prove accurate, one thing is clear: the consensus surrounding the idea of the Texas economic miracle may be unraveling.[30]

The People of Texas

 Explain how the population of Texas has changed over time

The population of Texas has grown rapidly since 1850, when it stood at a little more than 210,000 people, more than one-quarter of whom were African American slaves. According to the 1900 U.S. Census, there were only 470 American Indians still residing in Texas, the others having been driven out during the Indian Wars. Interestingly, today Texas is

FIGURE 1.4

The Changing Face of Texas, 1850–2016

*Latinos were not counted as a separate group until 1990 and were included in the white census count.

SOURCES: *Statistical Abstract of the United States: 1994* (Washington, D.C.: U.S. Department of Commerce. Bureau of the Census, 1994); see also *Texas Almanac* 2014–15 (Denton: Texas State Historical Association, 2014), 15; 2010 U.S. Census. *Texas Almanac* 2018–2019 also consulted. These are available online.

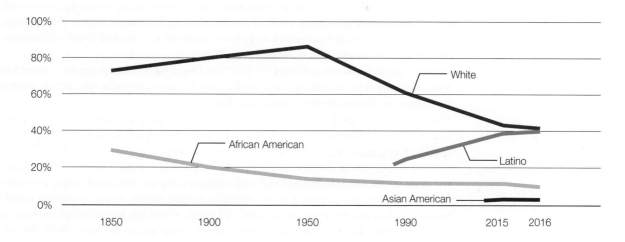

the home to over 65,000 American Indians. Although there are three recognized reservations, most live in urban areas, including over 20,000 in Dallas–Fort Worth.[31]

Texas in 1850 was an overwhelmingly rural state. Only 4 percent of the population lived in urban areas. By 1900 the population had increased to more than 3 million, with 83 percent living in rural areas. The 1980s began as boom years for population growth, with increases running between 2.9 percent and 1.6 percent per year from 1980 through 1986. With the collapse of oil prices, however, population growth slowed significantly between 1987 and 1989 to less than 1 percent.[32] Finally, with a recovering economy, population growth surged in the 1990s and has continued into the twenty-first century (see Figure 1.4).

Three factors account for the population growth in Texas: natural increase as a result of the difference between births and deaths; international immigration, particularly from Mexico; and domestic immigration from other states. The makeup of the growth in population shifted in significant ways in the late twentieth and early twenty-first centuries. In 1991 almost two-thirds of population growth was accounted for by natural increase. A little more than 20 percent was a result of international immigration, while less than 14 percent resulted from domestic immigration. By 2017 natural increase accounted for only a little over half the growth, while international immigration accounted for about 17 percent and domestic immigration for about 30 percent.[33] In the early decades of the twenty-first century, Texas was being redefined not by native-born

Texans but by outsiders coming to benefit from and contribute to the state's diversified economy.

In 2017, it was estimated that 400,000 new residents were added to the state, bringing the total population to 28.3 million people. The majority of this increase came from a natural increase. Of the 189,580 people who migrated into Texas during 2017, there was a sharp change in the numbers of integrational migrants (from outside the United States) and domestic migrants (from inside the United States). In 2016, 91,839 came to Texas from abroad while 125,703 came from other states. In 2017, the trend lines reversed: 110,417 migrated from abroad while 79,163 immigrated from other states. The immediate impact of this would mean that there would be more Latinos and fewer whites making up the Texas population in coming years.[34]

For a deeper understanding of the role that changing demographics have played in Texas's culture and politics, we must look closer at the major racial and ethnic groups that have constituted the population over time.

Whites

For most of the nineteenth and twentieth centuries, the largest ethnic group was non-Hispanic whites, also referred to as whites or Anglos. These whites comprise a wide range of European ethnic groups, including English, Germans, Scots, Irish, Czechs, and European Jews. The first wave of whites came to Texas before the break with Mexico. Encouraged by **empresarios** such as Moses Austin and his son Stephen F. Austin, who were authorized by the Spanish and later the Mexican leaders to bring people to Texas, these newcomers sought inexpensive land. But they brought along a new set of individualistic attitudes and values about democratic government that paved the way for the Texas Revolution. Following the revolution, a new surge of white immigrants came from the Deep South. Like their predecessors, they sought cheap land, but they brought with them new cultural baggage: slavery. By the time of the American Civil War, this group had come to dominate the political culture of the state. Although most Texas farmers did not own slaves themselves, the vast majority supported the institution as well as secession from the Union.

Defeat in the Civil War shattered temporarily the dominance of the traditional white power structure in the state. By the end of Reconstruction, however, it had reasserted itself, establishing the three patterns that defined Texas politics for the next hundred years: the one-party Democratic state, provincialism, and business dominance. Whites continued to dominate and define Texas's political culture throughout much of the twentieth century, but by the end of that century much had changed. As a percentage of the total, white population peaked at 74 percent in 1950. This percentage began to fall, reaching 42 percent in 2017, and will likely continue to fall (see Figure 1.5).[35]

Furthermore, numbers alone do not tell the whole story. Whites living in Texas in the early twenty-first century were not cut from the same cloth as those who had preceded them. A new wave of white immigration into Texas over the past 40 years has redefined the political culture of white Texans. No longer can one assume that a white Texan lives on a farm, holds culturally conservative values, and is firmly tied to the Democratic Party. On the contrary, he or she may not have been born in Texas and furthermore may be an urbanite with progressive values or a suburbanite who votes Republican.

empresario Spanish word for an individual who promotes, organizes, or helps to finance a particular endeavor

FIGURE 1.5

White Population in Texas Counties, 2014

SOURCE: QuickFacts, www.census.gov (accessed 6/21/16).

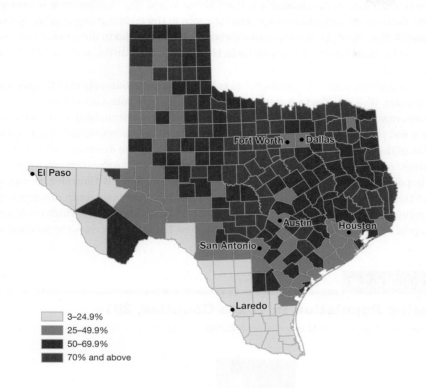

░	3–24.9%
▓	25–49.9%
▒	50–69.9%
■	70% and above

Latinos

The use of *Hispanic* and *Latino* can be confusing. The terms are often used interchangeably to refer to people of Spanish descent or people from Latin America. In asking about ethnic identity and reporting the results, the U.S. Census generally uses the term *Hispanic* in its databases, but we will generally use the term *Latino*.

Most Latinos in Texas are of Mexican descent.[36] Prior to independence from Spain, this group included people born of Iberian (Spanish) parents as well as mestizos (people of mixed Spanish and Native American ancestry). In the early nineteenth century, approximately 5,000 people of Mexican descent were living in Texas. Although their number fluctuated considerably over the years, by 1850 it was estimated that 14,000 Texans were of Mexican origin. Over the next 75 years, Texas became for many a refuge from the political and economic instability that troubled Mexico from the late 1850s to the 1920s. Subsequently, despite periodic attempts to curtail the growth of the Mexican American population in Texas, it grew from an estimated 700,000 in 1930 to 1,400,000 in 1960 and to 5.1 million in 2000. Immigration from other Latin American countries intensified as well. In 2015 there were 10.6 million Latinos residing in Texas, who constituted over 19 percent of all Latinos in the United States.[37]

Until 1900, Latinos were concentrated in south Texas, constituting a majority along the border with Mexico and in certain border counties of west Texas. During the first few decades of the twentieth century, many migrated to northwest Texas and the Panhandle to work as laborers in the newly emergent cotton economy. Labor segregation limited the opportunities available to them before World War II. After the war, however, many Latinos left agricultural work and took jobs in the rapidly growing urban areas of Texas. By the end of the century, Latinos constituted majorities in the cities of San Antonio and El Paso and sizable minorities in Houston, Dallas, Austin, and Fort Worth (see Figure 1.6).

The political status of Latinos in Texas has changed considerably over the past hundred years. Well into the twentieth century, their ability to vote, particularly among the lower economic classes, was tightly controlled or actively discouraged by the white primary and the **poll tax**. Only after World War II were Latino politicians able to escape some of the strictures that had been imposed on them by the dominant white political culture. A more tolerant atmosphere in urban areas enabled some to assume positions of importance in local political communities. In 1956, Henry B. Gonzalez became the first Mexican American elected to the Texas Senate since the nineteenth century. In the mid-1960s a political movement emerged in the La Raza Unida Party, which confronted many of the discriminatory practices that isolated Texas Latinos from the political and

poll tax a state tax imposed as a requirement for voting; poll taxes were rendered unconstitutional in national elections by the Twenty-Fourth Amendment, and in state elections by the U.S. Supreme Court in 1966

FIGURE 1.6

Latino Population in Texas Counties, 2014

SOURCE: QuickFacts, www.census.gov (accessed 6/21/16).

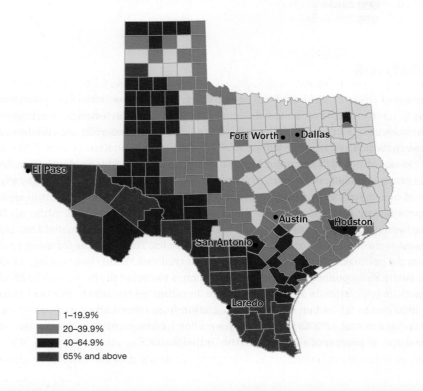

- 1–19.9%
- 20–39.9%
- 40–64.9%
- 65% and above

economic mainstream. By the 1980s, Latino political leaders were playing a growing role in state politics, and Latino voters were courted heavily by both political parties. The number of Latinos elected to public office rose from 1,466 in 1986 to 2,521 in 2011. In 2016 the National Association of Latino Elected and Appointed Officials reported that 1 Latino served in the U.S. Senate from Texas, 5 Latinos represented Texas in the U.S. House of Representatives, 7 Latinos were in the Texas Senate, and 35 Latinos were elected to the state legislature. In addition, the association reported that 2,477 Latinos served as local officials in Texas.[38]

African Americans

People of African descent were among the earliest explorers of Texas.[39] Most African Americans, however, entered Texas as slaves brought by whites from the upper and lower South. At first, antislavery attitudes among Spanish and Mexican authorities kept the slave population down. However, independence from Mexico lifted the restrictions on slavery, creating an incentive for southerners to expand the system westward. The number of slaves in Texas rose from 5,000 in 1845 to 58,000 in 1850. By the Civil War, over 182,000 slaves lived in Texas, approximately one-third of the state's entire population.

Emancipation for African Americans living in Texas came on June 19, 1865, a day now celebrated as "Juneteenth Day." Emancipation did not bring anything approaching equality. Between 1865 and 1868 both the state legislature and various cities passed a series of so-called Black Codes that restricted the rights of former slaves. But federal military occupation of the state and congressional reconstruction of its government opened new opportunities for former slaves, who supported the radical wing of the Republican Party. Ten African American delegates helped write the Texas Constitution of 1869, and 43 served in the state legislature between 1868 and 1900. The end of Reconstruction and the return to power of the Democratic Party in the mid-1870s, however, reversed much of the postwar progress made by black Texans. In 1900 over 100,000 African Americans voted in Texas elections. By 1903 the number had fallen to under 5,000, largely because of the imposition of the poll tax in 1902 and the passage of an early version of the white-primary law in 1903. In 1923 the legislature explicitly banned blacks from voting in the Democratic primary. Segregation of the races became a guiding principle of public policy, backed by the police power of the state and reinforced by lynching and race riots against African Americans. Between 1885 and 1942, 339 African Americans were lynched in Texas, with most lynchings taking place in the eastern portion of the state.[40] For all intents and purposes, African Americans had become second-class citizens, disenfranchised by the political system and marginalized by the political culture.

In the 1940s and 1950s federal court decisions offered some hope of relief to African Americans living in Texas. The U.S. Supreme Court decision in *Smith v. Allwright* (1944) outlawed the white primary. *Sweatt v. Painter* (1950) guaranteed African Americans admission to graduate and professional schools at state colleges and universities. Finally, *Brown v. Board of Education* (1954) outlawed the segregation of public schools.

Political progress was much slower. The Civil Rights Act of 1964 and the Voting Rights Act of 1965 helped to open the political system in Texas to African Americans, and in 1966 a small number of African American candidates began to win political office in the state. In 1972, Barbara Jordan became the first African American woman from Texas to be elected to the U.S. House of Representatives.

FIGURE 1.7

African American Population in Texas Counties, 2014

SOURCE: QuickFacts, www.census.gov (accessed 6/21/16).

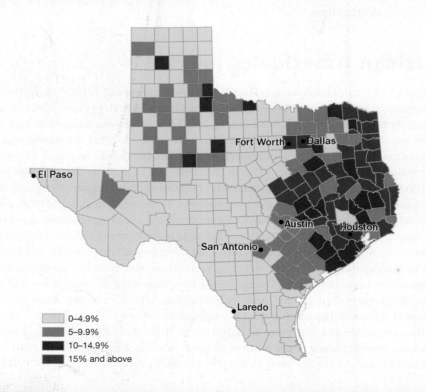

- 0–4.9%
- 5–9.9%
- 10–14.9%
- 15% and above

How Is the Texas Population Changing?

The face of Texas is changing rapidly and will continue to change well into the future. The figures below show projections of how the Texas population will change over the next 30 years. The state's population will continue to grow quickly, especially as the number of Latino Texans increases. Further, most of the population growth in the state will happen in metropolitan areas—Dallas–Fort Worth, Houston, San Antonio, and Austin.

Race and Total Population

= 250,000 people

	1980			2010			2050	
White	66%	Latino 21%	White	45%	Latino 38%	White	28%	Latino 54%
African American	12%	Other 1%	African American	12%	Other 6%	African American	10%	Other 8%

	1980	2010	2050
Total population =	14,229,191	25,145,561	41,311,221

Geography (projected population growth from the year 2010, by metropolitan area)

Area	2010	2020		2050	
San Antonio	2,142,508	2,481,286	+16%	3,445,603	+61%
El Paso	804,123	929,478	+16%	1,301,438	+62%
Dallas–Fort Worth	6,426,214	7,445,492	+16%	11,147,784	+73%
Houston	5,920,416	6,934,564	+17%	10,273,617	+74%
Brownsville	406,220	478,974	+18%	729,461	+80%
Austin	1,716,289	2,090,278	+22%	3,338,673	+95%
McAllen	774,769	953,069	+23%	1,589,783	+105%

SOURCES: Texas Demographic Center, demographics.texas.gov; (accessed 6/15/16).

NOTE: Numbers do not always add up to 100 percent due to rounding.

QUANTITATIVE REASONING

- Based on your reading of the data, how many Latinos were added to the state population between 1980 and 2010? How many whites? How is the projected 2050 population different from the population in 2010?

- Given the metropolitan population projections for 2020 and 2050, how might the balance of political power shift over the next 40 years?

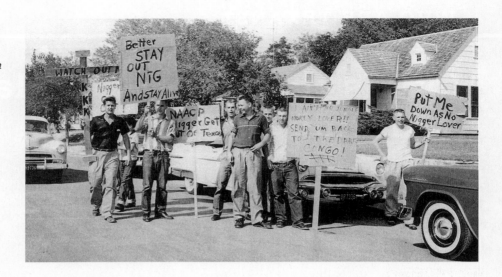

As in most former slave states, there was initial resistance to the civil rights movement in Texas. These signs appeared in Fort Worth's Riverside section in September 1956 during a protest over a black family's moving into a previously all-white block of homes.

The state's African American population remains concentrated in east Texas, where the plantation and sharecropping systems were dominant during the nineteenth century. Large numbers of African Americans have also migrated to Houston and Dallas, where they form sizable minorities in both central-city and suburban areas (see Figure 1.7). African American political leaders have come to play major roles in these areas as members of Congress, the state legislature, and city councils, as well as mayors of Houston and Dallas beginning in the late 1990s.

Asian Americans

Although considerably smaller than the groups already discussed, the Asian population has grown in Texas in recent years. It includes individuals from many countries, but particularly India, Vietnam, China, Pakistan, Korea, and Japan. In 2017 the U.S. Census Bureau estimated that over 1 million Asian Americans resided in Texas, or about 5 percent of the state's population.[41] Asian Americans tend to be concentrated in certain cities and their suburbs, particularly in west Houston and Fort Bend County, the western and northern suburbs of Dallas, Arlington, and Austin and its suburbs. Sizable pockets of Asian Americans also live along the Gulf Coast.[42]

Age

When compared with the rest of the nation, the population of Texas is younger. In 2017, 26 percent of the population was estimated to be under 18 years old, compared with 22.6 percent nationally. In addition, only 12.3 percent of Texans were 65 or older, compared with 15.6 percent nationally.[43] Its relatively young population presents Texas with a variety of both problems and opportunities, as we shall see in later chapters.

Poverty and Wealth

Younger populations tend to be poorer, as income and poverty statistics bear out. As noted above, even taking into account the Great Recession (2008–09), the late twentieth and early twenty-first centuries were a period of rapid economic growth in Texas. Although the state continued to lag slightly behind the nation as a whole, its per capita income rose from $17,366 in 1990 to $46,942 in 2017 (see Table 1.1). This was 93 percent of the national average per capita personal income of $50,393, ranking Texas at 25 among the 50 states.

The percentage of the population in Texas with incomes below the poverty level— as defined by the federal government—fell from 15.7 percent to 14.9 percent between 1990 and 2004 and rose to 17.2 percent in 2014. During the same period, the national poverty rate fell from 13.5 percent to 11.7 percent and rose to 14.8 percent in 2014.[44]

TABLE 1.1

Per Capita Personal Income in Texas and the United States

	1990	2000	2010	2017
United States	$19,611	$30,585	$39,366	$50,393
Texas	$17,366	$28,145	$37,896	$46,942

SOURCE: U.S. Department of Commerce, Bureau of Economic Analysis.

Urbanization

 Describe Texas's shift from a rural society to an urban one

Urbanization is the process by which people move from rural to urban areas. Suburbanization is the process by which people move out of central city areas to surrounding suburban areas. Much of Texas's history is linked to ongoing urbanization. By the twenty-first century, this process was largely complete, as 85 percent of the population now reside in urban areas (see Figure 1.8). Suburbanization, however, continues as city populations spill over into surrounding suburban areas.[45]

Most Texas cities are the result of American settlement and culture.[46] The Spanish influence on urban life in Texas grew out of efforts to extend territorial control northward out of Mexico through a series of presidios (garrisons), missions (churches), and pueblos (towns). The physical organization and planning of the towns reflected this imperial mission. For example, the largest Spanish settlement was San Antonio. Initially established as a supply depot to missions in east Texas, it later expanded as missions were established to convert local Native Americans to Roman Catholic Christianity and farms were cultivated to feed the local population. By the early nineteenth century, San

urbanization the process by which people move from rural to urban areas

FIGURE 1.8

Urbanization in Texas, 1850–2010

SOURCE: *Statistical Abstract of the United States: 1994* (Washington, D.C.: U.S. Department of Commerce. Bureau of the Census, 1994); Dallas Morning News, *Texas Almanac 2001–2002* (Dallas: Dallas Morning News, 2001); U.S. Department of Agriculture, Economic Research Service, U.S. Census Bureau, "Texas: 2010, Population and Housing Unit Courts, 2010 Census of Population and Housing" (September 2012), p. 16.

Antonio's population had reached 2,500. Other smaller settlements were located in east Texas, along the border with French and, later, American territory.

White American influence began with the arrival in 1820 in San Antonio of Moses Austin, soon followed by his son Stephen F. Austin. The Spanish offered the Austins and other empresarios grants of land to encourage the inflow of Americans into underpopulated regions of Texas. Small towns emerged as administrative units for impresario grants. There were considerably more economic and personal freedom (for whites) and dynamism in American urban areas than in Spanish ones. Americans brought with them a host of new cultural artifacts that would transform urban life in Texas, including a new language, slavery, Protestantism, and a commitment to free enterprise and democracy. The courthouse became a focal point of many American towns, often occupying a central location surrounded by shops.

Urbanization has transformed Texas political life. From Reconstruction through the first half of the twentieth century, Texas politics grew out of the state's rural-based economy centered on cotton, cattle, oil, and natural gas. The expansion of Texas's urban life began along the Gulf Coast and gradually moved west, particularly along rivers. New technologies played a key role in transforming the state's urban landscape. Dredging technologies stimulated the growth of port cities such as Houston, Galveston, Corpus Christi, and Brownsville, and railroad construction in the second half of the nineteenth century opened up new lands to regional and national markets as well as to economic development. In 1880 there were only 11 towns of 4,000 or more people in all of Texas. With the rapid expansion of the railroads in the 1880s and 1890s, the

SOCIAL RESPONSIBILITY: GET INVOLVED

• Based on the population growth, urbanization, and economic change of the last two decades, what do the next two decades hold for Texas? Which areas will grow in population, and will government be ready for that growth?

• If you wrote a letter to the governor or your state legislators, what advice would you give them to strengthen the Texas economy? Would you want them to focus on supporting rural or urban communities? Why?

How Does Texas's Population Compare to Other Major States'?

Texas is more diverse than many states in the country, which has important implications for the future of the state's politics. Also, the Texas population has increased dramatically, while some states are not growing as fast. In fact many states in the Midwest such as Ohio and Pennsylvania have seen population declines in recent years.

Racial Diversity

Texas		California		Florida		New York		Ohio	
White	44%	White	39%	White	56%	White	57%	White	80%
Black	13%	Black	7%	Black	17%	Black	18%	Black	13%
Latino	39%	Latino	39%	Latino	24%	Latino	19%	Latino	4%
Asian	4%	Asian	14%	Asian	3%	Asian	9%	Asian	2%

Percent Change in Population, 2000-2010

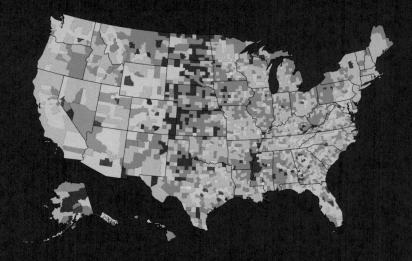

9.7%: overall U.S. change

Gain
- 50% +
- 25.1 to 49%
- 9.7 to 25%
- 0 to 9.6%
- -10 to -0.1%
- -50 to -10.1%

Loss

- Data not available

CRITICAL THINKING

- In what ways are California and Texas similar in terms of demographic makeup? How are they different?

- In what ways will Texas politics change in the future based on its racial and ethnic makeup?

SOURCES: U.S. Census Bureau, QuickFacts 2014, www.census.gov; demography.cpc.unc.edu.

NOTE: Numbers do not always add up to 100 percent. Black Latinos may be counted in both categories.

number rose to 36 by 1900. By 1910, when the railroad network of 13,110 miles was completed, Texas had 49 towns with a population of 4,000 or more. By 1920, 5 cities—Dallas, El Paso, Fort Worth, Houston, and San Antonio—had populations of more than 50,000. These population patterns would be reinforced by later technological breakthroughs in cars and air travel.

Urban Political Life

Understanding the complexity of the government and politics in Texas today demands having some sense of how Texas's major metropolitan areas compare with each other (see Table 1.2). We will look briefly at four of the most important.

Houston Houston, located in Harris County, is the largest city in Texas and—with a population of 2.3 million—the fourth-largest in the United States, behind New York, Los Angeles, and Chicago. Its metropolitan area encompasses eight counties, with an estimated population of 6.1 million in 2011. Houston grew by 7.5 percent during the first decade of the twenty-first century.

The city originated in 1836 out of the entrepreneurial dreams of two brothers, Augustus Chapman Allen and John Kirby Allen, who sought to create a "great interior commercial emporium of Texas."[47] It was named after Sam Houston, the leader of Texas's army during its war of independence from Mexico. Because its early settlers came from the South, bringing with them the institution of slavery, segregation was built into the social structure from the outset. For the first half of the twentieth century, African Americans were either denied or given limited access to a variety of public services such as parks, schools, buses, restrooms, and restaurants.

In the late nineteenth century, Houston's economic well-being depended on cotton and commerce. Railroads played an integral role in placing the city at the hub of the

TABLE 1.2

Race and Ethnic Breakdown of Texas and Its Largest Counties, 2017 (major cities indicated in parentheses)

	WHITE (%)	BLACK (%)	LATINO (%)	ASIAN (%)	MULTIPLE RACE (%)	TOTAL
Texas statewide	42.0%*	12.7%	39.4%	5.0%	2.0%	28,304,596
Harris (Houston)	29.7	19.7	43.0	7.3	1.9	4,652,980
Dallas (Dallas)	29.2	23.4	40.2	6.5	1.9	2,618,148
Tarrant (Fort Worth)	46.8	17.1	28.9	5.7	2.5	2,054,475
Bexar (San Antonio)	27.7	8.5	60.3	3.1	2.3	1,958,578
Travis (Austin)	49.0	8.9	33.9	7.1	2.6	1,226,698
Collin (Plano)	57.3	10.2	15.3	15.0	2.7	969,603
El Paso (El Paso)	11.8	3.9	82.8	1.3	1.5	840,410

*Columns may not add to 100 percent as a result of multiple counting. These are estimates projected from the 2017 Census.

SOURCE: 2017 U.S. Census Bureau.

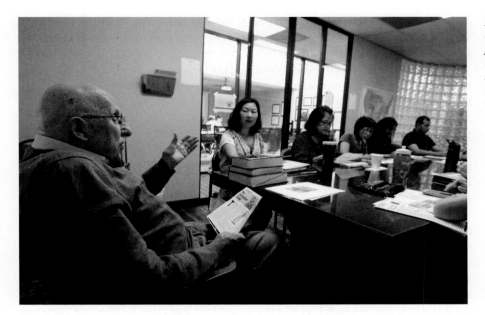

Texas economy, and the opening of the Houston Ship Channel further enhanced its position by helping to turn it into the second or third (depending on whose ranking is used) deep-water port in the United States. But it was oil that fundamentally transformed the Houston area in the twentieth century. Oil refineries opened along the ship channel and a petrochemical industry emerged, making Houston one of the leading energy centers in the world. Today, Houston continues to rank first in the nation in the manufacture of petroleum equipment.

By 1930, Houston had become the largest city in Texas, with a population of around 292,000 people. The population continued to expand in the next half century, assisted by a liberal state annexation policy that enabled the city to incorporate into itself many of the outlying suburban areas. Although the oil bust in the mid-1980s slowed the city's growth, that growth continued in the early twenty-first century.

Dallas–Fort Worth Metroplex The Metroplex is an economic region encompassing the cities of Dallas and Fort Worth as well as a number of their suburban cities, including Arlington (population 396,394 in 2017), Mesquite (143,949), Garland (238,002), Richardson (116,783), Irving (240,373), Plano (286,143), McKinney (181,330), Carrollton (135,710), Grand Prairie (193,837), Frisco (177,286), and Denton (136,268).[48] The major counties in the area are Dallas, Tarrant, and Collin. The Metroplex is joined together by a number of interlocking highways running north-south and east-west and by a major international airport strategically located in the national air system.

Dallas was founded as a trading post in 1841, near where two roads were to be built by the Republic.[49] By the 1850s it had become a retail center servicing surrounding rural areas, with a population that reached 3,000 by 1870. The coming of the Houston and Texas Central Railroad in 1871 and the Texas and Pacific Railroad in 1873 made Dallas the first rail crossroads in Texas and transformed forever its place in the state's economy. Markets now beckoned east and north, encouraging entrepreneurs and merchants to set up shop. As cotton became a major cash crop, the city's population more than tripled by 1880, to more than 10,000 people. By the turn of the twentieth century, Dallas had grown to more than 42,000 people.

As with Houston, the oil economy changed the direction and scope of the city's economic life. With the discovery of oil in east Texas in 1930, Dallas became a major center for petroleum financing. By the end of World War II, the economy had diversified, making Dallas a minor manufacturing center in the nation. In the 1950s and 1960s technology companies such as Ling-Temco-Vought (LTV) and Texas Instruments were added to the industrial mix, transforming Dallas into the third-largest technology center in the nation. The high-tech boom of the 1990s was built from the corporate infrastructure laid down in the 1950s and 1960s. Dallas grew from 844,401 people in 1970 to 1,341,075 in 2017.

Although locked together in important ways economically, Dallas and Fort Worth are as different as night and day. Whereas Dallas looks to the east and embodies a more corporate white-collar business culture, Fort Worth looks to the west. Fort Worth originated as an army post in 1849,[50] but by 1853 the military had abandoned it as new forts were built to the west. Although settlers replaced the soldiers, population growth was slow through the early 1870s. The spark that set off the town's prosperity was the rise of the cattle industry. Because Fort Worth was a convenient place for cowboys to rest on their cattle drives from southern Texas to Kansas, cattle buyers established headquarters in the city. By 1900, Fort Worth was served by eight railroad companies, most of them transporting cattle and related products to national markets.

The two world wars encouraged further economic development in Fort Worth. Over 100,000 troops were trained at Camp Bowie during World War I. World War II brought an important air force base and, along with it, the aviation industry. The Consolidated Vultee Aircraft Corporation, which was later bought by General Dynamics, became the largest manufacturer in the city. Between 1900 and 1950, Fort Worth's population grew from 26,668 to 277,047. By 2017 the population was 874,168. The overall metropolitan area of Dallas–Fort Worth included 6.954 million people in 2014.

San Antonio San Antonio, in Bexar County, grew out of the Spanish presidio San Antonio de Bexar, which was founded in 1718.[51] In 1773 it became the capital of Spanish Texas, with a population of around 2,100. Because of the threats posed by Native Americans and Mexicans after the Texas Revolution, this figure had declined to about 800 by 1846. On Texas's entry into the Union, however, the population took off, reaching 3,488 in 1850 and 8,235 in 1860. Immigrant groups from Germany added distinctive cultural (and language) styles to a rapidly expanding San Antonio. By the Civil War, San Antonio was the largest city in Texas.

Following the war, San Antonio continued to grow rapidly, stimulated by the building of the San Antonio Railroad in 1877. By 1880 the population was more than 20,000, mostly white Americans from southern states. By 1920 it had reached 161,000. Mexican immigration increased significantly following the Mexican Revolution of 1910 and the building of a city infrastructure that provided paved roads, utilities, water, telephones, and hospitals. By midcentury San Antonio had become a unique blend of Latino, German, and southern Anglo American cultures. Population growth slowed in the 1930s but picked up again during World War II, as major military bases came to dot the landscape around San Antonio. By 1950 the population topped 408,000, and by 1960 it topped 587,000.

Today, San Antonio is Texas's second-largest city (third if you consider Dallas and Fort Worth together). The population of the city was estimated to be 1,511,946 in 2017, and the metropolitan area had a population of 2,234,003 in 2014. San Antonio's population has become increasingly Latino. In Bexar County in 2017 approximately 60.3 percent of the people are Latino, 27.7 percent are white, and 8.5 percent are African American.[52]

Unlike Houston or Dallas, San Antonio lacks high-paying manufacturing jobs, and average metropolitan income is lower than in Houston and Dallas. The economy rests on four legs: national military bases, educational institutions, tourism, and a large medical research complex.

Austin Located in central Texas in Travis County on the eastern edge of the Hill Country, Austin had an estimated population of 950,715 in 2017. Demographically, Austin is 48 percent white, 35 percent Latino, 7 percent black, and 7 percent Asian. Per capita income is $39,103—40 percent higher than the state average. Median household income is $66,697—20 percent higher than the state amount. Almost half of adults living in Austin have a bachelor's degree or higher.[53] Along with Round Rock and San Marcos, Austin is part of the 31st largest metropolitan area in the country and 4th largest in the state (behind Houston, Dallas–Fort Worth, and San Antonio) with a population of 2,146,793.

Austin's economy rests on three solid foundations. First, as the state capital, Austin is the hub of governmental business in the state. Although the legislature only meets for 140 days every two years (and for special sessions when they are called) state agencies are a year-round activity as are the lobbying activities of special interests. Second, Austin is the location of the University of Texas at Austin, the flagship institution of the University of Texas system. Founded in 1883, UT Austin is today the home to more than 40,000 undergraduates, 11,000 graduate students, and 3,000 faculty members. In 2012–13, it was estimated that the school generated $8.8 billion in Texas business activity.[54] Third, Austin has a thriving high-tech industry. Grown from seeds planted by governmental and university activity, Austin's computer and electronics businesses are the core of one of the most vibrant regional economies in the country. Through them, the city continues to attract people and businesses at a remarkable pace.

The origins of Austin go back to the early years of the Republic.[55] Texas's capital moved five times in 1836 before Sam Houston settled on the city of Houston in 1837. However, Mirabeau Lamar, Texas's second president, wanted a site on the western frontier of the state, hoping that this new state capital would promote westward expansion. The Lamar administration settled on a site on the Colorado River near the hamlet of Waterloo. The Texas Congress convened in this location in November 1839, and Austin was incorporated by the Congress on December 27 of the same year. The population stood at 856, including 145 slaves and various foreign diplomatic representatives.

All was not well for the fledgling city. Sam Houston, who returned to the president's office following Lamar, felt that Austin was not a safe place for the national archives because of tensions with Mexico. He moved the capital back to Houston and then to Washington-on-the-Brazos until 1845. A fight broke out with Austin residents as Governor Houston tried to have the archives moved out of Austin (the so-called Archives War).[56] Chronic political instability and uncertainty caused the population of Austin to fall to below 200 by 1845. Annexation by the United States in 1845, however, turned Austin's fortunes around, and on February 19, 1846, the day Texas transitioned from nationhood to statehood, Austin became the permanent capital of the state.

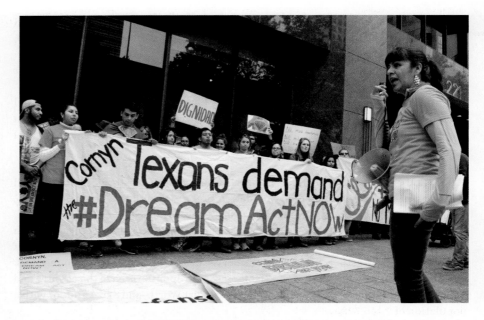

Urban areas like Austin, Houston, and Dallas have become bastions of liberal politics. Here, protesters rally in support of immigrant rights outside U.S. Senator John Cornyn's office in Austin.

Having settled its status as the government hub in the state, Austin began to gradually grow, reaching a population of 3,546 in 1860. The emergence of the Houston and Texas Central Railroad in 1871 linked Austin to the eastern part of the state and turned it into a trading center in central Texas. By 1880 the city's population had grown to 11,013.

Two events in the 1880s proved to be important benchmarks for Austin's future. First, Austin was selected in 1881 to be the site of the "Main University" for the state. Buildings were constructed in 1882, and the University of Texas opened on September 15, 1883. Although the University of Texas remained small for many years, the discovery of oil on university lands in west Texas in 1923 led to a financial windfall in the university's endowment, which fueled building construction in the city for decades. Second, in 1888 a new capitol was built in the center of Austin. Along with the university, the capitol would be the axis around which urban life in Austin would revolve.

Compared to Dallas–Fort Worth or Houston, Austin's economic base was narrow for the early decades of the twentieth century. Except for the benefits gleaned from the university's endowment, Austin missed out on much of the economic development flowing from the rise of oil and gas production. The population of the city was 22,258 in 1900, growing to 53,120 in 1930 and to 132,459 in 1950.[57] Austin's population began to surge in the second half of the twentieth century, growing to 186,5454 in 1960, to 345,890 in 1980, and to 656,962 in 2000. Driving this increase was a rapidly diversifying economy led by the high-tech sector. IBM located to Austin in 1969 and was soon followed by Texas Instruments (1969) and Motorola (1967). Other high-tech firms followed in the 1980s, including Dell Computers and Sematech. By the 1990s there were estimated to be 400 high-technology businesses located in Austin.[58]

In 2017, Austin's 100 largest digital tech companies employed almost 60,000 people, an 11 percent increase over 2016. The top three companies were Dell (13,000 employees), Apple (6,000), and IBM (5,416). Twenty-three of Austin's top 100 tech companies were launched within the last decade. Amazon and Facebook have increased their presence in the city with plans to expand.[59] Even though some experts believe that growth in Austin may be easing in 2017, most believe that the city's regional economy is strong.[60]

Immigration in Texas

IMMIGRATION has long been an important part of Texas culture. After the terrorist attacks of September 11, 2001, the U.S.–Mexico border tightened considerably. Traditionally, residents of areas near the border could cross it easily, but with increasing security concerns, crossings have become more difficult. The Paso del Norte bridge between El Paso and Ciudad Juarez (shown at right), the busiest cross-border footpath between the United States and Mexico, is one of several official international bridges in the state. One of Texas's ongoing debates is over the most effective ways to ensure border security while respecting the cultural diversity of the state.

In the 2014 campaign for lieutenant governor, Houston state senator Dan Patrick campaigned on a platform of stopping the "illegal invasion" of immigrants into Texas by spending more state money on border security. Patrick claimed that the federal government was not enforcing border security adequately and that illegal immigration had brought third-world diseases into the state.

In a debate between Patrick and then–San Antonio mayor Julián Castro about immigration reform, Castro accused Patrick of dog whistle politics, that is, using language that appealed indirectly to racism. Castro argued that there was no "invasion" of immigrants, that illegal immigration had dropped from its peak levels, and that undocumented immigrants were essential to the state's economy and should be allowed a path to citizenship, especially those in college or the military.

Patrick disagreed, arguing that those in the country illegally should go to the "back of the line" for legal immigration and wait their turns. He also suggested that granting "amnesty"—the opportunity to eventually become U.S. citizens—to illegal immigrants would only encourage more illegal immigration, which would strain the state budget on education and health care. In addition, Patrick opposed letting undocumented immigrants pay in-state tuition rates at state colleges, arguing that citizens should be given the priority.

The debate in Texas mirrors the national debate regarding how best to deal with immigration. There are approximately 11 million undocumented or "illegal" immigrants in the United States, and about 2 million of those immigrants are in Texas, mostly of Latino descent and mostly from Mexico.

The policies of the Trump administration have only intensified the issues raised in the debate between Patrick and Castro. Some claim Patrick's views will drive the growing Latino population away from the Republican Party because the harsh anti-immigrant rhetoric is perceived as anti-Latino. Patrick maintained that he supports legal immigration and just wants to stop illegal immigration. Castro and others have argued that the United States is a nation of immigrants and that there must be a comprehensive way to reform the immigration system. They say that businesses in Texas greatly benefit from the hard work of undocumented immigrants and that as long as jobs are available, immigrants will find a way to make it to the United States despite expensive border security efforts.

COMMUNICATING EFFECTIVELY: YOUR VOICE

- Do you agree with Dan Patrick or Julián Castro? Should illegal immigrants be given a pathway to citizenship or be sent back to their country of origin?

- Is compromise possible on immigration? Are the only two options deportations and amnesty? If you had to suggest a third option, what would it be?

★ ★

Political Culture and the Future of Texas

IN THIS CHAPTER we have studied the political culture of Texas and seen how the state has been transformed by economic and demographic shifts over the past hundred years. Three great technological revolutions have in turn reshaped the economic life of the state. Accompanying and fueling these economic transformations have been ongoing demographic changes, which have redefined who the "typical" Texan is and where this person lives. No longer can it be said that a "typical" Texan is simply an extension of white American culture rooted in southern tradition. No longer does this person reside in a small town, living life close to the land much as his or her ancestors did. Like the economy, the people of Texas have become diversified. Increasing numbers of Latinos from Mexico and farther south and whites from other parts of the United States as well as immigrants from Asia have created a new melting pot of cultures and concerns throughout the state, especially in the big metropolitan areas.

The future of Texas likely will continue to be defined by the economic and demographic changes that we have chronicled in this chapter. For almost 40 years, a diversifying economy fueled by international trade and a rejuvenated oil and natural gas industry has integrated the state more closely into a burgeoning world economy. President Trump's call to reevaluate international trade agreements, particularly NAFTA, and to rethink our trade relationship with China may negatively affect Texas's connection to the world economy. However, it is hard to imagine Texas in the twenty-first century without a thriving export-driven economy. Similarly, calls to build a wall to keep out undocumented workers may slow down the flow of Latinos into Texas, but it is hard to imagine Texas without a growing population fueled by loose immigration rules. Trump's initiatives aside, Latinos will come to play an increasingly important role in the economic and political life of the state as the Latino population ages and works its way through the educational system. Over the next 30 years, both political parties will have to adjust their expectations and ideologies to meet the demands of an electorate increasingly dominated by young Latino voters. ★

STUDY GUIDE

Use 🐰 INQUIZITIVE to help you study and master this material.

Texas Political Culture

> • Describe the defining characteristics of political culture in Texas (pp. 5–7)

Texas political culture can best be characterized as individualistic and traditional. Texans have great pride in their state and have adopted a famous phrase, "Don't mess with Texas," for those external forces wishing to change the state's way of doing things. Texas is a low-tax state with distrust for large government programs. Business plays a major role in defining the political culture of the state.

Key Terms
political culture (p. 5)
"traditionalistic individualistic" political culture (p. 5)
provincialism (p. 6)

Practice Quiz

1. In terms of area, how does Texas rank among the 50 states?
   a) first
   b) second
   c) third
   d) fifth
   e) seventh

2. *Provincialism* refers to
   a) a narrow view of the world.
   b) a progressive view of the value of diversity.
   c) a pro-business political culture.
   d) an urban society.
   e) a group of counties.

The Land

> • Explain how Texas's geography has influenced its political culture (pp. 7–10)

Because of Texas's immense size, the state's topography is diverse, with east Texas's flatlands, west Texas's arid climate, and central Texas's Hill Country all representing diverse ecosystems and land patterns.

Key Term
privatization of public property (p. 7)

Practice Quiz

3. Which of Texas's physical regions is characterized by the presence of many of the state's largest ranches?
   a) Gulf Coastal Plains
   b) Great Plains
   c) Interior Lowlands
   d) Basin and Range Province
   e) Rio Grande Valley

4. Which of Texas's physical regions is found in the westernmost part of Texas?
   a) Gulf Coastal Plains
   b) Great Plains
   c) Interior Lowlands
   d) Basin and Range Province
   e) Pine Belt

Economic Change in Texas

• Trace the evolution of Texas's economy
  (pp. 11–22)

The Texas economy has undergone a series of techno-logical transformations over the past 100 years. Once, the Texas economy was grounded in cotton and ranching. Oil production came to play an important role in the twen-tieth century. Today, high technology and international trade play important roles in the state's economy. Texas appears to have weathered the Great Recession better than most other states.

Key Term
North American Free Trade Agreement (NAFTA) (p. 17)

Practice Quiz
5. Creative destruction
   a) destroys both old and new economies.
   b) creates new economies and destroys old ones.
   c) maintains old economies and creates new ones.
   d) creates and maintains old and new economies.
   e) does not affect economies.

6. Which industry controlled the politics and economy of Texas for most of the twentieth century?
   a) cotton
   b) cattle
   c) railroad
   d) oil
   e) technology

7. Which of the following statements is true?
   a) Oil production in Texas is less today than it was 10 years ago.
   b) Oil production no longer plays an important role in the state's economy.
   c) Oil has been almost totally drained from Texas oil fields.
   d) The border region has become a major producer of oil in the early twenty-first century.
   e) Fracking and horizontal drilling have reinvigo-rated Texas's oil industry.

8. Unlike earlier eras, the Texas economy of the twenty-first century features
   a) computers, electronics, and other high-tech products.
   b) transportation, oil and natural gas, and banking.
   c) insurance, construction, and banking.
   d) ranching, oil, and tourism.
   e) education, the military, and agriculture.

9. NAFTA refers to
   a) an oil company.
   b) an independent regulatory commission.
   c) an interstate road network.
   d) an interest group.
   e) an international trade agreement.

10. What is meant by the "Great Recession"?
   a) the post–Vietnam War era in the mid-1970s when housing prices rose
   b) the period of high inflation during the early 1980s
   c) a time of chronic economic problems beginning in late 2007 that drew analogies to the Great Depression of the 1930s
   d) the time when Democrats lost control of the Texas House for the first time since Reconstruction
   e) a period of high unemployment in the early 1990s

The People of Texas

- **Explain how the population of Texas has changed over time (pp. 22–31)**

Texas demography has changed over the last century. Once dominated by whites, Texas now has a large Latino population that, when combined with the African American population and other minorities, makes Texas a majority-minority state. Despite considerable overall wealth in Texas, Texans tend to be younger and poorer than the average American.

Key Terms
empresario (p. 24)
poll tax (p. 26)

Practice Quiz

11. Which of the following accounts for most of Texas's population growth today?
- **a)** immigration
- **b)** natural increases as a result of the difference between births and deaths
- **c)** domestic immigration
- **d)** NAFTA
- **e)** movement from rural to urban areas

12. Which of the following is not true?
- **a)** Latinos are increasing as a percentage of the population in Dallas.
- **b)** More African Americans live in east Texas than in west Texas.
- **c)** San Antonio has a larger white population than Latino.
- **d)** Houston's largest minority population is Latino.
- **e)** The Latino population in Texas has grown rapidly in recent decades.

Urbanization

- **Describe Texas's shift from a rural society to an urban one (pp. 31–39)**

Initially a rural state, Texas has urbanized, with Houston, San Antonio, Dallas–Fort Worth, and Austin representing the largest metropolitan areas in the state. This process of urbanization has changed the state's economy from an agricultural powerhouse to a high-tech and innovative economy.

Key Term
urbanization (p. 31)

Practice Quiz

13. *Urbanization* refers to a process in which
- **a)** people move from rural to urban areas.
- **b)** people from the north and west move to Texas.
- **c)** people move out of urban centers to the suburbs.
- **d)** people move out of urban centers to rural areas.
- **e)** minorities assume political control of a city.

14. The four major metropolitan areas in Texas are
- **a)** Houston, Dallas–Fort Worth, San Antonio, and Austin.
- **b)** Houston, Dallas–Fort Worth, San Antonio, and El Paso.
- **c)** El Paso, Houston, Lubbock, and Austin.
- **d)** San Antonio, El Paso, Houston, and Brownsville-Harlingen-McAllen.
- **e)** San Antonio, El Paso, Dallas–Fort Worth, and Brownsville-Harlingen-McAllen.

The Texas Constitution has become a long and detailed document. Texans vote on constitutional amendments every two years, and most amendments pass.

The Texas Constitution

WHY THE TEXAS CONSTITUTION MATTERS The Texas Constitution is the legal framework within which government works in Texas, just as the U.S Constitution is the legal framework for our national institutions. Perhaps even more than the U.S. Constitution, however, the Texas Constitution has an immediate and enormous impact on citizens' everyday lives. Its Article 1 guarantees to Texans rights that go far beyond those guaranteed to Americans in the U.S. Constitution, addressing numerous specific issues related to Texans' private lives. For example, Article 1, Section 7, stipulates that no money will be appropriated or drawn from the treasury that benefits a sect, religious society, or religious seminary. Section 7 also clearly lists the conditions that the state must meet if it wants to take, damage, or destroy the private property of individuals. Section 30 provides a detailed list of the rights of crime victims, including the rights to be treated with dignity and privacy in the criminal process and to confer with representatives of the prosecutor's office. Section 31—now rendered inoperable by a U.S. Supreme Court decision in 2015—defines a marriage as consisting "only of the union of one man and one woman." Section 33 guarantees Texans a right to access and use public beaches. One could argue that each of these issues is more a matter of policy preference than of constitutional right. By being placed in the Texas Constitution, however, particular policy positions take on a protected status, because it is more difficult to change a right enshrined in a constitution than a policy backed only by ordinary, or statutory, law.

Given the length and detail of the Texas Constitution, the constitutional amendment process assumes a central role in the state's political process. There are some important differences between processes for amending the Texas Constitution and the U.S. Constitution. For example, voter approval is necessary for proposed amendments to the Texas Constitution to take effect. After passage during a regular or special session, the Texas legislature presents to the voters a list of proposed amendments for their approval. Whereas the U.S. Constitution has been amended 27 times since it was adopted in 1789, as of 2017 the Texas Constitution has been amended 498 times. The number of proposed amendments and their frequency of approval has varied over the years, although recently most have been approved. In 2013, nine amendments were proposed and passed; in 2014, one amendment was passed; and in 2015 and again in 2017, seven were put before the electorate and approved.

Occasionally, amendments deal with structural issues of government. In 1979, for example, an amendment gave the governor limited authority to remove appointed statewide officials. A 1995 amendment abolished the office of the state treasurer, placing its duties in the Texas Comptroller's Office. In such cases, amendments to the Texas Constitution function like those to the U.S. Constitution. There are many more amendments, however, that deal with technical problems in the Texas constitution, reflecting efforts to clean up specific language that has become out of date. In 2007, for example, an amendment passed that eliminated the county Office of the Inspector of Hides and Animals.[1] Although the office had been effectively abolished with the passage of a new Agricultural Code in statutory law,[2] the constitution needed to be brought up to date with the law. In 2013, Proposition 2 eliminated language relating to a State Medical and Education Board and a State Medical Education Fund, neither of which was operational.

Other amendments to the Texas Constitution grapple with pressing policy matters, and thus the electorate is asked to give its approval of certain policy initiatives directly, something that is inconceivable at the national level. In 2009 amendments were passed protecting certain private property from being taken by the state through eminent domain. In 2011 the Texas Water Development Board was allowed to issue bonds so that loans could be given to local governments for water projects. Among the amendments passed in 2013 and 2015 were ones creating funds to help finance important water and transportation projects. Without the passage of these amendments by the electorate, effective public policy in a variety of areas central to the future of Texas would have ground to a halt. While nothing as important as water or transportation project funding was proposed for voter approval in 2017, seven constitutional amendments were approved in November 2017. Far more than the U.S. Constitution, the Texas Constitution is involved with the nuts and bolts of public policy and must be taken into account frequently by Texas legislators seeking to address problems in new and innovative ways.

CHAPTER GOALS

- Identify the main functions of state constitutions (pp. 47–49)
- Describe the seven Texas constitutions and their role in Texas political life (pp. 49–64)
- Analyze the major provisions of the Texas Constitution today (pp. 64–73)
- Describe modern efforts to change the Texas Constitution (pp. 73–80)

The Role of a State Constitution

State **constitutions** perform a number of important functions. They justify and make legitimate state political institutions by clearly explaining the source of their power and authority. State constitutions also delegate power, explaining which political powers are granted to particular institutions and individuals and how those powers are to be used. They also are responsible for the establishment of local governments, including counties, municipalities, and special-purpose districts. They prevent the concentration of political power by providing mechanisms that check and balance the powers of one political institution or individual officeholder against another. Finally, they define the limits of political power. Through declarations of rights, state constitutions explicitly forbid the intrusion of certain kinds of governmental activities into the lives of individuals.

> **constitution** the legal structure of a government, which establishes its power and authority as well as the limits on that power

The idea of constitutional government in Texas since its first constitution has been heavily indebted to the larger American experience. Five ideas unite the U.S. and Texas constitutional experiences. First, political power in both the United States and Texas is ultimately derived from the people. The Preamble to the U.S. Constitution begins with the clear assertion that it is "We the People of the United States" who ordain and establish the Constitution. Echoing these sentiments, the Preamble to the Texas Constitution proclaims that "the People of the State of Texas, do ordain and establish this Constitution." In both documents, political power is something that is artificially created through the constitution by a conscious act of the people.

Second, the U.S. and Texas constitutions feature **separation of powers**. The legislative, executive, and judicial branches of government have their own unique powers derived from the people. Each branch has its corresponding duties and obligations.

> **separation of powers** the division of governmental power among several institutions that must cooperate in decision making

Third, the U.S. and Texas constitutions structure political power in such a way that the power of one branch is checked and balanced by the powers of the other two branches. The idea of **checks and balances** reflects a common concern among the framers of the U.S. Constitution and the authors of Texas's various constitutions that the intent of writing a constitution was not just to establish effective governing institutions but also to ensure that these institutions would not tyrannize the very people who established them. In this theory of checks and balances, both the U.S. and Texas constitutions embody the ideas articulated by James Madison in *The Federalist Papers*, nos. 10, 47, and 51. There, Madison argued that one of the most effective ways of preventing **tyranny** (the concentration of power in one branch of government) was to pit the self-interest of officeholders in one branch against that of officeholders in the other branches. Good intentions alone would not guarantee liberty in either the United States or Texas. Rather, constitutional means combined with self-interest would ensure that officeholders had an interest in preserving a balance among the different branches of government.

> **checks and balances** the constitutional idea that overlapping power is given to different branches of government to limit the concentration of power in any one branch

> **tyranny** according to James Madison, the concentration of power in any one branch of government

The concern for preventing the emergence of tyranny is also found in a fourth idea that underlies the U.S. and Texas constitutions: the idea of individual rights. Government is explicitly forbidden from violating a number of particular rights that the people possess. Some rights, such as freedom of speech, freedom of assembly, and freedom of religion, are guaranteed by both the U.S. Constitution and the Texas Constitution. Interestingly, the Texas Constitution also guarantees other rights not found in the U.S. Constitution, such as certain victims' rights and the right to have an "efficient system of public free schools."

federalism a system of government in which power is divided, by a constitution, between a central government and regional governments

The final idea embodied in both the U.S. and Texas constitutions is that of **federalism**, the division of government into a central government and a group of regional governments (see Chapter 3). Both kinds of government exercise direct authority over individual citizens, of both the nation or state and a particular region within it. The Tenth Amendment to the U.S. Constitution also recognizes the importance of the idea of federalism to the American political system. It reads, "The powers not delegated to the United States by the Constitution, nor prohibited by it to the States, are reserved to the States respectively, or to the people." According to the U.S. Constitution, enormous reservoirs of political power are thus derived from the people who reside in the states themselves.

supremacy clause Article VI of the U.S. Constitution, which states that the Constitution and laws passed by the national government and all treaties are the supreme law of the land and superior to all laws adopted by any state or any subdivision

However, some important differences distinguish the constitutional experience of Texas from that of the United States. Most important is the subordinate role that Texas has in the federal system. Article VI of the U.S. Constitution contains the **supremacy clause**, declaring the Constitution and the laws of the United States to be "the supreme Law of the Land." The supremacy clause requires all judges in every state to be bound by the U.S. Constitution, notwithstanding the laws or constitution of their particular state. In matters of disagreement, the U.S. Constitution thus takes precedence over the Texas Constitution.

One of the major issues of the Civil War was how the federal system was to be understood. Was the United States a confederation of autonomous sovereign states that were ultimately independent political entities capable of secession (much like the current European Union)? Or was it a perpetual union of states that were ultimately in a subordinate relationship to the central government? The results of the war and the ratification of the Fourteenth Amendment to the U.S. Constitution in 1868 ultimately resolved this debate in terms of the latter idea, an outcome that would have profound implications for constitutional government in Texas. A series of court cases determined that because of the language of the Fourteenth Amendment, much of the Bill of Rights to the U.S. Constitution applies to the states, a finding that became a dominant theme of constitutional law in the twentieth and twenty-first centuries. The Fourteenth Amendment thus effectively placed restrictions on Texas government and public policy that went far beyond those laid out in Texas's own constitution.

necessary and proper clause Article I, Section 8, of the U.S. Constitution; it provides Congress with the authority to make all laws "necessary and proper" to carry out its powers

Another major difference between the U.S. and Texas constitutions lies in the **necessary and proper clause** of Article I, Section 8, of the U.S. Constitution. Section 8 begins by listing in detail the specific powers granted to Congress by the Constitution. The Founders apparently wanted to limit the scope of national government activities. But Section 8 concludes by granting Congress the power "necessary and proper" to accomplish its constitutional tasks. The net effect of this clause was to provide a constitutional basis for an enormous expansion of central government activities over the next 200-plus years.

Drafters of Texas's various constitutions generally have been unwilling to grant such an enormous loophole in the exercise of governmental power. Although granting state government the power to accomplish certain tasks, Texas constitutions have generally denied officeholders broad grants of discretionary power to accomplish their goals.

Finally, Texas's power to establish local governments has no analogous feature in the U.S. Constitution. States such as Texas are sovereign entities unto themselves, deriving power directly from the people in the state through the state constitution. Texas is not created by the U.S. Constitution, although it is subject to it, as we shall see in Chapter 3. Local governments within Texas, on the other hand, derive their authority directly from the state constitution and the people of Texas as a whole, not from the people in the locality. Self-government for local governing bodies in Texas ultimately means self-government to the extent allowed by the Texas legislature under the state constitution.

The Texas Constitutions: 1836–1876

 Describe the seven Texas constitutions and their role in Texas political life

Many myths surround the origins of Texas as a state. Some trumpet its unique origins as an independent republic that fought to attain its own independence from an oppressive regime much like the United States did. Others suggest that Texas has a certain privileged position as a state given the way that it entered the Union or that it reserved for itself a right to break up into separate states or even to leave the Union. To separate the myth from the reality, it is necessary to understand how the constitutional regime operating in Texas today is the product of a long course of political and legal development in the state.

Texas has operated under seven constitutions: one when it was part of a state under the Mexican political regime prior to independence, one as an independent republic, one as a member of the Confederacy, and four as a state within the United States. Each was shaped by historical developments of its time and, following the first constitution, attempted to address the shortcomings of each previous constitution. To understand constitutional government in Texas today demands a clear understanding of the founding of Texas out of its war of independence with Mexico and the specific historical circumstances that gave rise to each constitution.

The Texas Founding

Political scientists refer to "the Founding" as that period in American history when the foundational principles of American political life were established, roughly the period of time from the Declaration of Independence in 1776 through the ratification of the Constitution (1790) and the Bill of Rights (1791). Texas too has a founding period, but one that is much longer and more convoluted.

On the face of it, Texas's road to independence appears to mirror that of the United States. Like the United States, Texas had a period of discontent with the governing regime that culminated in a Declaration of Independence. This document cataloged grievances against Mexico and announced the establishment of a new Republic of Texas.

But whereas Britain in the mid-eighteenth century was a stable and powerful empire, Mexico in the early nineteenth century was not. Mexico had only recently freed itself from Spain and was experiencing a lengthy period of domestic turmoil. In addition, while the American colonies had effectively been self-governing entities before their Declaration of Independence, Texas had never achieved such a status. The Texas Founding encompassed a number of phases of constitutional government, stretching from 1836, when Texas declared itself an independent republic, to 1876, when Reconstruction after the Civil War came to an end and a new (Texas's current) state constitution was put into place.

The Constitution of Coahuila y Tejas, 1827

Texas was part of New Spain until the Mexican War of Independence,[3] which grew out of a series of revolts against Spanish rule during the Napoleonic Wars. Burdened by debts brought on by a crippling war with France, Spain sought to extract more wealth from its colonies. The forced abdication of King Ferdinand VII in favor of Napoleon's brother Joseph in 1808 and an intensifying economic crisis in New Spain in 1809 and 1810 undermined the legitimacy of Spanish rule. Revolts broke out in Guanajuato and spread throughout Mexico, including its Texas province. Although these rebellions were initially put down by royalist forces loyal to Spain, by 1820 additional local revolts and guerrilla actions had helped to further weaken Spanish rule. On August 24, 1821, Mexico was formally granted independence by Spain.

The first federal constitution that Texas operated under was thus the Mexican Constitution of 1824. At the national level, it provided for two houses of Congress, a president and vice president elected for four-year terms by the legislative bodies of the states, and a supreme court. Although the Mexican Constitution mandated separate legislative, executive, and judicial branches, no attempt was made to define the scope of states' rights within the Mexican confederation, and local affairs remained independent of the central government. This constitution embodied many of the ideas found in the U.S. Constitution, but there was one important difference: Catholicism was established as the state religion and was supported financially by the state.[4]

Under the Mexican Constitution, the state of Coahuila and the sparsely populated province of Texas were combined into the state of Coahuila y Tejas, with Saltillo, in Coahuila, as the capital. More than two years were spent drafting a constitution for the new state. It was finally published on March 11, 1827.

The state of Coahuila y Tejas was formally divided into three districts, with Texas composing the District of Bexar. Legislative power for the state was placed in a **unicameral** legislature composed of 12 deputies elected by the people, including 2 representing Bexar. Along with wide-ranging legislative powers, the legislature was also empowered to elect state officials when no majority emerged from the popular vote, to serve as a grand jury in political and military matters, and to regulate the state's army and militia. Executive power was vested in a governor and a vice governor, each elected by the people for a four-year term. Judicial power was placed in state courts. The Constitution of 1827 formally guaranteed citizens the right to liberty, security, property, and equality. Its language also supported efforts to curtail the spread of slavery, an institution of vital importance to planters who were immigrating from the American South. The legislature was ordered to promote education and freedom of the press. As in the Mexican federal constitution, Catholicism was the established state religion.[5]

unicameral comprising one body or house, as in a one-house legislature

Political instability in Mexico in the late 1820s and early 1830s largely undercut the provisions and protections of both the federal and the state constitutions under which Texans lived. But these constitutions were important to political debate at the time as discontent against the central government built up. At least in the early stages of the Texas rebellion against Mexico, many Texans could, and did, see themselves as defending these constitutions and most of the political principles that they represented. The turn away from defending the Mexican Constitution of 1824 and the state constitution of 1827 to articulating a new constitutional regime relying more on American political and cultural values was a fundamental step on the road to independence for Texas.

The Constitution of the Republic of Texas, 1836

Texas's break with Mexico was in large part a constitutional crisis that culminated in separation. Americans had come to Texas for a variety of reasons. Some, like Stephen F. Austin, had come in the service of the Mexican state as *empresarios*, whose goal was to encourage American immigration into Texas by distributing land made available by the Mexican government. They saw themselves as Mexican citizens working with the constitutional regime of 1827. Americans who had come to Texas in the early 1830s still wanted the land and economic opportunities offered by Texas, but they, as part of America's move westward, were far less committed to integrating themselves into the Mexican political community. For these people, separation from Mexico, either as an independent republic or as part of the United States, was the ultimate political objective.

Recognizing the dangers to Mexican authority from Americans coming into Texas, Mexican officials made various attempts to limit the influx. These restrictions, along with other grievances, led to growing discontent among Texans over their place in the Mexican federal system. Ultimately, Texans called for political conventions in 1832 and 1833 to discuss new constitutional forms of government. Along with demands for a more liberal immigration policy for people from the United States and for the establishment of English- and Spanish-speaking primary schools, calls for separate statehood for Texas emerged from the conventions. The 1833 convention actually drafted a constitution and sent Stephen F. Austin to Mexico City to petition the central government for reform. Austin's mission failed and led to his imprisonment, which in turn pushed Texas closer to open rebellion.

On November 7, 1835, a meeting of Texas political leaders at San Felipe adopted a declaration stating the reasons Texans were beginning to take up arms against the Mexican government. The declaration proclaimed that Texas was rising up in defense of its rights and liberties as well as the republican principles articulated in the Mexican Constitution of 1824. But though it was one thing to call for a defense of republican principles under the Mexican Constitution of 1824, it was something else to call for separation from Mexico. In the end, the declaration was but a prelude to the formal Texas Declaration of Independence that emerged out of the Convention of 1836 held at Washington-on-the-Brazos.

Of the 59 delegates attending the Convention of 1836, only 10 had lived in Texas prior to 1830, and 2 had arrived as late as 1836. Two thirds of the delegates—39—were from southern slave states, 6 were from the border state of Kentucky, 7 were from northern states, 3 were from Mexico (including 2 born in Texas), and 4 were from other English-speaking lands.[6] The final products of the convention—the Texas Declaration of Independence and the Constitution of 1836—reflected the interests and values of these participants.

In their own Declaration of Independence, delegates to the convention proclaimed that the federal constitutional regime they had been invited to live under by the rulers of Mexico had been replaced by a military tyranny that combined a "despotism of the sword and the priesthood." Echoing the American Declaration of Independence, they presented a long list of grievances against the central government, including the failure to provide freedom of religion, a system of public education, and trial by jury.

The Texas Declaration of Independence Like the Founders during the American Revolution, leaders of the Texas Revolution felt they needed to justify their actions in print. Written by George C. Childress and adopted by the general convention at Washington-on-the-Brazos on March 2, 1836, the Texas Declaration of Independence stated why the signers believed it was necessary to separate from Mexico and create an independent republic (see Appendix, pp. A1–A3). Not surprisingly, the document draws heavily on the ideas of John Locke and Thomas Jefferson for inspiration. The description of the role of the government, "to protect the lives, liberty, and property of the people," repeated verbatim Locke's litany of the primary reasons for establishing government. And like Jefferson's Declaration, Texas's declaration catalogs a list of grievances against the Mexican regime. According to Texas's declaration, the existing government had abdicated its duties to protect the governed and had broken the trustee relationship that binds a people to those in authority. By dissolving civil society into its original elements, the government had forced the people to assert their inalienable right of self-preservation and to take political affairs into their own hands again. The "melancholy conclusion" of Texas's declaration echoed ideas that Locke and Jefferson would have understood well: any government that stripped a people of their liberty was unacceptable to those raised on principles of self-government. Self-preservation demanded "eternal political separation" from the very state (Mexico) that had invited them to settle in Texas (see Figure 2.1).

After declaring Texas a separate republic independent from Mexico, the convention proceeded to draft and pass a new constitution reflecting these republican sentiments. Resembling the U.S. Constitution in being brief (fewer than 6,500 words) and flexible, the 1836 Constitution established an elected chief executive with considerable powers, a **bicameral** legislature, and a four-tiered judicial system composed of justice, county, district, and supreme courts.[7] Power was divided among these three branches, with a system of checks and balances between them. The constitution also included complicated procedures for amendments, along with a bill of rights.

The values of American democracy percolated through the document in other ways as well, such as a guarantee that all white males could vote. Checks and balances were established between the three branches of government. On the other hand, a number of important provisions from Spanish-Mexican law were adapted for the Texas Republic in the constitution, including the idea of community property in which property acquired by either spouse during a marriage would be jointly owned, homestead protections in which one's home would be protected during bankruptcy proceedings, and debtor relief.

bicameral having a legislative assembly composed of two chambers or houses

FIGURE 2.1

The Republic of Texas 1836–45

This map shows the Republic of Texas with its large claimed territory. Texas's current boundaries were not established until 1850. Even then, minor controversies persisted along the Red River.

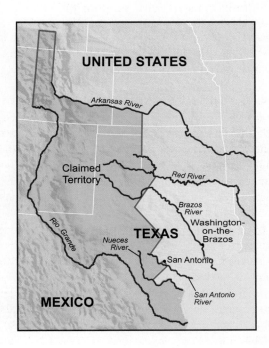

While giving these Spanish-American legal provisions constitutional status, Texas moved closer to the Anglo-American model of jurisprudence in other ways. By 1840 the Republic of Texas formally adopted the rules of English Common Law to replace Spanish Law in most civil and criminal matters. But there was one notable exception. Following Spanish and Mexican law, Texas initially retained ownership of all minerals under the ground even as land grants provided for individual ownership of the land itself. Until the Constitution of 1866, a consensus existed that the best model for developing Texas and its mineral resources was through direct government ownership of all mineral rights. Under the constitutions of 1866, 1869, and 1876, a new model was adopted granting ownership of mineral rights to the individuals who owned the land under which minerals were found. The state retained some claims to mineral rights, largely in western parts of the state, to fund public schools and higher education. But the new idea was that private entrepreneurs would do a better job developing the state's natural resources than would state officials. The complicated history of mineral rights and oil and gas law (as well as the entire oil and natural gas industry) in the nineteenth and twentieth centuries follows directly from the decisions made in later constitutions to replace the original mineral rights provisions of the constitutions of 1836, 1845, and 1861.

One of the most important aspects of the Constitution of 1836, at least from the perspective of newly immigrated Americans from the South, was its defense of slavery as an

The Texas Declaration of Independence was written by George C. Childress and adopted at the Convention of 1836. Childress modeled the document on the American Declaration of Independence (see Appendix, pp. A1–A3).

economic and political institution with constitutional protections. The Constitution of Coahuila y Tejas of 1827 had challenged, albeit unsuccessfully, the existence of slavery. Although the 1836 Constitution outlawed the importation of slaves from Africa, it guaranteed that slaveholders could keep their slaves as property and that new slaveholding immigrants could bring their slaves into Texas with them. The results of this constitutional protection were monumental. In 1836, Texas had a population of 38,470, including 5,000 slaves. By 1850 the slave population had grown to 58,161, over one-quarter of the state's population. By 1860 there were more than 182,566 slaves, accounting for more than 30 percent of the population.[8] The Constitution of 1836 not only saved slavery as an institution in Texas but also provided the protections needed for slavery to flourish.

Writing a constitution is one thing; putting it into effect is another. Only after the Battle of San Jacinto, where on April 21, 1836, Sam Houston's force of 900 men overran the 1,300-man force of Antonio Lopez de Santa Anna and captured Mexican dictator Santa Anna himself, did Texas really become an independent state with a working constitution. Many questioned whether the Lone Star Republic would survive given the dismal state of its finances, an army that couldn't protect the republic's sweeping land claims to the west and the south, a hostile Mexico that only reluctantly accepted Texas's secession, and a United States that appeared to be unwilling to bring Texas into the Union.[9] Annexation to the United States in 1845 ended such questions and brought into being a new constitution, this time a state constitution that would operate within the framework of the U.S. Constitution.

The Texas State Constitution of 1845

The next phase of Texas's Founding took place from 1845 to 1861. Although the 1836 Constitution called for annexation by the United States, Texas remained an independent republic for nine years. The reasons included American concerns that if Texas were admitted to the Union as a slave state, the move could alter the delicate balance between slave and free states and further divide the nation over the sensitive subject of slavery. Additionally, it was feared that annexation by the United States would lead to war with Mexico. Santa Anna had repudiated the Treaty of Velasco, which had ended the war between Texas and Mexico, and Mexico thus still claimed Texas as part of its territory.

Though both of these fears proved justified, hesitation over annexation was overcome by the mid-1840s. On March 1, 1845, the U.S. Congress approved a resolution that brought Texas into the Union as a state (see Appendix, pp. A5–A6). The annexation resolution had a number of interesting provisions. First, the Republic of Texas ceded to the United States all military armaments, bases, and facilities pertaining to public defense. Second, Texas retained a right to all "its vacant and unappropriated lands" as well as responsibility for its public debts. This was no small matter, because Texas claimed an enormous amount of land that extended far beyond its present state boundaries. The boundary issues were not resolved until Congress passed the Compromise of 1850, which among other provisions established Texas's present boundaries in exchange for a payment from the federal government, some of which was used to pay the state's debts. Finally, Texas was given permission to break up into four additional states when its population proved adequate. Considerable controversy surrounds this provision, and no serious attempt has been made to put it into effect.

On July 4, 1845, Anson Jones, fourth and final president of the Republic of Texas, called a convention in Austin to draft a state constitution. Drafters of the constitution relied heavily on the Constitution of 1836, although the final document ended up being almost twice as long. The familiar doctrines of separation of powers, checks and balances, and individual rights defined the basic design of government.

Under the Constitution of 1845, the legislature would be composed of two houses. The House of Representatives would have between 45 and 90 members, elected for two-year terms, and the Senate between 19 and 33 members, elected for four-year terms. (Half of the Senate would be elected every two years.) As in the U.S. Constitution, revenue bills would have to originate in the House. In a separate article on education, the legislature was ordered to establish a public school system and to set aside lands to support a Permanent School Fund. Another power granted to the legislature was the authority to select the state treasurer and comptroller in a joint session.

This 1844 cartoon satirized congressional opposition to the annexation of Texas. Personified as a beautiful young woman, Texas is holding a cornucopia filled with flowers. Though James K. Polk, elected to the presidency in 1844, welcomes Texas, the Whig Party leader Senator Henry Clay, with arms folded, warns, "Stand back, Madam Texas! For we are more holy than thou! Do you think we will have anything to do with gamblers, horse-racers, and licentious profligates?"

This constitution provided for an elected governor and lieutenant governor. The governor's term was set at two years, and a governor could serve only four years in any six-year period. Among the executive powers granted to the governor were powers to convene and adjourn the legislature, to veto legislation (vetoes could be overturned by a two-thirds vote of each house of the legislature), to grant pardons and reprieves, and to command the state militia. The governor also had the power to appoint the attorney general, secretary of state, and district and supreme court judges, subject to the approval of the Senate.

The Constitution of 1845 established a judicial branch consisting of a supreme court composed of three judges, district courts, and lower courts deemed necessary by the legislature. Judges on the higher courts were to be appointed to six-year terms and could be removed from office subject to a two-thirds vote of each house of the legislature.

Amending the Constitution of 1845 was difficult. After being proposed by a two-thirds vote of each house, amendments had to be approved by a majority of the voters and then by another two-thirds vote of each house in the next legislature in order to be ratified. Only one amendment was ever made, an 1850 provision for the election of state officials who were originally appointed by the governor or by the legislature.[10]

The Constitution of 1861: Texas Joins the Confederacy

While slavery had made it difficult for Texas to get into the Union in the early 1840s, slavery drove Texas from the Union twenty years later. By 1860 slavery, concentrated in east Texas and along the Gulf Coast, had become a vital institution to the Texas economy.

However, in large sections of the state, particularly in the north and west, the economy was based on ranching or corn and wheat production rather than cotton. There, slavery was virtually nonexistent. The question of whether Texas should secede from the Union along with other southern slave states was a controversial one that divided the state along regional as well as party lines.

Pressure to secede mounted following the November 1860 election of President Abraham Lincoln, who was committed to resisting the further expansion of slavery. A staunch Unionist, Governor Sam Houston refused calls to convene a special session of the legislature to discuss secession (see Appendix, pp. A7–A8). Seeking to bypass Houston, a number of influential political leaders in the state, including the chief justice of the Texas Supreme Court, called for a special convention in January 1861 to consider secession. Giving in to the pressure, Houston called a special session of the legislature in the hopes of undercutting the upcoming secession convention. The legislature, however, had other ideas, validating the call for the convention and turning its chambers over to the convention delegates.

Lawyers and slaveholders dominated the secession convention, with lawyers composing 40 percent of the delegates and slaveholders 70 percent. The Texas Ordinance of Secession, produced by the convention on February 2, 1861, reflected this proslavery membership (see Appendix, pp. A9–A10). In striking language, it proclaimed that the northern states had broken faith with Texas, particularly regarding the institution of slavery, and that Northerners had violated the laws and constitution of the federal Union by appealing to a "higher law" that trampled on the rights of Texans. The Ordinance of Secession proclaimed,

> We hold as undeniable truths that the governments of the various States, and of the confederacy itself, were established exclusively by the white race, for themselves and their posterity; that the African race had no agency in their establishment; that they were rightfully held and regarded as an inferior and dependent race, and in that condition only could their existence in this country be rendered beneficial and tolerable.[11]

The lowering of the Republic flag marked Texas's annexation to the Union on March 1, 1845. A state constitution was drafted shortly thereafter to reflect Texas's new role.

This image shows what the Texas State capitol, which burned in 1881, looked like in the 1870s. Texas's first constitution after joining the Union as a state was ratified in 1845. It lasted until 1861 when Texas seceded from the Union along with other southern states.

Texas voters approved secession from the Union on February 23, 1861. The secession convention then reconvened to enact a new constitution to guide the state as it entered the **Confederacy**. This constitution was surprisingly similar to the Constitution of 1845 except that references to the United States of America were replaced with references to the Confederate States of America. Public officials had to declare allegiance to the Confederacy, and slavery and states' rights were defended. A clause in the 1845 Constitution that provided for the possible emancipation of slaves was eliminated, and freeing slaves was declared illegal. But more controversial proposals, such as resuming the African slave trade, were rejected. The move out of the Union into the Confederacy may have been a radical one, but the new constitution was conservative insofar as it reaffirmed the existing constitutional order in the state.[12]

Confederacy the Confederate States of America, those southern states that seceded from the United States in late 1860 and 1861 and argued that the power of the states was more important than the power of the central government

The Constitution of 1866: Texas Rejoins the Union

Defeat in the Civil War led to the writing of another state constitution in 1866. The provisional governor, pro-Union Andrew Jackson Hamilton, called a constitutional convention on November 15, 1865, a little over six months after the surrender of Robert E. Lee's army in Virginia essentially ended the Confederacy's existence. Delegates were elected on January 8, 1866, and the convention was held February 7. Under the provisions of President Andrew Johnson's "**Presidential Reconstruction**," few former secessionists were excluded from voting. As a result, the convention was dominated by former secessionists, many of whom had held commissions in the Confederate army.

The delegates took a number of actions to bring the state into compliance with Presidential Reconstruction, including the rejection of the right to secession (see Appendix, p. A11), a repudiation of the war debt incurred by the state, and an acceptance of the abolition of slavery. Male freed slaves were granted fundamental rights to their persons and property as well as the right to sue and be sued and to contract with others. However, they were not allowed to vote and were banned from holding public office. The various amendments to the Constitution of 1861 passed by the convention came to be known as the Constitution of 1866.

Presidential Reconstruction a reconstruction plan for reintegrating former confederate states back into the Union and freeing the slaves that placed mild demands upon the existing white power structure

As in the two previous constitutions, the size of the House was set between 45 and 90 members, and that of the Senate between 19 and 33. Terms of office remained the same as under the 1845 and 1861 constitutions, although salaries were increased. Reapportionment was to be based on the number of white male citizens, who would be counted in a census every 10 years.

The salary was also increased for the governor, whose term was extended to 4 years, with a limit of 8 years in any 12-year period. The governor was also granted, for the first time, a line-item veto on appropriations. The comptroller and the treasurer were to be elected by the voters for 4-year terms.

Under the new constitution, the state supreme court was expanded from three to five judges, whose terms were increased to 10 years, and whose salaries were also increased. The chief justice was to be selected from among the five judges on the supreme court. District court judges were to be elected for 8-year terms, and the attorney general for a 4-year term.

Voters ratified the Constitution of 1866 in June in a relatively close referendum, 28,119 to 23,400. The close vote was attributed to a widespread unhappiness with the salary increases for the various state officers,[13] but there were other sources of opposition as well. Many unionists who had been driven from the state during the war rejected the constitution, arguing it was the product of a convention dominated by former secessionists. They appealed to the increasingly Radical Republican Congress in Washington, D.C., for redress, arguing that former secessionists should be disenfranchised and forbidden from holding office. Their arguments gained force when the first legislature elected under the provisions of the Constitution of 1866 passed laws including the Black Codes, which limited the social, political, and economic status of African Americans in Texas. In response, Radical Republicans in Washington passed the **Congressional Reconstruction** Acts of 1867.

The Reconstruction Constitution of 1869

Republicans in Congress had come to see the initial efforts of reintegrating Texas and other southern states back into the Union as a failure. Under the direction of Congress, General Winfield Scott, the commander of the Union military force that was still occupying Texas and Louisiana, summarily dismissed most state officials elected to office under the 1866 Constitution and called for a new convention to write a new constitution in Texas in 1868. This time, however, former secessionists would be banned from voting or holding office. Against limited Democratic opposition, **Radical Republicans** easily won the vote to hold a convention by 44,689 to 11,440. Of the 90 delegates to the convention, only 6 had served in the previous constitutional convention. Ten were African American. The vast majority represented the interests of various wings in the Republican Party. The convention was a rancorous affair as delegates argued over a wide range of issues, including railroad charters, lawlessness in the state, and whether laws passed during the war years were legal. In the final days of the convention, delegates finally got down to the constitutional matters and the challenges of accepting the Thirteenth and Fourteenth Amendments to the United States Constitution, which abolished slavery, provided full citizenship to African Americans, and restricted former secessionists from holding office. Although delegates never completed their task of reworking the Constitution of

Congressional Reconstruction the reconstruction program put forward by radical Republicans in Congress in 1866 that disenfranchised former Confederates and granted former slaves American citizenship and the right to vote

Radical Republicans a bloc of Republicans in the U.S. Congress who pushed through the adoption of African American suffrage as well as an extended period of military occupation of the South following the Civil War

1866, the results of their efforts were published under orders by military officials, without being submitted to the voters, and became the Constitution of 1869.

A number of features of the Constitution of 1869 stand out.[14] The U.S. Constitution was declared to be the supreme law of the land. As in the 1866 Constitution, slavery was forbidden. But now African Americans were given the right to vote. Fourteenth Amendment guarantees of the privileges and immunities of citizens, due process under law, and equal protection under the law were recognized. Additionally, the constitution altered the relationship among the three branches of government.

The House of Representatives was set at 90 and the Senate at 30 members. Senatorial terms were extended to six years, with one-third of the seats to be elected every biennium. Legislative sessions were to be held annually. The most critical changes, however, were in the executive branch and the courts. The powers of the governor were vastly expanded. Among other things, the governor was given wide-ranging appointment powers that included the power to appoint judges. The state supreme court was reduced from five to three judges, and their term was reduced to nine years, with one new judge to be appointed every three years. Salaries for state officials were increased.

Underlying and fueling the debate over the Constitution of 1869 was another deeper constitutional debate about the meaning of the Secession Ordinance of 1861, the Constitution of 1861, and the Texas government that had functioned under the Confederacy. From the perspective of the U.S. Constitution, had Texas ever "left the union"? Was the

TABLE 2.1

The Changing Texas Constitutions, 1845–1876

The common perception of major constitutional provisions is that they are fixed in time and never to be changed. In Texas, however, constitutional changes take place regularly.

	1836	1845	1861	1866	1869	1876
LEGISLATURE						
Session frequency	annual	biennial	biennial	annual	annual	biennial
House term length	1 year	2 years	2 years	2 years	2 years	2 years
Senate term length	3 years	4 years	4 years	4 years	6 years	4 years
SUPREME COURT						
Size	*	3	3	5	3**	3†
Term length	4 years	6 years	6 years	10 years	9 years	6 years
Method of selection	elected††	appointed†	elected	elected	appointed	elected
GOVERNOR						
Term length	2 years	2 years	2 years	4 years	4 years	2 years††

*Chief justice and district judges acting as associate judges. The constitution provides for 3–8 district judges.
**Increased to 5 in 1874 by constitutional amendment.
†Amended. Currently 9 members.
††Elected by joint ballot by the Texas congress.
†Election made selection method in 1850 by constitutional amendment.
††Amended. Currently 4 years.

Constitution of 1861 "illegal"? And what about the laws that had been passed by the legislature under the powers granted by the 1861 Constitution? Were they the law of the land, or did they have no legal force? Were all laws that had been written and all contracts that had been made during the period of rebellion "null and void"? This debate came to an end with the U.S. Supreme Court decision *Texas v. White et al.* (1869). Here, the court ruled that Texas had never left the Union, which was "perpetual, and as indissoluble as the union between the original states." The Ordinance of Secession of 1861 and all acts of the legislature that gave effect to that ordinance were considered to be "null" (see Appendix, pp. A11–A12).

The first governor elected under the Constitution of 1869 was Edmund Davis, a Republican affiliated with the Radical faction of the party and a former Union general. Davis had vast authority, since the constitution had centralized power in the executive while reducing local governmental control. The popular perception at the time was that he presided over a corrupt, extravagant administration that eventually turned to the state police and the militia to attempt to maintain its control. Closer to the truth may be the fact that Davis sought to maintain his rule by relying on former slaves who had become a bulwark of the Republican Party in the state, and by limiting the reintegration of former Confederates into state politics.

In 1872 the Democrats regained control of the legislature, and in 1873 the Democrat Richard Coke was elected governor. Davis attempted to maintain control over the governor's office by having his handpicked supreme court invalidate Coke's election. He refused to give up his office and surrounded himself with state police in the capitol. However, when Democrats slipped past the guards and gathered upstairs in the capitol to organize a government, Davis was unable to obtain federal troops to maintain him in office and finally had to leave.

The Constitution of 1876

The final phase of Texas's Founding began with the passage of the Constitution of 1876. To prevent another government such as Davis's, efforts were made to write a new constitution, but in 1874 a proposed constitution was rejected by the legislature.[15] Finally, in 1875, a new constitutional convention was called, with 3 delegates selected by popular vote from each of the 30 senatorial districts. The final composition of the convention included 75 white Democrats and 15 Republicans, 6 of whom were African American. Not one of the elected delegates had participated in the constitutional convention of 1868–69. Forty of them were farmers, and 40 were members of the **Grange**, a militant organization that had emerged to improve the financial plight of farmers.

Grange a militant farmers' movement of the late nineteenth century that fought for improved conditions for farmers

The document that emerged from this convention, the Constitution of 1876, is still the basis for Texas government today. In an era of agriculture when prices and incomes were low and when little was demanded or expected from government, much in the 1876 Constitution made sense. However, one might question whether a constitution designed primarily by white males for whites in a rural agrarian society—and for the purpose of keeping the likes of Edmund Davis from ever controlling the state again—is the best foundation for government in the modern era.

The framers were committed to a constitution with four major themes. First, they wanted strong popular control of state government; second, they believed that a constitution should seriously limit the power of state government; third, they sought economy

The example of Edmund Davis's reign motivated the revision of executive branch power in the Constitution of 1876. The framers of that constitution sought popular control of state government in order to limit the appointment powers of the governor as provided by the Constitution of 1869.

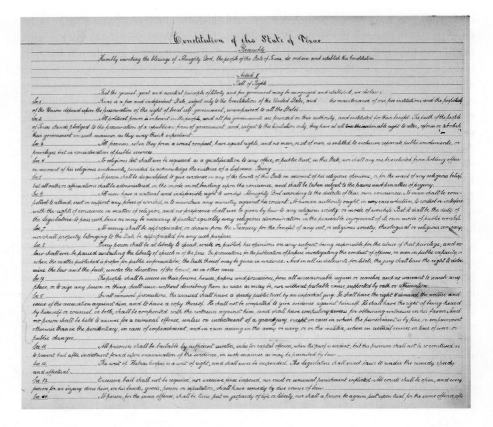

in government; and fourth, they sought to promote agrarian interests, particularly those of small farmers, who formed the basis of support for the Grange movement.

Popular control of state government meant that the governor's previously vast appointment powers were limited by making judges and other public officials subject to election. But it did not mean broadening the electorate. When the framers of the 1876 Constitution thought of popular control of government, they thought of control by white males.

In the effort to limit the powers of state government, the constitution placed great restrictions on governmental actions, restrictions that could be modified only through a complex constitutional amendment process. Executive authority was diffused among numerous officeholders, rather than concentrated in the hands of the governor. Although subsequently changed by constitutional amendment, an initial provision further limited gubernatorial power by setting a two-year term limit for the office. The legislature was part-time, ordinarily sitting for a prescribed time period every other year, in contrast to the annual sessions provided for in the 1869 Constitution.

Limiting the power of state government was accomplished in several other ways. The constitution restricted the extent of government debt and of government's power to tax. In addition, there were limits on the salaries of state officials, especially legislators. A major economic depression had begun in 1873, and many Texans were experiencing economic hardship. One way money was saved was by decentralizing public education.

The constitution provided for racially segregated schools and eliminated compulsory education laws. By gaining local control over education, white landowners could avoid paying taxes for the education of African American students.

Texas at that time was an agricultural state. Wishing to protect agrarian interests, the framers wrote provisions protecting homesteads from bankruptcy proceedings and restricting institutions that were perceived to be harmful to farmers, such as banks and railroads. There were also detailed regulations on railroad competition, freight and passenger rates, and railroad construction incentives.

The Constitution of 1876 was a conservative document with a distinctly populist flavor. On the one hand, it broke with the more activist government model laid out by the two reconstruction constitutions of 1866 and 1869. On the other hand, it sought to protect those being harmed by the social and economic changes that transformed Texas after Reconstruction. The debates of the Constitutional Convention of 1875

TABLE 2.2

A Constitutional Timeline, 1836–1876

DATE	MAJOR FEATURES
1836 The Constitution of the Republic of Texas following the revolution	• Adopted U.S. Constitution as a working model, including separation of powers, checks and balances, bill of rights. • Rejected Catholicism as state religion. • Defended slavery.
1845 The first Constitution of the State of Texas after annexation by the United States.	• Affirmed many of the institutional features of the U.S. Constitution and the 1836 Constitution of Texas. • Made amendment process difficult. • Provided for Texas to retain ownership of all public lands and minerals under these lands.
1861 The constitution following secession from the Union.	• Affirmed broad features of the 1845 Constitution. • Strongly defended slavery as an institution and the existing white-dominated political and economic system.
1866 Embodied values of Presidential Reconstruction. Suspended by military rule under Radical Reconstruction.	• Affirmed broad institutional features of the 1845 and 1861 constitutions. • Reflected values of former secessionists. • Accepted results of Civil War and an end to slavery. • Rejected equality before the law or the franchise for former slaves.
1869 The product of Radical Reconstruction. Never completed and went into effect without approval by the people.	• Affirmed U.S. Constitution as the "Supreme Law of the Land." • Affirmed 13th Amendment (ending slavery) and the 14th Amendment (granting equality under the law and due process to all former slaves). • Greatly expanded powers of governor. • Increased salaries of state officials
1876 Texas's current constitution. Amended 491 times.	• Backed away from radical features of Reconstruction, including the acceptance of the dominance of the national government over the state. • Reflected a break with activist constitutions of 1869. • Promoted traditional agrarian interests like the Grange in Texas. • Promoted values of "economy" and "efficiency." • Curtailed powers of governor and legislature. • Provided for election of judges. • Provided for future regulation of railroads.

drew attention to the fact that Texas was undergoing rapid change. New social and economic conditions, particularly the aggregation of capital in "immense railroad systems," gave rise to new social and political problems. These, in turn, demanded the institution of new restrictions on the powers of state government to prevent corruption. A new constitution with new provisions that restricted the activities of government became the bulwark of a conservative white social and political order in the state throughout the late nineteenth and early twentieth centuries (see Governor Richard Coke's Inaugural Address in 1876, Appendix, p. A13).

Even in its earliest stages, the Texas Constitution of 1876 was a lengthy, rigid, and detailed document, and purposely so. Regulations curtailing government power were placed not in statutes where they could easily be reversed, but in the body of the constitution. The goal of this design was to ensure that the Radical Republicans and Edmund Davis would never again be able to control the state. They never did, although over the years the constitution became an increasingly unwieldy document (see Tables 2.1 and 2.2).

The Constitution of Texas Today

 Analyze the major provisions of the Texas Constitution today

The U.S. Constitution has two great virtues: brevity and flexibility. Neither of these can be said to characterize the Texas Constitution. The U.S. Constitution is limited to 7 short articles and 27 amendments, and takes up only 8 pages of the *World Almanac*. Much in the federal document is left unsaid, allowing lawmaking to be accomplished by statute. In contrast, in 2016 the Texas Constitution contained 16 articles (see Table 2.3; another article that concerned Spanish and Mexican land titles was deleted from the constitution in 1969). Six hundred and seventy-three amendments have been proposed by the legislature. Four hundred and ninety-one have been approved by the electorate, while 179 have been defeated. (Curiously, three amendments were proposed by the legislature, but for obscure historical reasons never voted on by the electorate.[16]) Many of the articles are lengthy, complex affairs, taking up over 67 pages of text in one edition of the *Texas Almanac*. But it is not just the length that differentiates the two constitutions. There is a difference in tone. The Texas Constitution reflects the writers' fears of what government could do if the principle of **limited government** was not clearly established.

In addition to its severe limits on executive power, the Texas Constitution also addresses a number of specific policy problems directly in the text, turning what might appear to be matters of public policy into issues of constitutional authority. By granting a variety of boards and districts a special place in the constitution, the framers created

limited government a principle of constitutional government; a government whose powers are defined and limited by a constitution

TABLE 2.3

The Texas Constitution: An Overview

Article 1: The Bill of Rights

Article 2: Separation of Powers in State Government

Article 3: The State Legislature

Article 4: The Plural Executive

Article 5: The Judicial Department

Article 6: Suffrage

Article 7: Public Education

Article 8: Taxation and State Revenues

Articles 9 and 11: Local Government, Including Counties and Municipal Corporations

Article 10: Empowering the State to Regulate Railroads and to Create the Texas Railroad Commission

Article 12: Empowering the State to Create General Laws for Corporations

Article 13: Concerning Spanish and Mexican Land Titles, Now Deleted from the Constitution

Article 14: Creates the General Land Office to Deal with Registering Land Titles

Article 15: Impeachment Provisions

Article 16: General Provisions Covering a Wide Range of Topics

Article 17: Amendment Procedures

additional checks and balances that make it difficult for governors to exercise power effectively. Quite unintentionally, the Texas Constitution became a place where special interests could promote and protect their own agendas, even in the face of considerable political opposition.

The contrasts in character between the federal and Texas constitutions are a direct reflection of the differences in their framers' underlying goals. The U.S. Constitution was written to overcome the liabilities of the Articles of Confederation and create a government that could act effectively in the public welfare in a variety of policy areas. The Texas Constitution was written to prevent the expansion of governmental authority and the return of a system of political power that was perceived as acting against the interests of the people.

The Preamble

The Preamble to the Texas Constitution is surprisingly short: "Humbly invoking the blessings of Almighty God, the people of the State of Texas do ordain and establish this Constitution." This brevity is more than made up for in what follows.

Article 1: Bill of Rights

Article I of the U.S. Constitution establishes and delegates power to the legislative branch of government. One of the overriding concerns of the Founders was to create a legislature that could act effectively in public affairs. What came to be known as the Bill of Rights—the first 10 amendments to the Constitution—was added after the original Constitution was drafted and approved.

In contrast, the Texas Constitution puts its Bill of Rights up front as Article 1, well before any discussion of the legislature, the executive, or the courts. From the beginning, the purpose of the Texas Constitution was not simply to create a set of institutions that could wield political power. It was to limit the way political power is used and to prevent it from being abused.

Section 1 of the Bill of Rights proclaims that "Texas is a free and independent State, subject only to the Constitution of the United States, and the maintenance of our free institutions and the perpetuity of the Union depend upon the preservation of local self-government, unimpaired to all the States." On the face of it, this proclamation would seem to be relatively noncontroversial, as it appears to accept the Constitution of the United States and the perpetuity of the Union. Put into proper historical context, however, it meant something very different. The Constitution of 1869, written under the watchful eyes of Radical Republicans in Texas and in the U.S. Congress, had rejected the "heresies of nullification and secession" and explicitly acknowledged that the U.S. Constitution was "the supreme law of the land" and that the Texas Constitution was "subject to national authority." Article 1, Section 1—the product of a constitutional convention in 1876 that was hostile to many of the efforts of Reconstruction—concedes two very different things: (1) that Texas is free and independent, "subject" to the U.S. Constitution, and (2) that free institutions and the perpetuity of the Union depend upon local self-government that is "unimpaired." No mention is made of the supremacy of the U.S. Constitution over the state constitution. The idea of a "perpetual Union" is made to depend upon "the preservation of local self-government," meaning an independent and autonomous state government freed from an intrusive national authority. Texas may have lost the Civil War, but Article 1, Section 1, claims an autonomy of the state from outside forces that would have surprised many politicians outside the state. Such sentiments continue to resonate throughout parts of Texas today.

The Texas Bill of Rights embodies certain ideas captured in earlier state constitutions and the U.S. Bill of Rights. All "free men" are declared to have equal rights (Section 30) that cannot be denied or abridged because of sex, race, color, creed, or national origin (Section 3a). Freedom of religious worship is guaranteed (Section 6), and religious tests for office are prohibited (Section 4). Liberty of speech and liberty of the press are guaranteed (Section 8). Individuals are protected from unreasonable search and seizure of their homes and property (Section 9), from excessive bail (Section 11), from bills of attainder (imposing punishment for an action without holding a trial) and ex post facto laws (making an action into a crime retroactively) (Section 16), and from double jeopardy (being prosecuted twice for the same crime) (Section 14). Article 1 also guarantees an individual a right to trial by jury (Section 15) and the right to bear arms "in the lawful defense of himself or the State; but the Legislature shall have the power, by law, to regulate the wearing of arms, with a view to prevent crime" (Article 1, Section 23).

Article 1 also contains some ideas that move beyond those guaranteed by the first 10 amendments to the U.S. Constitution. The right to **republican government**, something

republican government a representative democracy, a system of government in which power is derived from the people clearly stated in the main body of the U.S. Constitution but not in the U.S. Bill of Rights, is powerfully articulated in the first two sections of Article 1. These sections declare that all political power is inherent in the people, and that the people of Texas have at all times the "inalienable right to alter, reform or abolish their government in such manner as they may think expedient" (Article 1, Section 2).

The differences between the Texas Bill of Rights and the U.S. Bill of Rights are not simply matters of where best to articulate a philosophy of republican government. They also involve very concrete matters of public policy. Section 26 of the Texas Bill of Rights, for example, forbids monopolies that are contrary to the public interest, and states that the law of primogeniture and entail (a law designed to keep large landed properties together by restricting their inheritance to the firstborn child) will never be in effect in the state. Although monopolies remain a public concern today, primogeniture and entail are not. Section 11 in the Texas Bill of Rights grapples with the complicated issue of bail and under what specific circumstances an individual can be denied it. Significantly, Section 11 has been the subject of three major constitutional revisions: in 1955, 1977, and 1993. Section 30, adopted in 1989, provides a long list of the "rights of crime victims," including the right to be treated fairly and with dignity, the right to be protected from the accused, and the right to restitution. Although these are important matters of public policy for Texas today, they could hardly be considered proper material for the U.S. Constitution.

Article 2: The Powers of Government

Like the U.S. Constitution, Article 2 divides the power of government in Texas into three distinct branches: the legislative, the executive, and the judicial. It also stipulates that no one in any one branch shall be attached to either of the other branches, except where explicitly permitted (as in the case of the lieutenant governor's role in the Senate). The article—one short paragraph of text—assures that a version of the separation of powers doctrine found in the U.S. Constitution will be embodied in Texas institutions.

Article 3: Legislative Department

Article 2 is one of the shortest articles in the Texas Constitution. Article 3 is the longest, making up almost one-third of the original text of 1876. Like Article I of the U.S. Constitution, Article 3 of the Texas Constitution vests legislative power in two houses: a Senate of 31 members and a House of Representatives of no more than 150 members. It stipulates the terms of office and qualifications: House members serve two-year terms, whereas senators serve four-year terms, half being elected every two years. House members must be citizens of the United States, must be at least 21 years of age, and must have resided in the state for two years and in their district for one year. Senators must be citizens of the United States, must be at least 26 years old, and must have resided in the state for five years and in their districts for one year. In addition, Article 3 provides for the selection of officers in both houses of the legislature, states when and for how long the legislature shall meet (Section 5), and explains how the legislative proceedings will be conducted (Sections 29–41) and how representative districts will be apportioned (Sections 25, 26, and 28).

Like Article 1 (Texas Bill of Rights), Article 3 moves well beyond the U.S. Constitution, putting limits on what the legislature can do. For example, it puts limits on legislators' salaries and makes it difficult to increase those salaries. Article 3 also creates a bipartisan Texas Ethics Commission, whose job, among other things, is to recommend salary increases for members of the legislature and to set per diem rates for legislators and the lieutenant governor. Article 3, Section 49a, also subjects the legislature to the actions of the comptroller of public accounts, whose duty is to prepare a report prior to the legislative session on the financial condition of the state treasury and to provide estimates of future expenditures by the state. This provision of the Texas Constitution effectively limits the state legislature to the financial calculations and endorsements of the comptroller, a check on the legislature all but unimaginable to the writers of the U.S. Constitution.

Putting constraints on certain legislative actions is only part of the story. The largest portion of Article 3 (Sections 47–64) is dedicated to addressing a variety of policy issues, including lotteries, emergency service districts, debt creation, the Veterans' Land Board and the Texas Water Development Board, Texas park development, the creation of a state medical education board, and even the establishment of an economic development fund in support of the now defunct superconducting supercollider.

Article 4: Executive Department

Article II of the U.S. Constitution concentrates executive power in the presidency. Under the U.S. Constitution, cabinet members such as the Secretary of State, the Attorney General, and the Secretary of Agriculture are appointed by the president (and confirmed by the Senate). "Executive power" is "vested" or placed in the hands of the president (see U.S. Constitution, Article 2, Section 1). Vested executive power, in this regard, is a broad-ranging term that covers a wide range of activities. The goal of the framers was to create a more effective and more responsible executive than had been possible under the Articles of Confederation.

In contrast, there is no "vesting" of executive power in any one executive office in Texas (see Table 2.4). Article 4 of the Texas Constitution states that the executive shall consist of six distinct offices: the governor, who serves as the chief executive; the lieutenant governor, who serves as the president of the Senate; the secretary of state, who keeps the official seals of the state; the comptroller of public accounts; the commissioner of the General Land Office; and the attorney general, who acts as the state's chief legal officer. With the exception of the secretary of state, who is appointed by the governor and approved by the Senate, all other offices are elected by qualified voters every four years. Besides creating a **plural executive** (see Chapter 8), Article 4 guarantees its members will have independent political bases in the electorate. This arrangement provides an additional check against any concentration of powers in the hands of any one person.

plural executive an executive branch in which power is fragmented because the election of statewide officeholders is independent of the election of the governor

Article 5: Judicial Department

Article III of the U.S. Constitution succinctly provides for a Supreme Court and empowers Congress to create any necessary lower courts. As such, it could not be further from the detailed discussion of the state courts found in Article 5 of the Texas Constitution.

TABLE 2.4

Major Constitutional Officers in Texas

OFFICE/POSITION	ELECTED BY/APPOINTED BY	DUTIES
LEGISLATIVE (ARTICLE 3)		
Speaker of the House	Elected by House members	Leads the House
President Pro Tempore of the Senate	Elected by Senate members. Most senior member of the Senate from either party.	Leads the Senate in absence of the lieutenant governor
EXECUTIVE (ARTICLE 4)		
Governor	Elected by Texas voters for 4-year term	Acts as chief executive of the state
Lieutenant Governor	Elected by Texas voters for 4-year term	Acts as governor in absence of the governor and presides over the Senate
Secretary of State	Appointed by the governor by and with advice and consent of the Senate	Acts as the chief election officer of Texas
Comptroller of Public Accounts	Elected by Texas voters	Acts as chief steward of state finances
Commissioner of the General Land Office	Elected by Texas voters	Manages state assets, investments, and mineral rights from state lands and serves as chair for numerous state boards and commissions
Attorney General	Elected by Texas voters	Represents the state in cases where it is a party
JUDICIAL (ARTICLE 5)		
Justice of Supreme Court	9 positions elected by Texas voters for 6-year terms	Decides on civil cases reaching the Texas Supreme Court
Judge of Court of Criminal Appeals	9 positions elected by Texas voters for 6-year terms	Decides on criminal cases reaching the Texas court of criminal appeals
Justice of the Court of Appeal	80 justices in 14 courts of appeal elected by Texas voters for 6-year terms from multimember districts	Decides on cases reaching the Texas court of appeal
District Court Judge	456 district court judges elected by Texas voters for 4-year terms from a mixture of multi- and single-member districts	Decides on cases in Texas district court

Other county-level court officials are also elected for 4-year terms on a county or precinct basis. Municipal court judges are usually appointed.

OFFICE/POSITION	ELECTED BY/APPOINTED BY	DUTIES
OTHER IMPORTANT OFFICES		
Texas Railroad Commissioner (Article 13, Section 30)	3 officers elected by Texas voters for 6-year overlapping terms	Regulates the oil and gas industry, gas utilities, pipeline safety, and surface coal and uranium mining (no longer regulates railroads)
State Board of Education Member (Article 7)	15 members elected by Texas voters from single-member districts for 4-year terms	Makes statewide policies for public schools
Agricultural Commissioner (office established under Agricultural Code, not the constitution)	Elected by Texas voters for a 4-year term	Regulates state agriculture and administers state agriculture policy

Besides creating a supreme court to hear civil cases and a court of criminal appeals to hear criminal cases, Article 5 provides for such lesser courts as courts of appeal, district courts, commissioner's courts, and justice of the peace courts, and empowers the legislature to establish other courts as deemed necessary. It also goes into such details as the retirement and compensation of judges, the jurisdictions of the various courts, and the duties of judges; it states what to do in the case of court vacancies; and it includes a series of discussions on particular issues involving the lower courts.

An even greater difference between the federal and the Texas constitutions in their treatment of the judiciary is the crucial role the latter gives to elections. Federal judges are appointed by the president and approved by the Senate. In Texas the people elect state judges. Nine supreme court and nine court of criminal appeals judges are elected at large in the state, and lower court judges are elected by voters in their respective geographic locations. Much like the U.S. Constitution, the Texas Constitution seeks to create an independent judiciary that can check and balance the other two branches of government. However, it seeks an additional check as well, in that it wants the people to in turn watch over the courts.

Article 6: Suffrage

Article 6 contains a short but detailed discussion about who may vote in Texas. It also empowers the legislature to enact laws regulating voter registration and the selection of electors for president and vice president.

Article 7: Education

The concerns found in the Texas Declaration of Independence over the need for public schools to promote a republican form of government are directly addressed in Article 7, which declares, "A general diffusion of knowledge [is] essential to the preservation of the liberties and rights of the people." Section 1 makes it a duty of the state legislature to support and maintain "an efficient system of public free schools." The Texas Supreme Court's interpretation of this provision as applying to school funding in the state has led to political battles over school finance for 40 years. Sections 2–8 provide for the funding of public education and the creation of a State Board of Education to oversee the operations of elementary and secondary education. Article 7 also provides for the establishment and funding of a "University of the first class" to be called "The University of Texas" as well as an "agricultural and mechanical college" (Texas A&M University). Provisions were later included to fund other state universities and colleges. State universities are the subject of over half of Article 7, where detailed discussions of the funding and operations of particular state institutions are put directly into the text.

Article 8: Taxation and Revenue

The complex issue of taxation is the subject of Article 8, where once again we find a highly detailed account of several important policy issues built directly into the text of the constitution. One of the most controversial sections of the Texas Constitution

Which State Has the Longest Constitution?

State Constitution Length (estimated)

- ● < 19,999 words
- ● 20,000–39,999 words
- ● 40,000–59,999 words
- ● 60,000–79,999 words
- ● > 79,999 words

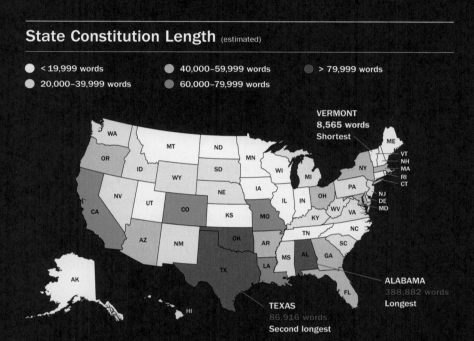

VERMONT
8,565 words
Shortest

ALABAMA
388,882 words
Longest

TEXAS
86,916 words
Second longest

The Texas Constitution is the second-longest state constitution in the United States. The framers of the Texas Constitution gave the state government very specific powers so that the government could not use ambiguity to expand its powers. As a result, the Texas Constitution requires frequent amendments to address situations not covered specifically in the original constitution. The Texas Constitution has been amended 498 times as of 2017, fourth most of any state.

SOURCE: Book of the States, 2017.
Council of State Governments.
Data for 2017 compiled by the authors.

Amendments Added to Constitution

- ● < 75 amendments
- ● 75–149 amendments
- ● 150–224 amendments
- ● 225–300 amendments
- ● > 300 amendments

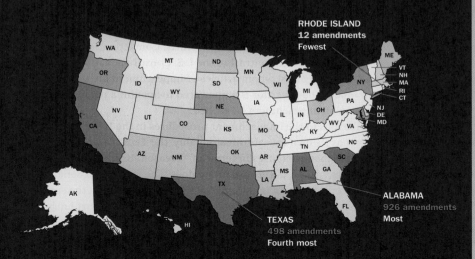

RHODE ISLAND
12 amendments
Fewest

ALABAMA
926 amendments
Most

TEXAS
498 amendments
Fourth most

CRITICAL THINKING

- After examining the two maps, do you see any relationship between the length of a state constitution and the number of amendments to the constitution? Why do you think that there might be such a relationship in some states?

- Do different regions in the country seem to favor short rather than long state constitutions? What factors might account for such similarities?

centers on the issue of the income tax. Section 1 of Article 8 enables the legislature to tax the income of individuals and businesses. This power, however, is subject to Section 24, adopted in 1993, which requires that a personal income tax be approved by the voters and that the proceeds from it be dedicated to education and tax relief. As with other portions of the constitution, the net effect of these provisions is to curtail severely what the state legislature can do and how it can do it. If Section 24 of Article 8 is any indication, the public fear of unresponsive and potentially tyrannical government is as alive today as it was in 1876.

Articles 9 and 11: Local Government

These articles provide highly detailed discussions of the creation, organization, and operation of counties and municipal corporations.

Articles 10, 12, 13, and 14

These heavily revised articles deal with a series of specific topics: the railroads (10), private corporations (12), Spanish and Mexican land titles (13), and public lands (14). Article 10 empowers the state to regulate railroads and to establish the Railroad Commission. Article 12 empowers the state to create general laws creating private corporations and protecting the public and individual stockholders. Article 13, now entirely repealed, dealt with the nineteenth-century issue of Spanish and Mexican land titles. Article 14 created a General Land Office to deal with the registration of land titles.

Article 15: Impeachment

impeachment under the Texas Constitution, the formal charge by the House of Representatives that leads to trial in the Senate and possible removal of a state official

In the U.S. Constitution, **impeachment** is one of the major checks Congress holds against both the executive and judicial branches of government. The House of Representatives holds the power to impeach an individual; the Senate is responsible for conducting trials. A two-thirds vote in the Senate following impeachment by the House leads to the removal of an individual from office.

A similar process is provided for in Article 15 of the Texas Constitution. The House has the power to impeach. The Senate has the power to try the governor, lieutenant governor, attorney general, land-office commissioner, and comptroller, as well as judges of the supreme court, the courts of appeal, and district courts. Conviction requires a two-thirds vote of the senators present. In contrast to the U.S. Constitution, the Texas Constitution rules that all officers against whom articles of impeachment are proffered are suspended from their office. The governor is empowered to appoint a person to fill the vacancy until the decision on impeachment is reached.

Despite these similarities to the impeachment procedures in the U.S. Constitution, the Texas Constitution has its own caveats. Most notably, the Texas Constitution does not explicitly define impeachable offenses in terms of "Treason, Bribery, or other high Crimes and Misdemeanors," as the U.S. Constitution does. The House and Senate (and the courts) decide what constitutes an impeachable offense.[17] In addition, the supreme court has original jurisdiction to hear and determine whether district court judges are competent to discharge their judicial duties. The governor may also remove judges of the supreme court, courts of appeal, and district courts when requested by the two-thirds vote of each legislature. Significantly, the reasons for removing a judge in this case need only involve a "willful neglect of duty, incompetence, habitual drunkenness, oppression in office, or other reasonable cause" (Article 15, Section 8). The barriers to removing a judge by political means are thus, at least on paper, much lower in Texas than in the national government.

In 1980, Section 9 was added to Article 15, providing a new way to remove officials appointed by the governor. With the advice and consent of two-thirds of the members of the Senate present, a governor may remove an appointed public official. If the legislature is not in session, the governor is empowered to call a special two-day session to consider the proposed removal.

Article 16: General Provisions

Article 16 is one of the lengthiest in the Texas Constitution and has no parallel in the U.S. Constitution. It is literally a catchall article tackling a variety of issues ranging from official oaths of office to community property to banking corporations and stock laws to the election of the Texas Railroad Commission to the state retirement systems. Here, perhaps more than anywhere else, we see the complexity and confusion of the philosophy reflected in the Texas Constitution.

Article 17: Amending the Constitution

Like the U.S. Constitution, the Texas Constitution explicitly delineates how it can be amended. Essentially, to be adopted, an amendment must undergo a four-stage process. First, it must be proposed by the legislature meeting in either regular or special session. Second, it must be approved by a two-thirds vote of all the members elected to each house. Third, a brief statement explaining it must be published twice in each recognized newspaper in the state that meets the publication requirements for official state notices. Finally, it must be approved by a majority of the state's voters in a statewide election.

Recent Attempts to Rewrite the Texas Constitution

Describe modern efforts to change the Texas Constitution

Given the difficulty of amending the state constitution, a surprising number of amendments have been proposed since 1876. A considerable number of these, however, have been turned down in the popular vote. As Table 2.5 shows, demands for amending the Constitution have intensified in recent years, as legislators have dealt with the problem

TABLE 2.5

Amending the Texas Constitution

The Constitution of Texas has been amended 491 times since its inception in 1876.

YEARS	NUMBER PROPOSED	NUMBER ADOPTED
1876–1900	31	17
1901–20	56	21
1921–40	71	47
1941–60	78	59
1961–80	151	98
1981–2000	180	148
2001–10	79	77
2011	10	7
2013	9	9
2014	1	1
2015	7	7
2017	7	7
Total	680	498

SOURCE: Texas Legislative Council and Texas Secretary of State.

of making changes in public policy while being constrained by an unwieldy constitutional document.

Sharpstown and the Failed Constitutional Reforms of 1974

A drive to rewrite the Texas Constitution grew out of a major stock fraud that broke in the early 1970s, involving the Sharpstown State Bank and the National Bankers Life Insurance Corporation. Following the 1970 elections, which had been dominated, as generally was the case at that time, by the conservative wing of the Democratic Party, a suit filed in Dallas federal court by the federal Securities and Exchange Commission alleged that a number of influential Democrats, including Governor Preston Smith, the state Democratic chairman and state banking board member Elmer Baum, Speaker of the House Gus Mutscher, and others, had been bribed. By the fall of 1971 Mutscher and two of his associates had been indicted. On March 15, 1972, they were convicted and sentenced to five years' probation.

The convictions fueled a firestorm in the state to "throw the rascals out." During the 1972 elections, "reform" candidates dominated the Democratic primary and the general election. One reformer, the politically conservative rancher-banker Dolph Briscoe, became governor, but only by a plurality, making him the first governor in the history of the state not to receive a majority of the popular vote. Other more liberal reform-minded candidates such as Lieutenant Governor William P. Hobby, Jr., and Attorney General John Hill were also successful. When the smoke cleared, half of the House seats were occupied by new members, and the Senate had witnessed a higher-than-normal rate of turnover. The elections had one other outcome: an amendment was passed empowering the legislature to sit as a constitutional convention whose task would be to rewrite the constitution and then present the new document to state voters for ratification.[18]

The constitutional convention met on January 8, 1974, in Austin. Originally scheduled to last 90 days, it was extended to 150 days, but even so, it did not have enough time. Bitter politics, coupled with the intense demands of highly mobilized special interests, made it impossible to reach agreement. In the end, proponents of a new constitution failed to achieve the necessary two-thirds majority by three votes (118 to 62, with 1 abstention).

The movement to rewrite the constitution did not die at the convention, however. During the next session of the legislature, eight constitutional amendments were passed that effectively would have rewritten the constitution through the normal amendment process. Each proposal, however, was turned down by the electorate in a special election on November 4, 1975. The Constitution of 1876 remained alive, if not well.

Land developer Frank Sharp was convicted of violating federal banking and security laws in 1972. The Sharpstown scandal rocked Texas politics and led to calls for constitutional reform.

Recent Amendments

One thing that is clear about Texas elections dealing with constitutional amendments is that voting participation is invariably low. "Who Are Texans?" compares the percentage turnout of registered voters in November special elections on constitutional amendments with the percentage turnout in presidential elections (which tend to produce the highest turnout). There are two likely reasons for the low voter turnout in constitutional amendment elections: First, constitutional amendment elections are usually held in "off" years—following the general session of the legislature (and most special sessions)—when there are no elections with candidates on the ballot. Without candidates to generate voter turnout, the political parties take a less active role in getting out their voters. As a result, advertising campaigns about the election are frequently limited to those of interest groups that support or oppose the issues on the ballot. Second, many of the amendments are relatively insignificant to most voters.

While most proposed constitutional amendments are uncontroversial, such was not the case in 2011 when 3 of the 10 amendments presented to the voters were turned down. The controversial ones were those that the Tea Party and other antitax groups saw as increasing the financial burden on Texans. For example, Proposition 4 was defeated because it would have expanded the ability of counties to issue bonds to finance the development of unproductive areas where those bonds were to be repaid with property tax revenues. Critics of the proposal argued that it would clear the way for new toll roads. Proposition 7 was defeated because it would have given El Paso new borrowing

TABLE 2.6

Passed Constitutional Amendments, 2017

Proposition 1	Authorizes the legislature to provide for an exemption from ad valorem taxation of part of the market value of the residence homestead of a partially disabled veteran or the surviving spouse of a partially disabled veteran if the residence homestead was donated to the disabled veteran by a charitable organization for less than the market value of the residence homestead and harmonizing certain related provisions of the Texas Constitution. (Passed 86.0%)
Proposition 2	Establishes a lower amount for expenses that can be charged to a borrower and removing certain financing expense limitations for a home equity loan, establishing certain authorized lenders to make a home equity loan, changing certain options for the refinancing of home equity loans, changing the threshold for an advance of a home equity line of credit, and allowing home equity loans on agricultural homesteads. (Passed 68.6%)
Proposition 3	Limits the service of certain officeholders appointed by the governor and confirmed by the Senate after the expiration of the person's term of office. (Passed 83.4%)
Proposition 4	Authorizes the legislature to require a court to provide notice to the attorney general of a challenge to the constitutionality of a state statute and authorizing the legislature to prescribe a waiting period before the court may enter a judgment holding the statute unconstitutional. (Passed 64.3%)
Proposition 5	Permits additional professional sports team charitable foundations conducting charitable raffles. (Passed 60.3%)
Proposition 6	Authorizes the legislature to provide for an exemption from ad valorem taxation of all or part of the market value of the residence homestead of the surviving spouse of a first responder who is killed or fatally injured in the line of duty. (Passed 84.6%)
Proposition 7	Authorizes the legislature to permit credit unions and other financial institutions to award prizes by lot to promote savings. (Passed 59.7%)

authority. Proposition 8, which passed the legislature with bipartisan support, was defeated because it would have given property owners the opportunity to opt out of agricultural or wildlife conservation property tax exemptions in favor of water conservation property tax exemptions. The Tea Party successfully opposed the proposition on the grounds that it would shift the tax burden to others.[19] While the Tea Party and other antitax groups could not defeat all of the propositions they opposed, low voter turnout enabled them to exert a significant influence. Indeed, their defeat of three proposals broke the modern pattern in which amendments are routinely approved. For example, between 2001 and 2010, 77 of 79 proposed amendments were approved. In the 2017 constitutional amendment elections, voters were asked to consider seven proposed amendments (see Table 2.6). All seven passed, although only approximately 5.7 percent of registered voters bothered to vote, down from 11.3 percent in the 2015 constitutional amendment elections.

Participation in the 2005 constitutional amendment election may appear to be abnormally high (see "Who Are Texans?" on p. 77). Most of the 2005 proposed constitutional amendments were, like the previously discussed propositions, of significance only to a narrow group of people. For example, one of the nine proposed amendments provided for clearing land titles in Upshur and Smith counties. Another authorized the legislature to

PERSONAL RESPONSIBILITY: WHAT WOULD YOU DO?

- Do you think that more people should participate in constitutional amendment elections? Why or why not?

- What do you think groups or political parties should do to increase turnout for constitutional amendment elections?

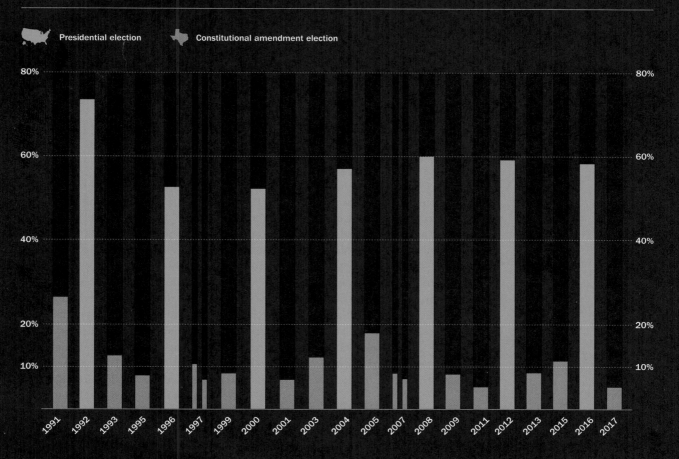

Who Votes in Texas Elections Amending the Constitution?

Turnout of Registered Voters in Texas Constitutional Amendment Elections Compared with Presidential Elections*

Presidential election   Constitutional amendment election

Since 1983, Texans have voted to amend the state's constitution dozens of times. Turnout in these elections is always low, even when well-publicized amendments are on the ballot. For example, in 2005, 17 percent of registered voters voted on Proposition 2, which banned same-sex marriage in the state.

* 1997 elections in August and November; 2007 elections in May and November.

SOURCE: Texas Secretary of State, www.sos.state.tx.us/ (accessed 3/18/18).

QUANTITATIVE REASONING

- What is the difference between participation rates in presidential elections and constitutional amendment elections? What might account for this difference?

- What could be done to increase turnout in constitutional amendment elections?

How Should We Balance Civil Rights and Religious Freedom?

Constitutional protections can clash with one another. The right to practice one's conservative religious beliefs can come into conflict with the civil rights of another person to get married. In Texas, Democrats, Republicans, and self-identified members of the conservative Tea Party movement disagree sharply on how these protections should be balanced with one another. In the context of controversies around same-sex marriage and transgender rights, a recent poll in Texas asked respondents to evaluate the following statement:

"A sincerely held religious belief is a legitimate reason to exempt someone from laws designed to prevent discrimination."

	AGREE (%)	DISAGREE (%)	DON'T KNOW (%)
ALL	30%	51%	19%
Republicans	40	39	21
Democrats	14	72	13
Tea Party	57	29	14

SOURCE: UT/TT Poll June 2017. Margin of error +/- 2.83 percent

provide for a six-year term for a board member of a regional mobility authority. Yet the turnout in this election was much higher than is typically seen in constitutional amendment elections. The reason was Proposition 2, which defined marriage in Texas as the union of one man and one woman. The proposition also prohibited the state or any political subdivision of the state from creating or recognizing any legal status identical to or similar to marriage. The proposition generated a strongly favorable vote—1,723,782 in favor versus 536,913 against. Unlike Proposition 12 in 2003, this was not an economic battle involving interests concerned with tort law; rather, this was an issue pitting social conservatives against those more sympathetic to gay rights. The strength of the social conservative vote in the state was, of course, remarkable, since the amendment carried by more than a 3-to-1 margin. Many churches and religious organizations strongly supported the proposed amendment. Their activities probably generated the relatively high voter turnout. The proposition was unusual in that people felt it was important to their lives because it affected their value systems. Although it is doubtful the amendment was necessary to support the traditional concept of marriage and although the ambiguity of the provision rejecting any legal status similar to marriage is disturbing, a significant part of the voting population apparently believed that it was important to vote their moral values, even if the proposal was largely symbolic.

Although most constitutional amendments are not of great importance, there are some notable exceptions. Table 2.7 identifies some of those amendments that, like Proposition 12 in 2003 or Proposition 2 in 2005, have had great significance in the public policy of the state.

Amendments to the state constitution affect many areas of Texans' lives. The amendments passed in 2017 included one providing property tax exemptions for the spouses of first responders killed in action. This amendment was first proposed in the legislature in memory of Little Elm police detective Jerry Walker, who was killed in action in January 2017.

Same-Sex Marriage and the Texas Constitution

RECENT controversy over same-sex marriage highlights the tensions that emerge between the federal and the Texas constitutions.

In November 2005, Texans went to the polls to vote on Proposition 2 to amend the Texas Constitution, a measure aimed at prohibiting same-sex marriages in the state. Supporters of Proposition 2 wanted the ban on such marriages enshrined in the state constitution in order to prevent any future legislation supporting gay and lesbian marriages. The measure passed, with nearly 76 percent of voters supporting it.

In *Obergefell v. Hodges* (2015), the U.S. Supreme Court ruled 5–4 that marriage was a fundamental right guaranteed to same-sex couples by the due process clause and the equal protection clause of the Fourteenth Amendment of the Constitution. Writing for the majority, Justice Kennedy explained the Supreme Court opinion clearly: "The Court now holds that same-sex couples may exercise the fundamental right to marry. No longer may this liberty be denied them." Although Texas was not one of the states involved in the *Obergefell* case, the ruling clearly applied to it.

One might have thought that the *Obergefell* decision would have ended debate over the legal status of same-sex marriage in Texas, superseding the provisions put into the Texas Constitution. But a few public officials sought to undercut the full effect of the U.S. Supreme Court ruling. In June 2015, Hood County Clerk Katie Lang said that she would refuse to issue same-sex marriage licenses because of her religious faith. Backtracking after a public furor broke out, she later agreed to allow staff members to issue the licenses. Attorney General Ken Paxton, a bitter opponent of same-sex marriage, advised county clerks in Texas that they could refuse marriage licenses to same-sex couples on religious grounds. According to Paxton, "Justices of the peace retain religious freedoms, and may claim that the government cannot force them to conduct same-sex wedding ceremonies over their religious objections." Threatened with a contempt citation from a federal judge, Paxton backed off, maintaining that he himself was not enforcing the laws that impeded gay marriage rights, only advising others about what courses of action could be pursued by public officials in Texas.

Additional complications arose in June 2017 when the Texas Supreme Court ruled that Texas courts could explore "the reach and ramification" of marriage related issues resulting from the *Obergefell* ruling, including whether spouses of gay and lesbian public employees in Houston were entitled to marriage-related benefits. Having extended benefits to gay and lesbian spouses following *Obergefell*, the city of Houston appealed the case to the U.S. Supreme Court, arguing that *Obergefell* demanded an extension of spousal benefits to all married employees. The U.S. Supreme Court chose in December 2017 not to review the Texas Supreme Court's decision.

Paxton's "advisory" opinion and the Houston spousal benefits case raise interesting questions. Should the personal religious values of

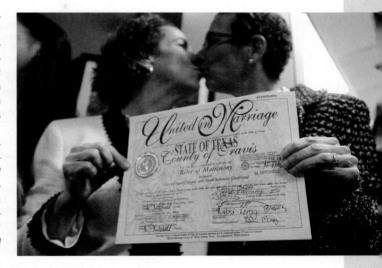

public officials allow them to not enforce the law? Should lawmakers bring the Texas Constitution in line with the *Obergefell* case by deleting the Proposition 2 provisions? Should spouses of gays and lesbians be offered the same benefits as spouses in heterosexual marriages? Should new provisions be added that protect the religious beliefs of state officials in the performance of their duties while upholding the principles of the U.S. Constitution?

COMMUNICATING EFFECTIVELY: YOUR VOICE

- Is Proposition 2 a violation of the equal protection clause of the U.S. Constitution? Should it be deleted from the Texas Constitution? Should provisions be made in the Texas Constitution for protecting spousal benefits for gays and lesbians?

- If you were writing a letter to the editor about this issue, what arguments would you make either in support of Paxton or in disagreement with him? How would you answer, or support, those who ask that they be allowed to listen to their "religious consciences" and not perform the duties for which they were elected?

TABLE 2.7

Some Important Constitutional Amendments

1894	an amendment providing for the election of railroad commissioners. In later years, when Texas became a major oil producer, the railroad commission gained the authority to regulate oil production and became the most powerful elected regulatory agency in the country.
1902	an amendment "requiring all persons subject to a poll tax to have paid a poll tax and to hold a receipt for same before they offer to vote at any election in this state, and fixing the time of payment of said tax." The poll tax required a payment of money prior to voting. The effect was to reduce the size of the electorate, limiting the opportunity of those with lower incomes to vote.
1919	state prohibition amendment, the same year the national Prohibition Amendment was ratified.
1935	repealed statewide prohibition, replaced it with a local-option policy whereby local communities chose whether alcohol could be sold there.
1954	an amendment requiring women to serve on juries if summoned. Previously, women were exempt on the grounds that they were needed at home as the center of home life.
1966	repealed the poll tax as a voting requirement in the face of pressures from the U.S. Supreme Court and from a national constitutional amendment that eliminated the poll tax in national elections.
1972	a constitutional amendment "to provide that equality under the law shall not be denied or abridged because of sex, race, color, creed or national origin." This amendment was seen as primarily banning sex discrimination, since federal civil rights statutes largely dealt with discrimination on other grounds. It was the state version of a proposed sexual equal rights amendment that was never ratified and made part of the U.S. Constitution.
2003	an amendment that placed limitations on lawsuits, reflecting the "tort reform" agenda. In "civil lawsuits against doctors and health care providers, and other actions," the legislature was authorized "to determine limitations on noneconomic damages."
2005	an amendment "providing that marriage in this state consists only of the union of one man and one woman and prohibiting this state or a political subdivision of this state from creating or recognizing any legal status identical or similar to marriage." The amendment was passed in response to the movement toward the recognition of civil unions and same-sex marriage in some states.
2009	an amendment establishing "the national research university fund to enable emerging research universities in this state to achieve national prominence as major research universities." The amendment was a recognition that the Texas economy would benefit by the development of more nationally recognized research universities in the state.
2009	an amendment "to prohibit the taking, damaging, or destroying of private property for public use unless the action is for the ownership, use, and enjoyment of the property by the State, a political subdivision of the State, the public at large, or entities granted the power of eminent domain under law or for the elimination of urban blight on a particular parcel of property, but not for certain economic development or enhancements of tax revenue purpose, passed in reaction to a U.S. Supreme Court decision involving eminent domain—the taking of private property for public use—that was seen as unsympathetic to property rights.

The Constitution and the Future of Texas

IN THIS CHAPTER, we explored the Texas Founding and the story of constitutional government in Texas. We analyzed the seven constitutions under which Texas has been governed and explained the similarities and differences between the U.S. Constitution and Texas's current constitution (the Constitution of 1876). We also discussed successful and unsuccessful attempts to amend the constitution and some of the constitutional issues that face Texas today.

It has been decades since there was any serious effort to change the Texas Constitution in any way other than by adding to its numerous amendments. This pattern likely will continue: more and more amendments will be added to an already lengthy and cumbersome document. Many of these amendments will address technical problems often related to the operations of various state agencies and local governments. Some may create additional funding sources for major state initiatives as we have seen recently in water and transportation policy. Other amendments might be adopted in response to such controversial social issues as abortion or the free exercise of religion. Turnout in constitutional amendment elections will remain low, unless there is a highly controversial amendment on the ballot. Though narrow interests have outsized influence on the proposing and passage of constitutional amendments, the constitution and its amendments will continue to reflect the values and goals of the people of Texas and the political system that the people have put into place through the constitution.

STUDY GUIDE

Use 🐰 inQuizitive to help you study and master this material.

The Role of a State Constitution

- **Identify the main functions of state constitutions (pp. 47–49)**

The state constitution is the governing document of the state much in the same way the U.S. Constitution sets up the framework for the nation as a whole. Many of the ideas found in the U.S. Constitution are also found in Texas's constitutions, including republican government, separation of powers, checks and balances, and individual rights.

Key Terms
constitution (p. 47)
separation of powers (p. 47)
checks and balances (p. 47)
tyranny (p. 47)
federalism (p. 48)
supremacy clause (p. 48)
necessary and proper clause (p. 48)

Practice Quiz
1. Which idea is contained in both the U.S. and Texas constitutions?
   a) separation of powers
   b) Keynesianism
   c) laissez-faire economics
   d) *Rebus sic stantibus*
   e) none of the above

2. Which of the following is *not* an important function of a state constitution?
   a) prevents the concentration of political power
   b) delegates power to individuals and institutions
   c) allows government to intrude in the lives of businesses and individuals
   d) legitimizes political institutions
   e) limits application of the U.S. Constitution

3. Which part of the U.S. Constitution reserves power to the states?
   a) Article I
   b) Article VI
   c) First Amendment
   d) Tenth Amendment
   e) Nineteenth Amendment

4. Under the U.S. Constitution, the government of Texas is most limited by
   a) Article IV of the U.S. Constitution.
   b) the implied-powers clause and the Tenth Amendment of the U.S. Constitution.
   c) the Fourteenth Amendment of the U.S. Constitution.
   d) all of the above equally
   e) none of the above

The Texas Constitutions: 1836–1876

- **Describe the seven Texas constitutions and their role in Texas political life (pp. 49–64)**

Texas has had seven constitutions reflecting the concerns of the historical periods in which they were written. The Civil War and Reconstruction played a major role in shaping Texans' attitudes toward the dangers of strong state government. The Constitution of 1876 sought to limit the powers that had been wielded under the previous constitution by Republican governor Edmund Davis. It remains, though much amended, the existing state constitution of Texas.

Key Terms

unicameral (p. 50)
bicameral (p. 52)
Confederacy (p. 58)
Presidential Reconstruction (p. 58)
Congressional Reconstruction (p. 59)
Radical Republicans (p. 59)
Grange (p. 61)

Practice Quiz

5. The Constitution of 1861
   a) generally accepted the existing constitutional framework.
   b) guided Texas's entry into the Confederate States of America.
   c) supported slavery.
   d) defended states' rights.
   e) all of the above

6. A unique feature of the Constitution of 1869 was that
   a) it explicitly rejected the power of the federal government in Texas.
   b) fewer than 1 percent of voters opposed it.
   c) it was less than four pages long.
   d) it was never submitted to the voters.
   e) it is considered the best of Texas's constitutions.

7. A new Texas Constitution was written
   a) when Reconstruction ended.
   b) when the Compromise of 1850 was adopted.
   c) at the start of World War I.
   d) in 1999.
   e) none of the above

8. The present Texas Constitution
   a) is well organized and well written.
   b) is considered to be one of the best of the 50 state constitutions.
   c) delegates a great deal of power to the governor.
   d) severely limits the power of the governor and other state officials.
   e) all of the above

9. The Constitution of 1876 was a reaction to the Reconstruction Constitution of 1869 because
   a) the 1869 Constitution was too short.
   b) the 1869 Constitution forbade slavery.
   c) the 1869 Constitution increased state officials' salaries.
   d) the 1869 Constitution was seen as giving the governor too much power.
   e) none of the above

10. When the framers of the Constitution of 1876 wrote of "the people," they meant
    a) all adult citizens of Texas.
    b) all adult male citizens of Texas.
    c) all men and women over the age of 21.
    d) all citizens except carpetbaggers and scalawags.
    e) none of the above

The Constitution of Texas Today

The Texas Constitution is composed of 16 articles (one of the original 17 articles has been deleted). The articles lay out the complex structures of power that define government in Texas.

Key Terms
limited government (p. 64)
republican government (p. 66)
plural executive (p. 68)
impeachment (p. 72)

Practice Quiz
11. The *separation of powers doctrine* refers to
    a) the idea that the United States is composed of 50 individual states.
    b) local government being autonomous from state rules and regulations.
    c) power being divided in Texas into three distinct branches of government: the legislature, the executive, and the judiciary.
    d) the process that sees the secretary of state appointed by the governor.
    e) none of the above

12. *Impeachment* refers to
    a) the power of the Court to declare a legislative act unconstitutional.
    b) the power of the House to charge a state official of inappropriate behavior leading to a trial by the Senate to remove him or her from office.
    c) the power of the governor to remove a judge from office.
    d) the result of an election.
    e) none of the above

Recent Attempts to Rewrite the Texas Constitution

• **Describe modern efforts to change the Texas Constitution (pp. 73–80)**

Practice Quiz

13. What did the Sharpstown scandal teach about constitutional reform in Texas?
   a) It is difficult to pass a wholesale revision of the state constitution.
   b) It is impossible to amend any provision of the constitution.
   c) Constitution reform has the support of the people but not the legislature.
   d) A governor can prevent constitutional reform from taking place.
   e) none of the above

14. The 1974 Constitutional Convention
   a) successfully rewrote the Texas Constitution.
   b) rewrote the Bill of Rights included in the Texas Constitution.
   c) contained articles of secession from the United States.
   d) failed to achieve any significant reforms of the existing Texas Constitutions.
   e) all of the above

15. Why is there such low participation in constitutional amendment elections?
   a) the elections are unimportant
   b) these elections are held in "off" years
   c) they are generally held before special sessions of the legislature
   d) they are held during a regular session of the legislature
   e) none of the above

The relationship between the state and federal governments has remained a key issue in Texas. Recently, Governor Greg Abbott called for a U.S. constitutional convention to amend the Constitution and strengthen the powers of states versus those of the national government.

Texas in the Federal System

WHY FEDERALISM MATTERS The issue of federalism—in the United States, how power is shared between national and state governments—has been a fundamental political concern since the nation's founding, and it continues to be a major political issue in Texas. Republican governor Greg Abbott is a major advocate of state power and a critic of the power of the national government. Abbott has called for a Constitutional convention which he believes will force the federal government to "take the Constitution seriously again." He wants Texas to be a leader in calling for a Constitutional convention to take power from a federal government that he believes has "run amok."[1]

A Constitutional convention is one of two ways to amend the U.S. Constitution. Congress can propose amendments that must be approved by two-thirds of the members of both chambers. Alternatively, two-thirds of state legislatures may call a convention to propose amendments. In both cases, three-fourths of the states must ratify the proposed amendments for them to become effective. No constitutional amendment has ever been generated by a constitutional convention, but Abbott sees the convention as the way to bypass Congress, insofar as Congress, as a part of the federal government, would be unwilling to return power to the states.[2] Abbott claims,

Indeed, the entire structure of the Constitution was premised on the idea that the States would be stronger than the national government. . . . And the Anti-Federalists' principal complaint with the Constitution was premised on their fear that it would turn the States into "useless and burdensome" relics. Madison passionately rebutted those concerns by insisting that the States would remain the most powerful and important organs of American government. If only we had heeded Madison's solutions to the Anti-Federalists' concerns, our Nation would not be mired in this constitutional conundrum today. But over the last 227 years, in fits and starts, through baby steps and giant leaps, our government lost its way; it left the Constitution in its rearview; and it pushed States into the roadside ditch.[3]

To strengthen the states and weaken the power of the national government, Abbott would like to require a balanced federal budget and prevent Congress from regulating activities occurring within a state, the latter which would likely prevent federal regulation of gun use and marriage. Among his other proposed amendments are ones that would allow federal laws and U.S. Supreme Court decisions to be overridden by two-thirds of the states and require a seven-justice supermajority for the Supreme Court to invalidate a state or national law.[4]

Abbott's proposal for a convention, while unlikely to be adopted, is one of the most comprehensive proposals for change that has been offered by Texans unhappy with the exercise of national governmental power. For the time being, rather than in a constitutional convention, the issues of federalism are being fought out in the federal courts where Texas and other states are involved in litigation involving immigration policy, voter ID, affirmative action, and environmental legislation.

Abbott's passion about national versus state power is nothing new in Texas politics. Major Texas political figures have been critical of the expanded role of the national government and the corresponding weakened role of the states going back at least to the administration of President Franklin Roosevelt in the 1930s and 1940s. In recent years, however, it has been Texas Republicans hostile to Democratic presidential administrations that have bemoaned the loss of state power to the national government. Reflecting the views of many conservative Texans, Governor Abbott has complained that, "For decades, the federal government has grown too big, too costly and too intrusive into our lives."[5] That hostility to the national government was identified by political scientist V.O. Key in 1949 in his classic book *Southern Politics in State and Nation*, where he argued that economic issues were the key divisions in Texas politics and that economic concerns affected Texans' views about national policies. Key wrote,

> Texans are coming to be concerned broadly about what government ought and ought not to do. In our times the grand issues of politics almost invariably turn on the economic policies of government. To what extent shall wealth and power, corporate or personal, be restrained for the protection of the defenseless? What services shall the government perform? Who shall pay for them? Such are the great questions that divide people and that politicians must solve provisionally from day to day to keep the wheels of our system turning.[6]

The economic conservatism of Texas that Key identified in 1949 remains today and puts modern Texas political leaders in conflict with liberal economic policies at the national level, particularly Democratic liberal economic policies. Added to that economic conservatism has been the emergence of a social conservatism on issues such as same-sex marriage, abortion, and transgender rights. Conservative views on these issues among Texas political leaders have produced still another area of conflict with national Democratic social policies.

Given that economic and social issues lie at the core of politics, a key question is: What difference does it make if the involvement of the national government in Texans' lives is reduced? What would be the effect on Texans' lives if state government had an enhanced involvement in governmental economic and social policies?

CHAPTER GOALS

- Understand the foundations of the U.S. federal system (pp. 89–94)
- Trace the major changes in national and state power over time (pp. 94–98)
- Describe the sources of, and tensions between, national and state power (pp. 98–109)

The Roots of American Federalism

Federalism is a system of government in which power is divided between a central government and regional governments. In the United States, the balance between the powers of the states and those of the national government has been the subject of intense political dispute since the American Revolution. States have always done much of the routine governance in the United States. State laws provide the regulations for birth, death, marriage, divorce, and most crime and punishment. Most commercial law is regulated by the states, and states manage education, prisons, highways, welfare, environmental issues, corporations, and professions. The many conflicts that have been fought over the proper roles of states versus the national government include disputes over the states' rights to leave the Union, the power of government to regulate business, the implementation of political reforms, and responses to problems of race, poverty, and abortion.

Roughly 40 percent of the world's population lives in countries that are organized around a federal principle where there is a national government and regional governments, each of which has the authority to maintain order, make laws, spend money, and provide services. The remaining countries have a centralized government where the regional governments are simply an arm of national governmental power. Federalist countries include the United States, Argentina, Australia, Austria, Belgium, Brazil, Canada, Ethiopia, Germany, India, Mexico, Nigeria, Spain, and Switzerland. The European

federalism a system of government in which power is divided between a central government and regional governments

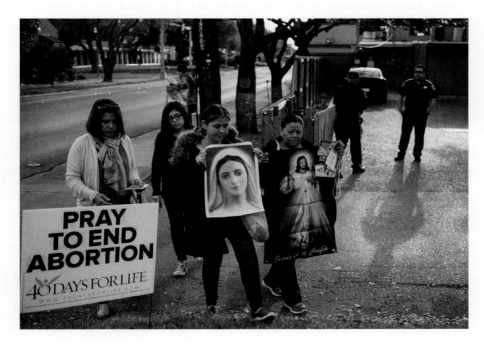

In recent years, Texas conservatives have clashed with the federal government's policies on key social issues, like abortion rights. Anti-abortion protesters demonstrated outside an abortion clinic in McAllen, Texas.

Union may be developing into a federalist system as well. Federalism exists because it is a method for bringing together smaller units to achieve larger goals—primarily the fostering of commerce and improving military security while allowing the smaller units some degree of autonomy in managing their internal affairs. In India, Belgium, and Spain, for example, federalism has been used to hold together nations that have serious geographical, ethnic, or cultural divisions. In these countries, the regional governments represent distinctive ethnic or religious groups and have unique powers of self-governance. In other federal systems, the national government consciously attempts to redistribute the country's wealth to the poorest regions, something not done in the United States. For whatever reasons, federalism has proven enormously flexible in the United States in comparison with other federal nations. It has adapted to vast changes in the geographic size of America, to large increases in its population, and to changes in the racial, religious, and ethnic background of its population. It has also adapted to vast economic changes in the nation.[7]

The Constitutional Roots of Federalism

For several years after the United States won its independence from Britain, the Articles of Confederation gave states the primary role in governance, and the national government was small and had limited powers. Its relative weakness meant that the states functioned as nearly independent entities rather than as a unified nation. By the mid-1780s, the states' diversity and self-serving policies appeared to be splitting the new nation apart. An economic decline in the 1780s worsened the divisions in the country. Daniel Shays led a rebellion of Massachusetts debtors who attacked towns and burned courthouses, and the new nation seemed on the precipice of revolt. George Washington criticized the state governments for the new nation's problems, saying the states' pursuit of narrow self-interest was making "the situation of this great country weak, inefficient and disgraceful."

It was hard for the national government under the Articles of Confederation to act. The Confederation Congress had limited powers, and the rules allowed a few states—in some cases a single state—to block congressional action. It took 9 states (out of 13) to enact any defense or economic policy. The Congress could not tax; it had to request money from the state governments, and it could not compel payment by them. The Confederation also had no executive or court system and could not defend the nation because it could not pay for an army or a navy. By 1786 the Congress was broke because states were not paying their share of expenses for the national government. Even though a majority of the states supported the Congress's efforts to tax imports, individual states killed these proposals. Moreover, the Articles of Confederation could not easily be amended, because a unanimous vote of the states was required for amendment.[8]

By 1786 it was becoming clear that something had to be done to increase the power of the national government. A meeting was held that year in Annapolis, Maryland, that called for a convention of states to meet in Philadelphia the following year to "render the constitution of the Federal Government adequate to the exigencies of the Union." That call led to the Constitutional Convention in 1787, where 55 delegates met and designed the new U.S. Constitution.[9]

Under the U.S. Constitution, a federal system was created in which the national government was **sovereign**, deriving its power directly from the American people. The

sovereign possessing supreme political authority within a geographic area

During the American Revolution, the lack of a strong central government made it difficult for the United States to fund a strong military, as exemplified by terrible conditions for the troops at Valley Forge.

immediate effect of the Constitution was to increase national power and to delegate to the national government distinctive powers and responsibilities such as national defense and foreign policy. Individual states were also sovereign, however, deriving their power from the people in their state through their state constitutions and having their own separate powers and responsibilities, such as protecting public safety.[10] Under this system, local governments were created by state governments, and their powers are granted (and can be revoked) by state governments. Rather than being a designated part of a federal system, local governments were the creations of states, and continue to be so today (see Chapter 10).

State interests were protected under the new Constitution in a variety of ways, and one of the most important was that each state would get equal representation in the Senate. At the time, state legislatures chose the U.S. senators from that state, and so the senators were agents of state interests in the national government. States also retained their power to tax and to maintain a militia, and they had commercial powers, such as the power to regulate commerce within states.

For its part, the national government had taxing authority, military powers, and commercial authority such as the power to regulate commerce between states. And it had flexible powers that could be expanded in the future through Congress's constitutional power "[t]o make all Laws which shall be necessary and proper for carrying into Execution the foregoing Powers, and all other Powers vested by this Constitution In the Government of the United States."[11]

The Tenth Amendment In the debates over ratification of the Constitution, there was great concern that the national government had been made too powerful and that, if ratified, the Constitution would foster a centralized tyranny that would destroy the rights of the people and the states. In an effort to alleviate these concerns, the Bill of Rights was added to the Constitution in the form of the first ten amendments. The Tenth Amendment, commonly called the States' Rights Amendment, says, "The powers not delegated to the United States by the Constitution, nor prohibited by it to the States, are reserved to the States respectively, or to the people." Although James Madison personally did not believe that the Tenth Amendment was necessary, he urged that it be adopted. The problem with the amendment is that it does not delineate national and state powers, and so rather than settle conflicts over federalism, the amendment has become a source of conflict over the meaning of federalism.[12]

Federalism in Early America

Controversy over the exact nature of the federal system divided Americans in the late 1820s and '30s. During the Nullification Crisis in 1833, South Carolina tried to assert the right to veto (or nullify) national legislation passed by Congress. The prominent South Carolina politician John C. Calhoun, then vice president under President Andrew Jackson, argued that a strong national government was a threat to the sovereignty of states and called for a federal system along the lines of the original Articles of Confederation. When Jackson responded by threatening to use military force in support of federal law, however, South Carolina backed down.

Although the national government had imposed its will successfully during the Nullification Crisis, the question of the exact relationship between it and individual states was still open. In spite of the forces of decentralization, most notably coming from the South, the Supreme Court under Chief Justice John Marshall (1801–35) issued a number of important opinions that promoted national power at the expense of state power.

In *McCulloch v. Maryland* (1819), for example, one issue was whether Congress had the power to incorporate the Second Bank of the United States. If it did have that power, a second issue was whether Maryland could tax the bank. Writing for a unanimous Court, Marshall noted that Article I, Section 8, of the Constitution enumerated the powers of Congress. Nowhere in Article I, Section 8, is specifically found the power to incorporate a bank. However, Article I, Section 8, also contains a provision that Congress has the power "[t]o make all Laws which shall be necessary and proper for carrying into Execution the foregoing powers, and all other Powers vested by this Constitution in the Government of the United States." Because a Bank of the United States could be a means to accomplish some of those enumerated powers, such as carrying out the power to borrow money, the Court found that Congress did have the implied power to incorporate the bank. Thus, the "necessary and proper" clause of Article I, Section 8, provided a source of implied powers for the national government. Marshall further noted in his opinion that unlike the Articles of Confederation, the U.S. Constitution had no provision that excluded the recognition of implied powers. He even made the case that the Tenth Amendment recognized that Congress had implied powers because it said "The powers not delegated to the United States" rather than "The powers not *expressly* delegated to the United States."

The Court also ruled that a state did not have the power to tax the Second Bank of the United States. For the states to have that taxing power, Marshall argued, would transfer the supremacy of the national government to the states. This was a vastly important decision favoring national power at the expense of state powers.[13]

Another major Marshall Court decision that expanded national power was *Gibbons v. Ogden* (1824), which dealt with a dispute over the operation of steamboats in New York waters. Robert Fulton and Robert Livingston obtained a monopoly from New York to operate steamboats in its waters, and they granted a license to Aaron Ogden to operate steamboats between New Jersey and New York. When Thomas Gibbons then obtained a license from the national government to operate steamboats between New Jersey and New York, Ogden went to New York courts to get an injunction against Gibbons. Marshall wrote that one of the powers of Congress in Article I, Section 8, was the "power to regulate commerce with foreign nations, and among the several states."[14] Ogden argued that such power was limited to the interchange of commodities and did not include navigation, but Marshall broadly defined commerce to include navigation and wrote that interstate commerce "cannot stop at the external boundary line of each state, but may be introduced into the interior." While the completely internal commerce of a state could be considered reserved to the states for regulation, he wrote, if commerce was not completely internal to a state, then it was interstate commerce and could be regulated by Congress, as the regulation of interstate commerce "does not stop at the jurisdictional lines of the several states."[15] This decision, providing a broad definition of interstate commerce, was to be the primary source of the most important regulatory power of Congress: the power to regulate interstate commerce.

A major power of the national government is the power to regulate interstate commerce. Gibbons v. Ogden (1824) was a key case that expanded national power. It held that Congress had the power to regulate interstate commerce, such as shipping between New York and New Jersey, pictured here.

Marshall was consistent when deciding cases in expanding the power of the national government and weakening the power of states. However, he was unwilling to make the Bill of Rights apply to the states as well as the national government, a step that would require the ratification of the Fourteenth Amendment in 1868. In Marshall's time, it was clear that the Bill of Rights was not a restriction on the powers of states; it was intended to limit the powers of the national government.

The Constitution was created out of a fear of disunity. Seventy-five years after the ratification of the Constitution, an observer of American federalism would have concluded that it was a failure. America faced a massive rebellion and a war that was immensely bloody.[16] Texas played a major part in the tensions between the North and the South that threatened the Union when Texas sought and was ultimately admitted to the Union as a slave state. Only sixteen years after its admission to the Union, Texas seceded and joined the Confederacy. With secession of southern states came the Civil War, which was, in part, a struggle over the meaning of the federal system and the proper relationship between the national and the state governments. Southern states, including Texas, feared that a national government controlled by northern states would move to end slavery, an institution that the southern states felt was essential to their social, political, and economic way of life. They saw the creation of the Confederacy as a movement back to the older system embodied in the Articles of Confederation, wherein the central government in Richmond was weak and the individual states were strong. This vision of a confederation effectively came to a close in 1865 with General Robert E. Lee's surrender to Union General Ulysses Grant at the Appomattox Court House.

Four years later, in 1869, Texas was a party to the case in which the Supreme Court resolved the debate over whether states can secede from the Union. The case, *Texas v. White*, dealt with the legality of a bond sale sponsored by the state that had occurred under its Confederate government. In rejecting the legality of the sale, Chief Justice

The United States and Texas flags that fly in front of many government buildings in Texas (including the Texas state capitol, pictured here) reflect the nature of federalism. Both the national government and the state government are sovereign.

Reconstruction the period after the Civil War when much of the South was under military occupation

dual federalism the concept of federalism that prevailed in the United States from 1789 to 1937, in which most fundamental governmental powers were strictly separated between the federal and state governments

layer-cake federalism a way of describing the system of dual federalism in which there is a division of responsibilities between the state and the national governments

Salmon Chase's opinion said that the Constitution "in all its provisions, looks to an indestructible Union, composed of indestructible states." Secession was void and Texas had remained a U.S. state during the Civil War; it had not had a lawful government during the Confederacy, and so the bond sale was void. Additionally, the Court ruled, the national government could create a government in Texas after the war where no legitimate government existed because Article IV, Section 4, of the Constitution provided, "The United States shall guarantee to every State in this Union a Republican Form of Government."[17]

Federalism: Texas and the Nation over Time

Trace the major changes in national and state power over time

Following the end of **Reconstruction** and into the early twentieth century, the court embraced dual federalism. **Dual federalism**, sometimes called dual sovereignty, was the idea that the national government had a limited sphere of powers which did not overlap or interfere with state powers. With dual federalism, the national government was relatively small in comparison to the states, and states did most of the governing. Citizens' daily lives were chiefly affected by their state governments, not the national government, whose role was more or less limited to providing for national defense and foreign policy and assisting in the development of commerce.

Prior to the late 1930s the Supreme Court was using dual federalism to strike down regulation of the economy by the national government. Congressional power to regulate interstate commerce was narrowly defined, Congress was powerless to forbid the distribution of the products of child labor in interstate commerce, and it could not regulate aspects of the manufacture of goods, such as monopolies on production or working conditions in factories.

Dual versus Cooperative Federalism

In **layer-cake federalism**, the responsibilities of the national government and state governments are clearly separated. In marble-cake federalism, national policies, state policies, and local policies overlap in many areas.

Dual federalism was described by political scientist Morton Grodzins as layer-cake federalism (see Figure 3.1). Like the layers on a cake, the powers of the national government and state governments were largely separate and, one might add, the layer that was the national government's powers and responsibilities was smaller than was the layer that represented the powers and responsibilities of state governments.[18] Under layer-cake federalism, there were still clear limits to the sovereignty of states. States could not nullify national legislation, nor could they secede from the Union. But states had a major role to play in governance that was quite distinct from the role of the federal government.

Dual federalism had tremendous effects on issues relating to economic regulations in Texas. For example, the Railroad Commission of Texas established rules that, among other things, limited the number of oil wells that could be drilled on a particular amount of land and the amount of oil that could be pumped from those wells. Such regulations were seen as a matter for state rather than national regulation until the discovery of the East Texas Oil Field in 1930, which then was the largest oil field in the world. As a result of this discovery, such overproduction of oil occurred that national legislation was needed to prevent an interstate market in oil produced in violation of state regulations.

Dual federalism was also used to prevent national intervention into acts of racial violence in Texas, because enforcement of criminal laws was seen as a state matter. Texas did pass an anti-lynching law in 1897 that was used to prevent some lynchings by authorizing the governor to call out the state guard. Nevertheless, Texas and other states were remarkably ineffective in preventing lynching. It is hard to identify the precise number of victims, but the Equal Justice Initiative has identified 3,959 lynchings between 1877 and 1950 whose purpose was to enforce racial separation and segregation laws. Of those, 376 occurred in Texas.[19] It was only in the 1960s that national laws began to be used to successfully prosecute these crimes.

Marble-Cake Federalism

With the presidency of Franklin Roosevelt (1933–1945)—when America faced the Great Depression and then World War II—the relationship between the national government and the states changed dramatically. The change came to what has been called

FIGURE 3.1

Dual versus Cooperative Federalism

In layer-cake federalism, the responsibilities of the national government and state governments are clearly separated. In marble-cake federalism, national policies, state policies, and local policies overlap in many areas.

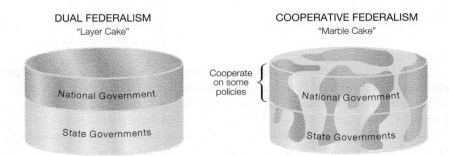

DUAL FEDERALISM
"Layer Cake"

National Government

State Governments

Cooperate on some policies

COOPERATIVE FEDERALISM
"Marble Cake"

National Government

State Governments

During the 1930s, Texans were affected by unemployment and drought that led to massive poverty across the state. The federal government stepped in to help, employing people in public works projects. Here, people make copper utensils for a Texas hospital.

marble-cake federalism a way of describing federalism where the boundaries between the national government and state governments have become blurred

cooperative federalism a type of federalism existing since the New Deal era in which grants-in-aid have been used to encourage states and localities (without requiring them) to pursue nationally defined goals; also known as intergovernmental cooperation

categorical grants congressionally appropriated grants to states and localities on the condition that expenditures be limited to a problem or group specified by law

marble-cake federalism, in which the boundaries between the national and state governments became blurred. The initial form of marble-cake federalism was **cooperative federalism**, wherein national and state governments worked together to provide services—often with joint funding of programs or state administration of programs mostly funded by the national government.

In fighting the Great Depression, Roosevelt pursued a variety of such programs. The Social Security Act of 1935, for instance, changed the existing system of federalism in a number of fundamental ways. First, it put into place a national insurance program for the elderly (now known as Social Security), wherein individuals in all states were assessed a payroll tax on their wages and upon retirement received a pension check. Second, the act put into place a series of state-federal programs to address particular social problems, including unemployment insurance, aid to dependent children, aid to the blind and disabled, and aid to impoverished elderly people. The basic model for these programs was that the federal government would make money available to states that established their own programs in these areas, provided they met specific administrative guidelines. Although the federal dollars came with these strings attached, the programs were state run and could differ from state to state. This type of funding system was common in the early days of cooperative federalism. The federal grants made using this model were called **categorical grants**.

During the New Deal period, the idea was abandoned that the Tenth Amendment was a barrier to national power and that the national government could not involve itself in areas that had previously been reserved only to the states. As the Supreme Court case *Wickard v. Filburn* (1942) suggested, the regulatory power of the national government under the interstate commerce clause was so broad that there seemed no boundaries on national power.[20]

In the 1960s, during the Great Society presidency of President Lyndon B. Johnson, a former U.S. senator from Texas, new programs were added to the Social Security Act. Medicare was established to provide health insurance for the elderly, paid for through a payroll tax on current workers. Medicaid was added to provide health care funding for individuals enrolled in the state-federal Aid to Families with Dependent Children (AFDC) program. Medicaid's funding and administration were based on the same

Federal Funds to Texas versus Other States

Many factors affect how much federal funding a state recieves. Federal money can go directly to individuals, such as Social Security or Medicare. Federal money can also go to the states, which then decide how best to use the funds to benefit their constituents, such as for highway funding. In the graph below, we can compare how much federal money Texas and Texans receive compared to California, Florida, New York, and Ohio.

Federal Funds Received by states, 2005–2017

Federal Funding as a Percentage of State Revenue, 2015

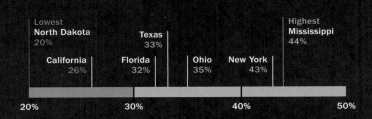

Lowest
North Dakota 20%

California 26%

Texas 33%

Florida 32%

Ohio 35%

New York 43%

Highest
Mississippi 44%

20%   30%   40%   50%

SOURCES: "Spending Map," USA Spending.gov, www.usaspending.gov, (accessed 12/01/17); John S. Kleman, "2015's States Most and Least Dependent on the Federal Government", Wallethub, wallethub.com (accessed 3/29/16).

CRITICAL THINKING

· What might explain why certain states receive more funding than others at different time periods?

· Florida and Texas received about the same amount of federal funding in 2015, even though the population of Texas is much larger. Why do you suppose Florida receives proportionally more federal funds than Texas?

state-federal principles as AFDC and unemployment insurance: the federal government provided funding for approved state programs. Federalism continued to evolve with the passage of civil rights legislation in the 1950s and '60s, when the role of the national government was expanded to protect the rights of minorities. In the process, the national government was often thrown into conflict with southern states such as Texas that persisted in trying to maintain a segregated society.

After his election in 1968, President Richard M. Nixon briefly tried a somewhat different version of federalism that he called **New Federalism**. In an attempt to reduce federal control, Nixon introduced a funding mechanism called **block grants**, which allowed the states considerable leeway in spending their federal dollars. In the 1980s, President Ronald Reagan adopted Nixon's New Federalism as his own, and block grants became an important part of state-federal cooperation.

New Federalism's biggest success, however, came during President Bill Clinton's administration, when in 1996 major reforms were passed that gave the states a significant decision-making role in welfare programs. By the 1990s liberals and conservatives were in agreement that welfare in America was broken. Replacing the state-federal system with a system of grants tied to federal regulations and guidelines lay at the heart of the Clinton welfare reforms, the most important since the New Deal.

New Federalism the attempts by Presidents Nixon and Reagan to return power to the states through block grants

block grants federal grants that allow states considerable discretion on how funds are spent

Coercive Federalism: Texas and the Federal Government

Describe the sources of, and tensions between, national and state power

coercive federalism federal policies that force states to change their policies to achieve national goals

In recent years some national actions have been described as **coercive federalism**, in which federal regulations are used to force states to change their policies to meet national goals. Until the 2012 Supreme Court decision involving the 2009 Affordable Care Act (commonly called Obamacare) struck down the provision, states were threatened with the loss of all Medicaid funding if they did not expand their Medicaid coverage to comply with the legislation.

unfunded mandates federal requirements that states or local governments pay the costs of federal policies

Perhaps most disturbing for states are the federal **unfunded mandates**, which are federal requirements that the state (or local) governments pay the costs of federal policies.[21] For example, the federal Americans with Disabilities Act requires that street curbs be accessible to wheelchairs, but the federal government does not pay for the curbs. That cost is passed on to state and local governments. The Congressional Budget Office reported that from 2006 through 2016 Congress passed 167 laws that imposed mandates on state and local governments, with 27 passed in 2015–2016. A study of the costs of unfunded mandates from 1994 through 1998 claimed they would cost states and localities $54 billion. In recent years, however, the costs of unfunded mandates have lessened. No mandate with costs exceeding $77 million has been imposed since 2010.[22]

preemption powers to act in a particular area are exclusively granted by the Constitution to the national government and cannot be interfered with by the states

Along with unfunded mandates, federal **preemption** is another aspect of coercive federalism. Preemption is based on the supremacy clause in Article VI of the U.S.

How Do Federal Funds Flow to Texas?

Federal grants provide states with money for programs that range from Medicaid and school lunches to tuberculosis control and immunization programs. As the chart below indicates, federal grants make up a majority of the money the state of Texas spends on health care and a large share of the money spent on natural resources, education, and general government.

2014–2015 Texas Budget

● = $1 billion

STATE FUNDS
$131.7B

FEDERAL FUNDS
$68.7B

Education
S: $63.6   F: $10.6

Health and human services
S: $31.5   F: $42.4

Business and economic development
S: $15.2   F: $11.1

Public safety and criminal justice
S: $10.3   F: $1.3

General government
S: $4.2   F: $0.7

Natural resources
S: $4.2   F: $2.6

Other (Regulatory, Judiciary, Legislature, General provisions)
S: $2.7   F: $0.04

SOURCE: Legislative Budget Board, "Fiscal Size-Up 2014–15 Biennium," pp. 2, 6.

QUANTITATIVE REASONING

- According to the data, what proportion of the Texas budget consists of federal funds? How might the presence of this federal money affect the relationship between the state and federal governments?

- Suppose federal funds for health and human services were eliminated. How might Texas reallocate state funds to avoid drastically reducing these services?

Constitution, which states, "This Constitution and the Laws of the United States which shall be made In Pursuance thereof; . . . shall be the supreme Law of the Land." Preemption does not force expenditures upon the states, but it does prevent the states from acting in areas that the Constitution exclusively reserves to the national government. In 2008 the city of Farmers Branch, Texas, passed an ordinance that prohibited persons who were not citizens or legally in the United States from renting a residence inside the city. Violations of the ordinance were criminal offenses which applied to both the renter and the landlord. The federal 5th Circuit Court of Appeals struck down the ordinance on preemption grounds, holding that the law interfered with the national government's constitutional power over immigration.[23]

The States Respond

States have begun to fight back against coercive federalism. The response to coercive federalism has often had a partisan tinge, in which Republican states opposed actions of the Democratic Obama administration. For instance, numerous state leaders have been highly critical of the Affordable Care Act. They have refused to initiate the state health insurance exchanges intended under the act, and a number of states, including Texas, have refused to expand Medicaid. During the Obama administration, politicians in Texas and elsewhere have also criticized what they call the federal government's weak efforts to enforce immigration laws, and thus states have become involved in aspects of immigration enforcement. State officials in Texas, Mississippi, and Oregon vowed to reject attempts by the federal government to impose new gun laws.[24] Reflecting this rebellion against coercive federalism, a number of states, including Texas, filed lawsuits against the federal government. As then attorney general Greg Abbott put it in defending such suits by his office, "When Texas challenges the federal government, it's about more than money. It's about principles—fundamental principles enshrined in the Constitution and recently reaffirmed by the U.S. Supreme Court when it said: 'The national government possesses only limited powers; the states and the people retain the remainder. The independent power of the states serves as a check on the power of the federal government.' Defending the constitutional principles that have made the United States truly exceptional: That's priceless."[25]

As coercive federalism became more common, concerns were increasingly expressed in the last few decades of the twentieth century, particularly among conservative Republicans, that the federal government was becoming too strong in the federal system. In response, not surprisingly, a more conservative Supreme Court rethought its doctrines on federalism. The effort to rethink the federal system is evident in Supreme Court decisions beginning in the 1990s. Although not dramatic reinterpretations of constitutional law, the court's rulings did begin to place limits on Congress's ability to legislate under the interstate commerce power, and the court resurrected the Tenth Amendment as a protection for the rights of states. The Tenth Amendment is now being used by some jurisdictions in an effort to prevent the federal government from forcing localities to end "sanctuary cities" and comply with federal immigration requirements.

Health care is a key federalism issue. Texas senator Ted Cruz has been among the key figures who have advanced states' opposition to the federal Affordable Care Act.

Major U.S. Constitutional and Statutory Restrictions on the States

The Thirteenth, Fourteenth, and Fifteenth amendments to the Constitution were ratified in the aftermath of the Civil War. The Thirteenth Amendment banned slavery and was important after the Civil War in ending slavery as a basis of the southern economy. It was the other Civil War amendments, the Fourteenth and Fifteenth, that even today have a dramatic effect on the nature of federalism in that they provide the basis for the major constitutional and statutory restrictions on the powers of states.

The Equal Protection Clause

The equal protection clause is a provision of the Fourteenth Amendment to the Constitution that bans states from denying equal treatment to persons. With few exceptions, in the nineteenth century the equal protection clause offered little promise of being a U.S. constitutional restriction on the states. Its importance in this regard began to increase early in the twentieth century due to two developments: (1) the Supreme Court's incorporation of the Bill of Rights into the Fourteenth Amendment and (2) the use of the equal protection clause in the Fourteenth Amendment to combat racial discrimination. The incorporation of the Bill of Rights meant that the Court ruled that some of the rights guaranteed in the Bill of Rights are fundamental—so essential they are incorporated in (held to be part of) the "liberty" guaranteed in the Fourteenth Amendment, which states, "nor shall any State deprive any person of life, *liberty* [emphasis added], or property, without due process of law." Over the years, more and more rights were found by the court to be fundamental ones that were held to apply to the states. Most recently, in 2010 the court held that the Second Amendment right to "keep and bear arms" applied

Heman Sweatt (right) walks with a white student at the University of Texas. Sweatt refused to attend a separate, all-black law school.

"separate but equal" an interpretation of the equal protection clause of the Fourteenth Amendment that held that states could segregate races as long as equal facilities were provided; it was overturned in 1954

to the states.[26] There are now very few rights in the Bill of Rights that have not been held to be fundamental.

In the 1930s the Supreme Court began to use the equal protection clause to chip away at state laws promoting racial discrimination. In 1950 a Texas case heralded the end of segregated higher education. Heman Sweatt was denied admission to the University of Texas Law School because he was African American. He refused to attend a black law school that Texas had set up to provide what the state claimed to be a **"separate but equal"** legal education for black Texans. Texas claimed that its provision of the two separate law schools complied with the Supreme Court's interpretation of the equal protection clause in *Plessy v. Ferguson* (1896), when it upheld a state requirement of racially segregated train cars in Louisiana. Sweatt's argument was that the black law school was not equal to the University of Texas Law School but was inferior and, therefore, to require him to attend it would deny him the equal protection of the laws. The Supreme Court agreed, pointing out that there were vast differences in the facilities as well as differences in the prestige of the schools, the reputation of the faculty, the experience of the administration, and the influence of the alumni. While the court stopped just short of declaring "separate but equal" requirements to be unconstitutional, after *Sweatt* it was hard to see how the doctrine could survive,[27] and it did not. In 1954, in *Brown v. Board of Education of Topeka*, the Supreme Court unanimously held that segregated public schools were inherently unequal.[28] The doctrine of "separate but equal" was dead, though resistance to the decision in many states, including Texas, would delay for decades the end of legally created segregation in public schools.

State Regulation of Voting

The federal Voting Rights Act was passed under Congress's authority under the Fifteenth Amendment to legislate to protect the right to vote where that right was denied or restricted on the basis of race or color. Section 4 of the act provided a formula that defined the jurisdictions covered under the act, and Section 5 required that federal officials—initially the U.S. Department of Justice—approve or preclear any changes in voting in those jurisdictions, which included Texas. Changes requiring preclearance included such things as establishment of voter identification laws, redrawing of political district boundaries, and changes in the times or locations of polling places. Texas had been subject to preclearance since 1975, and as in other covered jurisdictions, state officials chafed over the need to secure federal approval for changes they wished to make in voting in the state.

This is why an Alabama case decided by the U.S. Supreme Court in 2013 is so important to Texas and to federalism. The case, *Shelby County, Ala. v. Holder*, involved a challenge to Congress's decision to reauthorize the Voting Rights Act. Shelby County claimed that the act went beyond Congress's constitutional powers and that the law placed "substantial federalism costs" on the covered jurisdictions, costs so great that the Tenth Amendment rights of the states were violated. As a political unit of the state of Alabama, Shelby County had been covered by the preclearance requirement since 1965.

Voting Rights and Redistricting

IN 1965, President Lyndon Johnson made history by signing into law the Voting Rights Act. Its purpose was to eliminate racial discrimination in voting. One aspect of the law was Section 5, which required states covered under that provision, including Texas, to have any changes to their voting procedures approved by the Department of Justice or a federal court in the District of Columbia. The rationale behind what is termed "preclearance" was to ensure that the federal government would have oversight over voting in states that had historically excluded racial minorities from the political process.

The Voting Rights Act has been renewed periodically since 1965. During that time, the Department of Justice has required many states, including Texas, to redraw legislative districts to comply with the act. In recent years, however, there has been a backlash against the act by many state governments, including Texas. In 2013, Attorney General Abbott participated in a suit that challenged Section 5, claiming that preclearance was a violation of Texas state sovereignty. Abbott argued that the federal government singled out Texas for preclearance and that it was not fair to make some states, but not others, comply with the law. He also claimed that in 2013 voter discrimination in Texas was no longer an issue. The suit also claimed that the Voting Rights Act exceeded the bounds of federal authority, on the grounds that the Tenth Amendment to the U.S. Constitution reserves to the states powers that are not specifically enumerated as belonging to the federal government.

While the U.S. Supreme Court did not agree with Abbott's arguments in full, it did deliver a ruling striking down portions of the Voting Rights Act that establish a formula to determine which states are subject to Section 5 preclearance. Under this ruling, preclearance has been suspended, and it is unlikely that Congress will pass a new and constitutional formula. Civil rights groups are alarmed that without the protection of preclearance, Texas and other states will design legislative districts that will dilute the influence of minority voters and prevent them from electing candidates of their choice.

Part of the conundrum is that during redistricting political parties attempt to maximize their influence in elections and in Texas most minorities are members of the Democratic Party. Republicans claim that they are discriminating not against minorities but against Democrats, which is perfectly legal.

Although preclearance under Section 5 of the Voting Rights Act is no longer required, it is still possible to challenge districting by suing if plaintiffs allege that districting discriminates against minorities. In mid-August 2017 a panel of three judges decided *Perez v. Abbott*, which found that two Congressional districts were drawn by the Texas legislature with "racially discriminatory intent and effects." Those two districts are District 27 in the Corpus Christi area, which was then represented by Republican Blake Farenthold, and District 35 in the Austin area, which is represented by Democrat Lloyd Doggett. Redistricting those two districts would have, of course, affected other

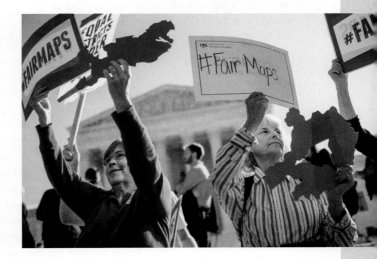

Congressional districts as well, and so the decision represents a significant political problem for Texas Republicans. Attorney General Paxton and Governor Abbott were quick to express their dismay with the decision and appealed to the U.S. Supreme Court.[a]

In April 2017 the same federal judges concluded that the 2011 Texas legislature diluted minority votes in drawing state house legislative districts.[b] In June 2018 the U.S. Supreme Court in a 5–4 decision largely upheld Texas's congressional and state legislative districts. With the exception of a state legislative district in Tarrant County, which the Court said was an illegal racial gerrymander, the Court reversed the lower court's findings that the districts discriminated against minorities.

COMMUNICATING EFFECTIVELY: YOUR VOICE

- **Does preclearance violate the Tenth Amendment and give the federal government too much power, or is it a necessary check on the states to make sure that minorities are not discriminated against?**

- **What are ways that Texas and the federal government can compromise on how best to ensure the rights of minorities in the electoral process?**

It viewed the act as outdated and as trying to remedy racial discrimination in voting that was far in the past.

Texas filed an amicus curiae or "friend of the court" brief in the Supreme Court litigation, a step often taken by states, groups, or individuals who have a strong interest in the outcome of the case but are not parties to it. Texas's brief supported Shelby County's claim that Section 5 of the Voting Rights Act went beyond Congress's powers and placed substantial enough costs on federalism that it violated the Tenth Amendment. Texas's brief noted that the act was based on voting conditions in Texas in the distant past. Unlike then, Texas now has bilingual ballots, and the brief pointed out that in every federal election between 1996 and 2004, African Americans in Texas had registered and voted at higher rates than whites, while between 1980 and 2002, Latinos in Texas had registered to vote at higher rates than Latinos in jurisdictions not covered by Section 5. The remainder of the brief essentially argued that the preclearance requirement created substantial costs to federalism because it had prevented the implementation of Texas's 2011 voter identification law. Under this legislation, to cast a ballot, a voter must provide one of the following forms of identification—a Texas driver's license, an election identification certificate, a personal identification card issued by the state, a U.S. military identification with a photo of the prospective voter, a U.S. citizenship certificate with a photo of the prospective voter, a U.S. passport, or a Texas concealed handgun license.[29]

In 2013 the court issued a 5–4 decision striking down the formula for determining the jurisdictions covered under the Section 5 preclearance requirement. Finding that the formula was based on decades-old data, the court held that Shelby County was correct in its position that they were too outdated to be valid. Congress could, the court said, draft another formula to cover jurisdictions under the act, but that formula must be based on current voting conditions. The court emphasized two important points about the federal system: (1) all states enjoy equal sovereignty, and (2) under the Tenth Amendment, states have broad power to regulate elections. Only exceptional conditions, it said, such as the racial discrimination in voting at the time of the initial passage of the Voting Rights Act, justified intrusion on the equality and the powers of states. The court's view was that the outdated data provided insufficient evidence that such conditions still existed and thus, absent a valid formula to determine which jurisdictions must go through a preclearance procedure, none had to do so.[30]

Given this decision, Texas no longer has to obtain preclearance to change aspects of its system of elections. However, under Section 2 of the Voting Rights Act, it is still possible to sue a state in federal court on the grounds that such a change negatively affects minority voters. That is what happened in *Veasey v. Abbott* (2014) where a federal district court in Corpus Christi, Texas, found that the state's voter identification requirement was intended to discriminate against minority voters and had a disparate impact on them. The district court decision was appealed to the federal Court of Appeals, which agreed in part with the district court's decision but sent the case back to that court for further evidence about whether the voter identification requirement had a discriminatory purpose. That first appeal was heard by a panel of 3 judges, but Texas sought and received a rehearing before the entire court of 15 judges. In a 9-to-6 decision, the

Court of Appeals held that the law had a racially discriminatory effect on those without identification and sent the case back to the district court to develop a remedy for this discrimination.

To prove that the law had a disparate impact on minorities and thus violated the Voting Rights Act (in the original case), the plaintiffs' lawyers presented statistical evidence to the court prepared by expert witnesses. The plaintiffs' experts included a prominent political scientist, Stephen Ansolabehere of Harvard University, who found that Latino and African American registered voters were 195 percent and 305 percent more likely than whites to lack the required voter identification. Perhaps even more destructive of the state's case was that even the expert witness for the state, in evidence the district court found to suffer from severe methodological problems, found that 4 percent of eligible white voters lacked the required voter identification, compared to 5.3 percent of eligible African American voters and 6.9 percent of eligible Latino voters.[31] After the case went back to the district court, Texas reached an agreement allowing voters without the required identification to vote in the November 2016 election if they signed a statement saying they were unable to reasonably procure it and if they provided alternative identification such as a voter registration certificate, a birth certificate, a utility bill, a bank statement, or a government document with their name and address (such as a government check).

These 2016 remedies were agreed to by the legislature in the 2017 session and were signed into law by Governor Abbott. The revised voter ID law was challenged successfully in district court and that decision was appealed to a panel of the federal 5th Circuit Court of Appeals. The appellate court, on April 28, 2018, held that the revised law was lawful and had successfully mitigated any racially discriminatory impact of the law.[32]

Flexibility for States under the Constitution

Although there are restrictions on the states imposed by the Fourteenth Amendment and by statutes passed under the authority of the Fifteenth Amendment, states do have some leeway to expand rights of their citizens through a concept known as **independent state grounds**. State constitutions can provide greater constitutional guarantees to a state's citizens than the U.S. Constitution. Independent state grounds are a characteristic of federalism in that states are free to add to the rights guaranteed at the national level. Some states, such as Massachusetts, have relied on their state constitutions to invalidate laws against same-sex marriage.[33] Under the U.S. Constitution, Texas's very inequitable property tax–based system for funding public education was held to be constitutional. In 1973 the U.S. Supreme Court held that education was not a fundamental right and so Texas only needed a rational justification—that is, local control of schools—for the funding system to be upheld.[34] However, in *Edgewood v. Kirby* (1989), the Texas Supreme Court relied on the Texas Constitution to strike down the system on the grounds that it did not provide "what the [Texas] constitution commands—i.e., an efficient system of public free schools throughout the state."[35]

In the 1970s there was a major effort to gain ratification of an Equal Rights Amendment to the U.S. Constitution. If ratified, the key part of the amendment would have stated, "Equality of rights under the law shall not be denied or abridged by the United States or by any state on account of sex." Although that amendment was never ratified

independent state grounds allow states, usually under the state constitution, to expand rights beyond those provided by the U.S. Constitution nationally, in 1972 Texas adopted its own version of the Equal Rights Amendment, which is Article 1, Section 3a, of the Texas Constitution: "Equality under the law shall not be denied or abridged because of sex, race, color, creed, or national origin." U.S. Supreme Court decisions have provided major protection against sex discrimination under the equal protection clause of the Fourteenth Amendment to the U.S. Constitution; however, it is the Texas Constitution, rather than the U.S. Constitution, that contains an explicit ban.

Texas and the Obama Administration

Texas's Republican political leadership and the Democratic Obama administration experienced frequent tension over what the Texas leaders believed was the administration's expansion of national power at the expense of the states. In fact, Texas sued the Obama administration 46 times over a variety of issues, including air quality regulations,

WHAT DO TEXANS THINK? ★

Is Texas headed in the right direction? Is the United States?

A recent poll suggests that Texans are more convinced that their state is moving in the correct direction than believe that the nation is moving in the right direction. Why do you think Texans are more supportive of the direction the state has taken than the direction of the national government? If state government was dominated by Democrats, how do you think these numbers would change? Why?

Is the state of Texas moving in the right direction? Or is it on the wrong track?

Right — 15%
Wrong — 36
Don't know — 48

Is the United States moving in the right direction? Or is it on the wrong track?

Right — 11%
Wrong — 50
Don't know — 39

SOURCE: University of Texas/Texas Tribune poll of 1,200 registered voters in Texas between February 1 and February 12, 2018. Margin of error is 2.83 percentage points.

business regulations, responses to climate change, education, health care, immigration, natural resources, voting, and same sex marriage.[36]

Among the most important of these cases was Texas's challenge to President Obama's actions on immigration policy. When it became clear that Congress would not pass comprehensive immigration reform, President Obama announced a new policy for undocumented immigrants who met two criteria: (1) they must have children who are U.S. citizens or lawful permanent residents, and (2) they must have been in the United States at least since January 2010. If they met these criteria, they would be allowed to stay in the country for three years and work legally. This policy could have allowed as many as 4,000,000 people to remain in the United States. Texas and 25 other states went to federal court to try to block this policy, and the district court issued an order to keep the policy from going into effect. A federal appeals court upheld the decision of the trial court, and the case was then appealed to the U.S. Supreme Court in *United States v. Texas*.[37] In 2016 the Supreme Court tied 4–4 in the case, which means that the appeals court's decision upholding the trial court's invalidation of the policy stands.

While the case presented a number of issues, Texas claimed that Obama's decision would increase costs for the state for services ranging from driver's licenses to education, and Attorney General Ken Paxton argued that the new policy, known as Deferred Action for Parents of Americans and Lawful Permanent Residents (DAPA), was "a crucial change in the Nation's immigration law and policy—and this is precisely why it could be created only by Congress, rather than unilaterally imposed by the Executive." In contrast, the Obama administration argued its actions were within presidential authority and that if the lower court decision was not overturned, it would allow states to "frustrate the federal government's enforcement of the Nation's immigration laws."[38]

Texas and the Trump Administration

Texas Attorney General Ken Paxton took pride in suing the federal government under the last two years of the Obama administration, but he has been less inclined to challenge Trump administration policies. Paxton has claimed that his more favorable approach to the Trump administration is because, "We just have a lot more cooperative administration to help try to resolve things in a positive way instead of constantly having to sue the federal government."[39] Of course, his more favorable approach to the federal government under President Trump is also due to a shared party affiliation and more of a shared ideology than under President Obama. The cooperative approach between Texas and the Trump administration was seen in Paxton's lead role in a 16-state coalition that filed an amicus brief in the Supreme Court in support of President Trump's first travel ban. Though changes in the travel ban led to dismissal of the case by the Supreme Court, the amicus brief argued that the travel ban was a lawful exercise of the President's power over foreign affairs and national security. States had an interest in the travel ban, argued the brief, because the states had a concern with public safety and national security that was related to presidential policies involving alien entry.[40]

The supportive relationship between Texas and the Trump administration is also seen in Trump's proposal for a border wall. Attorney General Paxton has long made support for private property rights a central theme of his administration. In a suit over contested land along the Red River between the federal government and Texas landowners, Paxton stressed that, "Washington, D.C., needs to hear loud and clear that Texas will

The Trump administration has proposed extending Texas's border walls to stretch the entire length of the state's border with Mexico. Here, Vice President Mike Pence tours an existing border wall in Hidalgo, Texas.

not stand for the federal government's infringement upon Texas land and the property rights of the people who live here." However, he has argued that taking private land in Texas for the border wall presents no problem as long as people are paid a fair price for the land since the taking of the land is for a valid public purpose.[41]

Some litigation has been initiated by Paxton against the Trump administration to deal with issues left over from the Obama administration. Texas has sued the federal government—including former Texas governor and now Secretary of Energy Rick Perry—over the federal government's failure to license a nuclear waste site in Nevada. The suit seeks a decision on licensing the site in the Yucca Mountains of Nevada and seeks to prevent the Department of Energy from spending billions of dollars received in fees from utilities in efforts to finalize another disposal site. The suit is important to Texas because Texas utilities have paid a large sum into a fund for a nuclear waste depository and because a temporary nuclear waste site in Andrews County, Texas, is rapidly filling.[42] On June 1, 2018, however, the federal 5th Circuit Court of Appeals dismissed Texas's suit at the request of the state of Nevada.

Texas pressured the Trump administration to rescind the DACA program, which shielded young undocumented immigrants from deportation. In a letter Paxton wrote to former U.S. Attorney General Jeff Sessions, Paxton noted that Texas and other plaintiff states had successfully challenged the DAPA program during the Obama administration and that Texas would sue the Trump administration unless by September 5, 2017, the administration rescinded the DACA program initiated by the Obama administration.[43] The Trump administration complied with Paxton's demand. The DACA program was ended, with President Trump urging Congress to pass a replacement for DACA before it was phased out in six months. President Trump's phaseout of DACA has led sixteen states to sue to stop DACA from being ended. The brief of the sixteen states uses President Trump's statements against Mexicans to show animus toward immigrant groups, but it also contains a section on Texas's role in phasing out DACA, noting that the state that pushed for ending the program was ". . . found to have discriminated against Latinos/Hispanics nine times since 2012."[44] The litigation against DACA is in process, but has so far been successful in at least delaying the phaseout of the program.

Federalism and the Future of Texas

LEADING TEXANS are now wishing to return greater power to the states. They argue that the national government is too distant, controlling, expensive, and unresponsive. National Democrats have a philosophical inclination to look to the national government for solutions to problems; Texas Republicans (and Republicans in general) prefer either no governmental action or to look to the states for solutions. The effect of this difference is, of course, a dispute over federalism. The United States originated in a dispute over national versus state power, and these battles have continued throughout U.S. history. The intensity of the disagreement over federalism will vary, however, depending on which political party controls state governments, Congress, and the White House. Though there remain points of tension, there has been and will likely continue to be far friendlier interaction between Texas and the national government than existed under the Obama administration.

Use 🐰 INQUIZITIVE to help you study and master this material.

The Roots of American Federalism

> • Understand the foundations of the U.S. federal system (pp. 89–94)

Along with many other countries, the American system of government has divided power between national and regional or state governments. That division of power has varied over time, and America's notion of federalism has evolved through a number of forms.

Key Terms

federalism (p. 89)
sovereign (p. 90)

Practice Quiz

1. *Federalism* refers to
   a) a system of government in which cities are strong.
   b) a system of government in which executive power is grounded in a committee of governors.
   c) a system of government in which there is a national government as well as a number of regional governments.
   d) a system of government dominated by business interests.
   e) a system of government with strong parliaments.

2. The Articles of Confederation
   a) were a loose confederation of independent states that operated in the 1820s.
   b) were never accepted by a majority of the states.
   c) derived their power directly from the state governments.
   d) replaced the U.S. Constitution of 1787.
   e) outlawed ineffective state constitutions.

3. The relationship between the states and the national government
   a) has been a matter of continuing controversy throughout the nation's history.
   b) was finally settled when the Articles of Confederation were rejected in favor of the U.S. Constitution.
   c) was resolved for all time by the Civil War.
   d) was resolved by Article I, Section 8, of the U.S. Constitution.
   e) was not a problem in a federal system.

4. The Supreme Court under John Marshall expanded national power partly through
   a) rejecting the Articles of Confederation.
   b) expanding the meaning of interstate commerce.
   c) expanding Congress's war-making powers.
   d) ignoring the Tenth Amendment.
   e) increasing the powers of the president.

5. Prior to the ratification of the Fourteenth Amendment, the Bill of Rights
   a) applied only to states.
   b) applied only to the national government.
   c) applied to states and the national government.
   d) was essential in protecting individual rights.
   e) was applied only in extreme cases of rights violations.

6. *McCulloch v. Maryland* (1819) was important
   a) in establishing that the national government had implied powers.
   b) in establishing that state governments had implied powers.
   c) in showing that the state and national governments could cooperate.
   d) in preventing national banks from operating.
   e) in destroying corrupt state banking systems.

Federalism: Texas and the Nation over Time

• **Trace the major changes in national and state power over time (pp. 94–98)**

American federalism has gone through major changes over the history of the country. In the late nineteenth century there was a strict division between the powers of the states and the powers of the national government. That division was called *dual federalism* or *layer-cake federalism*. During Franklin Roosevelt's New Deal, federalism was dramatically redefined and there was greater involvement of the national government in all areas of American life. Cooperative federalism or marble-cake federalism became the new approach to state and national relationships. In recent times, many believe federalism has taken a new form and has become coercive, with the national government compelling states to act in ways that achieve national priorities.

Key Terms
Reconstruction (p. 94)
dual federalism (p. 94)
layer-cake federalism (p. 94)
marble-cake federalism (p. 96)
cooperative federalism (p. 96)
categorical grants (p. 96)
New Federalism (p. 98)
block grants (p. 98)

Practice Quiz

7. *Dual federalism*
   a) refers to a system of government in which states do most of the governing.
   b) existed in the United States following World War II.
   c) rejected the idea that states were sovereign political entities.
   d) is the idea that there are two branches to the national legislature.
   e) drained all power from state governments.

8. Layer-cake federalism switched to marble-cake federalism
   a) after the Civil War.
   b) during World War I.
   c) during the New Deal.
   d) after the fall of the Soviet Union.
   e) because of President Ronald Reagan's efforts.

9. The use of categorical grants was a way of promoting
   a) cooperative federalism.
   b) dual federalism.
   c) coercive federalism.
   d) bipartisan federalism.
   e) civil rights.

Coercive Federalism: Texas and the Federal Government

• **Describe the sources of, and tensions between, national and state power (pp. 98–109)**

The incorporation of much of the Bill of Rights has limited the power of state governments by making them subject to restrictions under the U.S. Constitution. Additionally, the preemption doctrine has allowed the national government to prohibit state legislation in certain fields. An important constitutional provision that limits state action is the Fourteenth Amendment, particularly the equal protection clause of that amendment, which prohibits discriminatory actions by state governments. Until recently, a number of jurisdictions—including Texas—were limited by the 1965 Voting Rights Act in the legislation they could pass involving the electoral process, although a recent U.S. Supreme Court decision has made it possible for Texas to pass controversial voter identification legislation. Finally, while state governments cannot reduce the rights guaranteed by the U.S. Constitution, they can expand those guarantees under the concept of independent state grounds.

Key Terms
coercive federalism (p. 98)
unfunded mandates (p. 98)
preemption (p. 98)
"separate but equal" (p. 102)
independent state grounds (p. 105)

Practice Quiz

10. Hostility to modern federalism is partly a result of
  a) dual federalism.
  b) funded mandates.
  c) unfunded mandates.
  d) Tenth Amendment interpretations.
  e) high taxes.

11. States must adhere to most of the provisions of the Bill of Rights because of a process known as
  a) inclusion of the Bill of Rights.
  b) incorporation of the Bill of Rights.
  c) expansion of the Bill of Rights.
  d) ratification of the Bill of Rights.
  e) the Sanford dictum.

12. The equal protection clause of the Fourteenth Amendment
  a) makes it difficult for states to discriminate against minorities.
  b) is rarely used by federal courts.
  c) ensures that states will continue to have a republican form of government.
  d) mandates the right to vote for all adult citizens.
  e) requires all states to have an equal number of senators.

13. Independent state grounds
    a) allow states to provide fewer state constitutional protections.
    b) allow states to provide more state constitutional protections than does the U.S. Constitution.
    c) allow states to remain independent of the national government.
    d) prevent the national government from overriding the Tenth Amendment rights of states.
    e) limit the power of the national government to pass economic regulations.

14. The national government can preempt state laws because
    a) the national government is weaker than any state.
    b) the Tenth Amendment to the Constitution specifically allows state laws to be overridden by federal laws.
    c) the supremacy clause of the Constitution makes national laws supreme over state laws.
    d) the Sanford dictum established preemption.
    e) the Constitution was adopted mainly to do just that.

15. The Voting Rights Act
    a) ensured the right to vote for women.
    b) ensured the right to vote for 18-year-olds.
    c) approved photo ID requirements for voters.
    d) required that voters know how to read and write.
    e) was the major law providing the right to vote for African Americans.

Voters' support in the primary election for State Representative Sarah Davis, a rare pro-choice Republican, illustrates that the Republican Party in Texas may not be as united as it seems.

Political Parties

WHY POLITICAL PARTIES MATTER Sarah Davis is a moderate Republican who represents an urban, wealthy district in Houston that includes Rice University and the ritzy Galleria. Davis was first elected to the Legislature in 2010, narrowly defeating Houston city council member Ellen Cohen, a liberal Democrat. She was re-elected in 2012 against Democrat Ann Johnson. While in the legislature, Davis has toed an independent line, failing to cooperate with the Tea Party wing of the Republican party on issues ranging from the "bathroom" bill to abortion legislation. As the only pro-choice Republican in the Texas House, she has caught the attention of statewide elected officials, including Governor Greg Abbott. In an unprecedented move, Abbott endorsed Davis's Republican opponent in the March 2018 primary. He reasoned that Davis was not sufficiently supportive of his agenda in his first term as governor. Davis's opponent, Susanna Dokupil, had also worked under Abbott when he was attorney general of the state. Davis went on to defeat Dokupil in the primary and her Democratic opponent, Allison Lami Sawyer, in the November 2018 election.

What does this story about Sarah Davis tell us about the state of political parties in Texas? On the surface, Republicans dominate Texas politics. Since 1994 every statewide elected official has been a member of the Republican Party. Since 2002 the Texas legislature has been controlled by Republicans. Yet there remain intra-party tensions between the more conservative wing of the party and the few moderates remaining in the party. In a district such as Davis's, Republican divisions could possibly yield an opening for Democrats who could field a candidate that would be more in tune with the district, which voted for Hillary Clinton in the 2016 election.

In reality, there are three political parties in modern-day Texas politics: business-oriented mainstream Republicans, Tea Party conservative Republicans, and the Democratic Party. In the George W. Bush era during the 1990s, the Republican Party was dominated by business-oriented mainstream Republicans who were interested in low taxes, less regulation, and tort reform. By 2012 the party had become more conservative. That year the business-oriented Lieutenant Governor David Dewhurst lost the U.S. Senate primary to Ted Cruz, who positioned himself to the right of Dewhurst. This competitive primary resulted from the retirement of mainstream Republican senator Kay Bailey Hutchison.

In the most recent legislative session of 2017, the clash between factions of the Republican Party were readily apparent. Speaker Joe Straus, a moderate Republican, clashed with Lieutenant

Governor Patrick (Tea Party favorite) on a host of issues, including the bathroom bill as well as SB 4, a ban on sanctuary cities in the state. Governor Greg Abbott began his career as a mainstream Republican but arguably has moved to the right to avoid the fate of Dewhurst and other Republicans who were defeated in primaries by more conservative firebrands.

The Democratic Party has sought to gain power in the state by trying to capitalize on the internal divisions within the Republican Party. But based on the state's current voter profile, the Democrats face an uphill battle, at least in the short term. Democrats believed they had a chance to unseat Senator Ted Cruz in 2018 with the nomination of El Paso's U.S. representative Beto O'Rourke, a white liberal representing a heavily Hispanic district. They believed he would unite the party's urban, minority, and labor bases to unseat a relatively unpopular incumbent. Though O'Rourke lost, the margin was razor thin, with Cruz winning 51 percent of the vote to O'Rourke's 48 percent. Democrats might have more success, however, fielding candidates in suburban districts such as Davis's in Houston, Austin, San Antonio, and Dallas. Republican primaries might produce candidates in the general election who are too far to the right for these areas.

These examples demonstrate a couple of important facts about parties in Texas. All too often, we hear about Texas being a solidly Republican state, but this masks the internal diversity within the party. The observation that Republicans hold all statewide offices does not tell the whole story. In addition, internal divisions affect not only the Republican Party, with its Tea Party and mainstream business factions, but the Democratic Party as well. As the Democratic Party in Texas becomes more Latino, we might see more Democratic primary races pitting Latino candidates against white or African American incumbents.

Because parties play such a large role in government processes, we must know how parties are organized, how candidates are selected, and how partisanship influences public policy. This chapter will address the history of political parties in Texas, the current party system in the state, and what the future may hold for parties.

CHAPTER GOALS

- Describe the main functions and structure of state party organizations (pp. 117–29)
- Trace the evolution of the party system in Texas (pp. 129–36)
- Analyze how ideological divisions and demographic change affect Texas political parties (pp. 137–43)

The Roles and Structure of Political Parties in Texas

In the narrowest sense, a political party refers to an organization of people established to win elections. This can include people holding or running for office who identify formally with the party. It can also refer to the professionals and volunteers who actively work for the election of their party's candidates. In a broader sense, a political party can refer to those people in the electorate who identify with a particular party and vote for that party's candidates on a regular basis.

Political parties help candidates win elections and assist voters in making their electoral choices. Perhaps the most important function of parties in Texas is that they provide a label under which candidates can run and with which voters can identify. Each party develops a **party platform** by which voters can get a better sense of what the party stands for. While candidates can and often do deviate somewhat from their party platform, voters wishing to know a candidate's basic political philosophy can consult the state party platform. Because Texas elects large numbers of officeholders, it is unlikely that voters will be familiar with the views or the qualifications of every candidate. However, Texas voters overwhelmingly identify with or lean toward either the Republican Party or the Democratic Party.[1] Thus, for many voters, without other information, the party label becomes the standard they apply in casting a ballot for a candidate. Voters

> **party platform** a statement of principles and political philosophy that a political party promises to enact if elected to office.

One of the most important functions of political parties is to select candidates to run for office under the party label. Here, state senator and congressional candidate Sylvia Garcia (Houston) speaks at the Democratic Party's 2018 convention in Fort Worth, where the party officially announced its candidates for office.

often use the party label as a cue to the ideology of candidates. A voter may assume that, for example, a Republican candidate is a "conservative" and may vote for or against that candidate because of the ideology that a party affiliation implies.[2]

In addition, parties help in raising money for candidates' campaigns and in assisting candidates with legal requirements and training for a campaign. They sometimes recruit candidates for political races, although in Texas any candidate may run in a party primary and if victorious in the primary will become the party nominee. Parties also assist in "getting out the vote" for candidates through phone banks, door-to-door contacts, and other efforts.

Once a candidate is elected to office, party affiliation helps in organizing the government. Governors usually appoint members of their own party to positions within the government, and the Texas legislature is increasingly divided by party as well. Public officials may also feel a greater sense of loyalty and cooperation toward other public officials of their party. After all, they often campaign together and make appearances at the same political events, and their fortunes often rise and fall together based on the popularity of the party. In that sense, the banding together of officeholders with the same party affiliation provides voters an opportunity to hold the party accountable for its successes or its failures.

Texas Party Politics

As the nation has become more divided along party lines, voters have elected fewer moderates to office. This has had the result of creating more friction in government, including gridlock in Congress. If we only observed national politics, we would come away with the impression that politics at the state and local levels mirrors the national partisan battles. However, this has not always been the case. As explained in the introduction, in Texas the dominant Republican Party has its own internal divisions. Even though the majority party controls committee assignments, chairs of committees sometimes include a mix of Democrats and Republicans. This has historically been true in Texas. For example, the former speaker of the Texas House, Joe Straus from San Antonio, was considered a moderate Republican and owed his election to the speakership to many Democrats in the legislature who voted to elect him speaker. In recognition of their support, Straus made some Democrats committee chairs. This situation would never happen in the U.S. Congress, as parties are much more salient in national politics. In Congress the majority party gives leadership positions like committee chairs only to its own loyal party members. As the Republican Party in Texas has moved further to the right, the bipartisan tradition there will likely change to the partisan polarization prevalent nationally, as it already has in the state senate after Dan Patrick took over as lieutenant governor. Among his campaign promises—which he fulfilled—was to end the previous lieutenant governor's practice of appointing Democrats as committee chairs.

Why might these partisan divisions we see in Washington be less pronounced at the state and local levels? Tip O'Neill, the former Speaker of the U.S. House, used to say that "all politics is local," and this certainly rings true in Texas. Local issues are usually not ideological in nature. They often deal with who is most effective at creating jobs and providing public works projects within the district. Voters in state races are therefore likely to be influenced as much or more by these concerns than by hot-button issues such as abortion and same-sex marriage. Hence, partisanship is not always a major concern in running the everyday business of the state. To be sure, ideological issues might matter in certain state-level elections during some election years. In addition, **partisan polarization**, the degree to which Republicans have become more conservative and Democrats more liberal, is beginning to become more pronounced in the Texas legislature. Partisan polarization in politics means that it is increasingly difficult for politicians to compromise on important policy issues, since compromise becomes seen as a sign of weakness and caving in to the other side.

partisan polarization the degree to which Republicans have become more conservative and Democrats have become more liberal

Party politics in Texas is similar to that in some other southern states, but there are important differences in its racial and ethnic aspects. Historically, other southern states have had larger African American populations than Texas. African Americans, who are generally loyal Democrats, constitute nearly 30 percent of the population in Mississippi and Louisiana, for example. In Texas, they represent only 12 percent, and most are concentrated in east Texas and the state's major urban areas. Another major difference between Texas and some other southern states is Texas's large Latino population, which is about 40 percent of the state total. Like African Americans, Latinos tend to be Democrats, but not to the same degree.

To a certain extent, Texas is similar to New Mexico, Arizona, and Colorado in terms of its large Latino population. In contrast with the Latino population in Arizona, however, Tejanos (Texans of Mexican descent) are more likely to have resided in the state for generations. In Arizona, the Sonora Desert region is the largest U.S. gateway for Mexican immigration, and new immigrants in Arizona exhibit political behavior that differs from that of their Tejano counterparts in many ways. For example, they are more likely than Tejanos to identify as Democrats and to see the Democratic Party as more supportive of immigrant rights.

Public Attitudes about Parties

Texans, like many other Americans, are increasingly identifying as independent. However, in practice many self-identified independents lean toward either Democratic or Republican affiliation. What is the source of these political leanings? The process of **political socialization** occurs throughout our early years, when our parents, religious leaders, teachers, and others influence our partisan identifications. Although this identification can change over time, we often retain the same political beliefs as those of our parents. We are also profoundly shaped by our geographical environment. Texas has a long history of state pride, independence, and individualism. People growing up in the state become accustomed to these values and thus often incorporate them into their political ideologies and partisan preferences. Visitors to Texas are often surprised at how much state pride native Texans display. For example, the very notion of a state pledge of allegiance like the one recited by many Texas schoolchildren is a practice that surprises people from other states.

political socialization the introduction of individuals into the political culture; learning the underlying beliefs and values on which the political system is based

How does partisan affiliation affect Texas voters? According to a May 2012 *Texas Tribune* poll, 56 percent of respondents cited party affiliation as either very or somewhat important when deciding for whom to vote. For the most part, when we see an "R" or a "D" next to a candidate's name, we make certain assumptions about the positions the candidate takes. Of course, other characteristics of candidates matter too; in the same poll, voters also cited the candidate's record, stated positions on issues, and character as important considerations in their voting choices.[3]

The current strength of the Texas Republican Party is reflected in its advantage in partisan affiliation or leanings among voters. According to a 2016 *Texas Tribune* poll, 46 percent would support a generic Republican candidate for Congress, while roughly 39 percent of voters in Texas would support a generic Democratic candidate. This leaves a remainder of about 15 percent that are the "swing" voters who ultimately decide elections. Since their control of state government gives Republicans a built-in advantage, it is increasingly difficult for Democrats to win statewide.

At the conservative end of the spectrum, the Tea Party movement is particularly strong in Texas. In a June 2017 *Texas Tribune* poll, 16 percent of respondents said they would vote for a Tea Party candidate if the movement organized as a third party. When asked about the Tea Party's influence on the state Republican Party, respondents were split: 30 percent felt that the Tea Party had too much influence, 16 percent thought its degree of influence was about right, and 26 percent thought it had too little influence.[4]

The Contemporary Republican Party in Texas

Texas Republicans currently hold all of the major statewide elected offices. The governor, lieutenant governor, comptroller, attorney general, members of the state supreme court, the Court of Criminal Appeals, and railroad commissioners are all Republicans, as are both U.S. senators. Texas Democrats have attempted to recruit successful challengers for these offices but have come up short. The major competition for important statewide offices occurs during the Republican primaries, much in the same way the Democratic primaries used to fulfill this role when Texas was a Democratic state.

These primaries often pit conservatives against moderates, reflecting a major division that Texas Republicans are currently experiencing within their party. Pro-business "establishment" Republicans have dominated the party along with state politics in recent years, but the Tea Party movement has begun to influence state legislative races as well as major statewide races. Consider the lieutenant governor's race in 2014. In the Republican primary, incumbent lieutenant governor David Dewhurst had the endorsement of Governor Rick Perry and many of the state's other political leaders. However, state senator Dan Patrick, a darling of the Tea Party movement, and several other Republicans challenged Dewhurst because they sensed a weak candidate who had lost the U.S. Senate primary in 2012 to now senator Ted Cruz. Patrick ran to the right of Dewhurst and all the other candidates, especially on immigration issues. In a debate in early 2014, he called for an end to the "invasion" of illegal immigrants from the southern border. Patrick also criticized Dewhurst for being too moderate and a political insider, turning his endorsements from the state's political establishment against him. In a low-turnout primary, he forced Dewhurst into a runoff by winning 41 percent of the vote to Dewhurst's 28 percent, and in the runoff he received 65 percent to 35 percent for Dewhurst. (Patrick went on to win the general election over Democrat Leticia Van de Putte, a Latina state senator from San Antonio, with 58 percent of the vote.) It was remarkable that an incumbent lieutenant governor would be defeated so badly in his own party primary, but Patrick successfully positioned himself to the right of Dewhurst in an increasingly conservative party.

While running for lieutenant governor in 2014, Dan Patrick positioned himself as more conservative than his opponent, fellow Republican David Dewhurst. Here, Patrick celebrates his victory over Dewhurst in the primary on election night.

The Contemporary Democratic Party in Texas

The Republican Party and conservative politics have not always been so powerful in Texas. Prior to 1994, Democrats held many statewide offices, and many of those Democrats were liberals. Ann Richards, the state's last Democratic governor, was a proud liberal, as was former U.S. senator Ralph Yarborough, who championed the Bilingual Education Act in 1968. However, in recent years Democrats have had difficulty recruiting quality candidates for political office at the state level. In 2017 national Democrats were hopeful that former Health and Human Services Secretary Julián Castro would enter the race for governor but he decided against it. Democrats were scrambling to find a challenger to Governor Greg Abbott in 2018 and settled on Dallas County Sheriff Lupe Valdez. In the general election, Abbott defeated Valdez, winning 55 percent of the vote. Texas Democrats have been relegated to minority status in the state since the early 2000s, when they last controlled the Texas House. Most whites in Texas have settled into the Republican Party, and Republicans have won all recent statewide elections.

Most Texas Democrats today would be classified as liberal. The party's base is made up of African Americans, Latinos, and white liberals in urban areas. Most white liberals are located in Austin, Houston, Dallas, and San Antonio, and they have often moved to Texas from other parts of the country. This coalition, however, is currently not large enough to win elections in statewide races. Democrats hope to mobilize more Latinos to vote. Latinos are the fastest-growing minority group in the state. Sixty-nine percent of Texas Latinos are American citizens by birth, but a large proportion of these are under age 18 and cannot vote. Moreover, voter turnout rates among Texas Latinos are much lower than among their Anglo counterparts. To change this pattern will require extensive efforts to register Latino voters and bring them to the polls in force.

Recently, the Democratic Party in Texas has been shut out of statewide offices. Democrats continue to believe that mobilizing Latino voters and white urban liberals will help their chances. Here, U.S. representative Beto O'Rourke (D-El Paso) campaigns in Austin for the U.S. Senate seat held by Republican Ted Cruz.

No Democrat has won Texas in a presidential race since Jimmy Carter in 1976. In 2016, Republican presidential candidate Donald Trump won 52 percent of the vote in Texas, while Democrat Hillary Clinton won just 43 percent. This 9 percentage point margin in favor of the Republican candidate meant that Trump underperformed relative to Mitt Romney in 2012, who won the state by 16 percentage points. Democratic candidates have also fared poorly in recent U.S. Senate races. For example, in the 2012 election to replace retiring senator Kay Bailey Hutchison, Ted Cruz, the Republican nominee, won easily. Democrat Beto O'Rourke, a congressperson from El Paso, challenged Cruz in 2018, and narrowly lost to him in the most competitive statewide race in decades.

Texas Democrats do have influence in certain localities. In Travis County, the home of Austin, Democrats dominate city government. Other major cities, including Houston and San Antonio, have Democratic mayors and city councils. However, this influence does not extend to statewide elections. When Democrat Wendy Davis, a former state senator from Ft. Worth, ran for governor in 2014, she lost to Greg Abbott.

Eleven of the thirteen Democrats representing Texas in the U.S. Congress are either Latino or African American. Lloyd Doggett of Austin and Lizzie Fletcher of Houston are the only white Democrats representing Texas in Congress. This suggests that the majority of Texas Democrats are minorities, and the growth of the minority population in the state suggests that the party's makeup will become steadily more nonwhite. This demographic change in Texas is making the state more similar to its neighbors in the Deep South, where the Democratic Party is mostly an African American party. In contrast, in the Northeast and on the West Coast, white Democrats are a larger proportion of the electorate.

Democratic and Republican Party Organization

Although many Texans proclaim that they are "registered Republicans" or "registered Democrats," Texas does not have a system of party registration. Registered voters may vote in either the Democratic or the Republican primary. When they do vote in a primary, their voter registration card is stamped "Democrat" or "Republican" to prevent them from voting in the other primary as well.

One of the most important functions of political parties is to select candidates to run for office under the party label. During the nineteenth century, candidates were nominated at party conventions, but early in the twentieth century the state began using primary elections to select candidates. If several candidates are running for the party nomination in a primary, it may be that none receives a majority vote. In that case, the party holds a runoff election to determine its nominee.

To understand how the parties are organized, think first in terms of the permanent organization of the party and then in terms of the temporary (campaign) organization (see Figure 4.1). In each election **precinct**, a **precinct chair** is elected in the party primary. The precinct chair will head the precinct convention and serve on the party's **county executive committee**, whose main responsibility is to run the county primary and plan the county conventions. Also elected in the primary is a **county chair** to head

precinct the most basic level of political organization at the local level

precinct chair the local party official, elected in the party's primary election, who heads the precinct convention and serves on the party's county executive committee

county executive committee the party group, made up of a party's county chair and precinct chairs, that is responsible for running a county's primary elections and planning county conventions

county chair the county party official who heads the county executive committee

FIGURE 4.1

Party Organization in Texas

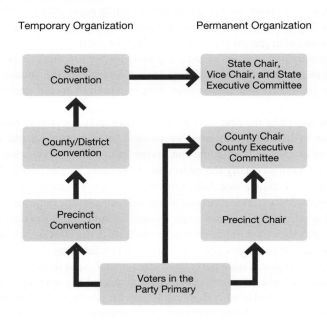

Temporary Organization | Permanent Organization

State Convention → State Chair, Vice Chair, and State Executive Committee

County/District Convention → County Chair County Executive Committee

Precinct Convention → Precinct Chair

Voters in the Party Primary

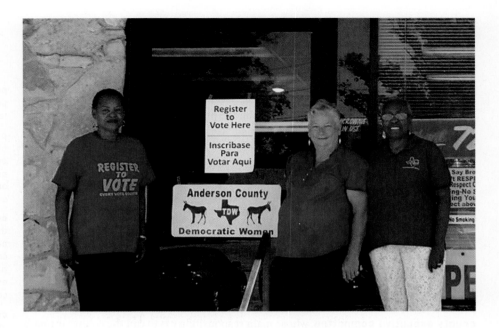

Political parties in Texas are organized at the precinct level, the county level, and the state level. This photo shows members of the Anderson County Democratic Party organization.

state chair and vice chair
the top two state-level leaders in the party

state executive committee
the committee responsible for governing a party's activities throughout the state

precinct convention a meeting held by a political party to select delegates for the county convention and to submit resolutions to the party's state platform; precinct conventions are held on the day of the party's primary election and are open to anyone who voted in that election

county convention a meeting held by a political party following its precinct conventions, for the purpose of electing delegates to its state convention

state convention a party meeting held every two years for the purpose of nominating candidates for statewide office, adopting a platform, electing the party's leadership, and in presidential election years selecting delegates for the national convention and choosing presidential electors

the county executive committee, which includes all the precinct chairs. There may be other district committees as well for political divisions that do not correspond to the county lines.

At the state level, there is a state executive committee, which includes a **state chair and vice chair**. These officers are selected every two years at the state party conventions. The **state executive committee** accepts filings by candidates for statewide office and also helps raise funds for the party and establish party policy. Both the Democratic and the Republican parties also employ professional staff to run day-to-day operations and to assist with special problems that affect the party.

The temporary organization of the party includes the **precinct conventions**. The main roles of the precinct conventions are to select delegates to the **county convention** and possibly to submit resolutions that may eventually become part of the party platform.

Delegates chosen by the precinct convention then go to the county conventions (or in urban areas, to district conventions), which elect delegates to the **state convention**. Both the Democratic and the Republican parties hold a state convention every other year. These conventions certify the nominees of the party for statewide office; adopt a platform; and elect a chair, a vice chair, and a state executive committee. In presidential election years, the state conventions also select delegates for the national party conventions, elect delegates for the national party committee, and choose presidential electors, who, if the party's choice for president carries the state in the election, will formally cast the state's electoral votes for the president in the electoral college.

Battles for control of a state party have often been fought in Texas politics, where rival ideological and other interest groups have struggled to control precinct, county, and state conventions and to elect their candidates for precinct chair, county chair, and state executive committee. In the 1950s struggles between liberals and conservatives for control of the Democratic Party were fierce. On the other hand, sometimes apathy has been so great that precinct conventions have been sparsely attended and offices such as precinct chair have gone unfilled.

Third Parties in Texas

In Texas, as in many other states, the two major parties have made it difficult for third parties to gain power, mostly through onerous requirements for ballot access. In essence, Democrats and Republicans agree that a third competitor is not a net positive for either of them. As a result of the major parties dominating the rules and processes of elections, third-party candidates rarely win elections in Texas. Since they are seen as inevitable losers at the ballot box, voters prefer to "go with the winner."

The third parties that have gained some success at certain points in Texas history have done so mainly because they emphasized a particular issue. In the late nineteenth century, two farmers' movements—the Grange and the Populists—provided alternatives to the two major parties in various elections. In 1948 opposition to racial integration led the States' Rights Party, or **Dixiecrats**, to rally behind segregationist Strom Thurmond for president instead of Democratic candidate Harry Truman. Interestingly, while Thurmond carried some southern states, they did not include Texas, which voted for Truman. Segregation spurred a third-party candidacy again in 1968 when Alabama governor George Wallace ran against the liberal Democratic candidate Hubert Humphrey. Echoing Thurmond's results, Wallace carried a number of southern states but failed to win Texas, which supported Humphrey.

The civil rights movement in the 1960s planted the seeds for an independent Latino movement named **La Raza Unida**, meaning "united race." José Ángel Gutiérrez led the party at its inception, which was concentrated in Zavala County. La Raza Unida developed into a third party that was able to win races in Crystal City and other small towns in south Texas by taking advantage of the system of nonpartisan elections used in many Texas municipalities. (Even today, many cities, such as Austin, conduct nonpartisan elections.) Actually, "nonpartisan" does not mean that the candidates for office do not belong to political parties; it just means that their party affiliation is not listed on the ballot. Reformers in many cities pushed for this change so that voters would choose candidates on the basis of their qualifications rather than their party. La Raza Unida won so many of these races in Zavala and surrounding counties that at one point the party was able to take control of some city councils, school boards, and even two mayor's offices. Statewide, in 1972 the La Raza Unida candidacy of Ramsey Muñiz nearly cost Democrat Dolph Briscoe the governorship. While the party ultimately faded away, as most third-party movements do, it marked the growing influence of Latinos in the state.

In recent years, the Libertarian Party in Texas has emerged as a third-party alternative to the two major parties. While running candidates for a wide range of offices across the state, the party has had little impact on Election Day. For the most part, it has been a party of protest through which people dissatisfied with politics in the state can express their discontent at the polls. Libertarians believe in limited government and can be considered fiscal conservatives and social liberals. Former U.S. representative Ron Paul of Lake Jackson, nominally a Republican, ran for president in 1988 as a Libertarian and subsequently as an unconventional Republican espousing libertarian views. His son, U.S. senator Rand Paul of Kentucky, has followed in the footsteps of his father by

Dixiecrats conservative southern Democrats who abandoned the national Democratic Party in the 1948 presidential election over the issue of racial integration

La Raza Unida Party former political party created in 1970 in Texas in order to bring attention to the concerns of Mexican Americans

Independent candidates face considerable challenges in elections. Although the musician and writer Kinky Friedman's 2006 candidacy for governor attracted major media attention, Friedman received only 12.4 percent of the vote.

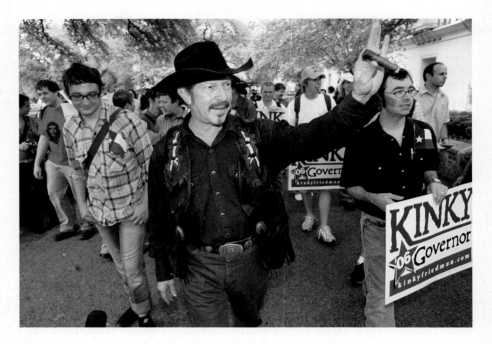

advocating libertarianism albeit as a Republican. Libertarians are particularly active in some of the major cities, including Austin. While they do not win very many elections, they can influence politics in other ways. For example, the major parties may adopt some of the positions promoted by Libertarians (or members of other minor parties) in order to win their support in runoff elections.

The most recent significant threat to major-party dominance of Texas politics came in the 2006 election for governor. Rick Perry was seen as a vulnerable incumbent, especially during a year that was not particularly favorable for Republicans. Chris Bell, a former Houston member of Congress, won the Democratic nomination, but two major independent candidates also ran for governor: former comptroller Carole Keeton Strayhorn and musician and humorist Kinky Friedman, whose slogan was "Why the hell not?" When all the ballots were counted, Perry was re-elected, but with only 39 percent of the vote. While it is not clear that a two-way race between Bell and Perry would have ensured a Bell victory, the candidacies of Strayhorn and Friedman damaged whatever mandate Perry could claim from a victory without a majority.

Why don't people vote for third parties? In general elections, Texas, like most of the United States, employs what is known as a **"first past the post," single-member district** electoral system. Under a first past the post system, only the candidate who wins the plurality of votes, that is, the most votes, is elected. According to **Duverger's Law**, this type of voting system tends to favor a two-party system because a vote for a third-party candidate generally does not result in a win. Consider the 2006 governor's race in which Perry won with less than an outright majority. Although Friedman and Strayhorn made good showings for third-party candidates, they still received only 12.4 percent and 18.1 percent of the vote, respectively. Even a runoff election would have been between the two major-party candidates, Perry and Bell. This is not to say that a vote for a third-party candidate is "wasted," because major-party candidates as well as the parties themselves

"first past the post" an election rule that states that the winner is the candidate who receives a plurality of the votes

single-member district an electorate that is allowed to elect only one representative for each district

Duverger's Law the observation that in a single-member district system of electing representatives, a two-party system will emerge

How Republican Is Texas?

The South has become a solidly Republican region, and Texas is no exception to this. Indeed, former President Clinton official Paul Begala, a native Texan, once called the state "South Carolina on steroids." Since the 1960s, South Carolina has been a reliable Republican state in presidential elections. On the other hand, California has become a solidly Democratic state since the 1990s largely due to its growing Latino population and its relatively high population of white liberals. How does Texas compare with other key states on political partisanship?

Percentage of Residents Who Identify as Republicans*

North Dakota 56%	Wyoming 56%	Utah 56%	Idaho 53%	South Dakota 52%	Alaska 52%	Montana 51%	Nebraska 50%	Alabama 50%
Oklahoma 49%	Kansas 48%	South Carolina 47%	Tennessee 47%	Missouri 45%	Kentucky 45%	Mississippi 45%	Arkansas 45%	West Virginia 44%
Indiana 43%	Louisiana 43%	Ohio 42%	Iowa 42%	Arizona 42%	Pennsylvania 41%	Wisconsin 41%	Texas 41%	New Hampshire 40%
Georgia 40%	Maine 39%	North Carolina 39%	Florida 39%	Nevada 39%	Michigan 38%	Virginia 38%	Minnesota 37%	Colorado 37%
Oregon 36%	New Mexico 34%	Washington 34%	New Jersey 33%	Delaware 33%	Illinois 33%	Connecticut 32%	Vermont 30%	California 30%
New York 29%	Maryland 28%	Hawaii 28%	Rhode Island 27%	Massachusetts 26%				

* Or who identify as independents but say they lean Republican.

SOURCE: 2017 Gallup Organization.

CRITICAL THINKING

- How does Texas compare with other states in terms of partisanship?

- How might demographic change, especially the growing Latino population, change Texas's political preferences?

proportional representation a multimember district system that allows each political party representation in proportion to its percentage of the total vote

Tea Party movement reaching prominence after Barack Obama's election, a political movement that advocates lower government spending, lower taxes, and limited government

often adapt their rhetoric and policies in response to voters who support a third-party candidate. Winning candidates often would like to appeal in future elections to constituents who might not have supported them in the past.

In contrast, some other countries use a system of **proportional representation** that encourages third-party voting because even if a party wins only 10 percent of the vote in an election, it will still win 10 percent of the seats in the legislature or other representative body. Voters in these countries are more likely to vote for third and minor parties because they will almost certainly be able to elect at least one of their preferred candidates.

Many American voters believe that their votes would be wasted if they voted for a third-party candidate. This expectation is rational, as the history of elections shows that a Republican or Democrat will almost always win. Most voters logically decide that it makes more sense to vote for the major-party candidate whose ideology is closest to their own.

The Tea Party Movement in Texas

The **Tea Party movement** became prominent nationwide and in Texas during the presidency of Barack Obama. Tea Party advocates have had a great deal of influence in Texas mainly because of their libertarian antitax message, which resonates with many Texans.

Rep. Dennis Bonnen (R-Angleton) was able to secure support from multiple factions of the Republican Party and ultimately win the race for Speaker of the Texas House.

The implications of these antitax policies in Texas mean less funding for K–12 and higher education and fewer social services such as children's health care programs.

Tea Party organizers have not sought to run a third-party candidate in elections, however. Instead, they have been successful at influencing Republican primary elections. They believe that they can have more influence in state politics if they become powerful within the Republican Party. Undoubtedly, this is a wise strategy given the history of defeat for third parties, not only in the state but nationwide. Tea Party groups have focused their efforts on key statewide races. They have campaigned against incumbents, such as Speaker Straus of San Antonio, whom they deem to be too moderate. Straus's retirement from the House in 2018 paved the way for a more conservative speaker, Rep. Dennis Bonnen (R-Angleton), who announced in November 2018 that he had secured enough votes from his colleagues to ensure his election as Speaker in early 2019. The Tea Party has had success in defeating incumbents and nominating preferred candidates, making it fairly clear that the Republican Party is dominated by this more conservative faction. Dan Patrick's re-election for lieutenant governor in 2018 suggests that the Tea Party movement has been co-opted by the Republican Party.

Parties and Digital Media

Traditionally, parties relied on newspapers, television, and radio to disseminate their messages to voters and to raise funds from and mobilize their supporters. However, in the digital age, parties have established active presences on social media platforms such as Facebook, Twitter, and Snapchat. They hire digital media professionals to monitor social media and respond to criticisms, publicize the other party's faults, and advertise for their candidates.

Social media are also an important fundraising tool. Before the Internet, parties relied on snail mail and phone calls to solicit campaign contributions, but now they can raise funds more easily and cheaply using email blasts and posts on social media.

Parties use digital media for voter mobilization as well. Parties can urge their supporters who follow them on Facebook or Twitter to turn out to vote. They can also encourage their friends to pass on these messages. In addition to social media, the Texas Democratic Party website (txdemocrats.org) and the Texas Republican Party website (texasgop.org) provide Texans an opportunity to learn more about party positions, contribute money, volunteer, and make inquiries.

Texas's History as a One-Party State

Trace the evolution of the party system in Texas

In order to understand the present partisan environment in Texas, let us look at the history of partisanship in Texas since the end of the Civil War. With the defeat of the Republican governor Edmund J. Davis in 1873, Texas entered a period of Democratic dominance that would last for over a century. Often the Republican Party would not contest major state offices, and other parties, such as the Populist or People's Party, exerted some influence for brief periods but lacked staying power. In general elections, it was a foregone conclusion that the Democratic nominee would win. Any meaningful election contest would have been in the Democratic Party primary.

Republicans tended to have a limited role in Texas politics. Most commonly, people remained Republicans in the hope of gaining political patronage (usually local postmaster or rural mail carrier positions) when Republican presidents were in office. Other Republicans were businesspeople unhappy with the liberal policies of Democratic presidents such as Franklin Delano Roosevelt or Harry Truman. However, Republicans were never numerous enough to make their party a threat to Democratic dominance in the state. Indeed, Republicans interested in patronage positions from the national government may have had an incentive to keep the party small, as the fewer the Republicans, the less the competition. When the father of the late U.S. senator Lloyd Bentsen first moved to the Rio Grande Valley, he visited R. B. Creager, then state chairman of the Republican Party, and told him that he wanted to get involved in the party because his father had been a devoted Republican in South Dakota. Rather than welcoming Bentsen Sr. as a Republican, however, Creager told him, "You go back to Mission [Texas] and join the Democratic Party, because what's best for Texas is for every [other] state in the union to have a two-party system and for Texas to be a one-party state. When you have a one-party state, your men stay in Congress longer and build up seniority."[5]

In 1952 and 1956, however, the conservative Democratic governor Allan Shivers led a rebellion within Democratic ranks, which became known as the **Shivercrat movement** and presaged a dramatic change in party alignments a quarter century later. Shivers, widely regarded as one of the most able Texas governors of the twentieth century, supported Republican Dwight Eisenhower for the presidency against the Democratic nominee, Adlai Stevenson. In addition, he and all statewide officeholders except the agriculture commissioner, John White, ran on the 1952 and 1956 ballots as both Democrats and Republicans. Stevenson opposed the Texas position on the Tidelands, offshore lands claimed by both Texas and the national government, which were believed to contain oil. Additionally, Stevenson was much more liberal than Shivers, and Eisenhower was a famous and popular hero of World War II. Nevertheless, the Shivercrats' party disloyalty was condemned by Texas Democrats such as Sam Rayburn, Speaker of the U.S. House of Representatives, and it led to much tension in the state party between liberal and conservative Democrats as well as between party loyalists and the Shivercrats.

The Shivercrat movement sent a strong message that many conservative Texas Democrats were philosophically opposed to the national Democratic Party and that, although unwilling to embrace the Republican Party fully, they found the Republican Party more compatible with their views. A pattern in voting known as **presidential Republicanism** was strengthening, whereby conservative Texas voters would vote Democratic for state offices but Republican for president. Those conservatives were more numerous and more closely aligned with the Republican Party. To be sure, the fact that some Democratic voters and leaders supported the Republican presidential candidate did not mean that candidate would always carry Texas. As the "Who Are Texans?" graphic shows, the fortunes of Republican presidential candidates fluctuated between 1944 and 2016. Nevertheless, presidential Republicanism would persist in Texas and other southern states until Republicans began to win state and local races in the 1990s and beyond.

Shivercrat movement a movement led by the Texas governor Allan Shivers during the 1950s in which conservative Democrats in Texas supported Republican candidate Dwight Eisenhower for the presidency because many of those conservative Democrats believed that the national Democratic Party had become too liberal

presidential Republicanism a voting pattern in which conservatives vote Democratic for state offices but Republican for president

When Did Texas Become Republican?

The Republican Party is the dominant party in Texas. However, this is a fairly recent development. Before the 1970s, Texans were less likely than the rest of the nation to support Republican presidential candidates. And it was only in the 1990s and the early 2000s that Republicans came to hold a majority of seats in the Texas delegation to the U.S. House and in the Texas legislature.

Republican Share of the Presidential Vote

■ Texas   ■ National

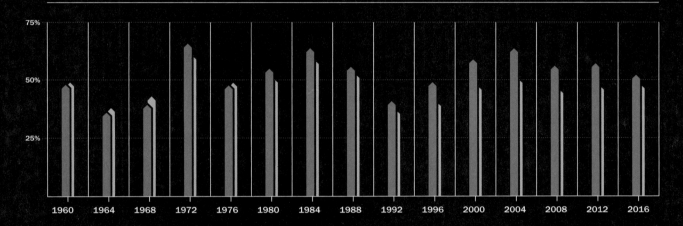

Republican Share of Offices Held

SOURCES: First figure: 1960–2004 data from the CQ Elections and Voting Collection. 2008 data from the Associated Press. Second figure: 1986–2002 data from Republican Party of Texas. 2004–18 data calculated by author from election results archived at the Texas Secretary of State.

Texas statewide offices
4% ... 100%

Texas House
37% ... 55%

Texas Senate
19% ... 61%

Texas delegation to U.S. House
37% ... 64%

1986 1990 1994 1998 2002 2006 2010 2014 2018

QUANTITATIVE REASONING

- Based on these data, how has the Republican share of the presidential vote in Texas changed compared to the rest of the nation? Why?

- Describe the trend in the growth of the Republican Party in Texas according to the data shown here. What factors might have shaped this trend? Do you think it will continue in the future?

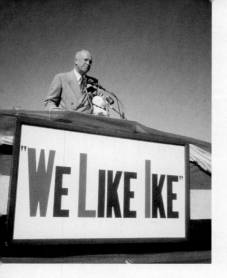

Though Democrats dominated Texas politics for decades, presidential Republicanism grew when Democrats supported Republican presidential candidate Dwight Eisenhower, who ran for president in 1952 and 1956. Here, Eisenhower is seen campaigning in Lubbock.

Still, in state elections from 1874 to 1994 the Democratic Party was overwhelmingly dominant despite pockets of Republican strength. Traditionally, in the post–Civil War era, the "German counties" in the Texas Hill Country, which were settled by German immigrants, showed Republican leanings. Dallas County, whose voters were influenced by a powerful group of conservative businesspeople and a conservative newspaper, the *Dallas Morning News*, also showed early Republican strength, electing a very conservative Republican member of Congress in the 1950s.

During this era, the Democratic Party was an umbrella party that held a variety of groups and interests. Both liberals and conservatives belonged to the party, as did members of labor unions, businesspeople, farmers, and city dwellers. Often, liberals and conservatives battled for control of the party and its offices, but what little political organization existed tended to be based on personal ties and the popularity of individual candidates. Until about the 1940s, politics inside the Texas Democratic Party was often chaotic and confused, with relatively few significant ideological divisions. Democrats were for the most part conservative during this time period.

By about the mid-1940s, however, a split occurred between liberals and conservatives in the Democratic Party. New Deal economic policies and civil rights measures divided the party, and liberals and conservatives battled in the Democratic primaries. Until the mid-1970s, the victor in these primary squabbles would then go on to win the general election fairly easily. However, by the late 1970s the winner of the Democratic primary had to face a significant conservative challenge from a Republican in the general election.[6]

The Era of Conservative Democrats

The Democrats who controlled Texas politics between Reconstruction and the mid-twentieth century were conservative on fiscal and racial issues and exerted a powerful influence in the region as well as in Congress. This may seem hard to fathom in today's political environment, wherein Democrats are liberal on these issues and Republicans conservative. But the Republican Party was started as an antislavery party and long remained identified with this legacy, whereas conservative Democrats in the early to mid-twentieth century were not particularly favorable to policies that would make it easier for African Americans to vote or participate in civic life in an equal manner.

In the many contests between conservative and liberal Democrats within Texas when the Democratic Party was the only game in town, the conservatives usually won because of the sheer fact that there were more of them in the state. However, some liberal leaders did emerge within the party, such as U.S. senator Ralph Yarborough, and to some extent, President Lyndon B. Johnson. They both held progressive views—unlike many of their white Texas counterparts. U.S. senator Lloyd Bentsen Jr. became the vice-presidential candidate for Michael Dukakis in 1988 but was unable to win the state for his running mate. Instead, Republican George H. W. Bush, who had moved to Texas from Connecticut, won the state and the presidency. By then the national conservative wave that began with the election of Ronald Reagan as president in 1980 had reached Texas, and from that point on, the Democratic Party in the state shrank to become the minority party.

The Growth of the Republican Party

Over the last fifty years, one of the most important developments in Texas politics has been the growth of the Republican Party (see Figure 4.2). This growth can be seen along three interrelated dimensions: in terms of those who identify with the party, those who vote for Republican candidates in primaries and general elections, and those Republicans who have been elected to office.

In the 1950s more than 60 percent of Texans identified with the Democratic Party and fewer than 10 percent identified as Republicans. The remainder considered themselves independents. In the 1960s, Republican identification in Texas rose above 10 percent, Democratic identification remained above 60 percent, and identification as independents dropped slightly. The 1970s saw a decline in Democratic affiliation and an increase in Republican affiliation, a pattern that accelerated during the 1980s and continued through the end of the century.[7] In 2016, Gallup reported that 37 percent of Texans identified as Democratic or leaning Democratic and 43 percent identified as Republican or leaning Republican. There is, however, clearly a difference between poll responses and election results. When one considers competition between the two parties in terms of actual voters in primaries or general elections, a different story emerges.

FIGURE 4.2

Party Composition of the Texas Delegation to the U.S. House of Representatives, 1845–2019

NOTE: Third-party data are not included.

SOURCE: Texas Politics Project at the University of Texas at Austin.

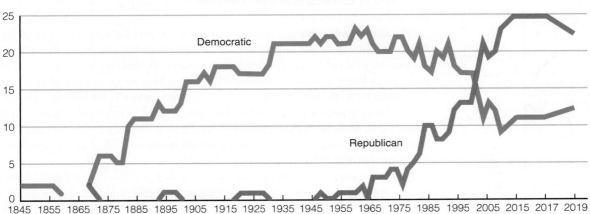

NUMBER OF REPRESENTATIVES

TABLE 4.1

Republican Officeholders in Texas, 1974–2018

YEAR	U.S. SENATE	OTHER STATEWIDE	U.S. HOUSE	TEXAS SENATE	TEXAS HOUSE	TOTAL
1974	1	0	2	3	16	22
1980	1	1	5	7	35	49
1990	1	6	8	8	57	80
2000	2	27	13	16	72	130
2010	2	27	23	19	101	172
2012	2	27	24	19	95	167
2014	2	27	25	20	98	172
2016	2	27	25	20	94	168
2018	2	27	23	19	83	154

By this measure, Texas is still a strongly Republican state, but Democrats have been making gains since 2014.

In the first quarter of the twentieth century, from 1903 to 1927, Republicans never held more than one seat in the Texas Senate or more than two seats in the Texas House. For the next quarter-century, from 1927 to 1951, there were no Republicans at all in the legislature, until in 1950 a lone Republican was elected from Dallas to serve only one term in the House. It was another decade before Republicans were again elected to the legislature; this time two Republican members served in the House. Then in 1962, six Republicans were elected to the House from Dallas County and 1 from Midland County. By 1963 there were ten Republicans in the House but still none in the Senate.[8]

As Table 4.1 shows, as late as 1974 there were very few Republican officeholders in the entire state of Texas. One of them was U.S. senator John Tower, and there were 2 Texas Republicans in the U.S. House of Representatives. No Republicans had been elected to state office in statewide elections. There were only 3 Republicans in the Texas Senate and only 16 in the Texas House.

Ronald Reagan's election as president in 1980 marked a significant change in how Texans began to vote not only in presidential elections but also in state elections. The Reagan era ushered in a period when conservative Democrats began to switch to the Republican Party in record numbers. This switch became more evident at the end of the George H. W. Bush presidency in the early 1990s, when Texas became a Republican state not only in presidential races but also in state races. In 2019 both U.S. senators from Texas and 23 of the 36 Texas members of the U.S. House of Representatives were Republican. In the state legislature, majorities of both the Senate (19 of the 31 members) and the House (83 of the 150 members) were Republican.

It was a record of remarkable Republican growth and Democratic decline. By 1999 every statewide elected official was Republican (and this remained true in 2018). That

Do Internal Divisions Spell Trouble for the Republican Party in Texas?

IN TEXAS, the majority of state legislators and all members of the executive branch are members of the Republican Party. However, in recent years, the conservative Tea Party movement has played an increasingly important and often divisive role in the Republican Party in the state. Now that the Tea Party has successfully garnered a large share of state and local offices, what does this mean for the Republican Party as a whole moving forward? Is this a sign of internal party dysfunction or minor debates within the major governing coalition?

The Tea Party faction within the Republican Party has pushed conservative policies and antitax sentiment. These more conservative Republicans in the legislature have challenged moderate Republicans, arguing that they were insufficiently conservative and unwilling to push these major reforms. They have also focused more heavily on social issues than in the past. For example, the more conservative wing of the Republican Party, led by Lieutenant Governor Dan Patrick, were strong advocates of the bathroom bill, which would have prevented transgendered Texans from using restrooms of their choosing. Additionally, they were strongly in favor of SB 4, the ban on sanctuary cities within the state. Speaker Joe Straus, the leader of mainstream Republicans at the state level, made no secret of his distaste for these two bills. The final result of these two major bills indicate a mixed record for the more conservative wing of the party. SB 4 passed and was signed by Governor Abbott, but the bathroom bill failed in the special session largely due to opposition from the state's business community.

Do these clear internal divisions within the Republican Party mean that there will be more opportunities for Democrats to gain power? There is no question that the path to victory in the state for Democrats is to mobilize and turn out Latino voters—who are not registered at the same rates as their Anglo counterparts and do not turn out to vote at the same rates. Democrats made a strong effort to oppose SB 4 and characterized the law as racially discriminatory against the state's large Latino population. State legislators such as Ana Hernandez of Houston and Rafael Anchia of Dallas have been outspoken about how SB 4 targets Latinos. Will legislation such as SB 4 mobilize Latinos to punish Republicans? This remains to be seen, as some commentators point to Donald Trump's election as evidence that Latinos did not realize their potential power in the 2016 election to stop his candidacy (which was driven in part by anti-immigrant rhetoric and policy proposals).

On the other hand, will Republicans weather this internal storm and adapt their policies to conform to the business community? Results of recent elections indicate that Republicans united after divisive primaries to elect Tea Party–backed candidates. For example, Senator Ted Cruz and Lieutenant Governor Dan Patrick did not have difficulty winning their respective elections after defeating the more moderate

David Dewhurst. An alternative explanation is that they benefited not so much from Republican unity as they did from weak Democratic candidates. Donald Trump, who represents the more conservative wing of the party, carried Texas in 2016, but by only nine percentage points, compared to Romney's 16-point victory over Obama in 2012.

COMMUNICATING EFFECTIVELY: YOUR VOICE

- How would you advise the Democratic Party to take advantage of Republican divisions and win more elections? Would you focus on recruiting stronger candidates or increasing turnout? Why?

- If you were advising the Republican Party on how to continue winning elections in Texas, would you argue for more Republican unity, or would you encourage the party to accept more voices and opinions? Why?

included the governor, lieutenant governor, attorney general, comptroller, land commissioner, agriculture commissioner, all three members of the Texas Railroad Commission, and all nine members of both the Texas Supreme Court and the Texas Court of Criminal Appeals. Only 20 years earlier, William Clements had been the first statewide official elected as a Republican since Reconstruction.

The Disappearance of Conservative Democrats

Blue Dog Democrats
another name for conservative Democrats, mostly from the South

Conservative Democrats, also known as **Blue Dog Democrats**, are becoming an endangered species in Texas and in the rest of the South. Such Democrats never left the party they grew up in, but they have become marginalized in the national party because of their social conservatism. Many of these Democrats are opposed to abortion while supportive of gun rights, positions that put them at odds with the prevailing consensus in the Democratic Party. Some of the few conservative Democrats elected to Congress in recent years even refused to support Nancy Pelosi of San Francisco as their party leader because of their divergence from her more liberal views.

By 2012 all of the conservative Democrats elected to represent Texas in Congress had retired, switched parties, or lost re-election contests. For example, Chet Edwards, who represented Crawford, the home of former president George W. Bush, lost his bid for re-election in 2010 to Republican Bill Flores. Ralph Hall of Rockwall became a Republican in 2004 after spending many years as a conservative Democrat. He switched parties in order to have more influence in what was then Congress's majority party, although just two years later, the Democrats retook control of the U.S. House. In 2014, Hall decided to run for re-election at the age of 91 but lost in a runoff with Tea Party–backed candidate John Ratcliffe, who went on to win the seat.

The biggest losses for conservative Democrats came following the 2003 redistricting cycle, spearheaded by Tom DeLay. As House majority leader, DeLay wanted to take advantage of the new Republican majority in the state legislature to redraw the boundaries of the state's congressional districts, which he thought were too favorable to Democrats. He therefore organized a dramatic though controversial redistricting session, which put many conservative Democrats from Texas at risk of losing their seats.

After this episode, two Democratic U.S. representatives, Charles Stenholm and Max Sandlin, lost their 2004 re-election bids to Republicans. Another Democrat, Jim Turner, decided not to seek re-election in his newly configured district in east Texas. Redistricting has left liberal Lloyd Doggett of Austin as the only white Democrat representing a majority white congressional district in Texas.

The pattern in Congress is also present at the state legislative level. Of the 55 Democrats in the Texas House of Representatives in 2013, only 11 were considered conservative in research conducted by Mark Jones of Rice University. This rating was relative to other Democrats, not Republicans; the most conservative Democrat in the Texas House is still more liberal than the most liberal Republican.[9] In the 2015 legislative session, however, Allan Ritter of Nederland switched to the Republican Party.

In today's political environment, the influence of conservative Democrats and liberal Republicans is very limited. Both nationally and in Texas, conservatives are disproportionately members of the Republican Party and liberals of the Democratic Party.

Recent elections have continued the trend toward greater strength of Republicans in Texas. Some conservative Democrats—like Representative Henry Cuellar of Laredo, pictured here—continue to serve in Congress.

Texas Party Politics Today

Analyze how ideological divisions and demographic change affect Texas political parties

Both Texas Democrats and Texas Republicans have factions within their party, and these factions emphasize different issues. For example, the Democratic Party in Texas has a large Latino base, which is very interested in the issue of immigration. The Republican Party has a strong and growing Tea Party contingent, which is making the party more antitax and fiscally conservative. Moreover, there are a shrinking number of truly independent voters who can swing elections. Often, both parties attempt to mobilize their own bases instead of trying to reach these swing voters. In this section, we will examine some of these conflicts both between and within the major parties.

Party Unity and Disunity

All groups have opposing factions within them, and political parties are no exception. When a party becomes dominant in a state, these factional battles become particularly important because the stakes are higher for the factions of the dominant party.

As discussed earlier, when the Democratic Party dominated Texas politics, factional battles were common between liberals and conservatives in the party. These conflicts were especially notable during the 1950s, in the struggles between the pro-Eisenhower conservative Democrats, led by Allan Shivers, and the pro-Stevenson liberal and loyalist Democrats, led by Sam Rayburn, Lyndon Johnson, and Ralph Yarborough. Now that the Republican Party dominates the state, its factions have fought major battles for control as well. One faction is the religious right, which is especially concerned with issues such as abortion, prayer in public schools and at school events, the teaching of evolution in public schools, and the so-called bathroom bill, which would have made it state law to only use restrooms corresponding to the gender on one's birth certificate. The other major segment of the party is composed of economic conservatives, who are primarily concerned with reduced government spending and regulation. At the end of the day, however, both these factions usually end up supporting the Republican candidate in the general election.

Starting in the 2006 primary, some Republicans, including two of the party's largest contributors in Texas, believed that some Republicans in the Texas House were insufficiently committed to conservative policies such as the bathroom bill and the sanctuary city ban and spent money to try to defeat them.[10] At least six Republican incumbents were aided by last-minute contributions from a political action committee that poured about $300,000 into their campaigns to help protect them from more conservative challengers. Nevertheless, two of the six were defeated in the primary and one had to win a runoff.[11] The 2014 primary battle between Dewhurst and Patrick shows that the ideological tensions in the Republican Party continue between what is essentially a conservative faction and an even more conservative faction, the latter identified with the Tea Party movement.

To maintain its political strength, the Republican Party has to keep these factional disputes within the party. For years, the Democratic Party battles between liberal and conservative wings were kept inside the party because there was no rival party to which one of the factions could go. Eventually the Republican Party emerged as a home where many conservative Democrats felt comfortable. Conceivably, the factional disputes in the Republican Party could lead one of the factions—the more moderate Republicans—to move to the Democratic Party.

Urban, Rural, and Suburban Influences on Partisanship

As in the rest of the country, one of the major divides in current political party affiliation in Texas is rural versus urban. Today's large suburban populations must be added to this equation. Since World War II, the growth of suburban enclaves around major cities such as the Dallas–Fort Worth metroplex, Houston, and San Antonio has profoundly changed politics. Prior to the growth of suburbia, people lived either in cities or in rural areas. Rural residents were often cattle ranchers or farmers. As cattle raising and farming became more mechanized and large companies bought out local farmers, family farms and ranches became less profitable, and many rural residents relocated to cities to work in banks, oil companies, or other industries.

During the 1950s the federal government embarked on a major project to connect cities through an interstate highway system. One consequence of this system was that for those who wanted to escape urban congestion, it became easier to move to the outskirts of the city and travel by car to their jobs. While mass transit facilitated suburban commuting in other parts of the country, Texas taxpayers were unwilling to fund these infrastructure investments. Interstate highways also encouraged the process of "white flight," the mass exodus of more affluent whites from urban to suburban areas, at least partly to avoid racial integration. This movement left urban areas with eroding tax bases and poorer minority populations, who often could not afford to purchase automobiles to commute between city and suburb.

The political result of this changing demographic is that cities have become more Democratic, even in Texas, where the urban strongholds of Austin, Dallas, El Paso, and Houston deliver the most Democratic votes in the state. Rural areas have remained solidly conservative and have become Republican, and suburban areas can best be described as hybrid areas with pockets of Republicans and Democrats, but an overall Republican majority. An important exception to these patterns is the Rio Grande Valley, which has large rural areas with Democratic dominance. However, voter turnout in the valley is substantially lower than in other parts of the state.

Voters also increasingly tend to settle in places with like-minded people; cities tend to attract more Democrats and suburban and rural areas more Republicans, reinforcing the political proclivities already established in such communities. A recent book, *Our Patchwork Nation*, by Dante Chinni and James Gimpel, explores this phenomenon nationwide, arguing that different communities have distinct political characteristics.[12]

The political shifts introduced by suburbanization are clearly seen in Dallas County over the last decade. In the early 1980s there had been a wholesale rush of incumbent

The Tea Party in Texas

With the election of many Tea Party–backed candidates and a more conservative turn in the Republican Party's positions on immigration, including the ban on sanctuary cities as well as increased border security, some have argued that the Republican Party has been taken over by the Tea Party. Do Texans think the Tea Party has too much influence, too little influence, or just the right amount? Where do you stand compared to your fellow Texans? Given the data here, why do you think the Tea Party has gained influence in the state in recent years?

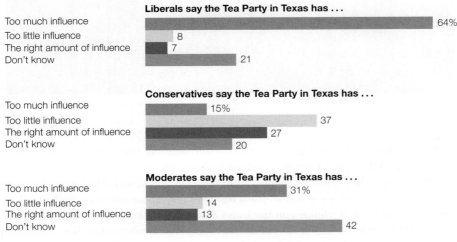

Liberals say the Tea Party in Texas has . . .

Too much influence	64%
Too little influence	8
The right amount of influence	7
Don't know	21

Conservatives say the Tea Party in Texas has . . .

Too much influence	15%
Too little influence	37
The right amount of influence	27
Don't know	20

Moderates say the Tea Party in Texas has . . .

Too much influence	31%
Too little influence	14
The right amount of influence	13
Don't know	42

SOURCE: The Texas Politics Project, "Tea Party Influence," February 2018, www.texaspolitics.utexas.edu (accessed 7/12/18).

Democratic judges in Dallas County into the Republican Party. Although varying explanations were given by the party switchers, perhaps the most honest and straightforward was by Judge Richard Mays: "My political philosophy about general things has nothing to do with me [*sic*] being a judge. . . . That's not the reason I'm switching parties. The reason I'm switching is that to be a judge in Dallas County you need to be a Republican." With Mays's switch in 1985, 32 of the 36 district judges in Dallas County were Republicans, though none had been Republicans before 1978.[13] By the late 1980s the only Democrat who could win a judicial race in Dallas County was Ron Chapman, who happened to share the name of the most popular disk jockey in the county. Only a few years later, all judges in Dallas County were Republican.[14]

As Dallas County became denser and the suburbs expanded to adjoining counties, Dallas transformed into a solidly Democratic county. This is illustrated by an almost overlooked judicial race in Dallas County in 2000. Only one article appeared in the *Dallas Morning News* about the puzzling results.[15] A three-term Republican judge, Bill Rhea, won re-election against a first-time Democratic candidate, Mary Ann Huey. On its own, that outcome was no surprise.[16]

What *was* remarkable about that district court race was that out of 560,558 votes cast, only 4,150 votes separated the two candidates. In other words, a three-term Republican

Former secretary of Housing and Urban Development Julián Castro (center) and congressperson Joaquín Castro of San Antonio (right) are two of a growing number of influential Latinos in the Democratic Party in Texas. Both have been touted as potential statewide or national candidates.

judge with no scandal or other controversy surrounding his name won with only 50.3 percent of the vote.[17] Even more astounding, his opponent had run with no money, no political experience, and no support from the legal community. She ran in the same year that Texas governor George W. Bush was the presidential nominee, with no other Democratic judicial candidates on the ballot at the county level, and with little more than audacity on her side. It is no wonder that Judge Rhea commented, "I'm thrilled to be serving again and duly humbled by the vote count."

Judge Rhea's humbling experience was caused not by his judicial performance but rather by demographic changes. By 2000 the voters who had made up the former Republican base in Dallas County had begun moving to places such as Collin, Denton, and Rockwall counties. That suburban growth changed those traditionally Democratic counties into Republican ones but left Dallas itself with a larger African American and an even larger Latino population and returned it to the Democratic column that it left a little more than 30 years ago.

In the 2004 elections, George W. Bush carried Dallas County by fewer than 10,000 votes (50.72 percent), and the county elected Democrats as sheriff and four countywide elected judges. The 2006 elections were truly a watershed in the county's politics. A Democrat was elected county judge, a Democrat was elected district attorney, and all 42 Democrats who ran for county judgeships were elected. Democrats continued their sweep of countywide elections in 2008, 2010, 2012, 2016, and 2018.

In 2008, Harris County (containing Houston) also dramatically shifted to the Democratic column, electing a large number of Democrats to county office. It seemed to be following in Dallas County's footsteps. However, the 2010 elections moved Harris back into the Republican column, and in 2012, it yielded a virtual tie between Obama and Republican presidential nominee Mitt Romney. In 2016, Hillary Clinton won Harris County by double digits, and Democrats swept the countywide races. In 2018, all countywide Republicans in Harris County were defeated by Democrats.

African Americans in Texas Political Parties

As noted earlier, about 12 percent of the Texas population is African American—roughly the same percentage as in the total U.S. population—and African Americans are concentrated in east Texas and in the major cities of Houston, Dallas, San Antonio, and Austin. In most elections, the vast majority of them cast their votes for Democrats. This is not unusual, as African Americans in other parts of the country are similarly loyal to the Democratic Party.

African Americans have been elected to represent Texas in Congress since Reconstruction. The first African American woman elected to Congress from Texas was Barbara Jordan, who played a major role in the investigation of Richard Nixon during the Watergate scandal. Her legacy remains strong among African Americans in Texas. In 2019, Texas was represented by six African Americans in the U.S. House: Republican Will Hurd of San Antonio and Democrats Eddie Bernice Johnson of Dallas, Al Green of Houston, Sheila Jackson Lee of Houston, Marc Veasey of Dallas, and Colin Allred of Richardson. In the state legislature as of 2019, 17 African Americans serve in the state House of Representatives and 2 serve in the state senate.

The influence of African Americans in the Democratic Party in Texas is high not only because they tend to vote Democratic but because they tend to vote at higher rates than other ethnic groups. During the 2014 statewide elections, 33.4 percent of African Americans turned out to vote, versus 30.7 percent of whites and only 16.2 percent of Hispanics (see Table 4.2).

This is not to say that all African Americans are Democrats. In 2015, Republican Will Hurd of San Antonio made history by becoming the first black Republican elected from the state to Congress. Former railroad commissioner Michael Williams became the first

TABLE 4.2

Turnout by Race: 2016 Presidential Year Versus 2014 Statewide Election Year

	NUMBER OF REGISTERED VOTERS IN 2016 (IN MILLIONS)	TURNOUT OF REGISTERED VOTERS IN 2014 STATEWIDE ELECTION YEAR (%)	TURNOUT OF REGISTERED VOTERS IN 2016 PRESIDENTIAL YEAR (%)	DIFFERENCE BETWEEN 2016 AND 2014 (%)
White*	89.3	30.7%	47.8%	17.1%
African American	1.7	33.4	54.9	21.5
Asian	0.4	11.9	30.4	18.5
Latino	4.8	16.2	28.0	11.8
Total	11.7	30.2	47.7	17.5

*White does not include whites who identify as Latino.
SOURCE: U.S. Census Bureau, "Voting and Registration in the Election of November 2014 and 2016—Detailed Tables."

black Republican to be elected to the statewide post. The former Texas Supreme Court chief justice Wallace Jefferson is also an African American Republican and was elected by voters to his position. Other than Williams and Jefferson, only two other African Americans have been elected to statewide office since Reconstruction.

African Americans have been elected mayors of the three largest cities in Texas. Democrat Ron Kirk became Dallas's first African American mayor in 1995, and Democrat Lee Brown became Houston's first African American mayor in 1997. In 2002, Kirk ran for the U.S. Senate but lost to white Republican John Cornyn. In 2015, Houston elected its second African American mayor, Democrat Sylvester Turner. In 2014, African American independent Ivy Taylor was elected San Antonio's mayor, but subsequently lost her re-election to Democrat Ron Nirenberg in 2017.

Latinos in Texas Political Parties

In the 2014 gubernatorial election, Republican Greg Abbott ran television ads in English and Spanish featuring his Latina mother-in-law's endorsement of his candidacy. Abbott's appeal to Latino voters in this way—if I am elected governor, Texas will have a Latina first lady—highlights at the very least the growing importance of this electorate.

Just 12 years prior to Abbott's election, Democrats had attempted to break the Republican lock on statewide offices by putting forward a "Dream Team" for the 2002 elections: a slate of nominees that aimed to mobilize minority voters to support the Democratic ticket while holding on to much of the party's traditional base of white voters. The team consisted of Tony Sanchez, a wealthy Latino businessman from Laredo who had been an appointee of Republican governor Rick Perry and had a record of not participating in many elections, running for governor alongside Ron Kirk for the U.S. Senate and John Sharp, a former state comptroller and white conservative Democrat, for lieutenant governor. The strategy failed dismally, as Sanchez lost to Perry (40 percent to 58 percent), Kirk lost to the Republican Cornyn (43 percent to 55 percent), and Sharp lost to the Republican Dewhurst (46 percent to 52 percent). Especially disappointing because Sanchez was the first Latino major-party nominee for governor, Latino voter turnout was only 32.8 percent. Sanchez had money and spent it with abandon, but he was a poor campaigner who could not even mobilize the Latino vote. Further, it appeared that negative campaigning, particularly directed at Sanchez, may have undercut support for the Democratic ticket among traditional white conservative voters.[18] The Democratic "Dream Team" became a nightmare.

Latinos have not fully realized their potential voting strength. Table 4.2 shows Latino voting population figures and turnout rates in comparison with those of other racial and ethnic groups in the state in 2016 (a presidential year) and 2014 (a statewide election year). This is an issue that we will explore in more depth in Chapter 5. For now, we should note that Latino voters have a significantly lower turnout rate than that of whites and African Americans in both presidential years and statewide election years. Moreover, a large number of the Latinos living in Texas—perhaps around 2 million—are not citizens and thus not eligible to vote, even if they are documented.[19] Such facts will likely depress the electoral power of the Latino population in Texas in the short and medium terms. However, many of the children of these noncitizens were born in the United States and thus are themselves citizens eligible to vote. It would be surprising if being brought up and educated in the United States did not lead to higher turnout rates among younger Latinos in the future. The full impact of the Latino demographic surge on political parties may not be felt until the next generation comes of age.[20] Exit polls released just after the 2018 election indicated Latinos were 26 percent of the state electorate, a 2 percent increase from 2016.

Political Parties and the Future of Texas

We often think of conflict in politics as occurring between the Democratic and Republican parties, especially in government. While this is certainly true, conflict can also occur within political parties among different factions. These factions usually compromise, however, to support their candidates during the general election. Political parties therefore provide a structure through which candidates strive to win office.

One of the most striking developments in Texas politics over the past 20 to 25 years is that though one-party dominance persists, control of government has moved from near-total Democratic to near-total Republican control. This change was fueled by many factors, including the disappearance of conservative Democrats and the sorting of conservatives into the Republican Party and liberals into the Democratic Party. Like other southern states, Texas has long been very socially conservative and religious. As the Republican Party became the conservative party while Democrats became the liberal party, Texas has remained solidly conservative and therefore has become Republican. What would it take for Democrats to regain even some significant power in the state? There are three factors to watch as partisan politics in Texas evolves: divisions within the Republican party, an influx of people from outside of Texas, and the effort put forth by the Democratic Party itself.

Divisions within the Republican Party could provide Democrats an opportunity to capitalize on what voters might perceive as dysfunction and extreme policies. If more Tea Party–backed Republicans are elected statewide and move further and further to the right, a centrist Democrat could possibly win a statewide race. Neighboring Louisiana elected a moderate to conservative Democrat as governor in 2015 by capitalizing on the state Republican Party's move to the right and a weak Republican candidate.

While Texas is becoming more racially and ethnically diverse and is now a majority-minority state (meaning that non-Hispanic whites are less than half of the population), it is also seeing a major influx of white residents from other states. Many of these are conservatives attracted to the state's low taxes and light regulation policies. If these individuals vote at higher rates than others, then they will complicate efforts by the Democratic Party to make inroads.

Finally, the Democratic Party has to appeal to Texans by adopting policies that are not too far to the left. To some extent, Wendy Davis tried to do this on the issue of guns in her campaign for governor in 2014, but her reputation as a defender of abortion rights overshadowed her other policy positions, and she lost resoundingly to Greg Abbott. This failure to move the needle even slightly toward Democrats might give pause to Democratic donors nationally, who might instead choose to invest their resources in states that show more promise of "swinging" away from the Republicans.

In early 2016 discussion about tapping former San Antonio mayor and Secretary of Housing and Urban Development Julián Castro as a possible running mate for Hillary Clinton led some to believe that this choice might mobilize Latino voters not only in Texas but nationwide. Even Castro's presence on the Democratic ticket, however, would probably not have moved Texas into the Democratic column in 2016. As Texas becomes more diverse, the Republican Party's lock on power is ebbing, especially in the state's urban and suburban areas. Rural areas have become more Republican, and urban areas have become more Democratic. The 2018 election led to Democratic gains in the Texas House and the loss of two suburban Republican incumbents in the U.S. House.

Clearly, a lot has to happen for Democratic power in Texas to increase, and while Beto O'Rourke did not win the Senate race, the very close margin indicates that Texas is moving slowly to a more competitive political environment statewide. The much closer margins in the statewide elections are evidence of this. We will see what the future holds.

Use ⬛ INQUIZITIVE to help you study and master this material.

The Roles and Structure of Political Parties in Texas

- **Describe the main functions and structure of state party organizations (pp. 117–29)**

In Texas, political parties serve as brand labels for voters to determine whom to vote for in elections that have little or no publicity. Texas political parties also have conventions and committees that help their members organize and mobilize in elections.

Key Terms

party platform (p. 117)
partisan polarization (p. 119)
political socialization (p. 119)
precinct (p. 123)
precinct chair (p. 123)
county executive committee (p. 123)
county chair (p. 123)
state chair and vice chair (p. 124)
state executive committee (p. 124)
precinct convention (p. 124)
county convention (p. 124)
state convention (p. 124)
Dixiecrats (p. 125)
La Raza Unida Party (p. 125)
"first past the post" (p. 126)
single-member district (p. 126)
Duverger's Law (p. 126)
proportional representation (p. 128)
Tea Party movement (p. 128)

Practice Quiz

1. Providing a label that helps voters identify those seeking office is an important function of
   a) the state.
   b) political parties.
   c) interest groups.
   d) regional and subregional governments.
   e) the president.

2. The process by which political parties become more distant from each other in terms of ideology is
   a) partisan convergence.
   b) partisan polarization.
   c) partisan conventions.
   d) partisan equilibrium.
   e) partisan deliverance.

3. All of the following groups constitute the Democratic Party base in Texas *except*
   a) business leaders.
   b) Latinos.
   c) African Americans.
   d) white liberals.
   e) urban residents.

4. Which minority group is the fastest growing in Texas?
   a) African Americans
   b) Latinos
   c) Asian Americans
   d) Native Americans
   e) All are growing equally

5. In the state of Texas, the highest level of temporary party organization is the
   a) state convention.
   b) state executive committee.
   c) governor's convention.
   d) civil executive committee.
   e) speaker's committee.

6. Which of the following third parties and movements had the most success in winning elections in post–World War II Texas?
   a) La Raza Unida Party
   b) the Dixiecrats
   c) the Green Party
   d) the Kinky Friedman movement
   e) the Constitution Party

Texas's History as a One-Party State

- **Trace the evolution of the party system in Texas (pp. 129–36)**

Texas has traditionally been a one-party state, meaning that one party has been in control of state politics for a long time. In the post–Civil War period, the Democrats held power in the state, but since 1994 the Republicans have won every statewide election and consequently dominate state politics.

Key Terms

Shivercrat movement (p. 130)
presidential Republicanism (p. 130)
Blue Dog Democrats (p. 136)

Practice Quiz

7. The Shivercrat movement was
    a) a group of conservative Democrats in Texas who supported Eisenhower for president.
    b) a group of liberal Democrats who supported equal rights for all Americans.
    c) a group of conservative Republicans who rejected the Obama administration.
    d) a group of liberal Republicans who rejected the Bush administration.
    e) a group of Libertarians.

8. In Texas, the Republican Party became the dominant party in
    a) the 1950s.
    b) the 1960s.
    c) the 1970s.
    d) the 1980s.
    e) the 1990s.

9. Blue Dog Democrats were
    a) northeastern Democrats with conservative views.
    b) southern Democrats with liberal views.
    c) southern Democrats with conservative views.
    d) northern Democrats with liberal views.
    e) western Democrats with liberal views.

10. Presidential Republicanism refers to which of the following?
    a) Texans voting for Republican local candidates
    b) Texans voting for Republican presidents and Democrats for state offices
    c) Texans voting for Republican presidents and Republicans for state offices
    d) Texans voting for Democratic local candidates
    e) Texans voting for third-party candidates at all levels

Texas Party Politics Today

• **Analyze how ideological divisions and demographic change affect Texas political parties (pp. 137–43)**

Texas is a diverse state with divisions between north and south and east and west. Latinos currently constitute nearly 40 percent of the state's population and currently favor the Democratic Party, although their registration and turnout rates are lower than those of the other major demographic groups.

Practice Quiz

11. Which of the following is *not* true?
    a) Cities in Texas have become more Democratic.
    b) Cities in Texas are dominated by third parties.
    c) Rural areas of Texas are solidly Republican.
    d) Texas suburbs contain pockets of both Democrats and Republicans.
    e) Democrats dominate elections in Dallas County.

12. African Americans in Texas
    a) tend to cast their votes for Democrats.
    b) are a large part of the Republican base.
    c) vote mainly for independent candidates.
    d) constitute less than 10 percent of the population.
    e) split their votes evenly between the Democratic and Republican parties.

The outcomes of elections shape political life in Texas. 2018 saw many statewide races, including a surprisingly competitive contest for the U.S. Senate between incumbent Republican Ted Cruz and former El Paso representative Democrat Beto O'Rourke (right). O'Rourke garnered strong enthusiasm from Democrats and raised twice as much money as Cruz but still lost, 51–48 percent.

Campaigns and Elections

WHY CAMPAIGNS AND ELECTIONS MATTER

Two high-profile statewide races captured the attention of Texas in 2018. Governor Greg Abbott and Senator Ted Cruz were up for re-election in a midterm year without a presidential race. Democrats hoped that dissatisfaction with President Trump would galvanize Democrats, especially Latinos, to flood the polls in support of their candidates. Democrats were able to recruit a strong candidate to take on Cruz in U.S. representative Beto O'Rourke (D-El Paso). O'Rourke ran a campaign that, by all accounts energized the state's young and minority populations. Although O'Rourke came up short and lost to Cruz, it was the tightest statewide race in over a decade. O'Rourke was seen as a hope for disaffected Democrats who had become disillusioned by Cruz's increasingly conservative voting record in Congress.

In the gubernatorial race, Governor Abbott, who previously served as attorney general of the state when Rick Perry was governor, decided to seek re-election in 2018. He ran his re-election campaign on his conservative record as governor and pointed to public policy successes, including border security, the ban on sanctuary cities, and fiscal restraint. He also ran on his record as governor during the floods of Hurricane Harvey, which devastated the Houston area and led to significant rebuilding.

Democrats were hoping that one of the Castro twins from San Antonio would enter the race to unseat Abbott. However, both Castros decided against running statewide, which left Democrats scrambling for a formidable candidate. Without any candidates with significant previous political experience and money, however, Democrats faced an uphill battle to recapture the governor's seat, especially considering Abbott's formidable war chest.

Both races presented challenges to the state's Democratic Party, which could not capitalize on the unpopularity of President Trump. If Trump could not turn the state blue, then who possibly could?

Why should it matter who is governor or U.S. senator? Governors and senators often have important national statures and sometimes move on to national offices, as did Rick Perry, the current secretary of the Department of Energy. The governor has the power to set the state political agenda, promoting or vetoing statewide legislation and influencing public policy in the state by other means. U.S. Senators also have important national profiles, and often are elected to the White House. Texan Lyndon B. Johnson was a U.S. senator before being selected by John F. Kennedy as his vice president. Sen. Ted Cruz ran unsuccessfully for president in 2016 but was able to raise his national profile in the process. Elections to the city council, school board, state legislature, governorship, and U.S. Senate all make huge differences in our lives. Education funding, health care policy, taxes, and environmental policy all hang in the balance.

CHAPTER GOALS

- Describe the types of elections held in Texas and how they work (pp. 151–55)
- Explain how the rules for voting affect turnout among different groups of Texans (pp. 155–67)
- Present the main features of election campaigns in Texas (pp. 168–77)

Features of Elections in Texas

Describe the types of elections held in Texas and how they work

Elections are the most important vehicles by which the people express themselves in the democratic process in Texas. At the national level, elections are limited to the selection of the president and vice president (via the electoral college) and members of Congress. In Texas, however, voters select candidates for various offices in all three statewide branches of government (the legislature, executive, and judiciary) and in numerous local elections. There are a multitude of elections: primary elections, general elections, city elections, school board elections, special elections, elections for community college boards and the governing boards for many special districts, and bond elections for city, county, and state governments.

With so many different elections held for various positions, city spending proposals, and other local issues, it is difficult for voters to process all of the information and make choices. Voters often rely on mental shortcuts to make voting decisions. Partisanship is the shortcut, or what political scientists call a *cue*, used by most Texans. Other shortcuts could be race, gender, ethnicity, or other demographic characteristics when selecting candidates. With regard to decisions on bonds or amendments, voters can rely on endorsements by elected officials as well as on condensed summaries from newspapers or political parties. Texans also vote on changes to the state constitution, which can alter public policy in the state. In theory, such elections are meant to enable the people to exercise some direct control over each branch. In practice, however, one-party dominance and low levels of voter participation have often told a different story, leaving the government exposed to special interests and big money.

Primary Elections

Primary elections are the first elections held in an **electoral cycle**. In Texas, primary elections are generally held on the second Tuesday in March of even-numbered years. Primary elections determine a political party's nominees for the general election. They are conducted by the party and funded jointly by the party and the state. Essentially, the party collects filing fees from those seeking its nomination and uses these funds to pay the costs of holding the primary election.

The Democratic and Republican parties both conduct primaries in nearly all of Texas's 254 counties. Within each county, voters cast ballots in precincts, with the number of precincts depending on the county's population. Less-populated counties such as Loving and Kennedy have as few as 6 precincts, whereas Harris County contains more than 1,000.

Those seeking their party's nomination file papers and pay a filing fee to their party. If several members of the same party are seeking the same office, such as governor, they compete against each other in the party's primary election, wherein one will be chosen to run in the general election. Winning the primary election requires an absolute majority: more votes than all opponents combined. If no candidate receives an absolute majority,

primary election a ballot vote in which citizens select a party's nominee for the general election

electoral cycle the process in which candidates run for office beginning with campaigns for the party primary and ending with the general election, usually in November

Texans vote in numerous elections each year. While November general elections ask Texans to cast their vote for a variety of offices, many local elections only have candidates for a handful of positions on the ballot.

runoff primary a second primary election held between the two candidates who received the most votes in the first primary election if no candidate in that election received an absolute majority

open primary a primary election in which any registered voter can participate in the contest, regardless of party affiliation

closed primary a primary election in which only registered members of a particular political party can vote

a **runoff primary** is held between the two candidates receiving the most votes. Voters who participate in the Republican Party primary cannot vote in a Democratic runoff; likewise, anyone who voted in the Democratic Party primary cannot vote in a Republican runoff. However, those who voted in neither the Democratic nor the Republican primary can vote in either the Republican or the Democratic runoff primary.

An **open primary** allows any registered voter to cast a ballot in either primary, but not both primaries. One can consider oneself a Republican and vote in the Democratic primary or can leave home intending to vote in the Democratic primary, change one's mind, and vote in the Republican primary.

The Texas Constitution and election laws call the Texas system a **closed primary** because one must declare one's party affiliation before voting, but in practice it is an open primary. Before receiving a primary ballot, the voter signs a roll sheet indicating eligibility to vote and pledging to support the party's candidates. By signing the roll sheet, the voter makes a declaration of party affiliation. However, because the affiliation is declared only a few moments prior to voting, the primary is closed only in the narrowest sense of the term. This declaration in no way legally binds a voter to support the party's candidates in future elections. Many other states have true closed primaries in that only voters who have registered as party members beforehand can vote in these elections.

General Elections

The **general election** to select members of Congress is held the first Tuesday following the first Monday in November of even-numbered years. The Democratic Party's nominee runs against the nominee of the Republican Party, and sometimes independent and minor-party candidates also appear on the general election ballot.

general election the election in which voters cast ballots to select public officials

Major state officials (governor, lieutenant governor, comptroller of public accounts, attorney general, and so on) are elected in nonpresidential election years. This arrangement seeks to prevent presidential candidates from influencing the outcomes of Texas races. For example, it is possible that a popular Republican presidential candidate might draw more than the usual number of Republican votes, and an unusually large Republican presidential vote might swing the election for statewide candidates running under the Republican banner. Likewise, it prevents an uncommonly popular statewide candidate from influencing the presidential election. If statewide elections were held in presidential election years, a Democratic candidate for governor, for example, might influence Texas's presidential voting by increasing the number of votes for Democratic candidates in general.

Members of city councils, school boards, and other local government entities are also selected by general elections; however, these usually take place at a different time of year than the national and state elections. These elections are "nonpartisan," meaning the political parties of the candidates are not listed on the ballot. In many cases, this timing translates into very low voter turnout. For example, in the San Antonio municipal elections in June 2015, only 14.12 percent of the city's registered voters participated. Leaders in some parts of the state have proposed moving municipal elections to November to encourage a larger proportion of voters to participate. In Houston's mayoral race in November 2015, the turnout was much higher, 27.5 percent, perhaps partly due to an open mayoral race (with no incumbent) and a controversial ordinance on the ballot. In 2018, Harris County broke voting records with a turnout exceeding the 2016 presidential election, leading to a sweep by Democrats of all countywide races.

Special Elections

In Texas, **special elections** are used to fill vacancies in office, to give approval to borrow money, or to ratify or reject amendments to the Texas Constitution. The dates for special elections are specified by the Texas legislature. If a Texas state representative or senator resigns, the governor will call a special election to fill the vacancy.

special election an election that is not held on a regularly scheduled basis; in Texas, a special election is called to fill a vacancy in office, to give approval for the state government to borrow money, or to ratify or reject amendments to the Texas Constitution

Texas laws require voter approval before any governmental agency in Texas can assume long-term debt. If the local school district wants to borrow money to build a new high school and repair three elementary schools, for example, a special election must be held for voters to decide on the issue.

The legislature proposes amendments to the Texas Constitution, and the voters in a special election then ratify or reject them.

Running as an Independent

It is unusual for a candidate to run for office in Texas as an independent. One reason is that there are substantial requirements for getting one's name on the ballot. Additionally,

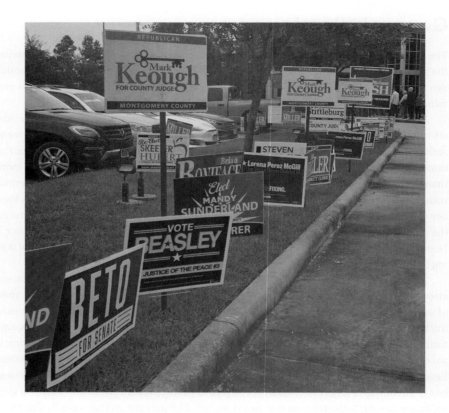

Some blame the relatively low voter turnout for Texas elections on the frequency of elections and the large number of candidates, as illustrated by the many campaign signs on an early voting day in The Woodlands. Also, state officials are not elected in presidential election years, when voter participation tends to be highest.

an independent candidate lacks the political support of party organizations and the advantage of having a party label on the ballot. Despite these obstacles, in 2006 two independent candidates ran for governor: musician and writer Kinky Friedman and former Austin mayor Carole Keeton Strayhorn, the state comptroller, who had been elected to that office as a Republican.

Both candidates were obviously hoping that an independent candidacy would attract the votes of Democrats who believed that a Democratic candidate for governor could not win in Texas. They also were hoping to get substantial votes from Republicans disaffected with the policies and performance of the Republican governor, Rick Perry. Strayhorn, in particular, seemed to have strong appeal to Democrats who usually contributed large sums to Democratic nominees. One study of her campaign contributions from July through December of 2005, for example, found that 52 percent of them were from people who had given exclusively or almost exclusively to Democrats over the previous five years.[1]

Each state decides its own requirements for getting on the ballot, and the process for independents to do so in Texas is relatively difficult. Friedman and Strayhorn, for example, had to meet the following requirements:

1. The candidates must obtain signatures on a petition from registered voters. The signatures must equal 1 percent of the total votes in the last governor's race. This meant that Friedman and Strayhorn each had to obtain 45,540 signatures.
2. The signatures must come from registered voters who did not participate in any political party primary election.

3. Signature collection cannot begin until the day after the last primary election. In 2018 this was June 21.
4. Voters may sign only one candidate's petition. If they sign both, only the first signature provided will count.[2]

The Democratic and Republican parties don't agree on much, but they do agree on keeping third-party competitors out. Making it difficult for independents to get their names on the ballot helps ensure that the two major parties will continue to dominate politics in the state well into the future. Elections may be open in Texas, but they work through the dominant political parties, helping to solidify their control over the political process and the major political offices in the state. The electoral performances of Friedman and Strayhorn also point to the difficulties of independent candidacy in that both of these candidates received only a small fraction of the overall vote.

Participation in Texas Elections

Explain how the rules for voting affect turnout among different groups of Texans

When we think of political participation, we often think of voting. Signing petitions, protesting, and writing letters to newspapers and elected officials are also forms of political participation, but voting is the most basic and fundamental duty citizens have in a democracy. Here, we begin by examining the history of voting in the state and the regulations and procedures surrounding voting rights. Issues include who can vote, how easy it is to register to vote, and why so few Texans vote.

Who Can Vote?

"The franchise" refers to the act of voting or the right to vote. For much of the period of one-party Democratic control that began in the late nineteenth century, there were restrictions on the franchise.

Early Restrictions on the Franchise
Women were allowed to vote in primaries and party conventions in Texas in 1918 and obtained the right to vote in all elections as a result of the **Nineteenth Amendment** to the U.S. Constitution in 1920. However, some of the most influential politicians in the state were opposed to the franchise for women. Joseph Weldon Bailey, for example, who had been Democratic leader in the U.S. House of Representatives and later the informal Democratic leader in the U.S. Senate, was a passionate opponent of women's **suffrage**, arguing that women could not vote because they could not perform the three basic duties of citizenship: jury service, *posse comitatus* service (citizens who are deputized to deal with an emergency), and military service. He believed that women's morals dictated their beliefs and women would force their beliefs on men. The result, he felt, would be prohibition of

Nineteenth Amendment ratified in 1919, amendment guaranteeing women the right to vote

suffrage the right to vote

alcohol.[3] Tinie Wells, the wife of Jim Wells, perhaps the most influential south Texas political leader of his day, was also an important and influential spokesperson for the anti–women's suffrage movement.[4] Governor "Farmer Jim" Ferguson was another opponent of women's suffrage, but when he was impeached, his successor, William P. Hobby, proved a key supporter of women's right to vote. It was Governor Hobby who called the legislature into special session in 1919 to consider the Nineteenth Amendment. Thus, Texas became the ninth state and the first state in the South to ratify the women's suffrage amendment.[5]

In the early twentieth century, one restriction on voting that affected poor people was the **poll tax**. Enacted in 1902, it required people to pay a fee before an election in order to vote in it, supposedly to cover the costs of elections. The tax was usually between $1.50 and $1.75—a small sum today, but one that in the first third of the century could be one, two, or even more days' wages for a farm worker. Thus, it tended to disenfranchise poorer people.

The south Texas political bosses used the poll tax to great advantage. They would purchase large numbers of poll tax receipts and provide those receipts to their supporters who did not have the means to pay for the tax themselves. They depended on the bosses for jobs and other economic, legal, and political assistance and therefore would vote as the bosses wanted.

Although the poll tax was made illegal in federal elections in 1964 by the passage of the Twenty-Fourth Amendment to the U.S. Constitution, it remained legal in state elections in Texas until 1966.[6] And even after its elimination, Texas continued to require **early registration**—more than nine months before the general election—for voting. Early registration was required on a yearly basis, a requirement that effectively prevented itinerant workers from voting. Texas even prohibited anyone who was not a property owner from voting in revenue bond and tax elections. Texas also required an unusually long period of residency for voting. Voters had to have lived in the state for at least one year and the county for at least six months prior to voting. All of these provisions were voided by the courts in the 1970s because they unduly restricted the franchise.[7]

The most oppressive restriction on the franchise in Texas, however, was designed to minimize the political strength of African American voters. It was the **white primary**. In 1923 the Texas legislature flatly prohibited African Americans from voting in the Democratic primary. Since Texas was a one-party state at this time, the effect, of course, was to prevent African Americans from participating in the only "real" election contests. Texas was able to do this because of a 1921 U.S. Supreme Court decision, *Newberry v. United States*, which stated that the primary election was "in no real sense part of the manner of holding the [general] election."[8] This ruling cleared the way for southern states, including Texas, to exclude African Americans from voting in the primaries of either party. Over the next two decades, this practice came under scrutiny by federal courts numerous times; yet each time, the Texas legislature and state parties found a way to maintain the white primary and exclude African American voters.

The Supreme Court first struck down the Texas white primary law in 1927, finding that the legal ban on black participation was a violation of the equal protection clause of the Fourteenth Amendment of the Constitution.[9] In response, the Texas legislature passed a law that authorized the state Democratic and Republican parties, through their executive committees, to determine the qualifications for voting in their primaries. That law, of course, allowed the parties to create white primaries. The legal argument behind it was that what a state could not do directly because of the Fourteenth Amendment, it

poll tax a state-imposed tax on voters as a prerequisite for voting; poll taxes were rendered unconstitutional in national elections by the Twenty-Fourth Amendment, and in state elections by the Supreme Court in 1966

early registration the requirement that a voter register long before the general election; in effect in Texas until 1971

white primary primary election in which only white voters are eligible to participate

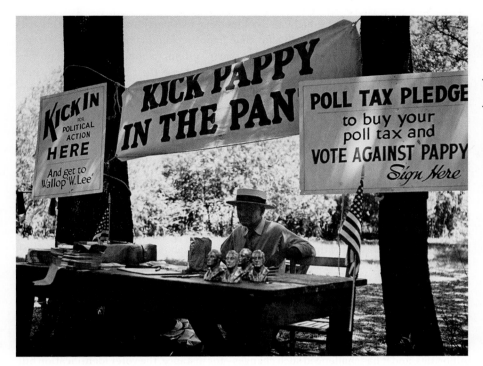

Participation in elections in Texas is low relative to that in other states. In the past, there were restrictions on the franchise. One such restriction that discouraged poor people from voting was the poll tax, which remained legal in Texas until 1966. Here, voters are asked to pay the poll tax and then vote against Pappy O'Daniel.

could authorize political parties to do. However, in *Nixon v. Condon* (1932), the Supreme Court held that the party executive committees were acting as agents of the state and were thus in violation of the Fourteenth Amendment.[10] As a result, the Texas Democratic Party convention, acting on its own authority and without any state law, passed a resolution that confined party membership to white citizens. That case was also appealed to the U.S. Supreme Court, and in *Grovey v. Townsend* (1935), the Court held there was no violation of the Fourteenth Amendment. The Court said that the requirement of "equal protection under the law" applied only to "state action," not action by private groups. Since there was no state law authorizing the white primary, the Court believed there was no "state action," only discrimination by a private organization, the Democratic Party, which is not banned by the Fourteenth Amendment.[11] Thus, the Court upheld the white primary until 1944, when, in *Smith v. Allwright*, it decided that the operation of primary elections involved so much state activity and so much public responsibility that the white primary did involve unconstitutional state action.[12]

Even after the *Smith* decision, at least one Texas county held unofficial primaries by a Democratic political organization that excluded African Americans, the **Jaybird Party**. The winners in the Jaybird primary then entered the regular Democratic Party primary, in which they seldom had opposition and were never defeated for county office. In 1953, in *Terry v. Adams*, the U.S. Supreme Court finally ruled that the Jaybird primary was an integral, and effectively the only, part of the elective process in the county. Thus, the Fifteenth Amendment (which deals with the right to vote) was applicable, and the white "preprimary" primary of the Jaybird Party was ruled unconstitutional.[13]

What made the white primary restriction work for Democrats during this era was the fact that Texas was a one-party state, where elections were essentially decided in the

Jaybird Party after the white primary was ruled unconstitutional, this offshoot Democratic Party preselected candidates for the Democratic primary and prohibited African Americans from participating

Democratic primary. If Texas had had a competitive two-party system during this era, the state might have had a more difficult time imposing and maintaining such restrictions on the franchise. In a competitive two-party system, to obtain and retain power, both parties have to search for ways to build and increase their base of support. In a one-party system, there is a greater incentive to restrict participation in the party in order to retain control over it. Losers in a battle for control of a one-party system essentially have no place to go. If they cannot maintain a place in the dominant party's councils, then they have no other avenue for expressing their political views.

Expanding the Franchise As discussed above, in the early twentieth century, African Americans were not allowed to vote in the all-white Democratic primaries. They could later vote in the general election, but since the winner of the Democratic primary always won the general election, African Americans had essentially no influence in state politics. At least since the 1940s there has been a gradual expansion of the franchise in Texas. Much of that expansion was brought about by litigation in the federal courts, often by African American and Latino civil rights organizations. For example, the National Association for the Advancement of Colored People (NAACP) filed lawsuits throughout the 1960s and '70s challenging laws that restricted or otherwise stunted African American political advancement. The Mexican American Legal Defense and Education Fund (MALDEF) has been active since the 1970s in monitoring any changes in electoral laws that might have the effect of suppressing the votes of Latinos and other minorities, and it has challenged such changes—for instance, the voter identification bill adopted by Texas in 2011.

New federal laws also played an important role in the expansion of the franchise. The most important of these was the **Voting Rights Act of 1965**, which was applied to Texas as a result of amendments after 1975. President Lyndon B. Johnson signed this new law, initially aimed at ensuring that African Americans were not discriminated against at the polls, even though he knew it would damage his political popularity in the South.

The Voting Rights Act has without question had an important influence on elections in Texas. One provision of the law was to send federal examiners to southern states to register voters. In many southern states, including Texas, blacks were systematically denied the ability to register to vote, much less attempt to vote. In Mississippi, only about 7 percent of blacks had been registered to vote prior to 1965, but by 1967 more than 67 percent were registered. In Texas, just prior to the Voting Rights Act, approximately 35 percent of blacks were registered to vote, but by 1971, the figure almost doubled to nearly 65 percent, according to the Southern Poverty Law Center. Section 2 of the Voting Rights Act involves a nationwide prohibition against the restriction of voting rights on the basis of race or ethnicity.

The Voting Rights Act has been renewed several times since 1965, and new provisions have been added. For example, bilingual ballots are now required in certain areas where more than 5 percent of voters speak a language other than English. In 2013, however, the Supreme Court ruled in *Shelby County v. Holder* that a key section of the Voting Rights Act was unconstitutional. This decision affects a provision requiring Texas to have any changes in its election districts or electoral procedures approved by the U.S. Department of Justice or a federal court in the District of Columbia before they go into effect. This provision was intended to make sure that the voting rights of minorities were not diminished.

Voting Rights Act of 1965
important legislation passed in order to ensure that African Americans would be guaranteed the right to vote. Renewed several times since 1965, the act also prevents the dilution of minority voting strength

Contracting the Vote? Highly partisan legislation passed in 2011 may make it more difficult for some people to vote in Texas. Over Democratic opposition, the Republican majority in the Texas legislature passed a voter identification law that requires a photo identification in order to vote. Republicans claimed that the requirement is necessary to prevent voter fraud. Democrats argued that evidence of such fraud is minimal and that the law will make it harder for low-income persons, students, and minorities (all of whom typically support Democrats) to vote.[14] The law specifies the acceptable forms of identification as a driver's license, an election identification certificate, a U.S. military ID, a U.S. citizenship certificate, a U.S. passport, and two items issued by the Texas Department of Public Safety: a personal ID card or a license to carry a concealed handgun.[15] A photo ID card issued by a college or university is not acceptable.

In 2015, however, a three-judge panel of a federal appeals court ruled that the Texas voter ID law violated the Voting Rights Act because it had a disparate impact on minority voters. Texas Republican leaders, such as Governor Abbott and Attorney General Paxton, have argued that Texas and other southern states should not be singled out for special scrutiny of their electoral practices and should be allowed to have a voter ID law without any approval process. They appealed the 2015 ruling to the full appellate court. Since other states have mounted similar legal challenges, the Supreme Court might ultimately decide on the constitutionality of voter ID laws. In the meantime, after a court order in 2016, Texas agreed that more forms of voter ID than its law authorized would be accepted at the polls (see Chapter 3). The "You Decide" section takes a closer look at this issue.

The assurance of voting rights has been a key debate for decades. It exemplifies the tensions between federal and state government. Here then U.S. attorney general Eric Holder speaks in Houston about his opposition to recent Texas voter identification laws and his support of the Voting Rights Act of 1965.

Qualifications to Vote Today

Meeting the qualifications to register to vote in Texas is relatively easy today. A voter must be

1. eighteen years of age.
2. a U.S. citizen.
3. a resident of Texas for 30 days.
4. a resident of the county for 30 days.

To be eligible to vote, one must be a registered voter for 30 days preceding the election and a resident of the voting precinct on the day of the election. Two groups of citizens cannot vote even if they meet all the preceding qualifications: felons who have not completed their sentences and persons judged by a court to be mentally incompetent.

According to the Texas secretary of state, 79.4 percent of the state's voting-age population (15.8 million citizens) was registered to vote in 2018.[16] The **motor voter law**,[17] which allows individuals to register to vote when applying for or renewing driver's licenses, is one factor in increased registration. Public schools distribute voter registration cards as students turn 18, and most colleges and universities sponsor drives to encourage their students to register. Cooperative efforts between the secretary of state's office and corporations also increase the number of registered voters.

Following the November 2016 election, a Census Bureau survey of Texans found that registration rates among citizens varied across racial and ethnic lines. Latino eligible

motor voter law a national act, passed in 1993, that requires states to allow people to register to vote when applying for a driver's license voters registered at a 38.3 percent rate, well below that of African Americans (70.2 percent) and non-Hispanic whites (71.6 percent).[18]

early voting a procedure that allows voters to cast ballots during a two-week period before the regularly scheduled election date

Early Voting

In Texas, **early voting** is a procedure that allows people to vote not just in a 12-hour period on Election Day but also for two weeks prior to the election. The legislature has allowed early voting in an effort to increase participation by accommodating those who have trouble getting to the polls between 7 A.M. and 7 P.M. on Election Day. For most elections, early voting begins on the 17th day before Election Day and ends four days before it. Voting early is basically the same as voting on Election Day. A voter appears at one of the designated early voting polling places, presents appropriate identification, and receives and casts a ballot.

Since it was introduced in Texas in the late 1980s, early voting has at best only modestly increased voting participation, and predictions that Democrats would benefit from it did not hold true after Texas moved strongly into the Republican column. Republican candidates for the highest office on the ballot get a much larger proportion of early votes than do Democratic candidates. In 2016, for example, 53 percent of the early votes for president in Texas were cast for Donald Trump, compared with 43 percent for Hillary Clinton. And in 7 of the 10 latest statewide elections, Republicans got a slightly smaller proportion of overall votes (votes cast in early voting plus Election Day voting) than early votes. On the other hand, in 6 of the last 10 statewide elections, Democrats got a slightly larger proportion of overall votes than early votes. Overall, in the most recent elections of 2014, 2016, and 2018 early voting has not benefited either party significantly (Figure 5.1).

straight-ticket voting a method of voting where a voter checks a box by one of the political parties on the ballot, which casts his/her vote for every candidate on the ballot with that political party affiliation

Straight-Ticket Voting

When voting, Texans can press one button and vote for every Republican or Democrat on the ballot. Known as **straight-ticket voting**, Texans had increasingly resorted to just voting the party line in many elections. In the 2016 election, nearly 64 percent of Texans in the state's 10 largest counties voted straight ticket.[19] State Republicans sought to eliminate straight-ticket voting in the 2017 legislative session mainly because Republican judges in some of the populous counties such as Harris were losing elections due to straight-ticket Democratic voting. For example, Lieutenant Governor Dan Patrick's son, a Harris county judge, lost his re-election bid and largely blamed straight-ticket Democratic voting for this loss. Governor Abbott signed the new law, which goes into effect starting with the 2020 elections.

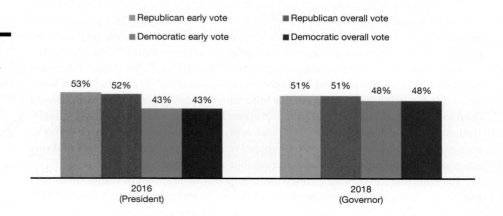

FIGURE 5.1

Early Voting and Overall Voting by Party in Texas

SOURCE: Texas Secretary of State.

■ Republican early vote   ■ Republican overall vote
■ Democratic early vote   ■ Democratic overall vote

2016 (President): 53% 52% 43% 43%

2018 (Governor): 51% 51% 48% 48%

Voter Identification Laws

IN 2011 the Texas legislature passed a law that requires all voters to produce photo identification when they present themselves to vote in an election. Prior to the law, Texans could present a voter registration certificate, which does not carry a photograph. Under the new law, not all forms of photo identification are considered valid for voting purposes. For example, state-issued concealed weapons permits are allowed, but student identification cards are not. A voter who shows up to the polls without appropriate photo identification may cast a provisional ballot but must return to the registrar's office with such identification within six days to make his or her vote count.

Supporters of the law argue that requiring photo identification is necessary to ensure the integrity of the election system and assure Texans that their elections are free from fraud. They claim that fraud is often undetected and difficult to prosecute; hence, the absence of high rates of prosecution does not mean that voter fraud is a problem that should be ignored. The potential of penalties for breaking the law, they argue, will deter any attempts to commit fraud. Former governor Rick Perry noted that the law "makes sense" since one needs to show photo identification to board airplanes and perform transactions with banks and other organizations.[a] Those in favor of the law also point to public opinion polls showing that the majority of Texans support the simple proposition that you must show photo identification to prove who you are in order to vote.

Opponents of the law claim that the measure is not really about preserving the integrity of the electoral system but is meant to minimize Democratic turnout in order to help the state Republican Party keep its hold on power. They argue that it puts an undue burden on populations who are less likely to possess photo identification (and who often vote for Democrats), such as elderly, disabled, minority, and poor voters, by making them go through additional steps to vote. Lubbock county commissioner Gilbert Flores noted that the bill's goal is to "weaken and deter the Hispanic vote."[b]

The law does provide for obtaining free photo identification from the state Department of Public Safety, but in some rural areas, opponents argue, the nearest DPS office is far away and not easily accessible. In addition, opponents suggest that the law is in essence a solution in search of a problem, pointing to studies that show there is no real problem of voter fraud in Texas.

Legitimate arguments can be made for and against the legislation, but one thing is clear: Republicans strongly support it and Democrats have attempted to block it. This fact alone suggests that Republicans believe they will electorally benefit from the law, while Democrats believe they will be harmed. In Wisconsin and North Carolina, federal judges agreed with challengers to those states' voter ID laws and declared them unconstitutional because of social science evidence suggesting that minorities were adversely affected by the new requirements. However, backers of the Texas law point to data

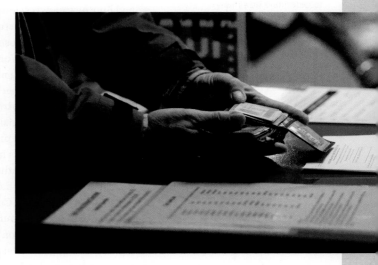

showing that turnout in the November 2013 off-year election was nearly double that of previous elections without the voter ID requirement, including in heavily Hispanic counties. This evidence suggests, they argue, that the law did not adversely affect minority turnout. However, turnout is consistently low in these off-year elections.

By the November 2016 election, the Texas law had been somewhat softened by a federal court. Voters without an authorized identification were allowed to vote, but they had to sign an affidavit indicating they had a legitimate impediment to obtaining an approved identification card. The legislature passed a revised voter ID law in the 2017 legislative session to address the concerns of the courts. It is still possible that a higher court will revisit Texas's law in future cases.

COMMUNICATING EFFECTIVELY: YOUR VOICE

- Do the arguments for the voter identification legislation outweigh the arguments against it?

- Do you think a student ID should be accepted for voting? Write a brief letter to the editor of your school or local paper arguing your position.

Redistricting: Where Do People Vote?

Every 10 years, the U.S. Census is charged with counting how many people live in the United States. The process of **reapportionment** involves recalculating how many U.S. representatives each state is entitled to based on its new population. For example, Texas gained four new congressional seats following the 2010 Census because of the explosive population growth of the state. (Since the House of Representatives is capped at 435 members, some states whose populations had increased more slowly during the previous 10 years, such as New York, lost some of their congressional seats.) The state legislature is tasked with drawing new congressional districts at least every 10 years to comply with the new overall number of seats allowed, as well as the principle of one person, one vote, a process called **redistricting**.

In 2011 the Texas legislature drew new congressional districts. Redistricting is always a blatantly political procedure in every state because the majority party uses it to retain power by creating as many friendly districts as it can. In 2011 the Republicans in charge of the Texas legislature attempted to draw as many Republican-voting districts as possible. (If Democrats had been in control, they would have tried to maximize their number of seats as well.) Complicating the Republicans' task was the fact that more than 67 percent of the population growth in Texas between 2000 and 2010 had been a result of Latino immigration and relatively high birthrates among both native-born and foreign-born Latinos. Given this, Latino leaders in the state wanted at least two of the new seats to be majority Latino. Most Latino-majority districts in Texas tend not to elect Republicans, however, putting the Republican-led legislature in a bind.

Further complicating the situation were the terms by which Texas—until the 2013 U.S. Supreme Court decision in *Shelby County v. Holder*—had to comply with the Voting Rights Act. As noted earlier, a section of the act required that any changes to election procedures, including the drawing of new district lines, must go through the process of **preclearance** by federal authorities. Districts that have previously been created to help minorities win cannot be dismantled in order to benefit a particular political party. For the most part, it is the southern states of the old Confederacy that were subject to this provision. The preclearance requirement was but one example of the conflict between Texas and the federal government on a number of issues (see Chapter 3).[20]

In the 2011 redistricting round, several lawsuits were filed by different parties challenging the districts created by the Texas legislature, and the federal court stepped in. Ultimately, the legislature and the court created one new congressional district with a majority Latino population that stretched from Bexar County to Travis County along Interstate 35 (see Figure 5.2). The three other new districts were designed to elect Republicans, a goal accomplished by splitting Travis County, centered on Austin, into five congressional districts in order to dilute the Democratic vote. Since most Travis County Democrats are white, there are no protections under the law against diluting their vote. The U.S. representative for Austin, white Democrat Lloyd Doggett, was forced to run in the new Latino majority district, since the other four districts were majority Republican (Doggett still won re-election). Because of the federal court's lengthy approval process for these districts, the 2012 Texas primary had to be pushed back to May 29, much later than the late March date originally scheduled.

One possible way to reform redistricting would be to take the process away from politicians who have a vested interest in protecting their seats and their parties. Critics often say that redistricting by legislatures is the only time when politicians choose their voters

FIGURE 5.2

Texas's 35th Congressional District

Texas's 35th district is one of the top ten gerrymandered districts in the United States. It stretches from San Antonio to Austin and is represented by Lloyd Doggett. In 2017 a panel of federal judges found that Texas's 35th congressional district was a racial gerrymander, but the 2018 Supreme Court case *Abbott v. Perez* allowed the district to stand.

SOURCE: U.S. Census Bureau.

115ᵗʰ Congress of the United States
Texas - Congressional District 35
Representative Lloyd Doggett

and not the other way around. Some states, such as Arizona, have taken the responsibility away from the legislature by creating an independent redistricting commission. Such a commission, supporters argue, would create fairer districts in Texas as well. According to a 2013 *Texas Tribune* poll, 43 percent of respondents voiced support in principle for such a system, while 28 percent were opposed, and 28 percent were unsure.[21] Changing the system of redistricting would be politically challenging, however, because legislators of both parties greatly benefit from their ability to influence how district lines are drawn.

In the court case *Evenwel v. Abbott* (2015), plaintiffs sued the State of Texas claiming that using the total number of residents in each district as the basis for creating state legislative districts violated the principle of one person, one vote and the equal protection clause of the Fourteenth Amendment. Instead, they argued, the state should use registered or eligible voters to draw districts, because voters living in districts with high numbers of undocumented immigrants, children, or prisoners had their votes unconstitutionally diluted compared with those of voters in other districts. The Supreme Court ruled, however, that states were justified in using total population in drawing legislative districts.

How districts are drawn can also have an important effect on political outcomes at the local level. For example, in many cities, council members are elected at large rather than from separate geographical districts. How does this create a barrier to voting? Consider a city that has 10 city council seats and is 20 percent African American, 25 percent Latino, and 55 percent white. In at-large races, the white majority could theoretically capture all of the seats for white candidates. If the city had a single-member district system, however, because of segregated housing patterns at least 4 of the seats could well be won by minorities. Austin changed its at-large system of electing city council members in 2014, and the city saw an increase in the number of minority council members.

Turnout: Who Votes?

In the most recent presidential election of 2016, according to the U.S. Elections Project, only 59 percent of U.S. voting eligible citizens voted.[22] Even fewer Texans exercise their right to vote, especially young Texans. In fact, Texas ranks last in the nation in voter participation. Figure 5.3 provides data on the abysmal turnout of registered voters in the various types of recent Texas elections. Considering the ease of registration and the ability to vote early, voter participation should be higher. Why do so few Texans vote? Several factors may contribute to the state's low participation rates:

1. low levels of educational attainment
2. low per capita income
3. high rate of poverty
4. location in the South
5. young population
7. lack of party competition
8. lack of media attention to substantive political issues
9. large numbers of undocumented residents and felons

Education and income appear to be the two most important factors in determining whether someone votes, and the combination of the two is often referred to as socioeconomic status (SES). In Texas low levels of education and high levels of poverty are the strongest predictors of low voter participation. In addition, the average age of Texans is less than the national average, and since young people are less likely to vote, this factor may also contribute to Texas's low turnout rate. Although college students and other young adults were mobilized by President Obama's campaign in 2008, in general voter turnout among this demographic is low.

Texas was part of the Confederacy, and its level of participation is consistent with lower levels of voting in the South than in other parts of the United States. That said, Texas differs from most other southern states because of its large Latino population, many of whom are not registered to vote or are not citizens. Although registration rates and voting rates among Latinos will likely increase in coming years, for now they remain lower than those for whites or African Americans.

There are other possible explanations for low voter participation in Texas. In keeping with the state's tradition of decentralized government, there are so many elections in Texas and so many candidates for office that voters simply feel overloaded. Note that as shown in Figure 5.3 (and discussed in Chapter 2), voter participation was much higher in the general election than in the special constitutional election. If there were fewer elections, the ballot might be longer, but voter turnout would likely be higher because more voters would be attracted to at least some races or issues on the ballot. Additionally, holding elections for state offices in nonpresidential election years decreases voter turnout because participation tends to be highest for presidential elections. A third problem is that most elections in Texas involve very low-visibility offices. Few voters know much about these positions or the candidates for them, and this lack of knowledge naturally discourages voting. Efforts have been made in a number of states, most notably Washington, to increase voter knowledge by having the state provide biographical information about

FIGURE 5.3

Turnout by Registered Voters in Texas Elections

SOURCE: Texas Secretary of State Division of Elections.

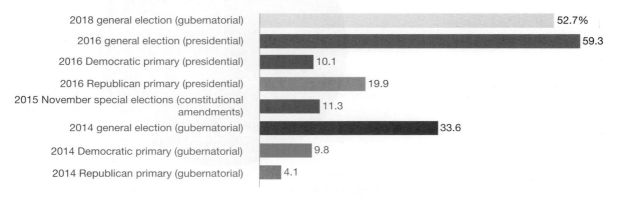

Election	Turnout
2018 general election (gubernatorial)	52.7%
2016 general election (presidential)	59.3
2016 Democratic primary (presidential)	10.1
2016 Republican primary (presidential)	19.9
2015 November special elections (constitutional amendments)	11.3
2014 general election (gubernatorial)	33.6
2014 Democratic primary (gubernatorial)	9.8
2014 Republican primary (gubernatorial)	4.1

candidates to voters, but Texas makes little effort of this kind. Independent groups such as the League of Women Voters often provide voter guides, but only readers of newspapers or those who actively seek out such guides benefit from this information. Finally, some suggest that the voter identification law has reduced voter turnout even more.

Racial and Ethnic Variations in Voting and Participation While non-Hispanic whites make up less than half the population of Texas, this does not mean that the majority of the state's voters are minorities. For example, in the November 2018 elections, Latinos composed only about 26 percent of the Texas electorate.[23] As a result of a variety of factors, including the large undocumented population and the lower rate of voter turnout by Latino citizens, non-Hispanic whites wield disproportionate influence in the state electorate. Because most whites tend to vote for Republicans, the balance of power in most state elections currently tilts toward Republicans.

While the days of poll taxes are over, in contemporary Texas there are still barriers to voting such as reducing the number of polling places in certain areas, giving misleading information to voters, and intimidating voters by threatening employment

WHAT DO TEXANS THINK?

Racial Bias in Voter ID Laws

After the passage of the state's voter identification law, some Texans argued that the election system was attempting to make it more difficult for racial and ethnic minorities to access the ballot box, the argument being that racial and ethnic minorities are less likely to have driver's licenses. Where do you stand relative to your fellow Texans?

Based on what you know, do you think Texas's election system discriminates against racial and ethnic minorities?

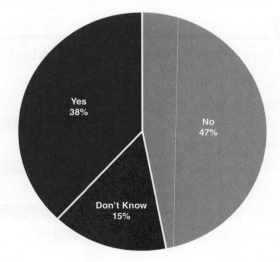

SOURCE: *Texas Tribune*, October 2017.

or other economic retaliation. While such practices are becoming less frequent, there are still reports of them in every contested election.

The Importance of the Republican Primary

In this era of Republican dominance in the state, the Republican primary has become the key to determining the winner of a statewide election. As shown in Table 5.1, only 10.16 percent of registered voters and only 7.79 percent of the voting-age population in Texas voted in the Republican primary in 2018, but since the 1990s the winner of that primary has gone on to win every statewide election. Of course, many of the Republican primaries for statewide offices are contested, and to be successful in winning office all that is needed is a majority of the vote in the primary. In the 2012 elections, theoretically a person could win statewide office with the votes of less than 5.546 percent of the registered voters in the state, assuming those voters cast ballots in the Republican primary.

TABLE 5.1

Percentage of Registered Voters and Voting-Age Population Voting in the Republican Primaries

YEAR	REGISTERED VOTERS	PERCENTAGE OF REGISTERED VOTERS VOTING IN REPUBLICAN PRIMARIES	PERCENTAGE OF VOTING-AGE POPULATION VOTING IN REPUBLICAN PRIMARIES
2018	15,249,541	10.16%	7.79%
2016	14,238,436	19.89	14.80
2014	13,601,324	9.98	7.18
2012	13,065,425	11.09	7.93
2010	13,023,358	11.40	8.00
2008	12,752,417	10.68	7.68
2006	12,722,671	5.15	3.94
2004	12,264,663	5.60	4.27
2002	12,218,164	5.09	4.01
2000	11,612,761	9.70	7.78
1998	11,159,845	5.35	4.24
1996	9,698,506	10.52	7.44
1994	9,041,906	6.16	4.26

Campaigns

The goal of the campaign is to attain sufficient support to win the primary election in March and then the general election in November. Some campaigns last a year or more; however, the more accepted practice is to limit the campaign to a few months before the election. For high-profile races such as governor, candidates often announce their intentions early in order to raise money. Candidates with more money are often taken more seriously by other campaign donors, as well as by the media, interest groups, and the national parties.

Candidates: Who Runs?

Candidates from all walks of life run for office in Texas. Business people, lawyers, stay-at-home mothers, teachers, retirees, and more have all run for office in Texas. The greater the prestige of the office, the more political experience candidates tend to have. Career paths for Texan officeholders usually begin with a run for a local office such as school board or city council. Many then decide to run for state representative, then state senator. Candidates for U.S. Congress usually have had prior political experience. For example, U.S. representative Randy Weber (R-Friendswood) previously served as a state representative.

Incumbents have the advantage in most races. Since there are no term limits in the Texas legislature, some members have served for many years. For example, Representative Tom Craddick (R-Midland) has served in the legislature for nearly 50 years. Challengers to incumbents rarely win, and many wait until a retirement to run for a seat.

Money

Campaigns involve attempts to reach the voters through print and electronic media, the mail, door-to-door campaigning, speeches to large and small groups, coffee hours, and telephone solicitation. Costs are enormous. In the 2018 gubernatorial race, Greg Abbott spent $46 million. There is no question, then, that money is important for candidate success in Texas. Candidates must continually raise funds by hosting events with donors, making phone calls to potential donors, and setting up websites that make it easy for ordinary citizens to contribute (see Tables 5.2 and 5.3).

Candidates who run in Texas for federal office such as the U.S. Congress are subject to federal campaign finance laws, which are stricter than state laws and impose limits for campaign contributions. (Recently, though, the federal laws have been greatly weakened by U.S. Supreme Court decisions that have held that parts of those laws unconstitutionally restricted free speech.) Candidates for state offices are subject to state laws enacted in 1991 when the Texas Ethics Commission (TEC) was established. State candidates and lobbyists must file quarterly reports with the TEC detailing expenditures and

Who Votes in Texas Statewide Elections?

Voter Turnout By Race, 2016

Texas Totals

Citizen Voting Age Population
16,844,000

Total Voter Turnout*
55.4%

Texas is now a majority-minority state. This means that the nonwhite population exceeds the white population. However, this does not mean that the majority of the state's voters are nonwhite. It is still the case that the Latino population is underrepresented compared with their population on the state's voter rolls.

White Voter Turnout

⬤ 10% voter turnout

Citizen Voting Age Population
13,693,000

62.9%

Latino Voter Turnout

Citizen Voting Age Population
4,878,000

40.5%

African American Voter Turnout

Citizen Voting Age Population
2,198,000

57.2%

Asian Voter Turnout

Citizen Voting Age Population
565,000

47.3%

* % of Citizen Voting Age Population who voted in 2016

Source: Non-citizen data from U.S. Census Bureau, Current Population Survey.
Racial group data from American Community Survey, US Census Bureau. Turnout data from U.S. Census Bureau.

QUANTITATIVE REASONING

- Some argue that minorities do not turn out to vote in Texas elections. Based on the data provided, is this true? How might you respond to such a statement?

- Based on the voter turnout data in the graph, what can you conclude about racial and ethnic differences in voter turnout?

TABLE 5.2

Money Raised by All Candidates in Texas, 2018

OFFICE	DEMOCRATIC ($)	REPUBLICAN ($)	THIRD-PARTY ($)
Governor	$2,067,292	$72,417,015	$37,299
Judicial	3,764,382	6,019,267	0
Other statewide	3,451,333	24,848,602	3,295
State House	13,400,562	36,567,487	103,612
State Senate	8,028,690	31,368,094	1,600

SOURCE: Calculated from Institute on Money in State Politics.

contributions, but with the exception of judicial campaigns there are no limits to campaign contributions for state races. The state imposes a moratorium on contributions to state legislators just prior to the beginning of a legislative session.

Payments for media ads account for the greatest expense in most campaigns. In metropolitan areas, television, radio, and print advertising are very costly. Full-page ads in metropolitan newspapers can cost as much as $40,000. Candidates for metropolitan districts in the Texas House of Representatives and Texas Senate need to reach only a small portion of the area's population, but they are forced to purchase ads in media that go to hundreds of thousands of people not in their districts. In rural areas, any individual ad is relatively inexpensive. However, candidates must advertise in dozens of small newspapers and radio stations, and the costs add up.

Partisan affiliation matters a great deal when it comes to raising money. For all statewide offices, Republican campaign contributions have overwhelmed Democratic campaign contributions. According to an analysis by the *Texas Tribune*, in 2018 total contributions in state races were far greater for Republicans than for Democrats. The report estimates that 86 percent of the $57 million in contributions went to Republican candidates for state offices.[24] Because Republicans are more likely to win statewide races, donors are more likely to donate to candidates who will hold positions of power.

Interest Groups

Interest groups (see Chapter 6) have recently become much more of a factor in state elections in Texas. For example, Empower Texans, a group backed by Michael Quinn Sullivan, spent millions of dollars in the 2016 Republican state legislative primaries to try to defeat backers of former Speaker Joe Straus, whom they considered insufficiently conservative. While they were unable to unseat Straus himself in 2016, they were able to help oust some of his lieutenants, including state representative Debbie Riddle (R-Tomball). Straus announced his retirement from the legislature in 2017, thus paving the way for a conservative replacement in his legislative seat as well as the speakership.

How Did Texans Vote in 2016?

	Race	Pop.%	= Clinton	= Trump		
National	White	61.1%			37%	58%
	Black	13.3%			88%	8%
	Latino	17.6%			65%	29%
	Asian	5.6%			65%	29%
	Other	4.0%			56%	37%
Texas	White	43.0%			26%	69%
	Black	12.5%			85%	11%
	Latino	38.8%			61%	34%
	Asian	4.7%			73%	27%
	Other		Note: Data on other groups were not available from Texas exit polls.			
California	White	38.0%			50%	45%
	Black	6.5%			88%	9%
	Latino	38.8%			71%	24%
	Asian	14.7%			73%	17%
	Other		Note: Data on other groups were not available from California exit polls.			

As expected, Republican presidential candidate Donald J. Trump carried Texas on Election Day and won the state's 38 electoral votes. However, Democratic presidential candidate Hillary Clinton outperformed Barack Obama, as the margin of victory was much closer in 2016 than in either 2008 or 2012. Racial divisions persisted between the parties, with Clinton winning large majorities of African American, Latino, and Asian voters.

SOURCE: 2016 CNN exit poll data.

CRITICAL THINKING

- Looking at the data, how does the national vote compare to California and Texas?

- Why do you think Latinos were more supportive of Trump in Texas than they were nationally?

TABLE 5.3

Campaign Contributions in Statewide Executive Offices: Texas General Elections, 2018

OFFICE	CANDIDATE	DOLLARS CONTRIBUTED	PERCENTAGE OF VOTE
Governor	G. Abbott (R) Lupe Valdez (D)	$72,412,015 1,253,688	55.8% 42.5
Lieutenant governor	D. Patrick (R) Mike Collier (D)	25,749,140 867,309	51.3 46.5
Agriculture commissioner	Sid Miller (R) Kim Olson (D)	1,797,867 386,223	51.3 46.4
Attorney general	Ken Paxton (R) Justin Nelson (D)	7,864,608 2,669,475	50.6 47.0
Comptroller	Glenn Hegar (R) Joi Chevalier (D)	3,746,306 59,282	53.2 43.4
Land commissioner	George P. Bush (R) Miguel Suazo (D)	3,780,944 93,955	53.7 43.1
Railroad commissioner	Christi Craddick (R) Roman McAllen (D)	5,471,872 22,298	53.2 43.9

SOURCE: Texas Ethics Commission Filings

Other interest groups have played important roles in shaping public policy in the state. For example, the Texas Association of Business and the Texas Public Policy Foundation have been very influential in advancing conservative legislation. These groups have helped sway Governor Abbott and other Republican officials to support laws that expand school vouchers, lower taxes, and reduce regulation in the state's economy. Because state legislators and other statewide officials are subject to only limited campaign regulations, the influence of interest groups in Texas politics will no doubt continue to grow.

Parties

In some places in the United States, political parties have a major role in the running of campaigns. That is not the case in Texas, where the candidates have the major responsibility for planning strategy, running their campaigns, and raising money. At times, party leaders will try to recruit individuals to run for office, especially if no candidates volunteer to seek an office or if the announced candidates appear to be weak ones. For the most part, the benefit of the party to a candidate in Texas is that it provides the label under which the candidate runs. That "Democratic" or "Republican" label is important because many voters use the party label in casting their votes, especially for low-visibility races. The party also contains numerous activists whom the candidate can tap for campaign tasks such as manning phone banks, preparing mailings, and posting campaign ads. Additionally, the party does provide some direct support for the candidate, most commonly through campaigns to get out the vote for the party's candidates. Campaigning in Texas, however, is generally left up to the candidate, and in that effort the parties take a secondary role.

Incumbents hold a distinct advantage in election campaigns, insofar as officeholders have many ways to achieve name visibility. They can mail out news releases, send newsletters to their constituents, appear on television and radio talk shows, and give speeches to civic clubs. Newspaper coverage and local television news coverage of the politician also increase name recognition. Challengers have a more difficult time getting this crucial name visibility, although newer media outlets such as Facebook and Twitter can help both incumbents and challengers gain name recognition, especially among young people, often in less expensive ways.

The case of William R. Clements illustrates the importance of name recognition. In 1978, Clements was a political unknown until he spent thousands of dollars of his own fortune to publicize his name. He leased hundreds of billboards throughout the state. Each had a blue background with white letters proclaiming "CLEMENTS." In the print media, his early ads bore the simple message, "ELECT CLEMENTS." The unprecedented scale of this advertising effort made Clements's name better known among Texas voters, and this recognition, in turn, stimulated interest in his campaign's message. Clements won the race for governor, becoming the first Republican to hold that office in Texas since the end of Reconstruction.

Strategy

As important as name recognition is, even more important is that a campaign be well designed and well executed. A slipup in a well-funded campaign can generate controversy, as Greg Abbott discovered in his first campaign for governor. While Abbott has made efforts to appeal to the Latino vote, his campaign received criticism when in February 2014 he referred to law enforcement tactics in the border region as resembling "third world country practices that erode the social fabric of our communities." A journalist for the *Monitor*, a newspaper in the Rio Grande Valley, called on Abbott to apologize for his comments, but he refused, saying they were directed not at Latinos but rather at the lack of border security in south Texas. Abbott sought to repair his relationship with Latino voters by emphasizing his Latina wife as the imminent first Latina first lady of Texas. While this slipup did not cost him the election (he received 44 percent of the Latino vote—a healthy number for a Republican candidate), it still raised doubts in the minds of many Texan Latinos about the state's Republican Party and its relationship with the growing Latino vote.[25]

Public Opinion and Campaigns

Political candidates in Texas campaigns hire pollsters to conduct surveys of their constituents. They do this in order to get a sense of what their constituents think on important issues. By doing this,

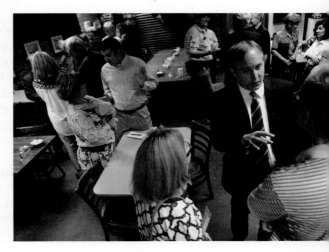

Candidates for statewide office in Texas routinely spend hundreds of thousands, if not millions, of dollars on their campaigns. Though much money goes to television advertising, candidates also spend time meeting voters one-on-one, as Republican attorney general candidate Ken Paxton does here at Joe Allen's Pit Bar-B-Que in Abilene.

they can better serve them—they want to make sure they are voting in line with what their constituents want so that voters will choose to support them in future elections. Opponents to elected officials may hire pollsters (if they have adequate funds) to craft messages they think might sway voters to support them. Once polls are conducted, politicians target voters based on information such as where they live, their age, or other factors and contact them with specific messages they think will inspire them to vote. In close elections, tailoring a message to a significant voter group—suburban women with children, college-educated men, senior citizens, etc.—might make a difference.

Media

Campaigns in Texas are covered mostly by local and statewide media. One of the more thorough statewide media outlets covering Texas politics is the *Texas Tribune*, founded in 2009. Based in Austin, the *Tribune* is a one-stop shop for all aspects of Texas politics, including statistical data, campaign news, updates on legislation, and coverage of statewide issues.

Of course, the major city newspapers, including the *Houston Chronicle*, the *Dallas Morning News*, the *San Antonio Express-News*, the *El Paso Times*, and the *Austin American Statesman*, cover state politics and campaigns extensively, especially local races in their respective readership areas. (See Table 5.4.) More important, they endorse candidates in primaries and general elections. These endorsements often carry important weight, especially in down-ballot races for local offices such as school board or city council, which do not attract significant attention from voters.

Television stations also play an important role in covering races by hosting programs and events aimed at informing the public about them. In Houston, Channel 2 KPRC hosts a weekly show called *Houston Newsmakers*. Hosted by Khambrell Marshall, this show often has political guests, hosts candidate debates, and informs the public on local political issues. Channel 13 KTRK in Houston hosts a public affairs show called *Viva Houston*, aimed at informing Latino viewers about local political issues. Local PBS stations in Houston, Dallas, and Austin also host programs with guests to help inform the public about local campaigns and elections.

Candidates promote their campaigns by running newspaper and television ads, meeting with newspaper editorial boards for endorsements, appearing on television shows, and any other means possible. Running a campaign can be expensive, and any opportunity for free airtime to increase name recognition can go a long way, especially in down-ballot races. In 2014 the Center for Public Integrity published a report indicating that nearly $39 million was spent by candidates and other organizations on political ads in Texas that year, a total second only to Pennsylvania.

Social Media Many, if not most, Texas candidates for all offices use Facebook and Twitter to push campaign messages, attack or defend themselves from opponents, and stay in touch with supporters and donors. While historically television was a very valuable tool for a Texas politi-

TABLE 5.4

Circulation of Texas's Top Five Daily Newspapers

Dallas Morning News	259,000
Houston Chronicle	236,000
San Antonio Express-News	99,000
Fort Worth Star-Telegram	98,000
Austin American Statesman	95,000

SOURCE: www.cision.com (accessed 12/19/17). (Estimates rounded) cal candidate, modern-day candidates have increasingly relied on social media to get their messages out. Former Texas Supreme Court justice Don Willett (@JusticeWillett) has been particularly active on Twitter, with over 110,000 followers. His tweets cover nearly every topic imaginable, with a particular emphasis on Texas themes. For example, one of his tweets in 2016 pictured freshly baked cornbread shaped like the state of Texas with the caption "when you are tired of cornbread shaped like Colorado or Wyoming."[26] His tweets captured the attention of another prolific tweeter, President Trump, who nominated him for the Fifth Circuit Court of Appeals in 2017.

Governor Abbott and other statewide leaders have relied on Facebook and Twitter to spread their messages and advertise with the public. Because officeholders do not have to pay for these messages, they are able to tout their accomplishments, policy proposals, and opinions about political situations more often. At times, however, elected officials can get in trouble if they tweet something that might be offensive. For example, during the 2016 presidential election, Agriculture Commissioner Sid Miller retweeted a tweet showing a poll in Pennsylvania substituting Hillary Clinton's name for an expletive. Miller apologized, blaming hackers and then a staff member for the tweet.[27]

Important Issues in Recent Texas Campaigns

The race for the gubernatorial seat in 2018 pitted Greg Abbott against former Dallas County Sheriff Lupe Valdez. With the state's economic challenges of the mid-2000s largely in the rearview mirror, both candidates fought hard to distinguish themselves on issues. Valdez struggled to distance herself from her record as sheriff in Dallas County in support of sanctuary city policies, and sought to expand her policy portfolio beyond this one issue. Abbott highlighted his record as governor, especially his policies on sanctuary cities (against), border security (in favor), education reform, and infrastructure improvements after Hurricane Harvey.

By far the more high-profile race, however, was the contest between incumbent Republican senator Ted Cruz and El Paso congressman Beto O'Rourke. O'Rourke ran a grassroots campaign emphasizing opposition to President Trump's policies and offering an unabashedly progressive vision. O'Rourke galvanized young voters across the state and stressed universal health care, justice for Dreamers, and standing with those who kneeled during the national anthem at NFL games. Cruz fired back at O'Rourke, claiming he was too liberal for Texas, given his support for these policies. At the end of the day, O'Rourke came up short in his race. However, he greatly expanded the electorate, and the enthusiasm for his candidacy no doubt helped elect Democrats across the state in local elections. Given his performance, some speculate he will run again for the Senate in 2020 when Senator John Cornyn's seat is up or perhaps seek the Democratic nomination for president.

Gun rights continues to be a salient issue in Texas, especially in recent debates about whether firearms should be allowed on college campuses. Texas has a concealed carry

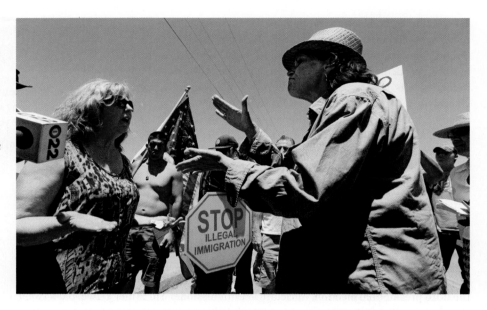

Immigration is a major issue in Texas elections, with Democrats and Republicans promoting starkly different plans for reform. Democrats tend to favor a path to citizenship for undocumented immigrants, while many Republicans emphasize stronger border security and stricter deportation measures.

law allowing licensed individuals to carry concealed firearms throughout the state, with some exceptions such as bars. As of 2016, Texas also allows permit holders open carry of personal firearms in most public places, although individual businesses can choose not to allow it. Gun safety in schools once again became a major issue in May 2018, when a high school student in Santa Fe, Texas, just outside of Houston, opened fire and killed ten classmates. Although Texas has traditionally not been open to gun control, Governor Abbott created a commission to study ways to improve school safety in the aftermath of the shooting. Valdez criticized Abbott for not supporting efforts to restrict the use of firearms at schools and for his close association with the gun lobby. The National Rifle Association, the nation's leading pro-gun lobbying group, gave Abbott an A+ and Valdez an F on their gun control policies.

Immigration policy also became a very salient issue in all of the statewide races in 2018. The two gubernatorial candidates also sought to distinguish themselves on these issues. Abbott called for more border security and a ban on sanctuary cities. Valdez, on the other hand, defended her record as Dallas county sheriff on these issues and claimed the governor was playing to anti-immigrant sentiment in his campaign. Republican candidates for all major elective offices pledged to enact strict border security measures and spend state resources on keeping illegal immigrants out of the state. This emphasis was a marked change from the 1990s, when then-governor George W. Bush appealed to the Latino vote in the state.

Tax policy also became a state campaign issue, especially the issue of property tax reform. Since Texas does not have a state income tax, property taxes are somewhat higher than in other states. The state relies on property taxes to fund public education and on sales taxes for other state spending. Sales taxes in Texas average 8.25 percent on most items, with the exception of medicine and groceries, and increasing them disproportionately affects lower-income Texans, since a higher percentage of their income is spent on purchasing goods and services. But Comptroller Glenn Hegar ran a campaign touting his conservative credentials and his desire for lower taxes in general, and he was ultimately elected comptroller of public accounts in the November election.

Though the issues above seem important ones, in recent statewide elections the distinguishing feature of the campaigns was actually the lack of emphasis on state issues. Instead, Republicans did not pivot from the positions they held in the primary, continuing to stress issues such as immigration and support for President Trump. Likewise, Democratic candidates in Texas, in attempting to attract support from the Democratic base, ran hard against President Trump and his policies. In particular, congressional Democratic candidates ran issue ads on health care, promising to protect people with pre-existing conditions and increase access to affordable health care. Although all statewide Republican candidates won their races, Democrats were heartened by the fact that the margins were some of the narrowest in recent memory. Most attribute these narrow margins to the presence of Beto O'Rourke, who energized and mobilized millennials, and to voters in the major cities and suburbs, which had become more Democratic.

One of the more interesting developments in 2018 in Texas was the deepening divide in voting patterns between urban/suburban areas and rural counties. Although cities have traditionally been more Democratic in Texas, the 2018 election witnessed growing shifts to Democrats in suburban areas, especially in Dallas and Houston. In the 7th congressional district, in the Houston suburbs, Democrat Lizzie Fletcher defeated longtime incumbent Republican John Culberson. This was an important pickup for Democrats, who capitalized on dissatisfaction with President Trump, especially among highly educated suburban white voters. Likewise, in the 32nd congressional district in the wealthy north Dallas suburbs, longtime incumbent Republican Pete Sessions lost to African American Democrat Colin Allred in a district largely populated by highly educated suburban white voters. In rural areas, Republican candidates fared well, thus intensifying the division in the state between strongly rural Republican areas and strongly Democratic urban areas. Meanwhile, suburban areas slowly shifted to Democrats.

After the 2018 elections, Republicans kept control of both chambers of the state legislature, although Democrats picked up twelve seats in the state House—the largest shift in seats since 2010—and two seats in the state Senate. These seats largely came from suburban areas in Dallas and Houston, where incumbent Republicans representing suburban districts were swept away by higher Democratic support that was due to President Trump's unpopularity in these areas.

One thing is clear after the 2018 election, however: Texas is not as solidly Republican as it once was. Republican political consultant Bill Miller noted after the election results, "It's a new day in Texas politics. The old way of doing things, just focusing on the extreme elements of the base, consider that nostalgia. That day is gone."[28] Many of the statewide races were much closer than in previous years. It remains to be seen whether Republican strength will return in the next cycle or whether Democrats will maintain and expand their gains into one or more statewide victories in the future.

★ ★

Campaigns, Elections, and the Future of Texas

ALTHOUGH REPUBLICANS have been winning statewide elections in Texas in recent years, the growing Latino population and increased diversification of the state may eventually change this pattern. Lupe Valdez had hoped to capitalize on these changing demographics in her bid for governor in 2018 but could not overcome countervailing winds against her candidacy, including the state's entrenched conservatism and Abbott's incumbency.

Campaigns—especially statewide campaigns—are very expensive in Texas, and gubernatorial campaigns can cost $40 million or more. For the most part, the candidates themselves must raise the money necessary to win an election. One effect of the high cost is that candidates are often wealthy individuals willing to use their own money in their campaigns. Such individuals, however, do not always prevail at the ballot box. Consider former lieutenant governor David Dewhurst, who invested millions of his own money in the Republican primary for a U.S. Senate seat in 2012 but suffered a bruising loss to Ted Cruz, leaving him vulnerable in his bid for re-election as lieutenant governor two years later. Insurgent senator Dan Patrick challenged Dewhurst from the right in the primary and forced him into a runoff, which Patrick won easily.

Although Texas once tried to restrict the right to vote, primarily through poll taxes and white primaries, in recent years it has tried to expand the franchise through the motor voter law and through early voting. Yet voter participation in Texas is the lowest in the nation. Turnout in 2014 was only 33.4 percent of eligible voters, which was less than the turnout in 2010. Turnout in the 2016 presidential election was only 51.1 percent of eligible voters, up slightly from 49.6 percent in 2012. These low figures are probably due to the demographics of Texas voters and the state's political culture, but they may also reflect the scheduling of elections in Texas, the vast number of elections, and the large number of low-visibility candidates for office. The competitive Senate race in Texas led to an increase in turnout from 2016. Nearly 53 percent of registered voters casted ballots in the 2018 election.

One of the biggest factors that could affect future Texas elections is the state's changing demographics. As we have discussed elsewhere in the text, the proportion of Latino voters in Texas is growing and that of white voters is shrinking. While not as strongly Democratic as African Americans, Latinos in Texas are more likely to identify as Democrats than Republicans. If this demographic trend continues, and if more Latinos register to vote and participate in state elections, Texas may once again become a competitive two-party state.

STUDY GUIDE

Use inQUIZITIVE to help you study and master this material.

Features of Elections in Texas

> • Describe the types of elections held in Texas and how they work (pp. 151–55)

Texas allows all registered voters the choice to vote in one party primary during an election season. Should a candidate not receive a majority of votes in a primary, a runoff is held to determine who the party nominee will be. The general election ultimately decides who is elected to office.

Key Terms

primary election (p. 151)
electoral cycle (p. 151)
runoff primary (p. 152)
open primary (p. 152)
closed primary (p. 152)
general election (p. 153)
special election (p. 153)

Practice Quiz

1. In a primary election,
   a) voters choose all local officials who will hold office in the following year.
   b) voters select federal officials for office.
   c) voters select their party's candidate for a general election.
   d) voters choose third-party candidates.
   e) voters cast ballots on proposed constitutional amendments.

2. Which of the following is *not* a type of election found in Texas?
   a) general
   b) primary
   c) distinguished
   d) special
   e) runoff primary

3. Officially, Texas has a
   a) joint primary.
   b) extended primary.
   c) open primary.
   d) closed primary.
   e) Jaybird primary.

4. The first Tuesday following the first Monday in November of even-numbered years is the day for which election?
   a) primary election
   b) runoff primary
   c) runoff for the general election
   d) secondary election
   e) general election

5. When are gubernatorial elections held?
   a) during presidential election years
   b) during odd-numbered years
   c) during even-numbered years that are not presidential election years
   d) every year
   e) every six months

Participation in Texas Elections

> • Explain how the rules for voting affect turnout among different groups of Texans (pp. 155–67)

Participation in Texas elections varies by election. Turnout is lowest in party primaries, followed by elections when a presidential candidate is not on the ballot. Latinos and those of lower socioeconomic status are also less likely to vote in state elections.

Key Terms

Nineteenth Amendment (p. 155)
suffrage (p. 155)
poll tax (p. 156)
early registration (p. 156)
white primary (p. 156)
Jaybird Party (p. 157)
Voting Rights Act of 1965 (p. 158)
motor voter law (p. 159)
early voting (p. 160)
straight-ticket voting (p. 160)
reapportionment (p. 162)
redistricting (p. 162)
preclearance (p. 162)

Practice Quiz

6. Which of the following is true?
- **a)** Poll taxes are legal.
- **b)** Women acquired the right to vote in the original 1876 Texas Constitution.
- **c)** The poll tax restricted the participation of poor people in the general election.
- **d)** You do not have to be a resident of Texas to vote in Texas.
- **e)** Latinos vote at higher rates than African Americans.

7. Who has benefited the most from early voting?
- **a)** Republicans
- **b)** Democrats
- **c)** All parties have benefited equally
- **d)** Independents
- **e)** Greens

8. The procedure by which certain states, such as Texas, are required to obtain approval every time they make changes to districts is called
- **a)** redistricting.
- **b)** reapportionment.
- **c)** preclearance.
- **d)** external validation.
- **e)** judicial review.

9. The two most important factors in determining whether someone will vote are
- **a)** income and education.
- **b)** education and family history of voting.
- **c)** income and gender.
- **d)** party membership and gender.
- **e)** ethnicity and race.

10. In which of the following elections is voter turnout the highest?
- **a)** presidential elections
- **b)** gubernatorial general elections
- **c)** city elections
- **d)** runoff elections
- **e)** off-year congressional elections

Campaigns

- **Present the main features of election campaigns in Texas (pp. 168–77)**

Because of Texas's size, statewide campaigns can be expensive. There are several major media markets, which makes television advertising very expensive. Grassroots efforts to mobilize voters are also costly because of the large territory. This means wealthy candidates are often on the ballot.

Practice Quiz

11. The most costly item for most political campaigns is
   a) travel.
   b) security.
   c) fund-raising.
   d) media.
   e) food.

12. Who is the first Republican to become Texas governor since Reconstruction?
   a) William Clements
   b) Rick Perry
   c) George W. Bush
   d) Ann Richards
   e) Kinky Friedman

13. Which of the following was *not* a feature of the 2018 campaigns in Texas?
   a) Voter turnout increased over previous midterm election years.
   b) Enthusiasm increased across the state, driven by anti-Trump sentiment and Beto O'Rourke's candidacy.
   c) Republicans lost control of the state legislature.
   d) Support for Democratic candidates increased in urban and suburban areas.
   e) Governor Greg Abbott was re-elected by a wide margin.

14. Which of the following was true of the 2018 elections in Texas?
   a) Democrats won control of the state Senate.
   b) Republicans won all statewide races.
   c) Women voted for Republicans in record numbers.
   d) Latinos voted for Republicans in record numbers.
   e) Voters in rural areas shifted sharply toward the Democratic party.

Dineen Majcher (right) was frustrated with the emphasis her daughter's school placed on standardized testing. She took action by helping to create an interest group and challenging Texas's education policies.

6

★ ★ ★ ★ ★

Interest Groups and Lobbying

WHY INTEREST GROUPS MATTER Dineen Majcher had had enough. A lawyer and mother of an incoming ninth grader in a prestigious Austin high school, she couldn't believe what she was hearing. Fifteen percent of her daughter's final grade in history would come from a new mandated statewide test, one that the teacher had never seen. This struck her as unfair and unreasonable. How could students prepare for such a test? Why 15 percent of the grade?

She went first to the principal to protest, but to no avail. This was after all a mandated state test, part of a 30-year effort by education reformers to bring testing and accountability to all elementary and secondary schools across the state. So Majcher raised the ante, getting the Austin School Board to request a waiver from the State Board of Education from the "15 percent rule." The request was denied. Raising the ante again, Majcher signed up to testify at legislative committee hearings that had been called for January 2012. During the hearings Majcher met others from across Texas who also were dissatisfied with the testing movement. Together these individuals established an interest group called Texans Advocating for Meaningful Student Assessment, or TAMSA. The group became known in the legislature as "Mothers Against Drunk Testing."

The goals of TAMSA were clearly articulated on its website: "to improve public education in Texas through the use of meaningful and effective student assessments that allow for more productive classroom instruction and more efficient use of public funds." On their face, these goals might seem to be relatively uncontroversial. In fact, however, they were questioning the philosophy of reform that had dominated education policy in the state for over thirty years.

TAMSA enabled people to join together and seek policy change in a number of ways: first, by providing like-minded individuals an organizational structure for discussing problems and offering solutions; second, by providing a vehicle for working with other organizations such as the Texas Association of School Administrators, who were also concerned with testing; third, by raising money to help pay for their efforts; and fourth, by educating the public and policy makers alike about the problems of testing across the elementary and secondary curriculum. TAMSA spearheaded the drive to change public policy regarding testing in the state. What had begun as a protest about unfair testing was morphing into an interest group with a clear political objective.

Since the early 1980s, testing had been seen as one of the best ways to ensure accountability by identifying schools that worked and those that didn't. Support for reform through testing and accountability came from a variety of sources inside and outside the legislature. Leading legislators from both parties, leaders at the Texas Education Agency, and business leaders all came to believe statewide testing was a key to higher performance. As governor, George W. Bush identified testing as a central part of his plan for educational reform in Texas and placed it at the heart of his "No Child Left Behind" initiatives as president. Key business interests, including the Texas Association of Business, supported expanded testing, seeing the tests as a way to ratchet up the quality of poorly performing schools across the state. Not surprisingly, the businesses involved in creating the tests also came to support expanded testing. As the debates over reform were proceeding in the legislature, Pearson publishers had a five-year contract with the state that was estimated to be worth $462 million. Testing itself had become big business with big interests seeking protection in the legislature.

Given the interests supporting testing and decades-old accountability initiatives, few thought at the beginning of the 2013 legislative session that change was in the wind. But it was. New legislators open to new ideas about reform were chairing the educational committees in both the House and the Senate. Entrenched interests in educational reform had lost their ability to control the agenda. On a paltry budget of under $100,000, drawing upon inexpensive social media and relying on the expertise of a few key members, TAMSA played a major role in getting the legislature to rethink what educational reform meant. In response to the efforts of TAMSA and other like-minded groups and individuals, the legislature dropped the number of end-of-year course exams from 15 to 5.

The story of Dineen Majcher and TAMSA highlights how interest groups matter in Texas politics. Interest groups provide support for existing policies in many areas of public policy, as well as for legislators in their electoral campaigns, and they help to articulate ideas from which policies can be crafted. In the case of TAMSA, interest groups have also challenged policies and advocated changes. Texas politics can be understood only with a clear understanding of the role that interest groups play in elections and in the legislative process.[1]

CHAPTERGOALS

- Define interest groups, and describe the major ways they try to influence Texas government (pp. 185–98)

- Describe the role of PACs in Texas elections (pp. 198–205)

- Explain how ordinary individuals can influence Texas government (pp. 205–7)

Interest Groups in the Political Process

Define interest groups, and describe the major ways they try to influence Texas government

It is probably true that all of us have political interests, goals, or objectives that can be achieved with governmental intervention. Many of us, however, will never act to achieve those goals. A few of us may speak privately to a legislator or other official. Some of us will join with others to try to convince the government to help us achieve our interests. When we do that, we have formed an **interest group**.

In Texas, as elsewhere, interest groups assume a variety of forms. A wide range of interests that are active in national, state, and local politics organize themselves into groups, including those concerned with business and labor (such as the real estate industry and the chemical workers' union), agriculture, the professions (such as law, medicine, and accounting), government affairs (such as state employees and cities), education (such as colleges and universities), and public interest causes (such as the environment). Interest groups can be established to serve the interests of a small number of people concerned with one particular interest, such as getting a road built in a county. They can also be established to serve the interests of a group of people with broader interests, such as those interested in reforming the school system by promoting vouchers, charter schools, home schooling, or better testing. A "peak association" is an interest group organized as an umbrella organization that seeks to coordinate the activities of member groups in a number of targeted areas.

interest group an organization established to influence the government's programs and policies

Resources and Strategies of Interest Groups

Political scientists have identified various resources that interest groups are able to mobilize in politics. First, interest groups have members. Groups can become influential because of whom they represent. The Texas Medical Association and the Texas Bar Association are excellent examples of groups representing influential people across Texas. Some people and industries clearly are more important to legislators than others. But numbers matter, too. In Texas, politicians who ignore the concerns of broad-based evangelical groups in discussions of abortion do so at their own peril. There are a lot of evangelical Christians in Texas and their votes, especially for Republicans, are very much needed.

Second, interest groups have the ability to raise money. Clearly, it is advantageous to have access to a few deep-pocketed individuals when trying to raise money in support of a particular cause. But in the age of the internet, it is also useful for there to be large numbers of members who are willing to give, if only a little.

Third, interest groups possess information about their membership and about the problems that concern their membership. In recent years, interest groups have begun to mine large databases of people who might be interested in particular policies or issues. Such information can become a valuable resource for politicians seeking to raise money or to promote a particular policy objective. Interest groups also offer advice on the best ways to address the concerns of their membership. Interest groups clearly are motivated by their self-interest, and the positions they present to legislators reflect this interest. The first drafts of bills introduced into the Texas House or Senate often come from interest groups seeking to promote their own particular perspective.

A fourth resource, one closely related to the third, is credibility. Providing information to a policy maker is important. But this must be good information if, over the longer run, an interest group or its representatives are to be taken seriously. Bad information about a problem or the concerns of a group's members can undercut an interest group's effectiveness quickly.

The resources available to interest groups are the foundation upon which groups develop various strategies to promote their concerns. Among the strategies that we will explore in this chapter are (1) explicit political strategies such as grassroots organizing, get-out-the-vote and electioneering campaigns, and campaign financing; (2) legislative strategies such as lobbying and testifying before legislative committees; (3) public awareness strategies such as drafting policy reports, writing editorials, and conducting educational campaigns in various public forums; and (4) the judicial strategy of supporting litigation that challenges existing policies in court. As we will see, the strategies adopted by various interest groups largely depend on the resources available to them at the time.

Interest Groups and Democracy

The rights to associate with others and to petition government lie at the heart of the rights guaranteed by the U.S. and Texas constitutions. These constitutional rights have helped to make the United States and Texas into what political scientists call a "pluralistic society" where individuals organize into groups to serve common interests and compete with one another for power and influence. Pluralism provides multiple access points for interest groups to try to influence public policy. Interest groups can lobby city councils, state legislatures, school boards, and other governmental bodies. In *Federalist 10*, an essay written in defense of the U.S. Constitution in 1787, James Madison discussed how a large republic comprising many interests competing with one another in the political arena could work to protect individuals from the abusive power of any one powerful interest. Drawing upon Madison for inspiration, later pluralist writers in the twentieth century would argue that groups could check and balance one another in the political process, much like different branches of government checked and balanced one another in constitutional government. The problem with this approach, however, is that having a common interest is one thing. Organizing that common interest into an effective group that can act to promote that interest is quite something else.

Overcoming the Free Rider Problem
In his groundbreaking book *The Logic of Collective Action,* Mancur Olson analyzed a collective action problem that lies at the heart of interest-group politics. People have an interest in organizing into an interest group that effectively represents their interests in politics. But people also

have an interest in getting someone else to pay for that group's organizational costs—so that in many groups people get the benefits of the group's activities despite the fact that others do the work. This is what political scientists call the **free rider problem**. If everyone acts as a free rider, everyone will be waiting for someone else to do the work, and an organization will never form. To use an everyday example, free riders are people who show up to potluck dinners without contributing a dish and then proceed to benefit by consuming everyone else's dishes. Ironically, the larger the common interest, the more difficult it may be to overcome the free rider problem and create effective interest groups. According to Olson's theory, for example, a small number of insurance companies are more likely to form a powerful interest group to affect health care policy than are the millions of poor people who lack quality health care. Similarly, business interests are more likely to form a common front in politics than are consumers because it is easier for the business interests to overcome the costs of collective action, that is, the costs of acting together as an organized interest group.[2]

free rider problem the incentive to benefit from others' work without making a contribution, which leads individuals in a collective action situation to refuse to work together

Interest groups engage in a number of activities to overcome the free rider problem. Sometimes, they offer people particular incentives to join a group. These selective benefits often cover a wide range of activities, from a subscription to a magazine, to access to special information on the internet, to invitations to special conferences, to special discounts. For example, AAA (the American Automobile Association), which advocates for road and vehicle safety, provides members with roadside assistance and travel discounts—strong incentives to join.

Interest groups also can provide people with what political scientists call solidary benefits, such as listing individuals' names as sponsors of an organization or offering free buttons, hats, or T-shirts that show their support for its activities. Such benefits, as well as the sense of belonging, strengthen the commitment an individual has to an interest group and help overcome the free rider problem.

Whose Interests Do Groups Represent?

One of the most important lessons to be drawn from the logic of collective action is that some interests do not get represented easily in the political process. Upper-class business interests are more likely to be well-represented than lower-class minority interests. A second lesson is that it is very difficult, even rare, for interest groups to emerge that protect the broad interests of large numbers of people or any vaguely defined public interest. Significantly, when such groups do emerge, as with the Prohibition (anti-alcohol) movement in the nineteenth and early twentieth centuries, or civil rights organizations in the 1950s and '60s, they can come to wield considerable power. Nevertheless, in the everyday politics in Texas as elsewhere, it is more likely for narrowly targeted interests to organize effectively in defense of their interests than it is for the public as a whole to organize. Even the above-mentioned "public interest groups" are not so much advancing the public good as a whole (whatever that may be) as advocating for the views that certain individuals have about the public good—such as increased awareness of climate change, or gun safety regulations.

Olson's theory of collective action provides an explanation of why it has often been claimed that business-oriented interest groups dominate the Texas legislature. Using campaign contributions, political pressure, and sometimes corruption, "the Lobby," as pro-business groups were called, was once purported to run Texas government. Some of the most influential business leaders of the state belonged to the "8F Crowd." At the Lamar Hotel in Houston, 8F was the number on a suite of rooms where George R. Brown held court. Brown was a founder of Brown and Root, one of the world's largest

PERSONAL RESPONSIBILITY: WHAT WOULD YOU DO?

- Do you think that business interests should have such a profound effect on Texas government and politics? Why or why not?

- Why do business interests have such a strong voice in Texas government and politics? If you were advising an environmental group on opposing business interests, what tactics would you suggest they take?

construction firms and until 2007 part of the even larger Halliburton Company, and now independently operating together with Wink Engineering. He met regularly in 8F and elsewhere with other fabulously wealthy Texans such as Jesse Jones of Texas Commerce Bank and Tenneco, Gus Wortham of American General Insurance, and James Elkins of the Vinson and Elkins law firm and First City National Bank. These men socialized together and worked together to promote their political interests. For 40 years they were considered the kingmakers in Texas politics who determined much of the important policy of state government.[3] Indeed, the convention center in Houston is named after George R. Brown, and Jones and Wortham have their names attached to performing arts centers in downtown Houston.

The 8F Crowd was, of course, an interest group—an elite, wealthy, powerful, pro-business interest group. Although the 8F Crowd is long gone from the Texas political scene, much of what it did is still done in Texas politics by other interest groups, though no modern-day group is ascribed the influence that the 8F Crowd allegedly had.

Texas is known as a state that has long had powerful interest groups. During the Texas Constitutional Convention of 1875, an important role was played by the Grange, a powerful farmers' organization, of which many of the constitution's framers were members. As Chapter 2 indicated, the Constitution of 1876 reflected many of the values of Grange members. It was a document for rural Texas that was pro–small farmer and opposed to a powerful state government.

With the development of a strong oil and gas industry in Texas in the first half of the twentieth century, this industry in turn began playing an important role in state politics. The interests of major oil companies such as ExxonMobil, who have their headquarters in Texas and employ millions of the state's residents, are well represented in the state legislature. While the oil and gas industry remains very important, the state's economy has also become more diversified in recent years. Interest groups representing newer industries such as telecommunications and high-tech companies in the Austin area have also begun to influence legislation. For example, when the legislature, in the 2017 legislative session, considered legislation to repeal city ordinances making background checks on Uber and Lyft drivers more stringent, both companies spent $2.3 million on lobbyists to help influence legislation. Their efforts were successful, as the legislature passed the new law.[4]

Interest Groups and Policy Makers

Interest groups want something from policy makers: policy that is beneficial for their groups. On the other hand, policy makers also benefit in a number of ways from developing relationships with interest groups. First, they gain information, insofar as interest groups can provide substantial expertise in areas that are their special concern. Additionally, interest groups can provide campaign funds to policy makers. In a state as large as Texas, with numerous media markets and with some party competition, considerable campaign funds are necessary to run and win elections. For example, in the 2014 gubernatorial race, according to the media project at Wesleyan University, interest groups favoring Democrat Wendy Davis spent $2.6 million in ads in Texas, while groups favoring Republican Greg Abbott spent $5.2 million. An interest group can help raise money from its membership for a candidate sympathetic to the interest group's goals.

Interest groups can also work to supply votes to the policy maker. Besides assisting in mobilizing their own members, they can supply campaign workers to distribute campaign leaflets and to operate phone banks to get out the vote. Interest groups can also publicize issues through press conferences, press releases, publications, workshops, hearings, and even by filing lawsuits. Finally, interest groups can engage in research and public education programs. It has become increasingly common for interest groups to run advertisements in the Texas media explaining why their particular approaches to a public policy problem would be more beneficial to Texans in general.

Newer companies associated with high-tech industries, including ride-sharing app Lyft, have begun to hire lobbyists to influence legislation in Texas.

Unlike a private citizen interested in and involved in politics, larger or better-funded interest groups have the advantages of time, money, expertise, and continuity. Although concerned individuals do have an impact on public policy in Texas, organized and well-funded interest groups have an advantage in affecting the policy process. It is difficult for a concerned citizen from McAllen to spend time in Austin developing relationships with policy makers and trying to convince them to support public policies compatible with the individual's goals. On the other hand, if that individual joins with like-minded people to create an organized interest group, the group may be more likely to achieve these policy goals. It might be possible to fund an office in Austin with a staff that could monitor events in state government on a daily basis and develop relationships with key policy makers. Additionally, although some individuals in Texas do have the money to provide substantial campaign support to policy makers, even they can get more "bang for the buck" if they join with others in **bundling** their funds into a larger contribution from a group. The creation of an organized interest group also allows for the development of a staff, who can gain in-depth knowledge of an area of policy far greater than could be gained by most individuals working alone. Finally, an individual may be intensely concerned with an issue in one legislative session but find it difficult to sustain that interest over a period of many more sessions. The larger, better-funded, more successful organized interest groups have continuity. They are in Austin developing relationships with policy makers and presenting the views of the organization day in and day out, year in and year out. The result is that legislators and other policy makers can develop long-standing relationships with the interest groups and their representatives in Austin.

bundling the interest-group practice of combining campaign contributions from several sources into one larger contribution from the group, so as to increase the group's impact on the candidate

Consider the role of Raise Your Hand Texas, founded by Charles Butt of the HEB Grocery store chain, located throughout Texas and parts of Northern Mexico. Raise Your Hand Texas is an interest group aimed at stopping school vouchers in Texas and promoting public education. In the 2013 legislative session, legislators were particularly influenced by the group. When Representative Ken King (R-Canadian) introduced a bill regarding education on the House floor, Representative Abel Herrero (D-Corpus Christi) asked his colleagues in the House whether Raise Your Hand Texas had taken a position on his bill.[5] At that point, one of them showed Herrero a text message showing that the group had supported the bill during the committee stage of the process. Herrero subsequently supported Raise Your Hand's position. This is but one example of how an interest group can have important influence over legislators.[6]

Types of Interest Groups and Lobbyists

lobbyist an individual employed by an interest group who tries to influence governmental decisions on behalf of that group

Interest groups strive to influence public opinion, make their views known to policy makers, and elect and support policy makers friendly to their points of view. To accomplish these goals, interest groups usually maintain **lobbyists** in Austin who try to gain access to policy makers and communicate their objectives to them. There are several types of lobbyists. Some interest groups have full-time staffs in Austin whose members work as lobbyists. One form of interest group is, of course, a corporation, and companies often have government relations departments that lobby for the companies' interests; others hire law firms to do so. Lobbyists may be employed by an interest group to deal with one issue, or on a regular basis to deal with a range of issues. Some lobbyists represent only one client; others have large numbers of clients. Often industries in a particular field have broad interests that need representation. For example, an insurance company may have one specific interest it wishes to have represented. However, the insurance industry as a whole also has a wide range of issues that need representation, and thus it will form an industrywide interest group.

Interest groups may also represent professional groups. One of the most influential professional groups in Austin is the Texas Medical Association, which represents the interests of doctors. Other professional groups represent accountants, chiropractors, opticians, dentists, lawyers, and teachers.

That teachers are an important interest group suggests still another type of interest group—public-employee interest groups. Public school teachers may be the largest and most effective of these groups, but firefighters, police officers, and even justices of the peace and constables all are represented in Austin.

Some interest groups are formed with a single issue in mind, as the introduction to this chapter illustrates. For example, a group may be concerned about the regulation of abortion or school vouchers or tort reform or the environment. Other interest groups are concerned with multiple issues that affect their members. Public school teachers, for example, are concerned about job security, professional qualifications, health insurance, pensions, salaries, and other matters that affect the lives of teachers.

Civil rights groups such as the National Association for the Advancement of Colored People, the League of United Latin American Citizens, and the Mexican American Legal Defense and Education Fund are concerned about civil rights issues affecting the lives primarily of African Americans and Latinos. Not only do these groups often try to influence public opinion and the legislature but they have had notable success in representing their members' interests through litigation, especially in the federal courts.

Other public interest groups promote consumer, environmental, and general public issues. Groups such as the Sierra Club focus on environmental interests, whereas Public Citizen and Common Cause work more broadly to promote more open government. These groups rarely have much funding, but they often can provide policy makers with information and expertise. In addition, they can mobilize their membership to support or oppose bills, and they can publicize matters that are important to their goals.

In recent years, the American Legislative Exchange Council (ALEC), a conservative policy group, has had a significant influence in Texas politics. ALEC provides funding and legislative assistance to conservative state legislators across the country. ALEC assists legislators by writing bills and pushing for their enactment all across the country. This organization has been accused by some liberal groups in Texas of having excessive influence. For example, Progress Texas compared the language in ALEC's documents proposing "model bills" with actual legislation before the Texas legislature and found in many cases word for word copies, indicating the extent of the organization's influence.[7]

Getting Access to Policy Makers

In order to communicate the goals of their interest groups to policy makers, lobbyists must first gain access to those policy makers. Such access, of course, imposes on the time of legislators, so lobbyists often spend significant sums entertaining them. That entertainment is one of the most criticized aspects of lobbying. But from the lobbyists' perspective, entertainment is an important tool for reaching policy makers and putting them in a congenial frame of mind. Entertainment by lobbyists can involve expensive dinners, golf, and other items and activities. For example, lobbyists for Texas Utilities (TXU) bought a $300 saddle for one state representative and a $200 bench for another, and treated a state senator to a trip to the Masters golf tournament, where they picked up the dinner tab as well. One House member received a gun as a gift, another received a jacket, and several got "deer-processing" costs paid for by TXU.[8] When former representative Lon Burnam (D–Fort Worth) proposed legislation to regulate consumer versions of "stun guns," the lobbyist for TASER International as a joke gave Burnam a gift of a pink "stun gun" valued at more than $150.[9] When Governor Abbott was attorney general, he received gifts ranging from hunting trips to college football tickets.[10]

In the 2015 legislative session, lobbyists spent more than $1.8 million on food and meals alone, with an additional $331,000 in entertainment and gifts for lawmakers and others in state government.[11] Texas lawmakers receive only $600 per month plus $190

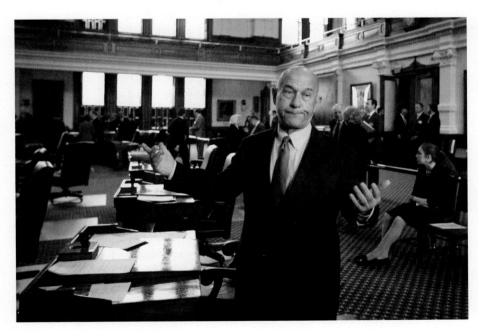

Senator John Whitmire (D-Houston) is well known for spending campaign contributions from interest groups on expenses that are not strictly campaign-related.

a day when on legislative business, but they are permitted to use campaign contributions for expenses associated with holding office. This policy allows interest groups to fund lavish benefits for them. For example, Senator John Whitmire (D-Houston) used his contributions to fund a car lease for a BMW totaling over $100,000 over ten years. In addition, he has spent nearly $300,000 in sports tickets for his hometown Houston Astros, Rockets, and Texans and classified the expenditures as "constituent entertainment."[12] Whitmire is not alone in spending campaign funds for these types of expenses, and recent efforts in the legislature to address these types of expenditures through ethics reform have failed.

The Texas Ethics Commission keeps a list of registered lobbyists as well as of their clients. In 2018 there were 1,927 registered lobbyists in Texas.[13] However, because of the loose nature of Texas reporting laws, it is unclear what these lobbyists were paid. The Texas Ethics Commission also collects information on how much lobbying firms spend to influence Texas lawmakers. In 2017, this sum reached an astonishing $4,644,634.98, and this is just the amount that was reported.[14]

Sometimes lobbyists have long-standing personal ties to policy makers, and those bonds can be invaluable to the lobbyists' clients. When lobbyist Andrea McWilliams celebrated her 40th birthday in California's wine country, six Texas lawmakers traveled to California for the party, including the chair of the House Appropriations Committee and the chair of the Senate Public Education Committee. In McWilliams's case, her personal ties to these lawmakers were probably strengthened by the fact that she and her clients had contributed more than $206,000 to their campaigns over the previous several years.[15] In the 2017 legislative session, McWilliams was one of the highest-paid lobbyists, with the largest number of clients and the largest revenue—$2.6 million.[16] *Texas Monthly* listed her among the most powerful Texans, and a friend described her as a "consigliere to the powerful and political."[17]

Andrea McWilliams is one of Texas's highest-paid and most successful lobbyists.

Registered Lobbyists: How Does Texas Compare?

While we often associate lobbyists with Washington, DC, the reality is that lobbyists are active at all levels of policy making. Some states, such as Texas, are larger and more populated, so it stands to reason that more lobbyists are active in those states and have a higher degree of impact on businesses and labor. The chart below compares Texas with five other states in terms of the number of registered lobbyists and the lobbyists per 100,000 people. The map compares all states in terms of how many lobbyists per 100,000 people are actively persuading government officials.

Number of Lobbyists in Selected States

● Registered lobbyists   ● Lobbyists per 100,000 people

	New York	Ohio	Alabama	Florida	Texas	California
Registered lobbyists	6,210	1,532	539	2,175	1,519	2,160
Lobbyists per 100,000 people	47	18	15	15	9	9
Voting eligible pop.	13,591,250	8,737,173	3,601,361	14,572,210	17,396,296	25,017,408

Lobbyists per Capita, Nationwide

Lobbyists per 100,000 people   ● < 15   ● 15–24.9   ● 25–34.9   ● 35–45   ● > 45

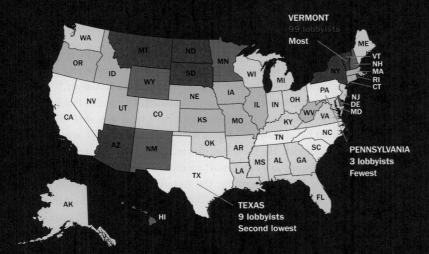

VERMONT
99 lobbyists
Most

PENNSYLVANIA
3 lobbyists
Fewest

TEXAS
9 lobbyists
Second lowest

SOURCES: Population data from www.electproject.org/2016g;
Lobbyist data from www.followthemoney.org, (accessed 3/10/18)

CRITICAL THINKING

· How does Texas compare with other states regarding the total number of lobbyists and the number of lobbyists per capita? Do you think Texas has too many, too few, or just the right number of lobbyists?

· Looking at the map, what can you conclude about the most populated states and the number of lobbyists per capita? Which states go against the norm? Why might this be?

Access to policy makers may also be gained by building support for an issue among their constituents. For example, interest groups might contact constituents to encourage them to write or call legislators about a bill and offer their opinions. Essentially, the interest group tries to mobilize interested voters to become involved in the political process on behalf of the group's goals.

Lobbying and Government's "Revolving Door" One important way of gaining access to those in government is to employ former officials as lobbyists. A lobbyist who is a former legislator often has friends in the legislature and can use that friendship to gain access. Additionally, a former legislator often is in an exceptionally good position to understand the personal relationships and informal power centers that must be involved in accomplishing a legislative objective. As a result, some of the best-paid lobbyists in Austin are former Texas state officials, who often are also former legislators.

In recent years, it has not been uncommon for former legislators to register as lobbyists. What they have in common is, as a writer for the *Texas Tribune* put it, knowledge of "how to pass bills, to kill them, whom to talk to, which clerks are friendly, whose birthdays are coming up—all inside stuff that makes the government machine whir."[18] Other especially valuable lobbyists have been former committee clerks for major committees and chiefs of staff of members who were on major committees.[19] In the 2017 legislative session, lobbyists included five recently retired lawmakers with a total of 31 lobbying contracts, allowing them to generate a total of $1.7 million in fees.[20] In 2013 former senator Tommy Williams of the Woodlands, who was chairman of the Senate Budget Committee, took a $300,000 per year job with the Texas A&M system after he left office. While he is not officially a "lobbyist," one of his duties is to advocate for Texas A&M in Austin. One gets a sense of the value of these ex-legislators-turned-lobbyists from the explanation Representative Jim Pitts gave for sponsoring an amendment pushed by an AT&T lobbyist and former legislator, Pat Heggerty. The amendment would have forced the state to pay for rerouting phone lines for road projects, and Pitts said, "I was just trying to help Pat out."[21] (The amendment failed to pass the House.)

It is not only former legislators who can move on to successful lobbying careers. During the fourteen-year governorship of Rick Perry, dozens of his aides either left the administration to become lobbyists or joined the administration after having been lobbyists. Some moved back and forth from administration to lobbying in a revolving door fashion.[22] In September 2017, for example, critics questioned the hiring of former lobbyist Luis Saenz as Governor Abbott's new chief of staff.

One former-legislator-turned-lobbyist reversed course and went back into the legislature. Todd Hunter had served in the legislature from 1989 to 1997. An active lobbyist as late as 2007, he was elected to the Texas House in 2008.[23] Jerry Patterson, former Texas land commissioner, was a state senator, became a lobbyist, and was able to move to his statewide office with little criticism of his role as a lobbyist. He then ran unsuccessfully for lieutenant governor in 2014 and most recently lost to George P. Bush in the 2018 primary for the Republican land commissioner nomination. However, David Sibley, a state senator who became a lobbyist and then tried to regain his old position, caught tremendous political flak for this decision and, to a considerable degree, lost the Republican primary because

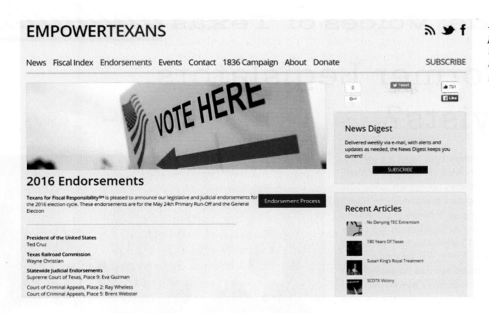

Empower Texans is a powerful political action committee that provides money to candidates, sometimes from undisclosed donors.

of it.[24] The issue of lobbying by former officials and their staffs is a significant one, as there is concern that policy decisions may be made with an eye toward future lucrative lobbying jobs.

Texas has only weak laws dealing with lobbying by former government officials. A former member of the governing body or a former executive head of a regulatory agency cannot lobby the agency for two years after leaving office. Senior employees or former officers of Texas regulatory agencies cannot ever lobby a governmental entity on matters they were involved in when employed by the government. However, there are no legal restrictions on lobbying by a former governor, former lieutenant governor, former legislator, or former aides to these officials.[25] In the 2015 and 2017 legislative sessions, Governor Abbott pledged action on ethics reform to address the problem of former legislators lobbying. Senator Van Taylor (R-Plano) introduced a bill that would impose a two-year limit before an outgoing legislator could lobby his or her former colleagues. The bill passed the Senate and a similar one passed the House, but Abbott vetoed the resulting legislation, claiming that it was not meaningful and included too many loopholes, including a provision to allow legislators to avoid reporting requirements by listing their assets and financial information under their spouse's name.[26]

What Lobbyists Do with Access The public perception of lobbying may be that interested groups bring bags of money to members of the legislature in exchange for their votes on important bills. While lobbyists have no doubt showered legislators with gifts, sports tickets, and fancy meals, the reality is much more complex and far less underhanded. Once lobbyists obtain access to policy makers, they provide information that may be useful. For example, they may explain how a bill benefits a legislator's district, or how it benefits the state, or how it is perceived as being unfair. Because the staffs of Texas legislators are small, lobbyists perform useful functions by explaining what numerous bills are intended to do. They may even write bills to be

Should Former Legislators Be Lobbyists?

LOBBYISTS come from different backgrounds. Most are lawyers, and many have not held elected office. However, in Austin as in Washington, D.C., the number of former legislators taking high-paying jobs lobbying their former colleagues has grown substantially in recent years. In fact, this practice is becoming so common that the term *revolving door* has emerged to describe it. An article in the *Dallas Morning News* estimated that in the 2013 legislative session, former legislators earned up to a collective $1.7 million in salaries.[a]

It is not surprising that interest groups such as corporations or labor unions would want to hire former legislators as lobbyists. Former legislators have cultivated relationships with their colleagues as well as with staff members; therefore, they can easily arrange meetings for their clients with important government leaders. Lobbying firms see former legislators as strong investments because of their ability to influence legislation.

Former legislators defend taking lobbying jobs by claiming that they have a right to make a living. Texas legislators point out that they make only $7,200 per year and that their experience should not go to waste once they leave office. Former legislators say they are uniquely suited to advise their clients because of their expertise in legislative politics. They also say they are employed not only to influence current legislators but also to educate them about the concerns of the lobbyists' clients, who are the legislators' constituents as well. As long as reporting requirements exist so that the public knows whom they are lobbying for, they argue, then there are no ethical issues with this practice. Former legislator and current lobbyist Cliff Johnson defends his experience by suggesting, "You have to hire somebody to get through the administrative minefield."[b] Lobbying firms will naturally gravitate toward hiring individuals who know the legislative process and so are able to best represent them.

On the other hand, opponents of the revolving door claim that this practice is unethical and should be curtailed because legislators are public servants who should not personally profit from their time in office. Representative Donna Howard (D-Austin) has proposed that former legislators should have to wait a period of time after their legislative service before they lobby. Senator Jane Nelson (R-Flower Mound) expressed her opposition to the revolving door in this way: "It just doesn't feel right. I don't want people questioning: Is she filing that bill because she hopes to cash in on that at some point in the future? I would rather be boiled in oil."[c] Governor Abbott and Lieutenant Governor Patrick have also proposed ethics reform in the legislature to address the issue of the revolving door. Nevertheless, a proposal to enact a two-session "cooling off" period before former

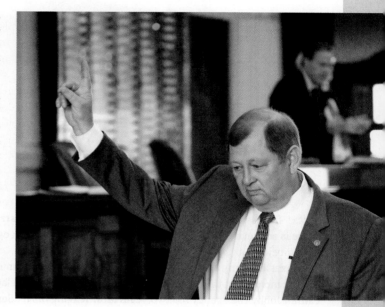

legislators could lobby failed in the 2017 legislative session. Ten states currently have revolving door laws, but Texas will have to wait until the next legislative session to even consider these bills to limit the practice.

COMMUNICATING EFFECTIVELY: YOUR VOICE

- Do you agree or disagree that former legislators lobbying their former colleagues is unethical? Why?

- Should Texas enact laws to limit the ability of former legislators to lobby? If so, what specific provisions should be enacted and why?

introduced by friendly legislators or write amendments to bills. Almost certainly, if a bill affects the interests of a lobbyist's client and reaches a point in the legislative process where hearings are held on it, the lobbyist will arrange for testimony to be given at the hearing explaining the interest group's viewpoint on the proposed legislation.

Lobbyists do not limit their activities to the legislative process, however. Rules proposed by the bureaucracy or the courts can also affect the interests of lobbyists' clients. Lobbyists will testify at hearings on rules and try to provide information to administrators in face-to-face meetings as well.

Corruption   There is always a concern that lobbyists may corrupt policy makers by bribing them in order to accomplish the interest groups' objectives. Early in the twentieth century, Sam Rayburn, later a famed U.S. representative and Speaker of the House, served in the Texas House of Representatives for six years. At that time, he was especially concerned with corruption and refused to accept free meals and entertainment from lobbyists. He called some of his fellow legislators "steak men." By that he meant that the legislators would sell their votes on a bill for a steak dinner at the Driskill Hotel in Austin. "Steak men" (and women) may still exist in Texas politics, but for the most part, lobbyists provide information, campaign contributions, and political support (or opposition) rather than bribes.

Still, some lobbying activities do seem ethically questionable. In 1989, "Bo" Pilgrim, a large poultry producer, distributed $10,000 checks to state senators in the capitol while he was lobbying them on workers' compensation reform. Perhaps even more troubling, some senators accepted the checks until media attention forced them to reconsider. Yet this practice of offering $10,000 while asking for a senator's vote on a specific bill was not illegal under state law. A year later, the Speaker of the Texas House of Representatives, "Gib" Lewis, got in trouble for his close relationship with a law firm that specialized in collecting delinquent taxes for local governments. In 1991, Lewis was indicted for receipt of an illegal gift from the firm. Ultimately, he plea bargained and received a minor penalty. The result of these scandals was legislation that created a state ethics commission. The legislation imposed additional lobbying reporting requirements and restrictions

WHAT DO TEXANS THINK?

Corruption in State and Federal Government

When interest groups have too much power in Austin, Texans can come to see this as political corruption. If interest groups get their way over the needs of everyday Texans, then some may see this as corruption. Do Texans see their state government as more or less corrupt than the federal government?

	TEXAS STATE GOVERNMENT	FEDERAL GOVERNMENT
Mostly Corrupt	33%	70%
Mostly Honest	42	15
Don't Know	25	15

SOURCE: *Texas Tribune* poll, October 2012.

on speaking fees that interest groups paid legislators and pleasure trips that lobbyists provided. By no means was the law a major regulation of or restriction on lobbying practices, but it did impose some limits.

Who Represents Ordinary Texans?

Another problem with lobbying was well described by Craig McDonald, the director of a public interest lobby: "Legislators are rubbing shoulders with . . . lobbyists, almost all of whom hustle for business interests. While corporate interests dominate our legislative process, there is virtually no counterbalancing lobby to represent ordinary Texans. Nowhere on the list of Texas's biggest lobby spenders will you find a single group dedicated to the interests of consumers, the environment or human services. No wonder these citizen interests repeatedly get steamrolled in Austin."[27]

The "Who Are Texans?" graphic on page 201 looks at campaign contributions to Texas legislators. Although the categories are very broad, it is clear that business interests dominate in Texas government. Of course, many issues considered by Texas government pit one business interest against another, and sometimes a business or professional organization may find itself aligned with consumer interests. For example, the Texas Trial Lawyers Association, an organization of plaintiffs' lawyers in Texas, frequently does so. Many of the clients of these lawyers are consumers who sue large businesses, and the interests of the lawyers and such clients are especially close since the lawyers are paid on a contingent fee basis, which means they don't receive payment unless their clients do.

It is also the case that lobbying is not all there is to the representation of interests in Austin. Interest groups without money may still mobilize their members in order to accomplish their objectives, or they may influence public opinion. Still, there is no question that money does help in politics. In this battle of mostly business interests, there may not be an objective voice, or at least a voice for the public interest, that reaches the ears of legislators.

Another Side to Lobbying

Describe the role of PACs in Texas elections

Although lobbyists for interest groups try to gain access to government officials and inform them of the legislative desires of their clients, interest groups are not simply information channels. They also promote the political interests of elected officials who support their viewpoints and oppose the interests of those who do not. One major way of doing so is by making campaign contributions. An interest group may encourage individual members to make contributions to candidates, or it may collect funds from members and "bundle" those funds as a donation from the interest group. With the second option, the interest group creates a **political action committee (PAC)** to make the contribution.

There are numerous reasons for forming a PAC. A candidate is more likely to notice a substantial contribution from a PAC than many small contributions from individual members of an interest group. Additionally, the lobbyist who delivers a substantial PAC check to a candidate can more likely gain political access than can a lobbyist who simply asks interest-group members to mail individual checks. The PAC becomes a way for the interest group to send a message to the candidate that its members care strongly enough about its agenda that they are prepared to back those goals with money. In some cases, a PAC can even serve as an intermediary to provide money to candidates that the interest group's members might not want to support publicly.

Instead of or in addition to giving money directly to the candidate, a PAC may engage in **issue advocacy** that might at times support the candidate but is independent of the candidate's control. The candidate need not report these independent expenditures on contribution disclosure statements. PACs may also spend money to support an issue rather than a specific candidate or to support such activities as "get out the vote" campaigns. In 2018 there were 2,037 active PACs in Texas that cumulatively spent just over $4 million. The Texas Association of Realtors was the state's largest PAC in the 2018 cycle, raising nearly $2 million to help candidates who support its preferred policies.[28]

issue advocacy independent spending by individuals or interest groups on a campaign issue but not directly tied to a particular candidate

Campaign contributions can be, to a considerable degree, classified in terms of the economic interests represented by the contributors. The "Who Are Texans?" graphic on page 201 shows that the largest contributor to candidates for the Texas legislature in 2017 was the finance, insurance, and real estate sector. This sector is a major part of the Texas economy and is subject to significant state regulation, characteristics that also apply to general business, energy and natural resources, construction, and health care. Compared with business, political parties, agriculture, and even candidates providing funds to their own campaigns, labor represents only a small amount of campaign spending.

Getting Out the Vote

Getting out the vote on Election Day is an important and difficult task. Both the Republican and the Democratic parties spend much time and money making sure that their voters get to the polls and vote for their candidates. In recent years, get-out-the-vote (GOTV) efforts by both parties have involved mining so-called big databases to identify people who are likely to vote for their candidates, then calling these people on the phone and visiting them at home. Battleground Texas is the latest attempt by the Democratic Party to identify potential Democratic voters, make them familiar with Democratic positions and candidates, and get them to vote. Similar efforts have been made by the Republican Party in recent years, particularly those identifying with the Tea Party movement.

GOTV initiatives also can be an important part of interest-group activity. The most successful GOTV campaign run by an interest group was that conducted in 1988 by the Texas Medical Association, which sought to elect its slate of candidates to the Texas Supreme Court. Physicians were encouraged to give to TEXPAC, the medical association PAC, as well as to make individual contributions to certain candidates. Additionally, they were given slate cards with recommended candidates, literature endorsing these candidates, and even expensively produced videotapes. They were asked to encourage not only their families and friends but also their patients to vote for the candidates. Of the five candidates TEXPAC supported, four won. The effort by the medical association was remarkable for its fund-raising success and for its reaching and mobilizing the grass roots.[29]

Most efforts by interest groups, however, are far less sophisticated. Generally, interest-group PACs simply provide resources for the candidates to get out the vote. In the 2010 primary campaign, Texans for Lawsuit Reform, which has had spectacular successes in forwarding its agenda over the past 15 years, suffered a remarkable failure. Although it contributed $602,290 to 28 candidates, 53 percent of this money was spent on 4 incumbent candidates who lost their primaries, and another 28 percent went to 3 candidates—2 of them incumbents—who were forced into runoff elections. Obviously, Texans for Lawsuit Reform thought these candidates were important for achieving its agenda, but it seemed questionable for an interest group to pump huge amounts of money into the campaigns of incumbent candidates who do not have the political strength to win even in their party's primary. And the high degree of financial support for candidates can be hurtful to the candidate. In one of these races, the winning candidate's main issue was that the defeated incumbent had received money from an organization known for giving huge sums to Republican candidates. This contribution, contended the winner, was proof that the incumbent Democrat was not a real Democrat but a Republican with a Democratic label.[30]

Nevertheless, Texans for Lawsuit Reform scored impressive victories in the 2012 general election. It gave more than $250,000 to Republican Donna Campbell to defeat moderate Republican state senator Jeff Wentworth and $463,393 to Republican James White to keep his seat.[31] In more recent elections, Texans for Lawsuit Reform has focused on supporting incumbents, rather than seeking to oust legislators. They were successful in defending Sarah Davis of Houston, a moderate Republican who was challenged by a more conservative Republican in the 2018 primary.[32]

Defeating Opponents

Generally, incumbents have a huge advantage over challengers in elections. Since they are officeholders, they usually have greater name recognition than challengers, and it is easy for them to get publicity by holding town hall meetings, by announcing the relocation of new businesses to the district, or simply by attending community events. Additionally, they usually have an established network of supporters who helped them get into office at least once previously.

Because of the incumbency advantage, it is far safer for interest groups to try to work with incumbents than challengers. Campaign contributions, for example, overwhelmingly go to incumbents (see Figure 6.1). In the 2018 campaign for the Texas legislature, candidates raised more than $90 million.[33] The total amounts contributed to some incumbent legislators are spectacularly large. Former Speaker of the House Joe Straus, for example, received $8,429,380 in contributions in 2015—no doubt in recognition that he was in a position to advance or hinder much legislation. In the Texas Senate in 2017, Senator Kel Seliger (R-Amarillo) faced a challenge from another Republican who lost to him in 2013 by only five percentage points. Seliger's $1.7 million proved to be enough

Which Interest Groups Contribute the Most?

Contributions to Texas Legislature Candidates, 2016

 = $250,000

Contributions to Democrats

Contributions to Republicans

79% (R)
21% (D)

Finance, insurance, and real estate
$11,549,214

80% (R)
20% (D)

Energy and natural resources
$7,299,565

51% (R)
49% (D)

Lawyers and lobbyists
$6,929,174

83% (R)
17% (D)

General business
$6,807,250

64% (R)
36% (D)

Health
$6,383,411

75% (R)
25% (D)

Construction
$3,146,752

43% (R)
57% (D)

Labor
$2,306,021

83% (R)
17% (D)

Agriculture
$2,181,590

73% (R)
27% (D)

Communications and electronics
$1,858,172

72% (R)
28% (D)

Transportation
$1,502,829

77% (R)
23% (D)

Defense
$185,975

Interest groups try to achieve favorable policies not only by lobbying members of the Texas legislature directly but also by influencing who becomes members of the legislature in the first place by donating to the election campaigns of favored candidates. The chart below breaks down contributions from employees of different industries by party in 2016.

QUANTITATIVE REASONING

- Which group contributes the highest percentage of contributions to Democrats? Republicans? Why might these groups provide strong support to a particular party?

- Which group provides the lowest total dollar amount to candidates of either political party? Why do you think this group provides less than other groups?

SOURCE: National Institution on State Money in Politics Industry Influence, www.followthemoney.org (accessed 3/10/18).

FIGURE 6.1

Contributions to Incumbents and Challengers for the Texas Legislature, 2018

SOURCE: National Institute on Money in State Politics.

to fend off a challenge from former Midland Mayor Mike Canon, whose campaign war chest was only $89,000.[34]

Of course, sometimes an interest group does not want to help a candidate or even pressure a candidate; it wants to defeat that candidate. Trying to do so can be a risky strategy, however, because if the candidate wins, then the interest group will be faced with a public official not only unsympathetic to its policy goals but also displeased with the interest group for its opposition. When that happens, the interest group will often "get well" or "get on the late train"—that is, make a substantial political contribution to the winning candidate whom it formerly opposed. Often, winning candidates have significant campaign debts after a grueling election battle, and they appreciate the late contributions of former enemies seeking to make amends.

Although "late-train" contributions may improve the relationship between officials and interest groups, usually candidates reserve a special loyalty for those supporters who backed them early. Without support at the very beginning of a campaign, it is hard for a candidate to build an organization and get the support necessary to make a decent campaign start. That is why early supporters are so valuable, and why the best lobbyists start early in trying to develop relationships with candidates and with new legislators. One national PAC, EMILY's List, is funded by women and provides early campaign contributions to female candidates. EMILY stands for Early Money Is Like Yeast, and yeast helps raise the dough—early money helps raise even more money. Legislators remember who was with them at the beginning of their political careers—and this memory can be immensely beneficial to the lobby that cultivated that early relationship.[35]

Sometimes PACs give to both candidates as a way to avoid alienating either one, though the possibility remains that such dual giving will wind up alienating both. At other times, interest groups simply don't care if they alienate a candidate. The 2010

Democratic primary election between state representatives Tara Rios Ybarra and Jose Manuel Lozano highlighted the lines that can clearly separate interest groups during a campaign. Texans for Lawsuit Reform contributed $256,610 to Ybarra, which was 56 percent of her campaign funds. Ybarra lost to Lozano, who was backed by trial lawyers completely unsympathetic to the goals of Texans for Lawsuit Reform.[36]

An extraordinary battle occurred in the 2012 Republican primary when Texans for Lawsuit Reform backed railroad commissioner Elizabeth Ames Jones in her challenge to Republican state senator Jeff Wentworth. Wentworth had served nearly five years in the Texas House before being elected to the state senate in 1992. He appeared to be well established and unbeatable, and an early poll showed him with a large lead. But although Wentworth had supported 21 of 23 bills designated by Texans for Lawsuit Reform as "major" legislation, he angered the interest group by criticizing a 2003 constitutional amendment that limited the amounts patients could receive in medical malpractice suits. While Wentworth was defeated, it was not by Jones, but by Donna Campbell, who had Tea Party backing. Nevertheless, Wentworth blamed his defeat on the "mammoth $2 million–plus negative campaign launched against me by Texans for Lawsuit Reform."[37] The defeat no doubt sent a message to Republican lawmakers that they had better not cross this particular interest group.

When an interest group is convinced that it cannot work with a public official toward its policy goals, it may undertake an all-out effort to defeat that official. As the examples above show, however, spending money by no means guarantees success. Dr. James Leininger is one of the biggest contributors to Republican candidates in Texas. In the 2006 election cycle, he gave over $5 million to Republican candidates in Texas, through both individual contributions and gifts to PACs that then made contributions. Leininger and some of the PACs he supports are strong supporters of school vouchers, and much of this money backed challengers to Republican incumbents unfavorable to vouchers. But the effort was unsuccessful, and the result, according to Texans for Public Justice, was a legislature "even less receptive to vouchers than its predecessor."[38]

A U.S. Supreme Court decision in 2009, *Citizens United v. Federal Election Commission*, allowed political contributors to create an organization that opposed powerful incumbents without having to disclose its donors. In the 2012 election cycle, Empower Texans moved several hundred thousand dollars through its nonprofit organization and thus avoided having to disclose its contributors. The nonprofit spent about $290,000 on mailers, about $40,000 on Internet ads, and about $18,000 on robo-calls. Another nonprofit that does not have to report donors is the Texas Organizing Project, which spent about $234,000 mostly supporting then–Harris County sheriff Adrian Garcia and 14 other local candidates. In the November 2018 elections, Empower Texans spent $4 million supporting Republican candidates for office in legislative races. In all, the group endorsed 42 candidates statewide. Only fourteen emerged victorious after the votes were counted. The group's heavy funds were not enough to counteract Democratic strength, especially in suburban areas around Austin, Dallas, and Houston.

In January 2018 the Texas Association of Business came under fire for funding its political action committee with money from these unknown sources. While the organization claims the money was only used for administrative expenses, critics have called for the Texas Ethics Commission to investigate and determine if proper procedures were followed.[39] These new funding structures in which donors do not have to be reported are known as sources of **dark money**.[40]

dark money political contributions whose donors are not legally required to be disclosed

Interest-Group Capture

interest-group capture process by which a government agency comes to serve the objectives of the interests that the agency is supposed to regulate

Interest-group capture occurs when an interest group has such influence over an agency of government that it is said that the agency primarily serves the objectives of the interest group. Interest groups representing particular industries can develop long-term relationships in a number of ways with the agencies that regulate the industries they represent. For example, interest groups can donate money to the election or re-election of agency officials who must seek election to their office. Subject to certain ethics rules, industries can also hire former agency officials to work for them as lobbyists. The closer the connection between the agency and the industry, the more complete is the capture.

Such interest-group capture may have occurred with the Texas Railroad Commission, which has the primary responsibility for regulating the state's oil and natural gas industry, pipelines, and coal and uranium surface-mining operations. The commission is run by three statewide elected officials who serve staggered six-year terms. Although one unsuccessful candidate included railroad safety in his campaign platform, the Railroad Commission's name is long outdated, and the commission today has nothing to do with railroads.[41]

In 2010, Public Citizen, a consumer advocacy group, published a highly critical report on the commission, in which it said "political spending is out of control, well over half of campaign donations coming from the very industries the commission is supposed to regulate. Real or perceived, this creates a conflict of interest. Railroad commissioner is seen as a springboard to higher elected office in the state, giving influence-peddlers more incentive to curry favor and sitting commissioners to amass campaign war chests. . . . Campaign donations coming from regulated industries present a very real problem, inserting the probability that regulatory decisions are made in favor of large donors rather than the public's interest."[42]

The Texas Railroad Commission regulates Texas's oil and gas drilling. Some say that this commission has been captured by those special interests, which sometimes advocates controversial procedures such as fracking.

A Public Citizen report pointed out that by 2010, 80 percent of donations to incumbent commissioners were from the industries they regulated, up from 45 percent in 2001, and that there had been nearly a tenfold increase in donations. Additionally, the size of individual donations had increased—in 2000, 80 percent of donations were $1,000 or more; in 2010, 92 percent were.[43] In the 2012 election an incumbent, Barry Smitherman, received $5,144,683 in campaign contributions, of which the oil and gas industry contributed the most among business/industrial interest groups. In a race for an open seat, Christi Craddick won with $2,850,158 in contributions. Again, contributions were led by the oil and gas industry.[44]

In the 2016 Republican primary for seats on the Railroad Commission, three candidates proposed banning donations from people or organizations that have business before the commission. These three candidates, however, raised very little funds for their campaigns and lost their primaries.[45] Of course, that so many contributions should come from the oil and gas industry should not be surprising, since the commission is the main regulatory agency for oil and gas. Other industries do not have the concerns about the commission's work that would cause them to make major contributions, and interest groups such as environmental organizations lack the resources to compete with the oil and gas industry in backing candidates.

The staff of the Sunset Advisory Commission prepared a report in 2012 that attempted to deal with some of the concerns that the Texas Railroad Commission had been captured by the oil and gas industry. Among other things, the report recommended that the commission's name be changed to realistically reflect its contemporary duties: the Texas Energy Resources Commission. It also recommended that solicitation and receipt of campaign contributions by commissioners or candidates seeking the office be limited to an 18-month period around the election rather than throughout the six-year term of office. It recommended that commissioners be banned from knowingly accepting contributions from those with contested cases before the commission, and that they be required to resign their office if they become candidates for another elected office. Further, it recommended that independent hearing examiners be used in contested cases involving oil and gas.[46]

House Speaker Pro Tem Dennis Bonnen was especially concerned that two sitting railroad commissioners had recently run for the U.S. Senate while retaining their offices and raising money from the oil and gas industry. While the efforts to reform the commission were publicly endorsed by the then-incumbent railroad commissioners, Bonnen claimed they were privately lobbying to weaken the proposals. In any event, the reform proposals failed in the 2013 legislature.[47] In 2017, Governor Abbott signed a bill reauthorizing the commission for another twelve years, despite criticisms that reforms suggested by the Sunset Commission were not implemented.[48]

Individuals as Lobbyists

 Explain how ordinary individuals can influence Texas government

Although interest groups clearly have an advantage in influencing the legislative process, sometimes ordinary individuals can have a remarkable impact on public policy. As we saw at the beginning of the chapter in the case of Dineen Majcher and school testing,

Occasionally, ordinary individuals can have a direct influence on policy. Tyrus Burks (right) lobbied the legislature to require landlords to buy and install visual smoke alarms for hearing-impaired tenants who requested them.

a persistent individual with a well-reasoned argument can make a difference. Another example involves Tyrus Burks, who lost his wife and two children in a late-night electrical fire in West Dallas. Burks did not awaken in time to save them because he is deaf and did not hear the audible smoke alarm. Texas's state property code required the installation of audible smoke alarms but not visual alarms. In 2009, Burks became an advocate for a bill that would require property managers to buy visual smoke alarms if hearing-impaired tenants requested them and to install the alarms in visible locations such as bedrooms. Supported by state senator Royce West, the Sephra Burks Law, named for Tyrus's wife, who was also deaf, went into effect at the start of 2010. Tyrus Burks was an active lobbyist for the bill and gave legislative testimony in support of it with the aid of a sign language interpreter.

Burks's efforts benefited from the support of the Texas Apartment Association, a major interest group representing apartment property interests, who backed the bill. Burks's story was tragic, and his argument was compelling. It would have been difficult for opposition to emerge against such a proposal. Still, his efforts resulted in a major victory for the deaf, who are protected by such a law requiring visual smoke alarms in only three other states and the District of Columbia.[49] Burks's achievement demonstrates that individuals can, at least sometimes, be successful lobbyists.

The problem is that relatively few Texans are engaged in their neighborhood, in their community, or in politics, and thus much lobbying is left to organized interest groups with professional lobbyists. Table 6.1 provides a number of measures of civic engagement, and all show Texas considerably lower than the national average on these measures. Texas is near the bottom of the nation in terms of measures of social connectedness that would lead to civic involvement, such as discussing politics with friends or family, group involvement, frequent communication with friends and family, and even trust in all or most of the people in the neighborhood. Nor, in comparison with other

TABLE 6.1

Measures of Texas Civic Health

	PERCENTAGE OF TEXANS AGREEING (%)	NATIONAL AVERAGE (%)	RANKING OF TEXAS AMONG THE STATES
Contacted or visited public official	9%	12%	49
Discuss politics with friends or family a few times a week or more	26	29	44
Communicate with friends and family frequently	78	79	41
Trust all or most people in the neighborhood	50	57	47
Donate $25 or more to charitable or religious organizations	47	52	43
Group involvement	38	39	37
Volunteer activity	25	27	42
Registered to vote	62	65	42
Voting	36	45	50

SOURCE: Regina Lawrence, Deborah Wise, and Emily Einsohn, *Texas Civic Health Index* (Austin: Annette Strauss Institute for Civic Life, 2013).

Americans, are Texans involved in volunteer activity or charitable donations. They tend not to contact or visit their public officials, vote, or register to vote. With such low levels of civic engagement, individual effects on the Texas political process are likely to be low.[50]

Interestingly, while in one survey 52 percent of Texans claimed they were very interested in politics and public affairs and 37 percent said they were somewhat interested, Texas has the lowest proportion of actual voters of any state. Texans give all sorts of reasons for not voting, the most common being that they are too busy or that work conflicts with voting and the next most common being that they either are not interested or believe their vote does not matter.[51] Of course, the low level of voting participation means that organized interest groups fill the void in political activity and can wield vast influence in the state's political process.

★ ★

Interest Groups and the Future of Texas

THOUGH NO SINGLE INTEREST group or coalition of interest groups dominates Texas politics, by far most lobbyists represent business interests, and the bulk of PAC money comes from them as well. Often, of course, businesses are pitted against one another in the political process. Also, public interest, civil rights, consumer, and environmental groups may still succeed by mobilizing public opinion and influencing the media. However, only a few interest groups offer alternatives to business perspectives on policy issues. Less frequently, ordinary individuals are able to influence public policy. Although they tend to be at a disadvantage in terms of money and other resources, dedicated individuals with a compelling argument sometimes succeed in lobbying for specific legislation. This is especially true when they are pursuing goals that do not put them in conflict with well-organized and well-funded interest groups.

The influence of interest groups in Texas shows no signs of diminishing. As long as federal and state law allow donations and the creation of PACs and other groups, we will see the strong influence of interest groups not only in Austin but also in Washington. Texas is a pro-business state, and the Texas Association of Business will continue to be a dominant interest group representing the concerns of corporations and entrepreneurs in Austin. At times, however, business interests might conflict with those of other groups, especially on the issue of immigration. Business leaders have often welcomed more immigrants because of the low-cost labor they provide. While the state is limited in what it can do to curtail immigration, the election of Lieutenant Governor Dan Patrick and his emphasis on curtailing immigration might pose a counter narrative to business interest groups. As Texas becomes more diverse and more immigrants settle in the state, the response by different interest groups will be something to watch.

Use 🐰 INQUIZITIVE to help you study and master this material.

Interest Groups in the Political Process

> • Define interest groups, and describe the major
> ways they try to influence Texas government
> (pp. 185–98)

Interest groups in Texas are organizations of interested citizens who band together to influence public policy. Lobbyists are hired to cultivate relationships with legislators and convince them of their clients' interests. The goal of lobbyists is to gain access to policy makers to persuade them to support the positions of the interest group.

Key Terms
interest group (p. 185)
free rider problem (p. 187)
bundling (p. 189)
lobbyist (p. 190)

Practice Quiz
1. The "8F Crowd"
   a) was a group of legislators who failed the eighth grade.
   b) was a group of extremely wealthy Texans who met in Suite 8F of the Lamar Hotel in Houston and controlled Texas politics for 40 years.
   c) were 25 legislators who boycotted the eighth session of the legislature in order to prevent the legislators from taking any action because it lacked a quorum.
   d) was made up of eight lobbyists who were close friends of the governor.
   e) were the eight most powerful officials in the state who met in Suite F of the Austin State Office Building.

2. Interest groups provide public officials with all the following *except*
   a) information.
   b) money.
   c) media coverage.
   d) votes.
   e) committee assignments.

3. The goals of interest groups include all *except*
   a) electing people to office in order to support the groups' goals.
   b) influencing those who control government.
   c) educating the public and members about issues of importance to the group.
   d) providing campaign funds for favored candidates.
   e) maintaining a heterogeneous membership.

4. Interest groups have an advantage over individuals in influencing policy because interest groups usually have
   a) more time to influence officials.
   b) greater expertise than individuals.
   c) more money to influence elections.
   d) more staff.
   e) all of the above

5. When interest groups combine small contributions from many sources to form one large contribution, it is called
   a) bundling.
   b) compacting.
   c) cracking.
   d) polling.
   e) packing.

6. The most important thing interest groups need to be effective is
   a) the support of a majority of Texans.
   b) office space in Austin.
   c) a variety of issues on which to lobby.
   d) a large, paid staff.
   e) access to politicians.

7. Trial lawyers are which type of interest group?
   a) professional group
   b) public employee group
   c) single-issue group
   d) consumer group
   e) business group

8. Interest groups often hire former legislators as lobbyists to
a) gain greater access to current legislators.
b) benefit from the policy expertise of former legislators.
c) benefit from the personal "insider" knowledge of the former legislator.
d) all of the above
e) none of the above

9. Lobbyists are
a) all corrupt.
b) all unethical.
c) important sources of information for legislators.
d) harmful to the democratic process.
e) never retired legislators.

Another Side to Lobbying

- **Describe the role of PACs in Texas elections (pp. 198–205)**

Political action committees (PACs) are private groups that raise and distribute funds for election campaigns. Interest groups play a major role in getting out the vote. Interest-group money can play a major role in defeating as well as electing candidates.

Key Terms
political action committee (PAC) (p. 199)
issue advocacy (p. 199)
dark money (p. 203)
interest-group capture (p. 204)

Practice Quiz
10. In Texas, the most powerful interest groups represent which interests?
a) consumer
b) civil rights
c) business
d) owners of oil wells
e) public employee

11. PACs are used to
a) stir the public's interest in politics.
b) raise money from individuals, which is then bundled and given to candidates.
c) create media campaigns to influence the course of government.
d) create grassroots campaigns.
e) all of the above

12. One of the most important grassroots tactics of interest groups is
a) to gain support from all the mayors of towns in a district.
b) to get out the vote.
c) to form political alliances with executive and legislative leaders.
d) to lobby the judicial branch of national and state government.
e) to interpret the needs of their members.

13. *Dark money* refers to
a) money that is illegally donated to politicians for their re-election.
b) money that cannot be used to pay typical campaign expenditures.
c) vouchers that candidates can use to fund their campaigns.
d) donated money that does not have to be reported by a campaign.
e) money that is printed on special dark green paper specifically formulated for campaigns.

14. *Capture theory* refers to the idea that
a) interest groups are controlled by politicians.
b) through long-term relationships, government interests come to serve the objectives of an interest group.
c) politicians work for the public good by controlling special interests.
d) labor unions are controlled by business.
e) business interests are captured by labor unions.

Individuals as Lobbyists

> • **Explain how ordinary individuals can influence Texas government (pp. 205–7)**

Citizens can lobby their legislators by calling, writing, or visiting their offices. Industries and well-financed interests can afford professional lobbyists to try to influence legislation, but legislators will listen to individual citizens, especially if they join together in large numbers.

Practice Quiz

15. Individuals have the best chance to influence public policy when they
    a) are not opposed by organized interest groups.
    b) are polite.
    c) entertain legislators.
    d) vote.
    e) live in Austin.

16. On the measures of civic health, Texas
    a) ranks higher than most other states.
    b) ranks lower than most other states.
    c) ranks about the same as other states.
    d) is stronger than average on some measures and weaker than average on others.
    e) ranks highly when it comes to Texans contacting elected officials, compared to other states.

Protesters against Texas's proposed ban on sanctuary cities rallied in the State Capitol as the legislature debated the bill. Discussions on the floor of the legislature were highly contentious and turned into a shouting match between two representatives.

The Legislature

WHY THE TEXAS LEGISLATURE MATTERS

During the tumultuous legislative session in 2017, something unprecedented happened on the Texas House floor. An escalation of tension between two legislators nearly led to what could have been a tragic situation. While members of the legislature have always had heated debates and vigorous disagreements about public policy, what occurred in the last legislative session was unusual and indicative of today's polarizing political climate.

During the debate on the controversial bill taking aim at sanctuary cities in Texas, Irving Republican representative Matt Rinaldi noticed a person in the viewing area of the legislature with a sign that read, "I am illegal and I am here to stay." Upon seeing the sign, Rinaldi reportedly called Immigration and Naturalization Services (INS) to report this individual as well as others for being in the country illegally. Upon hearing of this, his colleague, Representative Poncho Nevárez, a Democrat from Eagle Pass, became engaged in a verbal shouting match. Each representative threatened the other. Rinaldi reportedly threatened to shoot Nevárez in self-defense while Nevárez apparently suggested they settle their skirmish in the parking lot. The scuffle continued with other legislators intervening to settle the two men's escalation. While neither legislator was injured or harmed in any way, this episode highlights a growing tension in the Texas legislature on matters pertaining to public policy.[1]

Why is this story about the scuffle inside the legislature important? In many ways, the Texas legislature reflects the state of Texas and, more broadly, the country. As Texas—like the United States overall—has become more polarized, conflict has arisen not only inside the legislature, as the scuffle above shows, but also in town squares, city parks, and workplaces. The stakes are high, and the legislature is the place where important decisions about how Texas will be governed are made.

The Texas legislature has become less civil and more tense, especially with the introduction of deeply controversial bills such as the "bathroom bill" (see Chapter 10)

and abortion restrictions (see Chapter 12). In the past, legislators debated on the House floor, voted, and then proceeded to meet for dinner and conversation. This sense of camaraderie has become a relic in the Texas legislature, and it is not only the case that Democrats and Republicans are feuding. Republicans have internal divisions between moderates and more conservative members. All of these differences in the legislature reflect our increasingly tense political climate. What the Texas legislature does makes an important difference in the lives of everyone in Texas. Because the stakes are so high, passionate debates can arise and tempers can flare. As the state becomes more divided into different political factions, it is all the more important for Texans to know how the legislature works in order to elect representatives who will serve their interests and work to enact policies that reflect their vision for a safe and prosperous Texas.

CHAPTER GOALS

- Describe the organization and basic rules of the legislature (pp. 215–19)
- Outline the legislative and nonlegislative powers of the legislature (pp. 220–23)
- Trace the process through which law is made in Texas (pp. 223–34)
- Analyze how party leadership and partisanship affect power in the legislature (pp. 234–40)
- Explain the politics of redistricting (pp. 240–43)

Structure of the Texas Legislature

Describe the organization and basic rules of the legislature

The Texas state legislature is the most important representative institution in the state. Members share many of the duties and responsibilities that are taken up at the national level by members of the U.S. Congress. Like members of the U.S. Congress, the members of the Texas House and Senate are responsible for bringing the interests and concerns of their constituencies directly into the democratic political processes. But the important constitutional and institutional differences between the U.S. Congress and the Texas state legislature must also be taken into account to understand the role that the legislature plays in democracy in Texas.

Bicameralism

Like the U.S. Congress and all the states except Nebraska, Texas has a **bicameral** legislature, with two chambers: the Texas House of Representatives and the Texas Senate. The legislature's 150 House members and 31 senators meet in regular session for 140 days every odd-numbered year. Senators serve four-year terms, and House members serve for two years. Each represents a single-member district, with each House member representing approximately 168,000 people and each senator 811,000. A Texas state senator now represents more people than does a member of the U.S. House of Representatives. Elections are held in November of even-numbered years, and senators and House members take office in January of odd-numbered years.

Bicameralism creates interesting dynamics in a legislature. For one thing, it means that before a law is passed, it will be voted on by two deliberative bodies representing different constituencies. If a bill cannot be killed in one house, it can be killed or modified in the other body. In 2009, for example, the Texas Senate passed legislation to allow college students and faculty with concealed handgun licenses to carry their firearms on campus. That legislation, however, was killed in the Texas House of Representatives.[2] In 2011 the Senate again passed a bill with an amendment allowing guns on campus, a bill that was also supported by a majority of House members. However, this time the bill failed in the House because of a successful parliamentary objection that the gun amendment was not germane to the bill it amended, which dealt with scholarships.[3] In 2013 a bill allowing guns on campus passed the House, but the bill died in the Senate when it failed to get the two-thirds vote needed in that chamber for the bill to be brought to the floor for discussion and a vote.[4] In 2015, however, this bill to allow holders of concealed handgun licenses to carry firearms on campus was finally passed, and it led to public demonstrations and protests, especially at the University of Texas at Austin.

One distinctive aspect of bicameralism in Texas is that the author of a bill in one house that is then amended in the other body has the option of accepting or rejecting the amendment. If the author accepts the amendment, the bill moves forward; if the author rejects it, the bill is killed.

bicameral having a legislative assembly composed of two chambers or houses

Before becoming law in Texas, a bill must pass in both houses of the legislature. In 2013 the legislature passed a law forbidding guns on college campuses unless specifically authorized by the campus.

Bicameralism also allows a member of one body of the legislature to retaliate against a member of either body for not cooperating on desired legislation. For example, a "local and consent" calendar in the House is usually reserved for uncontroversial bills or bills limited to a localized problem. In order for a bill from that calendar to be passed, there has to be no objection to it from any member of the House. That requirement provides a perfect opportunity for members to retaliate against other members for perceived slights.[5]

Sessions of the Legislature

Not all state legislatures meet for the same time periods. Some meet every year, like the U.S. Congress. Texas's legislature generally meets every other year unless the governor calls it to meet between regular sessions.

regular session the 140-day period, occurring only in odd-numbered years, during which the Texas legislature meets to consider and pass bills

biennial occurring every two years

Regular Sessions   The Texas Constitution specifies that **regular sessions** of the Texas legislature be held for 140 days in odd-numbered years. The **biennial** legislative sessions have their origin in the nineteenth-century idea that legislative service is a part-time job and the belief that short, biennial sessions would limit the power of the legislature. For a few years, legislators were encouraged to end their work early by being paid for only 120 days of service.

Thousands of bills and resolutions are introduced into the legislature during a regular session, and the 140-day limitation places a considerable restriction on legislators' ability to deal with this workload. In the 2017 regular legislative session, for example, 6,631 bills were introduced and 1,211 passed. The governor vetoed 51 of the bills passed by the legislature.[6] Hundreds of bills pass in the last hours of a legislative session, most with little or no debate. More die in the end-of-session crush of business because there isn't time to consider them.

special session a legislative session called by the governor that addresses an agenda set by him or her and that lasts no longer than 30 days

Special Sessions   If the legislature does not finish its business by the end of the regular session or if problems requiring legislation arise between regular sessions, the governor may call a **special session**. Special sessions last no more than 30 days, but there is no limit to the number of special sessions a governor can call, and the governor sets their agenda. Texas has averaged one special session per year since 1876. Although years may go by with no special session, in some years there may be three or four.

The ability to call a special session and set its agenda provides the governor with control over which issues are discussed and what bills are passed (see Chapter 8). In many instances, the governor, the Speaker of the Texas House, the lieutenant governor, and various committee chairs will meet to decide what will be done to solve the problem at hand. Once the leaders address the issue and develop solutions, the governor calls the special session.

Once the session begins, the governor can open it to different issues. At times, the governor bargains for a legislator's vote in return for adding to the special session agenda an issue of importance to that legislator. In 2003, Governor Rick Perry called three special sessions of the legislature to address congressional redistricting. In 2004 a fourth special session was called to address school finance. In 2005 two special sessions addressed school finance. There was also a special session in 2006, 2009, and 2011. In

2013 two special sessions were called to deal with Texas abortion laws, and in 2017 one special session was called by Governor Abbott to deal with the "bathroom bill" as well as 19 other issues selected by the governor.

Between legislative sessions, members serve on interim committees that may require a few days of their time each month. Legislators are also frequently called on to present programs to schools, colleges, and civic clubs. They supervise the staff of their district offices and address the needs of their constituents. Special sessions, interim committee meetings, speeches, and constituent services require long hours with little remuneration. Many members devote more than 40 hours a week to legislative business in addition to maintaining their full-time jobs.

In the twenty-first century, Texas is a modern state with more than 80 percent of its population living in metropolitan areas. Population growth continues at a rapid rate, and the state's economic output exceeds that of many nations. Using part-time legislators serving biennial 140-day sessions may not work well anymore in allowing the legislature to respond quickly and effectively to problems that arise in such a large and complex state.

Representation in the Texas Legislature

There are 150 Texas House districts and 31 Texas Senate districts. One senator or one member of the House represents each district, a system called representation by **single-member districts**. Districts must be roughly equal in population. House districts each contain about 168,000 people, while Senate districts contain about 811,000. Some districts are geographically small, like House district 137, which is one of 29 districts in Harris County in the Houston metropolitan area. Some districts are large, like Senate district 19, which covers 35,000 square miles and parts of 17 counties in West Texas.

The constitutional requirements for becoming a member of the Texas legislature are minimal. A senator must be a U.S. citizen, a qualified voter, and a resident of the state for at least five years and of the district for at least one year. Additionally, the senator must be at least 26 years of age. Members of the House must be at least 21 years of age, U.S. citizens, qualified voters, and residents of the state for two years and of the district for one year. These requirements are in keeping with the political philosophy of those who wrote the Constitution of 1876. They believed holding public office required little or no formal training and should be open to most citizens.

In Texas, the typical legislator is white, male, Protestant, college educated, and affluent and has a professional or business occupation. This profile does not mean that others cannot be elected to the state legislature, but it does indicate that individuals with most of these characteristics have a distinct advantage. Members of the legislature must have jobs that allow them the flexibility to campaign for office and to work in the legislature for 140 days every other year, as well as in special legislative sessions and meetings of committees when the legislature is not in session. Thus, about one-third of the members of the legislature are attorneys. The legal profession is one of the few careers that both pays well and offers the flexibility a legislator needs. Lawyers who serve in the legislature may even gain increased legal business either from interests with legislative concerns or because of the enhanced visibility of a lawyer-legislator.[7]

Legislators have the power to get things done for or in the name of **constituents**. Efforts on behalf of constituents may involve legislative activity, such as introducing a

single-member district a district in which one official is elected rather than multiple officials

constituent a person who is represented by an elected official bill or voting on a resolution. Often, however, these efforts involve nonlegislative activity, such as arranging an appointment for a constituent with a government agency that regulates some aspect of the constituent's life, writing a letter of recommendation for a constituent, or giving a speech to a civic group in the legislator's district. These kinds of nonlegislative activities are called **constituent service**.

When the legislature is not in session, representatives are still actively involved in promoting their agendas. In the modern age, representatives have an increased presence in social media such as Facebook, Twitter, and Instagram. Unlike members of Congress, Texas legislators have to simultaneously make a living and continue to represent their constituents if they hope to to be re-elected.

"Who Are Texans: Who Are the Members of the Texas Legislature?" shows the proportions of minorities and women serving in the legislature. Although those numbers have increased over the years, they are not in proportion to the shares of these groups in the Texas population. Civil rights laws have increased voting by minorities by providing protection for political districts where minorities form the majority of the population. (The 2013 U.S. Supreme Court decision overturning part of the Voting Rights Act may lead to reduced legal protection for such districts.) Thus, more minority officeholders have been elected and, as the Hispanic population in Texas increases, additional Latino legislators are likely to be elected. Women have also had an increased role in politics, especially since the 1970s.

Republicans control both houses of the Texas legislature. In 2019 there were 12 Democrats and 19 Republicans in the Texas Senate and 67 Democrats and 83 Republicans in the Texas House of Representatives.

How Much Do Legislators Get Paid?

Legislators in Texas cannot expect to live on their legislative salaries alone. In keeping with the Texas constitutional tradition of a low-cost, part-time legislature, Texas legislators receive a salary of only $7,200 per year. Legislators also receive a payment of $190 a day when the legislature is in session. When the legislature is not in session, legislators may claim up to 12 days per month of **per diem** pay if they are in Austin on official business, or 16 days if they are committee chairs. The legislators themselves determine what qualifies as official business, and it is common to pay expenses from officeholder expense accounts and to pocket the per diem so that it becomes a salary supplement. Legislative retirement pensions are very generous. The pension is tied to district judges' salaries, which are $140,000 a year. That salary is multiplied by the years of service of the legislator times 2.3 percent. A legislator who has served 10 years thus would qualify for a pension of $32,200 per year, and one who has served 20 years for a pension of $64,400 per year. Lawmakers are eligible for pensions with at least 8 years of service. With 8 years of service, the lawmaker can start collecting a pension at age 60. With 10 years of service, a lawmaker can start collecting at age 50.[8]

Originally, per diem rates were set by the Texas Constitution, and a constitutional amendment was necessary to change this restriction. In 1991, Texans adopted an amendment allowing the Texas Ethics Commission to propose changes in legislative salaries, which then require voter approval. At the start of each regular session, the Ethics Commission sets the legislative per diem. In 2015 the commission authorized a per diem increase to $190.

constituent service
nonlegislative activities legislators perform to assist people living in their districts, including writing letters of recommendation, giving speeches to civic groups, or working to solve a problem for someone in their community

per diem daily payment to a public official engaged in state business

Who Are the Members of the Texas Legislature?

The Texas legislature is designed to be a representative body, which looks and sounds like the state as a whole. How well does the legislature represent Texas? In many ways, the legislature does not look like Texas. The state is evenly split between men and women, while the legislature is three-quarters male. While the state has no ethnic majority in its population, more than two-thirds of Texas legislators are white. Perhaps the biggest differences, though, relate to socioeconomic status. Over half of the members of the legislature hold graduate degrees, while only 9 percent of the population does.

Gender

	Texas pop.	Texas House	Texas Senate
Female	50%	21%	29%
Male	50%	79%	71%

Key

Texas population

Texas Senate

Texas House of Representatives

SOURCES: For Texas legislature, numbers calculated by author based on data from the Directory of Elected Officials of the Texas Tribune, www.texastribune.org/directory. State demographic data calculated from the U.S. Census Bureau American Community Survey, www.census.gov (accessed 11/10/18).

Race

	Texas pop.	Texas House	Texas Senate
White	43%	64%	70%
African American	13%	13%	7%
Latino	39%	21%	23%
Asian	5%	2%	0%

Education*

	Texas pop.	Texas House	Texas Senate
< HS diploma	19%	0%	0%
High school grad.	48%	7%	3%
Associate's degree	17%	3%	0%
Bachelor's degree	7%	53%	39%
Graduate degree	9%	37%	58%

QUANTITATIVE REASONING

- How much do you think the racial, gender, and socio-economic makeup of the Texas legislature matters to the type of laws that the legislature passes? If the legislature had more people of color, more women, or more middle-class members, would it pass different policies?

- Why do you think that members of the Texas legislature come from the more educated, higher socioeconomic groups? Does the structure of the Texas legislature encourage or discourage people from particular occupations to run?

Occupation*

- Business
- Attorney
- Community service
- Health care
- Education
- Other

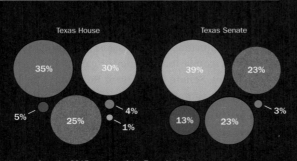

Texas House

35%   30%
5%   25%   4%   1%

Texas Senate

39%   23%
13%   23%   3%

* Education and occupation data are from the 2015 session of the Texas legislature.

Powers of the Legislature

Outline the legislative and nonlegislative powers of the legislature

The Texas legislature sets public policy by passing bills, but it also supervises the state bureaucracy through the budgetary process and the Sunset Act, an act that provides for the review and, when deemed appropriate, the termination of state agencies. This supervision is achieved using both legislative and nonlegislative powers. Legislative powers consist of passing bills and resolutions. Nonlegislative powers are those functions falling outside the lawmaking function.

Legislative Powers

bill a proposed law that has been sponsored by a member of the legislature and submitted to the clerk of the House or Senate

Bills Revenue bills must begin in the House of Representatives. All other bills may start in either the House or the Senate. For decades, a **bill** would be introduced in either the House or the Senate and work its way through the legislative process in that chamber before being considered by the other one. A bill introduced in the Senate would have to be passed by the Senate prior to going to the House. Today, it is customary for a bill to be introduced in the House and the same bill, a companion bill, to be introduced in the Senate at the same time. This simultaneous consideration of bills saves time in the legislature.

local bill a bill affecting only units of local government, such as a city, county, or special district

special bill a bill that gives an individual or corporation a special exemption from state law

general bill a bill that applies to all people and/or property in the state

There are three classifications of bills in the Texas legislature: (1) local bills, (2) special bills, and (3) general bills. **Local bills** affect only units of local government such as a city, a county, special districts, or more than one city in a county. A local bill, for example, might allow a county to create a sports authority such as the Harris County agency overseeing NRG Park or to establish a community college. **Special bills** give individuals or corporations an exemption from state law, and are less common than local bills. The Texas Constitution prohibits special bills for most purposes, since they can invite legal challenges. **General bills** apply to all people and/or property in the state. General bills define criminal behavior; establish standards for divorce, child custody, or bankruptcy; and address other matters affecting people and property throughout the state. There are a few standouts in the legislature in terms of high numbers of sponsorships. In the 2017 regular session of the legislature, for example, Senator Judith Zaffirini (D-Laredo) sponsored the most (376 bills). In the House, Representative Abel Herrero (D-Robstown) sponsored the most (488 bills).[9]

resolution an expression of opinion on an issue by a legislative body

concurrent resolution a resolution that is of interest to both chambers of the legislature and must pass both the House and Senate and generally be signed by the governor

Resolutions There are three types of **resolutions** in the Texas legislature: (1) concurrent resolutions, (2) joint resolutions, and (3) simple resolutions. **Concurrent resolutions** must pass both the House and Senate, and they require the governor's signature. These resolutions involve issues of interest to both chambers. They may request information from a state agency or call on Congress for some action. In the 2017 legislative session, Senate Concurrent Resolution 26, for example, called on Congress to review federal regulations on the oil and gas industry.

Joint resolutions require passage in both the House and Senate but do not require the governor's signature. The most common use of joint resolutions is to propose amendments to the Texas Constitution or to ratify amendments to the U.S. Constitution. Resolutions that propose amendments to the Texas Constitution require a two-thirds vote of the membership of both houses of the state legislature. Ratification of amendments to the U.S. Constitution requires a majority vote in both the Texas House and Senate.

Simple resolutions concern only the Texas House or the Senate, and they do not require the governor's signature. They are used to adopt rules, to request opinions from the attorney general, to appoint employees to office in the House or Senate, or to honor outstanding achievements by Texas residents. For example, in 2017, Senate resolution 159 by Senator Paul Bettencourt (R-Houston) commemorated the 150th anniversary of the Republican Party of Texas. That same year, HR 372 by Representative Oscar Longoria (D-Peñitas) recognized October 2018 as Texas Pecan Month.

Resolutions of honor or recognition are acted on without debate and without requiring members to read the resolution. Such resolutions are mostly symbolic acts that are designed to promote goodwill with voters. However, at times they can go terribly wrong. A Fort Worth doctor was twice honored by the Texas House of Representatives as the "doctor of the day." It was then reported, to the embarrassment of the House and the legislators who introduced him to the House, that the doctor was a registered sex offender who had been convicted of having a sexual relationship with a 17-year-old female patient.[10]

State senator Judith Zaffirini (D-Laredo) is an active sponsor of bills in the legislature.

Nonlegislative Powers

Nonlegislative powers include the power to serve constituents, electoral powers, investigative powers, directive and supervisory powers, and judicial powers. The functions of these powers fall outside the scope of passing bills and resolutions; however, the passage of legislation may be necessary to exercise these powers.

Electoral powers of the legislature consist of formally counting returns in the elections for governor and lieutenant governor. This task is accomplished during a joint session of the legislature when it is organized for the regular session.

Investigative powers can be exercised by the House of Representatives, by the Senate, or jointly by both bodies. The legislature can undertake to investigate problems facing the state, the integrity of a state agency, or almost anything else it wishes. A special investigative committee is established by a simple resolution creating the committee, establishing its jurisdiction, and explaining the need for the investigation. If the special committee is formed in the House, the Speaker appoints the members of the committee. The lieutenant governor appoints members for special committees in the Senate. The Speaker and the lieutenant governor share appointments for a joint investigation.

Directive and supervisory powers enable the legislature to have considerable control over the executive branch of government. Through the passage of the state budget, the legislature determines the size of the appropriation each state agency has to spend for the next two years. The amount of money an agency has determines how well it can

joint resolution a resolution, commonly a proposed amendment to the Texas Constitution or ratification of an amendment to the U.S. Constitution, that must pass both the House and Senate but that does not require the governor's signature

simple resolution a resolution that concerns only the Texas House or Senate, such as the adoption of a rule or the appointment of an employee, and that does not require the governor's signature

electoral power the legislature's mandated role in counting returns in the elections for governor and lieutenant governor

investigative power the power, exercised by the House, the Senate, or both chambers jointly, to investigate problems facing the state

directive and supervisory power the legislature's power over the executive branch; for example, the legislature determines the size of appropriations for state agencies

A Full-Time or Part-Time Legislature?

THE TEXAS legislature is a part-time, citizen legislature. It meets only once every two years for 140 days. Members of the Texas House are elected for two-year terms and are paid $7,200 per year. It is interesting to contrast the Texas legislature with a professional legislature, such as New York's. The New York legislature is considered professional because legislators are committed to being full-time representatives; they meet year-round, and members are paid $79,500 per year. Members of Congress also serve year-round.

Former governor Rick Perry campaigned for president on adapting the Texas model to the U.S. Congress. Perry argued that the Founders intended a "citizen" Congress similar to the one in Texas, with members serving for only a few terms and retaining their regular employment in the private sector. As far back as 2007, Perry remarked, "When you have a full-time legislature, they just feel pretty inclined to be doing something. So they are going to dream up new laws, new regulations and new statutes—and generally all of those cost money."[a] Perry's vision fits with the principle of limited government—the principle that Congress or a state legislature should have only a small role and the more legislators are in session, the more temptations they have to engage in corrupt practices and to pass laws restricting liberties.

Opponents argue that the Texas model is not one that should be adopted for the U.S. Congress or other legislatures. First, they point out, meeting only once every two years reduces the time to deliberate and make sensible policies. In Texas, critics argue, the legislative session is rushed, and legislators rely too heavily on staff who work year-round and are more familiar with the ins and outs of policy making. The rush of completing the legislation necessary to govern the state also often leaves important issues unresolved, leading to the need for more special sessions. Members who are not independently wealthy are unable to legislate effectively because they cannot just leave their jobs for 140 days at a time—plus any special sessions—every two years. In addition, legislators are not any less prone to corruption under the Texas model. Under either model, lobbyists attempt to influence policy makers, and the fact that legislators have private-sector jobs does not minimize this possibility. Former Houston-area congressman Chris Bell warns that state legislators in part-time legislatures are actually more susceptible to corruption because "unless they're retired or independently wealthy, [legislators are] in a tough spot. There aren't a whole lot of jobs that lend themselves to a legislator's schedule, so those in office become prime targets [for lobbyists]."[b] All of these factors result in a less productive legislature.

Your vision of the proper role of government will likely affect where you come down on this issue. Liberals, who prefer an active government, would probably prefer a full-time legislature that actively addresses social problems. Conservatives, who are not supporters of government activity in the economy, are more likely to support a minimal role for legislators so that citizens are free to make their own choices without governmental interference.

Why should citizens care about this issue? The political process matters, and how legislative institutions are designed makes a difference in terms of policy outcomes.

COMMUNICATING EFFECTIVELY: YOUR VOICE

- Are you more convinced by the arguments for a part-time legislature or those for a full-time legislature? What are the advantages and disadvantages of each approach?

- What sorts of compromises are possible between Texas's 140-day session and a full-time approach?

carry out its goals and objectives. A review of each agency of state government takes place every 12 years.

Judicial powers include the ability of the House to impeach members of the executive and judicial branches of state government. On **impeachment**, a trial takes place in the Senate. A majority vote of the House is required to bring charges, and a two-thirds vote of senators attending is necessary to convict an individual of the impeachment charges. Unlike the U.S. Constitution, the Texas Constitution does not explicitly define what constitutes an impeachable offense. This determination will be made by the House and Senate in the impeachment process itself.[11] Impeachment is rare in Texas. Governor Jim Ferguson was impeached in 1917, and a state judge was impeached in 1975.[12]

Each body can compel attendance of its members at regular and special sessions. More than once, Texas Rangers have handcuffed absent members and brought them to the legislature. On rare occasions, a chamber punishes nonmembers who disrupt legislative proceedings by imprisoning them for up to 48 hours. Finally, the House and Senate both judge the qualifications of members and can expel a member for cause. For example, either chamber can decide whether to seat members, but this has not been done since the Reconstruction era since it would require overturning the will of the voters in a district.

judicial power the power of the House to impeach and of the Senate to convict members of the executive and judicial branches of state government

impeachment according to the Texas Constitution, the formal charge by the House of Representatives that leads to a trial in the Senate and possibly to the removal of a state official

How a Bill Becomes a Law in Texas

Trace the process through which law is made in Texas

Anyone can write a bill, but only members of the legislature can introduce a bill. Bills may be written by members of the executive branch, by lobbyists, by constituents, or by local governmental entities. Legislators may also write bills, often with the help of legislative staff expert in drafting legislation. Revenue bills must start in the House of Representatives. Other bills can start in either the House or Senate. Figure 7.1 shows the flow of a bill from the time it is introduced in the Texas House of Representatives to its final passage and submission to the governor. A bill introduced in the Senate would follow the same procedure in reverse. This figure may suggest that the process of how a bill becomes law is long, detailed, and cumbersome. However, when the process is distilled to its basic parts, there are only six steps. For a bill that starts in the House these steps are (1) **introduction**, (2) **referral**, (3) **consideration by standing committee**, and (4) **floor action**. Steps (1) through (4) are repeated in the Senate. Step (5) is action by a **conference committee** and approval by both houses, and finally, step (6) is action by the governor.

Introduction in the House

A legislator introduces a bill by placing copies of it with the clerk of the House. In the Senate, the secretary of the Senate receives the bill. The clerk or secretary numbers the bill and enrolls it by recording its number, title, caption, and sponsor in a ledger. Similar information is entered into a computer.

introduction the first step in the legislative process, during which a member of the legislature drafts a bill and files a copy of it with the clerk of the House or secretary of the Senate

referral the second step in the legislative process, during which a bill is assigned to the appropriate standing committee by the Speaker (for House bills) or the lieutenant governor (for Senate bills)

consideration by standing committee the third step in the legislative process, during which a bill is killed, amended, or heard by a standing committee

floor action the fourth step in the legislative process, during which a bill referred by a standing committee is scheduled for floor debate by the Calendars Committee

conference committee a joint committee created to work out a compromise on House and Senate versions of a piece of legislation

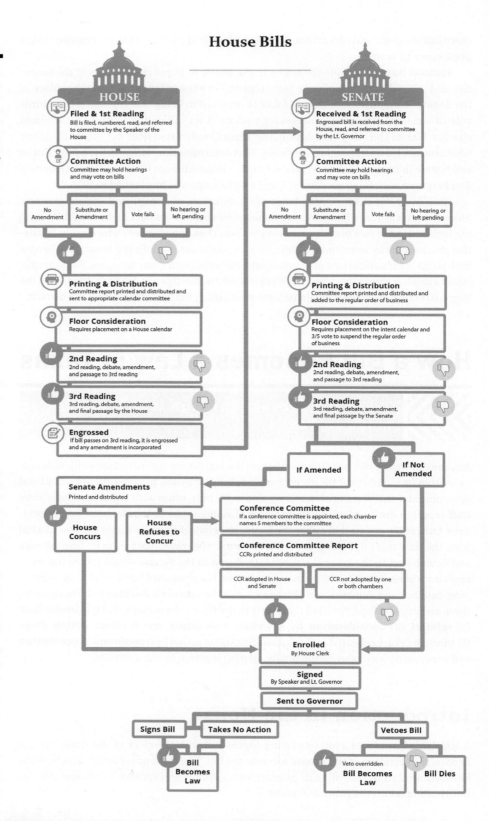

FIGURE 7.1

How a Bill Becomes a Law in Texas

Passing legislation in Texas is a complicated process. There are many points along the way where a bill can die.

House Bills

HOUSE

Filed & 1st Reading
Bill is filed, numbered, read, and referred to committee by the Speaker of the House

Committee Action
Committee may hold hearings and may vote on bills

No Amendment | Substitute or Amendment | Vote fails | No hearing or left pending

Printing & Distribution
Committee report printed and distributed and sent to appropriate calendar committee

Floor Consideration
Requires placement on a House calendar

2nd Reading
2nd reading, debate, amendment, and passage to 3rd reading

3rd Reading
3rd reading, debate, amendment, and final passage by the House

Engrossed
If bill passes on 3rd reading, it is engrossed and any amendment is incorporated

SENATE

Received & 1st Reading
Engrossed bill is received from the House, read, and referred to committee by the Lt. Governor

Committee Action
Committee may hold hearings and may vote on bills

No Amendment | Substitute or Amendment | Vote fails | No hearing or left pending

Printing & Distribution
Committee report printed and distributed and added to the regular order of business

Floor Consideration
Requires placement on the intent calendar and 3/5 vote to suspend the regular order of business

2nd Reading
2nd reading, debate, amendment, and passage to 3rd reading

3rd Reading
3rd reading, debate, amendment, and final passage by the Senate

If Amended | **If Not Amended**

Senate Amendments
Printed and distributed

House Concurs | **House Refuses to Concur**

Conference Committee
If a conference committee is appointed, each chamber names 5 members to the committee

Conference Committee Report
CCRs printed and distributed

CCR adopted in House and Senate | CCR not adopted by one or both chambers

Enrolled
By House Clerk

Signed
By Speaker and Lt. Governor

Sent to Governor

Signs Bill | Takes No Action | Vetoes Bill

Bill Becomes Law | Veto overridden **Bill Becomes Law** | **Bill Dies**

Senate Bills

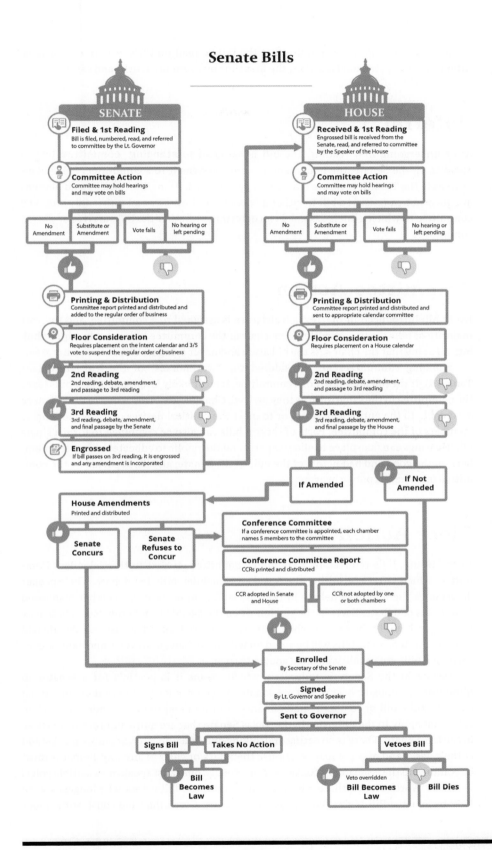

SENATE

Filed & 1st Reading
Bill is filed, numbered, read, and referred to committee by the Lt. Governor

Committee Action
Committee may hold hearings and may vote on bills

| No Amendment | Substitute or Amendment | Vote fails | No hearing or left pending |

Printing & Distribution
Committee report printed and distributed and added to the regular order of business

Floor Consideration
Requires placement on the intent calendar and 3/5 vote to suspend the regular order of business

2nd Reading
2nd reading, debate, amendment, and passage to 3rd reading

3rd Reading
3rd reading, debate, amendment, and final passage by the Senate

Engrossed
If bill passes on 3rd reading, it is engrossed and any amendment is incorporated

HOUSE

Received & 1st Reading
Engrossed bill is received from the Senate, read, and referred to committee by the Speaker of the House

Committee Action
Committee may hold hearings and may vote on bills

| No Amendment | Substitute or Amendment | Vote fails | No hearing or left pending |

Printing & Distribution
Committee report printed and distributed and sent to appropriate calendar committee

Floor Consideration
Requires placement on a House calendar

2nd Reading
2nd reading, debate, amendment, and passage to 3rd reading

3rd Reading
3rd reading, debate, amendment, and final passage by the House

If Amended

If Not Amended

House Amendments
Printed and distributed

Senate Concurs

Senate Refuses to Concur

Conference Committee
If a conference committee is appointed, each chamber names 5 members to the committee

Conference Committee Report
CCRs printed and distributed

CCR adopted in Senate and House

CCR not adopted by one or both chambers

Enrolled
By Secretary of the Senate

Signed
By Lt. Governor and Speaker

Sent to Governor

Signs Bill

Takes No Action

Vetoes Bill

Bill Becomes Law

Veto overridden
Bill Becomes Law

Bill Dies

Rules of the legislature require that the bill be read on three separate occasions. After enrollment, the bill is read for the first time by its number, title, and caption.

Referral

After undergoing first reading, the bill is assigned to **standing committee** by the Speaker. In the Senate, the lieutenant governor assigns it to a committee. Since committees in the Texas legislature have overlapping jurisdictions, the Speaker and lieutenant governor can assign a bill to either a friendly committee or an unfriendly one. The committee to which a bill is assigned can determine whether the bill survives or dies in committee.

Committee Action

Every bill introduced in the Texas legislature is assigned to a committee, and the vast majority of bills die in committee. The chair of the committee kills most by **pigeonholing**, meaning that the chair sets the bill aside and never brings it before the committee.

Standing committees are considered the "workhorses" of the legislature (see Table 7.1). If the bill does not die in committee, it most likely is amended. Few bills leave the committee in the same form as they arrived. Changes are made to make the bill more acceptable to the entire legislature or to meet the political desires of the leadership or members of the committee. Parts of several bills can also be combined to form a single bill. Hearings can take place to allow experts and the public to educate committee members on the good and bad points of the bill. In the Senate, all bills reported by the committee must have a public hearing.

Floor Action

In the House, bills referred by a standing committee go next to the Calendars Committee, which, after consulting the Speaker, schedules bills for debate. The Speaker determines the length of debate in the House. Customarily, each member is allowed 10 minutes of debate. Early in the session when the agenda is not crowded, debate may last longer. Later in the session when there is a crush of legislative business, debate will be more limited. Some bills will be voted on without debate; however, important or controversial bills are usually allocated adequate time.

Debate in the Senate is unlimited, which means it is possible for a senator to **filibuster**. A filibuster occurs when a senator talks for a lengthy period of time in an effort to kill a bill or to obtain amendments or other compromises. There are certain rules that apply to the filibuster in the Texas Senate that are quite different from those in the U.S. Senate. There is no eating or drinking during a filibuster. Senators must stand at their desks and may not lean, sit, or use their desk or chair in any way. Remarks must be confined to the issue under consideration. Finally, one must speak in an audible voice.

Since World War II, there have been more than 100 filibusters. The longest was in 1977 by Senator Bill Meier, who spoke for 43 hours. Given the time constraints under

TABLE 7.1

Standing Committees of the Texas Senate and House (85th Legislature), 2017

SENATE STANDING COMMITTEES

Administration	Finance	Nominations
Agriculture, Rural Affairs & Homeland Security	Health & Human Services	State Affairs
Business & Commerce	Health & Human Services	Transportation
Criminal Justice	Intergovernmental Relations	Veteran Affairs & Military Installations
Education	Natural Resources & Economic Development	

HOUSE STANDING COMMITTEES

Agriculture & Livestock	General Investigating & Ethics	Natural Resources
Appropriations	Government Efficiency and Reform	Pensions
Business & Industry	Higher Education	Public Education
Calendars	Homeland Security & Public Safety	Public Health
Corrections	House Administration	Redistricting
County Affairs	Human Services	Rules & Resolutions
Criminal Jurisprudence	Insurance	Special Purpose Districts
Culture, Recreation & Tourism	International Trade & Intergovernmental Affairs	State Affairs
Defense & Veterans' Affairs	Investments & Financial Services	Technology
Economic & Small Business Development	Judiciary & Civil Jurisprudence	Transportation
Elections	Land & Resource Management	Urban Affairs
Energy Resources	Licensing & Administrative Procedures	Ways & Means
Environmental Regulation	Local & Consent Calendars	

which the Texas legislature operates, even the threat of a filibuster may be sufficient to kill or force changes in a bill. In 2013 Senator Wendy Davis became famous nationwide for her nearly 24-hour filibuster against a bill requiring sonograms for women who wanted abortions. She went on to win the 2014 Democratic gubernatorial nomination but lost to Republican Greg Abbott.

Another tactic used in both the House and the Senate to prevent or delay passage of a bill is called "chubbing." Here, one or more members debate bills at length to slow down the legislative process. Like the filibuster, this is a particularly effective tactic as the legislative session draws to a close.

WHAT DO TEXANS THINK?

Approval of the Legislature

Voters across the country think very poorly of the performance of the U.S. Congress. At the same time, members of Congress are re-elected at very high rates. What about the performance of the Texas legislature? Thirty-seven percent of Texans disapprove of the legislature. For Congress, it is even worse: 69 percent of Texans disapprove of Congress and only 12 percent approve. Why do you think the Texas legislature has a higher approval rating than Congress among Texans?

Do you approve or disapprove of the Texas legislature's job performance?	
Approve strongly	5%
Approve somewhat	23
Neither approve nor disapprove	21
Disapprove somewhat	17
Disapprove strongly	20
Don't know	13

Do you approve or disapprove of the U.S. Congress's job performance?	
Approve strongly	2%
Approve somewhat	10
Neither approve nor disapprove	15
Disapprove somewhat	24
Disapprove strongly	45
Don't know	3

SOURCE: *Texas Tribune* UT Poll, October 2017.

Sponsors of a bill are expected to gather sufficient votes to pass it. In fact, before the Calendars Committee schedules the bill for floor debate, sponsors often assure the committee that they have enough votes for it to pass.

The Senate has limited time to consider bills, so the order of bills is important. The "regular order of business" is that bills are considered in the order they come out of committee. However, on highly salient issues, the Senate can suspend the rule and fast-track consideration of a bill. In the past, this rule could only be suspended if two-thirds of the Senate agreed. This made it difficult to pass controversial legislation because it meant that essentially two-thirds of the Senate would have to agree in order for a bill to proceed. Recently this has meant that Democrats (the minority party) could essentially block legislation they did not approve of. Lieutenant Governor Patrick changed this rule when he became lieutenant governor in 2015. Now a simple majority has to approve suspending the rule, thereby speeding legislation to the Senate floor.

Former state senator Wendy Davis, shown here during her filibuster of a Republican bill aimed at restricting abortion, later ran for governor in 2015 and lost to Greg Abbott.

Conference Committee

Bills must pass the House and Senate in exactly the same form. If their versions of the bill are different in any way, it is sent to a conference committee. Conference committees have 10 members: 5 members from the House appointed by the Speaker, and 5 members from the Senate appointed by

How Representative Is the Texas Legislature Compared with Other States?

	Texas	California	Florida	New York	Ohio
Gender	Female 20%	Female 23%	Female 26%	Female 28%	Female 22%
	Male 80%	Male 77%	Male 74%	Male 72%	Male 78%
Race	Latino 24%	Latino 23%	Latino 16%	Latino 8%	Latino 3%
	African American 10%	African American 8%	African American 16%	African American 15%	African American 14%
Education level*	H.S. diploma 2%	H.S. diploma 0%	H.S. diploma 4%	H.S. diploma 2%	H.S. diploma 3%
	Bachelor's degree 39%	Bachelor's degree 44%	Bachelor's degree 33%	Bachelor's degree 27%	Bachelor's degree 41%
	Graduate degree 54%	Graduate degree 44%	Graduate degree 51%	Graduate degree 58%	Graduate degree 44%

The Texas legislature is predominately white and male, even though the state population has become more diverse. The Latino and African American populations in Texas combine to form nearly half of the state's residents, although this is not reflected in the legislature. How does Texas compare with other states on the representation of women, minorities, and educational attainment?

*Education level data is from 2016.
SOURCE: National Conference of State Legislators, www.ncsl.org/research/about-state-legislatures (accessed 11/20/18).

CRITICAL THINKING

- How does Texas compare with the other states in the chart regarding the racial and ethnic composition of the legislature? What might explain any differences?

- How representative are the five legislatures presented in terms of educational level? How is Texas similar to or different from the other states in this regard?

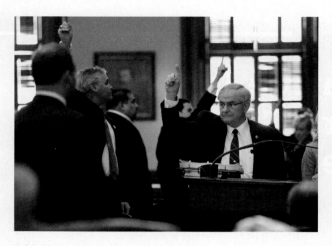

Before a law is passed in Texas, it is voted on by the two chambers of the legislature—the House and the Senate. Raising one finger means "yes" and raising two fingers means "no."

the lieutenant governor. Senate rules require that the latter group must include 2 members of the standing committee that considered the bill. Unless specifically instructed, the conference committee cannot change parts of the bill that are the same in both the House and the Senate versions. Changes are made and compromises reached only on parts that differ.

Once a compromise is reached, the report of the conference committee goes to the House and Senate. It can be debated in each chamber but cannot be changed. It must be either accepted or rejected as is. If either chamber fails to approve the report, the bill is dead. Although it is possible for the conference committee to try a second time to reach a compromise, it is unusual for conference committees to do so.

If the report is accepted in both chambers of the legislature, a final copy of the bill is prepared. The Speaker of the House, the clerk of the House, the president of the Senate (lieutenant governor), and the secretary of the Senate sign the bill. Signatures of the Speaker and lieutenant governor are required by Article 3, Section 38, of the Texas Constitution. The next stop is the governor's desk.

The Governor

veto according to the Texas Constitution, the governor's power to turn down legislation; can be overridden by a two-thirds vote of both the House and Senate

It is the governor's responsibility to sign or **veto** legislation. During the first 130 days of a regular session, the governor has 10 days from the time a bill arrives on his or her desk to sign or veto the legislation. If the governor neither signs nor vetoes the bill in the 10 days, it becomes law without the governor's signature. In the last 10 days of a session, the governor has 20 days from the time the bill arrives on his or her desk to sign or veto the legislation. Again, if the governor does neither, it becomes law without the governor's signature. The U.S. president may sometimes kill a bill without signing it through what is called a "pocket veto." The Texas governor, however, does not have this power.

The governor's veto can be overridden by a two-thirds vote of both the House and the Senate. Anytime the governor vetoes a bill, he or she attaches a message explaining why it was vetoed. It is then returned to the chamber that originated the bill. If the presiding officer chooses to allow a vote to override the veto, a vote is scheduled. Only two vetoes have been overridden in more than 70 years.

post-adjournment veto a veto of a bill that occurs after the legislature adjourns, thus preventing the legislature from overriding it

Many bills, including almost all important or controversial ones, arrive on the governor's desk in the last few days of a session. If the governor wants to veto a bill that comes to him or her from day 131 to day 140, the governor simply waits to do so until the legislature has adjourned, after which the veto cannot be overridden. Vetoing legislation after legislative adjournment is called a **post-adjournment veto**, or a strong veto, since the legislature has no opportunity to overturn it. The post-adjournment veto provides the governor with an excellent bargaining tool, since he or she can threaten a veto unless changes are made in a bill. Table 7.2 provides the total number of vetoes by Texas governors since 1991.

The governor also has a **line-item veto** that allows him or her to sign a bill but draw lines through specific items, deleting them from the bill. Except for the items that the governor has deleted, the bill becomes law. In Texas, the line-item veto applies only to the state's omnibus appropriations bill. Governor Abbott used the line-item veto in 2017 to cut $120 million from the state budget. Some of these cuts included funding to impoverished areas of South Texas known as colonias, as well as funding of environmental programs and a program meant to assist poor Texans repair their vehicles if they failed emissions tests.[13]

Other Ways in Which the Governor Influences Legislation

Message power is the governor's ability to communicate with the legislature. Early in each session, the governor delivers a State of the State message that is similar to the president's State of the Union message. In this address, the governor puts forth a vision for Texas and what legislation will accomplish that vision. In addition, if the governor chooses to submit an executive budget, a letter stating why this budget should be adopted accompanies it. The budget and this letter reveal the governor's priorities for the upcoming legislative session.

Periodically, the governor will visit with legislators to gain their vote on a bill. A personal visit can be persuasive, but increasingly, it is members of the governor's paid staff who are sent on these legislative visits. Like lobbyists for corporations and interest groups, the governor's representatives use their skills to encourage passage of bills the governor favors and to kill bills the governor opposes. However, there is a problem with this practice. The Texas Constitution forbids use of tax dollars to influence the legislature, and the governor's staff is, of course, paid through tax dollars. The governor's representatives avoid this ban by claiming they are simply providing needed information to the legislators.

TABLE 7.2

Total Number of Vetoes by Texas Governors, 1991–2017

YEAR	GOVERNOR	TOTAL VETOES
2017	Abbott	51
2015	Abbott	42
2013	Perry	26
2011	Perry	25
2009	Perry	38
2007	Perry	54
2005	Perry	19
2003	Perry	48
2001	Perry	82*
1999	Bush	33
1997	Bush	37
1995	Bush	25
1993	Richards	26
1991	Richards	36

*Record number of vetoes by a Texas governor.
SOURCES: Texas Legislature, "Legislative Statistics," February 2018; Legislative Reference Library of Texas, "Bill Statistics."

line-item veto the power of the executive to veto specific provisions (lines) of an appropriations bill passed by the legislature

Additional Players in the Legislative Process

In addition to the legislators and the governor, there are others involved in the lawmaking process. One official, the comptroller of public accounts, has direct involvement in the legislative process, while other players are involved indirectly.

The Comptroller of Public Accounts

The comptroller of public accounts issues revenue estimates to inform the legislature of the amount of money it can spend in the next two years. Texas's operating budgets must balance because the Texas Constitution forbids borrowing money to conduct the daily operations of government. The estimate provided by the comptroller sets the limit on state spending. If the legislature wants to spend more than the comptroller estimates, it must enhance revenue—that is, increase taxes and fees.

The comptroller's estimates can be political in nature. The comptroller can provide a low revenue estimate and tell the legislature that the estimate will remain low until it passes bills the comptroller wants. On passage of those bills, the comptroller can revise the estimate to increase the spending limit and allow the legislature to complete its business.

The Media The media can determine issues of legislative importance by the selection of stories they cover. If they cover more stories on crime, criminal justice issues will move toward the top of the legislature's agenda. A media focus on corporate fraud, rising homeowners' insurance rates, alcohol-related traffic deaths, or poor performance by Texas public school students will increase legislative attention to these issues.

The media also inform the public about the issues the legislature is considering and about the job it is doing during the session. Stories portraying the legislature as modern, efficient, and hardworking provide the public with a positive image of the legislature, whereas stories about legislators sleeping at their desks or killing legislation on technicalities provide a negative image.

Legislators also use social media such as Twitter, Facebook, and Instagram to communicate their messages. They advertise their positions and take credit for sponsoring bills. Followers on Twitter or fans on Facebook can then retweet or share legislators' concerns, which in turn helps them set an image for their constituents. While some legislators do their own tweeting or postings, others allow their staffs to update the legislators' social media profiles. As with other forms of communication, though, legislators must be careful not to make mistakes. When state senator Dan Patrick was running for lieutenant governor in 2014, he accidentally tweeted "Marriage=One Man and One Man," shocking supporters who had assumed he was for traditional marriage. Although he quickly deleted the tweet and updated it to "Marriage=One Man and One Woman," media outlets reported this blunder.

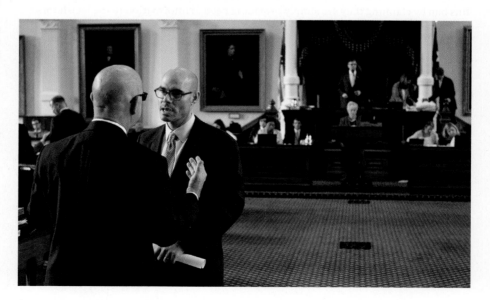

The media can influence the legislative agenda through the stories that they cover. Accordingly, legislators try to attract media attention that will support their positions. Here, likely incoming Speaker Dennis Bonnen (R-Angleton, right) speaks with Senator John Whitmire (D-Houston, left).

The Courts Federal and state courts influence the legislative agenda because the ability to rule acts of the legislature and actions of state agencies unconstitutional gives courts significant power over issues the legislature addresses. In recent years, subjects of the courts' scrutiny have included the Texas prison system, the state's treatment of patients in state mental hospitals, the funding of public education, and equality of funding for colleges and universities in South Texas. To a remarkable degree, state and federal courts have issued decisions that have forced the Texas legislature to act in areas it would have preferred to avoid—largely because action required a significant expenditure of money.

Lobbyists and Interest Groups During a regular session, roughly 1,800 individuals register as lobbyists and attempt to influence the legislature. As we saw in Chapter 6, a lobbyist's job is to convince legislators to support the interest the lobbyist represents. Lobbyists want legislators' votes on bills. And at the least, they desire access to legislators.

Interest groups in Texas have been actively involved in supporting legislation as well as stopping legislation they do not support. The Texas Association of Business is a very active interest group lobbying legislators to support its agenda of lower taxes and fewer regulations. Its leader, Bill Hammond, a former legislator, is one of the most influential powerbrokers in Austin. Other interest groups, such as the Texas Alliance for Life, have been very successful in passing abortion restrictions in the Texas legislature in recent years. Its leader, Joe Pojman, has been a powerful presence lobbying legislators and most recently has led the effort to defund Planned Parenthood from the state budget. Many more interest groups employ lobbyists to influence and educate legislators in Austin as well as in Washington, D.C.

The Public Individuals can influence legislators, who are evaluated at each election. If the people believe their elected officials are representing them well, legislators are re-elected. Legislators who fail to live up to expectations might not be re-elected.

The public can serve as lobbyists. Letters, emails, or telephone calls urging representatives or senators to vote a certain way constitute a lobbying effort. In many instances, the public will write to legislators when the media publicize a particular issue, or an interest group will make it easier for members to write to their legislators. Members of the public can also write legislation but must convince at least one legislator to sponsor it and introduce it for consideration by the legislature.

Some legislators also commission public opinion polls, especially right before an election. While most of the time the purpose is to find out where legislators stand in their districts, some polls ascertain how the public feels on important issues facing the district. The legislator can then choose to emphasize certain issues in the election. If, for example, the legislator does not personally place a high priority on a particular issue

The public and interest groups may also influence the legislature. During a special session in which the legislature dealt with tax reduction, these Houston-area real estate agents and others demonstrated in favor of property tax relief.

such as immigration, but polls show a majority of his constituents do, then he may well choose to emphasize this issue in his campaign.

Power and Partisanship in the Legislature

 Analyze how party leadership and partisanship affect power in the legislature

Among the most powerful political figures in Texas are the leaders of the House and Senate. They play a key role in structuring the committees of the legislature, setting the state's political agenda, and passing or defeating bills.

Leadership

Speaker the chief presiding officer of the House of Representatives; the Speaker is the most important party and House leader, and can influence the legislative agenda, the fate of individual pieces of legislation, and members' positions within the House

lieutenant governor a statewide elected official who is the presiding officer of the Senate; the lieutenant governor is one of the most important officials in state government and has significant control over legislation in the state Senate; the second-highest elected official in the state and president of the state Senate

The **Speaker** of the Texas House of Representatives and the lieutenant governor are two of the most powerful political figures in the state. Republican representative Dennis Bonnen (Angleton) is projected to be the Speaker of the House. Dan Patrick, who in 2014 was first elected **lieutenant governor**, leads the Senate. The Texas House and Senate endow both officials with considerable control over the legislative process. It is fair to say that both of them can usually kill legislation they oppose, and often they have the power to pass legislation they support.

Members of the House elect the Speaker at the beginning of the regular session. At the same time, the members also adopt rules that give the Speaker institutional powers sufficient to control the work of the House. Speakers usually are the dominant figures in the House and wield vast power.

One of the most interesting developments in modern times in the Texas legislature was the turmoil surrounding the 2009–2017 speakership of Republican Joe Straus. Straus represented the moderate wing of the Republican Party and became speaker because of moderate Republicans and Democrats coming together to elect him. As Speaker, he worked fairly well with Lieutenant Governor David Dewhurst during his first term, but when the more conservative Dan Patrick was elected lieutenant governor, tensions arose between the two on a variety of issues, especially the sanctuary cities and bathroom bills in 2017. While some more conservative Republicans tried to challenge Straus during his speakership, he retained his seat until announcing his retirement in 2017.

The lieutenant governor is elected statewide to a four-year term. His or her major responsibility is to serve as president of the Senate and to preside over it. Unlike the Speaker, who is a member of the chamber he presides over, the lieutenant governor is not a member of the Senate and may vote only to break a tie.

At the start of each regular session, senators adopt rules that the Senate will follow for the next two years. Article 22 of the Senate Rules requires a vote of two-thirds of the members present to suspend any rule of the Senate unless the rules specify a different majority. The rules also establish the office of president pro tempore of the Senate, who is a member elected by the Senate to perform the duties of the lieutenant governor in his or her absence or disability. These rules also give the lieutenant governor enormous control of the work of the Senate. Among those powers granted to the lieutenant governor under the rules are

- the power to decide all questions of order on the Senate floor (subject to appeal from members).
- the power to recognize members on the floor.
- the power to break a tie on a particular vote.
- the power to refer bills to committees.
- the power to appoint members to standing committees, subcommittees, special committees, and conference committees.

The Speaker of the House is one of the most powerful people in Texas politics. Despite being criticized by conservatives like Lieutenant Governor Dan Patrick (left), Joe Straus (right) was able to hold on to his position as Speaker until his retirement in 2018.

Centralizing Power: Sources of the Leadership's Power

The operation of the Texas legislature is significantly different from that of the U.S. Congress. In the U.S. Congress, the leader of the president's party in the House or the Senate often works closely with the president and White House staff. Additionally, the level of partisanship is high. Committee appointments are made in such a way that the majority party controls every committee, and chairs of those committees are always members of the majority party. Each house of Congress has majority party leadership and minority party leadership. Such divisions are not as rigid in the Texas legislature where, in the 2017 House, several Democrats were chairs of committees. Selecting someone from the other party to chair a committee would never happen in the U.S. Congress today.

The Texas legislature is not organized along party lines the way the U.S. Congress is. Leadership and power have become centralized in the Speaker and lieutenant governor. These presiding officers can make committee appointments with limited regard for party affiliation, thus ensuring that members will be loyal to them rather than to a party. Committee assignments and committee chair appointments cross party lines so that in the Texas House, for example, where the majority party is now Republican, a Democrat may chair an important committee and successfully sponsor important legislation. The bipartisan appointment of committee chairs, however, may be a declining tradition. With the retirement of Joe Straus and his coalition of Democrats and moderate Republicans, it remains to be seen whether this bipartisan tradition of sharing committee chairs will continue.

Besides the selection of committee chairs, other factors may also come to undermine the state legislature's tradition of nonpartisan politics. Because most of the powers of the Speaker and of the lieutenant governor are granted by the rules that each chamber's membership votes on at the beginning of the legislative session, these powers could potentially be greatly reduced if the members of the legislature so chose. One could, for example, imagine a future Republican Senate that would reduce the powers of the lieutenant governor over the Texas Senate if a Democrat were elected lieutenant governor.

The Republican congressional redistricting bill in 2003 led to abandonment of the two-thirds rule for that bill in the Senate so that a redistricting plan beneficial to Republicans could be passed. That bill would have been impossible to pass without this rule change, which allowed passage by majority vote. In the 2009 special session of the legislature, the Republican majority in the Texas Senate passed a highly partisan bill that required voters to show identification, an action possible only because the two-thirds rule is not used in special sessions.[14] Because the Texas House did not pass the bill, it was not until 2011, when the Texas Senate again abandoned the two-thirds rule, that the voter identification bill became law. The restrictions on abortion imposed in the second special session of the 2013 legislature were also made possible by the two-thirds rule not being in effect.

As the Texas Senate has become more partisan, it is not surprising that Lieutenant Governor Patrick was able to successfully change Senate rules to abolish the two-thirds rule altogether in 2015. Republicans did not want to rely on having to lure a single Democratic senator in order to pass their legislation.

The structure of the Texas legislature and the lack of formal lines of gubernatorial authority there are very important in centralizing power in the hands of the Speaker and the lieutenant governor. However, these officials have other important sources of power as well. One of those powers—especially important in the Texas House—is the power of **recognition**. In the House, the Speaker controls legislative debate, including who speaks and how long debate will last. On occasion, the Speaker ignores or skips a member seeking recognition to speak. Lack of recognition is a signal to other members of the House that this individual has fallen from the Speaker's good graces, and the ability to pick and choose among those desiring to speak on the House floor allows the Speaker to structure the debate and to affect the outcome of legislation. The Senate rule allowing unlimited debate decreases the lieutenant governor's power in this area.

As mentioned earlier, the Senate has a rule that for votes to be taken on bills, the bills must be taken in order. Given the vast powers of the lieutenant governor, on issues that are important to him, he can usually control the votes of at least one-third of the membership. Thus, if a bill is opposed by the lieutenant governor, he or she can frequently prevent it from being taken out of order for consideration.

recognition the power to control floor debate by recognizing who can speak before the House and Senate

PERSONAL RESPONSIBILITY: WHAT WOULD YOU DO?

- Who are the most important leaders in the Texas legislature? What are their powers?

- If you were the Speaker or the lieutenant governor, would you appoint committee chairs from the opposite party? Why or why not? What would be the likely consequences of your decision?

Appointment Power One of the most important duties and sources of power for the Speaker and the lieutenant governor is the power to assign members to standing committees and to appoint chairs of those committees. The committees on which legislators serve are important both to individual members and to the presiding officer. For members, assignments to powerful committees increase their prestige in the legislature. Committee assignment also affects how well constituents are represented.

As mentioned earlier, party affiliation and seniority are of only moderate importance in committee assignments. The most important factor is the members' relationships with the presiding officer. To maintain control over the

TABLE 7.3

Partisanship of House Committee Chair Appointments

	2009		2011		2013		2015		2017	
Speaker	Straus		Straus		Straus		Straus		Straus	
	DEM.	REP.	DEM.	REP.	DEM.	REP.	DEM.	REP.	DEM.	REP.
Standing committees	14	20	11	25	13	24	13	25	13	25
Select committees	1	5	0	3	1	3	1	4	1	3
Joint committee	—	—	0	1	0	1	0	3	0	7
Democratic House committee chairs (%)	38%		28%		33%		22%		29%	
Democrats in House (%)	49%		33%		37%		34%		37%	

NOTE: We are indebted to Sachi Dave for her work on this table for 2009–2011.
SOURCES: Legislative Reference Library and *Texas Tribune*.

legislature, the Speaker and lieutenant governor use their committee assignment powers to appoint members who are loyal to them and who support their legislative agendas. When chairs and vice chairs of important committees are appointed, usually only the most loyal friends and allies of the Speaker and lieutenant governor are chosen. Speaker Straus stated that one issue important to him when appointing chairs and members of committees is to ensure that the committees "reflect the geographic and demographic diversity of Texas."[15]

At the beginning of every legislative session, members of the House are asked to submit a list of committees on which they would like to serve. The Speaker then assigns committee memberships with consideration given to the members' seniority, their leadership skills, and their interest in particular issues. Chairs and other leadership positions are often given to more senior members with leadership skills and interests in the areas over which their committee has jurisdiction.[16] Straus, a Republican, was initially elected Speaker with Democratic votes in a successful challenge to the leadership of his predecessor, a more conservative speaker. As Table 7.3 shows, since being elected Speaker, Straus named Democrats as chairs of standing committees of the House roughly in proportion to their numbers in the House. Of course, some committees are more important than others, but in a purely partisan legislative body, no Democrats would be appointed chair of a committee by a Republican Speaker.

During his tenure as Republican lieutenant governor, David Dewhurst was in a far different position from Speaker Straus. Straus was elected from a House district like all other members and then was elected to the Speaker's office by the membership of the House; Dewhurst was elected to preside over the Texas Senate in a statewide election. In 2013, 6 of the 18 standing committee chairs in the Senate were Democrats, and thirteen of the 38 standing committee chairs in the House were Democrats. Nevertheless, like Straus (as Tables 7.3 and 7.4 show) Dewhurst maintained a practice of appointing Democrats to chair Senate standing committees roughly in proportion to the number of

TABLE 7.4

Partisanship of Senate Committee Chair Appointments

	2009		2011		2013*		2015		2017	
Lieutenant governor	Dewhurst		Dewhurst		Dewhurst		Patrick		Patrick	
	DEM.	REP.	DEM.	REP.	DEM.	REP.	DEM.	REP.	DEM.	REP.
Standing committees	6	12	7	12	7	11	2	12	2	12
Select committees	0	2	1	1	0	2	0	4	0	4
Democratic Senate committee chairs (%)	30%		38%		35%		11%		11%	
Democrats in Senate	39%		39%		37%		35%		35%	

NOTE: We are indebted to Sachi Dave for her work on this table.
*As a result of the death of a Democratic senator, there were only 30 senators during this session.
SOURCES: Legislative Reference Library and *Texas Tribune*.

Democrats overall in the Texas Senate. Since Dan Patrick's election as lieutenant governor, his appointments to Senate committees have all been Republicans.

Not only do the Speaker and the lieutenant governor have vast committee assignment powers, but committees in the Texas legislature also have overlapping jurisdiction. Although each bill must be assigned to a committee, there is more than one committee to which it can be assigned. Since the Speaker and the lieutenant governor assign bills to committees in their respective chambers, they use the bill assignment power to influence the fate of the bill. They can, for example, assign bills they oppose to committees they believe hostile to the bill and those they support to committees they believe will favor the bill.

Since bills must pass the House and Senate in exactly the same form, the Speaker and the lieutenant governor can exercise still another important influence on policy through their power to appoint conference committees. As we have seen, if any differences exist in a bill passed by both the House and the Senate, the bill goes to a conference committee that works out the differences in the House and Senate versions. By appointing the conference committee members, the Speaker and lieutenant governor can affect the language and even the fate of the bill.

Partisan Voting in the Texas Legislature

Between 1876 and 1980, the Democratic Party controlled both houses of the Texas legislature. The last 30 years of the twentieth century saw the growth of the Republican Party in both the House and the Senate, culminating in the Republican seizure of power in both houses in 2004. As conservative Republicans replaced conservative Democrats, particularly from rural and suburban districts, more traditional ideological splits appeared along partisan lines. When Representative Straus initially gained the speakership in 2011 with liberal Democratic and moderate Republican votes, some observers felt that the partisan rhetoric might become muted. As more conservative Republicans were elected in his second term and moderate Republicans either retired or were defeated, however, partisan divisions appeared with a vengeance. Ideological differences between Democrats and Republicans now play a major role in legislative politics (see Figure 7.2).

It is possible to show the increasing gulf between Democrats and Republicans by using roll-call votes cast by members of the Texas House over time. If one categorizes the votes along the dimension of liberalism-conservatism such that a score of –1.00 is extreme liberal and a score of 1.00 is extreme conservative, the average score of Republicans in the Texas House in 1973 was 0.44. The average score for Democrats was 0.01. In contrast, in 2009 the average Republican score was 0.67, a significant movement toward increased conservatism. Meanwhile, the Democrats in the Texas House became increasingly liberal. In 2009 the Democratic score was –0.34.

Another indication of the partisan gap between Democrats and Republicans in the Texas House is that in 1973 37 percent of Democratic House members were more conservative than the most liberal Republican in the House. In 1995 only 4 percent of

FIGURE 7.2

Ideological Differences in the Texas House of Representatives

Ideological differences between state legislators have grown in recent years. This graphic illustrates how ideology scores of Texas legislators have diverged over time.

SOURCE: Boris Shor and Nolan McCarty, "Aggregrate State Legislator Shor-McCarty Ideology Data, May 2016 update," Harvard Dataverse, V1.

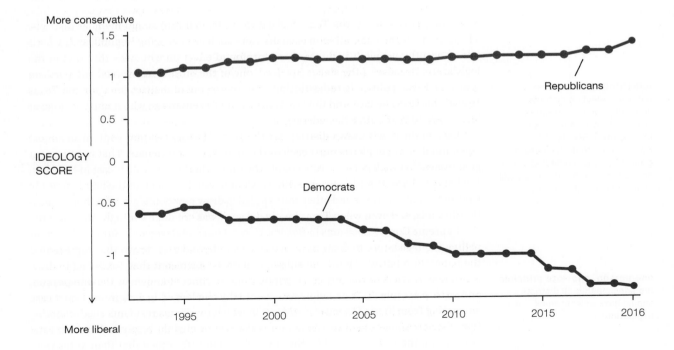

Democratic House members were more conservative than the most liberal Republican. Since 1999 there has been no Democrat in the House who has been more conservative than the most liberal Republican.[17] In a recent study of the 2015 Texas House, political scientist Mark Jones found that every Democrat was more liberal than any Republican.[18] Jones found the same pattern in the Texas Senate.[19] The ideological gap between Democrats and Republicans makes it harder to find common ground across party lines and produce a policy consensus. In that sense, the Texas legislature is becoming more like the U.S. Congress. As sociologist Paul Starr has pointed out regarding Congress,

> Traditionally, political parties in the United States have been broad coalitions that overlapped each other ideologically. The Republicans had included liberals . . . and the Democrats had included conservatives. But by 2009, the ideological alignment of the parties was nearly complete. . . . The growing ideological divergence between the two parties made cooperation between them more difficult.[20]

The pattern Starr saw in the U.S. Congress is now seen in the Texas legislature. With it we are seeing the end of the cooperation between Democrats and Republicans in Austin.

Redistricting

 Explain the politics of redistricting

As we discussed earlier, the Texas legislature is divided into single-member districts. The makeup of the population in each district—such as how many Republicans or Latinos or wealthy people it includes—has a profound effect on who wins that seat in the legislature. Because of the stakes involved, one of the most controversial and partisan issues in Texas politics is **redistricting**—the redrawing of district lines for the Texas House, the Texas Senate, and the U.S. House of Representatives, which must be done at least every 10 years, after the federal census.

Each of the newly drawn districts for the Texas House must now contain an almost equal number of people, as must each of those for the Texas Senate. That requirement guarantees that each person's vote counts the same whether the vote is cast in Houston, Big Lake, El Paso, Presidio, Brownsville, or Commerce. For much of the first half of the twentieth century, Texas and other states failed to draw new boundaries for their legislative districts, and even when Texas finally did so, it was not done willingly. Not until the U.S. Supreme Court's decisions in *Baker v. Carr* (1962) and *Reynolds v. Sims* (1964), compelling the legislature to draw new districts, were boundaries drawn that represented the population fairly.[21] These and subsequent decisions meant that Texas had to draw legislative districts of roughly equal populations—a concept known as the **one-person, one-vote principle**. This principle was eventually challenged in a Supreme Court case emanating from Texas (*Evenwel v. Abbott*) in which two Texas residents sued, claiming that districts should be drawn based on registered or eligible voters rather than total population, the standard used by the state. The plaintiffs argued that their votes were

redistricting the process of redrawing election districts and redistributing legislative representatives in the Texas House, Texas Senate, and U.S. House; this usually happens every 10 years to reflect shifts in population or in response to legal challenges in existing districts

one-person, one-vote principle the principle that all districts should have roughly equal populations unfairly diluted because they lived in a state legislative district with a smaller proportion of nonvoting residents, compared with districts containing many prisoners, felons, and/or immigrants ineligible to vote. The Court disagreed, siding with the state's argument that the historical practice of using total population to draw legislative districts was consistent with the Constitution.

Congressional redistricting is also a responsibility of the legislature. Once the U.S. Census proscribes how many seats each state is entitled to in the U.S. House of Representatives, the Texas legislature divides Texas into the appropriate number of congressional districts. According to the 1964 Supreme Court case *Wesberry v. Sanders*, each state's U.S. House districts must be roughly equal in population.[22] Depending on how the districts are drawn, the representation of the two political parties in the U.S. House can be significantly changed. Indeed, reapportionment and redistricting can so change the division of the parties that control of the House can be affected. Thus, maneuvering over redistricting is highly partisan.

If the legislature fails to redistrict at the first regular session after the census, the task falls to the Legislative Redistricting Board (LRB). The LRB has five members: the lieutenant governor, the Speaker of the House, the attorney general, the commissioner of the General Land Office, and the comptroller of public accounts. When the legislature adjourns without redistricting, the LRB convenes. The LRB must meet within 90 days of legislative adjournment and complete its responsibilities within another 60 days.

Texas redistricting plans must comply with the federal Voting Rights Act, although the U.S. Supreme Court has recently weakened that law. A federal court can temporarily redraw district lines if a redistricting violates this law by disadvantaging minority voters.

Partisan differences in the state legislature resulted in the failure to pass a redistricting plan during the regular 2001 session, transferring the responsibility to the Republican-dominated LRB. On a split vote, the board developed redistricting plans that appeared to favor the Republican Party. When the board's decision was appealed to the federal courts, a three-judge panel, composed of two Democrats and one Republican, approved the lines drawn for the state senate, noting that the U.S. Justice Department had determined that the plan did not violate the Voting Rights Act.[23]

The final plan approved by the court appeared to be a great victory for the Republican Party. Twenty-seven incumbent Democrats found themselves placed in districts with other Democratic incumbents. Four Democrats who chaired key committees announced that they would not seek re-election. Many observers felt that redistricting would make the Republicans the majority party in the House and would maintain their majority status in the Senate. Many also doubted that the Speaker of the House, Democrat Pete Laney, would be able to mobilize the votes needed for re-election to the speakership in the next session. After the 2002 elections, these observers were proven correct.[24]

In 2006 the U.S. Supreme Court upheld most of the new boundaries drawn in Republicans' controversial redistricting but found that some of the redrawn districts failed to protect minority voting rights. Here, Governor Perry displays the new redistricting map. The new map drawn by Republicans after the 2010 census again went to federal courts.

Power and Partisanship in the Redistricting Battle

Republican control of the Texas House and Senate in 2002 heralded more than simply a shift to unified party control of the legislature. With the partisan shift came a significant decline in the harmonious, bipartisan spirit that had largely governed the Texas legislature. The Republican leadership, especially House Speaker Tom Craddick, chose to govern in a more partisan fashion. Additionally, a number of Democrats in the House who saw their power slipping away chose a rebellious course. They worked to make Craddick's speakership a difficult one, obstructing Republican legislative efforts as much as possible.

This new partisan tension in the legislature rose to a fever pitch in 2003 when Republicans, with the support of their majority leader, Tom DeLay, sought to alter the Texas congressional districts for partisan advantage. The Republican goal was to increase Republican representation in the Texas congressional delegation and, in so doing, help ensure a continuing Republican majority in the U.S. House of Representatives. The Republican effort was unconventional in that it occurred in midcycle—that is, it was the second redistricting after the 2000 census. As a rule, redistricting occurs only once after each decennial census, although there is no legal requirement that this be the case.

The Republican congressional redistricting plan was not enacted without political turmoil, however. At the end of 2003, 51 Democrats from the state legislature walked out and gathered in Ardmore, Oklahoma, where the Texas state police did not have jurisdiction to bring them back to the state capitol. The result was that a quorum could not be reached to pass the plan. The Democratic legislators did not return to Austin until redistricting was taken off the agenda. A special legislative session was called to deal with redistricting, but the bill did not pass. In a second special session dealing with redistricting, 11 of the 12 Democratic members of the Senate fled to Albuquerque in order to prevent a Senate vote. Finally, a third special session produced a plan that passed both houses of the legislature.[25]

Most notable about the 2004 redistricting was that seven incumbent congressional Democrats were targeted for defeat. A lawsuit that challenged the redistricting on the grounds that it diluted minority votes stressed that the Democrats had been elected with minority support. The lawsuit also pointed out that these seven Democrats either had been paired so that they had to run against another incumbent or had been given a more Republican district.[26] For the most part, Republicans were successful in reshaping

Although the Texas legislature is not as susceptible to partisan squabbling as is the U.S. Congress, flare-ups between Democrats and Republicans do occur. For example, in this photo, Texas House Democrats celebrate their return to Texas in May 2003, after spending four days in Ardmore, Oklahoma, to kill a GOP-produced congressional redistricting plan.

the partisan composition of the Texas delegation to the U.S. House of Representatives. However, the 2006 election led to Democratic control of the U.S. House and to a Texas congressional delegation with vastly weakened power in Washington because of the loss of key Democrats in the redistricting.[27]

The 2010 census led to another round of redistricting for the Texas legislature and the U.S. House of Representatives. The overwhelmingly Republican legislature designed a redistricting plan strongly favorable to Republicans, but the plan ran afoul of a federal court, which held that it violated minority voting rights. The court ordered a redistricting plan that was more favorable to Democrats. Redistricting has seemingly become a perpetual issue before the Texas legislature, which in 2013 again voted on redistricting for the Texas House, the Texas Senate, and Texas's U.S. congressional districts. The legislature basically accepted the districting done by the federal courts prior to the 2012 elections, although there are legal challenges to the Texas House and the congressional district lines on the grounds that insufficient recognition of minority interests was given in developing the 2012 districts.[28] In June 2018 the U.S. Supreme Court ruled in a 5-4 decision that Texas did not demonstrate intentional discrimination when drawing most legislative districts in 2013. The Court did rule, however, that Texas impermissibly used race as the predominant factor in the creation of one district in the Fort Worth area, and that district would have to be redrawn. The decision did not affect the Court's previous ruling in *Shelby County v. Holder* (2013), which effectively eliminated the requirement that Texas had to have its new district lines approved by the Department of Justice. Future courts, however, can and most probably will revisit the drawing of legislative districts in Texas to ensure compliance with federal laws.

The Legislature and the Future of Texas

THE TEXAS LEGISLATURE has become more and more like the U.S. Congress in terms of political polarization and partisan division. When Democrat Bob Bullock was lieutenant governor during the late 1990s, he worked with then–Republican governor George W. Bush in a bipartisan fashion. Today, the legislature is completely controlled by Republicans, who are themselves internally divided between establishment and Tea Party factions. In November 2017, establishment Republican Speaker Joe Straus (R-San Antonio) shocked the Texas political world by announcing he would not seek re-election to the House. His retirement delighted some Republicans in the House such as the more conservative Matt Rinaldi, who was involved in the scuffle discussed at the beginning of this chapter. Rinaldi called Straus a "terrible Speaker . . . almost totalitarian. He silenced the voices of the majority in the House."[29] A Tea Party speaker would herald a more conservative direction in the House as well as the elimination of the little bipartisanship that exists there, in the form of some Democratic committee chairs and some cooperation that Straus had to employ with Democrats who helped elect him.

The end of the two-thirds rule in the Texas Senate also heralds a new era of partisanship. The rule required members of both parties to work together to pass legislation. Now that only a majority is needed, partisanship and rancor among Texas senators will probably increase.

The Texas legislature seems in some ways an archaic institution. Unless there are special sessions, it meets only once every two years, and it is a part-time body with very limited compensation for its members. The structure of the legislature has survived since the 1876 Constitution, however, and there seems little likelihood that it will soon change.

Especially notable regarding the legislature is the vast power held by the Speaker and the lieutenant governor. The 1876 Constitution showed its distrust of a powerful governor, and the result is that in Texas the governor must share political influence with two other major figures over whom the governor exerts no formal control. Still, the discontent exhibited by conservative Republicans against Speaker Straus reminds us that it is perilous for the Speaker to try to exert so much power that he becomes subject to rebuke from a constituency whose views he ultimately must reflect—the views of a majority of the members of the Texas House. With Straus's retirement, a new era in the Texas House will begin under a new speaker who will undoubtedly be more conservative and willing to work with Lieutenant Governor Dan Patrick to achieve the goals of the conservative elements of the Texas Republican Party.

STUDY GUIDE

Use 🐰 INQUIZITIVE to help you study and master this material.

Structure of the Texas Legislature

- **Describe the organization and basic rules of the legislature (pp. 215–19)**

The Texas legislature is bicameral. The leader of the House is the Speaker, and the lieutenant governor presides over the Texas Senate. Although the typical member of the legislature is white and male, women and minorities have increased their representation in recent years. Representatives use social media and other forms of communication to stay in touch with people in their districts.

Key Terms
bicameral (p. 215)
regular session (p. 216)
biennial (p. 216)
special session (p. 216)
single-member district (p. 217)
constituent (p. 217)
constituent service (p. 218)
per diem (p. 218)

Practice Quiz
1. There are ___ members of the Texas Senate, and state senators serve a ___-year term.
   a) 31/4
   b) 100/6
   c) 150/2
   d) 300/6
   e) 435/2

2. Texas House members differ from Texas Senate members because
   a) House members represent smaller districts and are subject to more frequent elections.
   b) House members represent people, and senators represent counties.
   c) House members are elected from single-member districts and senators from multimember districts.
   d) House members have term limits, and senators do not have term limits.
   e) House members must live in the state for 10 years before standing for election, and senators do not have a residency requirement.

3. The Texas legislature meets in regular session
   a) 90 days every year.
   b) 180 days every year.
   c) 140 days each odd-numbered year and 60 days each even-numbered year.
   d) 140 days each odd-numbered year.
   e) 180 days each even-numbered year.

4. The agenda for a special session of the Texas legislature is set by the
   a) lieutenant governor and the Speaker of the House.
   b) governor.
   c) Texas Supreme Court.
   d) chair of the joint committee on special sessions.
   e) agenda-setting committee.

Powers of the Legislature

- Outline the legislative and nonlegislative powers of the legislature (pp. 220–23)

The Texas legislature passes bills and resolutions and supervises the state bureaucracy through the budgetary process and sunset legislation.

Key Terms
bill (p. 220)
local bill (p. 220)
special bill (p. 220)
general bill (p. 220)
resolution (p. 220)
concurrent resolution (p. 220)
joint resolution (p. 221)
simple resolution (p. 221)
electoral power (p. 221)
investigative power (p. 221)
directive and supervisory power (p. 221)
judicial power (p. 223)
impeachment (p. 223)

Practice Quiz

5. The Texas legislature does not pass this type of bill or resolution:
   a) local bill.
   b) special bill.
   c) joint resolution.
   d) concurrent resolution.
   e) holiday resolution.

6. Texas legislators do not
   a) provide assistance to constituents.
   b) investigate wrongdoing by federal agencies.
   c) investigate wrongdoing in state agencies.
   d) pass bills and resolutions.
   e) count election returns for governor and lieutenant governor.

How a Bill Becomes a Law in Texas

- **Trace the process through which law is made in Texas (pp. 223–34)**

The process of a how a bill becomes a law is similar to that at the federal level. A key difference is the governor's use of the line-item veto by which the governor can eliminate individual appropriations or line items in the state budget. Additionally, the lieutenant governor and the Speaker of the Texas House have exceptionally strong powers. The committee system plays a major role in shaping the legislative process.

Key Terms

introduction (p. 223)
referral (p. 223)
consideration by standing committee (p. 223)
floor action (p. 223)
conference committee (p. 223)
standing committee (p. 226)
pigeonholing (p. 226)
filibuster (p. 226)
veto (p. 230)
post-adjournment veto (p. 230)
line-item veto (p. 231)

Practice Quiz

7. If a bill fails to pass the Texas House and Texas Senate in exactly the same form, the bill
   a) dies.
   b) is returned to the standing committee in the House or Senate that originally considered the bill.
   c) is sent to a conference committee.
   d) is sent to the governor, who decides which version of the bill will be signed.
   e) becomes a law.

8. The ___ provides the governor a powerful tool with which to bargain with the legislature.
   a) ability to introduce five bills in a regular session
   b) post-adjournment veto
   c) pocket veto
   d) message power
   e) initiative

9. Which state official, in large part, determines the total amount of money the legislature may appropriate?
   a) governor
   b) lieutenant governor
   c) treasurer
   d) comptroller of public accounts
   e) attorney general

Power and Partisanship in the Legislature

> • Analyze how party leadership and partisanship affect power in the legislature (pp. 234–40)

The Speaker of the House and the lieutenant governor are the most important actors in the legislature. Together they help to centralize power in the legislature, and they facilitate or prevent the passage of legislation. The legislature has become increasingly partisan.

Key Terms
Speaker (p. 234)
lieutenant governor (p. 234)
recognition (p. 236)

Practice Quiz
10. The two most powerful political figures in the Texas legislature are the
    a) governor and the lieutenant governor.
    b) governor and the attorney general.
    c) Speaker of the House and the governor.
    d) Speaker of the House and the lieutenant governor.
    e) chairs of the finance committee in each house.

11. The Speaker of the Texas House is chosen
    a) in a statewide election.
    b) in a party-line vote by members of the Texas House.
    c) by a majority of the members of the House, whether Democrat or Republican.
    d) by seniority in the House.
    e) by lot.

12. The lieutenant governor is the presiding officer of
    a) the Texas Senate.
    b) the governor's cabinet.
    c) the Texas legislature.
    d) the Legislative Conference committees.
    e) the treasury.

13. The chairs of the Texas House committees are
    a) of the same party as the Speaker.
    b) selected on the basis of seniority.
    c) chosen because of their experience.
    d) both Democrats and Republicans.
    e) independents.

14. The ability of the lieutenant governor and the Speaker of the House to control the final outcome of legislation comes from their power to
    a) appoint members of conference committees.
    b) refuse to approve the work of standing committees.
    c) exercise the legislative line-item veto.
    d) change up to three lines in any bill.
    e) control floor debate.

15. In recent years, the Texas legislature has
    a) become more partisan.
    b) become less partisan.
    c) become more experienced in lawmaking.
    d) been more inclined to let the governor make policy.
    e) been more respectful of county officials.

Redistricting

• Explain the politics of redistricting (pp. 240–43)

One of the most partisan activities of the legislature involves redrawing of district lines for the Texas House of Representatives and the Texas Senate. New districts must be drawn at least every 10 years to reflect changes in the population of the state. This process of redistricting provides the opportunities for the dominant political party to create districts for their partisan advantage. While there are some legal and constitutional restrictions on redistricting, generally as long as the districts reflect equal populations and racial or ethnic minorities are not disadvantaged, legislators have great freedom in drawing district boundaries.

Key Terms
redistricting (p. 240)
one-person, one-vote principle (p. 240)

Practice Quiz

16. An important issue for the legislature at least every 10 years is
    a) adopting a budget.
    b) deciding the order of succession to the office of governor.
    c) impeaching the lieutenant governor.
    d) redistricting.
    e) electing the president.

17. Legislative districts in Texas
    a) are created by a nonpartisan commission.
    b) are designed to benefit partisan interests.
    c) are voted on in a special election.
    d) are created in a cooperative effort between the two parties.
    e) are designed by the Center for Legislative Districts every 10 years.

Although the governor is the most visible leader in Texas politics, Texas governors have fewer powers than governors in many other states. Greg Abbott, first elected in 2014, succeeded one of the more powerful governors in Texas history, Rick Perry. Does Abbott use the power of the governor's office like Perry did?

The Executive Branch

WHY THE EXECUTIVE BRANCH MATTERS The late lieutenant governor of Texas Bob Bullock said that he did not want to be governor, because he claimed that all a Texas governor did was cut ribbons. Bullock was a remarkably powerful and effective lieutenant governor, and he gave weight to the view that real power in Texas government was not in the governor's office, but in the lieutenant governor's office. As one reporter put it, before the governorship of Rick Perry, "half the stories about the doings in the state Capitol were either about the inherent weakness of the governor's office or the ancient lore about how the lieutenant governor holds the state's most powerful office."

Texas certainly has had weak governors and powerful lieutenant governors, but Rick Perry's long tenure in the governor's office gave him remarkable power through his ability to appoint board and commission members who run the Texas bureaucracy. His successor, Greg Abbott, was elected to a second term in 2018, and while he has yet to dominate state government to the degree that Perry did, as he enters his second term of office, he will have more influence on state government through continued exercise of his appointment powers. Abbott has increasingly identified with the more conservative wing of the Republican Party and has pursued a very conservative policy agenda. He has, for example, supported legislation that restricted the availability of abortion and has supported legislation against so-called "sanctuary cities." As noted in Chapter 10, he has been a strong advocate of state preemption of local governmental powers—from restricting local government tree ordinances to limiting local tax increases. He has opposed state tax increases and the use of the state's Rainy Day Fund to supplement state revenues. He has been a vocal advocate of bathroom legislation, which would restrict persons to public bathrooms identified with the sex on their birth certificate. At the same time, he has endorsed a federal constitutional convention to amend the U.S. Constitution and return powers to the states.

Texas governors may take some political risks and become known as advocates for a particular policy agenda. Governor Mark White, for example, pushed educational reform as a major issue when he was governor. He largely succeeded in his reforms, although some of his proposals related to athletic programs in public schools were very controversial, such as "no pass, no play," which banned students' participation in extracurricular activities unless they maintained passing grades. Governor Rick Perry took some risk in advancing a tort reform agenda, which made it more difficult to sue physicians and hospitals for damages, and he succeeded in passing very controversial business taxes to aid in funding education. He advanced a proposal for a Trans-Texas Corridor, a massive new network of roads, railroads, and utility lines. That proposal was an utter failure, though to his credit he had a policy idea and was willing to take a risk promoting it.

Other governors, such as Dolph Briscoe, have primarily been caretakers who advance little in the way of new ideas and take few chances as governor. Greg Abbott so far has not taken many political risks nor has he advanced many innovative ideas. His is a program that could be the agenda of any Republican governor with a foreign border or issues with immigration. While Abbott in his first four years used the "bully pulpit" of the governor's office to preach a state's rights agenda, he has not initiated a major policy agenda like some of his predecessors. It seems more likely that Abbott will follow the lead of the Trump administration's policies rather than promote significant policy innovations of his own. Still, he was easily re-elected in 2018 and his favorability ratings while not high overall (47 percent) are very high among Republicans (80 percent).[1]

There is no question that Abbott is a skilled politician. He began his career in public service as a Houston district judge for three years. He was then appointed to the Texas Supreme Court by Governor George W. Bush and was elected twice. In 2001 he resigned from the Texas Supreme Court in order to seek the lieutenant governor's office, but when Texas Attorney General John Cornyn left his position to run for the U.S. Senate, Abbott switched to running for attorney general. He was elected attorney general three times and became the state's longest serving attorney general. As attorney general he won the hearts of conservatives by filing more lawsuits against the Obama administration than were filed by any other state. That record of lawsuits boosted his prospects of winning the governor's office for which he was initially elected in 2014. Perhaps in his second term as governor he will pursue a more daring policy agenda; however, his past electoral successes suggest that he sees his winning strategy as being a spokesman for conservative ideas and an advocate of Trump administration policies.

CHAPTER GOALS

- Describe the powers of the Texas governor and the limits of the governor's power (pp. 253–71)

- Identify the other elected officials who make up Texas's plural executive (pp. 271–81)

- Explain the roles played by boards, commissions, and regulatory agencies (pp. 281–87)

The Governor

At the national level, the president represents and is responsible to the American people as a whole. The president is the spokesperson for the government and the people in national and international affairs. Throughout the twentieth century, various presidents parlayed the powers granted them by the U.S. Constitution into what some commentators call the "imperial presidency." The governorship in Texas is not an analogous imperial one. Compared with the president, the governor of Texas is weak. Executive power in Texas is divided among a number of separately elected officials, all of whom are elected by and responsible to the people as a whole. This plural executive has important implications for political life in the Lone Star State.

Texas generally scores quite low on scales that compare the power of its governor with that of governors in other states. In a study by political scientists Thad Beyle and Margaret Ferguson, Texas tied with four other states for a ranking of 39th among the states in the overall institutional powers of the governor. The *2015 Book of the States* examined the formal powers of the office of governors throughout the United States and noted that the Texas governor, unlike governors of 30 states, has to share responsibility with others for budget making. Twelve states give governors the power to veto line items—specific provisions—in all bills; the Texas governor has the line item veto only on appropriations bills. Texas governors do have considerable power to have their vetoes upheld by the legislature, since a supermajority of two-thirds of each house is required to override a veto. But Texas is one of only 14 states where the governor cannot reorganize government without approval of the legislature.

To understand the restrictions placed on the office, it is necessary to remember that the Constitution of 1876 was a reaction to the Reconstruction government that existed in Texas following the Civil War. During Reconstruction, the governor was very powerful, and many Texans regarded state government as oppressive and corrupt. When a new constitution was drafted at the end of the Reconstruction era, Texans did their best to ensure that no state official had extensive power. The Texas Constitution of 1876 placed strict limits on the governor's ability to control the people appointed to office and almost eliminated the possibility that appointees to office could be removed. Power was further fragmented among other officeholders, who are collectively known as the plural executive. Each of these officeholders is elected and has separate and distinct responsibilities. Members of major state boards, such as the Railroad Commission and the State Board of Education, are also elected and are largely outside the control of the governor.

Governors who are successful in pushing their programs through the legislature and seeing them implemented by the bureaucracy are able to use the limited formal powers available to them, exercise their personal political power, exploit the prestige of the office of governor, and marshal various special interests to their cause. Former state representative Brian McCall, who has written a book about the modern Texas governorship, argues that Texas governors can be quite powerful in spite of the weaknesses of the office

George W. Bush was governor of Texas from 1995 until he was elected president of the United States in 2000. Here, Bush is seen campaigning for re-election as governor in 1998. Like Rick Perry, Bush was able to achieve a number of his political goals as governor, despite the limited powers of the office.

that are inherent in the Texas Constitution. He points out that governors can realize many of their goals if they are flexible, have a vision of what they want to accomplish, and are willing to motivate others to achieve that vision and work cooperatively with the legislature. McCall notes that when former governor Allan Shivers was asked about the weak governorship of Texas, he responded, "I never thought it was weak. I had all the power I needed."[2]

McCall, in stressing that capable individuals could parlay the Texas governorship into a position of power, noted that only the governor has the power to call special sessions of the legislature. The governor can pardon criminals and can permit fugitives to be extradited to other states. The governor appoints people to state governing boards and commissions. Only the governor can declare martial law. Only the governor can veto acts or specific appropriations passed by the legislature. Through the traditional State of the State address delivered at the beginning of every legislative session, the governor can outline his or her priorities for the state and convince others of their importance. Finally, the governor can be a major persuasive force in mobilizing interest groups, editorial boards of newspapers, and other opinion leaders to support his or her agenda.

Not all governors have the personal skills to turn the office into a powerful one. Some have been unable to develop a collaborative relationship with the legislature. Others have not had the interest or the ability to develop their own vision and political agenda. Still others have been unable to accomplish their goals because of economic downturns that have limited their resources. However, McCall argues that modern governors such as John Connally, Ann Richards, and George Bush have had the persuasive skills that have enabled them to achieve major political objectives in spite of the constitutional limitations on the powers of the office.[3]

Still, even many successful governors have not acted as if the job is a demanding one. George W. Bush, according to McCall, would typically arrive at the office by eight in the morning, leave for a run and a workout at 11:40 AM, return at 1:30 PM, and play video golf or computer solitaire until 3 PM.[4] Governor Perry was so detached from the operation of state government that he did not receive a full briefing on the raid on a polygamist cult that put 400 children in protective custody and involved a half-dozen state agencies and 1,000 state personnel until five days after the event. One review of Perry's schedule

How Much Power Does the Texas Governor Have?

Budget-Making Power

Full responsibility

California ★★★

New York ★★★   Illinois ★★★   Florida ★★★   Texas ★★★

Shared responsibility

Line-Item Veto

All bills

New York ★★★   Illinois ★★★

California ★★★   Florida ★★★   Texas ★★★

Appropriations bills only

Power to Reorganize State Government

Yes

California ★★★   Illinois ★★★   Florida ★★★

New York ★★★   Texas ★★★

No

Term Limits

Yes

California ★★★   Florida ★★★

New York ★★★   Illinois ★★★   Texas ★★★

No

Power Sharing

California
Texas
Florida
Illinois
New York

1   2   3   4   5

(1 = governor shares more power with other elected officials; 5 = governor shares less power)

Appointment Power*

Texas
Florida
Illinois
California
New York

1   2   3   4   5

(1 = weakest—other state officials have some appointment power; 5 = highest—governor's appointees need no other approval)

*Appointment power is measured in the areas of K–12 education, health, highways and transportation, public utilities regulation, and welfare.

SOURCES: U.S. Census Bureau, "Florida Passes New York to Become the Nation's Third Most Populous State, Census Bureau Reports," December 23, 2014, www.census.gov; Audrey Wall, "Table 4.4, The Governors: Powers," Book of the States 2016, knowledgecenter.csg.org; Thad Beyle and Margaret Ferguson, "Governors and the Executive Branch," in Politics in the American States, ed. Virginia Gray and Russell L. Hanson (Washington, DC: CQ Press, 2008), pp. 212–213.

Several institutional factors help to determine whether a state has a powerful governor. Powerful governors will often have full responsibility for budget making. They will also often have line-item veto powers on all bills, the ability to order governmental reorganizations, and no requirement to share their power with separately elected executive officials. Powerful governors are not restricted on the number of terms they may serve and they have broad appointment powers. How does the power of the Texas governor compare to other states'?

CRITICAL THINKING

- Compared with those of other large-population states, are the institutional powers of the Texas governor high or low? Explain your answer based on the data in this graphic.

- Would Texas government be more efficient and more responsive to public needs if it had a stronger governor? What enhancements in the powers of Texas governors would be most beneficial to the management of state government?

during the first four months of the 2011 legislative session showed that he averaged only 21 hours per week on state business and took six three-day weekends.[5]

Governor Abbott's schedule does not seem particularly grueling either. Of course, his formal schedule excludes phone calls and impromptu meetings as well as preparation time for meetings, but the schedule suggests the demands of the office are not stressful. On January 26, 2015, for example, Abbott's schedule started at 10 AM with a meeting with deputies and senior staff. From 11:30 AM to 1:00 PM, he had a working lunch, and from 2:00 PM to 4:00 PM, he had a budget meeting. From 4:00 PM to 4:30 PM, he had an interview with reporters from radio station KTRH, after which, at least according to his formal schedule, his workday ended. The following day was not any busier. From 3:00 PM to 4:00 PM, he had a budget meeting and briefing; at 4:30 PM, he met with state senator Charles Perry. Then his scheduled day ended with a meeting from 5:00 PM to 5:30 PM with Senator Perry and Representative Cecil Bell.[6]

Qualifications

Only three formal constitutional qualifications are required to become governor of Texas. Article 4 of the Texas Constitution requires the governor to (1) be at least 30 years of age, (2) be a U.S. citizen, and (3) have lived in Texas for five years immediately before election. Texas governors have tended to be male, white, conservative, Protestant, middle-aged, and either personally wealthy or with access to wealth, and they have had considerable prior political experience. Although women compose more than 50 percent of the population of the United States and Texas, only two women—Miriam Ferguson (1925–27, 1933–35) and Ann Richards (1991–95)—have served as governor of Texas.

Access to money is important because a campaign for the Texas governorship can cost tens of millions of dollars. The 2010 gubernatorial campaign set a record, costing about $91 million when all primary and general election candidates are considered. Tony Sánchez, the Democratic nominee for governor in 2002, spent over $66 million in that campaign, a record for an individual candidate. About $60 million of those funds came from his family's fortune in a losing effort for the governor's mansion.

Sam Kinch, a former editor of *Texas Weekly*, has suggested that prior political experience is an important consideration in selecting a governor. Kinch maintained that although experience may not mean that someone will be a better governor, it does mean he or she is more likely to know how to handle the pressures of the office.[7]

Election and Term of Office

Before 1974, Texas governors served two-year terms, and most were elected to a maximum of two consecutive two-year terms. As Table 8.1 shows, there have been exceptions, such as Coke Stevenson, Price Daniel, and John Connally, who each served for six years, and Allan Shivers, who served for eight years. In 1972, Texas voters adopted a constitutional amendment changing the governor's term to four years. In 1974, Dolph Briscoe was the first governor elected to a four-year term of office. George W. Bush was the first elected for two consecutive four-year terms, although he was elected president before completing the second. His successor, Rick Perry, served from 2000 through 2014, the longest tenure for a Texas governor.

Rick Perry's 14-year tenure as Texas's governor was the longest in the state's history. Here, Perry celebrates at the victory party for his successor, Greg Abbott.

TABLE 8.1

Governors of Texas and Their Terms of Office since 1874

Richard Coke	1874–76	Miriam Ferguson	1933–35
Richard B. Hubbard	1876–79	James V. Allred	1935–39
Oran M. Roberts	1879–83	W. Lee O'Daniel	1939–41
John Ireland	1883–87	Coke Stevenson	1941–47
Lawrence S. Ross	1887–91	Beauford H. Jester	1947–49**
James S. Hogg	1891–95	Allan Shivers	1949–57
Charles A. Culberson	1895–99	Price Daniel	1957–63
Joseph D. Sayers	1899–1903	John Connally	1963–69
S. W. T. Lanham	1903–07	Preston Smith	1969–73
Thomas M. Campbell	1907–11	Dolph Briscoe	1973–79†
Oscar B. Colquitt	1911–15	William Clements	1979–83
James E. Ferguson	1915–17*	Mark White	1983–87
William P. Hobby	1917–21	William Clements	1987–91
Pat M. Neff	1921–25	Ann Richards	1991–95
Miriam Ferguson	1925–27	George W. Bush	1995–2000††
Dan Moody	1927–31	Rick Perry	2000–2015
Ross Sterling	1931–33	Greg Abbott	2015–

*Impeached.
**Died in office.
†Term changed to four years with the 1974 general election.
††Resigned to become president of the United States.
SOURCE: Dallas Morning News, *Texas Almanac and State Industrial Guide 1998–99* (Dallas: A. H. Belo, 1999).

William Clements's victory over John Hill in the gubernatorial campaign of 1978 was the first time since Reconstruction that a Republican won the office. George W. Bush was the second Republican elected governor, in 1994, and his two successors have been Republican as well.

Gubernatorial elections are held in off-years (years in which a president is not elected) to minimize the effect of presidential elections on the selection of the Texas governor. The Texas legislature, controlled at the time by Democrats, designed the off-year system to eliminate the possibility that a popular Republican presidential candidate would bring votes to a Republican candidate for governor. Likewise, party leaders wanted to negate the chances of an unpopular Democratic presidential candidate costing a Democratic gubernatorial candidate votes. Unfortunately, because of this timing, voter turnout in gubernatorial contests is even lower than it is in Presidential years.

Campaigns

Just as with campaigns for president, Texas gubernatorial campaigns have become lengthy. For Greg Abbott's first election in November 2014, he announced in July 2013 that he would run for governor, and Wendy Davis, his Democratic opponent, announced her campaign in early October 2013. And even before their formal campaign announcements, both candidates, especially Abbott, were amassing campaign funds. Successful candidates must win their party's primary election in March. They then continue campaigning until the November general election. Successful candidates spend thousands of hours and millions of dollars campaigning. The money goes for staff salaries, travel, opinion polls, telephone banks, direct mailings, and advertisements in print, television, radio, and digital media.

Abbott announced his campaign for re-election on July 14, 2017. By then he already had a campaign treasury of $40 million. In contrast, Democrats had a difficult time fielding a serious candidate against Abbott, who looked unbeatable. Finally, on December 6, 2017, Dallas County sheriff Lupe Valdez announced her candidacy. Valdez and Andrew White, the son of former Democratic governor Mark White, were the most visible Democratic candidates, but by modern Texas gubernatorial standards both had a very late start in fund-raising and in the campaign.

In the 2010 Republican primary, Kay Bailey Hutchison spent over $14 million in her losing battle against Rick Perry, who spent nearly $13 million in the primary. Overall, Perry spent about $39 million and Bill White, the Democratic candidate, spent about $26 million in their 2010 campaigns. That amounted to $14.37 for every vote Perry received and $12.48 for every vote White received. In 2014, Abbott spent $47.4 million to Davis's $4 million. Incomplete data as of November 2018 show contributions of

Public debates give Texans the chance to see gubernatorial candidates face off over key campaign issues. In September 2018, Lupe Valdez and Greg Abbott held their first debate in Austin.

Who Elected Governor Greg Abbott in 2018?

Greg Abbott's support was widespread across the state. He had decisive support in nonborder rural counties. His greatest weakness was in border counties and the state's most urban counties.

2018 Election Results, by County

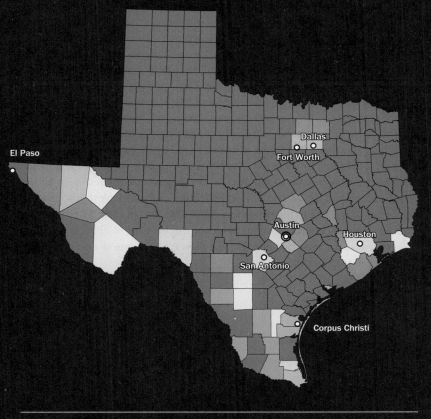

Margin of victory

Greg Abbott (R)
- > 30%
- 20–29%
- 10–19%
- 0.1–9%

Lupe Valdez (D)
- > 30%
- 20–29%
- 10–19%
- 0.1–9%

Map labels: El Paso, Dallas, Fort Worth, Austin, Houston, San Antonio, Corpus Christi

Vote Share

🐘 = Greg Abbott 🐴 = Lupe Valdez

	Abbott	Valdez
Urban and suburban	46%	54%
Rural and small town	77%	23%

SOURCE: Office of the Secretary of State, "2018 Election Night Returns," www.sos.state.tx.us (accessed 11/8/18).

QUANTITATIVE REASONING

- Lupe Valdez's strengths were in the counties along the Mexican border and in urban counties; Abbott was strongest in rural Texas, counties with smaller cities, and suburban counties. What do you think caused the differences in support for Valdez and Abbott?

- Given the election results, which parts of the state are likely to benefit the most from Governor Abbott's policies?

over $72 million to Abbott's campaign compared to less than $1.3 million to Lupe Valdez's campaign.

Removal of a Governor

impeachment the formal charge by the House of Representatives that leads to a trial in the Senate and the possible removal of a state official

In Texas, the only constitutional method of removing a governor from office is by **impeachment** and conviction. "To impeach" means to accuse or to indict, and impeachment is similar to a true bill (indictment) by a grand jury. The Texas Constitution notes that the governor may be impeached but does not give any grounds for impeachment. Possible justifications for impeachment are failure to perform the duties of governor, gross incompetence, and official misconduct.

The impeachment process in Texas is similar to the process for impeaching a president. Impeachment begins in the Texas House of Representatives. A majority vote of the House is required to impeach or to bring charges. If the House votes for impeachment, the trial takes place in the Texas Senate. One or more members of the House prosecute the case, and the chief justice of the Supreme Court of Texas presides over the trial. A two-thirds vote of the senators present and voting is necessary to convict. If convicted, the governor is removed from office and disqualified from holding any other state office.

Any member of the executive or judicial branch may be impeached. Once the House votes for impeachment charges against an official, that individual is suspended from office and cannot exercise any of his or her duties. Governor James Ferguson was the only Texas governor to be impeached and convicted. He had sought to remove several members of the faculty at the University of Texas at Austin whom he opposed and, when he failed to remove them, he vetoed practically the entire University of Texas legislative appropriation. After these actions led to broader investigations into Ferguson's conduct as governor, the Texas House voted 21 articles of impeachment against him, and the Texas Senate convicted him on 10 articles. Three charges were related to his actions regarding the University of Texas, five to misapplication of funds, one to his failure to enforce banking laws, and one to his secret receipt of $156,500 in cash. After impeachment, Jim Ferguson could no longer run for governor, but his wife, Miriam, ran with the slogan, "Two governors for the price of one." She served two terms as governor—from 1925 to 1927 and from 1933 to 1935.

Succession

The Texas Constitution provides for the lieutenant governor to become governor if the office becomes vacant through impeachment and conviction, death, resignation, or the governor's absence from the state.

In December 2000 a succession occurred when Governor George W. Bush became president-elect of the United States and resigned as governor. Lieutenant Governor Rick Perry immediately took the oath to become governor of Texas. The only time a Texas governor died in office was when Governor Beauford Jester suffered a fatal heart attack on July 11, 1949. Lieutenant Governor Allan Shivers became governor and, like Perry, was able to win later election to that office.

Should the governor leave the bounds of the state, the lieutenant governor becomes acting governor. If the governor is impeached, the lieutenant governor serves as acting governor before and during the trial. While serving as acting governor, the lieutenant governor earns the governor's daily salary, which is far better than the $26 earned as lieutenant governor. (However, a governor who is absent from the state still earns the same daily salary.)

Constitutionally, the governor's office is weak enough that when the governor is out of state, his absence does not seem to affect state operations. Former lieutenant governor Bill Hobby noted that about the only way he knew when he was acting governor was by a note his secretary left on his daily calendar.[8] In the first three months of 2000, Rick Perry, then lieutenant governor, served as acting governor more days than George W. Bush was in the state to serve as governor. Perry's press secretary commented that the added duties of being acting governor were not very noticeable and made little difference in Perry's schedule.[9]

Compensation

The governor's salary is set by the legislature. Texas pays its governor $150,000 annually. In addition to this salary, the governor receives use of an official mansion near the capitol grounds. The governor also receives use of a vehicle and a state-owned aircraft and the services of a personal staff.

Staff

The governor's staff consists of nearly 300 people organized into several divisions. The Executive Office, headed by the chief of staff, has overall responsibility for staff management and has primary contact with the governor. Governor Abbott's chief of staff is Luis Sáenz, who has worked in conservative politics for over twenty-five years. Sáenz started his career with the Heritage Foundation, a conservative think tank. He has worked as a congressional aide, was chief of staff to Texas comptroller Carole Keeton Strayhorn, was on Governor Perry's senior staff, was appointments director for Governor Abbott, and has been a lobbyist.[10] Under Sáenz's supervision are staff offices that deal with such matters as scheduling for the governor, political matters relating to the first lady, appointments to offices, legislative matters, budget, policy, and constituent communications.[11]

The staff keeps the governor informed about issues and problems facing the state, and it may suggest courses of action. In addition, during a four-year term, a governor makes about 3,000 appointments to various state posts. Since it is impossible for a governor to be acquainted personally with each appointee, some of the staff find qualified individuals for each post and recommend them to the governor. Other staff members track legislation. They talk with legislators, especially key people such as committee chairs, and let the governor know when his or her personal touch might make a difference in the outcome of legislation. For each bill that passes the legislature, a staff member prepares a summary with a recommendation that the governor sign or veto the bill.

Recent governors have used their staffs to make themselves more accessible to the public. Governor Abbott, like his immediate predecessors, encourages this accessibility through the Office of Constituent Communications, which reviews and responds to all communications to the governor.

Executive Powers of the Governor

Appointment Power To a substantial degree, the governor runs the state by appointing persons to supervisory positions over the state bureaucracy. To a great extent, Texas government is run through many boards and commissions, and the governor's power of **appointment** is the most significant executive power. Altogether, the governor makes appointments to over 400 multimember state boards or single-member commissioners that direct the operation of a broad array of state agencies (see Table 8.2). These agencies may be as obscure as the Texas Funeral Commission or the State Preservation Board or as well-known as the Public Utilities Commission of Texas or the Texas Department of Human Services, but each is important to its constituents. Governor Perry's long tenure allowed him to appoint every board member or commissioner that made policy for state agencies, and through these appointments he was able to exert significant control throughout state government.

The power of appointment enables the governor to exercise the power of **patronage**—rewarding supporters by appointing them to office. An April 2016 report found that roughly a quarter of Governor Abbott's appointees were campaign contributors. That was consistent with the proportion of appointees by Governor Perry who were campaign contributors.[12] Another report in May 2017 found that seventy-one of the nearly 800 appointees of Governor Abbott had donated a combined total of $8.6 million to Governor Abbott's campaign account since 2013. Top donors received appointments to university boards of regents, to the Higher Education Coordinating Board, and to the Texas Department of Parks and Wildlife.[13] Most of these offices pay no salary or small salaries, but they do offer supporters some prestige. The governor can also use the appointment power to repay political favors by appointing friends and associates of legislators to office as well as to garner political IOUs from other politicians (see "Appointment Controversies," below).

Most important, a governor can use the appointment power to influence agency policy. Of course, large donors generally share the same views as the governor, so their appointment can also be a way to influence agency policy in the direction sought by the governor. Sometimes a governor needs to appoint people who are highly competent at solving agency problems whether or not they were large donors. When Abbott talked Chris Traylor out of retirement to chair the Health and Human Services Commission, it was clear that he needed the widely respected Traylor, a former deputy executive commissioner, to lead the troubled commission out of its difficulties involving questionable contracts.[14] To a great degree, the effectiveness of a governor's appointees will determine the governor's success in office.

In some cases, the governor shares appointment power with others. For example, the State Commission on Judicial Conduct, which regulates the ethics and behavior of Texas judges, is governed by a 13-member board. Six of the members, appointed by the Texas Supreme Court, are judges representing various court levels. Two members, appointed by the state bar, are lawyers but non-judges. The governor appoints five citizen members. The Texas Ethics Commission promotes ethics rules for state officials and is where campaign finance data are reported. The commission has eight members—four appointed by the governor, two by the lieutenant governor, and two by the Speaker of the Texas House of Representatives. Some of the entities to which the governor makes appointments are advisory as opposed to policy-making. For example, the governor

appointment the power of the chief executive, whether the president of the United States or the governor of a state, to appoint persons to office

patronage the resources available to higher officials, usually opportunities to make political appointments to offices and to confer grants, licenses, or special favors to supporters

TABLE 8.2

The Governor's Appointment Power

The following are examples of some of the entities in Texas, in just four policy areas, where the governor has the power to appoint members. This power can provide the governor with significant influence over policy in these areas.

WATER

Angelina and Neches River Authority, Upper, Lower Central Colorado River Authority, Brazos River Authority, Canadian River Compact Commissioner, Board of Pilot Commissioners for Galveston County Ports, Guadalupe-Blanco River Authority, Upper Guadalupe River Authority, Gulf of Mexico Fishery Management Council, Gulf States Marine Fisheries Commission, Lavaca-Navidad River Authority, Nueces River Authority, Red River Authority and Red River Compact, Sabine River Authority and Sabine River Compact, San Antonio River Authority, San Jacinto River Authority, Trinity River Authority, Sulphur River Basin Authority, Western States Water Council, Evergreen Underground Water Conservation District, Drought Preparedness Council

HEALTH

Aging and Disability Services Council, Texas Council on Alzheimer's Disease and Related Disorders, Texas Council on Autism and Pervasive Developmental Disorders, Chronic Kidney Disease Task Force, Texas Council for Developmental Disabilities, Health Professions Council, Oversight Committee of the Cancer Prevention and Research Institute, Council on Cardiovascular Disease and Stroke, Sickle Cell Disease Advisory Committee

LAW ENFORCEMENT

Automobile Burglary and Theft Prevention Authority, Border Security Council, Task Force to Reduce Child Abuse and Neglect, Crime Stoppers Council, Crime Victims' Institute Advisory Council, Texas Board of Criminal Justice, Homeland Security Council, Commission on Jail Standards, Juvenile Justice Advisory Board, Juvenile Probation Commission, Commission on Law Enforcement Officer Standards and Education

PROFESSIONAL LICENSING

Texas Optometry Board, Board of Orthotics and Prosthetics, Board of Nursing, Board of Occupational Therapy Examiners, Board for the Licensure of Professional Medical Physicists, Medical Board, Board of Examiners of Marriage and Family Therapists, Board of Examiners in the Fitting and Dispensing of Hearing Instruments, Board of Podiatric Medical Examiners, Physician Assistant Board, Board of Plumbing Examiners, Board of Physical Therapy Examiners, Board of Pharmacy, Board of Veterinary Medical Examiners, Appraiser Licensing and Certification Board, Board of Architectural Examiners, Board of Chiropractic Examiners, Board of Dental Examiners, State Board of Examiners of Dietitians, State Board for Educator Certification

appoints the three-member Firefighters' Star of Texas Award Advisory Committee, which considers an award for firefighters killed or seriously injured in the line of duty.

Other entities are both advisory and appointed by several different officers. For example, the Oil-Field Cleanup Fund Advisory Committee has 10 members. One member is appointed by the lieutenant governor, one by the presiding officer of the Texas House of Representatives committee with primary jurisdiction over energy resources, one by the lieutenant governor from the academic field of geology or economics, one by the Speaker of the Texas House from the field of geology or economics, one by the governor, and one each by the executive officers (or the officers' designees) of the Texas Oil and Gas Association, the Texas Independent Producers and Royalty Owners Association, the Panhandle Producers and Royalty Owners Association, the Permian Basin

Producers Association, and the Alliance of Energy Producers. This committee meets with the Railroad Commission about oilfield cleanup issues and reports to the governor, the lieutenant governor, and the Speaker about any problems in the administration of oilfield cleanup funds and about any recommendations for legislation dealing with oilfield cleanup. Oilfield cleanup is not a top priority for most Texans, but it is a vital issue for oil producers and royalty owners. The governor has an appointive role in a number of these rather obscure advisory entities that provide input to state government for specialized issues. For example, there are the Nursing Facility Administrators Advisory Committee, the Advisory Committee to the Texas Board of Criminal Justice on Offenders with Medical or Mental Impairments, the Governor's Advisory Council on Physical Fitness, and numerous other such groups.

The governor also makes appointments to many commissions that have major policy impact. For example, the governor appoints all members to the governing boards of Texas public universities, which have considerable influence over the universities' governance and policies. Additionally, the governor appoints all of the nine members to the Texas Higher Education Coordinating Board, which oversees all public postsecondary education in the state, including determining when public colleges and universities start or continue offering degrees and what core class requirements all students in state colleges or universities must take. Another major agency for which the governor appoints the leadership is the Parks and Wildlife Commission, responsible for the management and conservation of the state's natural resources, with particular responsibility to provide for hunting, fishing, and outdoor recreation for Texans. The governor appoints the three members of the Alcoholic Beverage Commission, which regulates all aspects of alcoholic beverages within the state and collects $200 million a year in taxes and fees. Many of the other bodies over which the governor has supervision through the appointment process deal with water (its conservation, use, control, and navigation), health and aging, law enforcement, and professional licensing.

Appointment Controversies A governor must exert care in appointments, since failure to appoint responsible individuals can lead to serious political problems. In 2007 a scandal within the Texas Youth Commission, which has authority over institutionalized juveniles, revealed that not only was there a widespread pattern of physical and sexual abuse of juveniles in state facilities but also that authorities had tried to cover up the abuse. As a result, Governor Perry's appointees had to resign from the commission, which was then reorganized.

In the early stages of his administration, Greg Abbott ran into intense criticism for appointing Donna Bahorich as chair of the State Board of Education. Even some fellow Republicans were shocked when Abbott named Bahorich to head this agency, which makes policy and sets standards for the state's public schools, because Bahorich had home-schooled her three sons prior to sending them to private schools. They never attended public school. Thomas Ratliff, a Republican member of the board, said, "When 94 percent of our students in Texas attend public schools, I think it ought to be a baseline requirement that the chair of the State Board of Education have at least some experience in that realm, as a parent, teacher, something."[15] Bahorich's appointment was perhaps an act of political patronage; she managed now-lieutenant governor Dan Patrick's first campaign for the Texas Senate.

Of course, a governor makes so many appointments that some are bound to provoke criticism, but a governor may believe that a controversial appointment is necessary to

Josh McGee was a controversial Abbott appointee to chair the State Pension Review Board, since he had been outspoken in his criticism of governmental pensions.

deal with a particular problem. The State Pension Review Board oversees state and local retirement systems. It consists of seven members appointed by the governor. When Governor Abbott appointed Josh McGee as chair of the State Pension Review Board, the Combined Law Enforcement Association of Texas, which is the state's largest peace officer labor organization, and the Texas Retired Teacher Association objected. Both organizations feared McGee would harm their pensions since he had been critical of governmental pensions and had warned that cities faced financial disaster over their mismanagement of pensions. Given that a number of governmental pension funds, especially in Dallas and Houston, were in crisis and that the Dallas police and fire pension fund had been terribly mismanaged (see Chapter 10), it seemed reasonable for Abbott to appoint McGee in spite of the opposition to his appointment.[16]

The Senate's Role in Gubernatorial Appointments The governor appoints people to office, but the Texas Senate must confirm them. However, because the Senate may not be in session for almost two years after an appointment, the appointee takes office immediately and does not wait for Senate confirmation. Nevertheless, the governor cannot ignore how he or she thinks the Senate will react to appointees. Consider the appointment in 2011 of Eleanor Kitzman as Texas insurance commissioner. Insurance commissioner is a particularly important office in Texas, since it is a single appointed position rather than a board or commission and the commissioner has regulatory authority over insurance companies that operate in Texas. Kitzman came into strong conflict with the legislature. Her critics said she was too favorable to insurance companies. What seemed to sink her chances for approval by the Senate, however, was that Kitzman, who never blocked any large insurance premium hikes while she was commissioner, withheld insurance company profit data from the legislature. After this, it was clear that Kitzman would not be confirmed. Governor Perry did not even submit her name to the Senate Nominations Committee, and the Senate did not vote on her nomination. Kitzman had to leave office at the end of the regular legislative session.[17]

An important limitation on the power of the governor to appoint people to office is the informal requirement that the appointee's state senator must approve. This practice is known as **senatorial courtesy** and applies regardless of the party affiliation of the governor, senator, or appointee. Usually, if the appointee's senator concurs in the appointment, the remainder of the Senate will agree. However, if the appointee's senator opposes the appointment, the remainder of the Senate will also oppose it.

The process for removing an appointee is also complicated. The approval of two-thirds of the Texas Senate is required for a governor to remove one of his or her appointees who refuses to resign. Along with the practice of senatorial courtesy, this complex procedure for the termination of members of boards and commissions can be a significant limitation on the governor's power to influence the policies of state agencies. Chairs of boards, however, serve at the pleasure of the governor and so can easily be removed if they do something that displeases him or her.

Budgetary Power

Officially, the Texas governor is the state's chief budget officer. As such, governors submit an **executive budget** to the legislature. This budget suggests a plan for revenue and expenditure for Texas, but more important, it indicates the governor's priorities for the state in the next biennium.

In 1949, in an effort to gain more control over the state's budget, the legislature established the Legislative Budget Board (LBB), which is responsible for preparing a **legislative budget**. Thus, two budgets are prepared and submitted to the legislature: an executive budget by the governor and a legislative budget by the LBB. As a creation of the legislature, the LBB's budget proposal receives more consideration by the House and Senate than the governor's recommendations. In 1989, Governor Clements recognized the futility of submitting an executive budget and simply endorsed the recommendations of the LBB. Ann Richards followed Clements's precedent, but Governor Bush took a more active role in budget preparation, and Governor Perry was very involved in dealing with the state's 2011 budgetary shortfall. Governor Abbott also has shown involvement in budgetary policy making.

The governor has some control over the final appropriations bill through the use of the line-item veto. However, the governor must have the support of the LBB to impound funds or transfer funds from one agency to another if circumstances change from the time the money was appropriated. There is one exception to the constraint on gubernatorial power to transfer funds. Under a 1993 law, the governor can declare an emergency and bypass the other legislative members of the LBB. In 2014, Governor Perry declared an emergency and shifted $38.7 million from a Department of Public Safety fund to pay for the National Guard to patrol the Texas-Mexico border. Overall, however, the budgetary process does not provide the governor acting alone with a highly effective means of controlling state agencies.

Military and Police Power

The governor is commander in chief of the state's National Guard units when they are not under presidential orders. These units are headed by the adjutant general, who is appointed by the governor. The governor can

senatorial courtesy in Texas, the practice whereby the governor seeks the indication that the senator from the candidate's home district supports the nomination

executive budget the state budget prepared and submitted by the governor to the legislature, which indicates the governor's spending priorities. The executive budget is overshadowed in terms of importance by the legislative budget

legislative budget the state budget that is prepared and submitted by the Legislative Budget Board (LBB) and that is fully considered by the House and Senate declare martial law, which suspends most civil authority and imposes military rule over an area to protect lives and property. Martial law can be declared in the event of a riot, a flood, a hurricane, a tornado, or another disaster. In Texas, law enforcement and police power are primarily a local responsibility, and the governor has few responsibilities in this area. The governor appoints, with Senate approval, the three-member Public Safety Commission, which directs the work of the Department of Public Safety (DPS). The DPS is responsible for highway traffic enforcement (highway patrol), drivers' licensing, motor vehicle inspection, truck weighing stations, and the Texas Rangers (an elite, highly trained force of about 150 officers with 58 support staff). When circumstances warrant, the governor can assume command of the Rangers. If there is evidence of ongoing violence or corruption, the governor can use informal powers, the prestige of the governor's office, and appeals to the media to compel appropriate action from local law enforcement officials.

It is not often that the governor uses his or her military and police powers, but when he or she does, it usually makes news. Governor Perry ordered Texas National Guard troops to patrol the Texas-Mexico border in the summer of 2014 because of a surge of undocumented immigrants. Governor Abbott also used his military powers as governor to extend their service on the border. Additionally, Abbott used his powers over state police forces to order the DPS to team with the Texas Department of Parks and Wildlife to increase boat patrols on the Rio Grande as part of his border security efforts.[18]

In 2015, in what must be the most bizarre use of the governor's military power in modern times, Governor Abbott directed the Texas State Guard to monitor a U.S. military exercise code-named Jade Helm 15. Prodded by conspiracy theories hatched by talk radio hosts, people became convinced the exercise meant a federal takeover of Texas or at least the imposition of martial law and the confiscation of Texans' guns. Abbott received hundreds of letters and emails from people who demanded action from the

The Texas National Guard was instrumental in providing relief and assistance to communities struck by Hurricane Harvey.

governor. The effect of Abbott's order, however, was a strong political backlash from those who thought he disrespected the military and embarrassed himself and the state. Michael Hayden, a former CIA and NSA director, has stated that a Russian misinformation campaign also encouraged the Jade Helm 15 hysteria and that hysteria, coupled with Abbott's response, persuaded the Russians to begin a misinformation campaign in the 2016 elections.[19]

Governor Abbott did use his military powers for a real crisis in the wake of Hurricane Harvey when he activated the entire Texas National Guard to assist with relief efforts in south Texas as a result of Harvey's devastation. Approximately 12,000 Texas National Guardsmen assisted with hurricane relief.[20]

Legislative Powers of the Governor

The governor's legislative powers include message power, the power of the veto, and the authority to call special sessions and set their agendas. If a governor uses these powers effectively, he or she can have considerable control over the state's legislative business.

Message Power
Any communication between the governor and the legislature is part of the message power. Early in each regular session, the governor delivers a State of the State message. In this speech to a joint session of the legislature, the governor explains his or her plan for the state in the coming two years. The address, which may propose specific programs or simply set general goals, is covered by most news media and is often broadcast on public television and radio stations, analyzed on blogs, and discussed on social media.

If the governor submits an executive budget, he or she may address the legislature on the important items in the proposed plan of spending and revenue. At the very least, the budget proposal is forwarded to the legislature with a letter briefly explaining it.

Lobbying by governors is another part of the message power. Governors try to pass or defeat bills important to them. For example, in his 2017 State of the State address, Governor Abbott stressed the need to pass legislation restricting abortion and securing the Texas border with Mexico. He also stressed the importance of early childhood education and school choice programs, property tax reform, and he encouraged efforts to attract jobs while avoiding drawing money from the Rainy Day Fund. He voiced support for items he considered in need of emergency legislation: reform of the Child Protective Services program, which was failing in the state so badly that numerous children in the program had died in the previous year; a ban on sanctuary cities; ethics reform; and the passing of a resolution that called for a convention of states to amend the Constitution to reassert states' rights.[21]

veto the governor's power to turn down legislation; can be overridden by a two-thirds vote of both the House and Senate

Veto Power
Governors of Texas can sign or **veto** legislation, but in most cases they sign it. Rick Perry vetoed 301 bills during his gubernatorial career.[22] In his first legislative session, Greg Abbott vetoed 44 bills. Abbott signed about 1,300 bills, which means the veto was exercised in only about 3 percent of the cases in which a bill was presented to the governor for signature.[23] (In Abbott's second legislative session, he vetoed 51 bills.)[24] In modern times, vetoes are simply not overridden by the legislature. The state's Legislative Reference Library found that from 1876 to 2013 there

had been only 26 legislative overrides of vetoes, and ten of those occurred in 1941 during the administration of Governor W. Lee (Pappy) O'Daniel. No veto override has occurred since 1979.[25]

A veto of a bill after the legislature adjourns is called a **post-adjournment veto** (or strong veto). This veto cannot be overridden, because the legislature that passed the vetoed bill no longer exists.

Texas governors also possess the **line-item veto**, the ability to veto individual parts of an appropriations bill. To exercise this power, the governor signs the bill but strikes out particular lines in it. Items struck from the bill do not become law, but the remainder of the appropriations bill does.

The line-item veto allows the governor considerable control over appropriations to state agencies, and this power can be used to reduce state expenditures or to punish agencies or programs disfavored by the governor.[26] It is one important power of the Texas governor that is not available to the president of the United States. The U.S. Supreme Court has held that a presidential line-item veto violates the principle of separation of powers in the U.S. Constitution.

Governor Abbott issued two line-item vetoes among his 44 vetoes in the 2015 legislative session. One eliminated funding for numerous items in the general appropriations bill, which ranged from relatively small amounts such as a $193,000 appropriation for the Texas Education Agency to pay membership fees in the Southern Regional Education Board to a $132,000,000 appropriation to replace a state government building. His second line-item veto was of $500,000 in planning costs for a new Department of Motor Vehicles headquarters.[27] Still, Abbott faced an unusual challenge to some of his vetoes. The director of the Legislative Budget Board, Ursula Parks, wrote state comptroller Glenn Hegar, arguing that Abbott had not vetoed actual appropriations but rather items that were legislative statements of intent, direction, or conditions on the use of funds. Abbott's office responded that even if an appropriation was labeled something else, it was still an appropriation that could be vetoed. The comptroller sought an opinion from the Office of the Attorney General, which agreed with Abbott's position.

In the 2017 legislative session, Abbott used the line-item veto to cut about $120 million from the $217 billion two-year state budget. Claiming that the budget already included other funding sources for those living in colonias, Abbott vetoed $860,000 in aid to Texans living there. He cut funding for a Legislative Law Clinic at the University of Texas Law School, for state education employees who study dual-credit programs, and for "safety education" at the Texas Department of Public Safety. Using the attorney general's opinion, which expanded his veto powers by allowing the governor to veto directives to state agencies that were included in the budget but did not actually make an appropriation, Abbott line-item vetoed a number of environmental bills such as $87 million for the Low-Income Vehicle Repair Assistance Program, which he claimed had done little to improve air quality. He also cut $6 million for air quality planning at the Texas Commission on Environmental Quality and $2 million for a study of brackish ground water.[28]

Special Sessions As we saw in Chapter 7, the governor has the power to call special sessions of the Texas legislature, which may last for no more than 30 days and may consider only those items placed on the agenda by the governor. **Special sessions** are called to address critical problems as defined by the governor. Their nature allows the legislature to focus attention on specific issues.

post-adjournment veto a veto of a bill that occurs after the legislature adjourns, thus preventing the legislature from overriding it

line-item veto the power of the executive to veto specific provisions (lines) of an appropriations bill passed by the legislature

special session a legislative session called by the governor that addresses an agenda set by him or her and that lasts no longer than 30 days

From 1989 through 2017 the legislature met in 23 special sessions. Among other topics, these sessions considered the complicated and divisive issues of reform of workers' compensation laws, public school finance, reapportionment, and voter identification. The sessions ranged from 30 days to 2 days, with six of the sessions occurring in 1989–90 and five from 2005 through 2011. In 2013 three special sessions were called, two lasting 30 days and one lasting seven days. The issues involved redistricting, criminal sentencing, transportation, and abortion regulation, which received the most attention. In 2017 one special session was called that lasted 29 days and involved twenty-one topics on a wide variety of subjects, but many of which involved preemption of local legislation by the state.[29]

Judicial Powers of the Governor

Texas elects all of its appellate and district court judges, but when vacancies occur because of the death, resignation, or retirement of the incumbent or the creation of new courts, the governor is responsible for appointing people to fill these vacancies. The governor also fills vacancies (before an election) in the office of district attorney. Once

WHAT DO TEXANS THINK? ★★★★★★★★★★★★★★★★★★★★★★★★★

Governor Abbott's Job Approval

In eight polls from November 2015 to February 2018, Abbott's job approval has ranged from 41 percent to 48 percent, and his disapproval has ranged from 29 percent to 38 percent. However, Abbott has tremendous approval among Republicans, the dominant party in statewide elections. With such strong support from Republicans, why aren't Abbott's overall approval numbers higher?

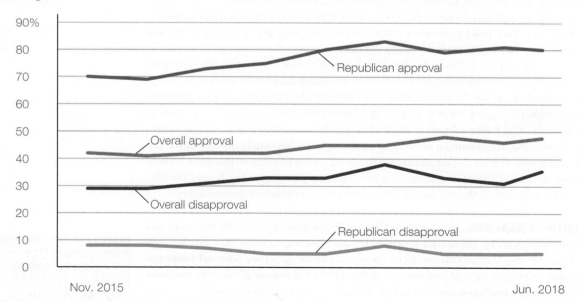

SOURCE: University of Texas/*Texas Tribune* polls from November 2015 to June 2018.

appointed to office, judges tend to remain in office. More than 95 percent of incumbents win re-election. Through this power to appoint judges, the governor has considerable influence over the Texas judicial system.

The governor has limited powers to issue clemencies for people convicted of crimes. Clemency normally includes the power to issue pardons, grant paroles, and issue reprieves. The governor's power in this area is severely limited, however, because of abuses by previous governors. Pardons can be granted only on the recommendation of the Board of Pardons and Paroles. Governors have the ability to grant each person condemned to death one 30-day reprieve. Additional reprieves and any other act of clemency must be recommended by the Board of Pardons and Paroles.

In 2017, Governor Abbott issued only seven pardons, most for relatively minor offenses. The pardon for the most serious offense involved a person who had been sentenced in 1992 to ten years' probation and a $500 fine on two charges of burglary of a habitation. Interestingly, in none of the cases where Abbott issued a pardon did the pardon release a person from imprisonment. Rather, it cleared their record of a crime from years in the past.[30]

The use of the pardoning power by governors has been criticized by criminal justice experts because governors usually issue pardons for minor crimes where the pardon has little impact on the life of the individual. If pardons are to have any real value, these experts argue, they should be issued for reformed felons who cannot rejoin the free world because of the felony on their record.[31]

Without question, the most surprising act of clemency by Governor Abbott was his February 2018 decision to spare Thomas Whitaker from the death penalty. Whitaker had planned the murder of his family with his roommate in order to collect inheritance money. His mother and brother died, and his father was wounded. After the Board of Pardons and Paroles unanimously recommended clemency for Whitaker, Abbott reduced his sentence to life imprisonment less than one hour before Whitaker was scheduled to be executed. There were a number of reasons Abbott, who has presented himself as a law-and-order official, granted clemency to Whitaker. One was that the roommate, who was the person who actually fired the weapon, had received a life sentence; another was that Whitaker waived any right to parole; and Whitaker's father had begged that his son be spared.[32]

The Plural Executive

Identify the other elected officials who make up Texas's plural executive

When Texans drafted a constitution in 1876, they chose to limit executive power and disperse it through several elected officials called the **plural executive**. Texans elect six of the seven people who make up the plural executive: the governor, lieutenant governor, attorney general, comptroller of public accounts, commissioner of the General Land Office, and commissioner of agriculture (see Table 8.3). The governor appoints the seventh person, the secretary of state. With the exception of the commissioner of

plural executive an executive branch in which power is fragmented because the election of statewide officeholders is independent of the election of the governor

TABLE 8.3

Elected Officials in Texas with Executive Responsibilities

SINGLE-ELECTED EXECUTIVES

Governor	Greg Abbott (R)
Lieutenant governor	Dan Patrick (R)
Attorney general	Ken Paxton (R)
Commissioner of the General Land Office	George P. Bush (R)
Agriculture commissioner	Sid Miller (R)
Comptroller	Glenn Hegar (R)

MULTI-MEMBER ELECTED EXECUTIVES

Railroad Commission (3 members)
State Board of Education (15 members)

APPOINTED EXECUTIVES

Secretary of state	David Whitley (R)

agriculture, whose office is created by statute, these offices are established by Article 3, Section 1, of the Texas Constitution. Except for the lieutenant governor, who receives the same salary as a legislator, salaries of members of the plural executive are set by the legislature.

The Railroad Commission of Texas and the State Board of Education also assume considerable executive authority in the state, although these offices are not formally part of the executive branch established under Article 4 of the Texas Constitution. Instead the Railroad Commission of Texas is created by the legislature under statutory law authority granted under Article 10, Section 2, of the Texas Constitution. The State Board of Education is created under Article 7, Section 8. This statutory-law origin is important because the constitution allows the legislature to decide in both cases how large the commission or board will be, whether its members will be appointed or elected, and how long their terms of office will be.

If the legislature wanted to change the way that the commissioner of agriculture, the Railroad Commission, or the Board of Education is selected, all it would have to do is pass a new law. To change the other executive offices' term or authority would demand a constitutional amendment. The ultimate result of all these constitutional nuances is vast fragmentation of responsibility for public policy in the state.

Elections are partisan, and each member of the plural executive may choose to operate independently of the others. At times, the members may be in competition with each other, often because of conflicting personal ambitions. That situation occurred when John Hill was attorney general and sought to take the governorship from Dolph Briscoe, and when Mark White was attorney general and sought the governorship from Bill Clements. Because of the difficulty of defeating incumbents, however, it is far more likely that members of the plural executive will wait for a vacancy in a more prestigious office before seeking that office. Champions of the plural executive believe that it limits the power of executive officials and makes them more accountable to the public. Opponents assert that the plural executive is inefficient and does not promote good government. The governor is a member of the plural executive, but this multipart executive limits the governor's control of the executive branch because he or she has little authority over this group.

One can get a sense of the importance of the various positions in the plural executive simply by looking at the campaign contributions received by winning candidates for these offices in the 2018 elections. Table 8.4 shows the contributions received by both the Democratic and the Republican nominees in 2018.

Two things are especially notable about these figures. One is the enormous amounts of money that are contributed to candidates. The Republican candidate for land commissioner, George P. Bush, had nearly $3.8 million in contributions, a large sum for a rather uncompetitive race for this office. George P. Bush is the son of former Florida governor and 2016 presidential candidate Jeb Bush, nephew of former president George W. Bush, and grandson of former president George H. W. Bush and is viewed as an up-and-coming Republican star. His family ties may explain Bush's success at fund-raising, but it is clear that large sums were given to all the Republican candidates for these offices.

The other thing that stands out about Table 8.4 is how lopsided the contributions are in favor of the Republican candidates. One explanation may be that all the Republican candidates were incumbents and incumbents usually have a fund-raising advantage. Part of the reason for the large sums contributed to Republican candidates may

TABLE 8.4

Campaign Contributions in 2018 for Statewide Elective Offices

OFFICE	WINNING CANDIDATE	CONTRIBUTIONS TO WINNER ($)	LOSING CANDIDATE	CONTRIBUTIONS TO LOSER ($)
Governor	Greg Abbott (R)	$72,412,015	Lupe Valdez (D)	$1,253,688
Lieutenant governor	Dan Patrick (R)	25,749,140	Mike Collier (D)	867,309
Attorney general	Ken Paxton (R)	7,864,608	Justin Nelson (D)	2,669,475
Comptroller	Glenn Hegar (R)	3,746,306	Joi Chevalier (D)	59,282
Agriculture commissioner	Sid Miller (R)	1,797,867	Kim Olson (D)	386,223
Land commissioner	George P. Bush (R)	3,780,944	Miguel Suazo (D)	93,955
Railroad commissioner*	Christi Craddick (R)	5,471,872	Roman McAllen (D)	22,298

*There was an election for one position on the three-member Railroad Commission.
NOTE: Contribution data is through election day, November 6, 2018.
SOURCE: National Institute on Money in State Politics.

be that some faced primary opposition. That, for example, was the case with the race for land commissioner, in which George P. Bush was opposed by the previous land commissioner, Jerry Patterson. For years, Republican candidates for statewide office have done exceedingly well against Democrats, which probably explains a large part of their fund-raising advantage. The electoral performance of Democrats in the 2018 statewide elections was the best in years, and so the Republican fund-raising advantage over Democrats will likely decline.

Lieutenant Governor

In 2014, Texans elected conservative state senator Dan Patrick to the powerful position of lieutenant governor. Here, Patrick presides over a session in the Senate that took up a bill to restrict access to abortions.

lieutenant governor the second-highest elected official in the state and president of the state Senate

The **lieutenant governor** has executive responsibilities, such as serving as acting governor when the governor is out of state and succeeding a governor who resigns, is incapacitated, or is impeached. The real power of the office of lieutenant governor, however, is derived from its place in the legislative process.

According to the Texas Constitution, the lieutenant governor is the "Constitutional President of the Senate" and has the right to debate and vote on all issues when the Senate sits as a "Committee of the Whole." The Texas Constitution also grants the lieutenant governor the power to cast a deciding vote in the Senate when there is a tie. Like the Speaker of the House, the lieutenant governor signs all bills and resolutions. The constitution names the lieutenant governor to the Legislative Redistricting Board, a five-member committee that apportions the state into senatorial and house districts if the legislature fails to do so following a census. Other powers of the lieutenant governor are derived from various statutes passed by the legislature. For example, the lieutenant governor is chair of the Legislative Budget Board and a member of a number of other boards and committees, including the Legislative Audit Committee, the Legislative Education Board, the Cash Management Committee, and the Bond Review Board.

The Texas Constitution grants the Senate the power to make its own rules, and lieutenant governors traditionally have been granted significant legislative power by the Senate itself. The Senate rules empower the lieutenant governor to decide all parliamentary questions and to use discretion in following Senate procedural rules. The lieutenant governor is also empowered to set up standing and special committees and to appoint committee members and chairs. The Senate rules, and not just the Texas Constitution, make the lieutenant governor one of the most powerful political leaders in the state. New Senate rules passed by a future Senate could, of course, substantially alter the power possessed by the lieutenant governor.

Political Style of Lieutenant Governors

In 2014 and 2018, Texas elected and re-elected a Tea Party–backed conservative Republican, Dan Patrick, as lieutenant governor. Patrick was a Houston AM radio talk show host, and he parlayed his talk show skills and his audience support into a state senate seat in 2006. In 2013 he was chosen as one of the worst Texas legislators by *Texas Monthly*, which claimed he was a bully and an ideologue who treated the committee he chaired, the Education Committee, as if it were part of his radio show. He lectured other legislators, interrupted witnesses, and assumed that those who disagreed with his bills did not understand them.

The only opinion that mattered to him, *Texas Monthly* claimed, was Patrick's.[33] Still, he ran (and won) an extraordinary race for lieutenant governor against three Republicans in the primary and against state senator Leticia Van De Putte, a very capable Democratic opponent in the general election.

Patrick's political agenda reflected his Tea Party/religious right support, which represents a different political faction and a different political orientation from the business-oriented agenda of previous lieutenant governors. Patrick changed the rules of the state Senate to make it easier for votes to be taken on bills opposed by the Democratic minority, and he sought to lessen the power of Democrats over committees by exercising his power to appoint committee chairs. He sought to restrict abortion as much as possible, to control the border, and to promote gun rights. In the 2017 legislative session Patrick continued to promote gun rights and religious liberty, to prevent public funds from being used to process union dues, and to weaken the influence of the federal Environmental Protection Agency.[34] One key issue for him was support for the "bathroom bill," which required persons to use the bathroom, showers, and locker rooms of public schools and other state and local buildings that matched the sex specified on their birth certificate as opposed to their gender identity. Much of his agenda in the 2017 session was stymied by Speaker Joe Straus, who represented the traditional, moderate-conservative, pro-business wing of the Republican Party.[35]

Attorney General

The **attorney general** is elected to a four-year term and acts as the chief lawyer for the state of Texas. Currently, the Texas attorney general oversees the work of more than 700 lawyers.

attorney general elected state official who serves as the state's chief civil lawyer

The attorney general is, in effect, head of Texas's civil law firm. The office is concerned primarily with civil matters. When a lawsuit is filed against the state or by the state, the attorney general manages the legal activities surrounding that lawsuit. Any time a state agency needs legal representation, the office represents the agency. In any lawsuit to which Texas is a party, the office has full responsibility to resolve the case and can litigate, compromise, settle, or choose not to continue the litigation.

One of the more important powers of the office comes from the opinion process. Any agency of state or local government can ask for an advisory opinion on the legality of an action. The office will rule on the question, and the ruling has the force of law unless overturned by a court or the legislature.

The office has little responsibility in criminal law but may appoint a special prosecutor if a local district attorney asks for assistance. This can happen when there is a potential conflict of interest—for example, if the district attorney is a friend of or works with a local official who is under criminal investigation. In one case, lawyers from the office prosecuted a state district judge in Collin County on bribery charges. Generally, criminal cases in Texas are prosecuted by district or county attorneys elected in each county. The county is usually responsible for the costs of the trial and for all appeals in state court. If a criminal case is appealed to the federal courts, the attorney general's office assumes responsibility.

Probably the most controversial and criticized aspect of the work of the office is child support collection. Almost one-half of its 4,000 employees are involved in collecting child support. However, this program is the subject of intense criticism because much child support remains uncollected.

In 2014 and 2018 Ken Paxton was elected and re-elected attorney general. Paxton had served in the Texas House from 2002 to 2012 and then was elected to the Texas Senate. He was elected with the support of the Tea Party in 2014 when the former attorney general, Greg Abbott, ran for and was elected governor. Taking a page from Abbott's political playbook as attorney general, Paxton emphasized suing the federal government. His biography on the attorney general's website notes, "In his first year in office, General Paxton hit the ground running, filing eight lawsuits against the federal government to protect Texas sovereignty on environmental issues, health care, religious freedom and immigration."[36] Though Texas attorneys general had battled in the past with the federal government over integration and off-shore oil ownership, Abbott and Paxton appear to have been the most litigious of Texas attorneys general when it comes to suits against the federal government.

A cloud has remained over Paxton for much of his administration as attorney general because he has been charged with two first degree felonies involving securities fraud and one third degree felony involving failure to register as a securities agent. (These charges stem from his time in the legislature in 2011–2012.) He has pled not guilty to these charges. He was also under investigation for a land sale in McKinney, Texas, that involved him, Collin County district attorney Greg Willis, and eight others. The group bought 35 acres of undeveloped land for $700,000, arranged to have the land rezoned, and sold half of it for $1,000,000 for construction of the Collin County Central Appraisal District building. A grand jury decided in 2016 not to pursue charges in this matter. In addition, Paxton was the subject of a disciplinary investigation by the State Bar of Texas for allegedly violating the rules of professional conduct by stating that county clerks could opt out of issuing marriage licenses to same-sex couples if they had religious objections to doing so. The State Bar did not ultimately discipline Paxton, who claimed that all the charges against him were politically motivated.[37] Paxton had no opponent in the 2018 Republican primary for attorney general, although he did draw a Democratic opponent with impressive legal credentials. Paxton's legal problems likely explain why he won re-election in 2018 with only 50.59 percent of the vote.

Commissioner of the General Land Office

land commissioner elected state official who is the manager of most publicly owned lands

The General Land Office (GLO) is the oldest state agency in Texas. Historically, the head of the agency, the **land commissioner**, gave away land. Today, the GLO is the manager for most publicly owned lands in Texas. Texas owns, or has mineral rights in, 13 million acres of land in the state, plus all submerged lands up to 10.35 miles into the Gulf of Mexico. All but 28 of Texas's 254 counties contain some of these public lands.

The GLO also awards rights for grazing and oil and gas exploration on this land. Thousands of producing oil and gas wells on state-owned land are managed by the GLO, and a significant portion of royalties on oil and natural gas produced by these wells goes to the state's Permanent School Fund and Permanent University Fund. These responsibilities make the office of land commissioner quite influential.

The commissioner also manages the Veterans' Land Program, through which the state makes low-cost loans to Texas veterans. The program includes loans for land, housing, and home improvements. In addition, the GLO was recently given authority over some environmental matters. The land commissioner is responsible for environmental quality on public lands and waters, especially along the Texas coast. All of Texas's Gulf Coast beaches are publicly owned and under the jurisdiction of the GLO.

The General Land Office is influential in large part because it awards oil and gas exploration rights for publicly owned lands. Here, Land Commissioner George P. Bush speaks in front of the Alamo, which is now under GLO supervision.

George P. Bush was elected commissioner of the GLO in 2014 and was re-elected in 2018 with 53.7 percent of the vote. Bush is generally believed to have sought the position as a stepping-stone to higher political office. However, he has taken an active and aggressive role in running and changing the GLO. He terminated two top-level GLO officials, and a third has resigned. In the wake of critical reports from the state auditor that found problems with the GLO's contracting process and internal audits that found numerous other problems, Bush undertook a complete restructuring of the organization.

Bush's major problem, however, was not related to his management of the organization, but with the Alamo. In the wake of fiscal problems with the Alamo and deterioration of the structure, Bush took over the Alamo from the Daughters of the Republic of Texas, its long-time managers. Litigation ensued between the GLO and the Daughters of the Republic of Texas. That was followed by opposition to redesign part of the facility. Conspiracy theorists objected when UNESCO gave the San Antonio missions, including the Alamo, a World Heritage designation. They claimed that Bush was allowing the United Nations to take over the Alamo. There was also opposition to the way Bush was handling state funding for Alamo improvements, the assertion being there was insufficient transparency in the use of these funds. Bush has further been criticized by his opponents for what was claimed to be his agency's inadequate response to Hurricane Harvey. He has also been criticized for receiving campaign contributions from those doing business with the GLO.

Jerry Patterson, Bush's predecessor at the GLO, was clearly displeased with Bush's management of the GLO, and he ran against Bush in the 2018 Republican primary. One factor in Patterson's decision to challenge Bush was that the Bush political name had lost much of its prestige in the state. George P. Bush's father, Jeb, had failed in his race for the presidency, his uncle George W. was long retired from the presidency, and his grandfather, George H.W., was now aged and infirm. Donald Trump, no friend of the Bush family, was in control of the Republican Party. As Patterson explained in 2018, "The Bush name is not an asset—it's a liability."[38] However, Bush did win the Republican primary—receiving 58 percent of the vote compared to Patterson's 30 percent, and he won by obtaining the endorsement of President Trump, a surprising development in light of the hostile relationship between Trump and the rest of the Bush political family.

Agriculture Commissioner

The **agriculture commissioner** is primarily responsible for enforcing agricultural laws. These include administration of animal quarantine laws, inspection of food, and enforcement of disease- and pest-control programs. Enforcement of the state's laws helps to ensure that Texas's farm products are of high quality and disease free.

Farming and ranching are big business in Texas. Although many small family farms still exist in the state, large corporate farms increasingly dominate Texas agriculture. These large agribusinesses are greatly affected by the decisions of the commissioner, which can increase or decrease the cost of production. Changes in production costs affect the profit margins of these agribusinesses and ultimately the price consumers pay for food products.

The Department of Agriculture is also responsible for checking weights and measures in the state. Each year a representative of the department checks each motor fuel pump to make sure that it dispenses the correct amount of fuel. Scales used by grocery stores and markets are checked to guarantee that they weigh products correctly.

The current agriculture commissioner, Sid Miller, was first elected in 2014 and quickly became an attention-getter within state government. He ran into trouble with the state legislature for his intense lobbying of them in behalf of his agency, for his extravagant proposal to renovate his office, for $413,700 in bonuses given to 146 of his employees, and for employing an ex-felon at the agency. Though he did not face criminal charges, he came under criminal investigation for using state funds to travel to a rodeo and to obtain an injection for pain treatment.

Commissioner of Agriculture Sid Miller bites into a cupcake at a press conference where he granted full amnesty to cupcakes in order to assure Texans it was legal to bring sweets to school.

Publicity seems to be a primary goal of Miller's administration. For his first official act as commissioner, he held a press conference in which he granted full amnesty to cupcakes. He said he wished to reassure Texans that it was legal to bring cupcakes and other sweets to school and that he would protect that right. He then took a large bite of a cupcake and said, "Let them eat cake." He also sent a cupcake to each member of the House and Senate. Subsequently, Miller's search for publicity has continued. He has threatened to slap anyone who wishes him "Happy Holidays" rather than "Merry Christmas"; has advocated dropping nuclear bombs on "the Muslim world"; and has spoken in favor of deep fryers and soda machines in public schools. During the 2016 Presidential election campaign Miller referred to Hillary Clinton with a vulgar term, then deleted the tweet and blamed it on an overzealous staff member. Miller has been criticized for the numerous false and misleading stories that he has posted on social media, which he has defended by saying, "I'm not a news source."[39]

Borrowing a political page from Governor Abbott and Attorney General Paxton, Miller has joined with Paxton in a suit against the federal Environmental Protection Agency and has argued, "Drought, hurricanes and tornadoes are not the biggest threats facing Texas, rather it is an overzealous federal government."[40] After the 2016 elections, Miller was mentioned as a possible nominee for secretary of agriculture in the Trump administration, although he was not chosen.

Miller's showmanship has not been unanimously supported, and he drew two Republican primary opponents in 2018. One opponent was Trey Blocker, who is an attorney and lobbyist. Blocker referred to Miller as an "embarrassment" and used Miller's antics as a campaign weapon against him. He also was highly critical of Miller's increases in the fees that his agency charges for some of its services. Miller, however, won the Republican primary with 56 percent of the vote, perhaps in part because he was endorsed by President Trump. He was successful in the general election, winning 51.3 percent of the vote.

Comptroller of Public Accounts

The **comptroller** is a powerful state official because he or she directs the collection of tax and nontax revenues and issues an estimate of anticipated state revenues before each legislative session. The taxes collected by the comptroller include the general sales tax, severance tax on natural resources, business franchise tax, motor fuel tax, inheritance tax, most occupational taxes, and many minor taxes.

comptroller elected state official who directs the collection of taxes and other revenues and estimates revenues for the budgeting process

Although collecting billions in revenue is important and more visible, estimating revenues provides the comptroller with more power. These estimates, issued monthly during legislative sessions, are vital to the appropriations process because the legislature is prohibited from spending more than the comptroller estimates will be available. Final passage of any appropriations bill is contingent on the comptroller's certifying that revenues will be available to cover the monies spent in the appropriation. Because most bills require the expenditure of monies, this certification function provides the comptroller with significant power over the legislative process. If the comptroller is unable to certify that monies are available to pay for the appropriation, the legislature must reduce the appropriation or increase revenues. More than just an auditor, accountant, and tax collector, the comptroller is a key figure in the appropriations process.

In 1996 the office of state treasurer was eliminated, and the comptroller assumed the duties of that office. Since then, the comptroller has been the official custodian of state funds, responsible for the safety of the state's money and for investing that money. To ensure the safety of Texas's money, funds are deposited only in financial institutions designated by the State Depository Board as eligible to receive state monies. Deposits are required to earn as much money as possible. The more money earned as interest on deposits, the fewer tax dollars are needed.

In 2014, Glenn Hegar was first elected comptroller. Hegar is a former state senator from Katy who campaigned for this office, which is largely financial in nature, as the "pro–Second Amendment," "pro-taxpayer," and "pro-life" candidate. Hegar faced the unenviable task of estimating the effect and duration of the dramatic decline in oil prices on tax revenues and on the Texas economy in general. Inaccurate estimates could force unnecessary budget cuts or bring about tax increases. While facing Democratic opposition in 2018, Hegar ran unopposed in the Republican primary and was re-elected in 2018 with 53.2 percent of the vote.

Secretary of State

secretary of state state official, appointed by the governor, whose primary responsibility is administering elections

Strangely, given Texas's fragmentation of power, the governor does appoint the Texas **secretary of state**, even though this office is an elective one in 37 other states. Though once considered a "glorified keeper of certain state records," the secretary of state is now an important officer with many responsibilities, and the appointment is one of the governor's most important tasks.

As Texas's chief election official, the secretary of state conducts voter registration drives. His or her office works with organizations such as the League of Women Voters to increase the number of registered voters. The secretary of state's office also collects election-night returns from county judges and county clerks and makes the results available to the media. This service provides media and voters with a convenient method of receiving the latest official election returns in Texas.

All debt and Uniform Commercial Code filings are placed with the secretary of state's office. When any individual borrows money from a financial institution, a copy of the loan agreement is placed in the secretary of state's office.

The Plural Executive and the Governor

The plural executive dilutes the ability of the governor to control state government. The governor appoints the secretary of state but has no control over other members of the plural executive. All its members are elected independently, and they do not run as a slate. The other elected members do not answer to the governor, and they do not serve as a cabinet. They tend to operate their offices as independent fiefdoms, and they jealously guard their turf. The plural executive can make state government appear as if it is going in several different directions at once. This is especially true when members of the plural executive are political rivals. For example, widely publicized tensions between Governor

Rick Perry and Comptroller Carole Strayhorn led to Strayhorn's unsuccessful campaign as an independent against Perry in 2006.

Boards, Commissions, and Regulatory Agencies

 Explain the roles played by boards, commissions, and regulatory agencies

The state **bureaucracy** in Texas has numerous state boards, commissions, councils, and committees as well as major agencies within the plural executive that have administrative or advisory functions. In addition to the governmental bodies under the direct control of the single executives who are part of the elected plural executive, there are also bodies (1) run by multimember boards appointed by the governor and confirmed by the Senate; (2) run by single executives appointed by the governor and confirmed by the Senate; (3) run by boards appointed by several members of the plural executive or even by legislative officers, and confirmed by the Senate; and (4) run by multimember boards elected by the people. Overall, the state bureaucracy employed 327,015 people in 2017,[41] compared to 289,515 ten years earlier.[42]

Appointment power coupled with long tenure gives a governor strong influence over the state bureaucracy. Governor Perry's lengthy service gave him enormous influence throughout state government, as he is the only Texas governor in modern history to have made every appointment in state government that a governor can make—and he also made numerous appointments to vacancies in office such as the Texas appellate courts and scores of district judgeships. The result, according to former state representative and author Brian McCall, is that "in this regard, [Perry] is by far the most powerful governor in Texas history. No governor has been able to do what he has done."[43] Perry placed many of his closest advisers in key positions, which spread not only his personal influence but also his personal political philosophy of a pro-business state government.

bureaucracy the complex structure of offices, tasks, rules, and principles of organization that are employed by all large-scale institutions to coordinate the work of their personnel

Multimember Appointed Boards

As we have discussed, most boards and commissions in Texas are headed by members appointed by the governor and confirmed by the Senate. Some commissioners are appointed by a variety of other people, including the lieutenant governor, the Speaker of the House, or leaders of professional organizations such as the state bar or state medical association. Multimember commissions with heads appointed by the governor include obscure agencies such as the Bandera County River Authority, the State Seed and Plant Board, the Caddo Lake Compact Commission, and the Texas Funeral Commission. Better-known agencies include the Texas Alcoholic Beverage Commission, the Department of Parks and Wildlife, the Texas Youth Commission, and the Texas Department of Corrections. Except in the case of a major controversy, such as the sexual abuse scandal

The Department of Parks and Wildlife is an agency in the Texas executive branch and is led by a board appointed by the governor. The department manages natural resources and fishing, hunting, and outdoor recreation in the state. Here, a researcher collects notes on fish caught in Matagorda Bay, Texas.

that embroiled the Texas Youth Commission in 2007, these agencies work in anonymity, although several of them have a direct effect on the lives of Texans. One such example is the Public Utilities Commission.

Appointed Single Executives

The Texas Department of Insurance is run by one commissioner appointed by the governor for a two-year term and confirmed by the Senate. The purpose of the Department of Insurance is to regulate the insurance market in Texas, a complicated task that affects most Texans.

Although insurance companies advocate less regulation, consumer groups argue that the insurance commissioner has inadequate powers to deal with insurance companies. Indeed, it is doubtful that the commissioner has sufficient power to force an uncooperative insurer to comply with his or her decisions. The commissioner is also faced with the seemingly intractable problem of keeping rates low and coverage available in hurricane- and flood-prone areas to which more and more people are moving.

Multimember Elected Boards

Members of two state agencies are elected by the voters: the Railroad Commission of Texas and the State Board of Education. The Railroad Commission has 3 members elected statewide to six-year terms of office. One of the 3 members is elected every two years. The Board of Education is a 15-member board elected to four-year terms from single-member districts.

A Plural or Single Executive?

THE TEXAS executive branch has similarities to the federal executive branch. The governor, like the president, is the chief executive. The governor is the commander in chief of military forces in the state, has the power to appoint people to various administrative offices, and is responsible for making sure that the laws are faithfully executed. But unlike the president and vice president, who run on the same ticket, the governor and lieutenant governor are elected separately. Moreover, the governor does not have a cabinet that he or she appoints and controls. The secretary of state is appointed by the governor, but the comptroller, the attorney general, the land commissioner, and the agriculture commissioner are all elected separately. We call this a plural executive system because executive power is divided among different officeholders. Current Governor Greg Abbott (at right, seated on the left), Attorney General Ken Paxton (center), and Lieutenant Governor Dan Patrick (right) are just a few of the people that today make up Texas's plural executive.

Many other states follow the federal model or single executive model, so that the governor and lieutenant governor are elected to office together. The governor then appoints all of the relevant officeholders to run the executive branch. In these instances, the attorney general, the secretary of state, the agriculture commissioner, and all other "cabinet" officials are appointed by the governor and serve at his or her pleasure.

Advocates of the plural executive model argue that a decentralized system of power within the executive branch helps guard against abuses of power. The Texas Constitution intentionally provides for a weak governorship, and the plural executive is one way to guarantee this. If the attorney general and other statewide officials are not beholden to the governor, they will not necessarily support the governor's agenda. Supporters of the Texas model also argue that it is more democratic in that the electorate has a larger role to play in the selection of executive officers.

Opponents of the plural executive model argue that it makes it difficult for the governor to govern effectively and creates a counterproductive tug of war among all of the separately elected officials. In the federal model, the president can decide who is best suited for a particular role and delegate power accordingly. The Texas governor, on the other hand, cannot give orders to the lieutenant governor or the attorney general, thus making it more difficult to run the state in a responsible manner.

In Texas's recent past, Republican governor George W. Bush had to work alongside Democratic lieutenant governor

Bob Bullock in order to pass his legislative agenda. Some observers saw this forced cooperation as a positive effect of the plural executive, because it required compromise for the good of the state. Opponents of the plural executive might have seen it as a negative effect, because it undermined the power of the governor to implement his agenda. Each form of governance has its benefits and its costs for democracy.

COMMUNICATING EFFECTIVELY: YOUR VOICE

- Is the plural executive more democratic than the single executive model? Does it lead to more efficient and accountable government? Why or why not?

- If you were to design a state executive branch, how would you decide whether to have a plural executive or a single executive? What are the arguments for and against each model?

Railroad Commission of Texas (RRC)

At one time, the Railroad Commission of Texas (RRC) was one of the most powerful state agencies in the nation. It not only regulated intrastate railroads, trucks, and bus transportation but also supervised the oil and natural gas industry in Texas. For most of the RRC's existence, in fact, regulation of the oil and gas industry was its primary focus.

Today, the RRC is a shadow of its former self. Court decisions, deregulation of the transportation industry, other state and federal legislation, and the decline in the nation's dependence on Texas's crude oil production have diminished the commission's power. In 2005 the RRC's limited authority over railroads was transferred to the Texas Department of Transportation; therefore, the RRC now has no authority over what was once its major reason for existence. During the RRC's heyday when Texas was a major oil producer, the commission limited production in order to conserve oil and to maintain prices. Consequently, the RRC was one of the most economically significant governmental bodies on the national and international stage. As oil production shifted to the Middle East, the RRC became the model for OPEC, the Organization of Petroleum Exporting Countries, which also seeks to limit oil production to maintain prices. At one time, members of the Texas RRC wielded such vast economic power that they were among the state's most influential politicians. More recently, renewed energy production in Texas as a result of fracking and horizontal drilling appears to be increasing the importance of the RRC, although it will never again be a major decision-making body for world oil and gas prices. There are now simply too many major oil and gas fields outside of Texas.

State Board of Education (SBOE)

The State Board of Education (SBOE) sets policy for public education (pre-kindergarten to 12th grade programs supported by the state government) in Texas. The education bureaucracy that enforces the SBOE's rules and regulations is called the Texas Education Agency (TEA). Together these two bodies control public education in Texas by determining licensing requirements for public school teachers, setting minimum high school graduation criteria for recommended or advanced curriculums, establishing standards for accreditation of public schools, and selecting public school textbooks.

The commissioner of education is appointed by the governor from a list of candidates submitted by the SBOE. He or she is administrative head of the TEA and serves as adviser to the SBOE. The commissioner of education is at the apex of the public education bureaucracy in Texas.

The SBOE is composed of 15 members. Because the board is elected from single-member districts, Democrats continue to be elected. Also, SBOE district lines are drawn in such a way that it is rare for a seat on the board to flip from one party to the other. In 2018, for example, there were seven seats up for election. In four of those seats an incumbent was running; three seats were open seats. Three of the incumbents were Democrats and one was Republican; they all won re-election. Two of the Democratic incumbents did not even have a Republican opponent. A Democrat won one of the open seats and Republicans won the two other open seats. SBOE incumbents of both parties are generally able to win re-election with little in campaign contributions compared with those for other elected executive offices—probably because SBOE offices are low visibility and each board member's district is one-fifteenth the size of the entire state. Typically, with the way the districts are drawn, there are about ten Republicans elected to the board and five Democrats.

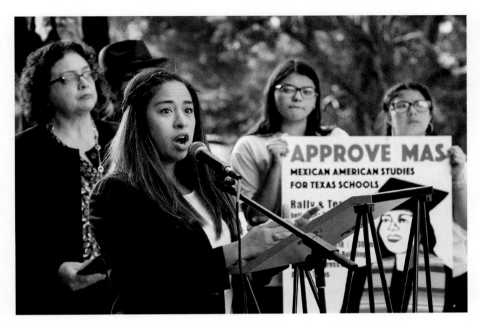

The State Board of Education sets policy for public education, from pre-kindergarten through 12th grade. In 2018, the board approved the inclusion of Mexican-American studies classes as elective courses in public school curriculums.

In recent years, the SBOE has become an ideological battleground. In 2009, for example, one such battle led the board to review how evolution was taught in public schools. In a partial defeat for religious conservatives, no longer are teachers required to teach the "strengths and weaknesses" of evolution, although they are encouraged to teach "all sides."

Other battles have broken out over other aspects of educational policy. For example, in late 2015 a Facebook posting that went viral brought the SBOE process for reviewing textbooks to widespread attention and led to a major effort to change it. Roni Dean-Burren, the mother of a 9th grader, posted what her son's geography text said about the Atlantic slave trade between the 1500s and 1800s: that it "brought millions of workers from Africa to the southern United States to work on agricultural plantations." One might conclude from this language that the slaves were voluntary paid plantation employees, and the publisher quickly apologized and promised to correct the terminology.

A larger issue raised by the controversy, however, was whether the process for reviewing textbooks was adequate. The existing process had led to numerous ideological struggles within the board over proper treatment of religion, the Civil War, and even climate change. Under that process, the board relies on citizen panels to review texts, with the panel members nominated by board members. Others can also review the texts and can testify during SBOE meetings about their objections to language or ideas in the texts. In the aftermath of the outcry over the use of "workers" rather than "slaves," one SBOE member proposed letting university experts fact-check textbooks. That motion failed by an 8–7 vote. However, another motion passed unanimously: in the future, review panels should have at least a majority of people "with sufficient content expertise and experience" to make judgments about textbooks. Whether this new policy reduces the ideological battles and factual errors in texts remains to be seen.[44]

An SBOE candidate in the 2015 Republican primary made some particularly provocative statements that suggest possible future intense ideological battles over educational policy. Mary Lou Bruner stated that she believed President Obama had been a male prostitute in New York, that humans and dinosaurs existed together, that health classes should avoid discussions of sexuality, and that Democrats had had John F. Kennedy killed because he was too conservative, among numerous other comments. Her statements were so bizarre that even though she almost won the Republican nomination for her seat without a runoff, once her statements were widely publicized she suffered an overwhelming defeat in the runoff primary.

Although many Texas voters may not be aware of them, the battles fought within the SBOE have wide-reaching effects. They affect not only the education of Texas schoolchildren but also that of children across the nation. Texas spends millions of dollars each year purchasing textbooks, and the state furnishes these books without charge to students. Books must meet stringent criteria, and because the state buys so many textbooks, publishers often print books with content designed especially for students in Texas. Even when this is not the case, the content of the textbooks used in Texas sets the tone for textbook content in other states that are less populous and therefore have smaller markets for textbooks.[45]

Making Agencies Accountable

In a democracy, elected officials are ultimately responsible to the voters. Appointed officials are indirectly accountable to the people through the elected officials who appoint them. Both are responsible to legislatures that determine responsibilities and appropriate money to carry out those responsibilities. In Texas, the plural executive is responsible to the legislature for its biennial funding and to the voters for re-election. The myriad state agencies look to the legislature for funding, and once every 12 years they must justify their existence to the **Sunset Advisory Commission (SAC)**.

Sunset Advisory Commission (SAC) a commission created in 1977 for the purpose of reviewing the effectiveness of state agencies

The 12-member SAC has 5 members from the Texas Senate and 1 public member appointed by the lieutenant governor, plus 5 members from the Texas House and 1 public member appointed by the Speaker of the Texas House. It was created in 1977 by the Sunset Review Act, which established specific criteria to be considered in evaluating the continuing need for an agency. One of several laws enacted in the mid-1970s to bring more openness and accountability to Texas government, the Sunset process establishes a date on which an agency is abolished unless the legislature passes a bill for the agency to continue in operation.

During its Sunset review, an agency must document its efficiency, the extent to which it meets legislative mandates, and its promptness and effectiveness in handling complaints, and it must establish the continuing need for its services. The review process is lengthy, lasting almost two years.

After a thorough study of an agency, the SAC recommends one of three actions to the legislature: (1) the agency continues as is, with no change in its organization or functions; (2) the agency continues but with changes (reorganization, a new focus for the agency, or merger with other agencies); or (3) the agency is abolished. If option 1 or 2 is recommended, specific action by the legislature is required before the date of the agency's abolition. Option 1 requires specific legislation to re-create the agency in its existing form. Option 2 requires the legislature to re-create the agency with some or all of the changes recommended by the SAC. If the legislature agrees the agency should be abolished, no action is necessary. It will expire at the Sunset deadline and the agency is no more.

Each state agency has been through the Sunset process. The legislature has allowed the sun to set on more than 37 agencies or programs, and 46 others have been merged with existing bodies. Since its beginning the legislature has accepted 80 percent of recommendations of the SAC, which the agency claims to have saved Texas taxpayers $981 million.[46]

★ ★

The Executive Branch and the Future of Texas

AT THE NATIONAL LEVEL, the president is elected, through the electoral college, by the people as a whole. The president is the spokesperson for the nation in the world and is the commander in chief of the armed forces. When there is a national crisis, the people look to the president for leadership. Throughout the twentieth century, the power and authority of the presidency increased significantly, often at the expense of Congress. American democracy has become an executive-led system, with a weakened Congress and a partially demobilized electorate.

Such is not the case in Texas. The fear of a strong executive who could ignore the wishes of either the legislature or the people, as was the case during Reconstruction in Texas, led in 1876 to a constitution that created a plural executive. The governor is the chief executive officer in the state, elected directly by the popular vote of all the people of Texas. People turn to the governor for leadership and direction during times of crisis. But compared with that of the president, the power of the Texas governor is more limited. Many key executive officials, including the lieutenant governor, the attorney general, the comptroller, and the land commissioner, are elected—like the governor—directly by the people. These members of the plural executive, along with other popularly elected statewide boards and commissions, possess power and authority that under other constitutional arrangements the governor might possess. As has been noted throughout this chapter, Governor Perry's ability to accumulate power in the governor's office is unprecedented in recent history. That his successors will be able to wield the limited powers of the governor as efficiently is by no means certain.

Abbott, following in the footsteps of an exceptionally powerful Texas governor, seems to be moving increasingly to the right in the Texas Republican Party. Land Commissioner George P. Bush is being heavily criticized for some of his campaign contributions and for his operation of the General Land Office. What once seemed like a bright political future has dimmed somewhat. Agriculture Commissioner Sid Miller seems to be the political publicity hound of the group, although his unusual behavior seems to have spawned political opposition. Lieutenant Governor Dan Patrick is pushing hard to be the leader of the right wing in state politics, and those efforts seem on the verge of success. Comptroller Glenn Hegar is simply trying to cope with the massive effects of the drop in the price of oil on state revenues and the state economy, while Attorney General Ken Paxton is trying to survive his indictments while joining with Abbott and Patrick in appealing to the right wing of the Republican Party. Paxton's political survival skills, however, are noteworthy since, in spite of his legal troubles, he had no opposition in the Republican primary. The mix of these competing roles, ambitions, and personal goals is what makes the plural executive of Texas so tumultuous.

There is no likelihood that the plural executive will see structural change. The candidacy of Beto O'Rourke for U.S. Senate and demographic changes in the state have provided some support for the view that the Democratic Party is on the cusp of coming back into power in state politics. The margins of victory for Republican statewide candidates were relatively low in 2018, and in some cases, such as the attorney general's race, the margin of victory was very low. It remains to be seen whether the new energy in the Democratic Party will continue and will increase in later elections. At least in the near future, the Republican Party remains in firm control of state-level politics. Still, the differences in the values, abilities, ambitions, and goals of these members of the plural executive will provide the fodder for the policies and controversies of the future.

Use **INQUIZITIVE** to help you study and master this material.

The Governor

> • Describe the powers of the Texas governor and the limits of the governor's power (pp. 253–71)

Although the Texas governor is considered weak compared with governors of other states, the power of appointing members to boards made Rick Perry the most powerful governor in state history, largely because of his long tenure. Among the executive powers the governor possesses are appointment, budgetary, military, and police powers. Among his legislative powers are message and veto powers and the ability to call special sessions of the legislature.

Key Terms
impeachment (p. 260)
appointment (p. 262)
patronage (p. 262)
senatorial courtesy (p. 266)
executive budget (p. 266)
legislative budget (p. 266)
veto (p. 268)
post-adjournment veto (p. 269)
line-item veto (p. 269)
special session (p. 269)

Practice Quiz

1. Which of the following is *not* necessary to become governor of Texas?
   a) A governor must be at least 30 years of age.
   b) A governor must have lived in Texas for at least five years.
   c) A governor must be a U.S. citizen.
   d) A governor must be a lawyer.
   e) A governor must have substantial campaign funding.

2. The election for governor of Texas is held in an off-year in order to
   a) increase voter participation in elections in odd-numbered years.
   b) influence the presidential vote in Texas.
   c) decrease the likelihood of voter fraud.
   d) give governors an opportunity to campaign for presidential candidates.
   e) prevent the presidential vote in Texas from influencing the election of state officials.

3. The only constitutional method of removing the governor is
   a) *quo warranto* proceedings.
   b) *ex post facto* removal.
   c) a vote of no confidence.
   d) impeachment.
   e) impeachment and conviction.

4. The governor's most effective power in controlling the executive branch of state government is the power
   a) of the veto.
   b) of appointment.
   c) of removal.
   d) of judicial review.
   e) to create a state budget.

5. The governor's veto is absolute when it is a
   a) line-item veto.
   b) special veto.
   c) budgetary veto.
   d) post-adjournment veto.
   e) select veto.

6. The governor can grant
   a) pardons.
   b) suspended sentences.
   c) probation.
   d) retrials.
   e) parole.

The Plural Executive

• **Identify the other elected officials who make up Texas's plural executive (pp. 271–81)**

Unlike the president of the United States, the governor of Texas does not appoint a cabinet. Voters in Texas elect the lieutenant governor and other major statewide offices in separate elections. This disperses power within the executive branch, which means that executive officers must compromise not only with the legislature but also within the executive branch.

Key Terms

plural executive (p. 271)
lieutenant governor (p. 274)
attorney general (p. 275)
land commissioner (p. 276)
agriculture commissioner (p. 278)
comptroller (p. 279)
secretary of state (p. 280)

Practice Quiz

7. Which member of the plural executive is appointed?
   a) secretary of state
   b) land commissioner
   c) lieutenant governor
   d) comptroller of public accounts
   e) attorney general

8. The attorney general is
   a) part of the governor's cabinet.
   b) elected independently of the governor.
   c) appointed by the Texas Supreme Court.
   d) the governor's lawyer.
   e) chosen by the State Bar of Texas.

9. The land commissioner
   a) records all property deeds.
   b) administers state land.
   c) surveys property in Texas.
   d) is appointed by the state senate.
   e) administers Big Bend National Park.

10. Members of the plural executive are accountable to the
   a) Sunset Advisory Commission.
   b) voters.
   c) constitution.
   d) state supreme court.
   e) Travis County district attorney.

Boards, Commissions, and Regulatory Agencies

• **Explain the roles played by boards, commissions, and regulatory agencies (pp. 281–87)**

The governor's most important power is the ability to appoint people to boards, commissions, councils, committees, and regulatory agencies. Such institutions have important powers to interpret state regulations and make a difference in the lives of everyday Texans.

Key Terms

bureaucracy (p. 281)
Sunset Advisory Commission (SAC) (p. 286)

Practice Quiz

11. The Public Utilities Commission
   a) regulates some electric rates.
   b) regulates local phone rates.
   c) maintains a website so consumers can compare electric rates.
   d) maintains a "do not call" registry.
   e) All of the above are features of the Public Utilities Commission.

12. The Texas Department of Insurance
   a) has limited power to regulate insurance rates.
   b) collects the penalties for not buying health insurance under Obamacare.

c) sells insurance for mold coverage.

d) is run by a five-member elected board.

e) All of the above are features of the Texas Department of Insurance.

13. The Railroad Commission of Texas

a) is responsible for the safety of the state's railroads.

b) issues bonds to support the state's transportation needs.

c) regulates oil and gas production in Texas.

d) approves mergers of railroads.

e) is the most powerful agency in the state.

14. The State Board of Education

a) has a major role in determining the books used in Texas public schools.

b) is appointed by the legislature.

c) reviews applications to state colleges and universities.

d) is responsible for school property tax rates.

e) governs local boards of education.

15. Which agency investigates the performance of state agencies and recommends whether an agency should be abolished, continued as is, or continued with changes?

a) Legislative Budget Board

b) Legislative Research Bureau

c) Texas Research League

d) Public Utilities Commission

e) Sunset Advisory Commission

George L. Allen, Sr. Courts Building

600
Commerce Street

The tragic story of Texas's 5th Court of Appeals
Justice David Lewis illustrates the politics of the
Texas judiciary as well as issues of discipline of the
state's judges.

The Judiciary

WHY THE JUDICIARY MATTERS On paper, David Lewis's qualifications for a judgeship were impressive. A graduate of Baylor Law School, he had been an assistant district attorney in Dallas County where he had handled death penalty cases, an assistant United States attorney, and then chief assistant United States attorney. He had been a deputy special prosecutor involving a scandal in the Dallas Police Department where police were knowingly arresting unauthorized immigrants for possessing drugs the police knew to be fake and which led to four Dallas police officers being convicted of crimes relating to the scandal. Lewis had even paid his political dues to the Republican Party by running unsuccessfully against an incumbent Democratic criminal district court judge in Dallas County in 2010. Although Lewis lost, his opponent only won by 51.89 percent of the vote with the advantage of being an incumbent in Dallas County, which had become a Democratic Party stronghold.

In 2012, Lewis ran for the Texas 5th Court of Appeals. Here, the district was more Republican and the seat on the Court of Appeals was open, so there was no incumbent who had an advantage. Lewis won the Republican primary and the general election and took office in January 2013.

In June 2016 a doctor made an evaluation of Justice Lewis and reported that Justice Lewis had started having physical and mental health problems as early as 2013. By 2014, the doctor reported, Lewis was experiencing "impaired cognition and . . . intense feelings of anger." Evaluating a 2015 brain scan, the doctor noted that Lewis displayed irreversible brain atrophy, and the doctor concluded that Justice Lewis ". . . was experiencing decreased functioning [and] . . . was trying to cover that up." Relying on a 2015 psychological evaluation, the doctor concluded that Lewis's "psychological testing showed a mix of disinhibited response patterns, poor psychological boundaries and lapses in reasoning and thought processes that bordered on psychotic processing." The doctor further concluded that Lewis was not then competent to return to work as a judge.

Lewis had not worked since September 2014. Since November 2015 he had been suspended without pay, but prior to that suspension he was receiving his $161,000 annual salary until a news channel reported that he was away from his job while still collecting a paycheck.

Lewis was suffering from uncontrolled diabetes, depression, and alcoholism. A month after Lewis had quit working—in October 2014—the chief justice of the 5th Court of Appeals filed a complaint with the State Commission on Judicial Conduct, which claimed Lewis was unfit to do the job, had been discourteous to other justices and staff, had delegated judicial decision making to staff, had failed to perform his duties, did not seem to understand the legal issues and law in cases, and had inappropriately used court computers. Another justice expressed fear for Lewis's safety and for the safety of court personnel because of Lewis's problems controlling his anger.

On October 11, 2016, Lewis resigned rather than face removal from office by the Texas Supreme Court. In June 2016 police found Lewis dead in his home. His death was due to chronic alcoholism complicated by heart disease and diabetes.

With the seat on the Court of Appeals vacant because of Lewis's resignation, Governor Abbott appointed Jason Boatwright for the remainder of Lewis's term. Boatwright would have the political advantage of being an incumbent in the next election and, as a Republican, would also have the advantage of running in a largely Republican region, although in 2018 all the Republicans running in the 5th Court of Appeals, including Boatwright, were defeated. Boatwright had lived in Austin but had moved to Dallas in 2014 as Lewis's problems had become clear. Whether his move to Dallas was in anticipation of Lewis's resignation and an appointment by Abbott is uncertain, but the timing of Boatwright's move was certainly convenient. Boatwright was close to Abbott, having worked for Abbott when Abbott was attorney general.

David Lewis's story is tragic. However, it illustrates key issues involving the Texas judiciary: Texas judges are elected in partisan elections, and thus judicial candidates make political calculations in seeking office just as candidates for other offices do. Additionally, even though Texas judges are elected, a substantial portion of those judges initially obtain that office as a result of appointment by the governor to new judgeships or to judicial vacancies brought about by the death, resignation, or retirement of incumbent judges. David Lewis's story also raises questions about judicial selection and judicial discipline. Would some alternative system of selection have led to the more rapid removal of an impaired judge? Finally, does Texas's system for disciplining judges move too slowly?[1]

As we attempt to answer these questions, we must keep in mind that, despite the popular myth of the dispassionate judge meting out justice based on strict, unbiased application of the law, the courts in Texas are deeply political institutions. They are made up of individuals with ideologies, party affiliations, political goals and connections, and, at times, personal problems. These facts greatly influence how laws in Texas are interpreted and how justice is handed down.

CHAPTER GOALS

- Describe how the Texas court system is organized (pp. 295–300)
- Explain the legal process and the differences between criminal and civil law (pp. 300–3)
- Evaluate the process for selecting judges in Texas (pp. 303–15)
- Assess the impact of recent changes related to tort reform, regulation of lawyers, and disciplining judges (pp. 316–20)

Court Structure

Describe how the Texas court system is organized

Texas has a large and complex court structure consisting of multiple courts with overlapping jurisdiction (see Figure 9.1). Additionally, some courts have specialized jurisdiction, whereas others have broad authority to handle a variety of cases. At the highest level for civil cases is the **Texas Supreme Court**, which consists of nine justices, including a chief justice. This court hears civil cases for which it is the final court of appeal at the state level. The only requirements for being a Texas Supreme Court justice are that one must be a citizen of the United States and of Texas, be at least 35 years of age and under 74 years, and have been either a practicing lawyer or judge for at least 10 years. The term of a justice is six years, with at least three justices being elected every two years. Justices on the Texas Supreme Court are paid $168,000 a year; the chief justice receives $2,500 a year more.

The **Texas Court of Criminal Appeals** is the highest appeals court in the state for criminal cases. This court also has nine judges, including a presiding judge. The pay, terms, and qualifications of Court of Criminal Appeals judges are the same as for the Texas Supreme Court. Perhaps the most important role of the Court of Criminal Appeals is its jurisdiction over automatic appeals in death penalty cases.

Both the Texas Supreme Court and the Court of Criminal Appeals have appellate jurisdiction. This means that they have the authority to review the decisions of lower courts to determine whether legal principles and court procedures were followed correctly. They also have the power to order that a case be retried if mistakes were made. Texas has 14 other appellate courts, located in various parts of the state, which have both criminal and civil jurisdiction. These **courts of appeal** are intermediate appellate courts that hear appeals from the trial courts. Usually, before the Texas Supreme Court or the Court of Criminal Appeals hears a case, the initial appeal has been heard by one of the courts of appeal. Currently, 80 judges serve on the 14 courts of appeal, which range in size from 3 to 13 judges. Although occasionally every judge on a court of appeal will hear a case, most appeals at this level are heard by panels of three judges. The requirements for a court of appeal justice are the same as those for justices of the higher courts. Courts of appeal justices are paid a base salary of $154,000 a year (which can be supplemented with additional funds and longevity pay), and the chief justice of each of the courts of appeal receives an additional $2,500.

The major trial courts in Texas are the **district courts**. Each county has at least one district court, although in rural parts of the state several counties may be served by one district court. Urban counties have many district courts. Harris County (Houston), for example, has 60 district courts, and Dallas County has 39. District courts usually have general jurisdiction, meaning that they hear a broad range of civil and criminal cases that include felonies, divorces, land disputes, election contests, and civil lawsuits. However, in urban counties, some district courts with specialized jurisdiction hear only civil, criminal, juvenile, or family law matters. District court judges receive $140,000 a year, and they may receive up to $18,000 in additional salary a year from county supplement payments to the state salary. All state judges, from district court judges through Texas

Texas Supreme Court the highest civil court in Texas; consists of nine justices and has final state appellate authority over civil cases

Texas Court of Criminal Appeals the highest criminal court in Texas; consists of nine justices and has final state appellate authority over criminal cases

courts of appeal the 14 intermediate-level appellate courts that hear appeals from district and county courts to determine whether the decisions of these lower courts followed legal principles and court procedures correctly

district courts the major trial courts in Texas, which usually have general jurisdiction over a broad range of civil and criminal cases

FIGURE 9.1

The Structure of the Texas Court System

SOURCE: Texas Office of Court Administration.

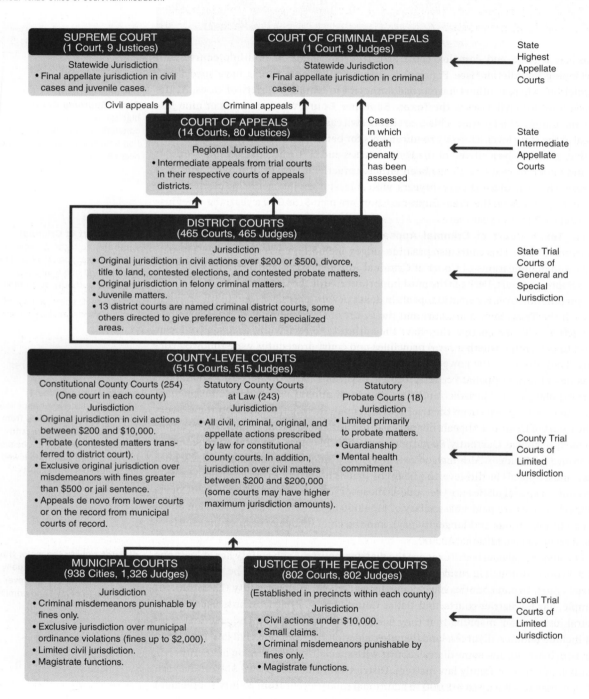

Supreme Court and Court of Criminal Appeals judges, also receive longevity pay of 3.1 percent of their monthly salary for each year of service after 16 years. Currently, there are 465 district judges, 9 state supreme court judges, 9 court of criminal appeals judges, and 80 courts of appeals judges.

Texas policy makers have recognized that there are many offenders who continually recycle through the system. As a result, **specialty courts** have been created to try to address particular crimes or serve particular populations. Rather than punishing offenders, these courts focus on rehabilitation and attempt to address the underlying causes of repetitive offenses. Among the most common specialty courts in Texas are veterans' courts. When a brain injury or mental issue from military service in a combat zone has affected a veteran, a veterans' court (which like other specialty courts is part of a district court dealing with criminal cases) can hear any criminal case in which a veteran is charged. The idea behind this court is to develop an individualized treatment plan for the veteran. Another specialized court focuses on encouraging prostitutes to leave that life by moving into residential counseling and later outpatient treatment. Counseling, education, and job training are also provided by the court. There are also DWI courts that deal with cases involving offenders who abuse alcohol and drive. Rather than imprisoning DWI offenders, the idea is to try to rehabilitate the offenders by focusing on the underlying alcohol problem.

By far the most common of specialty courts are drug courts, where regular monitoring of drug offenders occurs—far more intensive monitoring than in traditional probation—and where the courts work to stop offenders' pattern of drug abuse. Drug courts have been more intensively studied than other specialty courts, and it has been found that offenders who complete a drug court's program have far lower rates of recidivism than offenders who do not complete or who do not participate in a program.[2] Successful completion of a specialty court's program will result in dismissal of the charges against the offender.

In fiscal year 2016, 191 courts in Texas were specialty courts. These courts were located in fifty counties in the state. About 43 percent of these courts were drug courts. The development of specialty courts shows a recognition that for persons with recurring offenses, incarceration without dealing with the underlying causes of their repetitive behavior is not a solution. At least in reference to drug courts, the evidence does show that specialty courts can be a significant tool in preventing the criminal justice system from being a revolving door for offenders.[3]

Texas is unusual in having the office of **county judge** in each of its 254 counties. This official presides over the county commissioners' court and thus has responsibilities for administration of county government. But he or she also sometimes presides over a **county court**, which often has jurisdiction over uncontested probate cases and more serious misdemeanor criminal offenses, those involving fines greater than $500 or a jail sentence, as well as over civil cases where the amounts in dispute are relatively small, generally in the $200 to $10,000 range. The county court may also hear appeals from municipal courts or from justice of the peace courts. Thus, many county judges combine political-administrative functions with some judicial

specialty courts usually part of district courts and focusing on trying to resolve the underlying problems such as mental health, alcohol and drug abuse, and prostitution that lead to recurring criminal behavior

county judge the person in each of Texas's 254 counties who presides over the county commissioners' court, with responsibility for the administration of county government; some county judges carry out judicial responsibilities

county courts the courts that exist in some counties and that are presided over by county judges

The Texas Supreme Court is the highest civil court in Texas. The court consists of nine justices (pictured here as of 2018).

functions. However, in the more populated counties, statutory county courts at law, as well as statutory probate courts, have eliminated most and sometimes all of the county judges' judicial duties.

County court judges receive about $25,000 in extra compensation if they sign a one-page declaration at the start of every year in which they promise that 40 percent of their work will involve court cases. This extra compensation program for county judges has been in existence for over 20 years.

In a 2016 investigation by the *Austin American-Statesman*, it was found that this extra compensation amounted to nearly a 50 percent pay increase in some of the rural counties and that 219 of the 254 county judges claimed the extra money, even though it appeared many of them did not actually spend 40 percent of their time on court cases. The Kent County judge, for example, only handled about a half dozen court cases in 2015, although he received the extra pay. The county auditor in Austin County refused to pay the county judge the extra money because the auditor claimed the judge had performed negligible judicial functions. Some county judges took cases from statutory county court at law judges so that they would have a judicial caseload and be able to obtain the extra money.[4] In spite of the apparent abuse of this extra pay arrangement, nothing has been done by the state to increase supervision of the county judges' judicial work or to audit their activities.

statutory county courts at law courts that tend to hear less serious criminal cases than those heard by district courts; they usually hear civil cases that involve smaller economic claims than are heard by district courts

Since the **statutory county courts at law** were created by statute, often at widely different times, the jurisdiction of these courts varies significantly. Usually, they hear appeals from justices of the peace and from municipal courts. In civil cases, they usually hear cases involving sums greater than those in cases heard by a justice of the peace court. Typically, county courts at law hear civil cases involving less than $200,000. In comparison to district courts, county courts at law hear less serious criminal cases.

Some of the county courts at law have specialized jurisdiction; most commonly these are in the most urban counties, where some of the courts have only civil jurisdiction and others only criminal jurisdiction.

statutory probate courts specialized courts whose jurisdiction is limited to probate and guardianship matters

In the most urban areas of the state, the legislature has created **statutory probate courts**. These courts are highly specialized, as their primary activity involves matters relating to the disposition of property of deceased persons. They may also deal with guardianship of people unable to handle their own affairs and with commitments of people to mental institutions. In other parts of the state, depending on the statute, probate matters may be heard by the county court, the county court at law, or the district court.

justice of the peace courts local trial courts with limited jurisdiction over small claims and very minor criminal misdemeanors

Each county in Texas has between one and eight justice of the peace precincts, depending on population, although large urban counties have more than one judge in each precinct. Harris County, for example, has two in each of eight precincts. Within each precinct are **justice of the peace courts**, of which there are 802 in Texas. These courts hear class C misdemeanors, which are less serious crimes usually involving traffic offenses. They also have jurisdiction over minor civil matters, functioning as small claims courts where suits involving less than $10,000 can be heard. These suits can be handled informally as the rules governing suits may not be "so complex that a reasonable person without legal training would have difficulty understanding or applying the rules."[5] Justices of the peace may issue search and arrest warrants.

Justices of the peace mostly handle traffic misdemeanors. Of the more than 2.5 million cases added to justice of the peace court caseloads from September 2016 through

The Texas Court of Criminal Appeals is the highest court in the state for criminal cases. Like the Texas Supreme Court, it has nine justices (pictured here as of 2018). In November 2018, Michelle Slaughter was elected to Place 8 to replace retiring judge Elsa Alcala (left).

August 2017, almost 71 percent were state traffic law cases. In contrast, only 17 percent of the justice of the peace court caseloads involved civil cases.[6]

Justices of the peace have faced considerable criticism in recent years. Professor Barbara Kirby found that between 2008 and 2014, 28 to 62 percent of the disciplinary actions imposed on judges for inappropriate or unethical behavior by the State Commission on Judicial Conduct were on justices of the peace. Yet justices of the peace only constituted about 22 percent of the judges under the purview of the commission. Kirby found that between December 2002 and April 2015, 50 Texas judges had been suspended from their duties by the commission—one of the most severe punishments imposed. Of those 50 judges, 21 were justices of the peace and 19 of those justices did not have a law degree. One of the most common sanctions imposed on justices of the peace by the commission is a requirement that they undergo additional education because, the commission explained, "Legal and procedural issues are often complex, so it is not surprising that some judges, particularly non-lawyer judges, take judicial action that may exceed their authority or that is contrary to procedural rules."[7]

Only about 10 percent of the justices of the peace in Texas are lawyers, and the justices' lack of legal credentials has led to considerable debate in the state.[8] The office has existed in Texas since 1837, even before statehood. In the days of the frontier, justices of the peace provided legal authority where no other existed. The initial idea was that a justice of the peace would be a respected person in the community who was chosen for ability, judgment, and integrity. Today, as former Texas state bar president Frank Newton has pointed out, "in almost every large metropolitan area, there are some JPs [justices of the peace] who do virtually nothing and sort of get lost in the shuffle. People don't tend to get all excited about JP elections. Most people don't know what a JP does. JP is not a very prestigious job."[9]

Municipal courts have been created by the legislature in each of the incorporated cities of the state. There are 938 cities and towns in Texas that have these courts; larger cities have multiple courts. There are 1,326 municipal court judges in the state. Municipal courts have jurisdiction over violations of city **ordinances** and, concurrent with justice of the peace courts, have jurisdiction over class C misdemeanors, for which the punishment for conviction is a fine. Municipal judges may issue search and arrest warrants, but they have only limited civil jurisdiction. Municipal courts, like justice of the peace courts, function primarily as traffic courts. From September 2016 through August 2017, 5,187,007 cases were filed in municipal courts, of which 72 percent were traffic cases.[10]

municipal courts local trial courts with limited jurisdiction over violations of city ordinances and very minor criminal misdemeanors

ordinance a regulation enacted by a city government in each of Texas's incorporated cities and towns

The Legal Process

Explain the legal process and the differences between criminal and civil law

Just as the Texas Supreme Court hears civil cases and the Texas Court of Criminal Appeals hears criminal cases, it is useful to think of the law as divided into these parts. **Civil law** involves a dispute, usually between private individuals, over relationships, obligations, and responsibility. Though there are exceptions with a violation of the civil law, the remedy is often for the offending party to pay compensation to the injured party.

In contrast, **criminal law** involves the violation of concepts of right and wrong as defined by criminal statutes. In criminal law, the state accuses individuals of violations, and if found guilty the violator is subject to punishment. In some cases, that punishment may involve loss of liberty or even loss of life.

civil law a branch of law that deals with disputes, usually between private individuals over relationships, obligations, and responsibility

criminal law the branch of law that regulates the conduct of individuals, defines crimes, and specifies punishment for criminal acts

Civil Law

In civil law, an aggrieved person will usually obtain a lawyer and file a petition that details the **complaint** against the person accused of causing the harm. The petition is filed with the clerk of court, who issues a citation against the defendant. The defendant will usually file an **answer** explaining why the allegations are not valid. Depending on the issue, the amounts of money that may be awarded as damages, and the probability of success, the aggrieved person may be able to obtain the services of a lawyer on a contingent fee basis. This means that the lawyer will not charge the individual if the case is lost but will obtain a portion of the damages awarded if the case is won. It is not unusual for such **contingent fee** arrangements to involve one-third or more of the damages awarded plus expenses. Lawyers who handle cases on contingent fee agreements often handle personal-injury

complaint the presentation of a grievance by the plaintiff in a civil case

answer the presentation of a defendant's defense against an allegation in a civil case

contingent fee a fee paid to the lawyer in a civil case that is contingent on winning the case cases and are known as trial lawyers. Traditionally, these lawyers will contribute money to judicial candidates who are sympathetic to plaintiffs. They make money only if they win, so they have a strong economic interest in supporting judicial candidates who are sympathetic to plaintiffs and to the awarding of large damages.

The person being sued either will have to hire an attorney on his or her own or, if insured, will be represented by an attorney paid for by the insurance company. Fee arrangements vary for civil defense lawyers, but often they are paid by the hour, in which case they get paid whether they win or lose. Their economic incentives to contribute money to judicial campaigns may be different from the incentives trial lawyers have, but civil defense lawyers do contribute large sums to judicial campaigns in order to elect judges who support their views on **tort** law.

The court to which a civil case is taken depends on the type of case and the amount of money involved. Most commonly, a civil case will be settled, meaning the dispute is resolved without going to court. Settlements may, however, occur during trial, sometimes immediately before a jury renders its decision. If a case is not settled and goes to trial, it may be heard either by a judge or, if requested by either side, by a jury. Juries at the district court level consist of twelve jurors, whereas juries in lower level courts consist of six jurors. Civil jury verdicts do not have to be unanimous in Texas; five sixths of the jurors are sufficient for a verdict. The burden of proof is on the plaintiff. The standard of proof that the plaintiff must meet is **preponderance of the evidence**, meaning that the plaintiff must show that it is more likely than not that the defendant is the cause of the harm suffered by the plaintiff.

Civil cases may involve tiny amounts of damages or they may involve billions of dollars and have the potential of breaking huge corporations, such as happened in the 1980s when Pennzoil successfully sued Texaco in a dispute over the takeover of the Getty Oil Company.[11]

Civil case verdicts may, of course, be appealed. Appeals are usually from the trial court to the intermediate court of appeal and perhaps further to the state supreme court. Given the cost of appeals and the delay involved, it is not unusual for some settlement to be reached after the verdict but before the case goes through the appellate process. For example, a plaintiff might agree to settle for much less than the verdict in the case to avoid the expense and delay of further appeals.

Litigating a civil case is time consuming and expensive. As a result, in Texas and other states, it is increasingly common to try to negotiate a settlement through mediation or arbitration. With arbitration, the parties to the dispute agree to present their case to a decision maker and to be bound by the decision. With mediation, the parties to the dispute try to reach a compromise resolution of the problem without going to trial. Mediation is especially popular in civil disputes because the parties to the dispute are reaching the agreement and are not forced into a particular decision as they would be with arbitration. Mediation is also a very flexible process for resolving disputes where resolutions of disputes are contractual agreements between the opposing parties. To resolve the dispute, they may agree to any legal remedy. One of the most unusual such remedies occurred a number of years ago when Southwest Airlines and Stevens Aviation had a dispute over which company could use the slogan "Plane Smart." The two sides initially agreed to decide the issue by having an arm-wrestling match between Southwest's and Stevens Aviation's company chairmen. Lawyers later worked out another agreement, but the company chairmen went ahead and held their arm-wrestling event.

tort a civil wrong that causes harm to another; it is remedied by awarding economic damages to the injured party

preponderance of the evidence the standard of proof in a civil jury case, by which the plaintiff must show that the defendant is more likely than not the cause of the harm suffered by the plaintiff

Criminal Law

In criminal cases, the state alleges a violation of a criminal law and is represented in court by a prosecutor. Some prosecutors are career prosecutors with vast trial experience. These people will often prosecute the most difficult and complex cases, such as felonies and **capital cases**. However, because the pay of prosecutors is often much lower than that of private lawyers who do litigation in the private sector, it is common for prosecutors to be quite young and inexperienced. Once they gain trial experience, prosecutors commonly move into the private sector.

Defendants may hire criminal defense attorneys, who usually charge a flat fee to handle the case. Criminal defense lawyers do not work on a contingent fee basis. Since most criminal defendants are found guilty, criminal defense lawyers often prefer to obtain as much of their fee as possible in advance of the verdict.

Some parts of Texas have public defender offices where salaried lawyers provide at least some criminal defense services for low-income persons in a county. Bexar County has established the first public defender office for indigent criminal appeals. Travis County has a public defender office representing only poor people with mental impairments.[12] In west Texas, a public defender office represents indigents in capital cases.[13]

In Texas, poor criminal defendants are more commonly represented by lawyers appointed by the judge. Usually, the government-paid fees for court-appointed lawyers are less than would be paid to lawyers of nonindigent defendants. Thus, some lawyers are reluctant to fulfill court appointments; others may not put the time and energy into a court-appointed case that they would if they were privately paid; others take court appointments because they have a limited number of paying clients; and still others take court appointments to gain experience. Concern over the poor quality of legal representation provided indigent criminal defendants, especially in capital cases, led to legislation in 2001 to increase the pay and qualifications of court-appointed lawyers.

Serious crimes are **felonies**. In those cases, and potentially for lesser offenses known as **misdemeanors**, prior to the trial there will be an indictment by a grand jury. In Texas, a grand jury consists of 12 persons and two alternates who sit for two to six months. Depending on the county, a grand jury may meet only once or twice a year, or it may meet several times a week. Until recently, most Texas grand jurors were chosen by a commissioner system. A district judge would appoint several grand jury commissioners, who then selected 15 to 20 citizens of the county. The first 12 who were qualified became the **grand jury**.[14] New legislation now requires that grand juries be selected randomly from a pool of qualified citizens.

Grand juries can inquire into any criminal matter but usually spend most of their time on felony crimes. They work in secret and rely heavily on the information provided by the prosecutor, though in some rare cases grand juries will work quite independently of the prosecutor. If nine of the grand jurors decide a trial is warranted, they will indict a suspect. An **indictment** is also known as a "true bill." On the other hand, sometimes a grand jury does not believe a trial is warranted. In those cases, the grand jury issues a "no bill" decision.

Although a suspect has the right to trial by jury, he or she may waive that right and undergo a **bench trial** before the judge only. Most commonly, the suspect will engage in a plea bargain. With plea bargaining, a suspect agrees to plead guilty in exchange for a lighter sentence than might be imposed if the suspect were found guilty at trial. Approximately 97 percent of criminal convictions in Texas are the result of **plea bargains**.[15] If

capital case a criminal case in which the death penalty is a possible punishment

felony a serious criminal offense, punishable by a prison sentence or a fine; a capital felony is possibly punishable by death

misdemeanor a minor criminal offense, usually punishable by a fine or a jail sentence

grand jury jury that determines whether sufficient evidence is available to justify a trial; grand juries do not rule on the accused's guilt or innocence

indictment a written statement issued by a grand jury that charges a suspect with a crime and states that a trial is warranted

bench trial a trial held without a jury and before only a judge

plea bargain negotiated agreement in a criminal case in which a defendant agrees to plead guilty in return for the state's agreement to reduce the severity of the criminal charge or prison sentence the defendant is facing the suspect does choose trial by jury, felony juries will have 12 members; misdemeanor juries will have 6 members. There must be a unanimous verdict of guilty or not guilty. If the jurors are not unanimous, the result is a hung jury and a mistrial is declared. The prosecutor may then choose to retry the suspect. In addition to the requirement of unanimity in jury decisions, another important difference between civil and criminal cases is the standard of proof. In criminal cases, rather than the standard of preponderance of the evidence, the standard is **beyond a reasonable doubt**. This means that the prosecutor must prove the charges against the defendant, and they must be proven to a very high standard.

If a guilty verdict is returned, there will be a separate hearing on the sentence, which in Texas is sometimes also determined by the jury. At the sentencing hearing, factors such as prior record and background will be considered, even though these factors could not be considered at the trial portion of the proceeding.

Of course, a criminal defendant may also appeal a verdict. Usually, appeals are by a convicted defendant who alleges that an error in the trial may have affected the case's outcome. Criminal defendants will appeal their convictions to an intermediate appeals court and perhaps further to the Texas Court of Criminal Appeals. In capital cases, however, the appeal will be directly to the Texas Court of Criminal Appeals.

beyond a reasonable doubt the legal standard in criminal cases that requires the prosecution to prove guilt beyond a reasonable doubt

Judicial Politics

Evaluate the process for selecting judges in Texas

Like the federal courts, the state and local courts in Texas are responsible for securing liberty and equality under the law. However, the democratic mechanisms put into place in Texas to select judges and hold them accountable for their actions are quite different from those at the national level. Federal judges are appointed by the president and confirmed by the Senate. They have lifetime appointments. This means that federal judges, subject to good behavior in office, are free from the ebb and flow of democratic politics. They do not have to cater to public opinion and are empowered to interpret the law as they see fit, without fear of reprisal at the polls. In Texas, however, judges are elected. Although they may initially be appointed, sooner or later they are accountable to the voters. Election of judges brings not only the people but also interest groups into the selection and retention of judges. The influence of special interest money in judicial campaigns raises important questions about the relationship between the rule of law and the nature of democratic politics.

Initial Appointment of Judges by the Governor

Because the governor appoints district and appellate judges to the bench to fill vacancies prior to an election or to fill judgeships on new courts, a large percentage of judges initially get on the bench through appointment. Although some governors have been

Is justice for sale in Texas? Because statewide judicial races are expensive, candidates for judgeships have been forced to raise considerable amounts of money. This, in turn, has led to criticism that judicial decisions are, in effect, being bought.

criticized for the relatively small number of minorities they appointed, gubernatorial appointment of judges has generated little additional controversy.[16] As of September 2017 about 54 percent of appellate judges and about 33 percent of district judges initially got on the bench through appointment.[17] However, the controversial issue in Texas judicial politics deals with how the remaining judges obtained their seats and how all judges must retain their seats if they wish to remain in office. That controversy involves the partisan election of judges in Texas.

Judicial Elections Become Highly Partisan

Until 1978 the selection of judges in partisan elections did not create much concern. They were low-key, sleepy affairs. Texas was an overwhelmingly Democratic state, and judges were elected as Democrats. The only real competition occurred in the Democratic primary, and with the political advantage of incumbency, judges were rarely defeated even in the primary. Competition in judicial races occurred in those relatively rare cases where there was an open seat in which no incumbent sought office. One journalist aptly described the judicial elections of that era in this way:

> Justices' names seldom appeared in the press and were known only to the legal community. Most justices had been judges in the lower courts; a few had served in the Legislature. At election time, sitting justices almost never drew opposition. Some justices resigned before the end of their terms, enabling their replacements to be named by the governor and to run as incumbents. In the event that an open seat was actually contested, the decisive factor

in the race was the state bar poll, which was the key to newspaper endorsements and the support of courthouse politicians.[18]

Beginning in 1978, however, changes began to occur in Texas judicial politics. That year, William Clements, the first Republican governor since Reconstruction, was elected. The governor has the power to appoint judges to the district and higher courts when new courts have been created or when a judicial vacancy occurs as a result of death, resignation, or retirement. Unlike the previous Democratic governors, who appointed members of the Democratic Party, Clements began appointing Republicans. With that advantage of incumbency and with the increasing popularity of the Republican Party label, some of the Republican judges began to win re-election.

Helped by the popularity of Ronald Reagan in Texas, other Republicans began seeking judicial offices and winning. Thus, by the early 1980s, in statewide elections and in several counties in Texas, competition began to appear in judicial races. With that competition, incumbent judges began to be defeated. Sensing the growth of Republican strength, a number of Democratic judges changed to a Republican Party affiliation. At the same time, judicial elections became more expensive because judicial candidates needed money to run meaningful and competitive campaigns. In particular, campaigns that used television advertising became very expensive because of high media costs.

Judicial candidates needed money because judicial races tend to have low-visibility campaigns in which voters are unaware of the candidates. The races tend to be overshadowed by higher-visibility ones, such as the race for governor or U.S. senator. Money was needed to give judicial candidates some degree of name visibility to voters. However, in general, Texas voters do not give much money to judicial campaigns. Instead, it is lawyers and interest groups who tend to be donors in judicial races. Thus, by the early 1980s, there was a new and expensive competitiveness in Texas judicial politics that in turn fed a demand for reforms in the way Texas judges were selected.

Proposed Reforms of the Texas Judiciary

There have been numerous efforts to reform the Texas judiciary. In general, reformers are concerned with (1) changing the system for selecting judges, (2) increasing minority representation on the bench, or (3) restructuring the judiciary to make it more rational and efficient.

Changing the System for Selecting Judges
The reform movement focused on changing the method by which judges are selected has been concerned with the low visibility of judicial races in Texas. Voters are rarely aware of the qualifications and abilities of judicial candidates and, as a result, rely on party labels when electing judges. At other times, reformers claim, voters rely on the attractiveness of judicial candidates' names in voting, since they lack other knowledge of the candidates. Still another problem pointed out by these reformers is that in urban counties there are so many candidates on the ballot that it is impossible for voters to make informed decisions.

For decades efforts have been made to change the system of selecting judges in Texas. In some states judges are elected in nonpartisan elections, in which judicial candidates run for office without a party label; in some other states, judges are appointed by the executive; and in a couple of states, the legislature selects judges. By far the most frequently proposed reform nationwide, however, has been to switch to **merit selection** of judges. Under this system, a blue-ribbon commission solicits interest in a vacant judicial seat and screens possible candidates for that seat. The commission then recommends to the governor three to five persons who they believe are highly qualified for the position, and the governor appoints one of those recommended to the vacancy, subject to state senate confirmation. After serving for about one year, the appointed judge runs in a **retention election** where he or she has no opponent but voters decide if they wish to retain the judge in office. Thereafter, the judge would continue to run for re-election in a retention election. The result of adopting merit selection, in the view of its advocates, is a far greater likelihood that judges will be highly competent and will have little need to depend on lawyers and interest groups for funding to remain in office. Retention elections can be expensive campaigns, but in general they are very low-budget affairs.

Reformers advocate this plan because they believe voters lack sufficient knowledge of judicial candidates and rely too heavily on the party label in casting their ballots. As a result, they vote for the party rather than for the best-qualified person. In 2016, for example, 65 percent of Harris County voters cast a straight-ticket ballot, which meant that they voted the party label rather than for the individual candidate. Straight-ticket voting can sweep experienced judges out of office solely because of their party affiliation. That happened in the 2018 elections in Harris County where Republican judges lost office because of substantial Democratic straight-ticket voting. In response to his defeat, Harris County Juvenile Judge Glenn Devlin released almost all defendants that appeared before him the day after the election, only asking the defendants whether they intended to kill anyone before he released them. Seven juveniles were released including four facing aggravated robbery charges. Judge Devlin explained that in light of the election he believed that was what the voters wanted. While it seems doubtful that voters wanted juveniles charged with violent crimes to be released, it was the case that Republican judges running for re-election lost solely because of their political party affiliation.[19]

In 2017, Texas passed legislation that will ban **straight-ticket voting** in 2020. A voter will have to vote for individual candidates rather than cast a vote for all candidates with a party label. An argument for the new legislation is that voters who vote for individual candidates rather than voting a party label will be informed voters who are knowledgeable about the candidates. Democrats argued against this legislation because they believed that minority voters tended to vote a straight ticket for Democrats and that the legislation would therefore disproportionately impact minority voters and harm Democratic candidates. If the straight-ticket voting ban is not declared a voting rights act violation, far fewer votes are likely to be cast for judicial candidates.

The sheer number of candidates for judicial offices also leads to voter confusion and a lack of voter awareness of these candidates. In 2016 in Harris County, for example, voters were faced with casting ballots for 31 judges as well as 13 other offices.[20] Even voters who try to make a serious effort to learn about judicial candidates can have a hard time.

In the absence of voter awareness of judicial candidates, reformers are also concerned that voters will rely on irrelevant factors such as the perceived attractiveness

Elected or Appointed Judges?

IN TEXAS, members of the Texas Supreme Court and the Court of Criminal Appeals, as well as of all lower state courts, are elected in partisan elections. Texas is one of only seven states that elect judges this way. Other states use a variety of selection systems ranging from gubernatorial appointment to legislative selection to nonpartisan election. Many "good government" advocates support merit selection, which several states employ and which has been suggested many times as a possible alternative to the current system in Texas. Merit selection involves a commission that vets potential judges based on their character and temperament. A list of approved judicial nominees is then presented to the governor, who appoints one as judge. After a period of time, that judge runs in a retention election. The judge does not face an opponent, but the ballot question asks voters whether the judge should be retained in office.

Former Texas Supreme Court justice Wallace Jefferson has been a major advocate of merit selection. Partisan elections make little sense, according to Jefferson, when judges have so little to do with politics. He notes that what they do is "mundane, if nonetheless important. They probate wills and apportion divorcing spouses' assets. They determine child support and custody. They oversee trials and changes of pleas in criminal cases. They police discovery and preside over settlement conferences." Yet in every election, Jefferson argues, judges are swept out of office because of partisan voting, rather than decisions about judicial competence. Because of these concerns, Jefferson argues that the current system of selecting judges is one "in which an overwhelmed electorate ineffectually uses partisanship and name recognition as a proxy" for competence and integrity. "The result is the loss of good judges and a decrease in public confidence." Jefferson insists that "reform, beginning with merit selection followed by retention elections, is imperative."[a]

In response to Jefferson, Houston lawyer David Butts pointed out that Texas already has a system in which judges are appointed. The governor appoints judges to district and higher-level courts when new courts are created or when there are vacancies to fill. In fact, Governor Perry appointed more judges than any previous governor, and that included seven of the nine justices currently on the Texas Supreme Court. That appointment process is a political process, as was pointed out by a study of Perry's appointments done by the *Austin American-Statesman*. The study found that Perry "appointed reliably like-minded people—donors to his campaigns, one-time staffers in his office, former lobbyists—to dozens of boards, commissions and judgeships." If there is judicial reform, Butts argued, it should begin with restricting the governor's ability to appoint anyone he chooses. Butts noted that reformers always propose merit selection as a way to take politics out of judicial selection, but, he wrote, "the only

politics that are restricted from the selection of our judges are the voters'. The governor, the Legislature, the elite group of lawyers on the selection committee, and the special interest groups will continue to influence and decide who those select candidates are and who is chosen." In reference to retention elections, Butts noted evidence from retention elections in California, Wisconsin, and Iowa where judges were defeated because their decisions angered "deep-pocket special interests or ideological fault lines" and thus became as subject to defeat as if they were in a partisan election. There will always be politics in a selection system, claimed Butts, and Texans should "trust the voters with the final say. Voters will not always make the best choice, but they usually get it right."[b]

COMMUNICATING EFFECTIVELY: YOUR VOICE

- Should judges be elected or appointed? Is merit selection an effective compromise?

- Should the selection system vary according to type of judge?

of a candidate's name when they vote for judges. In 2008 there was heavy voting for Democrats in Harris County because of the popularity of presidential candidate Barack Obama. So many voters voted straight Democratic that all but four Republican judges were voted out of office. Interestingly, the four Republican judges who survived were all challenged by Democrats with more unusual names. As a result, the incumbent Republican judge Sharon McCally was able to defeat the Democratic challenger Ashish Mahendru; Mark Kent Ellis defeated Mekisha Murray; Patricia Kerrigan defeated Andres Pereira; and Joseph Halback defeated Goodwille Pierre.[21]

In the 2016 Republican Supreme Court primary, incumbent justice Paul Green was challenged by Rick Green. Paul Green had been an appellate court justice for 21 years and was a trial lawyer for 17 years. Rick Green had never been a judge, never tried a case, and never appealed a case. He had previously served in the Texas House, where he used his capitol office to film infomercials. He had also lobbied successfully to get a convicted swindler—who had earlier given him a $400,000 loan—out of prison after 3 years of a 16-year sentence. Moreover, Rick Green had received 6 months' probation for hitting the Democrat who defeated him for re-election to his House seat. Paul Green did win the primary with 52 percent of the vote, but the closeness of the race showed that his concern about voter confusion over similar names was a real one.

Another example of voter confusion over names occurred in the Republican primary race for a Place 5 (appellate courts have multiple members, and judicial candidates run for specific seats or places on those courts) on the Court of Criminal Appeals. No incumbent was running for re-election, and there were four candidates, including one with stellar credentials: Sid Harle had been a criminal defense attorney, a Bexar County prosecutor, and a longtime trial judge who had presided over more capital murder cases than any other judge in Texas, and he was a former chair of the State Commission on Judicial Conduct. His three opponents had no judicial experience, and one had civil rather than criminal law experience. Yet Harle finished fourth in the race with only about 18.5 percent of the vote. The candidate with the highest percentage of votes had limited criminal trial and appellate experience over an 18-year career and did not run an active campaign. He ran not as Richard Walker, but used his middle name, Scott, on the ballot—and "Scott Walker" happened to be the name of the then highly visible Republican governor of Wisconsin.[22] Walker later overwhelmingly won the Republican runoff primary and won in the general election.

Of special concern to reformers has been the role of money in judicial campaigns, insofar as campaign funds are seen as creating problems for the integrity of the judicial branch and for the appearance of fairness in judicial decision making. Contributions for judicial races in Texas can sometimes amount to several hundred thousand dollars, especially for hotly contested district court or appellate court races. In general, however, the most expensive races are for the Texas Supreme Court.

When Texas Supreme Court races are contested between Democratic and Republican candidates, a candidate can raise well over $1 million. However, hard-fought races are now rare, as these statewide elections have moved into the Republican column. Because these are statewide races and because this court sets the tone of tort law (civil lawsuits over harm to another) throughout the state, a great deal of money is needed and a great deal can be raised (see Table 9.1). One million dollars may seem like a small sum for a statewide race in Texas considering that in his 2014 campaign for governor, Greg Abbott alone raised over $47.4 million and that even the winning candidate for railroad

The high number of judicial elections makes it difficult for voters to be informed about each candidate. Most voters make their decision based on party identification and name recognition.

TABLE 9.1

State Supreme Court Elections in 2015–2016 with More Than $1,000,000 in Contributions

STATE	SYSTEM OF SELECTION	SEATS UP FOR ELECTION	TOTAL CONTRIBUTIONS
Pennsylvania	Partisan	3	$21,417,861
North Carolina[1]	Nonpartisan	1	5,419,151
West Virginia[2]	Nonpartisan	1	4,963,973
Louisiana	Partisan	2	4,912,154
Wisconsin (2016)	Nonpartisan	1	4,723,444
Michigan[3]	Nonpartisan	2	4,305,233
Texas	Partisan	3	4,205,358
Ohio[3]	Nonpartisan	3	4,453,641

[1] North Carolina changed to partisan judicial elections in December 2016.
[2] West Virginia changed to nonpartisan judicial elections in April 2015.
[3] Michigan and Ohio have partisan primaries, but nonpartisan general elections for judges.

SOURCE: Alicia Bannon, Cathleen Lisk, and Peter Hardin with Douglas Keith, Laila Robbins, Eric Velasco, Denise Roth Barber, and Linda Casey, *The Politics of Judicial Elections 2015–16: Who Pays for Judicial Races?* (New York: Brennan Center, undated), www.brennancenter.org/publication /politics-judicial-elections.

commissioner, Ryan Sitton, raised over $4 million.[23] Unlike other elected officials, however, judicial candidates are supposed to be neutral decision makers not reflecting the values of particular interests in the state. Yet winning Texas Supreme Court candidates overwhelmingly get their contributions from the oil and gas industry, lawyers and lobbyists, and the finance sector.

As the winners of Texas's statewide elections have become overwhelmingly Republican, the amounts contributed to supreme court candidates have dropped precipitously. In 1988, when Texas Supreme Court races were still competitive between Democrats and Republicans, total contributions for supreme court candidates came to over $11.4 million, with one candidate alone receiving over $2 million in contributions.[24] By 2014 far less money was contributed to or needed by Republican candidates, since they faced no serious threat from Democratic opponents. The Democratic candidate for the chief justice position against Republican incumbent Nathan Hecht could only raise $17,650. Hecht, on the other hand, raised $1,459,497.[25] To the extent that there is any real battle for a position on the Texas Supreme Court, it is now within the Republican primary. In 2018 all three of the incumbent Republican justices were unopposed in the Republican primary, faced Democratic opposition in the general election, and all three were re-elected.

In spite of decades-long efforts to change Texas from partisan election to merit selection, the attempts at such a comprehensive reform have failed. The only successful reform has been one dealing with judicial campaign finance, the **Judicial Campaign Fairness Act**. Texas is the only state with a campaign finance regulation of this type. Among the most important aspects of compliance with the act are campaign contribution limitations. For example, statewide judicial candidates must limit themselves to contributions of no more than $5,000 from any individual in any election. Additionally, statewide candidates can receive no more than $30,000 per election from any law firm. Although the amounts of money that can be donated are still quite high, there has been a significant reduction from contribution amounts in the 1980s when, prior to the act, some donors would give candidates $25,000, $50,000, and even more. These contribution limitations are imposed by law; however, judicial candidates may also voluntarily agree to campaign expenditure limitations specified in the law—for example, a $2 million expenditure limit for statewide judicial candidates and a $500,000 limit for candidates for courts of appeal in areas larger than one million persons.[26]

At least for the time being, it seems likely that not much will change in the way Texas selects its judges. Restructuring the system would be a major change, and such changes are always difficult to initiate. A major change might upset voters, who like being able to vote for judges, and it would surely upset the political parties, which like having large numbers of judicial candidates running under their party label. It might also upset lawyers accustomed to the traditional ways of selecting judges and even judges who have benefited from the present system.

In looking at the experience of other states, it seems clear that each state has developed a judicial selection system to reflect its own political objectives. While systems of judicial selections can roughly be classified as merit selection, partisan election, nonpartisan election, gubernatorial appointment, and selection by the legislature, states have great variations in selection systems within these broad categories. Illinois, for example, has partisan election of judges for their initial terms and then retention elections for subsequent elections. Missouri has merit selection for some courts and partisan election for others. New Mexico has merit selection for initial selection of judges, but in the

Judicial Campaign Fairness Act a judicial reform that places limits on judicial campaign contributions

Comparing How Texas Selects Its Judges to the Rest of the Country

Method of Initial Selection for State's Highest Court Judges

Gubernatorial appointment through nominating commission

Alaska	Hawaii	Nebraska	S. Dakota
Arizona	Indiana	New Hampshire	Tennessee
Colorado	Iowa	New Mexico	Utah
Connecticut	Kansas	New York	Vermont
Delaware	Maryland	Oklahoma	Washington, DC
Florida	Missouri	Rhode Island	Wyoming

Nonpartisan election

Arkansas	Nevada
Georgia	N. Dakota
Idaho	Oregon
Kentucky	Washington
Minnesota	Wisconsin
Mississippi	W. Virginia
Montana	

Legislative selection

S. Carolina
Virginia

Partisan election

Alabama	N. Carolina
Illinois	Ohio
Louisiana	Pennsylvania
Michigan	Texas

Gubernatorial appointment

California
Massachusetts
Maine
New Jersey

Texas is one of eight states that choose their state judges through partisan elections. Voters generally decide for whom to vote based on party affiliation. With so many offices on the ballot, it is simply easier for voters to use their party affiliation as a shortcut. Not all states select judges this way. Most states employ a merit selection method through nominating commissions that make recommendations to the governor. Other states have judges selected by the governor without nominating commissions. Thirteen states elect their judges in nonpartisan elections, meaning that the role of political parties in judicial elections is minimized. The state legislature chooses judges in the remaining two states.

Judicial Selection Methods: A Regional View

- ● Gubernatorial appointment through nominating commission
- ● Gubernatorial appointment
- ● Partisan election
- ● Nonpartisan election
- ● Legislative selection

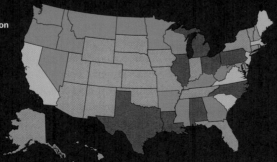

SOURCES: American Judicature Society, Judicial Selection in the States, www.judicial selection.us/ and IAALS, the Institute for the Advancement of the American Legal System at the University of Denver published in "Selection and Retention of State Judges," *Texas Bar Journal* (February 2016): 92–97.

CRITICAL THINKING

- What are the advantages of nonpartisan elections to select judges? Which method of selection do you think is the best and why?

- Are there regional patterns in how judges are selected? If so, why do you think that is?

next general election, the judge must run in a partisan election. The winning candidate serves the remainder of the term, at which time the judge runs in a retention election for another term. To be retained, the judge must receive at least a 57 percent affirmative vote. If the judge is not retained, the nominating commission presents another list of judicial candidates to the governor, who then appoints a new judge. Governors appoint judges in California, but a commission has the power to veto their appointment. When it comes to the details, there are almost as many ways to select judges as there are states. (See the "Texas and the Nation" graphic in this chapter.)

Increasing Minority Representation on the Bench A second group of reformers has been interested in increasing the numbers of African Americans and Latinos on the bench. In 1985, Professor Paul Brest wrote, "Judges are far from a representative cross-section of American society. They are overwhelmingly Anglo, male, well educated, and upper or upper middle class. They are also members of the legal profession. . . . Women, Blacks, and Hispanics are only the groups most notoriously under-represented on the judiciary."[27] What Brest wrote in 1985 is still true in Texas and throughout the nation. Although African Americans and Hispanics together make up about 50 percent of the Texas population, relatively few Texas judges belong to these groups.

The lack of diversity on the bench creates significant problems for the legitimacy of the courts and for the proper functioning of those courts within a diverse population. Professor Sherrilyn Ifill has argued that diversity among judges is necessary for impartiality in judicial decision making, public confidence in the court system, and the perception that society as a whole is represented on the bench. Ifill wrote, "First, the creation of a racially diverse bench can introduce traditionally excluded perspectives and values into judicial decision-making. The interplay of diverse views and perspectives can enrich judicial decision-making. . . . Second, racial diversity on the bench also encourages judicial impartiality, by ensuring that a single set of values or views do not dominate judicial decision making."[28]

Although women do not make up 50 percent of the Texas judiciary as they do of the population, there is a higher proportion of women in the Texas judiciary than of minorities. In Texas, the first woman to serve as a state judge was Sarah Hughes, who was appointed in 1935 and served as a district judge until 1961, when she was appointed to the federal bench. Famous for a number of her decisions, including one that forced Dallas County to build a new jail, she is probably best known as the judge who swore in Lyndon Johnson as president after the assassination of John F. Kennedy. By September 2017, 43 percent of appellate judges in Texas were women, and 35 percent of district judges were women. In contrast, only 2 percent of appellate judges and 7 percent of district judges are African American, and only 15 percent of appellate judges and 17 percent of district judges are Latino.[29]

Different interpretations have been offered for the low numbers of minorities on the bench. The lack of racial

PERSONAL RESPONSIBILITY: WHAT WOULD YOU DO?

- Few minorities hold judicial office in Texas. Although African Americans and Latinos make up about 50 percent of the Texas population, relatively few Texas judges belong to these groups. Offer at least three suggestions, including alternative election methods, to increase the number of minorities holding judicial office in Texas.

and ethnic diversity among the judiciary is a nationwide problem. Civil rights groups in several states with elective judiciaries, including Texas, have argued that judicial districts that are countywide or larger are dominated by whites who vote against minority judicial candidates. These groups have argued that for minorities to get elected as judges, there must be smaller judicial districts where minority voters make up the majority of the population. One problem with dividing judicial districts into areas smaller than counties, however, is that Latino and African American organizations have been unable to agree on the appropriate method of creating smaller districts. Both groups have sought to divide counties in different ways to reflect their group's respective interests. Additionally, the business community in Texas has been opposed to smaller judicial districts out of fear that they will lead to the election of judges whose largely minority constituencies might be hostile and favor individual plaintiffs in lawsuits against businesses.

In 2009, Rick Perry appointed Eva Guzman—the first Latina woman to serve on the Texas Supreme Court—to fill a vacancy on the court. Guzman was elected to a full term in the 2010 election.

An alternative perspective is that minority candidates in Texas, like minority voters, tend to be Democrats at a time when Republicans increasingly are winning judicial races. Thus, minorities do not get elected to judicial office because they run as Democrats. Still another argument is that there are few minority judges because there are few minority lawyers and, with the exception of county judges and justices of the peace, judges in Texas must be lawyers. Only 5 percent of lawyers in Texas are African American and only 9 percent are Latino.[30]

Restructuring the Texas Judiciary to Make It More Rational and Efficient
Texas judges may be elected, but they do not represent an electorate in the way legislators or county commissioners do. As a result, their districts are not subject to redistricting according to the one person–one vote standards used in redistricting legislative bodies. The result is that Texas judicial districts are a hodgepodge of jurisdictions. Things have not changed much since a 1993 report that criticized the structure of the Texas courts:

> The framers of our current Constitution deliberately designed a system to "localize justice," establishing a multiplicity of largely autonomous conveniently located courts across the state. With the passage of time, the organization of the courts has become more, not less, cumbersome. A case may frequently be eligible for filing in more than one court, either because of overlapping geographical boundaries or overlapping subject matter jurisdiction. Courts with the same name may have different responsibilities and similar places may have quite dissimilar court structures.[31]

As a state bar commission pointed out, the idea behind having justice of the peace courts, statutory county courts, constitutional county courts, and district courts was that each level of court was supposed to have its own jurisdiction that was to be consistent across each court at that level. That consistency has not come about because these courts have developed into a "patchwork array."[32]

Favorability Toward the Courts and Criminal Justice System by Race/Ethnicity

In February 2017 a University of Texas/*Texas Tribune* poll of 1,200 registered Texas voters asked their favorability toward the courts and the criminal justice system. Forty-two percent of white Texans had favorable attitudes, but only 28 percent of African Americans had favorable attitudes. What do you think explains the disparity in favorability ratings toward the courts and criminal justice system between white and African American Texans?

SOURCE: University of Texas/*Texas Tribune* poll, February 2017. Survey was conducted February 3–12, 2017, of 1,200 registered voters in Texas.

One illustration of this cumbersome court structure can be found in the district court structure in Anderson County in east Texas. There are four district courts in Anderson County. One of those courts also has jurisdiction in Henderson and Houston counties; one also has jurisdiction in Freestone, Leon, and Limestone counties; one has jurisdiction only in Houston County; and the fourth also has jurisdiction in Cherokee County. Bastrop County has three district courts—two of them have jurisdiction only in Bastrop County, but the third has jurisdiction in Bastrop, Burleson, Lee, and Washington counties.

The appellate courts in Texas are also plagued by a cumbersome structure, especially in the ten counties in the Houston area. These ten counties are served by two courts of appeal—the 1st and the 14th Courts of Appeal—that have overlapping jurisdictions, and cases are randomly assigned between them. The result is that at times the two courts render opposing decisions in cases that rely on the same facts, so that there is no precedent that lower courts and lawyers in the ten-county area can rely on. The effect of this situation is a lack of certainty and predictability, which one justice described as "practicing law on a guess and a gamble."[33]

These structural problems in the Texas judicial system are primarily a concern of the Texas legal community. While reforms have addressed some of the problems in the design of the Texas court system, such as the passage of a law in 2011 that allows justice of the peace courts to handle small claims with less formal rules of procedure, changes are rare and piecemeal rather than comprehensive.

Who Are Texas's Judges?

- By race
- By gender

● White ● African American ● Latino ● Other

● Male ● Female

Trial Courts

Trial courts include district courts, county courts at law, and probate courts

2%
17%
76%
6%
34%
66%

Appellate Courts

Appellate courts include the state Supreme Court, courts of appeal, and Court of Criminal Appeals

4%
18%
75%
3%
43%
57%

Texas Lawyers

6%
9%
80%
5%
35%
65%

Texas Population

8%
43%
39%
50%
50%
13%

Although the proportion of women and of Latino and African American judges is roughly representative of the proportion of women, Latino, and African American lawyers, the composition of the Texas judiciary is very unrepresentative of the Texas population as a whole. Should there be a rough proportionality between the racial/ethnic/gender composition of the judiciary and Texas as a whole?

QUANTITATIVE REASONING

- Are there more or fewer minority judges in Texas than in the state population overall? (Texas is 13 percent African American and 39 percent Latino.)

- What are some of the factors that might lead to an increase in the representation of minorities in the state's courts?

SOURCES: Texas Office of Court Administration, Profile of Appellate and Trial Judges as of September 1, 2017; State Bar of Texas, "State Bar of Texas Membership: Attorney Statistical Profile (2016-2017);" U.S. Census, "Quickfacts," July 1, 2016.

Issues in the Texas Court System Today

Assess the impact of recent changes related to tort reform, regulation of lawyers, and disciplining judges

One of the most important issues in Texas has been tort reform, which is the effort to change the system for awarding damages in lawsuits where harm is claimed. Tort reform has had important effects on the Texas judiciary.

Civil Cases and Tort Reform

Figure 9.2 shows the numbers of civil cases disposed of by the appellate courts and the trial courts in 2016–17. The Texas county court system and especially the district courts are handling huge caseloads. While the caseload of the Texas Supreme Court is quite low, it sets the tone for civil cases throughout the state. The most important type of civil cases, because of the large amounts of money involved, is tort law—cases in which one person has been harmed by the actions of another. For example, medical malpractice cases are a common type of tort case. In the early to mid-1980s, the Texas Supreme Court tended to be sympathetic to the plaintiffs' positions in tort cases. That is, the court tended to support the side in a case that was suing businesses, professionals, and insurance companies. However, in 1988 more justices began to be elected who favored the defendants in civil lawsuits. One reason for this change was that in 1988 Republican justices began to be elected, and they were more conservative than many of the previous justices, who were Democrats. Interest groups that were harmed by the pro-plaintiff tendencies of the court began to organize, raise and spend money, and elect justices more sympathetic to their perspective. Today the Texas Supreme Court is quite favorable to defendants in civil cases, in part because it is now an all-Republican and conservative court. Additionally, during Governor Perry's administration a number of laws were passed, most notably involving medical malpractice lawsuits, that make it much harder for the plaintiff to prevail over the defendant in a lawsuit.[34]

The Regulation of the Legal Profession

Lawyers occupy a crucial role in the legal process. In order to practice law, one must be a licensed lawyer, and in order to be licensed in Texas, it is generally necessary to complete a Juris Doctor (JD) degree at a law school accredited by the American Bar Association. Usually this degree takes three years beyond the bachelor's degree if the law student attends full-time. After completing law school, a prospective lawyer must take the state bar exam. After passing the Texas state bar, one may be sworn in as a lawyer in Texas. Texas has an integrated bar, which means that all licensed lawyers in the state must join and pay dues to the State Bar of Texas. That agency, which is under the administrative

FIGURE 9.2

Civil Cases Disposed of by Texas Courts, September 1, 2016–August 31, 2017

*Excludes civil cases related to criminal matters and family law cases.

SOURCE: Texas Office of Court Administration, 2017 Annual Statistical Report.

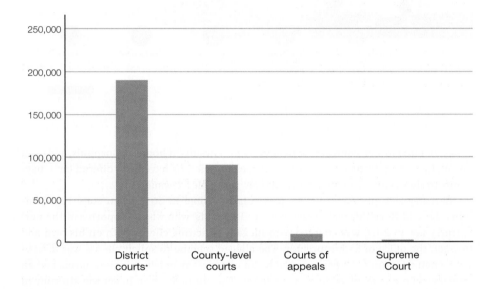

control of the Texas Supreme Court, offers a variety of services to lawyers such as insurance plans, a journal, and professional meetings. Since lawyers must undergo continuing education, the state bar authorizes continuing education credit for a number of educational programs.

The State Bar of Texas is unusual in that it is not only a professional organization of lawyers but also an agency of government that is charged with enforcing ethical standards for the profession. Lawyers can be disciplined for a variety of infractions, ranging from serious criminal behavior, to failing to keep a client informed of the status of a legal matter, to failing to promptly pay out funds from a legal settlement. The state bar may also enforce rules against illegal efforts to generate litigation. In 2016–17 the state bar exercised its enforcement power by disbarring 20 Texas lawyers, obtaining the resignations from legal practice of 28, suspending the legal practice of 126, publicly reprimanding 30, and privately reprimanding 89. The bar also offers what is known as the grievance referral program, where lawyers with problems such as substance abuse or mental health issues will be referred for assistance in dealing with those problems rather than face more severe sanctions. In 2016–17, 49 lawyers were referred for assistance.[35]

Illegal generation of litigation is commonly known as barratry, and the state legislature has become so concerned about lawyers' inappropriately generating legal business that in 2011 it passed new legislation that allows for a penalty of up to $10,000 and the recovery of attorney's fees. The goal of the legislation was to prevent what is commonly known as "ambulance chasing," which appears to remain a problem in spite of long-standing state bar rules against it. Some of the horror stories of barratry include people being solicited to sign contracts with lawyers for lawsuits at home, in hospitals, and even during funerals. At times the relatives of accident victims have been offered large payments to sign a contract with a particular lawyer to file a lawsuit.[36]

Barratry as a problem became particularly visible in 2012 when state representative Ronald Reynolds was arrested for it. Reynolds, who was a supporter of the new barratry law in 2011, was charged with illegally soliciting clients both on his own and through the office of a chiropractor. The alleged scheme to solicit clients was discovered when a "runner"—a person used by an attorney to solicit clients—approached an attorney who was involved in a car accident. The "runner" tried to get the attorney in the accident to hire Reynolds to represent her, but the accident victim instead reported that solicitation to authorities.[37] That charge against Reynolds fell apart when an investigator in the case was arrested for stealing evidence in another case. But Reynolds was arrested on another barratry charge for allegedly paying a man who would examine accident reports and then approach accident victims and persuade them to sign contracts for legal representation.[38] Altogether, eight lawyers were arrested in that barratry case, and seven of them made plea arrangements. Reynolds was the only one who went to trial, and he was convicted on five counts of barratry and sentenced to one year in jail. Reynolds is currently released on bail while appealing his conviction.[39] He has been suspended from practicing law and faces mounting legal problems. Reynolds owes creditors more than $1.3 million including $700,000 owed to clients in cases where he kept their part of legal settlements. No longer able to practice law, Reynolds has filed for bankruptcy. However, he was able to win re-election to the Texas House of Representatives in 2016 in spite of these problems.[40] However, in May 2018 the Texas Court of Criminal Appeals refused to review his conviction. Representative Reynolds is now serving a one-year sentence in the Montgomery County jail. He was re-elected unopposed in November 2018 and does not have to resign his office since he was not convicted of a felony. Unless he is released early from jail, he will miss the legislative session that begins in early 2019.

In order for the state bar to discipline a lawyer, a finding of wrongdoing is, of course, required. When a lawyer is charged with criminal offenses, he or she can practice until a court finds they are guilty of a crime. This can lead to bizarre situations. For example,

Rayan Ganesh graduated from South Texas College of Law and was licensed in 2012. In July 2016 he was arrested on two counts of indecency with a child. In February 2017 he was indicted on seven counts of barratry. Ganesh continued practicing law, and a local television channel reported that he was representing 650 clients, an astounding number in light of the fact that a typical criminal defense lawyer in private practice has a caseload of 50–100 clients. Ganesh was finally convicted in April 2018 of two counts of felony indecency with a child by exposure and sentenced to eight years of imprisonment. Between his arrest and his conviction, a reporter found him recruiting clients in the Dallas County courthouse. Despite Ganesh's serious legal problems, the state bar was unable to prevent him from practicing law until he was found guilty.[41]

In 2015–2017 there were almost 88,000 lawyers practicing in Texas,[42] or about 31.6 for every 10,000 people. With the decline in the number of legal jobs over the past decade, there has been much discussion about whether there is an oversupply of lawyers. Of course, lawyers trained in out-of-state law schools may take the bar exam and be licensed in Texas, but the state has a substantial number of law schools: the University of Texas, the University of Houston, Texas Tech, Texas Southern, St. Mary's, South Texas, Southern Methodist University, Baylor, and Texas A&M. The state's newest law school, the University of North Texas College of Law, opened in Dallas in 2014.

The legal process in Texas relies on lawyers. Constitutional county court judges and justices of the peace do not have to be lawyers, but all other judges must be "learned in the law," a term found in the Texas Constitution whose meaning has come to require a law degree. In civil and criminal litigation, it is possible for a layperson to pursue a case without a lawyer, but it is generally recognized that non-lawyers are at a significant disadvantage in either a civil or a criminal proceeding if they lack legal help.

Judicial Conduct

The State Commission on Judicial Conduct was created by a constitutional amendment in 1965 and charged with investigating allegations of judicial misconduct and disability and with disciplining judges. The 13 members of the commission serve six-year terms and are unpaid. The commission also has a staff of 14, and in 2017 its budget was slightly over $1.2 million, mostly for staff salaries. The commission is an unusual hybrid agency in that two attorney members are appointed by the state bar and six judicial members are appointed by the Texas Supreme Court. There are also five citizen members, who can be neither lawyers nor judges and are appointed by the governor. The state senate confirms the commission members.

In dealing with disciplinary issues involving Texas judges, the commission relies on complaints from the public, from attorneys, and from members of the judiciary. In 2017 the commission disposed of 1,333 cases. A common complaint is that the person disagrees with the judge's decision, but of course this is not a violation of the Code of Judicial Conduct, the ethical code promulgated by the Texas Supreme Court that is enforced by the commission along with certain legislative requirements on judges.

The commission's decision making is done behind closed doors and thus lacks openness and transparency. Still, other than impeachment by the legislature or criminal prosecution of judges—both rare and extreme measures—the commission is the only mechanism for regulating ethical and legal conduct of Texas judges.[43]

Justice Nora Longoria of the 13th Court of Appeals received a public admonition from the State Commission on Judicial Conduct due to her behavior during a traffic stop by McAllen police.

In 2017 the commission imposed 62 sanctions on judges. In 8 other cases, judges chose to resign rather than be sanctioned. The commission can recommend public censure or removal of a judge or the judge's involuntary retirement to a review tribunal composed of the chief justice of Texas and six appellate judges. The tribunal's decision can be appealed by the affected judge to the Texas Supreme Court. No such case occurred in 2016. Other decisions of the commission can be appealed to a court of review consisting of three appellate judges. In 2017 a court of review upheld a public reprimand against a Tarrant County justice of the peace.[44]

Many of the disciplinary actions of the commission involve private sanctions of the judge. In 2017, 24 sanctions were of a private nature and consisted of the commission providing a private admonition, warning, or reprimand (admonitions are less severe sanctions than warnings, which are less severe than reprimands). Often with private or public sanctions, judges are required to seek additional legal education. Twenty-seven disciplinary actions involved public sanctions, which are much more embarrassing to the judge and can be used in opposition to the judge in future campaigns for office. Three other actions by the commission were interim actions.

A sanction in 2015 received considerable media attention. It was against Justice Nora Longoria of the 13th Court of Appeals, who had been stopped by McAllen police for speeding. It became clear that she had been drinking, and she was emotional and uncooperative with the police. Among other things, she demanded to see the police supervisor, and she told the police she was a judge. She was charged with DWI. At trial she pled no contest to the speeding charge and was fined $500, and the DWI charge was dismissed. However, McAllen police released dashcam footage of the stop, which portrayed Justice Longoria very negatively, and it became a popular item on social media. The commission provided a public admonition to Justice Longoria.[45]

Although Justice David Lewis's suspension and later resignation in lieu of removal proceeding (discussed in the introduction to this chapter) received some statewide attention, the most widely publicized disciplinary case against a judge in recent years was against the presiding judge of the Texas Court of Criminal Appeals, Sharon Keller. In 2007, Judge Keller refused to keep the clerk's office at the court open beyond 5 PM to receive an appeal from death-row inmate Michael Richard. As a result, Richard was executed later that evening. Although Keller received a public warning from the State Commission on Judicial Conduct, she was successful in her litigation against the discipline by arguing that a warning cannot be a penalty following a formal proceeding against a judge.[46] Re-elected to another six-year term in 2012 with 55.49 percent of the vote, Keller remains the presiding judge of the court.

The Judiciary and the Future of Texas

TEXAS ELECTS its judges in partisan judicial elections. For many years, when the Democratic Party was dominant, Texas judicial elections were staid, low-budget, noncompetitive events. However, with the growth of the Republican Party, they became highly political, and large amounts of money have been raised for judicial candidates, especially in Texas Supreme Court races. Because the Texas Supreme Court sets the tone of tort law in the state, often these races pitted candidates backed by business interests against those backed by plaintiffs' lawyers. These elections have calmed down in recent years as the Democratic Party has weakened, and at least in statewide races judicial elections have become less competitive.

Because voters often don't know much about judicial candidates, they often decide on the basis of the candidate's party affiliation or name appeal. This tendency has caused problems, and numerous efforts have been undertaken to change the way judges are selected in Texas. There have been efforts to change to merit selection. Minority groups have pushed to reduce the size of judicial districts in order to increase the election of minority judges. However, no major change has so far been successful. No majority coalition can agree on appropriate changes in the judicial selection system, and significant opposition to change comes from groups such as the political parties and business interests. Additionally, Texans seem satisfied with the current system of selection and seem to prefer to elect their judges. The only change affecting judicial elections to date has been the Judicial Campaign Fairness Act, which provides limitations on campaign contributions to judicial candidates. Additionally, a recent change in Texas law that bans straight-ticket voting in 2020 will likely reduce the effect of judges' party affiliations on election outcomes, although the law will also reduce the numbers of people who vote in judicial elections and is legally questionable. Recent injustices in the Texas criminal system that are discussed in Chapter 13 do raise questions about how the system can be improved. One might speculate that a criminal justice system in which both judges and prosecutors are elected creates political pressures to gain convictions at all costs.

Because the Texas court system affects the liberty and especially the pocketbooks of Texans, it will continue to be an area of concern and controversy. And the most controversial area of Texas justice will continue to be the process by which judges are selected. Nevertheless, efforts to change the state's judicial system have been going on for decades with no result, and there seems no reason to believe change will occur in the near future. Even more minor changes in the judiciary, such as redistricting trial courts, seem to be a low priority in Texas. It is likely that the judiciary will continue "as is," at least for the next several years, with overlapping jurisdictions and a mishmash of courts. ★

Use **inQUIZITIVE** to help you study and master this material.

Court Structure

- **Describe how the Texas court system is organized (pp. 295–300)**

The appellate court system in Texas is divided into civil and criminal tracks with the Texas Supreme Court being the highest state-level court for civil cases and the Texas Criminal Court of Appeals being the highest for criminal cases. Texas has an intermediate appellate court system and trial courts that range from district courts for the most important criminal and civil cases, to county courts for less important criminal and civil cases, to justices of the peace and municipal courts for settling the lowest level of conflicts.

Key Terms

Texas Supreme Court (p. 295)
Texas Court of Criminal Appeals (p. 295)
courts of appeal (p. 295)
district courts (p. 295)
specialty courts (p. 297)
county judge (p. 297)
county courts (p. 297)
statutory county courts at law (p. 298)
statutory probate courts (p. 298)
justice of the peace courts (p. 298)
municipal courts (p. 300)
ordinance (p. 300)

Practice Quiz

1. The highest criminal court in the state of Texas is the
   a) Texas Supreme Court.
   b) Texas Court of Appeals.
   c) Texas Court of Criminal Appeals.
   d) county court.
   e) district court.

2. The major trial courts in Texas are the
   a) courts of appeal.
   b) justice of the peace courts.
   c) district courts.
   d) municipal courts.
   e) county courts.

3. Which of the following positions in the judiciary are filled primarily by non-lawyers?
   a) Texas Supreme Court justices
   b) district judges
   c) justices of the peace
   d) Texas Criminal Court of Appeals justices
   e) probate judges

The Legal Process

- **Explain the legal process and the differences between criminal and civil law (pp. 300–3)**

Civil law is dramatically different from criminal law, with the burden of proof relying on different standards. Plaintiffs are the initiators of legal actions in civil cases. Defendants in civil cases respond to accusations made against them. Civil cases may lead to trial or dismissal by a judge. They may also be resolved by a settlement between the parties. The state is a prosecutor in a criminal case, and the accused individual is the defendant. Criminal cases can result in a trial, a dismissal, or a plea bargain.

Key Terms

civil law (p. 300)
criminal law (p. 300)
complaint (p. 300)
answer (p. 300)
contingent fee (p. 300)
tort (p. 301)
preponderance of the evidence (p. 301)
capital case (p. 302)
felony (p. 302)
misdemeanor (p. 302)
grand jury (p. 302)
indictment (p. 302)
bench trial (p. 302)
plea bargain (p. 302)
beyond a reasonable doubt (p. 303)

Practice Quiz

4. Grand juries
  a) determine the guilt of defendants.
  b) decide whether a trial of an accused is warranted.
  c) agree to plea bargains.
  d) recommend that defendants undergo bench trials.
  e) hear appeals of convictions.

5. On conviction, the criminal's punishment is determined
  a) by the grand jury.
  b) in a separate hearing by the jury or judge that determined the person's guilt.
  c) by the prosecuting attorney.
  d) by the prosecuting and defense attorneys.
  e) by the Texas Court of Criminal Appeals.

Judicial Politics

- **Evaluate the process for selecting judges in Texas (pp. 303–15)**

Partisan elections make judges accountable to voters, but critics claim that unqualified judges are elected solely because of their party labels. These critics advocate alternatives for choosing judges such as merit selection. Minorities are not proportionately represented, possibly in part because most judges are elected from large districts that are non-minority.

Key Terms

merit selection (p. 306)
retention election (p. 306)
straight-ticket voting (p. 306)
Judicial Campaign Fairness Act (p. 310)

Practice Quiz

6. Civil defense lawyers often align themselves with
  a) business and professional groups.
  b) the grand jury.
  c) groups that support workers.
  d) judges supported by the Democratic Party.
  e) labor groups.

7. Texas's movement from being a Democratic to a Republican state led to
  a) defeats of large numbers of incumbent judges.
  b) party switching by incumbent judges.
  c) large campaign contributions to judges.
  d) election of more Republican judges.
  e) all of the above

8. In Texas, which event marked the rise of the Republican Party and partisan judicial elections?
  a) the election of President Ronald Reagan
  b) the impeachment of William Jefferson Clinton
  c) the appointment of Tom Phillips as chief justice of the United States
  d) the election of Bill Clements as governor of Texas
  e) the Shivercrat movement

9. How likely is Texas to change its method of selecting judicial candidates?
  a) Texas is scheduled to change to the Missouri Plan in January 2016.
  b) extremely likely in the next two decades
  c) likely in the next decade
  d) a 50–50 chance that change will soon occur
  e) unlikely

10. Which of the following sets campaign contribution limits for judicial candidates in Texas?
    a) Judicial Campaign Fairness Act
    b) Judicial Campaign Law
    c) Equal Justice Act
    d) Code of Judicial Conduct
    e) Federal Rules of Civil Procedure

11. Which of the following groups has the largest number of judges?
    a) African Americans
    b) American Indians
    c) Asian Americans
    d) Latinos
    e) women

Issues in the Texas Court System Today

- **Assess the impact of recent changes related to tort reform, regulation of lawyers, and disciplining judges (pp. 316–20)**

Texas courts make decisions affecting Texans on a variety of issues, including the ultimate penalty of death and tort cases such as medical malpractice.

Practice Quiz

12. Philosophically, in the past few years, Texas courts became
    a) more pro-defendant in civil cases.
    b) more liberal.
    c) more pro-defendant in criminal cases.
    d) more conservative.
    e) hostile to tort reform.

13. All lawyers who regularly practice in Texas
    a) must be members of the State Bar of Texas.
    b) must have graduated from a Texas law school.
    c) must appear in court at least twice a year.
    d) must volunteer to sit on grand juries.
    e) do not need any additional training once they have a law license.

14. The State Commission on Judicial Conduct
    a) screens judicial candidates to determine if they are qualified to be judges.
    b) offers continuing education courses for judges.
    c) investigates complaints of ethical violations by judges.
    d) recommends trial judges for promotion to appellate courts.
    e) makes rules governing the conduct of judges.

Hurricane Harvey drove people from their homes and inflicted damage throughout Houston and the surrounding areas. Local government played a critical, controversial role in the response.

Local Government

WHY LOCAL GOVERNMENT MATTERS Hurricane Harvey made landfall on August 25, 2017, as a Category 4 near Rockport, Texas. The storm moved around southern Texas for days, in the process dropping more than twenty trillion gallons of rain across Texas and Louisiana—enough water to supply New York City's water needs for more than five decades. Moody's Analytics estimated that $97 billion in property was destroyed, and other loss estimates were even higher. By September 1, 2017, the Texas Division of Emergency Management estimated 185,149 houses were damaged or destroyed and 364,000 persons had registered for FEMA assistance. At that time, 42,399 persons were in shelters, and FEMA had already distributed 1,900,000 meals in Texas. Houston, the largest city in Texas and the fourth largest city in the United States, with a population of 2.3 million, was flooded. At Cedar Bayou, on the outskirts of Houston, over 51 inches of rain were recorded in just under five days. This was a new record for the heaviest rainfall in the continental United States.

During the flooding, local government was inundated by rescue calls. There were cries for help from people flooded in their homes, cars, businesses, hospitals, and nursing homes. But somehow Houston and the surrounding area managed with a relatively small loss of life, given the overwhelming nature of the flooding. One estimate was that 107 persons died in the U.S. as a result of Harvey; in 2005 over 1,800 people died as a result of Hurricane Katrina. The combined governmental response coupled with the volunteer work of private citizens meant the response to Harvey was generally viewed favorably. A poll of 1,200 registered Texas voters found that 27 percent of Texans approved strongly of the local government response to Harvey and 34 percent approved somewhat. In contrast, only 5 percent disapproved strongly of the local response and only 6 percent disapproved somewhat.[1]

Houston mayor Sylvester Turner was criticized for not ordering an evacuation of Houston; Governor Abbott had said that if he were living in the area he would leave and head north. However, Turner and other local officials insisted it was best to stay put rather than evacuate, and most people did not leave. In 2005, Hurricane Rita headed toward Houston, and 3.7 million people left the Houston area. That evacuation was a disaster. Interstate 45 turned into a one-hundred-mile parking lot; cars ran out of fuel; no gasoline was available along the interstate. Dozens of people died in accidents and a bus fire, and of heat stroke. Hurricane Rita changed course and Houston was not severely hit. The evacuation was far more harmful than the storm. It is likely that Turner's decision not to evacuate Houston in 2017 was the correct one.

Though local government performed well in response to Harvey, the hurricane's damage would have been less had local government planned for Houston's rapid development with more regard for possible flooding. Developers paved over empty land that would have absorbed rainwater, which instead drained into streams and bayous that then overflowed. They also built in or near floodplains. FEMA maps of likely flood areas were infrequently updated and did not account for the effects of future development or climate change. Often developers did not comply with requirements to offset construction in wetlands with flood management measures. In 2008, when Houston banned new construction in floodways adjacent to bayous, opponents of the ban argued that the result was a reduction of property values. That ban was then reversed. Most homeowners were unaware of the danger of flooding, and an estimated 85 percent of them did not have flood insurance.

Local government is important to Texans. It was local government that made the decision, likely a wise one, that prevented the evacuation of the Houston area. And it was local government that played a major role in the rescue operations caused by the flooding disaster as well as in the feeding and sheltering of the victims of Harvey. On the other hand, it was largely the past decisions of local government—as in poor urban planning—that worsened the effect of the heaviest rainfall in the history of the continental United States.[2] Local government does not get the same level of media attention that the state and national government receive, but a crisis such as Hurricane Harvey emphasizes the vast importance of local government to our lives.

CHAPTER GOALS

- Explain the importance, role, and structure of county government in Texas (pp. 329–37)

- Describe the major characteristics of city government in Texas (pp. 337–50)

- Examine the role of special purpose districts in Texas government (pp. 350–57)

- Examine the financial problems facing local government (pp. 357–61)

County Government in Texas

Local government institutions play a major role in Texas. There are more than 5,147 general-purpose local governments, an average of about 20 per county,[3] which provide water, electricity, and sewer services as well as police protection and public education.

All but two states have governmental units known as counties (or parishes), but Texas has 254 counties, more than any other state.[4] County government in Texas is primarily a way of governing rural areas. Because Texas is so vast, with huge areas that are sparsely populated, county government remains an important aspect of local government. As was discussed in Chapter 2, however, the Texas Constitution places numerous restrictions on government, and many of those are restrictions on counties. Indeed, in Texas, counties have very constricted governmental powers. Unlike city governments, county governments usually do not have powers to legislate. Because they lack much of the power of self-government, they often function primarily as an administrative arm of the state government.

Texas counties have their origins in the "municipality" or "ayuntamiento," which was the local governmental unit under Spanish and Mexican rule. These municipalities were large and included settlements and surrounding rural territories. In 1835, Texas was divided into 3 departments and 23 municipalities. With the Republic of 1836, the 23 municipalities became counties. By the time Texas became a state in 1845, there were 36 counties, and when Texas entered the Confederacy in 1861, there were 122 counties. The number of counties increased steadily until 1921, when the 254th county was created. The underlying goal of the proliferation of counties was that any citizen could travel to the county seat—on horseback, of course—and return home in a day. Given the sparse population of west Texas, in particular, that initial plan for county organization was eventually rejected, but it does show that Texans believed that the local center of government, the county seat, should be accessible to the people.[5]

What Are the Functions of County Government?

The main functions of Texas county government are construction and maintenance of county roads and bridges, law enforcement, dispute resolution, record keeping, and administration of social services. Like most other aspects of county government in Texas, these five primary functions are performed with great variation among the counties.

County road and bridge construction and maintenance have traditionally been such important functions of county government that the county commissioners' court—those elected officials in charge of county government—are often called "road commissioners." County commissioners maintain more than one-half of the roads in the state,[6] including roughly 134,000 miles of rural roadways and 17,000 rural bridges. Maintenance of these roads and bridges is a major cost for county government.[7] For example, a 20-foot-wide

Counties have control over law-enforcement budgets, but sheriffs often decide how the money gets spent. Pictured here is the Montgomery County Sheriff's Department's $220,000 drone that quickly crashed because it was too heavy to fly.

asphalt road for lightweight traffic costs a county $45,000 per mile to resurface; a road of the same width for heavy trucks costs about $100,000 per mile.[8] Although a 1947 law allowed counties to place their road system under the authority of a county engineer, in most counties roads and bridges remain one of the most important responsibilities of the commissioners.

Law enforcement, another important responsibility of county government, is undertaken by constables and by the sheriff. The sheriff is the chief law-enforcement officer within county government. In rural counties with few city police departments, the sheriff may be the major law-enforcement official in the county. In addition to law enforcement and the provision of deputies for the district and county courts, sheriffs are responsible for the county jail and the safety of prisoners. In many counties, operating a county jail is an expensive and major undertaking. On September 1, 2018, for example, Harris County was guarding and supervising over 8,800 inmates in its county jail, and Dallas County had over 5,200. On the other hand, 23 counties had no jails. Overall, there were almost 69,000 inmates in Texas county jails.[9]

Although the law-enforcement budget must be approved by the county commissioners, sheriffs often have considerable influence in county government and develop their own law-enforcement styles. The sheriff of Montgomery County became the first sheriff in Texas to have an aerial drone, at a cost of $220,000, until it rose into the air about 18 feet, went out of control, and crashed into the sheriff's department's SWAT team armored vehicle.[10]

Traditionally in Texas, the office of constable has been an elective office with limited duties. Constables have served civil court papers and provided bailiffs for justices of the peace. However, some constables have transformed their offices into full-fledged police departments. Some constables' offices have traffic enforcement roles; some enforce truancy laws; and some have even formed heavily armed, tactical units that patrol high-crime areas. Since constables are elected officials, they are not subject to much oversight by other public officials, and they tend to function as law enforcement fiefdoms in larger counties in Texas.

County attorneys and **district attorneys** also perform a law-enforcement role by prosecuting criminal cases. Usually, the district attorneys prosecute the more serious criminal cases in the district courts, whereas the county attorneys prosecute the lesser criminal cases in the county courts. In more urban counties, the offices of county attorney and district attorney may be combined into one office that is usually called the office of criminal district attorney.

Record-keeping is another important function of county government. **County clerks** keep vital statistics for the county, issue marriage licenses and birth and death certificates, and maintain records for the commissioners' court and the county courts. Most important, the county clerk is responsible for records relating to property transactions. Sometimes the county clerk also maintains election and voting records. If there is a **district clerk**, he or she maintains records for the district courts, though in small counties this office is combined with the office of the county clerk. Tax records are maintained by the **county tax assessor-collector**, who in many counties also collects taxes, though in the smaller counties the sheriff often performs this job. Although in many counties constitutional amendments have eliminated the office of county treasurer, in those where the office still exists, the treasurer is responsible for receiving and spending

county attorney county official who prosecutes lesser criminal cases in the county court

district attorney public official who prosecutes the more serious criminal cases in the district court

county clerk public official who is the main record-keeper of the county

district clerk public official who is the main record-keeper of district court documents

county tax assessor-collector public official who maintains the county tax records and collects the taxes owed to the county

county funds. The **county auditor** now does much of the former work of the county treasurer. There are now 200 county auditors in Texas, who are appointed by the county's district judges. Not only do they audit the county's funds, but in large counties they will also often prepare the county budget for the commissioners' court.

Counties also have an important role in dispute resolution through their court systems. Civil law is a way to resolve disputes between people, and the justice of the peace court and the county and district courts deal with large numbers of civil disputes as well as criminal matters. County and district attorneys may also represent the interests of the county or state in disputes that involve governmental interests.

Finally, counties may perform a social service function. The services provided vary from county to county, but the most important ones involve providing emergency welfare assistance, which may include food, housing, rental assistance, or shelter. Larger counties have health departments to work on the prevention and control of communicable diseases. Some counties operate mental health services, and some provide parks, airports, fire protection, and sanitation facilities. One of the most important social services provided by counties is indigent health care.

Numerous County Offices: Checks and Balances or Built-In Problems?

As with the state government, one of the characteristics of county government in Texas is a multiplicity of elected governmental officials. Some argue that the large number of public officials at the county level is desirable because it creates a strong system of checks and balances, allowing no one official to dominate county government.[11] However, that system of checks and balances comes at a high price, in the form of problems in coordination of governmental activity, much as at the state level.

One of the most important bodies of county elected officials is the **county commissioners' court**, which is the main governing unit in the county. Although the commissioners' court is not a judicial body, it may have gotten its name from the Republic of Texas Constitution (1836–45), in which the county governing unit consisted of the chief justice of the county court and the justices of the peace within the county.[12]

The current structure of the county commissioners' court, shown in Figure 10.1, consists of a county judge and four commissioners. The **county judge** is elected countywide and serves for four years. He or she presides over the meetings of the commissioners' court and has administrative powers as well as judicial powers in rural counties. In those counties, the county judge hears minor criminal cases and handles some civil matters such as probate matters. In larger, more urban counties, the county judge is an administrator only, with the former judicial duties of the office now performed by probate judges, county-court-at-law judges, and others.

Each commissioners' court also has four **county commissioners**, each of whom is elected from a precinct that encompasses roughly one-fourth of the population of the county. In the late 1960s one of the great issues in American constitutional law involved malapportionment, the existence of election districts that did not represent equal population groupings. The malapportionment of Texas's county commissioners' courts became an important case before the U.S. Supreme Court because the courts' precincts tended to be drawn to represent equal land areas rather than equal population

county auditor public official, appointed by the district judges, who receives and disburses county funds; in large counties, this official also prepares the county budget

county commissioners' court the main governing body of each county; has the authority to set the county tax rate and budget

county judge the person in each of Texas's 254 counties who presides over the constitutional county court and county commissioners' court, with responsibility for the administration of county government; some county judges also carry out judicial responsibilities

county commissioner government official (four per county) on the county commissioners' court whose main duty is the construction and maintenance of roads and bridges groupings. In *Avery v. Midland County* (1968), the Court held that the principle of "one person–one vote" applies to commissioners' courts just as it applies to legislative districts. The result was that commissioners' precincts must now be drawn to reflect equal population groupings within counties.[13]

The main responsibility of county commissioners is the construction and maintenance of county roads and bridges. That aspect of a commissioner's work is, of course, very important to rural residents; it can be politically controversial and has sometimes been tinged with corruption.[14]

The commissioners' court also sets the county tax rate and the county budget. Related to its taxing and budgeting powers is its power to make contracts and pay bills. Other than road and bridge expenditures, perhaps the most important expenditure of most county commissioners' courts is building and maintaining county jails. Health care for people in poverty can be a significant cost for counties as well, along with, in some cases, fire protection and sanitation. Some counties also have costs associated with maintaining libraries and hospitals and providing emergency welfare measures, such as those brought on by natural disasters or fires. The commissioners' court can appoint certain county officials, and it can hire personnel as well as fill vacancies in county offices. It also administers elections in the county.

However, as noted earlier, there are numerous elected officials in Texas counties, each with an independent power base. It seems nearly inevitable that tensions would develop between the budgetary powers of the commissioners' courts and the needs and desires of other elected county officials. Such disputes among county officials can be mundane, as was the battle between Titus County commissioners and the county attorney over whether the commission could ban the county attorney's dog from the courthouse.[15] The disputes can also be far more serious and acrimonious, such as the litigation between the Galveston County commissioners and District Court Judge Lonnie Cox over the commissioners' firing of the county court administrator. After winding its

FIGURE 10.1

The County Commissioners' Court

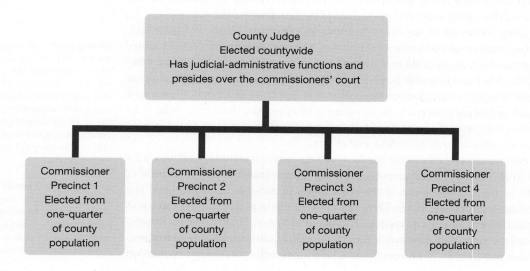

TABLE 10.1

Countywide and Precinct-Level Elected Officials

COUNTYWIDE OFFICIALS	PRECINCT-LEVEL OFFICIALS
County judge	County commissioners
Possibly county court-at-law judges, possibly probate judges, and district judges	Justices of the peace
County and district attorney or criminal district attorney	Constables
Sheriff	
County and district clerk or district clerk	
Possibly county treasurer	
Tax assessor-collector	
Possibly county surveyor	

way through the state courts, the Texas Supreme Court held that Judge Cox lacked the constitutional and statutory authority to compel the county commissioners to reinstate a county judicial employee at a specific salary. District court judges could not legislate from the bench nor could they replace the decisions of a legislative body of government. The bitter controversy between the county commissioners and the judge cost taxpayers over one million dollars.[16]

As Table 10.1 shows, other officeholders are elected at the county level and still others at the precinct level of the county. There is some variation in the numbers of officeholders, depending on the county. For example, larger counties will have more justices of the peace and more **constables** than smaller ones. In some counties, constables only serve legal papers, while in others, they also have a law-enforcement role with the authority to patrol, give tickets, and make arrests. Some counties use constables to check on truants from school, a niche duty that others in law enforcement do not seem to want.

constable precinct-level county official involved with serving legal papers and, in some counties, enforcing the law

Larger counties may have probate judges, numerous district judges, and county-court-at-law judges. Smaller counties may not have probate judges or even county-court-at-law judges and may share district judges and district attorneys with other counties. Some counties have county attorneys and district attorneys; others have criminal district attorneys that combine the county attorney and district attorney offices. Some counties have county clerks and district clerks; smaller counties may combine the offices in one person. Some counties have county treasurers; others do not.

The Challenges of County Government

Are Some Counties Too Small? The reason for the variation in offices is not simply that laws were passed at different times, thus sacrificing uniformity among counties. It is also the case that Texas is a large, diverse state with great variation among its counties. The result is great variation in the numbers of government

The county commissioners' court is the main governing unit at the county level, with control over the county budget and projects such as road construction. Here, Travis County Commissioner Brigid Shea presents a water conservation program to the community that would save the county millions of gallons of drinking water per year.

officials, the duties of officials, and the services provided by the different county governments. Brewster County has a population of only 9,173, but it covers a terri- tory of 6,193 square miles, about the size of Connecticut and Rhode Island combined. Rockwall County, in contrast, has only 149 square miles and a population of 87,809. Although Harris County has a population of 4,441,370, Loving County has a popula- tion of only 86, yet Loving County covers a huge land area—nearly 677 square miles.[17] Most employed residents of Loving County work for the county government, and this fact may be the main justification for Loving County's continuing existence as a gov- ernmental unit—although people with taxable property may also prefer the Loving County tax structure to that of another governmental unit.[18]

A small population may create a sense of community and closeness to local govern- ment, but it can place a huge strain on county resources when unusual events occur, such as an expensive murder trial or a natural disaster. For example, after suffering from flooding and a bad economy, Presidio County, with a population of less than 7,000, ran out of money to pay its bills. Several county phone lines were disconnected for lack of pay- ment, and the county had to cut its budget by 30 percent and raise taxes in order to con- tinue functioning.[19]

Polk County in east Texas (population of about 46,000) estimated that it had unan- ticipated costs of $200,000 when the U.S. Supreme Court overturned the sentence of Johnny Paul Penry, who had been convicted in the stabbing death of a woman in 1979, and sent the case back for another trial. Even with $100,000 in aid from the state to help pay the bill, the costs of this one trial represented a tremendous burden.[20] An even more severe situation faced tiny Franklin County (population 10,600) in 2007, when it needed to come up with a minimum of $250,000 for a murder trial.[21] Since capital murder cases were so rare in the county, the commissioners had no money at all budgeted for such a purpose. As in Presidio County, for small counties such as Polk and Franklin, expenses like these require either major cuts in other budget items or tax increases or both.

Very small counties in the Big Bend area of Texas are discovering that they cannot afford to prosecute the drug violations that are too small for the federal government to prosecute. In counties that have Border Patrol checkpoints, relatively minor drug cases have been prosecuted at the county level, although the federal government has provided some aid for funding these prosecutions. But Hudspeth County (population 3,300) has discovered that for every dollar it gets for handling federal border crimes and seized assets, it costs the county two dollars to detain, process, and prosecute the offenders. The cost has gotten so substantial that the county has chosen to no longer prosecute the federal drug cases sent to it. Brooks County (population 7,200) had previously stopped taking the federal drug cases from its Border Patrol checkpoint because the county found the costs too great, and Kenedy County (population 400) has recently made the same decision. Part of the problem is that the federal government has reimbursed local authorities only for prosecution costs and not for detention costs. For small-population counties such as Hudspeth County, that policy imposed too great a financial burden, since detention is the most expensive item in the county budget.[22]

Counties exist as they do for a variety of reasons. The original goal of making county seats easily accessible by horseback is, of course, no longer pertinent. Other reasons are political. For example, wealthy landowners may have urged the legislature to create counties so that they could control county government and hence the amount of property taxes they might pay. In modern times, there is arguably no practical reason for Texas to have so many counties. Even moderate-size counties by Texas standards may be too small to function adequately in unusual situations. It would take a state constitutional amendment to merge counties so that many of them would have a sufficient population to function efficiently and a sufficient tax base to deliver services adequately. But the issue of county mergers is not one that is on the political agenda. It would likely be controversial because of residents' traditional loyalties to a county, because county

Agents and drug-sniffing dogs at the U.S. Customs and Border Protection checkpoint in Hudspeth County, 85 miles east of El Paso. Smaller counties on the U.S.–Texas border, like Hudspeth, have found prosecuting smaller drug violations too costly.

officeholders would fear losing their jobs, and because voters might feel they would lose control over county government since a vote in a populous county is less influential than one in a small county.

Accountability of County Officials

County officials are made accountable to the public through elections. Generally every four years the voters get a chance to review county officials and make a judgment about their competence, efficiency, ability, and fitness to hold office for another four years. One question is whether having elections every four years is a sufficient mechanism to ensure the accountability of officials. In cases of inefficiency or incompetence, the only alternative to elections for the removal of county officials is a rarely used and generally unsuccessful judicial proceeding against an official believed incapable of performing duties.

One example of the problems of accountability of county officials involved Susan Hawk, the district attorney of Dallas County. A political superstar, Hawk had been a highly successful assistant district attorney in the county beginning at the age of 24. At 32, she was elected a state district judge, and in 2014 she resigned from the bench to run against incumbent Democrat Craig Watkins for district attorney. Hawk was the only Republican who won a countywide race in Dallas County that year. As the newly elected district attorney, Hawk was responsible for running an office with 260 assistant district attorneys and 190 support staff.

Even during her campaign, however, she began to have problems due to severe depression and an addiction to prescription pain medications. She became suicidal and paranoid and went into a rehabilitation facility, claiming she was going to have back surgery. After she became district attorney, her paranoia continued, and she became manic and forgetful, sometimes making impulsive decisions. She fired top assistant district attorneys, including people who were close associates. By the summer of 2015, she was again suicidal and was planning her resignation when she obtained treatment. After Hawk fired a lawyer who oversaw the budget of the D.A.'s office, the lawyer claimed Hawk had repeatedly tried to misuse public funds. A removal suit was filed against Hawk, but in early 2016 it was dismissed.[23] Hawk's mental health problems were not under control, however, and she was frequently in treatment. Finally, in September 2016 she resigned, waiting just long enough to prevent an election for her replacement, who in Democratic Dallas County would most likely have been a Democrat. In December 2016, Governor Abbott appointed Republican Faith Johnson as Dallas County's first black female district attorney. Johnson lost her re-election bid to John Creuzot in the November 2018 election.[24]

The descent of Susan Hawk into depression, drug abuse, and paranoia is a tragedy, but in the process of trying to gain self-control, Hawk damaged the careers of several employees in the district attorney's office and introduced considerable confusion and chaos into the office. Her story may be the most dramatic, but numerous other examples raise concerns about possible lack of accountability on the part of local governmental officials. Dallas County Commissioner John Wiley Price faced an 11-count indictment from the U.S. attorney on corruption charges; he is alleged to have received $950,000 in payments in money, cars, and land. Following a contentious and lengthy investigation and trial, Price was found not guilty on 7 of the 11 charges for bribery and fraud in April 2017. Federal prosecutors decided not to retry the tax fraud charges in May 2017. But questions about Price's actions continued to be raised in the media as late as October 2017.[25] Travis County district attorney Rosemary Lehmberg was arrested and convicted

David Wilson (right) misled voters in his campaign for Houston Community College trustee by mischaracterizing himself and his endorsements to appeal to African American voters. His actions are one example of many that cause some to question how to hold locally elected officials accountable.

on a drunk driving charge.[26] Houston Community College trustee Dave Wilson won his office with a questionable campaign that wrongly suggested to his heavily African American constituents that he was black. Wilson is white, but his campaign leaflets did not show his picture, instead featuring pictures of African Americans that were taken off the internet and shown beside the request, "Please vote for our friend and neighbor Dave Wilson." One leaflet said Wilson was endorsed by Ron Wilson—who it turns out was his cousin in Iowa rather than the African American former state representative who most voters would have assumed was meant.[27]

Local officials are supposed to be closest to the electorate, and therefore voters are supposed to be more aware of their strengths and flaws. But is this actually the case? Do voters have sufficient awareness of local officials when they elect them, and are future elections a sufficient control over the behavior of those officials once they are in office?

City Government in Texas

Describe the major characteristics of city government in Texas

Politics at the local level is often politics at its most basic. Unlike in presidential elections, in which the issues may well involve questions of war and peace, or state elections, which may involve issues such as whether a state should have an income tax, in local elections the most pressing issue may well be potholes in the city streets. Although pothole repair may not seem high in the hierarchy of political concerns, it is exactly such an issue that most directly and routinely affects most people's lives, and thus it becomes a prime issue for discussion among candidates. As mundane as such concerns are, these are the fundamental issues in most local elections because they reflect the needs and expectations that residents have of local government.

General-Law vs. Home-Rule Cities

In 2018 there were 1,214 incorporated municipalities in Texas, ranging in size from 18 in Los Ybañez to over 2.3 million in Houston (see Table 10.2). Like county governments, municipal governments are creations of the state of Texas. In the early years of the Republic of Texas, the Texas Congress was responsible for enacting laws that incorporated cities. Article XI, Sec. 4 of the 1876 Constitution provided for the incorporation of "general law" cities under 10,000 people, but was lowered to 5,000 in 1909.[28] The number of urban areas grew in the state in the late nineteenth and early twentieth centuries, making the management of local affairs a growing burden on the state legislature. In 1912 the legislature passed the Home-Rule Charter Amendment to the constitution that enabled cities of more than 5,000 inhabitants to adopt charters providing some degree of local self-government. Today there are 345 incorporated cities with more than 5,000 residents operating under home rule provisions and an additional 871 operating under general law. Table 10.2 lists the 10 largest of these. In contrast, California has only 121 home-rule cities and Illinois has only 209.[29]

The difference between a general-law city and a home-rule city is crucial not only because of the size of the city but the way in which self-government in the locality operates. Cities and towns of fewer than 5,000 people are chartered by general statute, as

TABLE 10.2

Texas's Largest Home-Rule Cities

NAME	2017 POPULATION ESTIMATES	FORM OF GOVERNMENT	FIRST CHARTER	PRESENT FORM ADOPTED
Houston	2,312,717	Mayor-council	1905	1994
San Antonio	1,511,946	Council-manager	1914	1951
Dallas	1,341,075	Council-manager	1889	1907
Austin	950,715	Council-manager	1919	1994
Fort Worth	874,168	Council-manager	1924	1985
El Paso	683,577	Council-manager	1873	2004
Arlington	396,394	Council-manager	1920	1990
Corpus Christi	325,605	Council-manager	1926	1993
Plano	286,143	Council-manager	1961	1993
Laredo	260,654	Council-manager	1848	1911

SOURCES: Compiled from *Texas Almanac 2006–2007* (Dallas: *Dallas Morning News*, 2006), 340–64; *Texas Almanac 2008–2009* (Dallas: *Dallas Morning News*, 2008), 8; Texas State Data Center; www.citypopulation.de; City Charter of the City of Laredo as Amended (2010); City of El Paso website; U.S. Census Bureau, "State and County QuickFacts, July 2017."

Favorability Toward Local Government

There is a widespread belief that government closer to the people is the most desirable. In a recent poll, favorability toward local government was far higher than unfavorable ratings among urban, suburban, and rural Texans. But many Texans said they were neither favorable nor unfavorable. Why? What could local officials do to change these numbers?

	VERY FAVORABLE	SOMEWHAT FAVORABLE	NEITHER	SOMEWHAT UNFAVORABLE	VERY UNFAVORABLE	DON'T KNOW/ NO OPINION
All Texans	14%	33%	25%	15%	9%	4%
Urban	16	31	24	16	9	4
Suburban	12	35	26	13	10	4
Rural	15	33	23	18	9	3

SOURCES: University of Texas/*Texas Tribune* poll of 1,200 registered voters in Texas between February 3 and February 10, 2017. Margin of error is +/− 2.83 percent.

was the case for all cities and towns prior to the 1912 home-rule amendments. Under the so-called "Dillon Rule" doctrine, "general-law" cities and towns may act or organize themselves only as explicitly permitted by statutory law passed by the state legislature.[30] The constitution also limits what they can do. For example, general-law cities may levy, assess, and collect taxes as authorized by statute. But the constitution sets a maximum property tax rate of $1.50 per $100 valuation, compared with $2.50 per $100 valuation for home-rule cities.

Home-rule cities, in contrast to general-law cities, work under a charter passed by the citizens. The **home-rule charter** essentially lays down the rules under which a city will operate.[31] The general principle for home-rule cities is that cities exercise power under the charter unless the state constitution or the legislature through law says otherwise. Unlike general-law cities, which look to the legislature for what they can do, home-rule cities look for guidance on what they can't do. The state legislature may "preempt" a particular policy passed by local governments when it perceives that the policy is not in the interest of the state.

Home-rule charters provide for the form of government that operates in the city and specify the number of members serving on the city's governing body. They also may grant the governing body the power to annex land adjacent to the city as well as to set property tax rates up to $2.50 per $100 valuation. Home-rule cities are also constitutionally authorized to borrow money in ways not available to smaller municipal entities. Home-rule charters must be consistent with the state constitution and any other relevant statutory provisions. For example, the state has mandated that most city elections take place on a date provided by the Texas Election Code. City elections must be conducted under the general guidelines set by the state. Nevertheless, home rule in Texas traditionally has delegated enormous power to local city governments. According to a report by the Advisory Commission on Intergovernmental Relations, the Texas Constitution allows cities more "home rule" than does any other state.[32]

home-rule charter the rules under which a city operates; local governments have considerable independent governing power under these charters

Preemption and Home-Rule While home-rule cities have substantial power to act independently of state control, the city of Denton discovered that there are limits on local control when home rule comes into conflict with the oil industry and state government. In 2014, Denton was the home of 277 gas wells. Concerned about the effects of the fracking drilling technique used for gas production, nearly 59 percent of the voters in Denton passed an ordinance on November 11, 2014, banning further fracking in the city. Immediately the petroleum industry sued the city over the ban, and the industry was joined in opposition by the Texas General Land Office. In May 2015 the legislature passed HB 40 preempting the fracking ban. By June 2015, Denton's city council was forced to repeal the ban. In the brief lifetime of the Denton anti-fracking law, the city spent over $842,000 trying to defend the ordinance. Oil interests meanwhile spent over $1.0 million challenging the ordinance.[33]

The 2015 fight over Denton's anti-fracking ordinances was only the first round in an intense debate that broke out early during the next legislative session over the wisdom of numerous city ordinances. Proclaiming that we are not the "United States of municipalities," Governor Abbott led the charge on a variety of initiatives to **preempt** or set aside local ordinances. Among proposed preemption initiatives were bills banning sanctuary cities in Texas and ending local regulation of ride-hailing services that originally drove Uber and Lyft out of Austin. Another bill that provided tax credit to offset local tree removal fees was vetoed by Abbott as not going far enough. (Abbott himself had experienced this inconvenience when he tried to remove trees on his property in Austin.) The special session of the legislature in the summer of 2017 was dominated by a host of preemption issues. Two popular preemption bills passed: a new bill limiting local regulations of tree removal and a second bill restricting the annexation powers of local government. Others were more controversial and failed to pass including

- a bill requiring transgender people to use the bathroom according to the sex on their birth certificate.
- a bill limiting the growth of local property taxes.
- a bill capping local government spending.
- a bill speeding up local permit processes.
- a bill preventing local rule changes midway through local construction projects.
- a bill preempting local restrictions on mobile devices in cars.
- a bill prohibiting local governments from sending money to Planned Parenthood.[34]

What was driving this debate over preemption and local self-government? There were many factors, but one stands out: the growing partisanship in the state legislature fueled by an aggressive conservative wing of the Republican Party. As noted in earlier chapters, the Democratic Party now dominates many of the large urban areas in the state. But an increasingly conservative Republican Party now controls most suburban, exurban, and rural parts of the state as well as the executive and state legislature. By expanding state preemption activity, the Republican Party effectively sought to impose its social conservative and free market ideology throughout the state, particularly into urban enclaves controlled by Democrats. The failure to pass more preemption legislation can be attributed to the fact that Speaker of the House Joe Straus, a moderate

preemption the legislature's power to overrule ordinances or actions of local home-rule cities

Republican, refused to join his conservative colleagues' efforts. But Straus's retirement as speaker of the house opens the door for new conservative Republican efforts to limit the scope of local government in Texas.[35]

Forms of Government in Texas Cities

Texas home-rule cities have had three major forms of city government: the mayor-council form, the commissioner form, and the council-manager form. The **mayor-council form of government** is the oldest. It consists of an elected mayor and city council. The mayor is usually elected from the city in an **at-large election**. The council may be elected either at large or from a group of **single-member districts**, or a mixture of the two. In the mayor-council form of government, the mayor is the chief executive officer of the city. He or she presides over council meetings and has a variety of appointment powers. The city council, meanwhile, serves as the legislative body in the city, passing local laws and watching over the executive departments.

There have been both strong mayor-council systems and weak ones, depending on the powers given to the mayor by the city charter or state statute. In the *strong mayor-council* variation, various executive powers, such as appointment and removal powers for boards and departments as well as veto powers, are concentrated in the office of mayor. These powers enable the mayor to establish effective control over various executive departments in the city and to control the legislative agenda of the city council. In the *weak mayor-council* variation, these executive powers are much more limited, fragmenting power between the mayor and other elected or appointed officials. Strong mayor systems reflect a perspective that having a strong executive in charge of city government makes it operate more efficiently. In contrast, weak-mayor systems diffuse power, with city council members retaining a great deal of power. Advocates of the latter say this system gives a greater voice to the various constituencies represented by the members.[36]

The mayor-council form of government is the dominant form of government in most general-law cities, although it is considerably less popular among home-rule cities. According to a 2017 survey by the *Texas Almanac* about 48 percent of Texas municipalities had mayors but not city managers or city administrators.[37]

A second form of city government is the **commissioner form of government**. Under this system, the city is run by a small commission, composed of between five and seven members generally elected at large. The commission acts in both a legislative and an executive capacity. As a group, commissioners enact laws for the city. At the same time, each commissioner is in charge of one of the executive departments. One commissioner is also designated as the mayor to preside at meetings.

The commission plan was developed as a response to the devastating hurricane that hit Galveston in 1900, claiming an estimated 6,000 lives. In the aftermath of the hurricane, wealthy business leaders known as the Deep Water Committee became convinced that the incumbent city council was incapable of bringing about economic recovery for the city. They proposed that the governor appoint a commission to govern the city during rebuilding, but opponents of the plan argued that appointed government was undemocratic; hence, the plan was modified so that two of the five commissioners would be elected. When court challenges to the idea of appointed commissioners persisted, the state legislature made all five commissioners elected. The commission plan, which came

mayor-council form of government a form of city government in which the mayor is the chief executive and the city council is the legislative body; in the *strong mayor–council* variation, the mayor's powers enable him or her to control executive departments and the agenda of the city council; in the *weak mayor–council* variation, the mayor's power is more limited

at-large election an election in which officials are selected by voters of the entire geographical area, rather than from smaller districts within that area

single-member district an electorate that elects only one representative for each district

commissioner form of government a form of city government in which the city is run by a small group of elected commissioners who act in both legislative and executive capacities to be known as the "Texas Idea," reflected a desire to bring to city government good business practices that would somehow escape the squabbles and inefficiency of traditional local government found in the mayor-council form. It was believed that commissioners with direct responsibility for operation of various departments would bring professional management to government.[38]

The commission plan was adopted by Houston in 1905 and by a number of other Texas cities in 1907, including Dallas, Fort Worth, and El Paso. Progressives across the country supported the plan, and other reform principles often integrated with it, including nonpartisan elections, merit selection of employees, and such direct democracy techniques as the initiative, referendum, and recall. At its peak in 1918 the commission form was used by approximately 500 cities across the country including 75 cities in Texas. Following World War I, the number of commission-form cities decreased. By 2000 no city in Texas had a pure commission form of government, although 26 still claimed to have some variation of it.[39] In practice, none of the "commissioners" in these cities exercised executive control over specific city departments as envisioned in the original commission system. Instead, they functioned more like council members under the council-manager system discussed below.[40]

Essentially the "Texas Idea" led to the third form of city government found in Texas, the **council-manager form of government**. A city manager replaced the commissioners because a single manager provided the professional management of city government without the squabbles and jurisdictional disputes that naturally occurred with the multiple managers of the various departments in the commission system.[41] As originally envisioned, a city council elected in at-large elections was to be the policy-making body. Council members generally received little or no pay and were intended to be publicly motivated citizens interested in serving the public good, rather than professional politicians. A mayor was selected from among the council members. The city manager was to

council-manager form of government a form of city government in which public policies are developed by the city council and executive and administrative functions are assigned to a professional city manager

The commissioner form of government was developed as a response to the devastating hurricane that hit Galveston in 1900.

be a professional public manager who served as the chief executive and administrative official in the city. As in the commissioner form of government, the goal of the council-manager form was twofold: to free local government from the seamier side of politics and to bring administrative expertise to local government.

In 1913, Amarillo became the first city to abandon the commissioner form of government for the council-manager system. In 1914, Taylor and Denton followed suit. By 1947 there were 47 council-manager systems in Texas. Today, almost 52 percent of the 1,216 incorporated Texas municipalities have some form of city manager government.[42] Across the United States, it has become the most popular form of government for cities of over 10,000 residents.[43]

Today, council-manager systems vary across the state in a number of ways. The desire for professional administration of local government remains high. Most city managers have graduate degrees and are paid high salaries like executive officers in the private sector. But a desire for more political accountability through traditional democratic processes has introduced some changes. The growing ethnic and racial diversity of some Texas cities has forced many political leaders to question the wisdom of freeing local government too much from democratic controls. In most cities, mayors now are elected at large from the population as a whole, rather than from among the council. Many cities also elect council members from single-member districts rather than at large. Many see at-large elections as undercutting minority representation by diluting minority votes. Only when Dallas moved from an at-large council to one elected from single-member districts in 1991 did minorities come to play a major role in the decision-making processes of city government. But most cities and towns under the council-manager system continue to view local political offices as part-time jobs. Mayoral and council salaries remain low (although a few cities, such as Austin, offer considerably higher salaries). The demand for more democratic accountability in local government will likely continue to lead to more changes in the council-manager system of government across Texas. Balancing professional efficiency in city government with democratic political processes will continue to be a problem as Texas's metropolitan areas grow and diversify in the twenty-first century.

Tales of Five Cities

Houston Houston is the largest city in Texas. It has over 2.2 million people and a strong mayor-council form of government. There are 18 elected officials in the city serving concurrent four-year terms, including a mayor, a controller, and 16 council members. The mayor serves as the chief executive. Much of the mayor's power stems from the authority to appoint department heads and members of advisory boards, subject to council approval. The mayor also presides over the city council and has voting privileges on it. The 16-member council is a legislative body composed of 5 at-large seats and 11 single-member district seats.

Unlike in most other cities, the controller in Houston is an elected official.[44] The controller is the city's chief financial officer. Besides investing city funds, conducting internal audits of city departments, and operating the city's financial management system, the controller is also responsible for certifying the availability of funds for city council initiatives. In the end, the office of the controller is both a professional and a political position. Not surprisingly, the controller often comes into conflict with the mayor and the council over important policy issues.

Although local politics in Houston is nominally nonpartisan, in recent years it has taken on a partisan flavor. Houston's current mayor is Sylvester Turner, a well-known Democrat who had previously served in the Texas legislature for 26 years and had major responsibilities for the state's budget while in that position. Turner had unsuccessfully sought the mayor's office in 1991 and in 2003 but won in 2015. He is the second African American to serve as Houston's mayor.

San Antonio

San Antonio, which has overtaken Dallas as the second-largest city in Texas, has a council-manager form of government. The council is composed of 10 members elected from single-member districts on a nonpartisan basis plus the mayor, who is the 11th member of the council and is selected at large. All members of the council serve for two-year terms. Until an election in 2015 that amended the city charter, the mayor's salary was a paltry $4,040 per year, and other council members were paid $20 per meeting, not to exceed $1,040 per year. Recognizing that service as an elected official in San Antonio had become a full-time job, voters raised salaries for council members to $45,722 a year and $61,725 for the mayor, currently Ron Nirenberg. This charter amendment was approved by 54.8 percent of those voting. Council members are subject to recall if 10 percent of the qualified voters in a district sign a petition of recall and a recall election is successful. The city charter also provides for initiatives and referendums that emerge from the voters.

The city manager in San Antonio serves at the pleasure of the council as the chief executive and administrative official in the city. He or she has wide-ranging appointment and removal authority over officers and employees in all city departments. The current city manager, Sheryl Sculley, supervises a budget of $2.4 billion and 12,000 employees.

Pictured here are the mayors of Texas's two largest cities. Sylvester Turner (left) is the current mayor of Houston. Prior to being elected mayor in the closest mayoral election in Houston history, he served in the Texas State House from 1989 to 2016. Ron Nirenberg (right) became mayor of San Antonio on June 21, 2017, after defeating the incumbent mayor Ivy Taylor in a runoff. Previously he had served two terms on the San Antonio City Council.

Houston's "Bathroom Ordinance"

TEXAS municipal governments may pass local laws known as ordinances, which govern behavior within the city limits. Generally, these ordinances do not generate much controversy, because their scope tends to be limited. Houston, however, held a referendum on an antidiscrimination ordinance in November 2015 that gained national attention and was one of the most bitter and costly local elections in Texas history.

Texas is one of 28 states with no statewide laws prohibiting discrimination based on sexual orientation or gender identity. In the absence of a state law, Houston's proposed ordinance would have prohibited bias in city housing, employment, city contracting, and business services on the basis of a number of criteria, including race, age, sexual orientation, and gender identity. The core of the political argument surrounding the ordinance was the ban on discrimination based on sexual orientation and gender identity.

Opponents reframed the political debate from one of civil rights for gay and transgendered persons to a claim that the law would allow sexual predators in women's bathrooms. Signs reading "No Men in Women's Bathrooms" were displayed outside polling places, and television ads showed a young girl being followed into a bathroom stall by an older man.[a] Opponents of the ordinance included Governor Greg Abbott and Lieutenant Governor Dan Patrick, who used the bathroom argument to support their position. Megachurches from the Houston area and former Houston Astros star Lance Berkman were strong opponents of the ordinance as well.[b]

Supporters of the ordinance included Houston's then mayor Annise Parker, who had been elected as the first openly gay mayor of a U.S. city and who argued that passage of the ordinance would show that "Houston does not discriminate."[c] Groups such as Equality Texas, the ACLU, and the Human Rights Campaign also strongly supported the ordinance. Actress Sally Field was a well-known celebrity supporter, and Hillary Clinton, President Obama, Vice President Biden, football player Michael Sam, and actors Eva Longoria, Jesse Tyler Ferguson, and Matthew Morrison used social media to show their support. Another actor, Matt Bomer, released a video calling on Houstonians to vote "yes," saying, "I was raised with the belief that everyone deserves to be treated equally. These are the same values I grew up with in Houston and they're the same values that I try to teach my kids."[d]

The ordinance failed overwhelmingly by a 61 percent to 39 percent margin in November 2015, but the issue did not go away. It returned during the 2017 legislative session when conservatives sought to pass legislation that would have restricted transgendered Texans from using restrooms, showers, and locker rooms. The debate was contentious and, at times, nasty. Big business, particularly large corporations with interests outside Texas, came out against the bill. In the end, the

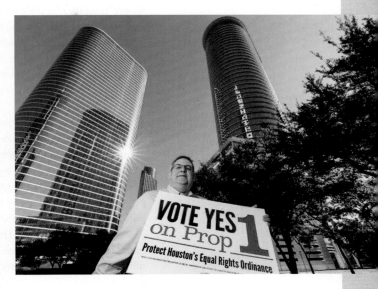

"Bathroom Bill" was killed in committee by Speaker Joe Straus. For his part, Straus believed that the bathroom bill could prove emotionally devastating to some transgender people. In no uncertain terms he stated, "I don't want the suicide of a single Texan on my hands."[e] No one would be surprised if the Bathroom Bill is resurrected for the next session of the state legislature in 2019.

COMMUNICATING EFFECTIVELY: YOUR VOICE

- Should cities' lawmaking powers be limited to local concerns such as traffic or animal control issues, rather than broader issues such as antidiscrimination laws?

- Why do you think the Houston bathroom ordinance failed? What arguments do you think the "pro" side should have made in order to persuade more people?

Indicative of the city manager's central role in running the city is her salary, which in 2017 was $475,000 plus a $75,000 bonus.

Dallas

Dallas also operates under a council-manager form of government. Until the late twentieth century, city politics had been dominated for years by the white business community. At-large nonpartisan elections tended to elect a council that was relatively united in its understanding of the problems facing the city and its vision of where the city should go. In the late 1980s and early 1990s, however, a bitter struggle over rewriting the city charter divided the city along racial lines.

The new charter, which went into effect in 1991, called for a 14-member council elected from single-member districts and a mayor elected at large. Members are limited to serving four two-year terms consecutively. Under the new charter, membership on the council was transformed as a significant number of African American and Latino members were elected.

As in other council-manager systems, the power of the mayor in Dallas is weak. The mayor—currently Mike Rawlings—presides over council meetings, creates council committees, and appoints members, chairs, and co-chairs. In many ways, however, the mayor is only first among equals on the council. The council as a whole is the legislative body for the city, approving budgets, determining the tax rate, and appointing key public officials, including the city manager, city attorney, city auditor, city secretary, municipal court judges, and various citizen boards and commissions. The city manager serves at the will of the council and is removable by a two-thirds vote of the members. As in San Antonio, the city manager's powers in Dallas are vast. As the chief administrative officer, the city manager has the power to appoint and remove all heads of departments

Mayor Mike Rawlings of Dallas was re-elected to a second four-year term in 2015. A popular mayor, he has spearheaded efforts to develop south Dallas and against domestic violence. He was previously the CEO of Pizza Hut.

and subordinate officers and employees in the city, subject to civil service provisions.

Despite the ideal of removing the city manager from the pressures of political life in Dallas, recent city managers have found themselves forced to accommodate the reality of an increasingly politicized city council. The political pressures emerging from Dallas's single-member district council may ultimately compel the city to reexamine the wisdom of retaining a council-manager system. As Dallas learned in the 1990s, efficient government and democratic governance are not as easy to balance as advocates of the council-manager system once thought.

Austin's mayor, Democrat Steve Adler, speaks at a celebration of same-sex marriage rights at a church in Austin.

Austin Austin, the 11th most populous city in the United States and the 4th most populous city in Texas, is the seat of Travis County and the capital of the state. In the November 2012 elections, Austinites adopted by more than a 60 percent margin a plan to change the method for selecting members of the city council. Under the old system, a mayor and a six-member city council were all elected citywide. A city manager served as chief administrative officer of the city. Austin continues to have a city manager; however, since 2014 only the mayor is elected citywide. The 10 city council members are elected from single-member districts. (Until this change, Austin was the largest city in the United States whose city council did not include at least some members elected from geographic districts.)[45]

Over the previous 40 years, Austin voters had rejected district plans six times. This time, however, there was a strong grassroots movement favoring the 10-district plan, with support from a broad coalition of groups such as the Travis County Republican Party and Hispanic groups. One important reason for the success of the proposal was that it appeared on the November ballot, when there was a larger and more diverse group of voters than in the prior six elections. The proposal required that the districts be drawn by a commission of citizens chosen through an application process overseen by the city auditor. The first elections under the new system were in 2014.[46]

El Paso El Paso, located in the far western part of the state, has a distinctive culture from its sister cities to the east. Home to over 679,000 people, El Paso is on the border with Mexico, which makes the city a center for international trade. The military is also important to the El Paso economy because of the presence of Fort Bliss. El Paso's ethnic composition is quite different from the state's other largest cities or the state as a whole. In 2010 only 3.4 percent of the city's population was African American—far smaller than the proportion of African Americans statewide. However, 80.7 percent of the city's population is Latino, far larger than the overall proportion of Latinos in Texas.

Until 2004, El Paso worked under a charter that provided for a strong mayor and eight district representatives who ran on a slate every two years.[47] Local politics was highly partisan and dominated by the Democratic Party. Turnover was high among all leadership positions. Between 1989 and 2004, El Paso had seven mayors. Because the mayor appointed the chief administrative officer in the city, there were frequent turnovers in the professional staff. Many felt that the process of city government had become

Poverty and unemployment continue to plague El Paso. The city government is trying to attract more jobs by developing the downtown area.

too politicized and lacked professionalism and accountability. While there was much sentiment for charter reform in the community as a whole and among groups such as the blue-ribbon City Charter's Citizen Advisory Committee, there was no clear advocate for changing the charter.

This changed in 2003 when Joe Wardy challenged and then beat the incumbent mayor on a platform that included charter revision. Along with four other council members who ran on a platform supporting charter change, Wardy was responsible for opening a public dialogue that educated the citizenry and key political leaders in the community. There was no organized opposition to the reform proposal. Some raised concerns about the accountability of an unpopular or ineffective city manager. But these were put to rest for the most part by the proposed revisions that enabled the council to remove a city manager with the support of five council members with the mayor's approval or six without the mayor's approval.

The charter revisions moving from a strong mayor form of government to a nonpartisan council-manager form were approved by the voters in February 2004. Turnout was low at 8 percent, although this was not out of the ordinary for typically low turnout local elections in El Paso. Under the new charter, the city manager would report directly to the mayor and city council. Elections would be nonpartisan, and city council members would serve four-year, staggered terms.

El Paso was the largest of 24 municipalities in the United States to adopt a manager-council form of government between 1998 and 2004. During the same period, nineteen other cities in the United States rejected adopting a manager-council form of government, and fourteen abandoned manager-council government for a strong mayor system. Among the large cities that adopted a strong mayor form were Oakland, California, and Miami, Florida.

Clearly there is considerable disagreement across the United States as to the best form of local government. Different political, economic, and cultural circumstances can

Who Governs Texas's Cities?

Racial and Ethnic Composition of Texas's Major Cities and Their City Councils

● White   ● African American   ● Latino   ● Other

Houston

City pop.	25.6%	23.7%	43.8%	6.8%
Council	56%		25%	12.5% 6.3%

Houston has an African American mayor and 16 city council members, 5 of whom are elected at large and 11 elected in single-member districts. Four of the five at-large members of the council are white.

San Antonio

City pop.	26.6%	6.9%	63.2%	3.4%
Council	30%	10%	60%	

San Antonio has a white mayor and a city council of 10 elected from single-member districts.

Dallas

City pop.	28.8%	25%	42.4%	3.6%
Council	57%	29%	14%	

Dallas has a white mayor and 14 council members elected from single-member districts.

Austin

City pop.	48.7%	8.1%	35.1%	7.3%
Council	60%	10%	30%	

Austin has a white mayor and 10 council members elected from single-member districts.

El Paso

City pop.	14.2% 3.4%	80.7%	2%	
Council	25%	12.5%	62.5%	

El Paso has a white mayor, and its eight city council members are elected from single-member districts.

Representation is an important issue at all levels of government. Who's in power can have a profound impact on what policies are enacted. A snapshot of representation at the municipal level raises critical questions: Can a community be properly represented when its elected officials do not reflect the racial and ethnic characteristics of the community? For example, does it make a difference that the city of Dallas city council is 14 percent Latino while the Dallas population is 42.4 percent Latino? Whom are the elected officials representing? Is it the population as a whole or the people who vote?

SOURCES: Data for city councils are from 2018, taken from each city's website; city populations are from 2014 Census data.

QUANTITATIVE REASONING

- Of these major Texas cities, which city council best reflects the racial/ethnic composition of its population? Which council diverges most from its city's racial/ethnic composition?

- Do you think it is important that the city councils do reflect the racial/ethnic composition of their communities? Why or why not?

lead cities to go in different directions. But in Texas, the dominant form of local government continues to be the manager-council form, with Houston as the sole holdout for the strong mayor system.

Special Purpose Districts

Examine the role of special purpose districts in Texas government

special purpose district a unit of local government that performs a single service, such as education or sanitation, within a limited geographic area

A **special purpose district** is a unit of local government that performs a single service in a limited geographic area. Special purpose districts can solve problems that cut across different units of government. Special purpose districts can be created to serve an entire county, part of a county, all of two or more counties, or parts of two or more counties. Nationwide, the number of special purpose districts has increased by 400 percent since the middle of the twentieth century.[48] In Texas, the number increased from 491 in 1952 to 2,600 in 2012. In addition, there were 1,079 independent school districts, which are also classified as special purpose districts.[49]

Special purpose districts can be created to do almost anything that is legal. Some are formed to provide hospital care, others to furnish pure water to communities, still others to provide mosquito control, navigation, flood control, sanitation, drainage, fire protection, ambulance services, and law enforcement. They can take in large amounts of tax monies to accomplish their purposes.

Types of Special Purpose Districts

school district a specific type of special district that provides public education in a designated area

There are two types of special purpose districts in Texas. The first is the **school district**, which consists of independent school districts in the state. These districts offer public education from pre-kindergarten through 12th grade. Almost all school districts offer the full range of elementary and secondary education; however, some small, rural districts provide education only through the 8th grade, the 6th grade, or the 4th grade. Those with limited offerings contract with nearby districts to complete the education of their students.

nonschool special district any special district other than a school district; examples include municipal utility districts (MUDs) and hospital districts

The second classification of special purpose districts is the **nonschool special district**. Everything except the school districts is included in this category. Municipal utility districts, economic development corporations, hospital districts, and fire-prevention districts are the most common examples.

In addition to county taxes a property owner in Upshur County, Texas, will pay taxes to two special purpose districts—the Union Grove Independent School District and the Emergency Services District No. 1 (fire protection). A property owner in Hopkins County will pay to the Sulphur Springs Independent School District and to the Hopkins County Hospital District. A property owner in Collin County will pay taxes to the Plano Independent School District and to the Collin College District. One property owner in Houston pays taxes to the Houston Independent School District, the Harris County Department

How Extensive Are Texas's Local Governments?

Number of Local Governments in Each State, 2012

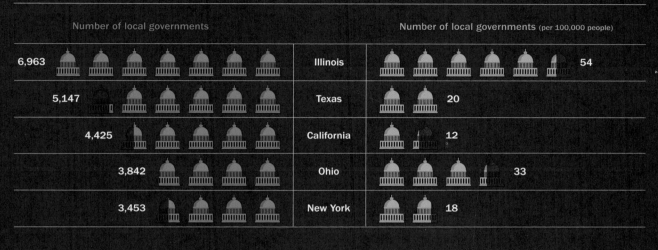

Number of local governments		Number of local governments (per 100,000 people)	
6,963	Illinois		54
5,147	Texas		20
4,425	California		12
3,842	Ohio		33
3,453	New York		18

	Total local govs.	Per 100K people		Total local govs.	Per 100K people		Total local govs.	Per 100K people		Total local govs.	Per 100K people		Total local govs.	Per 100K people
IL	6,963	54	CO	2,905	56	AK	1,556	53	TN	916	14	UT	622	22
TX	5,147	20	MI	2,875	29	OR	1,542	40	NM	863	41	NH	541	41
PA	4,897	38	IN	2,709	41	GA	1,378	14	MA	857	13	LA	529	12
CA	4,425	12	ND	2,685	384	NJ	1,344	15	ME	840	63	VA	518	6
OH	3,842	33	NE	2,581	139	KY	1,338	31	WY	805	140	MD	347	6
KS	3,826	133	SD	1,983	238	MT	1,265	126	VT	738	118	DE	339	37
MO	3,768	63	IA	1,947	63	AL	1,208	25	SC	678	14	NV	191	7
MN	3,672	68	WA	1,900	28	ID	1,168	73	AZ	674	10	AK	177	24
NY	3,453	18	OK	1,852	49	MS	983	33	WV	659	36	RI	133	13
WI	3,128	55	FL	1,650	9	NC	973	10	CT	643	18	HI	21	2

Local governments include county governments, school board districts, special districts, and municipal utility districts. One would expect that Texas's political culture would lead it to have fewer local governments than other states with traditions of more governmental involvement. Is this the case?

NOTE: Different sources provide different numbers of local governments, but Texas does have somewhat more than 4,800 local governments.

SOURCE: Governing, "Number of Local Governments by State." www.governing.com (accessed 7/21/16).

CRITICAL THINKING

- What are some of the characteristics of states with large numbers of local governments?

- Does the picture change when we factor in population? Which states have larger numbers of local governments per capita? What might explain these differences?

of Education, the Harris County Flood Control District, the Port of Houston Authority, the Harris County Hospital District, the Lone Star College System, Emergency Service District No. 13 (fire protection), and Emergency Service District No. 11 (EMS).

School Districts

Every square inch of land in Texas is part of a school district, and the state contains 1,265 school districts. Some school districts in east and west Texas cover an entire county. In metropolitan counties, there may be a dozen or more school districts. Each is governed by an elected board of trustees composed of five to nine members. The board employs a superintendent to oversee the daily operation of the school district. On the recommendation of the superintendent, the trustees

- set overall policy for the school district.
- adopt the budget for the school district.
- set the tax rate for the school district. (The maximum rate is $1.04 for each $100 of the assessed property value unless voters approve a higher rate.)
- select textbooks for classroom use.
- hire principals, faculty, and support staff.
- set the school calendar.
- determine salaries and benefits for employees.

Educating millions of students is a daunting task. By localizing public education, the state places much of the burden on the local school districts but also allows local residents to participate in governing them. Unfortunately, few people vote in the elections to select members of the board of trustees. Even fewer individuals attend meetings of the school board.

Nonschool Special Purpose Districts

Nonschool special purpose districts include a vast number of types. Larger counties tend to have many different special purpose districts. Dallas County, for example, has 13 nonschool special purpose districts. Harris County is the record-holder for special purpose districts in Texas, with a total of 436 nonschool special purpose districts.[50] Some of the most common types are as follows.

municipal utility district (MUD) a special district that offers services such as electricity, water, sewage, and sanitation outside the city limits

Municipal Utility Districts

Municipal utility districts (MUDs) offer electricity, water, sewer, and sanitation services outside the city limits. These governments might offer all utility services or only one or two, depending on the needs of the special district. Though MUDs are located throughout Texas, the vast majority are found in the Houston metropolitan area.

MUDs can be a financial blessing for developers. Entrepreneurs who build new housing outside city limits must furnish utilities to these homes, but few developers can afford to do this over a long period of time.

Banks and finance companies, legislators, and land developers maintain a warm and snug relationship with each other. Banks and finance companies willingly lend developers millions of dollars to establish residential subdivisions, build new homes, and run water and sewer services to these houses. When a few houses are sold, the developer asks the residents to establish a MUD. Enabling the legislation is seldom a problem because of the close relationship between developers and local legislators.

Once the MUD is up and running, the board of directors sets a tax rate and determines how much to charge residents for its services. One of its first activities is to borrow money by issuing bonds (interest-bearing financial instruments that are sold in financial markets to fund government projects). The bond proceeds are used to purchase the utilities from the developer, often at a premium. Using the proceeds from the sale of the utilities, the developer is able to repay loans. By establishing the MUD, residents agree to pay a property tax to retire the bonded indebtedness. In addition to the property tax, residents pay a monthly fee for the water, sewer, and sanitation services.

Community College Districts Community college districts are classified as nonschool special purpose districts because the public education they offer is not from pre-kindergarten through 12th grade but postsecondary academic and vocational programs. Community colleges are governed by an elected board of regents. Residents of the district pay a property tax to the district and in return pay lower tuition. The board employs a president or chancellor, who operates the college on a daily basis. The regents set policy on the recommendation of the president or chancellor. Among the regents' responsibilities are to

- set overall policy for the district.
- set the tax rate.
- set the cost of tuition and fees.
- build new buildings and repair older ones.
- hire teachers, counselors, administrators, and nonprofessional staff.
- set the school calendar.
- determine salaries and benefits for employees.

Hospital, Emergency Services, and Flood Control Districts A number of counties have hospital districts, some of which are designed to serve the poor and uninsured and supplement the costs of indigent medical care through taxes imposed by the hospital district. Emergency services districts provide fire and ambulance services to areas not served otherwise. The districts can be of varying size—Harris County has more than 30 emergency services districts, though most counties in Texas contain only one or two such districts.[51] Flood control districts are established to solve a multicounty problem, since flooding is seldom confined to a single county.

Creating, Governing, and Paying for a Special Purpose District
Special purpose districts are created by voters of the area to be served. Creating a special purpose district requires

- a petition signed by the residents of the area to be served, requesting the legislature to authorize a special election to create a special district.
- enabling legislation in the form of a law that authorizes such an election.
- approval by a majority of those voting in the special election.

Most special purpose districts are governed by boards elected by the voters of the district. The board of a school district is called the board of trustees; the governing board of a community college is often called the board of regents; and the governing boards of other special purpose districts are usually known as boards of directors. Each board is the policy-making group for its district. The directors set the tax rate and establish rules and policy for the operation of the district, which often employs an individual to run it on a day-to-day basis.

property tax a tax based on an assessment of the value of one's property, which is used to fund the services provided by local governments, such as education

user fee a fee paid for public goods and services, such as water or sewage service

Property taxes are the primary source of revenue for special purpose districts. This was not always the case. In 1949 school districts received 80 percent of their income from the state, and the school district furnished 20 percent, primarily from property taxes. Today, property taxes constitute as much as 90 percent of revenues for some districts. The second-largest source of income is **user fees**, raised from providing goods and services. Water districts, for example, sell water, sewer, and sometimes sanitation services. State and federal aid furnish the remainder of special district funding.

Property tax rates and user fees are set by governing boards. Hospital districts set fees for room occupancy, dispensation of medicine, use of surgical suites, taking and evaluation of X-rays, nursing and laboratory service, and myriad other charges. The board of trustees of a school district sets the local tax rate for property, which funds pre-kindergarten through 12th grade education. Tuition paid by in-district and out-of-district students, building fees, student fees, and technology and lab fees are determined by the board of regents of a community college district.

Problems with Special Purpose Districts

Hidden Governments
Everyone in Texas lives in at least one special purpose district, their school district. Most people live in several, have the opportunity to vote for people to represent them on the governing board of each district, and pay property taxes to these agencies of government. Yet few people are aware these agencies exist, thus their reputation as **hidden governments**.

hidden government a term that refers to special purpose districts of which many citizens are unaware

Special purpose districts provide needed services in specific geographic areas, where existing governments may lack authority to provide the service or funds to finance the project. In theory, special purpose districts are an example of democracy at work. They are created by a vote of the residents of the area to be served, and their governing boards are elected by the voters. Board meetings, at which decisions on policy, taxing, and fees are made, are open for attendance by any interested residents. However, fewer than 10 percent of eligible voters cast ballots in special purpose district elections, and fewer than 1 percent of district residents ever attend a board meeting.

Abuses of Power
There is a potential for abuse in the creation of special purpose districts. Many of them were originally authorized by the Texas legislature to develop the economies of poor, rural counties. More recently, however, developers of large tracts of land began creating these districts to place the burden of developing the property's infrastructure on future owners of the property. In order to comply with the law, all the developers must do is create the district and hold an election in which at least one short-term resident must vote. These short-term residents then approve bonds in the millions of dollars that must be paid for with the taxation of

The creation of special purpose districts by real estate developers has sometimes been controversial. Recent investigations have charged developers with abusing the process in order to circumvent inconvenient laws and to give the developers greater control over taxes and other government functions in the district.

future homes and property owners. In the 1980s this kind of special purpose district creation in Harris County led to defaults on bond issues after a housing bust.

In 2001 a major investigation of special purpose districts created by developers in Dallas found unusual and questionable practices. Some developers drew district boundaries to exclude existing residents of an area. The developers then moved people into rent-free mobile homes within these boundaries shortly before the special district election, in which these newly established "residents" were the only ones eligible to vote. After approving large bond sales for the construction of roads, water lines, and sewers, the voters for the new district would often move away. Future homeowners in the area were then expected to pay for the bonds with property taxes on their homes. The investigation found that sometimes a single voter—and always fewer than 10 voters—approved the bonded indebtedness that helped the developers create an infrastructure for their properties. In the Lantana subdivision near Flower Mound, for example, a family of three voted to authorize $277 million in bond sales by two water districts. That bond proposition rivals the biggest bond proposals by the city of Dallas.[52] Similar schemes have been especially prevalent in Travis, Harris, and Denton counties.

One danger is that development will not proceed as planned in the areas covered by these special purpose districts, which can lead to exceptionally high charges to existing homeowners to cover the debt or bankruptcy of the special purpose districts. In this case, the holders of the bonds lose all or part of their investment. One such outcome occurred in the Grimes County Municipal Utility District No. 1, which defaulted on its $1.86 million in water and sewer revenue bonds. The district could not hope to make payments on the bonds when it ended up providing services to only three customers.[53]

The pervasiveness of special purpose districts is shown by one study of Texas special purpose districts that addresses water issues. The study found that about 1,000 MUDs were engaged in supplying water, 48 special

PERSONAL RESPONSIBILITY: WHAT WOULD YOU DO?

- Why are there so many special purpose districts in Texas? Do you feel cities and counties should do the jobs that special purpose districts do? Why don't they?

- Do you think cities and counties should more closely monitor the activities of special purpose districts? Who do you think should be in charge of that oversight?

purpose districts existed to deal with water drainage issues, and 66 special purpose districts existed solely to supply fresh water. Others had the following purposes: 91 to conserve groundwater, 25 to provide for irrigation, 46 to improve levees, 42 to manage municipal water, 26 to deal with navigation, and 31 to deal with rivers. Finally, 55 special utility districts dealt with general water issues, 221 were water control and improvement districts, and 18 were water improvement districts. Of course, this hodgepodge of special purpose districts dealing with all aspects of water makes a coherent approach to statewide water policy virtually impossible.[54]

Special purpose districts are among the least-studied areas of Texas politics, but their use as an instrument of private gain and as a way for developers to minimize their financial risks suggest the need for much greater scrutiny. Of course, developers may defend this system as a way to improve property and enhance the tax base of communities. On the other hand, the extent to which special purpose districts have acquired governmental taxing powers with little public scrutiny or accountability is disturbing. And if the huge bond issues floated by these entities default, thousands of people could suffer the financial consequences.

Councils of Government (COGs)

council of government (COG) a regional planning board composed of local elected officials and some private citizens from the region

The Regional Planning Act of 1965 initially provided for the creation of regional **councils of government (COGs)** to promote coordination and planning across all local governments in a particular region. Councils of government are not special purpose districts, as

---

Regional Councils of Government in Texas

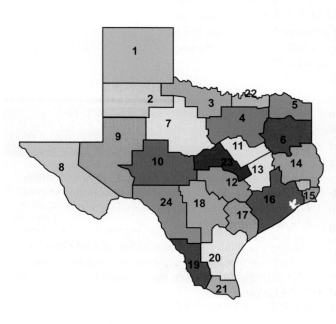

Region Name	Number
Alamo Area Council of Governments	18
Ark-Tex Council of Governments	5
Brazos Valley Council of Governments	13
Capital Area Council of Governments	12
Central Texas Council of Governments	23
Coastal Bend Council of Governments	20
Concho Valley Council of Governments	10
Deep East Texas Council of Governments	14
East Texas Council of Governments	6
Golden Crescent Regional Planning Commission	17
Heart of Texas Council of Governments	11
Houston-Galveston Area Council	16
Lower Rio Grande Valley Development Council	21
Middle Rio Grande Development Council	24
Nortex Regional Planning Commission	3
North Central Texas Council of Governments	4
Panhandle Regional Planning Commission	1
Permian Basin Regional Planning Commission	9
Rio Grande Council of Governments	8
South East Texas Regional Planning Commission	15
South Plains Association of Governments	2
South Texas Development Council	19
Texoma Council of Governments	22
West Central Texas Council of Governments	7

---

they do not tax or impose user fees. Still, they play an important role at the regional level in providing planning and coordination across numerous local government boundaries. Major water, airport, or highway projects, among others, involve many local governments, and councils are necessary to work across these many local entities.

There are 24 regional councils in Texas today, each with its own bylaws or articles of agreement. At least two-thirds of the governing body of a regional council must consist of local elected officials of cities and counties, but it may also include citizen members and representatives of other groups. Figure 10.2 provides a map and listing of the 24 regional COGs in Texas.

The basic responsibilities of regional councils include planning for the economic development of an area, helping local governments carry out regional projects, contracting with local governments to provide certain services, and reviewing applications for state and federal financial assistance. Originally, COGs focused considerable attention on meeting federal mandates for water and sewer provision, open space, and housing planning. More recently, activities have focused on comprehensive planning and service delivery in such policy areas as aging, employment and training, criminal justice, economic development, environmental quality, and transportation.[55]

Financial Issues Facing Local Government

Examine the financial problems facing local government

As noted earlier, there are many different forms of local government in Texas, including county governments, municipal governments, school districts, and nonschool special purpose districts. These governments manage money through special financial mechanisms that rely on their ability to tax. Two of these mechanisms, capital appreciation bonds and local government pensions, raise important opportunities and problems for local government.

Capital Appreciation Bonds

A **capital appreciation bond (CAB)** is a method by which local governments borrow money. Its main use is by school districts to raise revenue for development in times of rapid population growth.[56] Local governments often sell bonds to obtain funds for projects, but unlike traditional government-issued bonds, capital appreciation bonds do not make periodic interest payments to bondholders over the course of the bond; instead, the local government promises to pay back the initial investment in the bond and all accrued interest when the bond reaches maturity. The bond is usually sold for an amount that is far less than the lump sum payment the local government has to make when the

capital appreciation bond (CAB)
a long-term, high-interest-paying bond that pays off both principal and interest in one lump sum when the bond reaches maturity

bond matures. Essentially, this type of bond is a way for local government to get money now for a promise to pay back much more money in one lump sum far into the future. This type of bond has been causing a great deal of controversy, especially in California and Texas. But despite the controversy, CABs are becoming more and more common in Texas. According to the nonpartisan group California Watch, "in Texas, 590 districts and other government entities have issued these bonds over the past six years—more than any other state."[57] Combined, Texas's local governments issued more than $2.3 billion in CABs in over 700 separate issuances between 2007 and 2011—debts that will eventually cost more than $20 billion to repay.[58] The per capita debt of Texas's state government ranks 45th in the nation. However, when local debt is taken into consideration, it jumps to 15th highest in the nation.[59]

CABs are extremely long-term bonds. In many cases they do not have to be paid by the local government until 40 years after they are issued.[60] During this entire time period, the issuer does not have to pay a dime to investors—meaning that local government officials can promise new education facilities to voters without raising current taxes.[61] CABs also tend to pay high interest to bond investors.

An analysis of the numbers provided by the *Austin American-Statesman* shows that Texas municipalities will owe, on average, nearly $9 for every $1 they have borrowed using CABs.[62] In extreme cases, the ratio of money owed to money borrowed can reach 35 to 1.[63] As with most municipal bonds, the interest accrued by capital appreciation bonds is tax exempt. Essentially what this all means is that the debt burden facing local government is considerably more than is found on the books.

The dilemma of entities that use these bonds is well illustrated by the Anna Independent School District in Collin County. In the early twenty-first century, Anna was undergoing tremendous population growth, changing from a rural to a suburban school district as the Dallas metropolitan area grew to the north. In 2002–03, the district had about 1,000 students; in 2012–13, it had about 2,500. By issuing CABs, Anna could build schools to accommodate its rapid growth. Meanwhile, regular interest payments over the course of the bond are not required as they would be by traditional bonds. Additionally, state law caps the school district tax rate on property, the primary funding source for public schools, but CABs do not count against the cap until the payment is due many years later. The cap requires that when school bonds are issued, total repayments from property taxes cannot exceed a tax rate of 50 cents per $100 of assessed property value. In 2008, Anna had reached the 50-cent limit, which ruled out any more traditional bond funding. The only way to get more funding was through CABs. The upside, of course, was that CABs skirted the state cap and got money to the school district immediately—the schools could deal with the district's burgeoning growth. The downside was the long-term costs. When these bonds mature, Anna's taxpayers will have to pay back about five times the amount borrowed. Other districts in rapidly growing areas have followed Anna's lead.[64]

During the 2015 regular session, the state legislature considered a number of bills related to capital appreciation bonds, but only one passed. This bill prohibited local governments (including school districts) from issuing CABs for terms longer than 20 years and from refunding CABs to extend their maturity dates. CAB debt was also limited to 25 percent of the outstanding bond debt of the local governmental entity. CABs may be the only way that school districts can obtain the funding to pay for rapid growth, but the incautious use of them could have dire long-term consequences for local government finances.[65]

Local Government Pensions

Another area of concern with local government involves the cost and financial health of pension plans. Several municipal bankruptcies throughout the United States in 2012 brought attention to the instability of a number of state and local public pension plans.[66]

Pension shortfalls became a major issue in Texas in December 2016, just before the opening of the 2017 legislative session. Texas has 81 different local governmental pension plans that cover nearly 184,000 persons and that have net assets of over $28 billion. Unfortunately, not all these pension plans have sufficient funds to meet their obligations to pay retirees.

A report by Moody's released in late November 2016 found that Dallas and Houston had two of the largest unfunded liabilities of local governments in the United States. Dallas ranked second in the nation (behind Chicago) with a liability 549 percent of annual operating revenues, while Houston ranked fourth with a 414 percent liability of operating revenues. The problems did not stop there. Austin ranked ninth, and San Antonio ranked twelfth with liabilities as a percentage of annual operating revenues of 267 percent and 188 percent respectively.[67]

Houston's city workers have three major pension systems—the Houston Police Officers Pension System, the Houston Firefighters' Relief and Retirement Fund, and the Houston Municipal Employees Pension System. Houston expected its contributions to pensions to rise to 17.1 percent of all city expenditures by 2017.[68] The city's pension costs in 2015 for the Firefighters' Relief and Retirement Fund were 34 percent of the fire department's annual payroll.[69] Bill King, while running for mayor of Houston in the 2015 election, claimed that if the problem with city employee pensions was not fixed, "it's game over" for city finances.[70]

The Fort Worth Employees' Retirement Fund began having serious funding issues in the 1990s when the city's contributions to the fund were decreased while plan benefits were increased. Additionally, investment returns to the fund were wiped out in the 2008 Great Recession. In 2011, Fort Worth's pension problems led to a reduction in benefits for new hires other than public safety workers, which included increases in the minimum retirement age, reduction of the multiplier used to calculate benefits, elimination of cost-of-living adjustments, and removal of overtime earnings from benefit calculations. In spite of these reductions, Fort Worth's funding of its pension system remains inadequate.[71]

Probably the most extreme example in Texas of a failing pension system was the Dallas Police and Fire Pension System. Its problems were so severe that Dallas has imposed immediate and drastic reforms to the system. Reforms were necessary because of overly generous benefits and remarkably poor management, which put pension benefits for Dallas police officers and firefighters at risk. According to one accounting of the fund, it had $3 billion in assets and $8 billion in liabilities and without changes would have been broke in 15 years. One reason is that pensioners in the fund got an automatic 4 percent annual cost of living increase. Given low inflation and the fund's low returns on investments, such an increase is not sustainable.

Another problem was the **deferred retirement option plan (DROP)**. Dallas police and firefighter base salaries are low in comparison to those of Fort Worth and neighboring suburbs, and since police and firefighters can retire after 20 years of service, the DROP plan was created in 1993 to discourage them from leaving employment after only two decades. Under the plan, if a 20-year veteran chose to stop contributing to the

deferred retirement option plan (DROP) retirement plan in which local government employees who are eligible to retire have their retirement benefits deposited in an account in which the benefits draw interest until actual retirement. Some of these plans pay high interest and cost-of-living adjustments and may be coupled with very early retirement ages

SOCIAL RESPONSIBILITY:
GET INVOLVED

- What are the tradeoffs in local governments' cutting back pension benefits to their employees?

- Should taxes be raised in order to fully fund these pension plans? Why or why not?

pension plan and entered DROP, it was as if the police officer or firefighter had retired, but that person could continue working. Instead of being paid out to the person, his or her pension checks would be deposited in a DROP account paying between 8 and 10 percent interest.

Still another problem with the Dallas system was that fund managers appeared to have tried to maximize returns by investing in speculative real estate deals, such as paying $34 million for some Arizona desert land that later sold for $7.5 million. Managers also overvalued real estate and made rosy assumptions, such as 8.5 percent yearly returns on investment, which did not ultimately come to pass.

Taxpayers in Dallas already contributed $100 million per year to the pension fund. It would have been difficult to get them to contribute much more, although the alternative had to be pension reductions for police and firefighters. In the meantime, the credit rating for Dallas bonds had been reduced, in part because of concerns about the problems with the police and firefighter pension fund. A lower credit rating for bonds issued by a governmental entity means that the entity has to pay a higher interest rate to borrowers.[72]

The Dallas pension problems were so severe that in the November 2016 election 69 percent of Dallas voters approved changes that should reduce the pension's liabilities by $2.15 billion over the next 30 years. Voters usually tend to be uninterested in and unaware of problems associated with government employee pension plans, but the effects on a government's financial stability and tax system can be enormous.

Bailing out the pension plans of Houston and Dallas was a major issue confronting the 2017 legislative session. Actuarial projections at the end of 2016 forecast that the Dallas pension fund would run out of money in 10 years while the Houston pension fund would fail in less than 15 years. Separate bills were passed during the session addressing the specific problems confronting each city's plan. In general, though, the solutions were the same: there were reductions in future pension accruals for workers and retirees and provisions were made for the plans to receive additional contributions from their respective cities. Financial benchmarks were also laid down for future years that would have to be met or there would be more benefit cuts. The Dallas bill also banned lump sum withdrawals under the DROP program.

All in all, the actions of the legislature in 2017 brought some stability to the pension plans of Houston and Dallas and helped to protect the credit rating of each city, at least in the medium term. But it did nothing to address the funding problems facing other city pension plans in the state, particularly those in Austin, San Antonio, and Fort Worth.[73]

Future Pension Policy Pensions have a huge effect on state, county, and local governments. And for some local governments, employee pensions have already become unmanageable. Some pension administrators have recognized that their plans were no longer economically viable and have instituted significant plan changes.

One example of significant pension plan changes has come in El Paso, which has increased the standard age of retirement for city employees, increased the years of service required to receive a pension, and changed the formula for calculating pension amounts to be less favorable to the employee. As an example, prior to the pension changes, assume an employee chose to retire at age 60 with 25 years and 5 months of service with the city and that the employee's final wages were $2,000 per month. That employee's pension would be $1,270.85 per month. Under the new plan, that employee would receive $1,143.76, or $127.09 a month less, a 10 percent reduction.[74] For that employee, this no doubt seems a drastic cut in retirement pay, but such changes make pension systems viable.

The complex financial issues involved in providing pensions to local government workers may seem tiresome to try to understand. But they cut to the core of the problems facing government officials in the early twenty-first century. If local governments in Texas are to thrive in the coming decades, they must not be burdened with debts that cannot be paid.

Local Government and the Future of Texas

IN THIS CHAPTER, we have investigated the role of local government in Texas government and politics. In many ways, local government affects the average citizen's life much more than either the federal or the state government. Local government generally works well in Texas in providing basic services. It picks up the trash, provides water, provides fire and police protection, and maintains local roads. However, in some ways local government may not be functioning as well as we might hope. As Texas has become more diverse and as Latinos and African Americans have gained political power, there is a greater demand for democratic responsiveness from local government. That demand is most clearly seen in the movement away from at-large city councils and toward single-member city council districts. But is local government sufficiently responsive? Special purpose districts have been described as "hidden governments," suggesting a real lack of democratic accountability for their actions. It is unclear that there is sufficient democratic accountability even for high-level county officials such as district attorneys. As Texas looks to the future, the issue of expanding democratic accountability in local government looms as increasingly important.

One issue, currently far from the minds of Texas policy makers, is the way local government is structured in Texas. Should real estate developers support a handful of persons in a special district to incur millions in debt for that district and for future residents of that district? In terms of county governments, does Texas need 254 counties? Many of these counties are too small to deal with important concerns such as supporting the costs of a capital punishment trial. Though consolidation of governments in Texas and greater regulation of special purpose districts are matters that are not currently on the state's political agenda, demands for a more transparent and efficient government should lead to consideration of such issues.

Finally, there are potential financial disasters facing local governments in their pension systems and in their methods of borrowing money. These problems must be dealt with in the near future to avoid financial calamity at the local level in the next few decades. Financial mechanisms other than risky capital appreciation bonds must be found to fund the infrastructure needed for Texas's growth. And many employee pension plans are currently costing local governments more and more of their resources while the ability of those funds to pay future pensions is becoming less likely. For Texas's urban centers, the crisis in local pension funds will become increasingly apparent and, as time goes by, harder to resolve. Most likely, this crisis cannot be resolved only with a tax increase. It will require pension reductions and ultimately a rethinking of how local employees receive support in retirement.

Use 🔖 INQUIZITIVE to help you study and master this material.

County Government in Texas

- **Explain the importance, role, and structure of county government in Texas (pp. 329–37)**

There are more counties in Texas than in any other state. County governance in Texas affects the lives of everyday Texans in ways ranging from hospital care to trash pickup.

Key Terms
county attorney (p. 330)
district attorney (p. 330)
county clerk (p. 330)
district clerk (p. 330)
county tax assessor-collector (p. 330)
county auditor (p. 331)
county commissioners' court (p. 331)
county judge (p. 331)
county commissioner (p. 331)
constable (p. 333)

Practice Quiz
1. Which of the following is *not* a type of local government found in Texas?
   a) city
   b) council of government
   c) county
   d) special district
   e) municipal

2. The basic governing body of a county is known as
   a) a council of government.
   b) a county council.
   c) a city-manager government.
   d) a county commissioners' court.
   e) a county governing committee.

3. How many counties are there in Texas?
   a) 25
   b) 56
   c) 110
   d) 254
   e) 500

4. All county commissioners' precincts must be equal in population according to
   a) Article 1 of the Texas Constitution.
   b) the Civil Rights Act of 1964.
   c) the Voting Rights Act of 1975.
   d) *Avery v. Midland County.*
   e) *Marbury v. Madison.*

5. A county judge
   a) only hears appellate cases from JP courts.
   b) is an appointive position from the governor.
   c) presides over the constitutional county court and the county commissioners' court.
   d) implements all the decisions of the Supreme Court affecting the county.
   e) judges juvenile cases.

6. Which county officials are responsible for the jail and the safety of the prisoners?
   a) sheriff
   b) county council
   c) county commissioners' court
   d) council of mayors
   e) city manager

City Government in Texas

- Describe the major characteristics of city government in Texas (pp. 337–50)

Municipalities in Texas vary in terms of how they are governed. Some cities have strong mayors who run the city, while other cities have weak mayors where the day-to-day running of the city is delegated to city managers. Mayors and city councils often decide issues that directly affect the lives of everyday people.

Key Terms

home-rule charter (p. 339)
preemption (p. 340)
mayor-council form of government (p. 341)
at-large election (p. 341)
single-member district (p. 341)
commissioner form of government (p. 341)
council-manager form of government (p. 342)

Practice Quiz

7. To adopt a home-rule charter, a city must have a minimum population of
   a) 201.
   b) 5,000.
   c) 10,000.
   d) 50,000.
   e) There is no minimum.

8. The two legal classifications of Texas cities are
   a) local and regional.
   b) general law and home rule.
   c) tax and nontax.
   d) charter and noncharter.
   e) big and small.

9. The form of city government that allows the mayor to establish control over most of the city's government is called the
   a) commissioner form of city government.
   b) council-manager form of city government.
   c) council of government form of city government.
   d) strong mayor–council form of city government.
   e) none of the above

10. A city controller
   a) works directly for the governor.
   b) controls and manages the election in a city.
   c) is a city's chief elected official who presides over the city council.
   d) is independent of all political control in a small statutory city.
   e) is a city's chief financial officer.

11. Cities that have home rule
   a) make ordinances and regulations without interference by the state.
   b) have considerable freedom to make ordinances and regulations, but the state legislature can preempt their actions.
   c) have rules that prevent homes from being taxed.
   d) are allowed great leeway by the state legislature because they are heavily Republican.
   e) are concentrated in West Texas.

Special Purpose Districts

- Examine the role of special purpose districts in Texas government (pp. 350–57)

Special purpose districts often span different cities and counties. They are tasked with operating such things as school districts or water utility districts. They have the authority to levy property taxes to fund the operation of services essential to the lives of many residents.

Key Terms

special purpose district (p. 350)
school district (p. 350)
nonschool special district (p. 350)
municipal utility district (MUD) (p. 352)
property tax (p. 354)
user fee (p. 354)
hidden government (p. 354)
council of government (COG) (p. 356)

12. Which local government provides a single service not provided by any other local government?
    a) special district
    b) council of government
    c) police district
    d) city
    e) county

13. What are the two types of special purpose districts found in Texas?
    a) school and nonschool
    b) home rule and general law
    c) tax and nontax
    d) statutory and constitutional
    e) none of the above

14. A special district
    a) must be limited to under 150,000 people.
    b) covers the entire state to provide a particular service.
    c) is a unit of local government that provides a special service to a limited geographic area.

    d) temporarily combines two congressional districts.
    e) none of the above

15. A MUD
    a) serves the needs of developers.
    b) is generally opposed by banks and real estate developers as being too expensive.
    c) provides ambulance service inside a city's geographic limits.
    d) delegates the setting of tax rates in a particular geographic area to the state legislature.
    e) provides funding for special purpose districts.

16. Comprehensive planning and service delivery in a specific geographic area are the function of a
    a) special district.
    b) council of government.
    c) city.
    d) county.
    e) town.

Financial Issues Facing Local Government

- **Examine the financial problems facing local government (pp. 357–61)**

Local government in Texas is facing a looming financial crisis as a result of widespread issuance of capital appreciation bonds, which allow funds to be raised in the present while interest and payments on the principal are paid far into the future, and the liabilities imposed on local government by generous retirement plans for governmental employees.

Key Terms

capital appreciation bond (CAB) (p. 357)
deferred retirement option plan (DROP) (p. 359)

Practice Quiz

17. Capital appreciation bonds
    a) are long-term bonds on which local governments pay back principal and interest on a yearly basis.
    b) are short-term bonds on which local governments borrow money for emergencies.

    c) are bonds on which interest is paid quarterly by local governments but the principal is not paid back for 40 years.
    d) are bonds on which principal and interest are not paid back until the end of a lengthy term while local governments can use the borrowed money immediately.
    e) create such long-term financial risks that they are illegal in Texas.

18. Some governmental employee retirement plans in Texas
    a) impose huge financial liabilities on government.
    b) need to be increased to support needy retired employees.
    c) have not kept up with inflation.
    d) will soon be merged into the Social Security retirement program.
    e) are so minimal that it is hard to recruit employees at the local level.

The way the state raises and spends money affects many aspects of life in Texas, including tuition and fees at public colleges and universities.

Public Finance

WHY PUBLIC FINANCE MATTERS For college students, the state budget might appear to be pretty far removed from everyday life and things such as attending class, preparing for an exam, or getting everything in order for a timely graduation. But like it or not, the budgetary decisions made by legislators every two years affect students where they matter most: in the pocketbook.

In 2003 state political leaders found themselves staring at a $10 billion shortfall in the upcoming budget period. Mandated by the state constitution to maintain a balanced budget, they needed to find new ways to close the budget gap without raising taxes. One method was to cut higher education funding.

Prior to 2003 tuition and fee rates for state universities had been set by the state legislature, and in Texas they tended to be low when compared to tuition in other states. Costs ranged from $2,870 per year at Texas A&M at Texarkana to $4,912 per year at the University of Texas (UT) at Austin. General revenues funded a large portion of the state university's education budget. In 2003, as a trade-off for a 2 percent cut in the higher education budget, the legislature gave the regents of the various state schools the authority to raise tuition to make up the difference.[1]

Tuition skyrocketed across the country in the first decade of the twenty-first century. Tuition and fees for Texas A&M at Texarkana rose 132 percent between 2003 and 2016 to $6,649 per year. At UT Austin, they rose 100 percent to $10,570 per year. The average tuition and fees for a four-year public university in Texas in 2016 reached $8,670. Although this was below the national average, higher education had become an expensive commodity in Texas.[2] Following the 2017 legislative session additional tuition and fee increases were put into effect across the state. In the spring of 2018 the University of Texas System Board of Regents approved increases to all system schools.

As universities and colleges lined up in 2015 and 2016 to present a new round of tuition increases, many lawmakers expressed serious concerns about the wisdom of the 2003 decision to give over control of tuition and fees to the universities. Spiraling student debt coupled to higher tuition and fees was making it difficult for Texans to attend college. Moreover, state leaders believed that college spending was out of control. If universities could not hold the line on costs, then perhaps the legislature would have to take action.

University leaders across the state did not take the challenge to their control over tuition and fees lightly. Supporting continued deregulation, Deputy Chancellor David E. Daniel of the University of Texas System argued that each university or university system was better equipped to make decisions about tuition and fees than the legislature. Others argued that the universities had kept increases in tuition and fees lower than the legislature had.[3]

Constituent pressure to keep higher education prices down likely will continue over the next few years. But three factors related to public finance will work against a return to highly regulated tuition and fees. First, state political leaders want costs held down, but few appear to want to return all decision making about tuition back to the legislature. Deregulation, after all, freed the legislature from having to choose between higher costs and lower quality. Second, most political leaders also recognize that if Texas wants to build high-quality universities, someone has to pay for them. But the third factor may be the most important. Over the past 25 years, the legislature has been unwilling to allocate more general revenue monies directly to fund higher education, even in an era of rapidly escalated costs in the industry. Appropriated dollars per student have actually fallen approximately 15 percent since the Great Recession in 2008. Until the state is willing to invest more in higher education or is willing to accept lower-quality institutions of higher education, tuition, fees and public discontent will continue to rise.[4]

The debate over tuition and fees is one example of how matters of public finance lie at the heart of Texas government. Passing a balanced budget is the most important task presented to the state legislature during its regular session every two years. Priorities must be identified and money must be allocated across a wide range of governmental activities through a variety of financial mechanisms. Difficult decisions must be made about how to fund governmental activities through increased taxes and fees. Understanding public policy demands a mastery of public finance. That is the subject of this chapter.

CHAPTER GOALS

- Explain the purpose of the state budget and what is typically included (pp. 369–71)

- Describe the general pattern of state spending in Texas and where state revenue comes from (pp. 371–80)

- Describe how the money in the budget is organized into specific funds (pp. 380–84)

- Outline the constitutional provisions that affect how the state budget is made (pp. 384–88)

- Identify the steps, players, and political tensions in making the state budget (pp. 388–96)

What Is the Budget?

Explain the purpose of the state budget and what is typically included

One of the most distinguishing characteristics of public finance in Texas is that the state constitution mandates that the legislature operate within a "balanced budget." On its face, this idea is straightforward: a balanced budget would exist whenever the projected income from tax revenues is equal to or exceeds the projected expenditure. But public finance is a complicated business. There are actually a number of different ways to talk about the funds that constitute the "budget." One way is to divide them into the following five broad and overlapping categories.[5]

- The **General Revenue Funds** includes "dedicated" and "nondedicated" general revenue funds flowing into the budget. The "nondedicated" portion of the General Revenue Fund (funds not directed toward specific purposes) serves as the state's primary operating fund in the General Revenue Fund. It also includes three large educational funds (the Available School Fund, the State Instructional Materials Fund, and the Foundation School Fund). Appropriations from General Revenue Funds totaled $106.6 billion for the 2018–19 biennium.

- The **General Revenue–Dedicated Funds** is a subset of the General Revenue Fund and includes over 200 funds dedicated to specific purposes, such as the State Parks Account and the college operating accounts (which hold tuition funds). Generally speaking, the legislature can appropriate money from these accounts only for their dedicated purposes. The balances in this budget are used to certify that the constitutional pay-as-you-go limits (discussed below) are being met. Appropriations from the General Revenue–Dedicated Funds amounted to $6.3 billion for the 2018–19 biennium.

- **Federal Funds** includes all grants, payments, and reimbursements received from the federal government by state agencies and institutions, including those from the Medicaid program, Title 1 Grants to Local Educational Agencies, transportation grants, and the Children's Health Insurance Program. Seventy-two billion dollars were appropriated from Federal Funds for the 2018–19 biennium.

- **Other Funds** consists of all other funds flowing into the state treasury that are not included in the other methods of financing. These include, among others, the State Highway Fund, the Texas Mobility Fund, the Property Tax Relief Fund, and the Economic Stabilization Fund. For the 2018–19 biennium, $31.8 billion was appropriated from Other Funds.

- **All Funds** is the aggregate of all these ways of financing government and refers to all revenue that goes through agencies, including federal and state programs.

Some important things must be noted about this complicated system of public financing through these various budgets. First, the state budget involves huge amounts of money (see Table 11.1). Second, much of this money lies outside the direct control

General Revenue Funds a nondedicated revenue account that functions as the state's primary operating fund

General Revenue–Dedicated Funds budget composed of funds for dedicated revenues that target money for specific purposes

Federal Funds includes all grants, payments, and reimbursements received from the federal government by state agencies and institutions

Other Funds consists of all other funds flowing into the state treasury that are not included in other state budgets; this includes the Texas Highway Fund, various trust funds operated by the state, and certain revenues held for local higher education accounts

All Funds the aggregate of all these ways of financing government and refers to revenue that goes through agencies, including federal and state programs

TABLE 11.1

Summary of All Funds State Budget Allocation by Biennium (in millions of dollars)

ALL FUNCTIONS	2016–17	2018–19*	PERCENTAGE CHANGE
Article I: General Government	$7,046	$6,243	–11.4%
Article II: Health and Human Services	80,872	78,872	–2.5
Article III: Agencies of Education	79,140	80,998	2.3
Public Education	58,896	60,510	2.7
Higher Education	20,244	20,488	1.2
Article IV: The Judiciary	813	831	2.1
Article V: Public Safety and Criminal Justice	12,575	12,306	–2.1
Article VI: Natural Resources	4,538	4,455	–1.8
Article VII: Business and Economic Development	29,650	31,842	7.4
Article VIII: Regulatory	956	675	–29.4
Article IX: General Provisions	0	0	N/A
Article X: The Legislature	401	388	–3.3
Total, all articles	**$215,992**	**$216,608**	**0.3%**

*Appropriated.

SOURCE: Texas Legislative Budget Board, *Fiscal Size-Up: 2018–19 Biennium* (September 2018), p. 2.

FIGURE 11.1

Trends in State Government Expenditures

*Appropriated.

SOURCE: Texas Legislative Budget
Board, *Fiscal Size-Up: 2018–19
Biennium* (September 2018), p. 24.

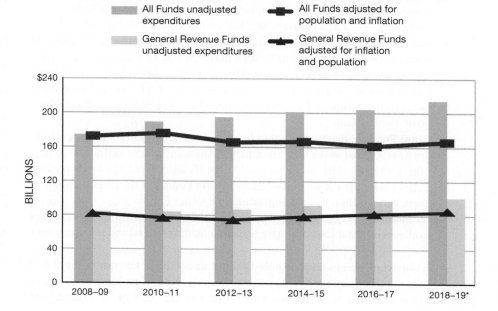

Legend:
- All Funds unadjusted expenditures
- General Revenue Funds unadjusted expenditures
- All Funds adjusted for population and inflation
- General Revenue Funds adjusted for inflation and population

of the legislature. Trust funds and other dedicated funds exist for particular purposes and are hard to manipulate for other budgetary purposes. As a result, legislators seeking to balance the budget are often left with relatively few places to cut expenditures. Given its large share of the General Revenue Funds budget, education is often at the top of the list. Third, federal expenditures have a very important role in shaping the overall direction of the state budget. The bulk of federal expenditures is in two areas: health and human services, and education. Strings are often attached to these monies: if legislators want federal dollars, they must spend state dollars first. Figure 11.1 highlights the increasingly important role that federal dollars have played in spending patterns in Texas. Expenditures from the All Funds budget (which takes into account federal spending) have exploded recently. The pressure to maximize federal dollars flowing into Texas is one legislative goal. But legislators also desire to minimize state spending and not raise taxes.

Spending and Revenue in Texas

Describe the general pattern of state spending in Texas and where state revenue comes from

Texas has a reputation of being a "low service, low tax" state that seeks to maintain a favorable environment for business. In this section, we will look at the general pattern of state spending in Texas, as well as taxes and other sources of revenue in the state.

Trends in State Spending

For the most part, Texas's reputation as a low-spending state is well earned. On a variety of measures, Texas spends less than other states. A 2015 Kaiser Foundation Study found that among the 50 states, Texas ranked 44th on per capita state government expenditures, with $4,350 spent per capita.[6] On a per capita basis, Texas ranks 27th in educational spending, 44th in highway spending, 25th in hospital spending, and 41st in public welfare spending.[7] Conversely, Texas ranked high when compared with other states on the per capita federal dollars flowing into the state. In 2012, Texas took in $10,647 per capita from the federal government, ranking it 11th among the states, above the national state average of $8,844.[8]

The trend in overall spending reveals a similar story, particularly in recent years (see Figure 11.1). In unadjusted dollars (that is, not taking into account inflation or population increases), state spending (General Revenue Funds) in Texas rose from $81.9 billion in the 2008–09 biennium to over $106.6 billion in the 2018–19 biennium. However, in real per capita dollars (that is, controlling for inflation and population increases), state spending actually declined by 0.7 percent.[9]

When considering state and federal spending in Texas together (see All Funds in Figure 11.1), the story is a little different. Unadjusted spending for all funds (state and federal) in Texas rose from around $187.5 billion in 2010–11 to over $216.6 billion in 2018–19. But in real per capita dollars, spending over the same period actually decreased by 10.6 percent. Because of the Great Recession in 2008, the federal monies available to the state increased for a few years but then fell off. Still, though the federal government has backed away from its 2008 efforts, a lot of federal money continues to flow into Texas.[10]

Revenue in Texas

Spending is only part of Texas's "low service, low tax" reputation. The taxes that fund government are the other dimension. It is difficult to compare the state tax burden Texans face with that of citizens in other states. There are a variety of taxes that individuals can pay to state governments, including state income taxes, general state sales taxes, specific state sales taxes, local sales taxes, and property taxes. Moreover, some kinds of taxes can be lower in one state than another but be offset by higher local taxes.

Two measures are often used to compare tax burdens across states: state and local tax burden per capita and state tax collections per capita. On both measures, Texas's low tax reputation seems to be well earned. According to a 2017 Tax Foundation Study, Texas ranked 46th in state and local tax burden per capita (at $3,340), well below the national average of $4,420. In addition, Texas state tax collections per capita was $2,005 compared to a national average of $2,694, ranking Texas 42nd among the 50 states.[11]

Texas is one of seven states that do not have a personal income tax. (Two other states, Tennessee and New Hampshire, only tax income from dividends and interest.) On the other hand, Texas has a sales tax of 6.25 percent, the 13th highest in the nation. Combined general state and local sales taxes in the state can reach 8.25 percent. As we will see later in this chapter, a variety of specific sales taxes also raise revenue to fund government, including ones on cigarettes, alcohol, and gasoline.

Although Texas state taxes are low compared with other states' taxes, local taxes are a different story. In 2011, Texas ranked 14th among the states in terms of property taxes paid per capita, at $1,560. When state and local taxes are taken together, however, Texas remains a fairly low-tax state. Combined state and local taxes were $3,863 per capita in 2013, ranking Texas 30th in the nation. A 2016 study conducted by the Tax Foundation concluded that Texas had the 10th most business-friendly tax system.[12]

Besides sales taxes, government and public policy in Texas are funded from a variety of sources, including severance taxes on oil and natural gas produced in the state, licensing income, interest and dividends, and federal aid (Table 11.2). Many of these taxes are based on complex formulas, and people often are unaware they are paying them. Nevertheless, they are important sources of state revenue.

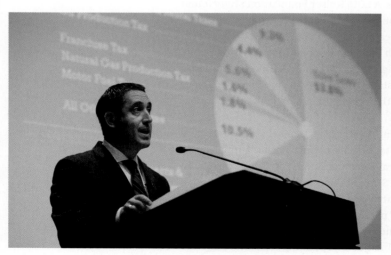

After the legislature passes the biennial state budget, the state comptroller certifies the budget, confirming that it is within current revenue estimates for the period. Here, state comptroller Glenn Hegar certifies the 2018–19 budget.

TABLE 11.2

State Revenue by Source, 2016–17 and 2018–19 Bienniums (in millions of dollars)

REVENUE	2016–17	2018–19*	PERCENTAGE CHANGE
Tax collections	$98,120	$107,114	9.2%
Federal receipts	77,840	74,915	–3.8
Licenses, fees, fines, and penalties	12,386	12,632	2.0
Interest and investment income	3,054	3,166	3.7
Lottery	4,273	4,155	–2.8
Land income	2,834	2,820	–0.5
Other revenue sources	23,971	19,747	–17.6
Total net revenue	**$222,476**	**$224,549**	**0.9**

*Estimated.

SOURCE: Texas Legislative Budget Board, *Fiscal Size-Up: 2018–19 Biennium* (September 2018), p. 31.

Sales Tax The most important single tax financing Texas government is the sales tax. Today, the general sales tax in Texas is 6.25 percent of the retail sales price of tangible personal property and selected services. Together, county, city, and metropolitan transit authorities are allowed to impose up to an additional 2 percent sales tax. For the 2018–19 biennium the sales tax is expected to account for 58.4 percent of the total tax collections in the state (see Figure 11.2).

Oil Production and Regulation Taxes The oil severance tax (incurred when oil is removed from the ground within a taxing jurisdiction) is 4.6 percent of the market value of a barrel of oil produced in the state. (There is also an oil regulation tax of three-sixteenths of one cent per barrel of oil produced in Texas.) The tax revenue from oil production fluctuates with the price of oil and the volume of oil produced in Texas. In fiscal year 2014, 903.0 million barrels were produced in Texas for an average price of $96.56 per barrel. Fracking and horizontal drilling, new technologies lying behind Texas's latest oil boom, likely rescued the state budget during the 2014–15 biennium. Unstable prices and uncertain tax revenues beginning in 2016 are posing new challenges to officials trying to project revenues from oil taxes during the 2016–17 biennium when revenues were $3.8 billion. Increased oil production in Texas along with rising prices have resulted in a projected increase in tax revenues to $4.9 billion in 2018–19, an increase of 29.7 percent from the 2016–2017 biennium.

Natural Gas Production Tax There is a 7.5 percent tax on the market value of all natural gas produced in the state. As with the oil tax, the tax raised from natural gas depends on the price and the amount produced. Revenues from natural gas

FIGURE 11.2

State Tax Revenue Sources, 2018–19 Biennium

*Percentages calculated based on constitutionally and statutorily dedicated tax revenues and appropriations in the 2018–19 General Appropriations Act, as modified by other legislation.

SOURCE: Texas Legislative Budget Board, *Fiscal Size-Up: 2018–19 Biennium* (September 2018), p. 32.

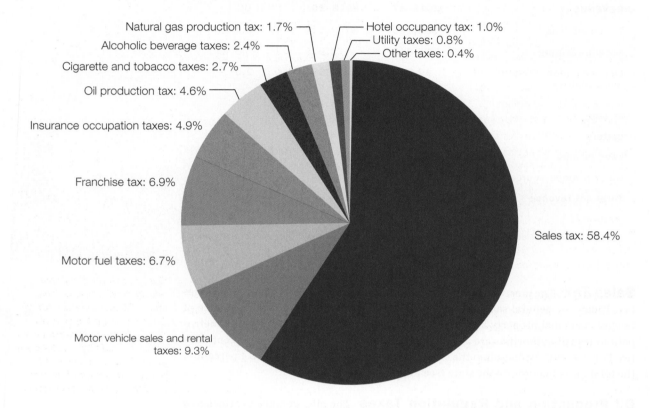

Natural gas production tax: 1.7%
Alcoholic beverage taxes: 2.4%
Cigarette and tobacco taxes: 2.7%
Oil production tax: 4.6%
Insurance occupation taxes: 4.9%
Franchise tax: 6.9%
Motor fuel taxes: 6.7%
Motor vehicle sales and rental taxes: 9.3%
Hotel occupancy tax: 1.0%
Utility taxes: 0.8%
Other taxes: 0.4%
Sales tax: 58.4%

have fluctuated considerably over time. The Comptroller's Office estimates that natural gas revenues will rise to $1.8 billion in 2018–19 from $1.6 billion in 2016–17, for a gain of 16.4 percent.

Motor Fuels Tax The motor fuels tax in Texas is 20 cents per gallon of gasoline and diesel fuel. There is a 15-cents-per-gallon tax on liquefied gas. The comptroller is expecting the motor fuels tax to generate approximately $7.3 billion in 2018–19, 2.8 percent greater than the previous biennium.

The revenues flowing from the motor fuels tax are "dedicated," meaning that they can be used only for purposes specified by the legislature. About three-quarters of these monies are appropriated to the Texas Department of Transportation and the Texas Department of Public Safety and are dedicated to the construction, maintenance, and policing of public roads. Most of the remaining one-quarter of the revenues are dedicated to public education.

Motor Vehicle and Home Sales Tax A 6.25 percent tax is charged on the sales price of all motor vehicles in the state. There is also a 10 percent tax on all rental vehicles up to 30 days and 6.25 percent thereafter. Newly manufactured homes are taxed at 5 percent of 65 percent of the sale price. Because of the effects of the Great Recession, motor vehicle sales and rental taxes declined by 5.6 percent in the 2010–11 biennium to $5.6 billion. The economic recovery since then increased the revenues from these taxes up to $8.7 billion in 2014–15. The Great Recession caused this tax revenue to decline to $5.6 billion for the 2010–11 biennium. But it has recovered in recent bienniums and is projected to generate $9.9 billion for the 2018–19 biennium.

Franchise Tax The so-called franchise tax is imposed on all corporations in Texas for the privilege of doing business in the state. Prior to 2008 the tax was imposed on taxable capital (net worth) and on earned surplus. The franchise tax is a complicated (and controversial) tax on businesses based upon earnings. The Comptroller's Office projects that this tax will generate $7.4 billion in the 2018–19 biennium. For the first year of the biennium, $2.7 billion of these revenues went directly into the General Revenue Fund with the remaining $0.5 billion allocated to the Property Relief Tax Fund. Similar proportions will be distributed during the second year.[13]

Gas prices have fluctuated widely in recent years. The state of Texas collects a tax of 20 cents per gallon on motor fuels. The federal government collects an additional 18.4 cents per gallon, but Texans still pay less tax for gasoline than residents of many other states.

Tobacco Taxes Texas imposes a variety of taxes on cigarettes and tobacco products. For example, every pack of 20 cigarettes has a $1.41 per-pack tax. The comptroller projects that tobacco taxes will generate $2.88 billion in revenues for 2018–19, a 1 percent decrease from the previous biennium.

Like the franchise tax reforms, a portion of the tobacco taxes has been linked to property tax relief. The share of revenues generated by the tax rate in place before 2007 goes directly into the General Revenue Fund, and the amount generated by the increase goes into the Property Tax Relief Fund. A portion of the other tax increase on tobacco products put into effect in 2007 goes to a Physician Education Loan Repayment program, and the remainder into the Property Tax Relief Fund.

Alcoholic Beverage Taxes As with tobacco, a variety of taxes are imposed on alcoholic beverages. The revenue generated by the Alcohol Beverage Tax in 2018–19 is expected to be $2.9 billion, 8.9 percent above the previous biennium.

Insurance Occupation Taxes A complex schedule of tax rates is applied to insurance premiums. For example, life, health, and accident insurance is taxed at the rate of 1.75 percent on gross premium receipts. For the 2018–19 biennium, insurance premium taxes are expected to be $4.6 billion, an increase of 14.7 percent from the previous biennium.

Utility Taxes Utility tax revenue flows from three sources in Texas. First, there is a tax on the gross receipts of gas, electric, and water utilities. Rates vary from 0.581 percent to 1.997 percent based on the size of the city population. Taxes are also imposed on the gross receipts of utilities and on gas utility pipelines. In 2018–19, utility taxes are estimated to take in $894 million, representing a 2.4 percent increase from the 2016–17 biennium.

Hotel and Motel Tax This state tax is 6 percent of the hotel and motel occupancy bill paid by the occupant. This tax revenue fell during the Great Recession but has rebounded along with increased tourism during the economic recovery over the past four years. It is expected to generate $1.1 billion.

Other Taxes Taxes on a few other items such as attorney services, cement, sulfur, coin-operated machines, and bingo rental receipts are expected to generate $458.1 million, up 17.1 percent from the previous biennium.

The Question of the Income Tax in Texas

Many commentators have complained that the tax system in Texas is too **regressive**.[14] By this they mean that the tax burden in the state falls more heavily on lower-income individuals. Sales and use taxes such as those found in Texas are generally considered to be regressive. Property taxes on individuals and businesses are also generally considered somewhat regressive, insofar as poor homeowners and renters generally pay more of their income in property taxes than do the wealthy. A 2015 study conducted by the Institute on Taxation and Economic Policy found that among the states Texas had the third most unfair tax system in the nation. The study estimated that in Texas people with incomes in the bottom 20 percent paid 12.5 percent of their income in state and local taxes, while those with incomes in the upper 1 percent paid only 2.9 percent of their income.[15]

There have been occasional calls for the institution of a state income tax in Texas. Supporters argue that the income tax is not only a more reliable source of revenue for the state but that it can also be made fairer. Unlike sales and use taxes, which are applied equally to everyone whatever their income, income taxes can be made **progressive**. With a progressive income tax, people with lower income pay a lower tax rate than people with higher income. Progressive income taxes thus place a higher tax burden on the rich than on the poor.

Few Texas politicians, however, have been willing to support an income tax, the absence of which has always been one of the state's most attractive features to business. It was not until the late 1980s that the first serious attempt to put a state income tax in place was undertaken. Responding to mounting budgetary pressures, the retiring lieutenant governor, Bill Hobby, came out in favor of an income tax in 1989. Bob Bullock, Hobby's successor, announced in 1991 that he would actively campaign for an income tax. A blue-ribbon panel chaired by former governor John Connally was charged with looking into new revenue sources for the state. The committee ended up recommending to the legislature

> SOCIAL RESPONSIBILITY: GET INVOLVED
>
> • Do you think sales and use taxes are a fair way for the state to generate revenue? Why or why not?
>
> • If you were writing a letter to the editor on behalf of a group advocating for poor Texans, how would you argue that the state change tax policy to help your supporters?

Who Pays the Highest State Taxes?

Texas is one of a handful of states that do not tax income, which means that Texans pay income taxes only to the federal government. Where does the state get its money? Through a variety of taxes including sales, property, severance, and franchise taxes, the state is able to fund roads, schools, prisons, and other needs. Critics of this approach argue that states without income taxes fail to distribute tax burdens fairly and that they underfund essential government services. Proponents argue that businesses are attracted to Texas because it does not tax personal income.

Top State Marginal Income Tax Rates, 2018

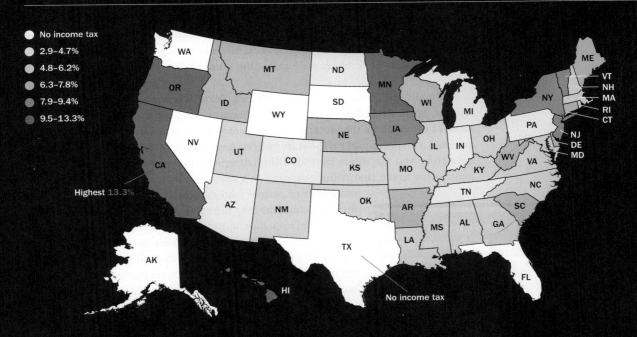

- No income tax
- 2.9–4.7%
- 4.8–6.2%
- 6.3–7.8%
- 7.9–9.4%
- 9.5–13.3%

Highest 13.3%

No income tax

Number of States in Each Tax Bracket

No income tax   2.9–4.7%   4.8–6.2%   6.3–7.8%   7.9–9.4%   9.5–13.3%

SOURCE: Tax Foundation, taxfoundation.org (accessed 6/13/18).

CRITICAL THINKING

- Which states have the highest income tax rates? Which have the lowest? What might explain this?

- What are the advantages and disadvantages to having no state income tax in Texas?

both a corporate and a personal income tax, but not without generating an enormous amount of controversy.[16]

Connally himself opposed the income-tax recommendations, as did Governor Ann Richards. By the 1993 legislative session, Bullock was backing off. He proposed a constitutional amendment requiring voter approval of any personal income tax and specifying that the revenue from it be used to support public education. The amendment quickly passed the legislature and was overwhelmingly approved by voters. As it effectively gave the electorate veto power on the issue, it is unlikely that Texans will have a personal income tax in the foreseeable future.

Other State Revenue

matching funds federal monies going to a state based on state spending for a program

The largest source of revenue for Texas is the federal government (see Table 11.3). Historically, Texas spends relatively little, compared with other states, for jointly funded state-federal programs. As a result, federal grants and **matching funds** (federal monies going to a state based on the state's spending for a program) also have been relatively low. For the 2018–19 biennium, federal funds accounted for $74.9 billion, about 33.4 percent of the total state revenue, down from 3.8 percent during the previous biennium. Much of the increase in these federal funds in recent years can be attributed to Medicaid, a state-federal program providing funds to finance health care delivery to the poor.[17]

In addition to taxes and federal monies, Texas has a number of other revenue sources, as shown in Table 11.4, including licenses, fees, and fines, sales of goods and services provided by the state, and land income. In recent years, two other sources have had a major impact on the state budget. A state lottery was approved by the state legislature and the voters in 1991. Although voters endorsed the lottery overwhelmingly, some argue that using gambling as a source of state revenues unfairly takes money from people who can least afford it by fooling them into thinking that they too can strike it rich if only they have a little luck. Large numbers of people from all social classes continue to play the lottery. In fiscal year 2017 lottery ticket sales totaled $5.1 billion. Of those sales, $3.3 billion was paid to players and $276.3 million was paid to retailers for commissions, bonuses, and incentives. In addition, $1.2 billion was transferred to the Foundation School Fund and $17.8 million to the Texas Veterans Commission, and $75.8 million of unclaimed prizes were transferred to the state.[18]

A second major source of nontax revenue is a result of the settlement the state reached with tobacco companies in 1998 over false and misleading statements about the safety of tobacco products. Under the settlement, Texas was to receive over $17.3 billion over the next 25 years and an additional $580 million every year thereafter from the tobacco industry. The Texas Comptroller's Office projects that Texas tobacco settlement receipts will total $916 million in 2018–19, down from the $966.4 million received in 2016–17. This drop is the result of a projected decline in cigarette sales.[19]

TABLE 11.3

Estimated State Revenue Collections, 2018–19 Biennium

Total	$224,549 million
Federal funds	33.4%
Sales tax	27.8
Other receipts	13.3
Motor vehicle sales and rental tax	4.4
Licenses, fees, fines, penalties	5.6
Other taxes	5.9
Franchise tax	3.3
Motor fuels tax	3.2
Severance tax	3.0

Who Pays the Most State Taxes in Texas?

Taxes as a Percentage of Income in Texas, 2015*

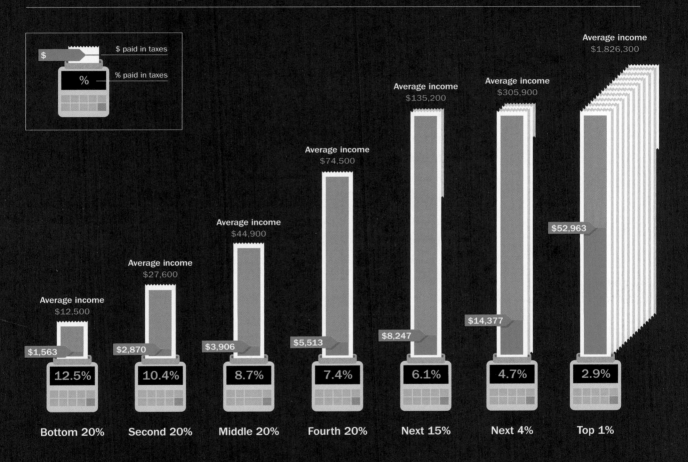

$ paid in taxes

% paid in taxes

	Bottom 20%	Second 20%	Middle 20%	Fourth 20%	Next 15%	Next 4%	Top 1%
Average income	$12,500	$27,600	$44,900	$74,500	$135,200	$305,900	$1,826,300
$ paid	$1,563	$2,870	$3,906	$5,513	$8,247	$14,377	$52,963
% paid	12.5%	10.4%	8.7%	7.4%	6.1%	4.7%	2.9%

Texas has no state income tax, which does keep overall individual tax rates down. However, this means that the state's revenues rely heavily on sales and property taxes. These taxes are regressive—those with less income pay a higher share of their income in taxes; those with higher incomes pay a lower share of their income in taxes.

QUANTITATIVE REASONING

- Which group pays the highest percentage of its income in taxes in Texas?
- How would the proportions paid in taxes change across all incomes if a progressive state income tax was instituted?

*Based on family income for non-elderly taxpayers.

SOURCE: Institute for Taxation and Economic Policy, www.itep.org (accessed 6/13/16).

TABLE 11.4

Tax Collections Biennial Comparison by Source, 2016–17 and 2018–19 (in billions of dollars)

	2016–17	2018–19*	PERCENTAGE CHANGE
Sales tax	$57.1	$62.5	9.4%
Oil production taxes	3.8	4.9	29.7
Natural gas production tax	1.6	1.8	16.4
Motor fuels tax	7.1	7.3	2.8
Motor vehicle sales and rental taxes	9.1	9.9	8.5
Franchise tax	7.1	7.4	3.5
Cigarette and tobacco taxes	2.9	2.9	−1.0
Alcoholic beverages taxes	2.4	2.6	8.9
Insurance occupation taxes	4.6	5.3	14.7
Utility taxes	0.9	0.9	2.4
Hotel occupancy tax	1.1	1.1	3.9
Inheritance tax	0	0	0
Other taxes	0.4	0.5	17.1
Total tax collections	**98.1**	**$107.1**	**9.2%**

NOTE: Biennial change and percentage change have been calculated on actual amounts before rounding in all tables and graphics in this chapter. Totals may not sum as a result of rounding. *Estimated.

SOURCE: Texas Legislative Budget Board, *Fiscal Size-Up: 2018–19 Biennium* (September 2018), p. 31.

State Funds

 Describe how the money in the budget is organized into specific funds

Money comes into state coffers from a variety of sources and is dispersed to a wide range of activities. But this money doesn't flow into and out of just one pot. There are, in fact, 400 funds in the state treasury whose monies are directed to a wide variety of functions. Understanding how money flows into and out of these funds lies at the heart of mastering the state budget. We examine some of the most important funds here.

As previously mentioned, the *General Revenue Fund*s consists of two parts: nondedicated General Revenue and General Revenue–Dedicated accounts. The nondedicated revenue is the state's primary operating fund and the place where most state taxes and fees flow. Expenditures may be made directly from the nondedicated funds and may be transferred to other special funds or accounts for allocation.

The **Permanent School Fund (PSF)** was created in 1854 with a $2 million appropriation by the legislature to fund primary and secondary schools. The Constitution of 1876, along with subsequent acts, stipulated that certain lands and sales from them would constitute the PSF. The second-largest educational endowment in the country, the PSF is managed primarily by the state board of education. The fund distributes money to school districts across the state on the basis of attendance and guarantees bonds issued by local school boards, enabling them to borrow money at lower interest rates. At the end of 2017 the fund was guaranteeing about $72.9 billion in school district bonds across the state.

The value of this fund fluctuated throughout the turbulent first decade of the twenty-first century, dropping to a little over $20 billion in 2009. At the end of fiscal year 2015, the fund balance had recovered to $33.8 billion. The fund provided $838.7 million to help fund public education in 2015.[20]

The **Available School Fund (ASF)** is a dedicated fund established by the constitution for the support of public education in the state. The ASF is funded through distributions of the Permanent School Fund and 25 percent of the state's motor fuels tax revenue. The ASF also provides funds for another fund, the Instructional Materials Fund, which funds state purchases of instructional materials. Revenue flowing into the ASF for the 2018–19 biennium from the motor fuels tax and PSF together is projected to be $3.01 billion.

The **State Highway Fund** comes from a variety of sources, including motor vehicle registration fees, the federal highway fund, and the sales tax on motor lubricants. A significant portion of the motor fuels tax is initially deposited in the General Revenue Fund and then allocated to the State Highway Fund. The purposes of the State Highway Fund are constructing, maintaining, and policing roadways in Texas and acquiring rights of way for them. Constitutional amendments in 2014 and 2015 provide for diverting billions of dollars into this fund from the Economic Stabilization Fund (discussed below) and state sales and use taxes. The Comptroller's Office estimates that $24 billion will flow into the State Highway Fund for the 2018–19 biennium.[21]

The **Economic Stabilization Fund (ESF)**, commonly known as the Rainy Day Fund, was established through constitutional amendment in 1988 to provide relief during times of financial distress. The fund is generated by a formula involving the base year of 1987. If collections from oil and gas taxes in any year exceed the 1987 amount, 75 percent of the excess is transferred to the fund. Half of any "unencumbered" general revenue—that is, revenue not already targeted for a specific purpose—also goes into the fund. The legislature has the authority to contribute additional funds but never has.

Under certain extraordinary circumstances, ESF monies can be appropriated with a three-fifths vote of members of both houses of the legislature. These circumstances include when a budget deficit develops in a biennium or when the comptroller estimates that revenue will decline from one biennium to the next. Money can also be appropriated from this fund for other purposes at any time with the support of two-thirds of members present in both houses.

Permanent School Fund (PSF) fund created in 1854 that provides monies for primary and secondary schools

Available School Fund (ASF) dedicated fund established by the constitution for the support of public education in the state

State Highway Fund fund that supports the construction, maintenance, and policing of roadways and acquires rights of way; funded through a variety of taxes such as motor vehicle registration fees, the federal highway fund, and the sales tax on motor lubricants

Economic Stabilization Fund (ESF) fund established by constitutional amendment in 1988 to provide funds for the state during times of financial stress; commonly known as the Rainy Day Fund

Few thought that large sums would accumulate in the fund. The first transfer of funds from oil and gas tax revenues, $18.5 million, took place in 1990, and the ESF account balance remained below $100 million until 2001, when more than $700 million was transferred into the account. In 2003 the ESF was depleted to help solve the impending $10 billion budget shortfall. That year and in 2005 the legislature appropriated ESF monies to a variety of agencies, including the Teachers' Retirement System, various health and human service agencies, the governor's office, and the Texas Education Agency.

Rising tax revenues from oil and gas production in the first decade of the twenty-first century flooded the ESF with cash. In 2014 and 2015 constitutional amendments transferred rainy day funds to water and transportation initiatives in the state. The fund is expected to generate $1.9 billion in revenues in the 2018–19 biennium and to grow to $11.2 billion (see Table 11.5). This fund contains more cash than similar funds in any other state. Only Alaska, also awash in oil and gas revenues, had a fund whose size approached that of its Texas counterpart. The debate over whether or how to use the Rainy Day Fund to close a budget shortfall was a major issue during the 2011 and 2013 legislative sessions and likely will be so again whenever the economy falters and the state revenues decline.[22]

To appreciate the importance of the operations of Texas's 400 funds and the complexity that they introduce into the budgetary process, one need only look at a few funds lying at the heart of higher education. Specific legislative goals are met through the creation of these funds and the allocation and reallocation of money to and from

TABLE 11.5

Economic Stabilization Fund History, Fiscal Years 2002 to 2019 (in billions of dollars)

BIENNIUM	REVENUES	EXPENDITURES	ENDING BALANCE
2002–03	$0.8	$0.4	$0.4
2004–05	1.0	1.5	−0.1
2006–07	2.5	1.2	1.2
2008–09	5.5	0.1	6.7
2010–11	1.5	3.2	5.0
2012–13	3.0	1.9	6.2
2014–15	4.3	2.0	8.5
2016–17	1.8	0.0	10.3
2018–19*	1.9	1.0	11.2

*Projected estimates.
NOTE: These are reported figures. Columns and rows may not add because of rounding.

SOURCE: Comptroller of Public Accounts, 2015 Certification Revenue Estimate. See also Texas Legislative Budget Board, *Fiscal Size-Up: 2018–19 Biennium*, pp. 40–41.

them. Some funds, such as the Permanent University Fund or the Higher Education Fund, were established to channel money directly to certain institutions of higher education. Others, like the National Research University Fund, are intended to encourage universities to behave in certain ways and to achieve a specific set of legislative objectives.

The **Permanent University Fund (PUF)** contributes to the support of most institutions in the University of Texas (UT) and Texas A&M University systems. Originally established in 1876 by a land grant of 1 million acres, the fund now contains approximately 2.1 million acres in 24 West Texas counties. Under the state constitution, all income from surface leases of this land goes into the Available University Fund (AUF), a fund set up to distribute PUF monies. Income from mineral leases and proceeds from the sale of PUF lands go into PUF and are invested. In 1999 an amendment to the constitution authorized the UT Board of Regents to channel investment income into the AUF. Two-thirds of the monies going to AUF go to the UT system; one-third goes to the Texas A&M system. The first obligation of any income earned by PUF is to pay the debt service on outstanding PUF bonds. The estimated market value of the PUF on August 31, 2017, was $19.1 billion.[23]

The **Higher Education Fund (HEF)** was established by a constitutional amendment for universities that did not have access to PUF monies. It is funded through the General Revenue Fund. Appropriations for the HEF are projected to be $787.5 million for the 2018–19 biennium. An advisory committee made up of member institutions provides input to the Texas Higher Education Coordinating Board, which in turn makes recommendations to the legislature for budgetary allocation to each school out of the HEF.

The **National Research University Fund (NRUF)** was established through a 2009 constitutional amendment to provide a source of funding for universities seeking to achieve national prominence as research institutions. Under the amendment, money was transferred from the HEF to the NRUF. UT Austin and Texas A&M are already considered national research institutions and therefore do not qualify for this fund. Eligibility criteria as well as distribution rules were established in 2011 by the legislature. An institution must be identified as an emerging research university by the Higher Education Coordinating Board and must spend at least $45 million per year in specifically defined types of research. In addition, universities must meet at least four of the following criteria to qualify: (1) maintain an endowment of at least $400 million in the two preceding academic years; (2) produce 200 Ph.D. degrees during the previous two years; (3) have a freshman class of high academic achievement; (4) be designated as a member of the Association of Research Libraries, have a Phi Beta Kappa chapter, or be a member of Phi Kappa Phi; (5) have a certain number of tenured faculty who have demonstrated excellence by winning a Nobel Prize or other prestigious fellowships, or have been elected to one of the National Academies; and (6) have a demonstrable excellence in graduate education. In 2015 the value of the fund was over $630 million.

In 2011 seven universities were designated as emerging research universities, each of which could have access to these funds if certain criteria were met. They were Texas Tech University, the University of Texas at Arlington, the University of Texas at Dallas, the University of Texas at El Paso, the University of Texas at San Antonio, the University of Houston, and the University of North Texas. In 2012, Texas Tech and the

Permanent University Fund (PUF) fund established in 1876 and funded from the proceeds from land owned by the state; monies go to various universities in the University of Texas (UT) and Texas A&M systems

Higher Education Fund (HEF) state higher education fund for universities not having access to PUF monies

National Research University Fund (NRUF) fund established in 2009 to provide funding to universities seeking to achieve national prominence as research institutions

University of Houston were identified by the Coordinating Board as being eligible to receive some of these NRUF monies subject to meeting a state audit. The University of Texas at Dallas also became eligible for NRUF funds. Appropriations from the fund are estimated to total $46.3 million for the 2018–19 biennium.[24]

The Texas Constitution and the Budget

 Outline the constitutional provisions that affect how the state budget is made

A number of constitutional factors affect the way the budget is made in Texas. Probably the biggest constraint on the budgetary process has to do with time limits. As noted in Figure 11.3, the legislature is compelled to write a two-year, or biennial, budget because of the constitutional provision that the legislature may meet in regular session only once every two years. One of the effects of this restricted time frame is to force government agencies to project their budgetary needs well in advance of any clear understanding of the particular problems they may be facing during the biennium. In addition, the legislature can meet for only 140 days in regular session. This seriously limits the amount of time that the legislature can spend analyzing the budget or developing innovative responses to pressing matters of public importance.

Another important factor is that a large portion of the biennial budget is dedicated for special purposes by federal law or by the Texas Constitution or state statute. These dedicated funds include federal monies earmarked for financing health care for the poor (Medicaid), as well as state funds for highways, education, teachers' retirement, and numerous other purposes. The purpose of dedicated funds is not difficult to understand. Supporters of particular programs want to create a stable revenue source for them. But in protecting their own programs, supporters encourage other interests to do likewise, with the result that the legislature loses control of a large portion of the budget.

Finally, a number of specific constitutional provisions constrain the legislature's control of the budget.[25] Two of these—the Pay-as-You-Go Limit and the Spending Limit—limit the appropriations process in very specific ways.

Article 3, Section 49a (Pay-as-You-Go Limit) portion of the Texas Constitution that requires the state to maintain a balanced budget

appropriations authorization by the legislature to a government agency or body to spend up to a particular amount of money

The Pay-as-You-Go Limit **Article 3, Section 49a (Pay-as-You-Go Limit)**, of the Texas Constitution requires the state to maintain a balanced budget. Under this provision, the General Revenue Fund budget is not allowed to exceed the projected available revenue. All bills that get as far as **appropriations** in the legislative process must be sent to the comptroller of public accounts so that the comptroller can certify the bills are within available budget limit projections. One of the most important consequences of the pay-as-you-go limit is to put the comptroller at the heart of the budget process.[26]

FIGURE 11.3

Texas Biennial Budget Cycle

SOURCE: Senate Research Center, *Budget 101: A Guide to the Budget Process in Texas* (January 2011), p. 5.

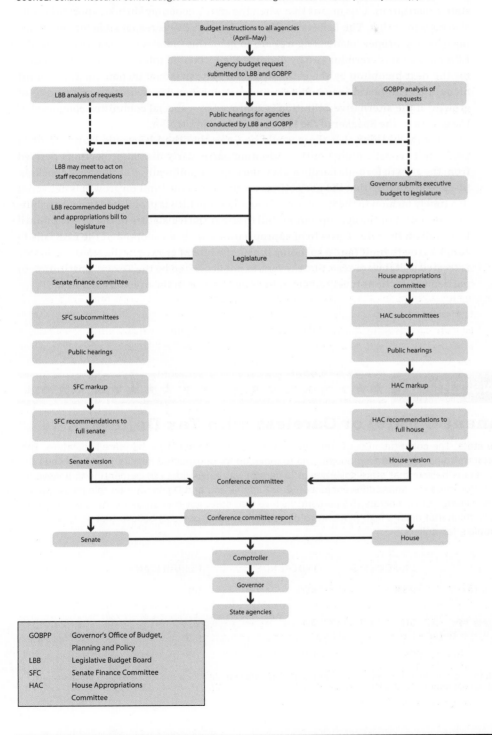

GOBPP	Governor's Office of Budget, Planning and Policy	
LBB	Legislative Budget Board	
SFC	Senate Finance Committee	
HAC	House Appropriations Committee	

The Spending Limit, or the Limit on the Growth of Certain Appropriations Article 8, Section 22, of the Texas Constitution, which was passed in 1978, specifies that the growth in appropriations cannot be more than the growth of the state's economy, not counting dedicated spending as specified in the state constitution. This means that when the state's economy shrinks, appropriations also have to shrink. The Legislative Budget Board (LBB) is responsible for determining what the proper financial figures are to meet this mandate. Under Texas law, the LBB makes this determination by dividing the estimated total state personal income for the next biennium by the estimated total state personal income for the current biennium. The board may adopt "a more comprehensive definition of the rate of growth" if the alternative definition is approved by a special committee composed of the governor, the Speaker of the House, and the comptroller.[27]

One might think that there would be times that the LBB would be reluctant to perform its constitutional duties. Adopting particularly dismal projections derived from the growth formula hardly makes one popular politically. But there are checks in place to make sure that the projections are made and the limit on growth is delivered in a timely fashion to the legislature. Under law, the LBB is prohibited from distributing the budget or the appropriations bill to either the legislature or the governor until this limit on the rate of growth of appropriations has been adopted. If the LBB fails to adopt a growth limit (and a spending limit), the rate of growth in the state's economy is treated as if it were zero. State revenues not dedicated by the Texas Constitution to particular functions must remain at the same level as in the previous biennium.

WHAT DO TEXANS THINK?

Is State Government Careful or Careless with Tax Dollars?

Texas is a fiscally conservative state. The constitution puts limits on how money can be spent by the state legislature. The budgetary process forces legislators to pass a balanced budget and to make up for unexpected deficits in the previous budgetary cycle. Overall, more Texans believe that state government is careful with tax dollars (44 percent) than believe it is mostly careless (37 percent). But there are sharp differences between Republicans and Democrats on this issue. Why do you think that such a high percentage of Democrats (56 percent) believe that state government is mostly careless with people's tax dollars? Why do you think that such a high percentage of Republicans (66 percent) believe that state government is mostly careful with people's tax dollars?

	DEMOCRATS	INDEPENDENTS	REPUBLICANS	ALL TEXANS
Mostly careful with people's tax dollars	23%	40%	66%	44%
Mostly careless with people's tax dollars	56	40	20	37
Don't know	21	21	14	18

SOURCE: UT *Texas Tribune* Poll, Texas Politics Project, texaspolitics.utexas.edu/set/state-government-careful-or-careless-tax-dollars-october-2017#party-id, October 2017. Margin of error is =/- 2.83%.

For 2018–19, these two spending limits worked in the following way (see Table 11.6). The comptroller calculated the available revenue to be $0.1 billion, above appropriations after some technical adjustments. Meanwhile, the LBB calculated that the spending limit was $99.7 billion, $7.7 billion above the biennial appropriations. Both constitutional provisions were thus met.[28]

Along with the Pay-as-You-Go Limit and the Spending Limit, three other constitutional provisions affect the budgeting process.

The Welfare Spending Limit

Article 3, Section 51a, provides that the amount of money the state pays for assistance to or on behalf of needy dependent children and their caretakers shall not exceed 1 percent of the state budget in any biennium. This article sets a constitutional limit on the amount of money that the state may pay out to welfare beneficiaries under the Temporary Assistance for Needy Families program (TANF). As defined by the Texas Human Resources Code, the 2018–19 biennial budget was $216.6 billion, creating a welfare spending limit of $2.2 billion. State funds appropriated for TANF, however, were only $96.5 million, far below the 1 percent limit. State expenditures on Medicaid are not included in this spending limit.[29]

TABLE 11.6

Two Ways to Calculate the Constitutional Spending Limit

Pay-as-You-Go Limit	
2018–19 General Revenue Funds appropriations	$107.2 billion
2018–19 Comptroller projection for revenue	108.6 billion
Remaining spending authority	0.1 billion
Spending Limit	
2016–17 appropriations (not dedicated)	$92.3 billion
LBB adopted growth rate	8%
2018–19 spending authority	99.7 billion
2018–19 appropriations (not dedicated)	92 billion
Remaining spending authority	7.7 billion

Limitation on Debt Payable from the General Revenue Fund The state constitution also limits the amount of debt the state can incur. Under a 1997 amendment to Article 3, Section 49j, the legislature cannot authorize additional debt if the resulting **debt service** is greater than 5 percent of the average General Revenue Fund revenue for the three preceding fiscal years (this excludes dedicated spending). Essentially, Texas state debt payments cannot be more than 5 percent of state revenue.

debt service money spent by the state to pay off debt; includes interest and principal payments

One of the consequences of this constitutional debt limit is that compared with other states (as well as with the federal government), the Texas debt burden is relatively low. A 2015 Tax Foundation study calculated that Texas's per capita debt burden was $1,509, as contrasted with $6,935 in New York, $4,997 in Illinois, and $4,944 in California. Texas's per capita state debt was ranked 45th out of the 50 states.[30]

Budget-Execution Authority Under a constitutional amendment passed in 1985 (now Article 16, Section 69), the legislature was empowered to establish rules for the expenditure of funds by state agencies. Today the rules provide that between legislative sessions, the governor or the LBB may propose (1) that an agency stop spending money appropriated to it in the budget, (2) that money be transferred from one agency to another, or (3) that the purpose for an appropriation to a particular agency be changed. If the governor proposes the changes, the LBB must approve or amend the proposal. If the LBB proposes the changes, the governor must approve or amend the proposal.

The Budgetary Process

 Identify the steps, players, and political tensions in making the state budget

In theory, Texas has a "dual-budget" system. This means that responsibility for preparing an initial draft of the budget is shared by the governor through the Governor's Office of Budget, Planning, and Policy (GOBPP) and the legislature through the LBB. In practice, the budget is primarily the responsibility of the legislature.

The GOBPP is responsible for advising the governor, the chief planning officer of the state, regarding fiscal matters. It prepares the governor's budget recommendations for the legislature, monitors state appropriations and operations, provides analysis on fiscal and economic matters, coordinates federal programs in the state, and assists in the operations of various regional and state planning councils.

Before 1949 there was little coordination in public budgeting. Financial procedures varied, and state agencies were funded by individual appropriations. In 1949 a law was enacted to establish the 10-member LBB, whose primary job would be to recommend appropriations for all agencies of state government. The board is chaired by the lieutenant governor. The vice chair is the Speaker of the House. Other members include the chairs of the House Appropriations Committee, the House Committee on Ways and Means, the Senate Finance Committee, and the Senate State Affairs Committee. Two additional members from the Senate and the House are chosen by the lieutenant governor and the Speaker, respectively.

The LBB appoints a budget director, who brings together budgeting requests from the various state agencies and prepares appropriations bills for them. The LBB is also responsible for evaluating agency programs and developing estimates of the probable costs of implementing legislation introduced in a legislative session. The LBB's draft budget, not the governor's, is the basis for final legislation. Table 11.7 summarizes the duties of key players in the budgetary process.

TABLE 11.7

Key Players in the Budgetary Process

The Legislative Budget Board (LBB)

1. adopts a constitutional spending limit

2. prepares a general appropriations bill

3. prepares agency performance reports

4. guides, reviews, and finalizes agency strategic plans

5. prepares fiscal notes regarding costs and impacts of proposed legislation

6. engages in "budget execution actions" in conjunction with the governor by transferring money from one assigned purpose to another purpose or to another agency

The governor and the Governor's Office of Budget, Planning, and Policy (GOBPP)

1. develop a strategic plan for the state

2. help to develop agency Legislative Appropriation Requests (LARs)

3. hold LAR hearings, often in conjunction with the legislature

4. deliver a governor's appropriations budget and a general appropriations bill at the beginning of the legislative session

5. exercise a line-item veto after an appropriations bill is passed by the legislature

6. engage in "budget execution actions" in conjunction with the LBB by transferring money from one assigned purpose to another purpose or to another agency

The comptroller of public accounts

1. submits a statement regarding the estimated anticipated revenues for the coming biennium

2. certifies that an appropriations bill is in balance with projected state revenues

3. collects state taxes

4. tracks 600+ separate revenue and spending funds and makes sure that agencies stay within their budgets

Estimation and Planning

Preparing and implementing a budget are complex matters. The budgetary process involves two stages. In the first stage, the LBB develops a draft budget based on requests supplied by state agencies. This draft budget follows a series of steps. First, each agency develops a strategic plan, which includes (1) a mission statement, (2) a statement about the goals of the agency, (3) a discussion of the population served by the agency, (4) an explanation of the means that will be used to achieve the goals, and (5) an identification of the measures to be used to assess the agency's success in meeting these goals. This information provides the basis for LBB funding recommendations for each agency. In the spring or early summer prior to the legislative session, the LBB sends out detailed Legislative Appropriation Request (LAR) instructions to the agencies. The LBB and the GOBPP then hold hearings with each agency where the agency's strategic plan and LAR are discussed. LARs become the starting point for the appropriations bill that is prepared by the LBB. *Legislative Budget Estimates* is a publication of the LBB that contains information on the proposed appropriations bill, including expenditures for previous bienniums and proposed expenditures for the next biennium.[31]

While the draft budgets are being prepared, the comptroller's office prepares the Biennial Revenue Estimate (BRE), a detailed forecast of the total revenue that the state is expected to take in over the next biennium. The Texas Constitution requires that the BRE contain "an itemized estimate of the anticipated revenue . . . to be credited during the succeeding biennium." The BRE includes other information to assist legislators in the budget process, including (1) statements about the anticipated revenue from different sources, (2) an analysis of the economic outlook facing Texas and the nation, and (3) a detailed accounting of the funds in the state treasury. Through this forecast, the comptroller effectively sets a ceiling on what the state legislature may spend. Although the legislature can override the comptroller's estimates with a four-fifths vote of each house, this has never happened. The BRE is updated by the comptroller when economic conditions change significantly or special sessions of the legislature are called.

The difficulty of making accurate projections about tax revenue over the next biennium has been a concern in recent years. A study conducted by the Comptroller's Office in 2015 highlighted how frequently actual tax revenues undershot or overshot its projections. Interestingly, the study found that over the past 40 years overestimations of tax revenue were a result of an unexpected recession or a "precipitous" decline in energy prices. Underestimations were associated with soaring energy prices, the implementation of new technologies in the oil and gas industry (such as fracking), and boom periods in the economy that led to higher employment rates and an expansion of the housing market. One thing was clear from the study: making accurate predictions about tax collections over a two-year period is difficult, if not impossible.[32]

The Legislative Process

The second stage of the budget process involves the legislative process. By the seventh day of each regular session, appropriations bills are submitted by the LBB to the House Appropriations Committee and the Senate Finance Committee. Tradition-

The Legislative Budgeting Board is a key player in the budgeting process in Texas. Here, the Texas House appropriations committee hears from Ursula Parks, Director of the LBB.

ally, the bills are introduced to these committees by their respective chairs, although any member may do so. The bills then work their way through the committee system of each house separately and are subject to hearings, debates, and revisions. This process of drafting the bill is referred to as a "markup." Final versions of the budget are prepared by the House Appropriations Committee and the Senate Finance Committee. Each house then votes on the bill. Differences between the two versions of the bill are reconciled in a conference committee.

The conference committee is composed of representatives from the Senate and the House. Senate members are selected by the lieutenant governor or the president pro tempore of the Senate. The senator sponsoring the bill, traditionally the chair of the Senate Finance Committee, appoints the chair of the Senate conferees. At least two members from the Senate Finance Committee must sit on the conference committee. The Speaker of the House appoints all conferees from the House as well as the chair of the House conferees. Traditionally, Senate and House representatives alternate each session in chairing the conference committee.

Specific rules govern how disagreements between the Senate and House versions of the appropriations bills are to be handled.[33]

- Items that appear in both versions of the bill must be included in the final conference committee report.
- Items that appear in both versions of the bill with identical amounts allocated to them may not be changed by the committee.
- Items that appear in both versions of the bill with differing amounts allocated to them cannot be eliminated. The committee has the discretion to fund these items at a level not larger than the larger allocation or smaller than the smaller allocation.
- Items that appear in one version of the bill but not the other can be included or eliminated from the final bill subject to the discretion of the committee.

However, no more money may be allocated to that item than is found in the original version of the bill.

- Items found in neither version of the bill may not be included in the final conference report. However, the conference committee has the discretion to propose the appropriation of money for bills that already have been passed by the legislature.

While constraining the discretionary authority of the committee to a degree, these rules still leave considerable room for political maneuvering. Membership on this important committee is a highly prized commodity. Once the bill passes the conference committee, it is returned to both houses for final passage.

Under Article 3, Section 49a, of the Texas Constitution, the comptroller has the formal authority to "certify" the budget. This means that the comptroller confirms that the comptroller's office has analyzed the budget and concluded that it is within the current revenue estimates. For all intents and purposes, the budget is being declared balanced. If the general appropriations bill is not certified by the comptroller, it is returned to the house in which it originated. The legislature normally must then either decrease expenditures or raise revenues to make up the difference. According to provisions set out in Article 3, Section 49a, under conditions of "imperative public necessity" the legislature may with a four-fifths vote in each house decide to spend in excess of anticipated revenue.

After certification, the budget moves on to the governor, who can sign, not sign, or veto the entire bill or exercise the line-item veto. With the line-item veto, in particular, the governor has the power to unravel some of the compromises that legislators may have forged to get the bill through the committee system. The line-item veto also potentially gives the governor enormous power to limit expenditures in certain targeted areas. Of course, line-item vetoes exercised too vigorously in one session can come back to haunt the governor's legislative agenda in the next session.

The appropriations bill takes effect on September 1 in odd-numbered years. All agencies are bound by it. Monitoring agency compliance with the budget is the job of the LBB and the **state auditor's office**. The governor and the LBB have the authority to execute the budget, which includes the power to shift funds between agency programs or between agencies if necessary when the legislature is not in session. This power to execute the budget is an important one. It has been a tool used by the governor and the LBB to cope with unanticipated shortfalls in the budget by ordering state agencies to cut their expenditures in the middle of a biennium.

As noted in Chapter 8, the governor is also able to move funds from one account to another without permission of the LBB if he or she declares an emergency. Such a situation has only occurred once—in the summer of 2014—when Governor Perry declared an emergency and transferred funds to pay for the deployment of National Guard troops along the border with Mexico to cope with illegal immigration into Texas.

The Challenge of Budgeting in Texas

Unlike the federal government, the Texas state government cannot approve a budget deficit and must pass a balanced budget every two years. The budgetary process is a complicated process full of uncertainty. Projecting expenditures in programs such as Med-

state auditor's office develops independent audits of state agencies, including institutions of higher education. These audits are used to evaluate agencies icaid, public education, and higher education is difficult. Predicting future tax revenues is even more problematic. An unexpected recession or bust in oil prices can drive revenues down significantly, throwing the projected state budget into a deficit that must be resolved before it can be passed. And the reverse can be true: an unexpected economic boom or surge in oil prices can drive up revenues unexpectedly, creating an unexpected surplus. Not surprisingly, the specifics of the politics surrounding budget surpluses in Texas in the twenty-first century can be quite different from those involving deficits. Comparing the situations facing the legislature in 2015 when there was a projected surplus with 2017 when there was a projected deficit is useful.

Confronting a Budget Surplus   As noted in the "You Decide" box on p. 394, the comptroller presented the 2015 state legislature with a revenue estimate that far exceeded expected expenditures. A budget surplus was brought on by the comptroller having underestimated revenues flowing into state coffers for the 2014–15 biennium by $11.3 billion. This was the worst estimate in 40 years of budgeting.[34] Special interest groups and think tanks debated the costs and benefits of managing the surplus either by cutting taxes or by creating new programs or expanding old ones. But in the Republican-dominated state legislature there was never any doubt of the course of action to be pursued. Taxes were going to be cut. The only real issues were what taxes to cut and by how much.

The budgetary surplus also made possible some new programs. During the regular session, the legislature established small programs related to education, including a High-Quality Prekindergarten Grant Program for public and charter schools. The largest new initiative centered on a constitutional amendment to address transportation needs by transferring state sales tax and motor vehicle sales tax revenues from the General Revenue Fund to the State Highway Fund. This amendment was approved by the voters in November 2017 and began adding money to the State Highway Fund in 2018.[35]

Confronting a Budget Deficit   The state legislature faced a very different budget scenario in 2017 when an ever-widening deficit was projected. Part of the problem lay in the legislature's responses to the surpluses in the 2015 session just discussed. The oil and gas fracking boom had led to a massive tax infusion into the state coffers. But this began to slow down in 2016 as prices dropped and production fell. Less severance tax revenue than had been originally projected was coming into the state. In addition, the rededicated sales tax revenues to the newly created transportation fund removed an estimated $5 billion from the General Revenue Fund. In January 2017, Comptroller Glen Hegar estimated that the biennial revenue would be $3 billion less than the previous session. Creative solutions had to be found to address both the revenue and the expenditure sides of the budget.

After considerable controversy as to how to raise revenues, the House and Senate reached a compromise: get $1.8 billion in one-time revenue by delaying the sales tax transfer, and withdraw $989 million from the Rainy Day Fund, but only for capital and nonrecurring items. An additional $668 million became available through another bookkeeping trick: Comptroller Hegar allowed a number of dedicated accounts with the general revenue to be available for certifications through a funds consolidation bill. Hegar also made available another $500 million for spending certification by speeding up the sales of state-owned financial assets.

What to Do with a Budget Surplus?

TEXAS STATE government must pass a balanced budget every two years. Sometimes, legislators confront a budgetary deficit when projected expenditures exceed projected revenues. At other times, they face a budgetary surplus when projected revenues exceed projected expenditures. Debating what to do when facing a budgetary surplus tells us much about the choices politicians and special interests face in the politics of the budget.

In the 2015 legislative session, state lawmakers faced a budget surplus. Previous comptroller Susan Combs had underestimated the revenues flowing into state coffers for the 2014–15 biennium by $11.3 billion, the worst estimate in 40 years of budgeting.[a] The budgetary windfall led to a lively debate about what to do with the surplus funds. On the one hand, some policy makers, such as Chuck DeVore of the Texas Public Policy Foundation, a conservative think tank in the state, argued that the surplus meant that Texas taxpayers had overpaid the state and should receive refunds.

On the other hand, Dick Lavine and Eva DeLuna Castro of the Center for Public Policy Priorities, a progressive think tank in Austin, argued that cuts to education and health care from the last session should be restored so that the state could better prepare for an uncertain economic future.

DeVore countered that education money is spent not on the classroom but on bureaucratic overhead, and he pointed to the fact that the student-teacher ratio in Texas is better than the national average. He also contended that as the legislature spends more on new programs, a sense of entitlement would develop, making it difficult to make cuts later during times of economic difficulty. Lavine and Castro, in turn, responded that Texas was simply not spending enough in real dollars, given the state's rapid growth. With new residents on highways, in classrooms, and in hospitals, the state would need to maintain these public goods for future generations. Spending the same amount of money as when the state's population was smaller, they argued, would not lead to a prosperous state.

After considerable wrangling over the best level of funding for existing programs, the legislature passed a two-year budget that represented a 3.6 percent increase from the previous budget. Funding increased for education and border security. The final budget left a surplus of $6.4 billion and did not touch the estimated $11 billion in the Rainy Day Fund. Most importantly for conservative Republicans, property and franchise taxes were cut by $3.8 billion.[b]

COMMUNICATING EFFECTIVELY: YOUR VOICE

- How should policy makers deal with a projected budgetary surplus? Should taxes be cut or spending increased? If the latter, where should it be increased first?

- Suppose your state representative thought that taxes should be reduced but you think spending for public education should be increased. What argument would you make to try to bring your representative around on the issue?

On the expenditure side, $1.3 billion in cuts were put into place in the 2018–19 budget compared to the 2016–17 budget. Public education was cut by $600 million, health and human services by $100 million, and public safety by $200 million. Additional miscellaneous programs were cut to the tune of $600 million. Higher education received a paltry increase of $200 million across the state, and state health insurance was increased by $400 million. Cuts were particularly controversial in public education, where maintaining current levels of funding would have cost an additional $4 billion in state expenditures. Significantly, the final state Medicaid appropriation did not fund for medical inflation or an increased demand for Medicaid services. And more ominously, caseload growth was funded only through the first year of the biennium. A supplemental appropriation of up to $2 billion could be needed to fund Medicaid in 2019.

Essentially, legislators had met the formal challenges of the deficit—passing a balanced budget certified by the comptroller—but only by pushing some financial decisions into the future, where they would still need to be confronted. The Texas Taxpayers and Research Association calculated there was a potential budgetary shortfall for the next biennium of up to $7.9 billion. The $2 billion Medicaid shortfall could be addressed by the Trump administration's reworking (or elimination) of Obamacare. But that still left the structural gap brought on by the bookkeeping tricks and the use of the Rainy Day Fund to balance the budget during the 2017 session. There will also be additional costs from Hurricane Harvey. Clearly more revenue was needed from somewhere. But where?

Lurking in the background in the debate over the deficit in 2017 was the belief that buying time might be a good thing for responsible public finance. After all, a return to $80 a barrel oil prices would lead to a surge in oil production that, in turn, would fill the state's coffers with oil severance taxes. For tax weary Republican Party leaders or their supporters in the state, raising revenues through increased oil and natural gas production was not as controversial as raising sales taxes or property taxes on individuals.[36]

The Budget Process Today

The politics of budgetary surpluses and deficits in Texas today are contentious but predictable. First, as long as conservative Republicans are in power, cutting taxes will always be high on the agenda as will minimizing tax increases. Expanding social welfare or educational programs will not likely take priority even during times of surplus, and cuts are always high on the agenda during deficit times. Moreover, those programs that are expanded or added, such as transportation, will likely address the needs of the business community or the economy as a whole. Second, not all tax cuts or tax increases are the same. Different interests are served by different tax cuts or increases. Sales tax cuts create different winners and losers than do franchise tax cuts. Property tax cuts can benefit the taxpayer but adversely affect the schools that rely on those taxes. Hence, while property tax cuts may seem to have universal support they may nevertheless not be popular in expanding suburban communities trying to raise money to build new schools to educate a rapidly expanding population. Third, grappling with a budgetary surplus or deficit is complicated not only because of the politics surrounding the budgetary process but also because of the difficulty in projecting a budget both on the revenue side and the expenditure side two years into the future. Individuals have trouble estimating their income and spending two years into the future. Given the complexity of the budgetary process, why should the legislature be expected to do much better? Passing a meaningful balanced budget is hard work, involving many compromises and sacrifices. It is the hardest and most important work that the legislature engages in during every regular session.

Public Finance and the Future of Texas

PUBLIC FINANCE in Texas will continue to be a troubling issue for political leaders in Texas in the future. Uncertainty remains about the future course of the national and international economies. Texas's economy is tied inextricably to the booms and busts of the U.S. economy as well as the world economy. Moreover, the revenue mechanisms that support policy initiatives in Texas are sensitive and can move down quickly when the national and international economies falter. A declining economy can cut back on consumer spending, which affects the sales tax revenue. Falling housing prices can adversely affect property tax revenue. Falling prices for oil and natural gas can cut into severance tax revenues and the revenue flowing into the Rainy Day Fund. But the reverse is also true: an expanding international and domestic economy and rising wages can lead to steady increases in sales tax revenue. Higher oil and natural gas prices can drive up severance tax income on oil and natural gas production, leading to additional growth in the Rainy Day Fund. Such are the rules that govern public finance in Texas in the early twenty-first century.

State budgetary policy ultimately depends on the successful implementation of a national economic policy that works. As was noted in Chapter 1, Texas is no longer, and maybe never was, an island apart from national and international economic trends. In 2018 most leaders in the Texas Republican Party are confident of the direction of the national economy under the Trump administration. Tea Party Republicans see Texas as the cutting edge of the national economy. Indeed, they view the budgetary and policy initiatives of the state to be enlightened, freed from the tax more and spend more policies of the Democratic Party. These ideological commitments will likely dominate public finance in Texas well into the next ten years.

Four factors will continue to define public finance in Texas over the next biennium. First, economic conditions look favorable in the short run, assuring the state a healthy flow of revenues from its complex structure of state and local taxes. Second, there will be increased demands from the federal government for paying for expanded federal initiatives in health care (see Chapter 12). Third, increased population will lead to increased demands on state agencies for services ranging from health care to roads, to water, and to public education. All other things being equal, a larger population demands more from government, and that costs money. Fourth, there is a growing antigovernment feeling among portions of the population in Texas that state government is too big already. For Tea Partyers and other conservative Republicans, "No new taxes" is a successful mantra for winning office. Whether it will be a successful one for legislating and leading is another question. Navigating a passage between the rock of intensifying demands for expanded services and the hard place of "No new taxes" may be the most difficult problem legislators face in the foreseeable future.

STUDY GUIDE

Use ⚙ INQUIZITIVE to help you study and master this material.

What Is the Budget?

- **Explain the purpose of the state budget and what is typically included (pp. 369–71)**

Texas is required to operate within a balanced budget. The budget can be considered in light of five revenue streams: the General Revenue Funds, the General Revenue–Dedicated Funds, Federal Funds, Other Funds, and All Funds.

Key Terms
General Revenue Funds (p. 369)
General Revenue–Dedicated Funds (p. 369)
Federal Funds (p. 369)
Other Funds (p. 369)
All Funds (p. 369)

Practice Quiz
1. The Texas Constitution requires that the Texas budget be
   a) balanced.
   b) approved by the governor's cabinet.
   c) funded only from sales taxes.
   d) approved by the governor, the legislature, and the state treasurer.
   e) funded only from federal grants.

2. Federal expenditures primarily affect the state budget in which two areas?
   a) energy and law enforcement
   b) health and human services and education
   c) business development and highways
   d) interstate highways and airports
   e) Medicare and transportation

Spending and Revenue in Texas

- **Describe the general pattern of state spending in Texas and where state revenue comes from (pp. 371–80)**

Texas spends less than the national average in a variety of policy areas, including education and highway spending. Although Texas does not have an income tax, it has one of the highest sales taxes in the nation. However, the per capita revenue from those sales taxes is among the lowest in the nation. Property taxes in Texas are among the highest in the nation. Among other important state taxes are the natural gas production tax and the oil production and regulation tax. Although a controversial issue in the past, a state income tax has little support either in the legislature or in the population as a whole. Texas also has on average fewer state employees per capita than other states.

Key Terms
regressive tax (p. 376)
progressive tax (p. 376)
matching funds (p. 378)

Practice Quiz
3. Texas has the reputation for being
   a) a low-service, low-tax state.
   b) a high-service, high-tax state.
   c) a low-service, high-tax state.
   d) a high-service, low-tax state.
   e) an average-service, average-tax state.

4. One major revenue source for Texas is the sales tax, which is
   a) 8.25 percent for state government and 2.25 percent for local government.

b) 4.25 percent for state government and 2 percent for local government.

c) 6.25 percent for state government and 2 percent for local government.

d) 5 percent for state government and 1.25 percent for local government.

e) none of the above

5. A Texas personal income tax
   a) used to exist but was repealed because of new taxes on oil production.

b) would have to be approved by the voters, and the revenues from it would have to support public education.

c) would have to be passed through a constitutional amendment.

d) could only be imposed on incomes greater than $250,000 per year.

e) would be unlikely to raise much revenue.

State Funds

- **Describe how the money in the budget is organized into specific funds (pp. 380–84)**

Money flows into and out of a variety of over 400 different funds controlled by the state. Among the most important are the General Revenue Fund, the Permanent School Fund, the State Highway Fund, and the Economic Stabilization Fund (the Rainy Day Fund). The existence of these funds makes budgeting a complicated process.

Key Terms
Permanent School Fund (PSF) (p. 381)
Available School Fund (ASF) (p. 381)
State Highway Fund (p. 381)
Economic Stabilization Fund (ESF) (p. 381)
Permanent University Fund (PUF) (p. 383)
Higher Education Fund (HEF) (p. 383)
National Research University Fund (NRUF) (p. 383)

Practice Quiz
6. The Rainy Day Fund
   a) provides funds for flood victims.
   b) was designed to provide funding for the state during times of financial distress.
   c) contains only a small amount of state funds.
   d) is used to promote oil and gas development.
   e) can only be spent by the Texas comptroller.

7. The National Research University Fund
   a) pays for university-level research at all state universities.
   b) provides the funding for the University of Texas at Austin.
   c) funds Texas universities seeking national prominence as research institutions.
   d) only provides funds to universities with Nobel Prize winners.
   e) will not provide funds if more than 20 percent of students fail to graduate in four years.

The Texas Constitution and the Budget

- Outline the constitutional provisions that affect how the state budget is made (pp. 384–88)

There are many constitutional restrictions on the budget, including the requirement of a biennial budget, a pay-as-you-go limit, a welfare spending limit, a limit on the growth of some appropriations, rules on the spending of funds by state agencies, and limitations on debt payable from the General Revenue Fund. These restrictions play important roles in shaping the budget policy-making process.

Key Terms

Article 3, Section 49a (Pay-as-You-Go Limit) (p. 384)
appropriations (p. 384)
debt service (p. 388)

Practice Quiz

8. Which of the following is *not* a constitutional constraint on the budgetary process in Texas?
   a) the annual budget
   b) a welfare spending limit
   c) a pay-as-you-go limit
   d) a limitation on the debt payable from the General Revenue Fund
   e) All are constitutional limits

9. What is meant by "the budget-execution authority"?
   a) the power to execute the laws of the land
   b) the legislature's power to establish rules for the expenditure of funds by state agencies
   c) the governor's power to veto the budget
   d) the LBB's power to create the budget for the judiciary in Texas
   e) none of the above

The Budgetary Process

- Identify the steps, players, and political tensions in making the state budget (pp. 388–96)

In theory, Texas has a dual budget system with budgeting shared by the governor and the legislature. In reality, the budget is the responsibility of the legislature. There are a series of steps that the budget must go through to be passed by the legislature. Among the most important is the requirement that the Texas comptroller certify the budget as being balanced. At the beginning of the budgetary process the legislature can be faced with projected surpluses or projected deficits that call for very different responses. In recent sessions, budgetary politics has been dominated by the Republican Party's desire to lower taxes and, when necessary, cut program spending.

Key Term

state auditor's office (p. 392)

Practice Quiz

10. Who is the chief planning officer of the state of Texas?
    a) the lieutenant governor
    b) the Speaker of the House
    c) the comptroller
    d) the governor
    e) the state treasurer

11. The principal job of the Legislative Budget Board is
    a) to keep track of the expenses of the executive.
    b) to monitor the operations of the House.
    c) to raise taxes.
    d) to recommend appropriations for all agencies of state government.
    e) to conduct audits of state expenditures.

12. A budgetary surplus is best defined as
    a) a budgetary situation wherein the comptroller believes that taxes are too high.
    b) a budgetary situation wherein projected revenues exceed projected expenditures.

c) a budgetary situation wherein projected revenues are less than projected expenditures.

d) a budgetary situation wherein the governor discovers that more money is available for the state to spend than the legislature initially thought.

e) a budgetary situation wherein the federal government provides emergency funds to address a problem in Texas.

13. What is one of the causes of the recent projected deficit that dominated budgetary politics during the 2017 session of the legislature?

a) declining oil prices

b) declining demand for Medicaid services

c) increased sales tax receipts

d) decline in the Rainy Day Fund

e) the comptroller getting rid of accounting tricks to balance the budget

Child Protective Services in Texas plays a major role in ensuring the well-being of many children. However, the program has come under scrutiny in recent years due to underfunding, overburdened caseworkers, and thus poor outcomes for the children under the government's charge. Here, the CPS program director hugs a child before he is adopted by his grandparents.

Public Policy

W **HY PUBLIC POLICY MATTERS** One of the most important responsibilities of the state is protecting those who can't protect themselves. In Texas, this massive task falls to the 13,000 employees of the Texas Department of Family and Protective Services (DFPS). One of the most sensitive programs run by DFPS is Child Protective Services (CPS). CPS's job is to investigate cases of child neglect or abuse and, when necessary, remove a child from parents' custody and place the child in a relative's home or in a foster home. One might think that CPS would be a backwater issue, the province of policy wonks and interested family members. But by the 2017 session of the legislature, CPS had become one of the top concerns of the governor and the legislative leaders.[1] Why and how this happened says much about why public policy matters.

Advocates for children in Texas have long bemoaned the underfunding of CPS. The state employs too few caseworkers to watch over the foster care program, and turnover is too high. In 2004, DFPS calculated that a caseload of 25 clients per worker would theoretically allow caseworkers to have meaningful contact with all children in their charge. In reality, the actual caseload per worker was around 34. The state made disturbingly little effort to look at the workload of caseworkers or evaluate the effects of the high average caseloads or caseworker turnover on the children themselves.

In 2011 a New York–based advocacy group brought a class action suit on behalf of all children in long-term care in Texas. In a 260-page ruling, U.S. District Judge Janis Jack of Corpus Christie found that "excessive caseloads and overburdened caseworkers cause an unreasonable risk of harm" to foster children.[2] The court found that almost 3,000 children considered to be at risk each day were either seen by caseworkers outside of the required 24-hour period following a report of possible abuse, or not seen at all. Things were so bad that the judge concluded the state had violated a "substantive due process right" under the Fourteenth Amendment of the U.S. Constitution that foster children had to be free from "an unreasonable risk of harm caused by the state."[3] The court ordered DFPS to implement reforms that protected children and directed the agency to hire enough caseworkers to ensure that caseloads were manageable.

The court ruling, in addition to the $40 million deficit that CPS faced in 2017, placed CPS reform high on Governor Abbott's legislative agenda for the 2017 session. Lieutenant Governor Patrick and House Speaker Straus called upon DFPS Commissioner Hank Whitman to immediately develop a plan to hire and train more caseworkers. They also called upon the agency to "create a culture of accountability."[4] As a result, four major bills were passed during the regular session that addressed the child protective service crisis.

If one of the goals of this legislation was to get the court out of the business of reforming child welfare, the legislature failed. In January 2018 Judge Jack ruled that CPS would remain under the "watchful eye" of a court-appointed special master. Years of inaction led the judge to argue that Texas officials could not be trusted to act in the best interests of children under the care of the state. Texas, represented by Attorney General Paxton, appealed the ruling on the grounds that unelected judges should not be allowed to assume control of state institutions.[5] A second federal court ordered a temporary stay of Jack's final ruling and asked for more information about the case.[6] By the late spring of 2018 no one was quite sure how the case would be resolved, and it was possible that the legislature would have to return to the issue in the 2019 session. One thing is clear: the state will no longer be allowed to ignore the needs of children in its charge, and changes are coming to the structure and operations of CPS. The responses of the legislature to the court's findings and rulings will redefine the duties and obligations that the state has to some of its most vulnerable members. The failures of Child Protective Services to protect its wards, and the legislative and judicial responses to the CPS crisis, demonstrate all too clearly why public policy matters to Texans in the twenty-first century.

CHAPTER GOALS

- Describe the key steps and concepts in the policy-making process (pp. 405–8)

- Describe the major issues that have shaped education policy in Texas (pp. 408–19)

- Describe the state's role in addressing poverty and how it is affected by national policies (pp. 419–25)

- Explain why Medicaid in particular and health care policy in general have been so controversial in Texas (pp. 426–35)

The Policy-Making Process

Describe the key steps and concepts in the policy-making process

In broadest terms, public policy refers to the outputs of governmental institutions. More narrowly, public policy can be defined as the expressed goals of a governmental body backed by incentives or sanctions.[7] Public policies can be found in laws passed by legislative bodies as well as in the rules, regulations, and orders from properly authorized public agencies. The incentives or sanctions can include a wide range of strategies, from subsidies that reward individuals for acting in a certain way, to admonitions, to monetary or criminal penalties that punish people for engaging in particular actions.

One way that political scientists have approached the study of public policy is by focusing attention upon the different stages of the policy-making process: the political and administrative process through which governmental goals are identified, formulated, articulated into law, and evaluated.[8] Analyzing stages of the policy-making process does not mean giving a step-by-step description or explicit road map of how public policy is made within institutions such as a legislature or a bureaucracy. Public policy is not made in a simple linear way. The real world of policy making is, in fact, much messier; there, stages in the process may overlap or even collapse into one another. Nevertheless, the idea that there are stages of the policy-making process has proven to be a useful analytical framework for understanding the various factors that go into the making of public policy.

Problem Identification The first stage is problem identification. Here, society at large and actors in the political system develop an understanding of how we must think about and address a particular problem. Roger Cobb and Charles Elder refer to this set of ideas as a "systemic agenda" where an issue is "commonly perceived by members of the political community as meriting public attention and as involving matters within the legitimate jurisdiction of existing governmental authority."[9] This systemic agenda is used by citizens and policy makers to understand the nature of public problems and to shape and direct the way policy makers will develop public policy aimed at them. For example, if we view the problem of poverty as fundamentally one of limited income, we might conclude that the best solution is increasing welfare payments to the poor. However, if we consider the problem to be behavior that causes people to be poor, such as unwillingness to work or poor job skills, we might conclude that policies directed toward encouraging work or subsidizing education are better courses of action. In the problem identification stage, our ideology—that is, our ideas, concepts, and visions about the way society works—plays a major role in defining public-policy making.

Policy Formulation Policy formulation is the second stage of the policy-making process. Here, the more general ideas that the public and lawmakers have about social and political problems become clarified, and strategies for dealing with these specifically defined problems are developed. Policy formulation involves the detailed procedures that guide the passage of legislation and the development of administrative rules and regulations. Here, institutional agenda setting takes place. As we noted in our earlier discussion of interest groups, one of the goals of interest groups is to gain access to policy discussions inside legislatures and agencies. Access provides interest groups with the opportunity to help set the institutional agenda in the policy formulation stage. Setting the agenda on what problems will be discussed, how these problems will be understood, and what concrete measures will be taken to address them lies at the heart of all policy formulation.

Implementation The third stage in the policy-making process is implementation. At this stage, the goals of public policy along with the incentives or sanctions to support them are put into effect by a particular government agency. Identifying the appropriate agency to implement a program is crucial at this stage. Similarly, budgetary policy plays a major role in the implementation stage and can determine the success or failure of a particular public policy. A well-formulated public policy can be dashed by poorly executed or poorly funded implementation.

Evaluation The fourth stage of the policy-making process is evaluation. At a certain point all public policies must be evaluated for their effectiveness. In the best of all possible worlds, evaluation procedures would assess the stated goals of a particular policy against the actual outcomes of the implemented policy. Good evaluation would lead to a rethinking of the policy in light of the problem being addressed and the solutions formulated to address it. Similarly, good evaluation could lead to a rethinking of the strategies being used and the resources being committed to implementing the policy. Closing the loop between problem identification and program evaluation is one of the most difficult problems facing policy makers.

Some political scientists identify policy legitimation as another stage in the policy-making process. Legitimation—the establishment and recognition in the political community of the legality and constitutionality of a particular policy initiative—is probably better understood not as a separate stage but as something that takes place throughout the entire policy-making process. Legitimation can include a wide range of activities: open discussions of a problem in the press, committee investigations and oversight investigations, following the appropriate rules for passing a bill in the legislature or making a rule in an administrative agency, and judicial review of the policy. Establishing the legitimacy of a public policy throughout the various stages of the policy-making process is an essential part of any democratic political system.

Rationality in Policy Making

rationality the idea in public-policy making that we have clearly identified goals and that we seek to achieve these goals in an optimal or efficient manner

An often-stated goal of policy makers is to make public policy more rational and more efficient. **Rationality**, in this regard, generally refers to the idea that we have clearly identified the goals that we wish to achieve and have formulated and implemented policies that address these problems in an optimal or efficient manner. Optimality or efficiency refers to the idea that policy should maximize the outputs of government with a minimum commitment of resources. Given this commitment to rationality in policy making, people are often surprised by how irrational and inefficient public policy can seem in a democracy. Part of the problem lies in the fact that the policy-making process is highly complex. Writing reports, holding committee hearings, and passing legislation

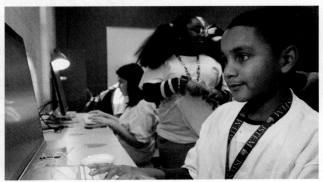

As shown here, education policy involves the four key stages in the policy-making process. Clockwise from top left: A policy issue such as school funding is identified. Politicians, such as former state senator Wendy Davis, who filibustered a bill to lower school funding, create policies to address the issue. Bureaucrats implement policy changes (for example, adding more computers in classrooms). Finally, policies are evaluated and changes are considered. Here, the Texas Education Commissioner Michael Morath visits a middle school classroom in Dallas.

often involve political compromises that muddy the waters of policy making. Vagueness in the problem identification stage along with compromises made among competing parties in the policy formulation stage can work against the development of rational and efficient solutions to problems.

Additional factors tend to work against rationality and efficiency in the making of public policy. The first is the fact that governments tend to work incrementally. Neither legislators nor government agencies begin their work on a particular problem from ground zero every year. Year in and year out, there is a general agreement among policy makers on the nature of a public problem and on how it should be addressed. Unless measures are taken to compel agencies to reassess what they are doing and why, programs, policies, and budgets tend to grow incrementally from one policy cycle to another. And even when such measures are taken, as in the Sunset process (as discussed in Chapter 8), or when major changes are initiated in the fundamental direction of public policy, incrementalism governs the decision-making process.

A second factor is that policy makers and other politically active individuals may not behave strictly rationally or efficiently. The economist Herbert Simon has argued that individual rationality is limited by a number of factors, including the expense of getting information about a problem, the cognitive limitations of the human mind, and the time constraints that all individuals face in making a decision.[10] Policy makers' rationality may be a **bounded rationality**. Rather than seeking to rationally understand everything that is involved in a particular policy problem or optimize every action taken to address this problem, they may simply seek to "satisfice." Essentially, satisficing means to reach

bounded rationality the idea that in policy making decision makers may seek solutions to problems that are satisfactory to them but not necessarily optimal or efficient a decision that is satisfactory rather than optimal to the decision maker. From the perspective of the policy process as a whole, satisficing by many individuals and groups can lead to less-than-rational and less-than-efficient public policy.

To appreciate the intricacies of policy making, we will turn to a discussion of three policy areas shaping political life in Texas: education, welfare, and health care.

Education Policy

 Describe the major issues that have shaped education policy in Texas

Education policy is a complex field. There is no one education "problem" that has been identified to drive education policy, nor is there just one formulated solution to this problem. Education policy in Texas involves a large number of overlapping problems, each of which has spawned a variety of solutions.

Education is big business in Texas. For the 2018–19 biennium, a projected $40.3 billion in state General Revenue monies went to public education. Local property taxes are projected to contribute $59.5 billion in revenue to local school districts. The federal government contributed an estimated $10.4 billion to fund a variety of education-related programs, including Child Nutrition Grants, No Child Left Behind Grants, disabilities funding, and other formula grants.[11]

There are 1,023 regular school districts in Texas, with over 8,096 public schools as of 2018. Almost 5.5 million students were enrolled in public schools in Texas in 2018, second only to California. Enrollments increased by 15.7 percent between 2005 and 2015, the fastest growth rate of the 15 most populous states. The student-teacher ratio of 15.1 students per teacher compares favorably with the national average of 15.9. But the average expenditure of $9,336 per student is far below the national average of $11,984. Texas ranked 36th in per capita student expenditure in 2016–17, a fall from 24th in 1998.[12]

Along with the regular school districts there are over 707 open-enrollment charter school campuses serving 296,323 as of 2016–17. Although funded with public monies, charter schools have been set up as an alternative to traditional public schools, often because the public schools have failed to meet the needs of certain groups of students. Charter schools are in many ways more flexible than public schools, but they must meet the standards set by the state for public schools.[13]

More than half the state's school districts and charter schools—825—had fewer than 1,600 students in 2014. A large number of these were in rural areas. Eighteen districts enrolled over 50,000 students each, and together they accounted for 62 percent of all students in the state. The largest school districts are Houston (215,627), Dallas (158,604), Cypress-Fairbanks in Harris County (113,936), and Northside in Bexar County (105,110).[14] Over 323,373 students graduated from Texas high schools in 2017.[15]

State school districts employ over 342,000 teachers. According to a *Texas Tribune* study, in 2015 salaries ranged from a beginner's salary of $44,540 to $59,787 for teachers with 20+ years' experience. Not surprisingly, there was considerable variation across different school districts. The race and ethnicity of teachers differed considerably

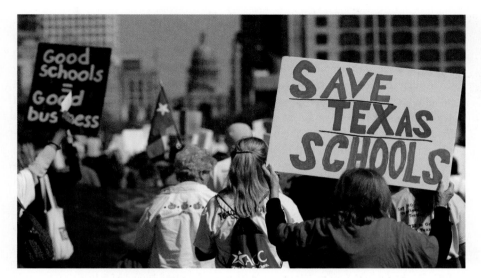

Texas has a large and complicated public school system fraught with nearly constant public-policy battles, including that over the level of funding for public schools.

from those of the student body: 59.8 percent of teachers were white, 26.6 percent were Latino, and 10.1 percent were African American, whereas 28.8 percent of students were white, 52.4 percent were Latino, and 12.6 percent were African American. The districts also employed almost 26,000 administrators and almost 70,000 professional support staff (such as counselors, librarians, and nurses). On top of that, they employed another 235,000 educational aides and auxiliary staff. Today, total staffing in elementary and secondary schools in Texas exceeds 674,000 people.[16]

The challenges facing educational policy in Texas are great, but a few stand out. First, there is the above-noted low level of public spending per pupil. Second, the demographics are not only increasingly minority but also increasingly disadvantaged.[17] Of all students, 18.2 percent had "limited English proficiency," 58.8 percent were considered "economically disadvantaged" (meaning they were poor), and 51.2 percent were considered "at risk" (meaning that given their circumstances, they were more likely to fail academically). Not surprisingly, these demographic characteristics often lead to lower performance on national and state tests. Third, Texas students have high dropout rates,[18] particularly among Latinos and African Americans, which affect state and federal efforts to address the problem of poverty. To understand how policy makers are dealing with these challenges, we must look deeper into the making of educational policy since the founding of the state.

The Roots of Education Policy in Texas

One of the indictments of the Mexican regime contained in the Texas Declaration of Independence was that the government had failed to establish a public system of education. Later, the Constitution of the Republic of Texas required a public system of education, but a bill actually establishing a public-school system did not pass the legislature until 1854. Public education was to be financed with a part of the $10 million given to Texas by the U.S. government to settle outstanding land claims in parts of what are now New Mexico, Colorado, and Oklahoma. Unfortunately, the fund was diverted to a variety of other purposes, including the purchase of railroad stock and the building of prisons. When Democrats returned to power following Reconstruction, an effort was made to protect the fund and commit its use solely to education.[19] The Constitution of 1876 also had provisions to support public education through various state and local taxes.

Through the first half of the twentieth century, public education remained largely a local affair. Schools were funded by local taxes, and decisions such as what to teach and how long the school year would be were made at the local level. Many school systems were chronically short of funds, facing such problems as a shortage of supplies and textbooks, inadequate facilities, and poorly trained teachers. In 1949 the state legislature tried to address some of these problems by passing the **Gilmer-Aikin Laws**, under which school districts were consolidated into 2,900 administrative units, state equalization funding was provided to supplement local taxes, teachers' salaries were raised, and a minimum school year of 175 teaching days was established. In addition, the laws established the Texas Education Agency (TEA), originally known as the State Department of Education, to supervise public education in the state.

The Gilmer-Aikin Laws also established bureaucratic institutions responsible for public education in the state. The elected 21-member State Board of Education became the policy-making body for public education, selecting budgets, establishing regulations for school accreditation, executing contracts for the purchase of textbooks, and investing in the Permanent School Fund. The board also has the power to appoint a commissioner of education, subject to confirmation by the Texas Senate, who serves a four-year term as the chief executive officer for the TEA. The TEA is responsible for setting standards for public schools and for handling federal funds related to public education. For the next 70 years, educational policy in the state would work through the overall institutional framework established by the Gilmer-Aikin Laws.[20]

Since 1949 the State Board of Education has undergone occasional restructuring. It became a 15-member appointed body in 1984, but in 1988 it reverted to an elected body of 15 members serving four-year terms.

Three specific problems have played a major role in Texas educational policy over the last 50 years: desegregation, equity in funding, and the search for educational excellence. Each has its own set of policy formulations, implementation procedures, and evaluative processes.

Desegregation

Few problems have troubled educational policy in Texas, and given rise to such controversial policy formulations or implementations, as much as desegregation.

Segregation of the races was provided for under the Texas Constitution of 1876 and upheld by the U.S. Supreme Court in *Plessy v. Ferguson* (1896) through the now-infamous "separate but equal" doctrine. In Texas, as elsewhere across the South, segregated schools may have been separate, but they were far from equal. In the 1920s and '30s, for example, Texas spent an average of one-third less per student on the education of African American students than on white students.[21]

The U.S. Supreme Court overturned *Plessy v. Ferguson* in the 1954 case *Brown v. Board of Education*, ruling that state-imposed segregation in schools violated the **equal protection clause** of the Fourteenth Amendment. School districts were ordered to desegregate their school systems "with all deliberate speed." In Texas, the San Antonio

Gilmer-Aikin Laws education reform legislation passed in 1949 that supplemented local funding of education with public monies, raised teachers' salaries, mandated a minimum length for the school year, and provided for more state supervision of public education

equal protection clause provision in the Fourteenth Amendment of the U.S. Constitution guaranteeing citizens the "equal protection of the laws"; this clause has been the basis for the civil rights of African Americans, women, and other groups school district became one of the first in the nation to comply with the order, but other districts in the state, such as Houston's, were much slower.

The desegregation of public schools was hampered by political opposition at both the local and state levels. In 1957 the Texas legislature passed laws encouraging school districts to resist federally ordered desegregation, although then-governor Price Daniel, Sr., chose to ignore them.[22] By the late 1960s legally segregated schools were largely a thing of the past. Nevertheless, de facto segregation remains a problem, particularly in urban areas with large minority populations. As in many other urban areas across the country, many middle- and upper-income whites in Texas abandoned urban public school systems for suburban public schools or private schools.

Equity in Funding

In addition to *Brown v. Board of Education*, two later court cases have played a major role in shaping education policy and politics in Texas over the last 50 years: *San Antonio v. Rodríguez* and *Edgewood ISD v. Kirby*. These cases forced policy makers to look at the problems of education in a new light and to formulate new solutions to address these problems.

San Antonio v. Rodríguez *San Antonio v. Rodríguez* was a landmark case involving the constitutionality of using property taxes to fund public schools.[23] Lawyers for eight children in the poor Edgewood independent school district (ISD) in the San Antonio area argued that the system of financing public schools based on local property taxes was unfair. The Edgewood school district had one of the highest property tax rates in the country, but it could raise only $37 per pupil. Meanwhile the neighboring school district of Alamo Heights was able to raise $413 per pupil with a much lower property tax rate. The reason was that the value of the property subject to taxation in Alamo Heights far exceeded that in Edgewood.

In 1971 a federal district court ruled that the Texas school finance system was unconstitutional under the equal protection clause of the Fourteenth Amendment to the U.S. Constitution. However, on appeal to the U.S. Supreme Court, the decision was overturned. In 1973 the Court ruled 5–4 that the clause did not require states such as Texas to subsidize poorer school districts. The question of equity in public school funding would have to be addressed later in terms of Texas's state constitution and in Texas courts.

Edgewood ISD v. Kirby The second landmark case involving the financing of public schools was *Edgewood ISD v. Kirby*. Unlike *Rodríguez*, *Edgewood* considered whether the system of funding public schools through local property taxes fulfilled the Texas State Constitution's provisions on education. Much of the litigation over the next few years would center on Article 7, Section 1, of the 1876 Constitution, which read:

> A general diffusion of knowledge being essential to the preservation of the liberties and rights of the people, it shall be the duty of the Legislature of the State to establish and make suitable provision for the support and maintenance of an efficient system of free public schools.

A key constitutional issue would be exactly what constituted a "general diffusion of knowledge" and an "efficient system of free public schools."

On behalf of the Edgewood ISD, the Mexican American Legal Defense and Education Fund sued William Kirby, the state commissioner of education, in 1984. Initially, only 8 school districts were represented in the case. By the time the case was finally decided, however, 67 other districts had joined the original plaintiffs. The plaintiffs argued that the state's reliance on local property taxes to fund public education discriminated against poor children by denying them equal opportunities in education. One month after the original case was filed, the legislature passed a modest reform measure that increased state aid to poor districts. In 1985, however, the plaintiffs filed an amended lawsuit arguing that the legislature's action was far from satisfactory.

A state district judge ruled in favor of the plaintiffs, a decision that was reversed by the state appeals court. But in 1989, in a 9–0 decision, the Texas Supreme Court held that the funding system was, indeed, in violation of the state constitution. The court held that education was a fundamental right under the Texas Constitution and that the "glaring disparities" between rich and poor schools violated the efficiency clause of the constitution. Although it did not demand "absolute equality" in per pupil spending, the court did require a standard of "substantially equal access to similar revenues per pupil at similar levels of tax effort."[24] It ordered the legislature to implement an equitable system by the 1990–91 school year.

The ruling touched off a political firestorm that swept through Texas politics throughout the 1990s and into the first two decades of the twenty-first century. Over the years, various courts held various funding provisions for public education to be unconstitutional, and the legislature responded with various fixes, one of which was dubbed the "Robin Hood" plan because it transferred funds from rich to poor districts.

The back and forth wrangling over funding public education came to a head in 2013 when state district judge John Dietz ruled that the state had violated the constitution by underfunding schools during the 2011 session,[25] but his ruling was not the last say in the matter. On May 13, 2016, the Texas Supreme Court overruled Judge Dietz's decision and declared the existing funding system to be constitutional. Acknowledging that the system was "Byzantine," "undeniably imperfect," and open to improvement, the all-Republican court held, with no dissents, that it met the minimum constitutional provisions for the "general diffusion of knowledge." Further, the court stated that its job was not to second-guess the legislature when it came to the best funding of public education.[26]

The importance of this decision to public education policy cannot be stressed enough. The Democratic Supreme Court of the 1980s had focused on the constitutional issues of fairness and "efficiency" in the funding of public schools. In contrast, the Republican court of 2016 focused on whether or not the funding provided a constitutionally acceptable "general diffusion of knowledge" throughout the state. This decision had two immediate effects. First, state courts were taken out of the policy-making process regarding financing public education for the first time since the original *Edgewood* decision in 1989. Second, the debate over equity and financing public education was pushed firmly into the legislative budgetary process.

The New Debate over Funding Public Education

Giving the legislature primary responsibility to resolve funding questions has not been without its challenges. During the 2017 legislative session, legislators cut $600 million from general revenue funding of public education in the face of a looming budget deficit. This cut came on top of the legislature's refusal to spend an additional $4 billion to keep funding levels per student equal to those of the previous biennium. Legislators

Who Attends Public School in Texas?

Two factors have played a role in shaping the demographics of the children attending Texas urban public schools since *Brown v. Board of Education.* First, the state has become more diverse, with a growing Latino presence in large urban areas. Second, while African American attendance has remained steady, white attendance has not. In major cities like Houston and Dallas, whites have moved to suburban school districts, leaving the largest urban school districts to serve minority populations, particularly Latinos. While Texas schools are legally desegregated, there is de facto segregation in public education across much of the state.

Demographics of Selected Houston-Area School Districts, 2014–2015

District	White	African Am.	Latino	Other	Total students
1. Aldine	1.9%	24.5%	71.3%	2.3%	69,533
2. Alief	3.7%	29.6%	52.6%	14.2%	47,174
3. Channelview	8.5%	11.8%	77.2%	1.7%	9,130
4. Cypress–Fairbanks	27.5%	16.5%	44.0%	11.3%	112,640
5. Friendswood	73.8%	2.0%	15.5%	8.4%	6,087
6. Houston	8.3%	24.9%	62.1%	5.7%	214,462
7. Huffman	77.0%	2.0%	19.0%	2.8%	3,381
8. Spring	10.2%	39.9%	43.1%	5.5%	36,781

Percentage of White Students in Houston-Area School Districts

| Under 5% | 5.1–10.0% | 10.1–25.0% | 25.1–50.0% | Above 50.0% |

Public School Enrollment by Race vs. Texas State Population, 2014–2015

Latino

Enrollment
52.0%

State population
38.8%

African American

Enrollment
12.6%

State population
12.5%

White

Enrollment
29.0%

State population
43.0%

Other

Enrollment
6.4%

State population
5.7%

SOURCES: schools.texastribune.org/districts; Texas Education Agency, Enrollment Trends, tea.texas.gov.

QUANTITATIVE REASONING

- Drawing upon the data and the map, develop an argument that, despite *Brown v. Board of Education*, public schools in Texas are still segregated.

- What factors might account for this segregation? Should policy makers be concerned about de facto segregation of public school districts? What should policy makers do?

expected that increases in local property taxes of up to 7 percent per year would bridge the state spending shortfall. This shift from state to local funding of public education reflects a long-term trend. In 2008 the state covered 48.5 percent of the cost of public education. By 2019, state support had dropped to 38 percent.[27]

The shifting burden of public school funding from state general revenues to local property taxes has, in turn, sparked a new controversy: bringing rising property taxes under control. Lieutenant Governor Patrick and Governor Abbott both came out in favor of legislation that would preempt local governments from raising taxes significantly without the support of a referendum vote (see Chapter 10). A special finance commission was set up to hold hearings around the state and deliver a report on the problems of funding public education before the next legislative session in 2019. There appeared to be no easy fixes on the horizon that would provide either an "efficient" public education system or one that promotes the "general diffusion of knowledge throughout the state."[28]

Educational Excellence and Accountability in Texas

Whereas the debate over equity in public education was touched off by litigation, a different set of factors has driven the debate over the quality of education in the state and how best to promote educational excellence. The beginning of the debate in Texas over these issues was actually part of a larger national debate over the state of education in the United States.[29] A 1983 report by the National Commission on Excellence in Education, *A Nation at Risk*, identified a number of crises in the nation's educational system. Test scores were declining, and functional illiteracy was on the rise. Students were simply not equipped with the intellectual skills required in the modern world. If steps were not taken soon to reform education in the United States, the report argued, the nation was at risk of falling behind in the rapidly changing world of international competition.[30]

Educational reform was put on the state agenda in 1983 when the legislature established the Select Committee on Public Education (SCOPE),[31] which was intended both to figure out how to fund pay raises for teachers and evaluate the entire system of public education in the state. One of the most important decisions was Governor White's appointment of the Dallas businessman Ross Perot to chair the committee. To the surprise of many, Perot took an active role in SCOPE, mobilizing the committee in private and in public to take on what he considered abuses in the public education system.

Perot was particularly scornful of athletic programs and what he considered the misplaced priorities of the existing Texas educational system. In the end, SCOPE presented 140 recommendations for reform in its final report on April 19, 1984. Among the most controversial was "No Pass, No Play," under which students who failed to earn a passing grade of 70 could not participate in any extracurricular activities for the next six-week grading period. But "No Pass, No Play" was only the tip of the iceberg. Other proposals created new standards for students' attendance and performance; annual school performance reports and tighter accreditation standards, with schools that did not meet the standards losing state funds; a longer school year—extended from 175 to 180 days; and a professional career ladder for teachers that tied pay raises to performance.[32] In July 1984 many of the reform proposals were put into place in a 266-page education reform bill, along with the necessary accompanying tax increases.

One means of encouraging educational excellence has been to allow students to transfer from low-performing to high-performing schools. Charter schools are promoting competition among the schools and allowing parents more choices.

A second round in the debate over excellence and accountability in the public school system opened during the 1995 legislative session. There was strong business and bipartisan support for reforms that supported increased accountability through testing. But there were some important differences from the so-called Perot reforms in the reform package finally signed by Republican governor George W. Bush. The Perot reforms had generally centralized control over education policy in the state. The Bush reforms, in contrast, gave more discretion to local school districts to achieve the educational goals the state was mandating. Some of them were symbolic. The controversial "No Pass, No Play" rule was relaxed, cutting the period of nonparticipation from six to three weeks and lifting a ban on practicing while on scholastic probation. But other changes were more substantive. Local control of public schools was increased by limiting the power of the TEA. Local voters were empowered to adopt home charters that could free their school districts from many state requirements. The 1995 reforms also enabled students under certain circumstances to transfer from low-performing schools to high-performing schools in their districts, thus promoting competition among schools by holding them accountable for the performance of their students.[33]

One of the most controversial aspects of the reform movement was the development of statewide assessment standards. "Testing," as assessment came to be known, was first instituted in 1986 with the Texas Educational Assessment of Minimal Skills (TEAMS) exams, which sought to certify that students from all districts met certain minimum academic expectations. Students had to pass TEAMS to be eligible to receive a high school diploma. In 1990, TEAMS was replaced with the Texas Assessment of Academic Skills (TAAS) test, which focused on minimum academic skills in reading, writing, and math at grade 10. The implementation of Texas Assessment of Knowledge and Skills (TAKS) in 2003 pushed statewide testing across the state-mandated curriculum, requiring students to pass exit-level tests in English, math, science, and social studies. TAKS, in turn,

Efforts to improve the quality of the Texas public school education and student outcomes have taken different forms over the years. Statewide testing and methods of school evaluation have met with backlash from teachers and legislators alike. However, schools continue to innovate to achieve better outcomes for students, like using special desks (pictured here) to keep children active while learning.

was replaced by the State of Texas Assessments of Academic Readiness (STAAR), 15 end-of-course exams across the curriculum for grades 9 through 12 beginning in 2011. The idea was to have passing standards increased with subsequent administrations of the exam. Schools would be held accountable for their student performances. In the process, it was hoped that public education in Texas would ratchet upward in quality.

Unfortunately, high-minded expectations were dashed as failure rates stayed stubbornly high. In 2012 the TEA reported that passing rates on five of the STAAR end-of-course exams ranged from 87 percent in biology to 55 percent in English writing. Although failing students were allowed to retake the test, fears began to mount about the impact that failure rates would have on retention and graduation rates. In addition, a storm brewed up out of the classrooms as teachers and administrators complained about the growing need to teach to the tests.[34]

Support among business and political elites for an expanded, intensified set of tests to reform public education collapsed during the 2013 legislative session. As we discussed in the introduction to Chapter 6, new groups with different interests emerged to challenge the consensus around accountability and testing that had driven educational reform policy for 25 years. Under House Bill 5, the state legislature cut the number of required end-of-course tests from 15 to 5. The idea of testing to promote academic excellence was not abandoned completely, but it no longer held center stage for reformers. As state senator Dan Patrick, the chair of the Senate Public Education Committee, noted, "By the elimination of 15 [tests] to 5 . . . that could save 40 or more days of testing, give teachers more time to teach, be innovative and creative."[35]

In 2015 the state legislature moved toward an accountability system that would evaluate schools on an A–F scale, replacing the old pass/fail system. Many educators rejected the scale, arguing that it relied too much on the standardized tests that were still being given, rather than how schools were improving. In 2017 the legislature tried again and finally passed a compromise bill on the last day of the session that proposed to evaluate schools on three dimensions: student achievement, student progress, and a "closing the gaps" measure. Elementary and middle schools would focus on the results of standardized state exams while high schools would look at graduation rates and the rates of students taking advanced courses. No one was completely satisfied with the final results, and many interest groups were upset that they were not able to weigh in on the final version of the compromise bill. Most interested parties expected that the issue of accountability and testing would come up again in the next legislative session.[36]

Education Policy in a New Era

One might have hoped that the educational reforms of the past 30 years would have ushered in an era of rising educational attainment in Texas in the twenty-first century. Such has hardly been the case. New problems identified by policy makers in recent years have led to new initiatives to overhaul education in the state. Despite the efforts of policy makers, teachers' salaries and overall state and local spending on public education have remained low compared with those in other states, as have graduation rates. In 2017 the average SAT scores in Texas were 513 in reading and 507 in math, compared with a national average of 533 in reading and 527 in math.[37] Although the dropout rate in grades 7 through 12 has been declining since the 1990s, it has remained high among minorities.

For a few years at the turn of the century, scores on standardized tests such as the TAAS test improved across the state, leading many to think that developing new assessment tests would succeed in holding teachers and schools more accountable. But with the implementation of the more rigorous STAAR assessments, overall student performance stayed flat or fell on various tests. More disturbingly, there appeared to be a growing "achievement gap" as minorities and at-risk students failed at higher rates than whites in consecutive iterations of the tests.[38]

Vouchers and Charter Schools The perceived failure of reform efforts based on testing and accountability led some to advocate new ideas in public education. One new idea—actually an old idea from the early 1960s—being offered up by conservatives, particularly in the Tea Party wing of the Republican Party, is vouchers. The basic idea of vouchers is simple: increase competition in the school system by letting funding follow the students. If a public school doesn't work, let parents and students opt out of it and take their funding with them.[39] Among the recurring criticisms of voucher-based reform is that middle- and upper-middle-income students will leave poorer students behind in poorly funded public schools.

An alternative to vouchers has been available to some in Texas through open-enrollment charter schools. Like vouchers, the idea of charter schools is to make more options available to parents and students, particularly in places where schools are underperforming. As part of a larger 1995 reform package, the legislature authorized the establishment of charter schools that would have increased flexibility to deliver education to student populations with special needs. Working under their own charters and granted the freedom to manage their own schools, charter schools operate under the TEA and receive their own accountability ranking based on test scores. While they receive state monies, as of 2019 they do not receive local tax revenue or, in most cases, funding for facilities. Charter schools are able to receive privately raised funds.

The criticisms of charter schools resemble, in some ways, the criticisms of vouchers. Opponents fear that charter schools will drain money from public schools. While serving the needs of their specially identified student bodies, some suggest that they will distract attention away from the needs of other, possibly more needy groups. In addition, there is some concern that charter schools will not be able to meet the challenges of educating youth any better than traditional public schools. In 2016 some larger public school districts began to challenge the wisdom of diverting public monies to charter schools. For example, Michael Hinojosa, superintendent of the Dallas

SOCIAL RESPONSIBILITY: GET INVOLVED

- Do you think that Texas should increase investment in charter schools, provide increased funding for vouchers that can be used for private schools, or increase funding for traditional public schools? Why?

- Think about your high school experience. What was good about it? What could have been better? Draft an email to your state representative explaining how you would like to see your high school improved. If you are arguing for spending more money on teachers, sports, the arts, or other programs, where would you suggest policy makers save money to compensate?

Independent School District (DISD), charged that the DISD had acted "fat, dumb, and happy" as it watched students move to Dallas-area charter schools. In 2016, DISD enrollment had dropped by 2,000 students, costing the DISD over $10 million in state funding. Significantly, about half of those students were kindergarteners attending charter schools. In Hinojosa's mind, the DISD had to respond to the challenges posed by an aggressive charter school movement.[40]

WHAT DO TEXANS THINK? ★

Does the state spend too much, too little, or about right on primary and secondary education in Texas?

How much state money should be spent on elementary and secondary education? How are educational spending priorities to be balanced against other budgetary priorities such as health care or higher education? When addressing these questions, legislators often look to public opinion for guidance. As the following table shows, there is a partisan dimension to preferences on funding public education. Republicans think differently from Democrats when it comes to evaluating whether the state spends too much, too little, or the right amount on primary and secondary schools. Given this data, do you think the legislature will spend more on education in the future?

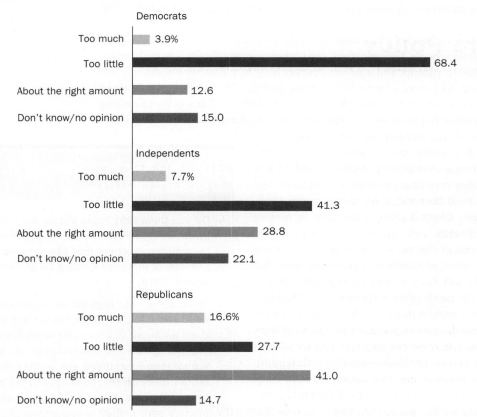

SOURCE: The University of Texas/*Texas Tribune* Poll, The Texas Project at the University of Texas at Austin, June 13, 2017, p. 427.

Increased Funding A third alternative to current education policy is rather simple: spend more money, a lot more money. Here, the idea is that Texas schools fail because they are woefully underfunded. Salaries of teachers are too low, and state regulations on the curriculum and classroom are too great. Get the best teachers in the classroom, some argue, and the problem of public education will be able to right itself. Vouchers and charter schools are seen as threats to this alternative.

New interest groups have emerged over the last two sessions of the Texas legislature to champion approaches to educational reform far different from the business-led bipartisan efforts of recent years that championed testing and accountability. Groups such as Texans for Educational Reform, Texans Deserve Great Schools, and Raise Your Hand Texas will change the direction of the debate on education policy in the future.[41]

Interestingly, the public appears to be in favor of increased expenditures going to public education, but it splits along partisan lines. A poll conducted by the University of Texas in 2014 found that 74 percent of Texans believed that increasing pay to teachers would be an effective way of improving public education in Texas, including 87 percent of Democrats and 65 percent of Republicans. Even 52 percent of self-identified Tea Partiers agreed. But when respondents were asked if increasing overall funding would be effective, a different story emerged. Eighty-nine percent of Democrats agreed that increased overall funding would improve public education, but only 51 percent of Republicans did. One of the problems facing policy makers in the future will be formulating reform proposals amid a divided electorate.[42]

Welfare Policy

Describe the state's role in addressing poverty and how it is affected by national policies

Another long-term policy issue in Texas has been how to provide for the basic needs of poor people in the state. This issue raises fundamental questions about the state's role in helping people in poverty and the extent to which national policies determine the state's response to the needs of the poor. Welfare policy is a clear example of how changes in problem identification and formulation can lead to an overhaul in policy implementation and evaluation.

Poverty in Texas

Poverty has never been an easy topic to talk about in Texas. The idea that some individuals have trouble taking care of themselves or meeting the basic needs of their families seems to fly in the face of Texas's individualistic culture. In light of the booming Texas economy, many policy makers may have hoped that the poverty problem would go away. It hasn't.

Policy makers define "poverty" in very specific terms: it is the condition under which individuals or families do not have the resources to meet their basic needs, including food,

Though poverty in Texas afflicts many different social groups, Latinos currently make up the majority of Texans living below the poverty line. The border counties in Texas are by far the poorest in the state.

shelter, health care, transportation, and clothing. The U.S. Department of Health and Human Services' "poverty index" calculates the consumption requirements of families based on their size and composition. The poverty index is adjusted every year to account for the rate of inflation. Although there is considerable controversy as to whether it adequately measures the minimal needs of a family, the poverty index is the generally accepted standard against which poverty is measured.

In 2016, 15.6 percent of Texans lived below the poverty line. The five counties of more than 10,000 residents with the highest percentage of people living in poverty were along the border: Willacy County (38.8 percent), Starr County (35.4 percent), Cameron County (34.5 percent), Hidalgo County (33.5 percent), and Zapata County (32.6 percent). The counties with the lowest were three in the Dallas–Fort Worth area, Rockwall County (6.8 percent), Collin County (7 percent), and Denton County (8.7 percent); one north of Austin, Williamson County (7.8 percent); and one north of San Antonio, Kendall County (8.3 percent). In addition, in March 2016 a total of 4,065,627 people (approximately 14.7 percent of all residents of Texas) were enrolled in Medicaid, the federally financed, state-operated program providing medical services to low-income people. Poverty remains one of the most intractable problems facing the state.[43]

In 2018 the federal poverty guideline was $12,140 a year for one person and $4,320 a year for each additional person in the family. A study conducted by the Henry J. Kaiser Foundation in 2016 found that over 23 percent of Latinos, 22 percent of African Americans, and 10 percent of whites in Texas are poor. Of those over age 65 in Texas, 11 percent are poor compared with 10 percent in the nation as a whole. Poverty among children under age 18 is much higher in Texas (24 percent) than in the United States as a whole (21 percent).[44]

Texas uses these federal poverty guidelines to determine eligibility for a variety of social programs. For example, a family of three is eligible for reduced-price school meals if the family is at no more than 185 percent of the poverty level. A family of three is eligible for free school meals and food stamps (the Supplemental Nutritional Assistance Program or SNAP) if the family is at no more than 130 percent of the poverty level.

The Texas Health and Human Services Commission (HHS)—which since 2003 has overseen the Department of Family and Protective Services, the Department of Assistive and Rehabilitative Services, the Department of Aging and Disability Services, and the Department of State Health Services—is responsible for coordinating, determining eligibility for, and administering the major welfare and antipoverty programs in Texas (see Table 12.1). These programs include Temporary Assistance to Needy Families (TANF), a welfare program for families with dependent children; Medicaid, a state-federal program providing health coverage to the poor; SNAP; and other programs to address family violence, provide disaster relief, and settle refugees. The appropriated budget for HHS programs in 2016–17 is almost $77.2 billion, 36.9 percent of all state appropriations. HHS agencies employ almost 56,000 state workers at more than 1,000 locations.[45]

Poverty is a complicated policy issue in Texas. There are more than 200 programs administered by HHS that are aimed at different problems related to poverty. We will now focus attention on two of the most important of these initiatives: welfare, in this

TABLE 12.1

Agency Budgets for the 2018–19 Biennium, All Funds	
Health and Human Services Commission	$71.8 billion
Department of Family and Protective Services	$4.1 billion
Department of State Health Services	$1.6 billion
TOTAL	$76.4 billion

SOURCE: Texas Legislative Budget Board, *Fiscal Size-Up: 2018–19 Biennium*, p. 157–9.

section, and health care financing, in the following section. Understanding how these programs evolved over time and the reforms that have been put into place over the past 20 years will shed considerable light on public-policy making in the state.

Welfare in Texas, 1935–1996

The origins of modern welfare policy lie in President Franklin Delano Roosevelt's **New Deal**.[46] Prior to the 1930s welfare was considered a state and local responsibility. The Great Depression overwhelmed many state and local welfare arrangements, however, causing the federal government to expand its role in addressing the needs of the poor and the unemployed. The Social Security Act of 1935 transformed the way in which welfare policy was implemented in the United States. Along with two social insurance programs (Old Age Insurance and Unemployment Insurance), the Social Security Act established a number of state-federal public assistance programs: Aid for Dependent Children (ADC, later **Aid to Families with Dependent Children (AFDC)**, Old Age Assistance (OAA), and Aid for the Blind (AB). States administered and determined the benefit levels for these programs; however, in exchange for federal assistance in funding, the programs had to meet certain minimum federal guidelines.

The Department of Public Welfare was established in Texas in 1939 to run the state's various public assistance programs.[47] Until the early 1960s the basic strategy adopted by welfare-policy makers in Texas was to minimize the cost to the state while maximizing federal dollars. Some programs were expanded during these years. In 1950, ADC became AFDC as mothers were included in the program. Other new social-service programs were added. Much of the initiative for this expansion of welfare came from the federal government. One of the major issues with enlarging welfare coverage in Texas was the constitutional ceiling on welfare spending, which had to be raised repeatedly.[48]

Welfare policy in Texas transformed fundamentally in the 1960s. Federal court decisions between 1968 and 1971 effectively ended a series of state-level policies such as residency requirements and bans on men

New Deal President Franklin Delano Roosevelt's 1930s programs to stimulate the national economy and provide relief to victims of the Great Depression

Aid to Families with Dependent Children (AFDC) a federally and state-financed program for children living with parents or relatives who fell below state standards of need; replaced in 1996 by TANF

The Texas Department of Public Welfare was established in 1939 during the New Deal. This photo shows farmers receiving support from the government at the time.

Medicaid a federal and state program financing medical services to low-income people

Supplemental Security Income (SSI) a national welfare program passed in 1972 that provides assistance to low-income elderly or disabled individuals; replaced the federal-state programs that had offered assistance to the blind, the permanently and totally disabled, and the aged

in the houses of mothers receiving welfare, both of which had been used by states to keep welfare rolls low. In 1965, Congress established **Medicaid**, a state-federal program to finance health care for the poor. President Lyndon Johnson's "War on Poverty" also expanded the number of social service programs available to the poor. Increasingly, it was argued, the solution to alleviating poverty was through expanded federal control over welfare programs.

In 1965 the Texas Department of Public Welfare was authorized to work with the federal government's new antipoverty programs. Among the welfare programs administered by the department were four public assistance programs: AFDC, Aid for the Blind, Aid to the Permanently and Totally Disabled, and Old Age Assistance. The latter three programs were taken over entirely by the federal government in 1972 in the form of the new national **Supplemental Security Income (SSI)** program. Along with these programs, the department ran the Texas Medical Assistance Program (Medicaid), the national food stamp program, and various other social-service programs.

In 1977 the Department of Public Welfare became the Department of Human Resources. It was renamed again in 1985 as the Texas Department of Human Services, and in 2003 as the Health and Human Services Commission. The name changes reflected policy makers' ongoing desire to think of the agency less as a welfare provider and more as a service agency to the poor. By 1980 the department was reorganized to focus on the major client groups it served: families with children and aged and disabled people. In 1981 the constitutional ceiling on welfare spending was replaced with a more flexible standard: welfare expenditures could not exceed 1 percent of the total state budget.

Between 1967 and 1973 participation rates and expenditures for welfare in Texas exploded. The number of children on AFDC more than quadrupled, from 80,000 to 325,000, while the number of families on AFDC more than quintupled, from 23,000 to 120,000. Rates leveled off in the late 1970s but began to push upward again in the 1980s. Liberal attempts to nationalize AFDC, turning the state-federal program into a national program like SSI, failed throughout the 1970s. Conservative attempts to compel welfare recipients to participate in job-training programs, such as the Work Incentive Program of 1967, had limited success. A frustrating political stalemate set in. Few were happy with welfare policy as then conducted, but no consensus had emerged as to what would be a better alternative. Meanwhile, welfare rolls and expenditures continued to increase in both Texas and the nation.

The Idea of Dependency and Welfare Reform in the 1990s

By the mid-1980s a new critique of welfare programs had begun to emerge, which led to a new understanding of what the problem of poverty was and how solutions might be developed to address it. At its heart lay the idea that the well-intentioned policies of the 1960s had backfired and created a dysfunctional underclass of people dependent on welfare. Programs such as AFDC may have helped people financially in the short run, but in the long run, some argued, they had robbed people of the character traits and moral values that would enable them to succeed in a market economy.[49] These critics believed that the skyrocketing rate of children born to poor, unwed mothers was in part the result of a perverse set of incentives created by welfare programs. Under the existing welfare system, at least to a point, the more children one had, the higher one's welfare payment. Because some states, including Texas, did not provide welfare to families with fathers in the home, fathers were actually being encouraged to abandon their families so that the families might qualify for welfare. According to critics, the poor needed encouragement and proper incentives to become independent workers rather than have a permanent source of income from the state.

At the national level, the deadlock over welfare reform was broken in 1988 with the passage of the Family Support Act, which mandated that all state AFDC programs cover families with two parents in the home. It also established a number of new "workfare" programs intended to get people off welfare and into the workforce, and set standards requiring parents to participate in these programs or lose their benefits.[50]

Much hyperbole surrounded the passage of the Family Support Act. Although it did break new ground in formulating programs to help people make the transition from welfare to work, it also was an important expansion of the existing AFDC system. Far from declining, welfare roll expansion continued in the early 1990s. In Texas, this expansion was especially rapid, and total federal and state expenditures on AFDC in Texas almost tripled from 1984 to 1994. Food stamp costs also rose rapidly during this period, and Medicaid costs were escalating at a rate of more than 20 percent a year. Soaring costs of AFDC, food stamps, and Medicaid provided the backdrop to the welfare reforms that Texas policy makers would put into place in 1995.

Growing discontent over welfare policy across the country encouraged many states, including Texas, to seek waivers from federal regulations so that they might experiment with reform.[51] Some states sought to modify AFDC rules to eliminate some of the incentive structures in the welfare system. Other states set caps on benefits and on how long one could continue to receive welfare. Welfare became an issue during the 1994 state elections. The winner of that year's governor's race, Republican George W. Bush, echoed the conservative critics of the welfare system, arguing that it was robbing people of their independence. Among the changes he called for were

In August 2018, 3.89 million Texans participated in the food stamps program (now called SNAP), which allows low-income people to buy groceries with a special debit card. SNAP benefits are paid by the federal government, but the state and federal governments share administrative costs.

- strengthening child-support procedures and penalties.
- imposing a two-year limit on benefits for recipients able to work.
- requiring individuals receiving welfare to accept a state-sponsored job if after two years they were unable to find work.
- creating new child-care and job-training programs.
- requiring unwed mothers to live with their parents or grandparents.
- moving family support systems from the state to the local level.

Data released by the office of the comptroller, John Sharp, a Democrat, lent support to Bush's contention that there were serious problems with the existing system of welfare in Texas. Over one-quarter of all welfare recipients in 1993 were "long-term" recipients who had remained on the rolls for five years or more. The publication of *A Partnership for Independence: Welfare Reform in Texas* by the comptroller's office helped to set the legislative agenda for the debate over welfare policy. The report documented how welfare often failed to help those most in need and how it encouraged those already on it to become dependent on government largesse. Among the report's 100 proposals were many of the reforms that had been implemented by conservative reformers in other states.

A bipartisan legislative coalition ultimately supported major welfare reform in Texas. On May 26, 1995, the vote on House Bill 1863 was 128 to 9 in the House and 30 to 1 in the Senate. The law provided a number of "carrot and stick" incentives that sought to mold the character of welfare recipients in positive ways and wean them off welfare. Among the carrots were expanded education and job-training programs, as well as pilot studies involving transitional child care and medical benefits. Among the sticks were a limitation on benefits to 36 months, alimony for ex-spouses in poverty who couldn't support themselves, and a five-year ban on reapplying for benefits once they ran out. To implement the state reforms, Texas secured a waiver that freed the state from various federal regulations regarding welfare programs. In granting the waivers to Texas and other states, President Bill Clinton's administration hoped to stimulate innovative reforms that might be duplicated elsewhere.

Texas was ahead of the welfare reform curve in 1995. In 1996, Clinton signed into law the most important reform in federal welfare policy since the New Deal. The Personal Responsibility and Work Opportunity Reconciliation Act essentially rethought the assumptions that had guided the expansion of welfare programs for 60 years. Under the legislation, AFDC, JOBS (a work-related training program), and the Emergency Assistance Program were combined into one block grant titled **Temporary Assistance for Needy Families (TANF)**. As with the welfare reforms instituted in Texas and other states, the primary purpose of TANF was to make families self-sufficient by ending the cycle of dependency on government benefits. States were given great flexibility in setting benefit levels, eligibility requirements, and other program details.

Temporary Assistance for Needy Families (TANF) a welfare program passed in 1996 to provide temporary assistance to families with needy children; replacing the AFDC program, TANF sought to make poor families self-sufficient and to give states greater flexibility in setting benefit levels, eligibility requirements, and other program details

Today in Texas, TANF provides temporary financial assistance to families with needy children when one or both of the parents are missing or disabled.[52] The program also provides a onetime $1,000 payment to individuals in certain crisis situations. To qualify, a recipient's income must be below 17 percent of the poverty income limit based on family size. In addition, the combined equity of the family may not exceed $2,000 ($3,000 for the elderly and disabled). People participating in TANF receive a monthly assistance payment based on the size of their family. They cannot receive this assistance for more than 36 months, but they are also eligible for Medicaid benefits, food stamps, and child day-care services. Unless legally exempt, recipients are also required to participate in an employment services program, attend parenting skills classes, get vaccines for their children, make sure their children go to school, and agree not to abuse drugs or alcohol.

The maximum monthly grant available to a household of three under TANF is low, only $290 a month for a home with one parent. For the 2016–17 biennium, TANF expenditures will be $131.8 million in the All Funds budget, including $101.8 million in General Revenue Funds and $30 million in federal funds.

Evaluating Welfare Reforms

Texas is now into its third decade of welfare policy as reformed by the state and federal government in the 1990s. The success of the welfare reforms in Texas has been evaluated along a number of dimensions, of which two stand out. First, the reforms have been evaluated in terms of the degree to which they have helped lower the number of welfare recipients in Texas. Second, the reforms have been evaluated based on the degree to which they have succeeded in taking people off welfare and moving them into the workforce as productive, independent members of society.

Judged by changes in the number of people on welfare, the reforms appear to be a success. The average monthly number of people on welfare in Texas rose from a little more than half a million in 1989 to a peak of more than three-quarters of a million in 1994, then began to fall after the 1995 reforms. The decline in the number of people on welfare continued over the next decade, falling to approximately 156,000 people in 2006 and to 55,475 in early 2018. Of these recipients, 83 percent are children.[53]

Judged by a second measure—the number of people moving from welfare to work—the reforms of 1995 have been more mixed in their success. Studies over the past decade have found that the caseload for TANF has fallen and that the workforce in Texas has grown as the Great Recession has faded from memory. Fewer individuals are relying on TANF for their income. Poverty measures have also fallen in Texas, as the percentage of those in Texas living in poverty fell to 15.6 percent. Jobs have generally seemed to be available for people willing and able to work.

But some statistics trouble policymakers as they evaluate the success of the welfare reforms. In 2016, Texas's poverty rate of 15.6 percent ranked 11th highest among the states. The percentage of children under the age of 18 in poverty stood at 22.2 percent, ranking Texas 12th highest in the nation.[54] Though the welfare reforms instituted in the 1990s and reaffirmed over the next 20 years may have curtailed welfare expenditures to poor people, this simply means that fewer people in poverty are getting cash assistance. In 1995–96, 43 percent of poor families in Texas received TANF funds, compared to 68 percent nationwide. In 2015–16, the numbers had dropped to 4 percent in Texas and 23 percent nationwide. One study found that of the 619,400 families living in poverty in Texas and 282,400 families living in deep poverty in Texas, only 26,400 received TANF in 2015–16.[55]

Public spending on monetary assistance programs such as TANF has declined sharply over the last 20 years as the number of people enrolled in the program has declined. At the same time, however, funding for non-cash assistance programs has more than tripled during the same time period and is now over $700 million in Texas. As welfare rolls and expenditures have declined, Texas has used the federal block grant funds allocated to it to fund antipoverty initiatives to cover a wide range of other programs, including Child Protective Services, a program we discussed in the introduction to this chapter. Other block grant monies have gone to early childhood intervention services and mental health state hospitals. In the 2018–19 budget, $3 million of this block grant money will go to an alternative to abortion programs, and $4 million a year will go to the Texas Education Agency for "school improvement and support programs." The welfare reforms of the 1990s have not eliminated poverty by making the poor more independent. But the reforms have clearly redirected the way in which Texas addresses the needs of poor people in the state, away from cash assistance and toward social services.[56]

PERSONAL RESPONSIBILITY: WHAT WOULD YOU DO?

- If you were advising public officials on welfare policy, what programs would you urge them to adopt today to reduce poverty? What assumptions about poverty are you making in recommending these policies?

- What are the stereotypes about people on welfare? In your experience, are these stereotypes accurate? If not, why do you think they persist?

Medicaid and Health Care Policy

Explain why Medicaid in particular and health care policy in general have been so controversial in Texas

Health insurance is a major policy problem facing Texas. People get health insurance from a variety of sources, including employer-provided policies, individually purchased policies, Medicare (a federal program for the elderly), and Medicaid (a state-federal program for the poor). In 2016 an estimated 15 percent of Texans were uninsured, the highest percentage of any state and much higher than the 10 percent figure for the U.S. population as a whole. Figure 12.1 shows the breakdown of this uninsured population by age group and race/ethnicity. Approximately 1.2 million children under age 18 (16.3 percent) were without insurance, far above the national average of 9.8 percent.[57]

Medicaid

Other than health insurance programs established for state employees, Texas's principal policy initiative regarding health care and health insurance is Medicaid, a program closely linked to poverty programs. Medicaid, which provides for the health care of poor people, particularly poor children, is an especially costly program for the state. The caseload for Medicaid has exploded in recent years, pushed up by the Great Recession. For the 2018–19 biennium, $61.8 billion in federal and state funds have been appropriated for the Medicaid program in Texas. Of these funds, $36.1 billion is from the federal government sources, while the remaining $25.7 is from state sources. These appropriations are a $2.5 billion decrease from expenditures during the 2016–17 biennium. Most of the decrease is due to cuts in client services. Funding Medicaid is a major issue in the broader debate over the state and national governments' roles in providing health care.[58]

Medicaid is a joint state-federal program established under the Social Security Amendments of 1965 as Title XIX of the Social Security Act. This act requires that Texas and other states follow certain principles and meet certain standards if they are to receive federal money to help fund the program. First, Medicaid services must be available on a statewide basis. Second, the same level of service must be available to all clients throughout the state. Children are entitled to a broader range of services than adults. Third, participants must be allowed to use any health care provider who meets program standards. (Providers, of course, must be willing to accept Medicaid recipients.) Fourth, the amount, duration, and scope of medical services must be "sufficiently reasonable." Exactly what kind or how much of these services are considered "sufficiently reasonable" is vague and often contested, and Medicaid reimbursement rates for providers tend to be much lower than those under conventional private insurance plans. While Texas may limit the services provided to adult clients, it may not arbitrarily deny services for specific conditions or illnesses.

Federal law also allows states to be granted waivers from these principles to create programs directed toward particular clients. In this approach, federal Medicaid policy mirrors the initiatives in welfare policy that give states more freedom of action in developing pro-

FIGURE 12.1

Texas's Uninsured Population by Age and Race/Ethnicity (Estimated)

SOURCE: Texas Health and Human Services Commission, *Texas Medicaid and CHIP in Perspective*, 9th ed. (February 2015), and Henry J. Kaiser Family Foundation, kff.org.

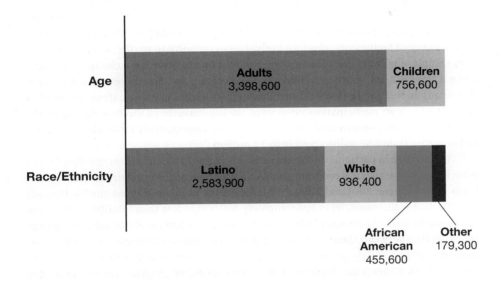

grams to serve clients. For example, Texas has been granted the authority to enroll clients in managed care programs. In traditional fee-for-service programs a doctor or a hospital provides a service directly to the patient and is paid a fee for that service. In the managed care organization (MCO) model, by contrast, programs such as health maintenance organizations or doctor-hospital networks act as intermediaries between the patient and the doctor and negotiate discounted fees for services. In addition, MCOs reimburse their member health care providers with a monthly payment, which is known as a *capitation payment* because it has a limit or "cap" based on medical expenses calculated for the average patient. The State of Texas Access Reform program (STAR) is the managed care program run by the Texas Health and Human Services Commission, under which the state contracts with MCOs to provide health care in various areas to poor populations in Texas.

Another model, found primarily in rural areas in Texas, is now referred to as traditional Medicaid and enables Medicaid recipients to receive medical services from a primary care provider. As a noncapitated plan, it does not set any average dollar amount per patient per month that the state pays for the cost of health care service. Primary care providers receive fee-for-service reimbursement and a small monthly management fee directly from the state. A recent initiative, Medicaid Rural Area STAR, has been implemented to provide managed care to clients in 164 mostly rural counties. Its goal is to move rural clients away from traditional fee-for-service delivery as much as possible.

Managed care programs under the umbrella of Texas Medicaid have been growing in popularity since the early 1990s and became an essential part of cost containment measures instituted by the legislature over the next 20 years. In 1994, 2.9 percent of Texas

Medicaid recipients were in state-sponsored managed care programs. By 2014 this figure had risen to almost 82 percent.[59]

Medicaid Participation
Over the last five decades, Medicaid has grown from a narrowly defined program targeting low-income people on public assistance to a large, complex program serving a variety of special groups. In the late 1980s and early 1990s Medicaid was expanded to include older adults not fully covered by Medicare, people with disabilities, and pregnant women. Individuals participating in TANF and SSI automatically qualify for Medicaid, as do others who meet these other criteria.

A variety of factors can affect an individual's eligibility to participate in Medicaid. For example, eligibility can change when a parent or caregiver has a change in income, when a child is born, or when a child reaches a certain age. For these reasons, there is significant fluctuation in Medicaid enrollment from month to month. However, one fact is strikingly clear: participation rates went up significantly in the first decade of the twenty-first century. Between 2001 and 2009 the average monthly Medicaid enrollment in Texas rose from 1.87 million people to 3.1 million.

The increase in participation is not caused by a rise in participation through Texas's principal public assistance program, the TANF program. As the number of monthly caseloads grew between 2001 and 2009 for Medicaid, the number of those eligible through TANF actually decreased, from approximately 500,000 to less than 350,000 in 2009 and to 75,000 in 2016. Although Medicaid and public assistance are still joined together, the close link between them that existed at the founding of Medicaid has largely been severed.

Figure 12.2 shows participation today in Medicaid by gender, age, and ethnicity. Seventy-seven percent of those on Medicaid are under the age of 20. Fifty-one percent on Medicaid rolls are Latino, 19 percent are white, and 15 percent are African American.

Administration and Financing of Medicaid in Texas
In Texas, Medicaid is administered through the Texas Health and Human Services Commission. At the federal level, the Centers for Medicare and Medicaid in the Department of Health and Human Services monitor Texas's Medicaid program and establish basic services, delivery, quality, funding, and eligibility standards. Through Medicaid, Texas and the federal government together pay for a variety of health care services for a number of low-income populations. The acute services paid for include physicians' bills, inpatient care in a hospital, outpatient care, and pharmacy, lab, and X-ray services. Medicaid also provides for selected long-term and support services, including home- and community-based services for the disabled, home-health and personal care, and nursing services.

The federal portion of the financing for the program is determined every year by comparing average state per capita income to the average national per capita income. Poorer states receive a larger share of federal assistance than richer states. Each state thus has its own FMAP (federal medical assistance percentage). In 2018 the FMAP for Texas was 56.88 percent, which means that 43.12 percent of all Medicaid expenditures were state funded.[60]

A program related to Medicaid is the Children's Health Insurance Program (CHIP), which provides coverage for children in families with incomes too high to qualify for Medicaid. Established in 1997 under Title XXI of the Social Security Act, CHIP is administered like Medicaid through the Centers for Medicare and Medicaid Services in the

FIGURE 12.2

Texas Medicaid Recipients by Gender, Age, and Race/Ethnicity (Estimated)

NOTE: Total numbers fluctuate month by month based on total number of clients.

SOURCE: Texas Health and Human Services Commission, *Texas Medicaid and CHIP in Perspective* (The "Pink Book"), (February 2015), Chapter 5, pp. 5–14 to 5–15.

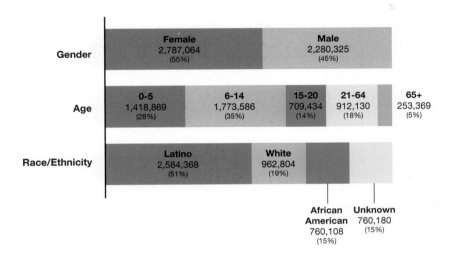

U.S. Department of Health and Human Services. The 2010 federal allocation to Texas for CHIP was more than $925 million. The average monthly caseload for CHIP was 497,666 in 2002. After falling to 312,101 in 2007 before the Great Recession, enrollment in CHIP has fluctuated between 500,000 in early 2010 and 600,000 in early 2013. Participation numbers were falling throughout the first half of 2014 as the economy continued to improve, dropping below 500,000 in April 2014. The bulk of the increase in Medicaid caseload in the 2014–15 biennium mentioned in Chapter 11 will come because of the transfer of children from CHIP to Medicaid under the Affordable Care Act.

Medicaid and CHIP expenditures have become an increasing part of both the national and the state budgets. In 1996 the total Texas Medicaid budget (both federal and state dollars) was $8.2 billion. By 2014 this had risen to $32.2 billion. By 2014 federal expenditures on Medicaid nationwide encompassed $475.9 billion.[61] Figure 12.3 shows the average increases in Medicaid spending between 2000 and 2015.

Broader Health Care Issues in Texas

Medicaid policy is embedded in a larger national discussion over health care in America and the proper way to fund it. Numerous controversies divide the public and politicians at all levels of government. Is health care fundamentally a private or a public issue? How can exploding health care costs, including the costs of private insurance such as Blue Cross Blue Shield or public insurance such as Medicare and Medicaid, be brought under control? Should individuals be compelled to purchase health care insurance? If so, how

FIGURE 12.3

Percentage of Medicaid Expenditures in Texas's State Budget

Source: Texas Health and Human Services Commission, *Texas Medicaid and CHIP in Perspective*, 11th ed. (February 2017), Chapter 14.

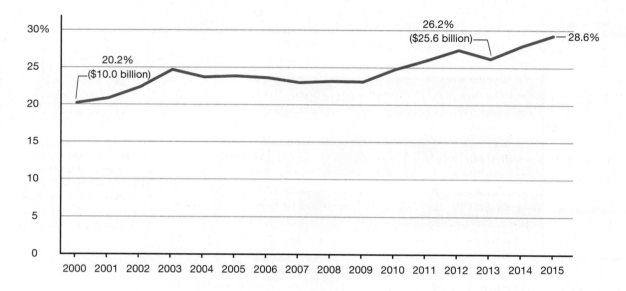

much and what kind of insurance? Who should foot the bill for individuals who cannot afford to pay for private insurance? What is the proper role for the state and federal governments in the delivery of health care across the nation?

As in other state-federal programs, federal money for Medicaid is accompanied by federal rules and regulations with which the state must comply to maintain this funding. This sometimes breeds tremendous political controversy between the state of Texas and the federal government. One such controversy broke out in early 2012 over provisions relating to Texas's Medicaid Women's Health Program.[62]

The Medicaid Women's Health Program in Texas serves more than 100,000 women and is funded by $35 million from federal funds and $7 million from state funds. Through subsidized clinics located across the state, the program helps pay for birth control, health screening, and family exams for a select group of women on Medicaid. Planned Parenthood offers these services as well as abortion services at its various clinics across the state. Conservatives in Texas, including Governor Perry, were unhappy with any state monies being used to subsidize groups supporting abortion and moved to cut program funds from going to these clinics. But federal regulations clearly state that patients in the program, not state officials, decide where money from the program is spent.

By March 2012 an impasse had been reached. On one side were Governor Perry and the Republican-dominated state legislature, who ordered an end to Medicaid funding of Planned Parenthood clinics. On the other side were the federal government and supporters of Planned Parenthood, who insisted on strictly following federal rules and guidelines. Interestingly, some moderate Republicans, including Senator Kay Bailey Hutchison, broke with the governor and backed Planned Parenthood in the dispute. By early March 2012 all federal funding of the Texas Women's Health Program had been pulled. Governor Perry claimed he would find new funding for the program at the state level that would exclude Planned Parenthood.

In early May 2012 the issue became even more complicated. Eight Planned Parenthood clinics that did not provide abortion services sued the state, claiming their rights to freedom of speech and freedom of association had been violated. A federal appeals court ruled on August 22, 2012, that Texas could ban Planned Parenthood from receiving funds. Texas solicitor general Jonathan Mitchell reiterated the state's opposition to providing taxpayer money "to entities that affiliate with abortion-promoting entities."[63] The conflict over the funding and administration of the Texas Women's Health Program signals the emergence of a new set of conflicts over Medicaid in Texas and a new round in the debate over the relationship between the national and the state government in the federal system.

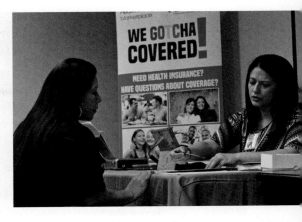

Health care remains a controversial issue in Texas. While Texas holds as the state with the highest rate of uninsured individuals, many have used the Affordable Care Act to sign up for health care.

Cost, however, is the single most important issue confronting policy makers regarding Medicaid in Texas. Now encompassing more than 25 percent of state expenditures, Medicaid in Texas as in other states threatens to overwhelm the budget. In the spring of 2012, Texas comptroller Susan Combs began referring to Medicaid as "The Big Red," the program that was going to push an otherwise healthy state budget into the red. She claimed that by 2023 "Big Red is going to be over a third of state spending."[64] Medicaid expenditures, many mandated by the federal government, would begin to crowd out other forms of spending from the state budget.

Policy makers are forever looking for ways to make the program less costly. Two strategies have predominated over the past 20 years: first, to bring more efficiency into the program by expanding managed care initiatives across the state, and second, to institute cost controls and cutbacks to providers. Both efforts have had limited success, and at the same time have sparked concern over the quality of care being offered to Medicaid participants across the state. As cost containment efforts intensify, Texas policy makers inside and outside the legislature will be compelled to increase their monitoring of the delivery of the program.

The Affordable Care Act

In March 2010, Congress passed two bills, the Patient Protection and Affordable Care Act and the Health Care and Education Reconciliation Act of 2010, which together became known as the Affordable Care Act (ACA), often referred to as Obamacare. The passage of the ACA transformed the debate over health care policy in the United States. Passed on a party line vote by Congress, the legislation requires individuals not covered by existing plans to pursue health insurance or pay a penalty. Along with this "individual mandate," as the mandatory coverage came to be called, the act also increased coverage for preexisting conditions and expanded medical insurance to an estimated 30 million people at the time.[65]

When fully implemented, the ACA was expected to bring significant change to the health insurance market in Texas as well as to Texas's Medicaid program.[66] Initial estimates in 2012 projected that under the ACA insurance coverage in Texas would rise to 91 percent, with almost 40 percent of the remaining uninsured being undocumented persons. The expansion of Medicaid in Texas would be funded through a complicated set of subsidies based on family income. For the first three years of the expansion (2014–16), the federal

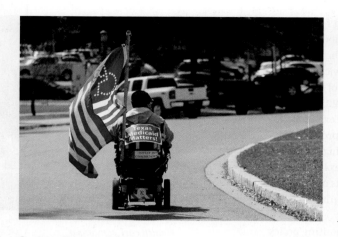

In 2013, Governor Rick Perry elected to not expand Medicaid in Texas, which has denied insurance to many of the state's poor population. Many Texans have protested this decision, urging the government to expand Medicaid throughout the state and insure close to 1 million citizens.

government would cover all costs for newly eligible participants in Medicaid and CHIP. Thereafter, the percentage would slowly decline, committing Texas to a larger portion of the funding. The long-term effect of the ACA for Texas would be a budgetary one. Increased expenditures on Medicaid and health care in Texas are all but inevitable.

The ACA sparked a national controversy. A majority of the states (including Texas) and a number of private individuals and groups challenged the constitutionality of the act in court, focusing on the mandatory coverage provisions. For three days in March 2012 the U.S. Supreme Court held oral arguments on the case, *National Federation of Independent Business v. Sebelius*. A complicated decision was delivered by a divided Court on June 28, 2012. Four liberal justices believed that most features of the ACA were constitutional. Four conservative justices countered that they were not. Representing the decisive vote, Chief Justice Roberts rejected the idea that people could be mandated or forced to buy insurance under Congress's power to regulate commerce, but he nevertheless concluded that a tax penalizing people who did not get medical insurance met constitutional muster. Regarding the expansion of Medicaid, he supported a conservative position, arguing that states could not be bullied into expanding medical insurance coverage for poorer segments of the population. Chief Justice Roberts wrote that for federalism to thrive, states had to have a meaningful and real choice as to whether or not they would participate in federally sponsored programs.

The complicated U.S. Supreme Court decision opened the door for a new round of political posturing around the health care issue in Texas. Governor Perry announced that Texas would refuse to participate in the expanded Medicaid program, giving up millions of federal dollars for not having to incur new financial responsibilities at the state level. The state legislature, supporting Governor Perry, has refused to expand Medicaid in Texas. An estimate by the Kaiser Family Foundation in 2014 concluded that over 1 million uninsured adults in Texas, 17 percent of the uninsured in the state, would not be brought under the ACA provisions to expand Medicaid because of Texas's actions (or inactions).[67] Perry also decided that the state would not go into the business of designing an insurance exchange in the state. Texas would let the federal government sell federally designed insurance policies in the state on its own. Tax reform in 2017 under the Trump Administration further muddied the waters surrounding provisions of the ACA. Originally, the ACA required individuals to prove that they were insured when they filed their federal income taxes or they would incur a tax penalty. As noted above, this provision was held constitutional by the United States Supreme Court, upholding the mandate as a tax, not interstate commerce, in *NFIB v. Sebelius*. However, the Trump-inspired 2017 tax reconciliation act removed the tax penalties while keeping the mandate beginning in 2019. This effectively undercut an important part of the ACA's initiatives to lower the number of uninsured people through tax penalties.

As if things weren't complicated enough in the emerging discussion over what to do about Medicaid and health care coverage in Texas, a 2012 survey was released by the Texas Medical Association that found only 31 percent of Texas doctors were accepting new patients who relied on Medicaid for insurance coverage, down from 42 percent in 2012 and 67 percent in 2000. Low payment and excessive red tape were cited as the reasons

Abortion Policy in Texas

ABORTION LAWS are among the most contentious public policies in the United States. In 1973 the U.S. Supreme Court ruled that a woman's right to privacy extended to her decision to have an abortion. This right was balanced, however, by the state's interest in guaranteeing safe and effective medical regulations. The balance has led to considerable controversy over the last 40 years as many state legislatures tried to limit the opportunities for women to have an abortion. Texas passed legislation in 2013 that effectively would have shuttered three-fourths of the abortion clinics in Texas. These laws, requiring abortion facilities to be like surgical facilities and requiring doctors providing abortions to have admitting privileges at a nearby hospital, were invalidated by the U.S. Supreme Court in 2016. In the decision *Whole Woman's Health v. Hellerstedt*, the Court reaffirmed a woman's right to abortion services without facing an undue burden imposed by the state.

Significantly, *Whole Woman's Health v. Hellerstedt* has not rejected all state regulations of abortion procedures. Earlier, in 2011, the Texas legislature passed and the courts upheld a law requiring doctors who perform abortions to provide a sonogram to women before carrying out the procedure.

The law requires doctors to provide with the sonogram "a simultaneous verbal explanation of the results of the live, real-time sonogram images, including a medical description of the dimensions of the embryo or fetus, the presence of cardiac activity, and the presence of arms, legs, external members, and internal organs." Doctors are also required to make the fetus's heartbeat audible to the woman. Pregnant women affected by the law may choose not to view the sonogram, listen to the doctor's explanations, or listen to the heartbeat. However, doctors who refuse to comply with the law are subject to losing their licenses to practice medicine. Doctors are not required to perform the sonogram procedure for women who were impregnated as a result of rape or incest.

Proponents of Texas's law argue that because abortion involves a nascent human life, efforts to make women think twice about going forward with an abortion should be implemented. They believe that the state has a compelling interest to protect the lives of what they consider to be human beings in the earliest stages of development. Supporters emphasize that women can still go forward with a legal abortion if they so choose, but they should have full and complete information about the consequences of the decision they are making. Elizabeth Graham, the director of Texas Right to Life, adds, "This paternalistic attitude, that we're saddling women with too much information, really does an injustice . . . It underestimates the capability of women to make a decision with more information, not less."[a]

Opponents of the law argue that abortion is a constitutional right that has been protected by the Supreme Court and that, through forcing women to take the extra step of having a sonogram, the state is making it more difficult for women to exercise this right. They cite the

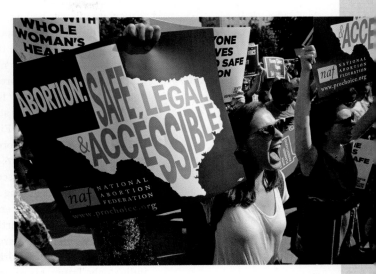

Court's argument that no abortion law can place an undue burden on women who choose to obtain an abortion, and they note that the law makes women come into a medical office twice—once for the sonogram and again for the abortion after the 24-hour waiting period. In particular, opponents argue that vaginal ultrasounds invade a woman's privacy, as they necessarily involve an invasive procedure that women should not be required to endure. Jenni Beaver, assistant director at the Southwestern Women's Surgery Center in Dallas, argues that the sonogram law "treats women as if they are stupid and don't know what is in their uterus . . . The law just creates hoops and barriers and drives up the cost for the women. And we have not had anyone decide not to have an abortion because of a sonogram."[b]

COMMUNICATING EFFECTIVELY: YOUR VOICE

- Do you believe abortions should be curtailed in Texas, and if so, is the sonogram law an effective way to achieve this goal?

- Do you believe that the sonogram policy presents an "undue burden" on the right of a woman to choose to have an abortion? Why or why not?

for the declining acceptance of Medicaid as a form of medical insurance.[68] Further complicating matters, officials from the Texas Health and Human Services Commission released a new estimate of the costs of the ACA in Texas based upon new, more conservative assumptions about how quickly newly eligible people might apply to participate in the program. The new estimates were 42 percent less than the original ones. In July 2012 state officials believed that if Texas opted into the new ACA Medicaid programs, by 2023 the state would spend $15.6 billion of state money and bring in $100.1 billion of federal money. Despite these projections, neither the Health and Human Services commissioner Tom Suehs nor Governor Perry believed that Texas should opt into the new ACA programs. Before Texas should participate in an expanded program, they believed the act should be "fixed" by Congress.[69]

Although the ACA was still in effect, it is unclear what that will mean for poorer Texans over the long run (see Figure 12.4). Health insurance coverage overall has increased in Texas since 2013. The percentage of uninsured in Texas dropped from 22.1 percent in 2013 to 16.6 percent in 2016, still the highest rate of uninsured in the nation.[70] According to a 2016 study by the Episcopal Health Foundation, the number of uninsured in Texas fell by 34.9 percent among 18- to 34-year-olds, by 8.2 percent among 35- to 49-year-olds, and by 53.2 percent among 50- to 64-year-olds. This success story may be short lived. Texas's refusal to participate in the optional state-federal expansion of Medicaid has effectively denied insurance coverage to many poor people.[71] And then there is the issue of undocumented workers in Texas, who compose a growing portion of uninsured individuals. Trump tax reforms have raised even more questions about the future of the ACA and health care in Texas. One thing is clear: few individuals are willing to argue that Texas has solved the problem of providing health care to the poor.

FIGURE 12.4

Where Do Texans Get Their Insurance? (2016)

SOURCE: Henry J. Kaiser Family Foundation, kff.org.

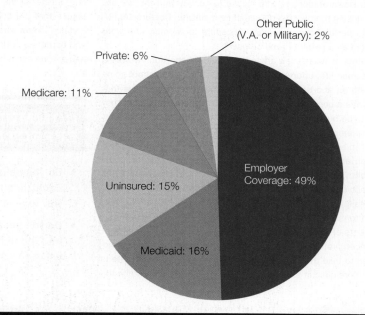

Other Public (V.A. or Military): 2%

Private: 6%

Medicare: 11%

Uninsured: 15%

Medicaid: 16%

Employer Coverage: 49%

What Are the Trade-Offs in Texas Public Policy?

The contemporary Texas government tends to pass conservative policies (low taxes and lower levels of social services). The figures below show these policies compared with those of other states. Texas collects the sixth-lowest share of taxes of any state. But when government lacks revenue, it cannot spend money to address social problems, such as providing health insurance to those who cannot afford it.

State Taxes (as a percentage of state income)

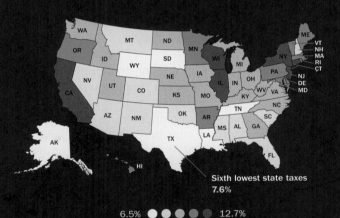

Sixth lowest state taxes
7.6%

6.5% ●●●●● 12.7%

Percentage without Health Insurance

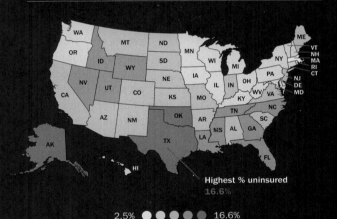

Highest % uninsured
16.6%

2.5% ●●●●● 16.6%

SOURCES: Tax Data: 2012 tax data from TaxFoundation.org (accessed 7/7/18). Uninsured Data: 2016 uninsured data from U.S. Census Bureau, Current Population Survey, Annual Social and Economic Supplements, www.census.gov (accessed 7/7/18).

*States with the same percentage of uninsured individuals are given the same rank.

State Taxes Compared with Percent Uninsured*

	Low tax rank	Uninsured rank		Low tax rank	Uninsured rank		Low tax rank	Uninsured rank
Alaska	1	2	North Dakota	18	40	Delaware	35	42
South Dakota	2	28	Georgia	19	4	Hawaii	36	48
Wyoming	3	18	Iowa	20	46	Maine	37	27
Tennessee	4	18	Nebraska	21	29	Pennsylvania	38	36
Louisiana	5	7	Idaho	22	11	Massachusetts	39	50
Texas	6	1	Missouri	23	22	Oregon	40	29
New Hampshire	7	32	Virginia	24	23	Vermont	41	49
Nevada	8	6	Washington	25	32	Minnesota	42	47
South Carolina	9	11	Michigan	26	36	Rhode Island	43	43
Mississippi	10	8	Indiana	27	20	Maryland	44	40
Oklahoma	11	5	Kansas	28	26	California	45	16
Alabama	12	17	Kentucky	29	36	Illinois	46	29
Montana	13	10	Utah	30	15	Wisconsin	47	44
New Mexico	14	8	North Carolina	31	14	New Jersey	48	23
Arizona	15	11	Ohio	32	39	Connecticut	49	45
Colorado	16	25	West Virginia	33	35	New York	50	34
Florida	17	3	Arkansas	34	21			

CRITICAL THINKING

- What appears to be the relationship between state taxes and insurance rates in a state?

- When Obamacare is fully implemented, will the numbers of uninsured change? Why or why not?

Public Policy and the Future of Texas

IN THIS CHAPTER, we examined various aspects of social-policy making in Texas. We focused particular attention on the complex issues that have driven the various stages of the policy-making process in public education, welfare, and health care. Looking at these matters with a critical eye to the future demands that we pay attention to a number of key political questions: How are problems identified by policy makers and the public at large? What kinds of solutions are formulated to address these problems? Who benefits by a particular public policy? Who pays for the policy? What ideas are used to justify or legitimate a particular program? How are programs evaluated? How do particular public policies evolve and change over time to address new problems? How do they alter the relationship between individual citizens and the government that represents them in Austin?

In earlier chapters, we saw how the high-tech revolution transformed Texas's economy in the 1980s and '90s. We also traced how social and political changes have restructured the political party system in the state and increased the power of the Republican Party. In this chapter, we have seen how many of these shifts resulted in important changes in public policy in the twentieth and twenty-first centuries. These policy changes are occurring as the Texas political economy moves from an oil, cattle, and cotton economy into an era of computers, high technology, and globalization.

What will be the future of public policy in the areas of education, welfare, and health care? What issues will be seen as problems? What policies will be formulated to address these problems? How will those new policies be implemented, evaluated, and legitimated?

Funding and fairness issues in public education will be dominated by the legislature now that the courts have pulled out of the business of figuring out what was meant in the constitution by "efficiency." Charter schools likely will continue to expand, challenging the dominance of traditional public schools. Poverty policy will continue to be the poor child of public policy as the state continues to find ways to reform welfare by ending dependency and by putting people back to work.

The wild card for the state may be health care policy. Will the state ever accept the expansion of Medicaid and insurance services provided under the Affordable Care Act? What will be done to address the continuing problem of the uninsured? Must the poor be allowed to fend for themselves, even those who are too young to do much fending? There is a chance that the state will punt on these issues, leaving segments of the poor and uninsured exposed.

Use **INQUIZITIVE** to help you study and master this material.

The Policy-Making Process

- **Describe the key steps and concepts in the policy-making process (pp. 405–8)**

Public policies are the outcomes of governmental institutions. There are a number of stages in the policy-making process. One stage is problem identification, where political actors and society at large develop an understanding of a problem and how that problem can be addressed. The second stage in the process is policy formulation, where strategies for dealing with specifically defined problems are developed. The third stage is policy implementation, where the goals of public policy along with sanctions to support them are put into effect by a particular government agency. A fourth stage of the process is evaluation, where efforts are made to evaluate the effectiveness of a policy. Some political scientists argue that still another stage in the process is policy legitimation, where the legality of a particular policy initiative is determined.

Key Terms
rationality (p. 406)
bounded rationality (p. 407)

Practice Quiz
1. *Satisficing* means that decision makers are seeking
   a) the optimal means of solving a problem.
   b) a satisfactory way for solving a problem.
   c) policies that will satisfy voters.
   d) the easiest policies to adopt.
   e) policies that satisfy the courts.

2. Among the factors that work against rationality and efficiency in the making of public policies is that
   a) politicians are more interested in votes than in effective policies.
   b) administrators of policies often seek the easiest ways of administering laws rather than the most efficient ways.
   c) governments work incrementally.
   d) rational and efficient policies are often difficult to legitimate to a broader public.
   e) all of the above

3. An example of policy legitimation is when
   a) the courts uphold the constitutionality of a law.
   b) the governor vetoes a particular bill.
   c) the governor appoints an official to run a bureaucracy.
   d) political scientists research the effectiveness of a law.
   e) the legislature does not repeal a law during the legislative session following its passage.

Education Policy

- **Describe the major issues that have shaped education policy in Texas (pp. 408–19)**

One of the most important functions of state government is providing and funding public education. Under the Gilmer-Aikin Laws, Texas extended its control over financing and administering public education through local school districts. As in many southern states, segregation of public schools was a major problem that was not dealt with until federal courts forced Texas to desegregate in the 1950s and '60s. Equity in the funding of public education remains a major issue in Texas. State courts continue to play an important role in addressing the equity issue. Concerns over excellence and accountability in public education persist today.

Key Terms
Gilmer-Aikin Laws (p. 410)
equal protection clause (p. 410)

Practice Quiz
4. The Gilmer-Aikin Laws
    a) regulate schools in the Gilmer-Aikin ISD.
    b) were major educational reforms passed in 1949.
    c) established an office of elected state superintendent of public instruction.
    d) allowed for homeschooling of children.
    e) required that money raised from the poll tax be spent on public education.

5. State courts tried to address the issue of equity in the funding of public schools
    a) in the case of *Edgewood ISD v. Kirby*.
    b) in the case of *Brown v. Board of Education*.
    c) in the case of *San Antonio v. Rodríguez*.
    d) by appointing Ross Perot to recommend changes to the property tax in Texas.
    e) by abolishing the office of the State Board of Education.

6. Among the reforms in public education in Texas to improve the quality of education was
    a) "No Pass, No Play."
    b) "No Play, No Pass."
    c) a shorter school year.
    d) more flexible standards for accrediting schools.
    e) tying teacher pay raises to student grades.

Welfare Policy

- **Describe the state's role in addressing poverty and how it is affected by national policies (pp. 419–25)**

Texas has large numbers of people living in poverty who have received governmental assistance since the New Deal, when the Social Security Act of 1935 was passed. Texas's most important welfare program was AFDC. President Lyndon Johnson's War on Poverty expanded social welfare programs for the poor in the 1960s. But compared with other states, welfare benefits remained low in Texas. Concerns over the problem of welfare dependency led to major reforms at the national level in 1996, when AFDC was replaced with TANF. Since these reforms, welfare rolls have declined, although poverty has remained a chronic problem among a significant portion of the Texas population.

Key Terms
New Deal (p. 421)
Aid to Families with Dependent Children (AFDC) (p. 421)
Medicaid (p. 422)
Supplemental Security Income (SSI) (p. 422)
Temporary Assistance for Needy Families (TANF) (p. 424)

Practice Quiz
7. Poverty among those over age 65 and those under age 18 in Texas
    a) is almost nonexistent because of the welfare reforms of the 1990s.
    b) is at a level above the national average.
    c) is at a level below the national average.
    d) was largely eliminated by the Social Security Act of 1935.
    e) was largely eliminated by Lyndon Johnson's War on Poverty.

8. The welfare reforms of the 1990s
a) resulted from a belief that the welfare policies of the 1960s had failed.
b) led to a 36-month limitation on welfare benefits in Texas.
c) led to a five-year ban on reapplying for benefits once benefits ran out.
d) expanded education and job-training programs.
e) all of the above

9. Two presidents who had major roles in welfare policy are
a) Franklin Delano Roosevelt and Lyndon B. Johnson.
b) Dwight Eisenhower and Herbert Hoover.
c) Harry Truman and John F. Kennedy.
d) Woodrow Wilson and Franklin Delano Roosevelt.
e) Lyndon B. Johnson and George H. W. Bush.

Medicaid and Health Care Policy

- **Explain why Medicaid in particular and health care policy in general have been so controversial in Texas (pp. 426–35)**

One major welfare program that has become increasingly costly is Medicaid, a state-federal program that finances health care for the poor. Reforms instituted under the Obama administration have significantly expanded health care coverage for the poor. Texas, however, is not participating in that expansion. The rising cost of Medicaid is seen by many conservatives to be a growing threat to the financial integrity of the state's budget.

Practice Quiz

10. Which of the following statements is *true* about Medicaid in Texas?
a) Medicaid is a program that was part of the New Deal.
b) Texas policy makers make all the major decisions regarding the principles and standards directing Medicaid in Texas. There is no federal oversight.
c) Texas can apply for a waiver with the federal government, enabling it to create programs directed toward particular clients.
d) Medicaid employs doctors and nurses as members of the Department of Health and Human Services hired to provide medical care to the poor.
e) Medicaid is funded entirely by the state.

11. Managed care programs
a) are not found in the Texas Medicaid program.
b) provide medical care to an increasing number of Medicaid clients in Texas.
c) provide medical care to a small number of Medicaid clients in Texas.
d) provide direct fee-for-service care for Medicaid recipients.
e) have declined in popularity since the 1990s.

12. The Affordable Care Act
a) was part of the War on Poverty.
b) merged Medicare and Medicaid into a single program.
c) will increase health insurance coverage to millions of Texans.
d) was declared unconstitutional by the Texas Supreme Court.
e) originated in the Texas legislature.

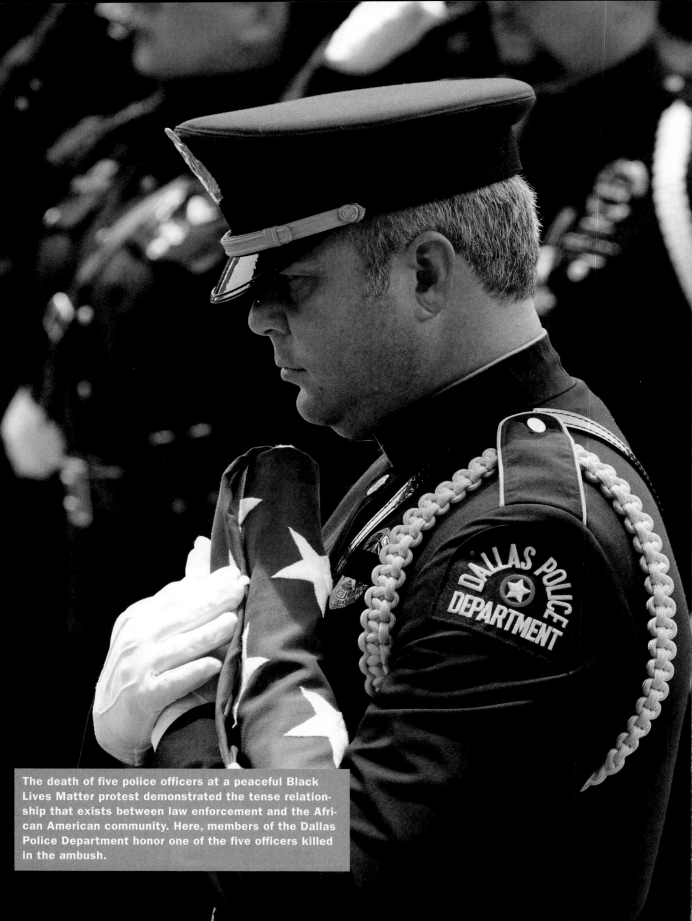

The death of five police officers at a peaceful Black Lives Matter protest demonstrated the tense relationship that exists between law enforcement and the African American community. Here, members of the Dallas Police Department honor one of the five officers killed in the ambush.

Crime, Corrections, and Public Safety

WHY POLICIES AROUND CRIME, CORRECTIONS, AND PUBLIC SAFETY MATTER On July 7, 2016, there was a peaceful march of about 800 people through downtown Dallas. The march was one of several throughout the country that were held to protest recent police shootings of African American men in Baton Rouge and in a Minneapolis suburb. About one hundred police officers were on hand to monitor the march.

The marchers were chanting "Hands up, don't shoot!," which was a chant that had been used by protestors since the shooting death of Michael Brown in Ferguson, Missouri, in 2014.

Suddenly, shots rang out. There was so much gunfire that police initially believed there were multiple snipers. The protestors scattered and shouted, "Go, go, go . . . run, run, run! Someone's shot! . . ." Massive confusion erupted. A total of twelve police officers returned fire in a fast-moving series of gun battles that took place over several blocks. Three people were arrested who ultimately were determined to have nothing to do with the shooting. Instead, the shooter was a heavily armed single sniper who was cornered in a garage at El Centro Community College. Negotiations with the sniper and exchanges of gunfire with him went on for hours. Finally, police killed him by detonating explosives near him that had been carried there by a robot.

The sniper told a hostage negotiator that he was upset about the Black Lives Matter movement and the recent police shootings of black men. He had claimed that "the end is coming" and that bombs were planted throughout the area. That claim was false, but a search of his home led to the discovery of bomb-making material, ballistic vests, and additional rifles and ammunition along with a journal of combat tactics.

Five police officers died. Seven officers and two civilians were wounded. It was the deadliest day for law enforcement since September 11, 2001. More Texas law enforcement officers have died in the line of duty than in any other state since 1980 and, while the data is less complete, it appears than more Texas law enforcement officers have died in the line of duty from the early 1800s to the present than in any other state.

The horrific shootings in Dallas underscore the dangerousness of police work and the fact that at any moment a situation can flare into a life-threatening situation. Then–Dallas police chief David Brown commented shortly after the killings, "All I know is that this must stop, this divisiveness between our police and our citizens."[1]

The peaceful demonstration from which the police killings emerged was over a fundamental issue in policing in Texas and throughout the country. How do police who must enforce laws and who must frequently deal with lawbreakers, as well as with citizens who are often in very tension-filled situations, maintain a positive relationship with the communities they police while providing for their own personal safety?

Policing, however, is only part of the criminal justice process in Texas. It is within the criminal justice process that the power of the state is greatest. The criminal law can take away an individual's liberty and even life. Texas has long been the poster child for its harshness in criminal punishment. No state executes more prisoners than Texas, and no state has a larger correctional population than Texas. Texas has 681,900 people in prison or jail or on probation or parole. To give a sense of the importance of criminal corrections to an understanding of Texas politics and policy: although Texas has 8.6 percent of the nation's population, it has 10.9 percent of its correctional population. For every 100,000 people age 18 and older in Texas, 3,290 are in prison or jail or on probation or parole. In contrast, 2,500 people for every 100,000 people age 18 and older are in the correctional system in the states as a whole.[2] In this chapter, we will look both at the basics of the criminal justice system and at recent issues related to criminal justice in Texas.

CHAPTERGOALS

- Describe the characteristics of policing in Texas and analyze the controversies surrounding it (pp. 443–48)

- Identify the major classifications of crime under Texas law and the types of punishments that may be imposed (pp. 448–51)

- Outline the procedural steps that occur after a person is arrested (pp. 451–57)

- Describe prisons and corrections policy in Texas (pp. 458–68)

- Explain why Texas's criminal justice system is often controversial (pp. 468–71)

- Consider recent proposals to improve Texas's criminal justice system (pp. 471–72)

Policing in Texas

Describe the characteristics of policing in Texas and analyze the controversies surrounding it

Law enforcement officers have the power of arrest and the power to use force in the conduct of their duties. It is an awesome responsibility that is carried out by a multiplicity of police organizations such as the Texas Department of Public Safety, city police departments, sheriff's departments, constables' offices, independent school district police departments, and college police departments.

Police Departments

The size of police departments in Texas ranges from about 5,200 in the Houston Police Department—a department to which the mayor wishes to add 540 more officers by 2020 but which needs, according to one academic who has examined the department, 1,174 more officers—to tiny one-officer departments.[3] The small town of Anton, Texas, population 1,200, has one such department—a single police officer who, in case of trouble, has as his nearest backup the Hockley County Sheriff's Office, which is 25 miles away. There are 25 city police departments in Texas with only one officer, and 25 police departments have closed in the Panhandle and South Plains since 2000 because of the costs of operating a police department. Those towns without a police department rely on assistance from county sheriff's departments.[4]

Along with differences in the size of police departments (from 1 to 5,200), there are vast differences in specialization, equipment of officers, contact with the community, and response times. One of the biggest problems facing police departments is their response time to calls for assistance. The Dallas Police Department, in particular, has faced criticism for slow response times. The Dallas Police Department has a four-category system for responding to calls. Priority 1 is a response to an emergency call, and the average time of these in 2017 was 8.12 minutes. Priority 4 is a response to a noncritical call, and the average time of these in 2017 was 74.49 minutes. One reason for the slow response times is that over the past 6 years the size of the department has dropped from 3,700 officers to 3,077, a loss of nearly 700 officers.[5]

A problem with the recruitment and retention of police officers in large urban departments is that nearby suburban departments pay much more, which encourages officers to move to higher-paying positions in areas where policing demands are likely to be less than in more populated urban areas. Starting pay for a Dallas police officer is $44,659 a year. In contrast, in the nearby suburb of Rowlett, the starting salary is $44,659; and in nearby Plano, it is $63,757. At the same time, it is difficult for very small police departments to have the tax base sufficient to support a police department. Often, small departments offer such a meager salary that officers are encouraged to move elsewhere. In 2017 the Kent County Sheriff's Department, with three full-time officers including the sheriff, advertised for a patrol deputy with a starting salary of $35,000.[6]

Small-town police officers do have advantages over urban officers, however. One major advantage is that they know the communities they serve. The single officer in Anton, Texas, for example, has lived in the town for 32 years and knows almost everyone. When people in Anton call the police, they rarely call the dispatch office, but instead call the officer's cell phone.[7] In contrast, officers in Texas's urban areas are unlikely to have much of a personal relationship with the communities in which they patrol. Diversity training is now required of police officers, and some departments pay a bonus for officers who speak languages common in the community, such as Spanish. Nevertheless, urban police are rarely the friendly neighbor that officers in small towns and rural counties in Texas are.

Texas Commission on Law Enforcement

The major state regulatory agency that develops and enforces law enforcement standards is the Texas Commission on Law Enforcement. It was established in 1965, though it was not until two years later that it received any state funding. Initially a small agency with only a director and a staff of three, it has grown substantially—as has its responsibility in **licensing** those in law enforcement. Beginning in 1969, the commission was responsible for certifying all peace officers with the exception of those peace officers who were elected officers under the Texas Constitution. Those duties were expanded in 1979 to the certification of county jailers and in 1989 to the certification of those in telecommunications. In 1997 the commission's duties were again expanded to Texas private prison jailers who are responsible for federal prisoners or for prisoners from other states. Once the commission licenses these persons, it requires that they undergo continuing education. The commission revokes licenses if standards are not met, and it also monitors police training academies.

The commission is governed by nine commissioners who are appointed by the governor and confirmed by the Senate. They are chosen for six-year terms, and terms expire for three members every two years. Commissioners are selected from three categories. Three are chief administrators of law enforcement agencies such as sheriffs, constables, or chiefs of police; three must be licensed by the commission, and two of those must be peace officers in nonsupervisory positions; and three must be private citizens.[8]

Controversies Surrounding Policing in Texas

Police have not only the power of arrest but also the power to use reasonable force in doing so. It is the **use of force** by police that is the most controversial issue involving police in both Texas and the nation. Rarely, however, does the use of force result in major consequences to police. The *Texas Tribune* examined 656 police shootings in the largest cities in Texas between 2010 and 2015. Thirty-eight percent of these shootings were fatal, and 41 percent of those shot were African American. Of these 656 shootings, twenty-five officers were subject to disciplinary action and ten were terminated as police officers. Seven were indicted for criminal charges, though none of those were charged with murder, and none were convicted.[9]

licensing (of law enforcement officials) in order to be a Texas peace officer, one must meet the requirements imposed by the Texas Commission on Law Enforcement, the regulatory body for peace officers and certain other officers in the state

use of force peace officers may use reasonable force to effect an arrest or to protect themselves or others

More recently, two police officers have been charged with murder, and both have been convicted. One officer has been sentenced to ten years in prison and ten years of probation for a charge of aggravated assault. That officer was with the Farmers Branch Police Department and was off duty and in plain clothes when he chased two teenagers he saw breaking into his vehicle. After a short vehicle chase in which he rammed their vehicle off the road, he quickly began shooting at the teens. He fired sixteen times, killing one and wounding the other. The officer claimed he saw one of the teens reach down after the crash and pull a weapon. A box cutter was found in the vehicle, but it was a tool used in the dead teen's work. No gun was found.[10]

The other officer was with the Balch Springs Police Department. He killed a 15-year-old high school freshman who, with his friends, was driving away from a party that police had been called to investigate. The officer opened fire on the vehicle with an AR-15 rifle. The department initially defended the officer, claiming that the driver of the car had attempted to back over the officer. Video of the incident, however, showed the car was moving away from the officer.[11] That officer was sentenced to 15 years in prison and a $10,000 fine.

Prior to the conviction of the Farmers Branch officer, the last time a police officer was convicted of murder was 1973. In that case, Dallas police officer Darrell Cain held a gun to the head of a 12-year-old boy and, on the second pull of the trigger, killed him while the boy was handcuffed inside a patrol car. Although Cain claimed the shooting was an accident, he was convicted, sentenced to five years, and served half of that time.[12]

Police shootings generally do not go to trial. One example of such a shooting occurred in 2016 in Beckville after a Texas Department of Public Safety (DPS) trooper attempted to pull over a 23-year-old for speeding. Rather than stopping, a vehicle chase ensued, followed by a foot chase. The trooper drew his gun and repeatedly shouted for the 23-year-old to stop and put his hands up. Instead, the suspect continued running until he tripped and fell. The trooper claimed he believed the young man had a gun and shot him in the back five times because he failed to show his hands. The young man was unarmed, and the trooper at the time had no reason to suspect the young man of any crime other than speeding. The Texas Rangers investigated the shooting and reported to the grand jury information about previous traffic tickets and a drug charge that were unknown to the trooper at the time of the shooting. The grand jury refused to return an indictment.[13]

It is, of course, difficult to second-guess a police officer who must make a split-second decision about whether to fire a weapon. If a suspect makes a sudden movement, the officer must act quickly, and in some cases the suspect's actions are later determined to be unrelated to use of a weapon against an officer. Still, police use of force has become a major issue in Texas, in part because of a concern that police use of force may be indicative of racial bias. Between September 2015 and May 2017, 302 officer-involved shootings occurred in Texas. Fifty-three of the persons involved were unarmed, and twenty-two were African Americans.[14]

One potential remedy for concerns over the appropriateness of police use of force is the increased use of video cameras in police vehicles and on police officers. It was video of the incident involving the Balch Springs police officer, for example, that showed, contrary to the initial explanation for the shooting by the department, that the car was not going toward the police officer but away from him.

Ken Johnson, a Farmers Branch police officer, is the first police officer in Texas to be charged with murder since 1973. After shooting two teenage boys while off duty, killing one and injuring the other, he was sentenced to ten years in prison.

Favorability Toward the Police

Republicans have more favorable attitudes toward the police than Democrats and Independents. Why would that partisan difference exist? Whites and Latinos have far more favorable attitudes toward the police than do African Americans. Why do you think there are racial differences in attitudes toward the police?

	VERY/SOMEWHAT FAVORABLE	NEITHER FAVORABLE NOR UNFAVORABLE	VERY/SOMEWHAT UNFAVORABLE	DON'T KNOW/NO OPINION
All	64%	15%	18%	3%
Democrat	48	22	27	3
Republican	82	7	8	2
Independent	49	18	38	3
White	73	11	13	2
African American	30	31	39	1
Latino	60	15	20	5

SOURCE: University of Texas/*Texas Tribune* poll of 1,200 registered voters in Texas between February 3 and February 10, 2017. Margin of error is +/− 2.83 percent.

Beginning in September 2017, a law went into effect requiring police departments to report officer-involved shootings to the state and imposing a substantial financial penalty if the department does not do so. Amazingly, there was no accurate central repository for information on officer-involved shootings, and some police departments were unwilling to report that information. The new legislation should offer a better sense of the extent of officer-involved shootings in the state along with the causes of these shootings.

One concern has been the potential for bias in the investigation of officer-involved shootings. A hint of such investigation bias occurred in the Beckville shooting when the Texas Ranger report to the grand jury mentioned the shooting victim's traffic record and drug charge, although the DPS trooper did not have knowledge of this record when the shooting occurred. While no such proposal is currently being considered, an independent investigation body solely focused on the examination of officer-involved shootings might provide a remedy for concerns about bias in the investigation of these shootings.

The Sandra Bland Case The Sandra Bland case is probably the most recent and most highly publicized case that involved questionable police practices in Texas unrelated to officer-involved shootings. In 2015, Bland returned from Naperville, Illinois, to her alma mater, Prairie View A&M, to start a new job working with the university's alumni association. A DPS trooper stopped Bland for failing to signal a lane change. The encounter escalated when Bland refused a request to extinguish her cigarette and the trooper threatened to use a Taser on her. The trooper claimed Bland was combative and uncooperative and that he removed her from her car to conduct a safer traffic investigation. He then arrested her for assaulting a public servant. She was taken to the Waller County jail where she remained because she was unable to pay the $500 bail. After being in the jail for three days, Bland was found dead in her cell. A medical examiner ruled the death a suicide. While an investigation of her death led to no criminal charges at the jail, the trooper was indicted for perjury and was terminated from his position. Later, an agreement was made between prosecutors and the trooper that led to the perjury charge being dropped in exchange for the trooper never again seeking a law enforcement position. DPS claimed the trooper had violated its courtesy policy, had prolonged the stop beyond the time reasonably necessary, and had failed to follow procedure for interviewing traffic violators. The key question was, of course, how a simple traffic stop could possibly escalate into a death in a county jail. Bland was African American, and there were questions about whether her race played a role in her treatment. Additionally, there were questions about how frequently simple police stops unnecessarily escalated, particularly in the absence of police dashboard camera video coverage.[15]

In 2016, Bland's family agreed to a settlement in a civil suit in which they would be paid $100,000 by the Department of Public Safety and $1.8 million by Waller County. Additionally, the county agreed to provide emergency nurses on all shifts at the jail, use electronic sensors to ensure timely cell checks, and seek state funds for jail improvements. However, in 2017 the proposed **Sandra Bland Act** was largely gutted in the legislature because of opposition by police groups. The bill would have required officers to acquire signatures or recorded consent before they conducted a search and would have

Sandra Bland Act legislation in response to the arrest and jailing of Sandra Bland, who died in jail; the law requires independent investigation of jail deaths and alternatives to jailing those with mental or substance abuse problems

Sandra Bland was stopped for a minor traffic violation that escalated and led to her being jailed. Bland subsequently died in the county jail, which led to a national outcry. In response to national attention over Sandra Bland's case, major political figures such as Lieutenant Governor Dan Patrick spoke to the press about her death.

prevented jailing persons for offenses in which the maximum punishment was a fine. The law that did pass does, however, mandate diversion of persons with mental health or substance abuse problems to treatment and does require an independent agency to investigate jail deaths.[16]

Categorizing Crime in Texas

 Identify the major classifications of crime under Texas law and the types of punishments that may be imposed

Crimes, of course, are classified by legislation into different levels of seriousness, and punishments vary according to the seriousness of the crime. In the Texas criminal justice system, crimes are classified as felonies or misdemeanors. Table 13.1 shows the punishment range for the various classifications of crime in Texas.

Felonies and Misdemeanors

felony a serious criminal offense, punishable by a prison sentence or a fine. A capital felony is punishable by death or a life sentence

A **felony** is a serious criminal offense that subjects a convicted person to a fine of up to $10,000 and/or prison punishment ranging from six months to the death penalty. The right to vote, to have a gun, or to have certain occupational licenses can also be taken away, although in Texas voting rights for felons are restored after the sentence has been fully discharged. There are degrees of felonies, with more severe sentences attached to higher degrees. The most serious felony is capital murder, for which the penalty can be death or life imprisonment without parole.

misdemeanor a minor criminal offense usually punishable by a small fine and/or short jail sentence

Misdemeanors are less serious crimes, for which the penalty is a fine of $4,000 or less and/or a sentence of up to one year in the county jail. The right to vote, to possess a weapon, or to have some occupational licenses is not lost as a result of a misdemeanor conviction. There are three classes of misdemeanors, again with more severe sentences attached to more serious crimes (see Table 13.1).

Punishing Crime

probation punishment where an offender is not imprisoned but remains in the community under specified rules and under the supervision of a probation officer

In some cases, especially if it is the defendant's first conviction, the judge may allow **probation** or community supervision rather than a jail or prison sentence. Probation is a suspension of the jail or prison sentence with the understanding that the defendant will meet certain requirements imposed by the court. These usually include reporting to a probation officer on a regular basis, holding a steady job, paying fines or restitution, and abstaining from alcohol or drug use. Generally, community supervision can run up to 2 years for misdemeanors and up to 10 years for felonies, although if a probationer complies with the rules, it is possible to obtain early release from probation after serving one-third of the term.[17]

TABLE 13.1

Classification of Crimes

FELONY CRIMES	EXAMPLES	PENALTIES*
Capital murder	killing a peace officer or firefighter in the line of duty, killing a small child, murder for hire, death occurring during the commission of certain crimes	Death or life without parole
First degree	Aggravated (using a weapon) assault on a public servant, aggravated kidnapping, aggravated sexual assault, arson of a habitation	5 to 99 years in state prison; fine up to $10,000
Second degree	Arson, bigamy, bribery, robbery, sexual assault, manslaughter, possession of 50 to 2,000 pounds of marijuana	2 to 20 years in state prison; fine up to $10,000
Third degree	Stalking conviction, third driving while intoxicated (DWI) charge, third offense of violation of a protective order	2 to 10 years in state prison; fine up to $10,000
State jail	Burglary of a building, DWI with a child as a passenger, forgery of a check, possession of less than one gram of a controlled substance	180 days to 2 years in a state jail; fine up to $10,000

MISDEMEANOR CRIMES	EXAMPLES	PENALTIES*
Class A	Burglary of a vehicle, second DWI offense, public lewdness, possession of two to four ounces of marijuana	No more than 1 year in county jail; fine up to $4,000
Class B	Prostitution, terrorist threats, first DWI charge, criminal trespass, possession of two ounces or less of marijuana	No more than 180 days in county jail; fine up to $2,000
Class C	Public intoxication, disorderly conduct, minor's possession of alcohol	Fine up to $500

*In many cases, probation is a possible substitute for serving jail or prison time. If jail or prison time is imposed, it is possible to obtain parole or early release.
SOURCES: "Texas Criminal Laws & Penalties," Texas Criminal Defense Lawyer; Fred Dahr, "Crimes and Punishment in Texas State Court," texasdefenselaw.com.

Violation of probation requirements can result in being sent to jail or prison to serve out the sentence behind bars. Often, prosecutors know that people with lengthy probation sentences will find it difficult to comply with all of the requirements. So, in cases where they believe it will be difficult to get a conviction, they might agree to a plea bargain allowing community supervision for a long period. They expect that the defendant will violate probation and spend time in jail or prison.

People who are sentenced to prison may be released on **parole** after a period of time behind bars. The decision to grant parole is made by the Texas Board of Pardons and Paroles, composed of a chair and six members who serve six-year staggered terms. Besides determining grants of parole, conditions of parole, and revocation of parole, the board makes recommendations to the governor about sentences and clemency. In order

parole the conditional release of an offender who has served some prison time, under specified rules and under the supervision of a parole officer

Cite and Release: Necessary Cost-Savings or Soft on Crime?

EIGHT STATES have legalized the recreational use of marijuana. In Texas, however, possession of less than two ounces of marijuana is a class B misdemeanor, and possession of two to four ounces is a class A misdemeanor. The maximum punishment for a class B is 180 days in the county jail and a $2,000 fine, and for a class A it is one year in jail and a $4,000 fine. Such punishments are unlikely—far more likely is a substantial fine and probation. However, until 2007 a person arrested with less than four ounces of marijuana would be taken to jail and booked and then likely spend hours in jail until he or she could post bond (and far longer in jail awaiting trial if unable to post bond). To ease jail crowding and to free police officers to deal with more egregious offenses, in 2007 the Texas legislature gave police the option to cite and then release a person arrested for possession of less than four ounces of marijuana. The citation would be much like a traffic ticket. The person would have to appear in court and would be subject to criminal punishment but would not be arrested, booked, or put in jail until bail was paid.

The theory behind this change was that jail space would not be taken up by minor offenders, police resources would be saved (police in Dallas make 100 to 120 arrests per month for small amounts of marijuana), and counties would save money (on average it costs taxpayers $120 to arrest and book someone in an urban Texas county, and it costs taxpayers about $53 a day to keep a prisoner in jail).[a] Despite these benefits, most counties proved unwilling to use the cite and release option. By 2017, however, some counties such as Hays, Williamson, Travis, Harris, and Bexar counties were frequently using it.[b]

Counties such Collin have rejected "cite and release." District attorney Greg Davis said his county did not adopt the policy because "it may . . . lead some people to believe that drug use is not more serious than double parking."[c] Prosecutors also claimed they lacked a system for dealing with misdemeanor tickets. Another concern was that without a booking process where all ten fingerprints are taken, police would have difficulty establishing a person's identity, and it would be easier for an offender to avoid showing up for trial. In response, supporters of cite and release point out that the offender is still subject to criminal punishment. Additionally, they point to a study of Hays County, where 95 percent of those cited and released did show up for trial.[d]

Other police departments, such as in the city of Denton, are looking into beginning cite and release primarily as a way of keeping police on patrol rather than having them tied up with booking persons on minor drug charges. City police officers in Denton, Texas,

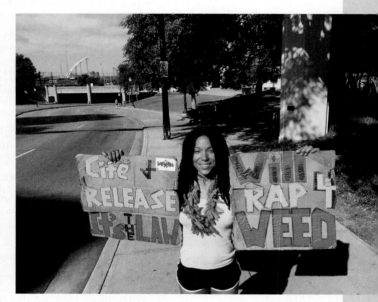

for example, made 224 marijuana possession arrests in 2016 and 261 in 2015. Each arrest and booking in Denton takes police two to three hours when they could be patrolling and answering other calls. The city of Dallas is in the early stages of implementing a cite and release program.

COMMUNICATING EFFECTIVELY: YOUR VOICE

- Why is there sudden interest in cite and release, which has been allowed since 2007?

- Consider the advantages and disadvantages of cite and release programs. If you could voice your opinion on this issue to local law enforcement, what would you say? What arguments would you use to support your opinion?

for the governor to alter a prisoner's sentence or grant clemency, a majority of the board must support the change.

People serving time for capital crimes are not eligible for parole, and generally those convicted of other violent crimes must serve at least half their sentence before being considered for parole. People convicted of nonviolent crimes must serve at least one-fourth of their sentences or 15 years, whichever is less, before being considered. The Board of Pardons and Paroles uses a complex formula that considers such factors as the offender's prior record, previous parole violations, employment history, prison disciplinary record, the severity of the current offense, the age of the offender, educational or vocational opportunities taken during confinement, and whether the offender is a gang member. If a prisoner is granted parole, he or she must comply with the requirements imposed or, like probation violators, he or she can be sent to prison for the remainder of the sentence.[18] In the 2017 fiscal year, over 5,600 persons had their parole revoked and were returned to prison, and 17,377 persons successfully completed parole and were discharged.[19]

There are also sentencing enhancements—certain circumstances, such as previous convictions—that increase the classification of or penalties for the crime. For example, a DWI offense is a class B misdemeanor, but a second DWI is a class A misdemeanor, and a third DWI is a third degree felony. That means, of course, that a second or third DWI conviction will result in more serious penalties than will the first DWI offense.

Texas enhances sentences for repeat felony offenders as well. If a person convicted of a third degree felony has a prior felony conviction, that person is sentenced for a second degree felony. Similarly, a second degree felony is punished as a first degree felony if the person had a prior felony conviction. A person convicted of a third felony can be sentenced to life imprisonment based on a **"three strikes" provision** in the penal code, and in some cases, such as sexual assault cases, two felony convictions are sufficient for life imprisonment.

"three strikes" provision a law that allows persons convicted of three felonies (or in some cases two felonies) to be sentenced to life imprisonment

The Criminal Justice Process

 Outline the procedural steps that occur after a person is arrested

Several procedural steps occur after a person is arrested and before guilt or innocence is determined. In Texas, as in most other states, this process may take months or even years. The major steps are listed below.

Arraignment and Posting Bail

Generally, when a person is arrested for a felony or misdemeanor and jailed rather than ticketed, he or she will be arraigned before a judge. At the arraignment, the charges will be explained to the accused, and he or she will be reminded of their due process rights—such as the right to remain silent and the right to an attorney.

bail payment of money to the state as an assurance that an accused person who is released from jail pending trial will appear for trial; if the accused does not appear, the bail is forfeited

After being charged, a defendant may be offered the chance to be released from jail on bail until the trial, and the amount of bail is generally set at the arraignment. **Bail** is money paid to the state to ensure a defendant's future appearance in court. Usually, if the defendant does not show up for trial, the bail is forfeited. If the defendant appears as required, the bail money is returned. Often, bail is more than the accused can pay, and so he or she will arrange with a bail bondsman to pay the bail in exchange for a nonrefundable payment that is often 10 percent of the amount, but can be higher. Even a defendant who cannot provide bail or pay a bondsman to do so can possibly be released on personal recognizance, which is a personal promise to appear. This possibility is most likely if the accused has ties in the community such as a family or employment and does not have a criminal record. If an accused cannot provide bail or be released without bail, he or she usually will be held in jail until the trial.

Recently, a federal court declared the operation of the money bail system in Harris County for indigent misdemeanor arrestees to be unconstitutional. The court found that keeping poor misdemeanor defendants in jail had detrimental effects on their employment, made it more likely that they would be found guilty than persons released on bail, and encouraged those indigents who were jailed to plead guilty. Also, there seemed no good reason to jail indigent misdemeanor defendants. The court found that there was not a significant difference in failure to appear for trial between those who provided money for bail versus those who were released without bail. A three-judge appellate panel ruled that the Harris County bail system was indeed unconstitutional, though it returned the case to the trial judge for implementation of the decision that was less broad than had been ordered by the trial judge, who had wanted very rapid release from jail of indigent misdemeanor defendants. Dallas County has also been sued over its bail practices and, as with Harris County, is having to change its bail practices. The decision has enormous implications statewide and throughout the nation. A likely effect is that misdemeanor arrestees will often be released on personal recognizance rather than being required to pay bail.[20]

After being charged, a defendant may be released on bail. If the individual does not have enough money to post bail, he or she may make arrangements with a bail bondsman, who posts bail in exchange for a nonrefundable payment.

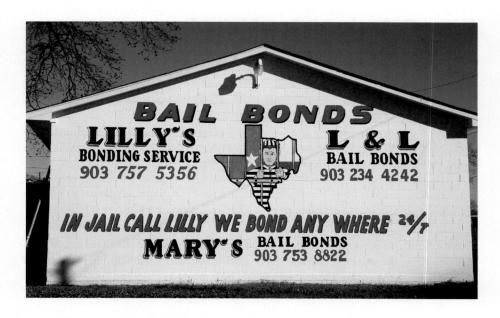

Grand Jury Indictment

Although the procedure can vary, after arraignment a felony case will generally be presented to a **grand jury**—12 persons who will determine if there is sufficient evidence to hold the accused for trial. Grand juries do not find people guilty or not guilty but instead will vote a "true bill," meaning that they find probable cause that the accused has committed the crime, or a "no bill," meaning that they do not find probable cause. A person would, of course, be held for trial only if there is a "true bill." A grand jury indictment is far from conviction, as all a grand jury determines is the existence of probable cause, and usually the decision is based only on a presentation by the prosecutor. For a conviction in a trial, there must be a finding of guilt "beyond a reasonable doubt," which is a demanding standard of proof for a prosecutor. At a trial the defense is also heard. It has the opportunity to cross-examine witnesses and present its version of events. The major criticism of the grand jury is that it usually hears only what the prosecutor chooses to let it hear and that it serves as a "rubber stamp" for the prosecutor's decision.

On September 1, 2015, a major change occurred in the way grand juries are selected in Texas. Texas was the last state to use what was commonly called the "pick-a-pal" or "key man" system, in which a district judge appointed commissioners who chose persons to serve on grand juries. One problem with this system was that those who were chosen tended to be unrepresentative of the community. The new system selects 12 grand jurors and 4 alternates in a random selection process such as the one for trial juries.

> **grand jury** jury that determines whether sufficient evidence is available to justify a trial; grand juries do not rule on the accused's guilt or innocence

Pretrial Hearings

After indictment for a felony, there will likely be a number of pretrial hearings in which the accused will formally plead guilty or not guilty, the trial is scheduled, and various motions may be presented, such as ones to move the trial or exclude certain evidence. These hearings vary in length but in most cases are quite brief. In a criminal trial, a common motion is one to exclude certain evidence on the grounds that it was illegally seized in violation of the Fourth Amendment to the U.S. Constitution. In these instances, the judge examines the facts of the seizure and determines whether the evidence was legally seized and therefore can be used at trial.

Plea Bargaining

Although **plea bargaining** can occur during a trial and even after a finding of guilt but before sentencing, the prosecution and the defense will often discuss a punishment in exchange for a guilty plea and reach an agreement before the trial. The prosecutor's offer might involve reducing the charge, dropping some of the charges, or recommending a lighter sentence than the defendant might get at trial if found guilty.

Plea bargaining is one way that prosecutors maintain high conviction rates. But plea bargaining is not only necessary politically; it is also crucial in managing the limited resources of the prosecutor's office and the courts. Prosecuting a case that goes to trial after a defendant pleads not guilty can cost thousands and even hundreds of thousands of dollars. A trial also uses up the limited time employees have. If plea bargaining were

> **plea bargain** negotiated agreement in a criminal case in which a defendant agrees to plead guilty in return for the state's agreement to reduce the severity of the charge or prison sentence the defendant is facing

suddenly abandoned in Texas, the criminal justice system would quickly come to a halt as a result of a massive overflow of trials. Defense lawyers often have an incentive to plea bargain as well. In many cases, they can generate more income by representing numerous defendants (who often have limited resources) in plea negotiations than by engaging in a few time-consuming trials. And plea bargains can benefit defendants, even innocent ones, in that they get an assured sentence that may be less than they would receive if they went to trial and were found guilty and then sentenced by either a judge or a jury.

The judge with jurisdiction over the case will almost always agree with a plea bargain made by the district attorney's office. For one thing, plea bargains reduce the crowded dockets of judges. Without a trial, the judge cannot be aware of the strengths and weaknesses of the state's case and so will generally recognize that the district attorney is in a far better position to determine the appropriate sentence.

Trial and Sentencing

If the case does go to trial, a defendant may choose to waive the right to a jury trial and instead have the judge determine guilt. Such cases include those where a judge is perceived as inclined to favor the defendant or where the crime is believed to be one that would inflame jurors' emotions against the defendant. A defendant may also have a jury trial but waive the right to sentencing by a jury, so that the judge determines the sentence if there is a guilty verdict. In Texas, felony juries are composed of 12 people, and misdemeanor juries are composed of 6. Decisions by criminal juries must be unanimous, and for both felonies and misdemeanors the standard of proof must be "beyond a reasonable doubt." If the jury's decision in either a felony or misdemeanor case is not unanimous, the case results in a mistrial, and the prosecutor must decide whether to retry the defendant.

If the defendant is acquitted (found not guilty), he or she is, of course, set free. If the defendant is found guilty, there will be a jail or prison sentence or probation and/or a fine. A defendant may appeal a guilty verdict by asking a higher court to reconsider the lower court's decision. Very minor criminal cases that are heard by municipal courts or by justice of the peace courts can be appealed to the county courts. More serious misdemeanors and felonies, however, are heard by county or district courts, and appeals from those courts go to one of the 14 courts of appeal in Texas. Any further appeal will be to the highest criminal court in Texas, the Texas Court of Criminal Appeals. Death penalty cases are appealed directly from trial courts to the Texas Court of Criminal Appeals. In rare events where a question of U.S. constitutional or statutory law is raised, it may also be possible to appeal to the federal courts.

Does the Criminal Justice System Create Criminals?

In some cases, the requirements of the Texas criminal justice system can be quite burdensome on individuals. For some people, complying with the rules of the process can be difficult and even financially impossible. One common crime in Texas, especially among younger offenders, is possession of less than two ounces of marijuana. Although a few Texas counties treat this crime as the equivalent of a traffic offense where the police officer tickets the offender, in other counties offenders will be taken to jail to be held until the bond hearing and until they can make bail. Although a recent federal court decision is in the process of changing bail requirements for misdemeanors in Harris County and potentially throughout Texas, for the time being in much of Texas, bail on such a charge would be $500, which means that either the full $500 will have to be posted with the county, or a bail bondsman will have to be retained for roughly a $50 nonrefundable fee. After bail is posted, the defendant will eventually have to go to trial in a county-court-at-law. Some defendants hire an attorney, which may cost $1,000 to $3,000 for the entire process in this type of case; others may appear in court without an attorney. It would not be unusual for a first offense to result in at least a $500 fine plus court costs, a sentence of 30 hours of community service, a sentence of 15 hours in an approved drug education course, and nine months' probation during which the defendant would pay a fee for each visit to the probation officer and any drug testing required by the probation officer. After court costs, probation costs, and the fine, the offender will probably have spent about $1,000 to $1,200, plus legal fees.

While on probation, the offender will not be allowed to use drugs or alcohol and will be subject to testing. There will be a required visit with a drug counselor and regular trips to a probation officer. Travel will be restricted. If the offender is in compliance, he or she will probably get early release from probation. If not, probation could be full length and jail time is possible. Additionally, because this is a drug case, the offender's driver's license will be suspended for six months. If the offender must drive in order to get to and from work or to care for family matters, he or she must go to court and obtain an occupational driver's license. Filing this paperwork can easily cost nearly $300, not counting possible attorney's fees. In order to drive legally, the offender will also have to purchase an SR-22 automobile insurance policy for two years. This high-risk policy, in which the insurance company reports directly to the state that the offender has automobile insurance coverage, can cost twice as much as a regular policy.

Thus, an arrest for possession of a marijuana cigarette can easily cost more than $5,000 to $7,000 overall in fines, court costs, insurance charges, probation fees, and attorney costs, not to mention time in jail after arrest and, if the marijuana was found in the offender's vehicle, towing and impoundment charges. Failure to comply with all probation requirements can lead to violation of probation and other criminal charges such as driving with a suspended license or driving without proper insurance. The structure of the criminal justice process even for minor crimes such as class B misdemeanors may deter future crimes because of the severity of punishment, but the cost and penalty structure also seem to encourage failure and further criminality by the offender.

Crime and Texas District Attorneys

Ordinarily when we think of the criminal justice system, we think of the police who make arrests and the courts that adjudicate those cases. The most important actors in the Texas criminal justice system, however, are probably the prosecuting attorneys. Some counties have an elected **county attorney** whose office represents the state in misdemeanor

county attorney an elected official in some counties who prosecutes misdemeanor cases

Greg Willis's campaign website shows how candidates for district attorney must emphasize how they are "tough on crime." Willis was re-elected Collin County district attorney in 2018.

district attorney public official who prosecutes the more serious criminal cases in the district court

criminal cases. The county attorney usually provides legal advice to the county commissioners as well, although generally the county attorney does not represent the county in civil cases. Counties with elected county attorneys also have elected **district attorneys**, who represent the state in felony cases. Some counties have merged the offices of county and district attorney into an office that represents the state in both misdemeanor and felony cases and is often called the office of the criminal district attorney.[21]

In urban counties in Texas, the office of the district attorney is huge, encompassing several hundred lawyers, investigators, and support staff. In 2016 the Harris County district attorney's office employed 310 prosecutors and a total of about 700 employees. In most rural counties, the district attorney's office includes only one or two lawyers. The head of every district attorney's office in Texas is an elected officer who runs under a party label for a four-year term. As the chief prosecuting officers of a county or district, district attorneys generally campaign as "tough on crime" and brag about high conviction rates. If they appear too lenient or their conviction rates are too low, political opponents will emerge who will accuse them of not doing their job appropriately. Because prosecutors often deal with people who have committed terrible crimes, they often see the worst aspects of humanity, and this also may lead to a "tough on crime" approach.

The district attorney has prosecutorial discretion, which means the power to charge or not charge a person with a crime. Even when a case is presented before a grand jury to determine if a criminal indictment should be issued, the grand jury is dependent on the prosecutor to present the evidence that may lead to an indictment, and a prosecutor has great discretion in choosing both whether to go before a grand jury and whether to accept or not accept the decision of a particular grand jury.

Crime and Criminal Defense

Persons accused of crime may represent themselves or may retain a criminal defense lawyer to represent them. Since the famous Supreme Court case *Gideon v. Wainwright*, persons too poor to hire a lawyer have had a constitutional right to have an attorney appointed to represent them in serious cases. As mentioned in Chapter 9, in Texas that representation is generally provided by **assigned counsel**—that is, the judge will appoint a lawyer to represent people who cannot afford one. However, in some counties in at least some types of cases, such people will be represented by a **public defender**, a lawyer who is paid a salary by the government to represent indigent defendants. With assigned counsel, usually judges appoint a private attorney on a case-by-case basis for a fee that varies according to the county and the legal service performed. One concern with this system is that the fee may be so small that the assigned attorneys do not do an adequate job in representing their clients. The issue of the quality of representation provided to indigents in Texas is an important one because large numbers of cases are tried and substantial amounts of money are spent in providing this representation. Table 13.2 specifies the 2017 costs of indigent defense in the state and the numbers of cases involving poor people whose lawyers are paid by the state.

Some of the fees counties pay for assigned counsel seem remarkably inadequate. As examples, Bexar County pays appointed counsel $75 an hour for trial work involving a state jail felony, $100 an hour for a second degree felony, and $125 an hour for a first degree felony. Harris County pays $300 a day for trial work in a state jail felony, $400 a day for a second degree felony, and $500 a day for a first degree felony. The joint Jack and Wise County judicial district pays lawyers $400 for each half day of trial work for felonies and $250 for each half day of trial work for misdemeanors to a maximum of $1,000.[22]

Public defenders are far rarer in Texas than are assigned counsel. However, a statewide public defender program is available for capital cases and serves participating small and midsize counties. There are a small number of other public defender offices in Texas, and they are regional or countywide in scope. Some of those have specialized caseloads such as mentally ill defendants, rural areas, appeals, or juvenile defendants. The public defender program for capital cases has been evaluated by comparing it with assigned counsel in capital cases, and several interesting findings have emerged from the study. For one thing, in rural areas of the state, few lawyers are qualified to handle capital cases. In an area of Texas spanning over 80,000 square miles, for example, only 13 private lawyers are qualified for these cases. For such an area, death penalty specialists who are public defenders are particularly useful, and they also have the necessary support team that would be difficult to organize in the more rural and isolated parts of the state. For many smaller counties, the cost of death penalty cases is prohibitive—defense costs alone often exceed $100,000. Participating in a public defender program with death penalty specialists can greatly reduce costs for these counties. The public defenders were also more likely than assigned counsel to avoid a death penalty and to get better dispositions for their clients overall.[23] Death penalty work is very specialized and complex, but the success of public defender programs over assigned counsel in such cases suggests that an expansion of public defender programs in other areas may be beneficial to indigent defendants.

assigned counsel private lawyers appointed by judges to provide legal representation for indigent defendants in serious criminal cases; the lawyer's fee is determined by and paid by the county

public defender salaried lawyer who is funded by the government or by grants who represents indigents in Texas in some counties or for some types of cases

TABLE 13.2	
Indigent Defense in Texas, 2017	
Costs of indigent legal services	$265,131,386
Number of noncapital felony trials	$211,877
Number of misdemeanor trials	$217,000
Juvenile hearings	$39,635
Appeals	$2,666
Capital cases	$551

SOURCE: Texas Indigent Defense Commission, "Indigent Defense Data for Texas."

Crime, Corrections, and the Texas Prison System

Describe prisons and corrections policy in Texas

It has long been claimed that Texas does things in a big way, and that is certainly true of its levels of crime and the way it deals with criminals. As of August 31, 2017, there were 145,341 offenders incarcerated in the state's prisons, state jails, and substance abuse facilities.[24] These numbers exclude those incarcerated in municipal and county facilities. In 2016 the average cost per day for each bed in the state's correctional facilities was about $53. It costs about twenty-six times more to imprison someone than to place that person on probation and about eighteen times more to keep him or her in prison than on parole.[25]

History of the Prison System

Shortly after Texas joined the Union, construction was authorized for a state penitentiary in Huntsville. The 225-cell facility opened in 1849. It confined prisoners in single cells at night and congregated them during the day to work in silence. From 1870 to 1883 the entire prison system was leased to private contractors who used the labor of inmates in exchange for providing maintenance and prisoner supervision. After 1883 convicts were leased to railroads, planters, and others who provided the prisoners with food and clothing and paid a stipend to the state. These leasing arrangements were abandoned in 1910 as a result of scandals and abuses of the system.[26]

Under the new state-run system, however, abuses continued. In 1924 an investigation found inadequate care and brutal treatment of prisoners as well as inefficient management. That investigation led to the creation of a state prison board, which supervised the work of a general prison manager. Still, abuses continued, and by the mid-1940s the Texas prison system was considered one of the worst in the nation. In 1974 the Joint Committee on Prison Reform submitted findings to the legislature that found serious fault with numerous aspects of the system's operation—from inmates' living and working conditions to their classification, and from medical care to staff training. Still, no significant reforms were made.[27]

The event that had the most dramatic effect on the system's operation in modern times was a federal court case, *Ruiz v. Estelle*.[28] Lawsuits filed by prisoners are nothing new. During the tenure of W. J. Estelle, Jr., the prison director from 1973 to 1983 and the defendant in the *Ruiz* case, prisoners filed 19,696 cases in the federal courts in Texas, a caseload amounting to about 20 percent of the federal court docket in Texas during that period.[29] However, the *Ruiz* case was exceptional. A class-action suit on behalf of inmates that began in 1972, it focused on issues of crowding in the system, security and supervision, health care, discipline, and access to the courts. In 1980 a federal court concluded that inmates' constitutionally guaranteed rights had been violated. Texas joined several other states in having its prison system declared unconstitutional.

Who Is in Prison in Texas?

Prison Population in Texas by Race, 2016*

■ % of Texas population   ■ % of Prison population

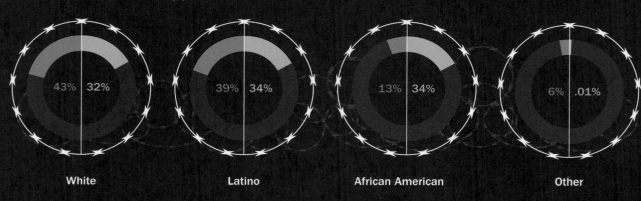

White	Latino	African American	Other
43% 32%	39% 34%	13% 34%	6% .01%

Death Row Population in Texas, 2017*

% of Texas population   % of death row population   Total death row inmates

White	Latino	African American	Other
43%	39%	13%	6%
28% — 66 inmates	26% — 61 inmates	44% — 102 inmates	2% — 5 inmates

While Texas does not lead the nation in its incarceration rate, it is still the seventh highest in the United States. A disproportionately high number of African American men, for example, are serving in the state's prisons compared with their percentage of the population in the state. In fact, 7 out of every 10 prisoners in Texas are either African American or Latino.

*May not add to 100 percent due to rounding.

SOURCES: U.S. Census, Quick Facts, July 1, 2017; Texas Department of Criminal Justice, Statistical Report, Fiscal Year, 2017; Texas Department of Criminal Justice, "Death Row Information," December 15, 2017.

QUANTITATIVE REASONING

- The Texas population is 39 percent Latino, 13 percent African American, and 43 percent white. According to the data shown here, how does the Texas prison population compare?

- What might help explain the racial/ethnic makeup of the prison population in Texas?

David Ruiz (right) and other Texas prison inmates filed a class-action lawsuit demanding stronger rights for prisoners. The case resulted in changes in how Texas prisons operated.

The result was the appointment by the court of a special master, a court officer, to oversee the system to eliminate constitutional violations such as overcrowding, improper supervision, and improper care of inmates. This massive reform had to be imposed by the federal courts because the state seemed unwilling or unable to reform its own prison system. Federal court supervision of the system ended in 2002.

For a long time, many in Texas government resisted federal court supervision of the prison system, arguing, for example, that the *Ruiz* decision amounted to judicial activism and interfered with the rights of the state. To reduce the overcrowding in state prisons to comply with *Ruiz*, the state encouraged the early release of prisoners, some of whom then committed more crimes. *Ruiz* did, however, help turn the criminal justice system into a major public policy issue in Texas.

The Prison System Today

The Texas prison system is operated by the Texas Department of Criminal Justice. This agency is run by a nine-member board appointed by the governor, and members serve staggered six-year terms. The board hires an executive director to lead the sprawling agency, and it is responsible for developing the rules and regulations that govern the entire state prison system.[30] Since 1993 the Department of Criminal Justice is responsible not only for the massive prison system in Texas, where convicted felons are incarcerated, but also for the much smaller state jail system. State jails are minimum security facilities, and they hold low-level drug and property crime offenders who are sentenced to serve 180 days to two years. Unlike county jails, no one in the state jail system is awaiting trial; they have all been convicted and are serving a sentence.[31]

The Department of Criminal Justice also runs a small program called Substance Abuse Felony Punishment Facilities (SAFPF), which provides assistance to offenders who need treatment for substance abuse problems. Offenders may be sentenced to this program by a judge, or the Board of Pardons and Parole may require substance abuse services as a condition of parole. Typically, offenders receive a six-month in-prison treatment program, as much as three months additional treatment in a residential treatment facility, six to nine months of outpatient treatment, and up to twelve months of support groups and supervision.[32]

In the wake of estimates in 2007 that Texas would need 17,000 new prison beds costing $1 billion by 2012, the Texas legislature increased the capacity of prison alternatives such as drug treatment and halfway homes, much cheaper alternatives to prison.[33] Until 2007, when the Texas legislature began to seriously address alternatives to imprisonment, the state government had significantly increased the incarceration of offenders by building more prisons, especially in the early 1990s. In 2011, however, for the first time in Texas history, the state actually closed a prison—the century-old Central Unit in Sugarland. After that, seven other prisons closed, making a total of eight prison closings in a six-year period.[34]

From 1976 to 1990 the rate of property crime in Texas rose 38 percent, and the rate of violent crime rose 113 percent. Since prison expansion in this period did not keep up with these increases, generous early-release policies were used to make room for newly convicted inmates. With prison expansion, however, early-release policies were reduced. In 1990, for example, 38,000 prisoners were given early release; in 1997, with a much larger prison population, only 28,000 were.[35] The steady lengthening of sentences is shown in Figure 13.1. In 1994 prisoners on average were released after serving one-third of their sentences. In 2017 prisoners were serving about 61.1 percent of their sentences before being released. Inmates at state jails served on average 99.5 percent of their sentences.[36]

As shown in Figure 13.2, the Texas prison population reached its peak in 2000 and then dropped off. In 1980, at the time of the *Ruiz* case, there were fewer than 30,000 inmates in the state. By 2002, the number had jumped to over 150,000, then dropped to 133,600 by 2017.[37]

For much of the 1980s the rates of violent and property crime in Texas were especially high.[38] By the mid-1990s, however, those rates had dropped. While some observers argued that the drop was due to increased incarceration of offenders, there may also be other causes, such as demographic change. The most prison-prone group in society is males between the ages of 20 and 29. If that demographic group is large, then we would expect the prison population to also be large.[39] Indeed, 93 percent of Texas prisoners are male, and the average age of male prisoners is 39.4 years.[40] Of course, changes in laws and treatment practices also affect the crime rate and the incarceration rate. Long sentences for habitual criminals, for example, are relatively new, as are long sentences for the use of a firearm in the commission of a crime.[41] The number of prison inmates per 100,000 total population in Texas in 2017 was 568. Only six states, including Louisiana with an astounding incarceration rate of 760 per 100,000, beat the Texas per capita rate. (See the "Texas and the Nation" graphic, which presents the incarceration rate for the adult population.) Texas had 12.4 percent of the nation's total state prison population in 2016, and no other state had more inmates in its prison system than Texas.[42] Nevertheless, the state ranked high in crime rates. Texas ranks 15th among the states in violent crimes per 100,000 persons.[43]

FIGURE 13.1

Percentage of Prison Sentence Served by Texas Inmates

SOURCE: Criminal Justice Policy Council, "Percentage of Prison Sentence Served for All Release Types, Fiscal Years 1994–2004"; Texas Department of Criminal Justice, Fiscal Year 2006 Statistical Report; Texas Department of Criminal Justice, Fiscal Year 2008 Statistical Report; Texas Department of Criminal Justice, "Fiscal Year 2011 Operating Budget and Fiscal Years 2012–2013 Legislative Appropriations Request," August 16, 2010; Texas Department of Criminal Justice, Fiscal Year 2012 and 2014 Statistical Reports; Texas Department of Criminal Justice, Fiscal Year 2016 Statistical Report.

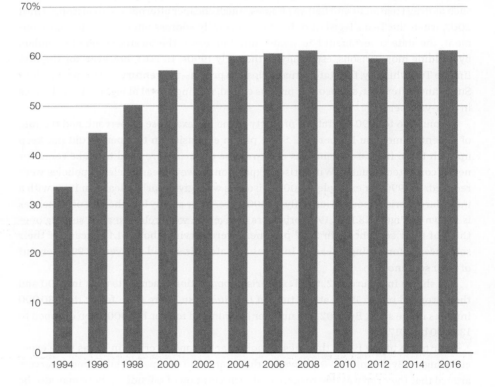

As Figure 13.3 shows, Texas imprisons mostly violent offenders. In 2017, 60 percent of Texas prison inmates had been convicted of violent offenses, 11 percent of property offenses, and 14 percent of drug offenses.[44]

It is especially difficult for felons to gain legitimate employment after their release—so much so that the federal government offers a large tax credit to employers who give jobs to people who have served a felony sentence. This difficulty makes it more likely that former prisoners will commit further crimes. Another problem is that the average sentence in a Texas prison is 19.4 years. After such a substantial time in prison, it is hard to readjust to life in the free world, and support structures such as family members have often died or removed the inmate from their lives. Still another problem is that the average educational achievement of an inmate in Texas prisons is only 8.4 years.[45] Finally, frequent drug and alcohol addiction among felons makes employment difficult and encourages criminal behavior. The problem of addiction was recognized during

FIGURE 13.2

Texas Inmate Population, 1980–2017

SOURCE: Associated Texans against Crime Annual Report, 1998; Texas Department of Criminal Justice, "Fiscal Year 2004 Statistics"; Criminal Justice Policy Council, "Texas Department of Criminal Justice State Incarcerated Population, Fiscal Years 1988–2002"; Texas Department of Criminal Justice, 2006, 2008, 2010, 2012, and 2014 Statistical Report; and Texas State Library and Archives Commission, "United States and Texas Populations 1850–2015"; 2016 and 2017 Statistical Reports and U.S. Census, Quick Facts.

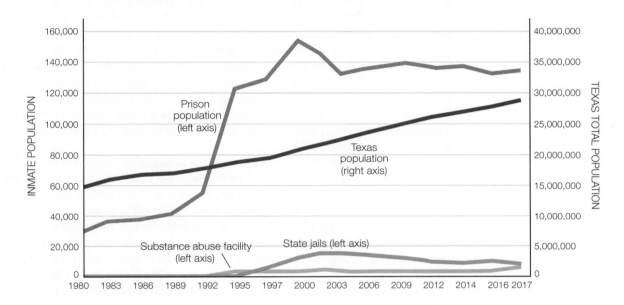

FIGURE 13.3

Prison Population by Offense, 2017

SOURCE: Texas Department of Criminal Justice, FY 2017 Statistical Report.

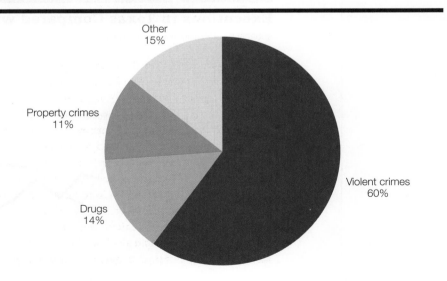

Other 15%

Property crimes 11%

Drugs 14%

Violent crimes 60%

Governor Ann Richards's administration, and drug and alcohol treatment efforts begun at that time have continued and expanded.

The Death Penalty

Texas is one of 31 states that have the death penalty. Of the 20 states that do not impose the death penalty, five have banned it since 2010. As of April 1, 2018, there were 2,743 people on death row throughout the nation, although over 60 percent of them are in five states—California with 740, Florida with 354, Texas with 235, Alabama with 188, and Pennsylvania with 160.[46] In Texas, one is subject to the death penalty for the murder of a public safety officer, fireman, or correctional employee; murder during commission of a kidnapping, burglary, robbery, aggravated rape, or arson; murder for hire; multiple murders; murder during a prison escape; murder by a prison inmate serving a life sentence; or murder of a child under the age of 6. Texas executed 555 people from 1976 through October 2018.[47]

As Figure 13.4 shows, though Texas has led the nation in the number of executions since the death penalty was reinstated by the Supreme Court, the imposition of the death penalty has declined in Texas and other states. National polling data show an increase in opposition to the death penalty—from 28 percent in 2000 to 37 percent in 2015. That 343 people have been exonerated from 1989 through June 2018 and that 11 death row inmates have been exonerated during that time period has perhaps contributed to reducing the number of executions in Texas.[48] More important is that death penalty cases have become very expensive and time-consuming for the state. A life without parole sentence is far less costly, while ensuring that the defendant will not pose a future danger to the public.

FIGURE 13.4

Executions in Texas Compared with Other States

SOURCE: Death Penalty Information Center.

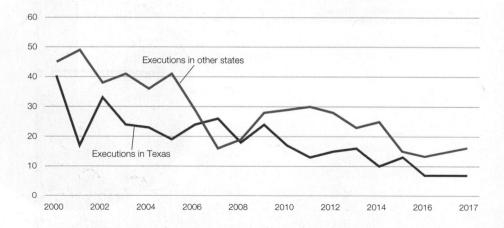

How Does Criminal Justice in Texas Compare with Other States?

Incarceration Rate, 2016 per 100,000 adult residents

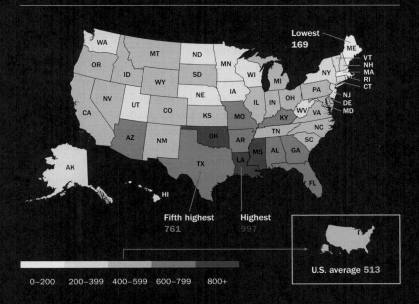

Lowest
169

Fifth highest
761

Highest
997

0–200   200–399   400–599   600–799   800+

U.S. average 513

Although the incarceration rate in Texas has declined in recent years, it still has a high rate—the fifth highest in the nation. In 2016, Texas incarcerated 761 out of every 100,000 persons, which is far higher than the national average and other large states such as California, Florida, and New York. Texas is also known for its use of the death penalty. Since the U.S. Supreme Court reinstated the death penalty in 1976, 37 percent of all executions within the United States have occurred in Texas, although the number of executions in Texas has declined.

SOURCES: E. Ann Carson, "Prisoners in 2016," U.S. Bureau of Justice Statistics, January, 2018; "Executions by State Since 1976," Death Penalty Information Center.

Total Executions, 1976–2017

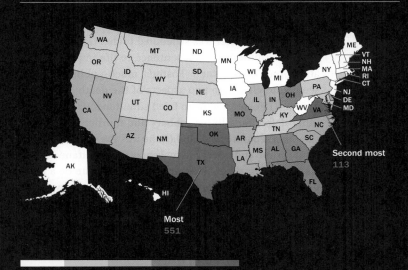

Second most
113

Most
551

0   1–10   11–50   51–100   100+

CRITICAL THINKING

- Which elements of Texas political culture or public opinion may contribute to the willingness to use the death penalty and to have high incarceration rates?

- Examine the regional patterns on the two maps. Do certain regions of the country have higher incarceration rates and death penalty usage? What do you think explains these regional patterns?

Political scientists Paul Brace and Brent Boyea found that judges tend to affirm death penalty sentences in states where judges are elected and where there is strong public support for the death penalty.[49] This finding may explain why Texas appellate courts are so supportive of the death sentences imposed by juries at the trial court level. Texas judges are elected, and polls show strong public support in the state for the death penalty. One 2018 poll, for example, showed that 65 percent of Texas voters either somewhat or strongly supported the death penalty and that only 25 percent were opposed.[50]

A stay on death row can be a lengthy one, even in Texas. In Texas, over the period 1974–2017, the average time spent on death row prior to execution was 10.87 years, although the time varied considerably. One inmate waived his appeals and spent only 252 days. On the other hand, David Lee Powell spent 31 years on death row before his execution in 2010.[51]

One of the issues involving the death penalty is whether all offenders are treated fairly and equally. Racial and ethnic minorities, especially African Americans, are disproportionately represented on death row. As of September 27, 2017, 102 death row inmates were African American, 63 were Latino, 64 were white, and 5 were classified as "other."[52]

From December 7, 1982, to July 27, 2017, 238 whites, 199 African Americans, 102 Latinos, and 4 members of "other" racial and ethnic groups have been executed.[53] A bias may exist in the criminal justice system that makes minorities disproportionately subject to the death penalty, although a counterargument is that the murder rate is higher among minorities. When the bias issue was presented to the U.S. Supreme Court, the Court refused to strike down the death penalty on the basis of statistical generalizations—essentially saying that there had to be evidence of racial bias in the specific case presented to the Court.[54]

The Texas Board of Pardons and Paroles votes on clemency for death row inmates. The board was originally created as a remedy for possible corruption in clemency granted by the governor. Prior to 1936 the governor essentially had unlimited power to grant clemency—a power often abused, especially by Governor Miriam Ferguson, who granted 4,000 requests for commutations of sentences in 1922 alone. It was widely believed that payments were made for many of these acts of executive clemency. In reaction, a constitutional amendment was passed in 1936 that charged the board with giving the governor recommendations on clemency. Without such a recommendation, the governor can grant only a single 30-day reprieve. No other state so limits the powers of the governor.

In 2007 the board recommended commutation of Kenneth Foster's sentence to be executed—only seven hours before Foster was scheduled to die. Governor Rick Perry commuted Foster's sentence to life imprisonment about one hour later.[55] Foster's much-publicized case seemed to challenge two aspects of the death penalty in Texas: (1) Foster had been tried simultaneously with the other defendants in his robbery and murder case rather than in a separate trial, and (2) he was the getaway driver in the crime and not the actual shooter. Simultaneous trials with other defendants in murder cases can be a huge disadvantage for a defendant like Foster, who was not the shooter but was nevertheless tried with the shooter.

Foster was tried in this way because Texas has the law of parties—a person involved in a crime that leads to a murder is guilty of murder even though that person is not actually the person who committed the murder.

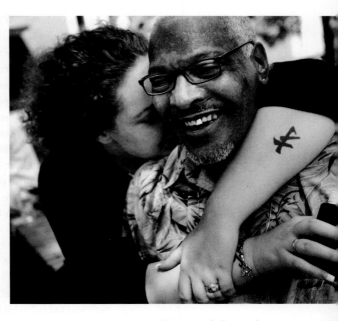

Self-Defense and Concealed/ Open Carry of Handguns

In any examination of crime in Texas, the enormous concern Texans have with self-defense cannot be ignored. One of the most controversial issues in the state over the past few years has concerned concealed and open carry of handguns. Advocates of concealed and open carry argue that the U.S. Constitution's Second Amendment provides them with a constitutional right to bear arms. Article 1, Section 28, of the Texas Constitution provides a similar right with the caveat that carrying arms is subject to state regulation. It states:

> Every citizen shall have the right to keep and bear arms in lawful defense of himself or the state; but the Legislature shall have the power, by law, to regulate the wearing of arms with a view to prevent crime.

Kenneth Foster's father and wife celebrate after hearing that Governor Perry had commuted Foster's sentence only hours before Foster was to receive the death penalty. Foster was convicted of murder despite only driving the getaway car.

To a large degree the wording in the Texas Constitution sums up the long-standing political debate over carrying firearms: does it provide protection against crime, or does it lead to crime?

In 1871, during Reconstruction, Texas passed legislation against both concealed and open carry. That law was not substantially changed until, in 1995, the legislature passed its first bill legalizing concealed carry, which was signed by Governor George W. Bush in fulfillment of a campaign promise. In the 2011 legislative session, concealed carry of handguns on college campuses became a major issue, and there clearly were enough votes to pass a bill allowing it, but the bill failed because of a parliamentary challenge. At the same time, legislation was passed and signed into law that prohibited employers from banning guns secured in employees' vehicles in company-owned parking lots.[56]

In the 2015 legislative session a bill allowing open carry of firearms passed despite concern that it would increase violence and lead to intimidation of others. The handgun must be in a hip or shoulder holster but no longer needs to be concealed. A concealed handgun license is still required, however, which means the license holder must be 21, pass a criminal and psychological record check, and undergo classroom and shooting training.[57] In 2015 campus carry was also passed, which allowed licensed gun holders to conceal carry on parts of Texas's public universities.

Campus carry has been one of the most controversial aspects of Texas handgun legislation. It required public universities to allow concealed handgun license holders to carry, except in some restricted locations, on their campuses. Some faculty, especially at the University of Texas at Austin, expressed concern that campus carry would lead to campus violence. At least one senior professor resigned over the policy, and three professors filed a lawsuit in an unsuccessful effort to stop it. Public opinion about campus carry has been only slightly favorable. One 2015 poll found that 47 percent of Texans favored campus carry, 45 percent opposed it, and 8 percent did not know.[58]

To date, however, campus carry, concealed carry, and open carry have not led to the violence their opponents predicted. Open carry has proven rare in the state's urban centers, and the number of students who can carry handguns on campus is limited by the requirement that concealed carry license holders be 21. The greatest problems have been in determining the specific locations where bans on carrying handguns can be legally implemented. During the shootings of Dallas police officers on July 7, 2016, bystanders and the police had some difficulty in distinguishing the shooter from demonstrators who were carrying long guns, but carrying a long gun in Texas has long been lawful and has never been part of the debate over concealed carry, open carry, or campus carry of handguns.

What is clear is that Texas's handgun legislation has led to a large number of concealed carry licenses being issued. In 2017 there were 1,200,747 concealed carry license holders in Texas.[59]

Currently, some lawmakers are pushing for legislation commonly called "constitutional carry," which would make the licensing process and the gun training classes optional. Supporters of constitutional carry argue that bearing arms is a constitutional right and that licenses and training classes burden that right.[60]

The Integrity of the Texas Criminal Justice System

 Explain why Texas's criminal justice system is often controversial

In recent years, numerous controversial issues and cases have raised questions about how criminal justice works in Texas. Here, we consider whether the integrity of the criminal justice system is compromised. At the end of this section, we consider some of the reforms designed to improve the fairness of the criminal justice process.

How Fair Is the Criminal Justice System?

Ideally, the criminal justice system should hold the guilty accountable and protect the innocent from punishment. That has not always been the case in Texas. There seem to be problems with the fairness of the system. The question is how common those abuses are and what, if anything, can be done about them.

Texas is the home of more verified wrongful convictions than any other state.[61] There is a registry that lists wrongful convictions, generally known as exonerations,[62] in Texas and throughout the nation from 1989 through June 2018. Two thousand two hundred and forty exonerations have occurred nationally, and 343 of those exonerations have occurred in Texas. Many of the exonerations have resulted from scientific advances in DNA technology, and a number of wrongful convictions have received widespread public attention. Randell Dale Adams, for example, was the subject of an acclaimed movie, "The Thin Blue Line." Adams was sentenced to death in 1977 for the murder of a police officer. In 1989, largely as a result of the 1988 movie, Adams was released from prison. His conviction was the result of perjury, mistaken witness identification, and official misconduct.[63]

Still another widely publicized exoneration was that of Tim Cole, who was convicted in 1986 of sexual assault. Though his conviction was for one rape, he was believed to be the "Texas Tech rapist," a serial rapist who had assaulted women near Texas Tech University. He was sentenced to twenty-five years in prison and died in prison in 1999. In 2009 he was exonerated—the first posthumous exoneration in the state. Largely owing to efforts by Cole's mother and brother, Texas enacted the Timothy Cole Act, which increased compensation for exonerated persons to $80,000 per year wrongfully served in prison and which expanded services to exonerated persons. In addition, the Timothy Cole Advisory Panel on Wrongful Convictions was created in 2009 to study the causes and prevention of wrongful convictions.[64] In December 2016, the panel issued an extensive final report detailing numerous recommendations on how wrongful convictions could be prevented.[65]

One of the most recent highly publicized exoneration cases involved Michael Morton, who was convicted of murdering his wife. On August 13, 1986, Christine Morton was beaten to death at her home in Austin. Her husband, Michael Morton, was charged with the murder and was prosecuted by Williamson County district attorney Ken Anderson. Michael received a life sentence for the murder, though he persisted in claiming his innocence and argued that some unknown intruder must have killed his wife after he had gone to work. The day after the murder, Christine's brother had found a bloodstained blue bandana near the crime scene, and he had turned it over to detectives. In 2005, Michael asked for DNA testing on several items including the blue bandana.

John Bradley, the district attorney at the time, and known as a tough prosecutor, opposed the requests for DNA testing, claiming there was no way the testing would lead to some "mystery killer." He said that Michael Morton's lawyers were "grasping at straws." Morton's lawyers suspected that key evidence had been withheld, and so they sought investigative materials in the case. Bradley opposed those requests as well. In 2008, Bradley was forced to turn over the investigative materials, and Morton's defense lawyers discovered that Eric Morton, who was three years old at the time of his mother's murder, had seen the murder and described the killer as a "monster" who had red gloves and a big mustache. He also had said that the killer was not his father.

Defense lawyers discovered other information as well from the newly released files of the case. Police reports noted there was a check to Christine that was cashed with a forged signature after her death. There were reports of fraudulent use of her credit card after her death. There were also neighbors' statements to police that a man was seen parked in a green van near the Morton home on several occasions before the murder. Contrary to a legal requirement that prosecutors share exculpatory materials, this information had not been provided to the defense lawyers.

Then, in 2010, DNA testing on the blue bandana was allowed. DNA was found on the bandana to belong to the victim, Christine, and to a man whose DNA was in a national database as a result of an arrest in California. That man was Mark Alan Norwood. On

In 2011, Michael Morton was released from prison based on new DNA testing in his case. He served nearly 25 years in prison before another man was arrested for the crime. DNA evidence has revealed a series of wrongful convictions raising questions about criminal justice in Texas.

October 4, 2011, Michael Morton was released from prison—he had been convicted in 1987. Mark Alan Norwood was convicted of the murder of Christine Morton on March 27, 2013. He is believed to have murdered another woman in 1988.

High-profile exonerations like Morton's can have political consequences. District Attorney Bradley was defeated for re-election in the Republican primary in 2012. His opponent, Williamson County attorney Jana Duty, hammered Bradley for blocking the postconviction DNA testing for Morton and won with 55 percent of the vote. Bradley's resistance to that testing meant that Morton spent six additional years in prison.[66] Judge Ken Anderson, the original district attorney, was sentenced to 10 days in jail, a $500 fine, and 500 hours of community service for criminal contempt in telling the Morton trial judge that he had no evidence favorable to Morton.[67] He has also lost his judgeship and law license. Morton is free and will receive financial restitution from the state for the quarter century that he spent in prison for a murder he did not commit. He was present when the Texas legislature passed a bill, the Michael Morton Act, which established a uniform policy for district attorneys to make material that can help defendants' cases available to defense attorneys.[68] Perhaps even more important than the Michael Morton Act, for the first time in Texas a prosecutor was held criminally responsible for actions that resulted in a wrongful conviction, and another prosecutor was held accountable by the electorate for his actions that delayed Morton's efforts to prove his innocence.

Reforms

Consider recent proposals to improve Texas's criminal justice system

Despite widely publicized abuses, improvements in the Texas criminal justice system have occurred. Texas is no longer handling its crime problem solely by incarceration. The number of drug treatment programs has increased, and there is greater emphasis on imprisonment as a last response to criminal behavior and more emphasis on alternatives such as requiring increased reporting to probation officers, community service, electronic monitoring of offenders, and mandatory treatment for alcohol or drug addiction. The result has been a decline in prison construction and even the beginning of prison closings. Texas has the most generous compensation system in the nation for exonerated persons.

Some police departments are modifying their procedures for obtaining eyewitness evidence. For example, the Dallas Police Department has changed the way photographic spreads for identification of suspects are conducted so that the police officer handling the photographs does not know who the actual suspect is and thus cannot provide cues to the witness as to which photo to pick. Prosecutors often call on scientific experts, such as arson investigators, to help prove their cases. However, fields such as arson science are rapidly evolving, and some scientific theories used to convict defendants in the past have now been debunked. Certain indicators once considered signs of arson are now known to appear in accidental fires.[69] Similarly, the Texas Forensic Science Commission has recommended that testimony that connects bite marks to a specific defendant's teeth is junk science and should not be used as evidence against a defendant. A new Texas law makes it much easier for an inmate to challenge a conviction if it was based on bad science.

Some Texas district attorneys have recognized the problem of wrongful conviction and have appointed prosecutors who review wrongful conviction claims and take a cooperative approach toward lawyers working with the claimants. In 2016 the Harris County district attorney announced major programs to divert first time felony drug offenders into treatment programs rather than jail; to divert class B theft offenders to treatment programs; and to provide treatment rather than jail for the mentally ill.[70] These changes are a recognition that not all crimes are best handled by jailing the offenders.

For the first time in Texas, prosecutors are suffering significant consequences for actions that deny rights to defendants. Michael Morton's prosecutor lost his law license and served brief jail time for his actions in the Michael Morton case, in which he failed to turn

Does Texas's criminal justice system need to be reformed? Some observers feel that, beyond problems with wrongful convictions, the emphasis on imprisonment and the large number of inmates in Texas are major concerns, though incarceration rates are declining.

over exculpatory evidence to the defense. Since then, the former district attorney of Burleson County has failed in his effort to retain his law license. He had used false testimony and withheld evidence from the defense in a case where the defendant was sent to death row and later exonerated.

During the 2017 legislative session, one of the recommendations of the Timothy Cole Advisory Panel on Wrongful Convictions was made law. The law, the strictest in the nation regarding jailhouse informants, was in response to the recognition that one of the biggest causes of wrongful convictions was an inmate falsely testifying against another inmate in exchange for leniency in reference to his own crime. Such false testimony by inmates will become much more difficult because prosecutors will now be required to document their use of jailhouse informants, and they will have to share with defense lawyers information about the jailhouse informants' criminal histories. Additionally, prosecutors will have to notify defense lawyers of anything offered to the jailhouse informants in exchange for their testimony.

★ ★

Criminal Justice and the Future of Texas

PERHAPS THE CRIMINAL justice system in Texas works well overall, but is the system working as well as it should?

Will Texas decide, for example, that the accused need higher-quality legal representation so that problems in the system can be identified and resolved before a person is convicted and imprisoned? Former Dallas County district attorney Craig Watkins received national acclaim by offering a new perspective on his role of prosecutor, which he saw as not only convicting the guilty but also protecting the innocent charged with crime.

While Texas remains the major death penalty state and the state that holds the most offenders within its criminal justice system, its correctional policies are changing notably. The death penalty is imposed far less often than in the past—in large part because of a new alternative punishment of life without parole—although politically it remains unassailable. Texas is also sending fewer people to prison than in earlier years. Today, the old corrections model of "lock 'em up" seems to have been replaced by a more economically efficient approach in which nonviolent offenders, especially, are often given alternatives to prison, such as community supervision. The state is recognizing the strong connection between alcohol and drug addiction and crime, and more resources are being expended in addiction treatment programs. The issue of the future will be whether Texas will continue pursuing alternatives to prison for offenders. Finally, many states are reducing penalties for crimes such as possessing small amounts of marijuana. Will Texas join the movement toward decriminalization? Crime and corrections have always been a major issue in Texas politics, and the state appears on the cusp of major changes in this area.

STUDY GUIDE

Use **InQUIZITIVE** to help you study and master this material.

Policing in Texas

- **Describe the characteristics of policing in Texas and analyze the controversies surrounding it (pp. 443–48)**

Law enforcement in Texas is a dangerous occupation with a large number of peace officers spread throughout a large number of local, county, and state agencies. The size and resources of these police agencies vary widely. Additionally, there are problems with public impressions of the fairness of police behavior and the use of violence by the police.

Key Terms
licensing (of law enforcement officials) (p. 444)
use of force (p. 444)
Sandra Bland Act (p. 447)

Practice Quiz
1. The agency responsible for licensing peace officers is the
   a) Texas Peace Officers Association.
   b) Police Licensing Board.
   c) Texas Commission on Law Enforcement.
   d) FBI.
   e) Texas Department of Public Safety.

2. One important requirement of the Sandra Bland Act is that
   a) jail deaths must be investigated by an independent agency.
   b) families of those who die in jail will have the right to sue for monetary damages.
   c) jailers will be legally liable if a person dies in a county jail.
   d) persons cannot be jailed if their offense is only punished by a fine.
   e) persons must give written consent for their vehicle to be searched by the police.

3. Officer-involved shootings in Texas
   a) create questions of racial bias in the use of violence by police.
   b) have never involved shootings of unarmed suspects.
   c) are always examined by the Texas Commission on Law Enforcement to determine if correct procedure was followed.
   d) are rarely controversial.
   e) will lead to the arrest of the police officer who did the shooting.

Categorizing Crime in Texas

- **Identify the major classifications of crime under Texas law and the types of punishments that may be imposed (pp. 448–51)**

Crimes are categorized along a number of dimensions. The more serious crimes are felonies. The less serious crimes are misdemeanors. Within each classification are various degrees of crime based upon the severity of the offenses. The more serious the crimes, the greater the penalties.

Key Terms
felony (p. 448)
misdemeanor (p. 448)
probation (p. 448)
parole (p. 449)
"three strikes" provision (p. 451)

Practice Quiz

4. The most serious crimes are classified as
   a) felonies.
   b) misdemeanors.
   c) trial-eligible crimes.
   d) grand jury felonies.
   e) county-court-at-law crimes.

5. Probation refers to
   a) a judge's initial term in office.
   b) a suspension of the jail or prison sentence.
   c) a court in the local state court system.
   d) release into the community after time in prison.
   e) failure to pay bail.

6. Which of the following is true?
   a) Parole is granted by the governor.
   b) Members of the Texas Board of Pardons and Paroles are chosen by the legislature every two years.
   c) People convicted of capital crimes are not eligible for parole.
   d) The death penalty is required in all serious felonies.
   e) Texas does not enhance the sentence of repeat felony offenders.

The Criminal Justice Process

• **Outline the procedural steps that occur after a person is arrested (pp. 451–57)**

There are a number of stages in the criminal justice process, including arrest, arraignment, possible posting of bail, possible grand jury indictment, pretrial hearings, and either plea bargaining or trial. If a person is found guilty, he or she will be sentenced, after which there may be appeals. Within this process, the most important actor is probably the district attorney, who is the key decision maker with regard to charging a suspect, presenting evidence to a grand jury, plea bargaining, or recommending a sentence to a jury or judge.

Key Terms

bail (p. 452)
grand jury (p. 453)
plea bargain (p. 453)
county attorney (p. 455)
district attorney (p. 456)
assigned counsel (p. 457)
public defender (p. 457)

Practice Quiz

7. Grand juries
   a) review all decisions made by a trial judge.
   b) determine if witnesses are telling the truth by voting "true bills" or "false bills."
   c) determine if there is probable cause to prosecute an individual for a crime.
   d) hear trials involving the death penalty.
   e) hear trials in district court.

8. District attorneys may have the most important roles in the criminal justice process because
   a) they have the power to charge people with crimes.
   b) they have the power to plea bargain with defendants.
   c) they usually make the only presentation before grand juries.
   d) all of the above
   e) none of the above

9. Which of the following statements about plea bargaining is true?
   a) Plea bargaining threatens to overwhelm the limited resources of a prosecutor's office.
   b) Plea bargaining does not benefit defendants.
   c) Plea bargains are made by defendants with district attorneys and agreed to by a judge.
   d) Most Texas district attorneys oppose plea bargaining.
   e) Most Texas criminal defense attorneys oppose plea bargaining.

10. Indigent defendants charged with serious crimes in Texas
   a) must represent themselves.
   b) are represented by private attorneys pro bono as part of their ethical obligation to help others.
   c) most commonly are represented by public defenders.
   d) most commonly are represented by assigned counsel.
   e) are usually represented by legal clinics at law schools.

Crime, Corrections, and the Texas Prison System

Describe prisons and corrections policy in Texas (pp. 458–68)

- **Describe prisons and corrections policy in Texas (pp. 458–68)**

The Texas prison system is one of the largest in the nation. A major federal court decision (*Ruiz v. Estelle*) found serious overcrowding in the prison system. A series of reforms have been implemented to address the concerns raised by the decision. There has been an effort to lessen the number of people in prison through community supervision. While Texas remains the death penalty capital of the United States, fewer death penalties have been imposed recently than in earlier years.

Practice Quiz

11. The Texas prison system
    a) was vastly affected by a federal court decision, *Ruiz v. Estelle*, which declared that the overcrowded system was unconstitutional.
    b) holds mostly persons convicted of violent crimes.
    c) is a very costly way of dealing with crime as opposed to community supervision such as drug and alcohol programs, and probation and parole.
    d) is beginning to contract in size after a long period of expansion.
    e) All of the above are true of the Texas prison system.

12. The Texas Department of Criminal Justice
    a) is run by a nine-member board appointed by the governor.
    b) is run by an elected body.
    c) runs the court system for felony murder.
    d) establishes sentencing guidelines for crimes.
    e) grants probation to those convicted of crimes.

13. The death penalty
    a) has now been banned in Texas.
    b) has been imposed less frequently since Texas allowed juries to sentence a defendant to life without parole.
    c) is opposed by most Texas voters.
    d) is carried out disproportionately against whites.
    e) is imposed by a majority vote of the Texas Board of Pardons and Parole.

The Integrity of the Texas Criminal Justice System

- **Explain why Texas's criminal justice system is often controversial (pp. 468–71)**

Texas has had a significant number of people who have been wrongfully convicted. Numerous recent cases in which convictions were overturned have raised questions about the criminal justice system in Texas.

Practice Quiz

14. People have been wrongfully convicted in Texas because of
    a) police misconduct.
    b) bad or outdated forensic science.
    c) mistaken identifications.
    d) prosecutorial misconduct.
    e) All of the above are reasons for wrongful convictions.

15. An advance in which technology has conclusively proved the innocence of a large number of convicted people is
    a) drug testing.
    b) ballistics testing.
    c) DNA analysis.
    d) fire science.
    e) fingerprinting.

Reforms

- **Consider recent proposals to improve Texas's criminal justice system (pp. 471–72)**

Recent reforms that have been enacted may help reduce the number of wrongful convictions in Texas and improve the fairness of the criminal justice system. Reforms also may rely more on rehabilitation programs and less on incarceration as a solution to crime.

Practice Quiz

16. Reforms in the criminal justice process include
    a) financial compensation for people wrongfully convicted.
    b) changes to suspect lineups so that the police officer in charge of the lineup does not know who the actual suspect is.
    c) expanding drug treatment programs.
    d) showing photos in photo identifications to witnesses sequentially rather than at the same time to reduce the danger of witnesses comparing photos and choosing the one that best fits their memory of the assailant.
    e) All of the above are reforms to the criminal justice process.

17. Probation costs are
    a) about the same as prison costs.
    b) 10 percent higher than prison costs.
    c) considerably less than prison costs.
    d) extremely expensive because of costs of drug treatments.
    e) double the cost of prison.

The Santa Fe Bridge is a busy border crossing between Ciudad Juárez, Mexico, and El Paso, United States. Immigration to Texas from Mexico, Latin America, and elsewhere has transformed the state's demographics and increased its population in urban centers. What effects does this change have on the culture, politics, and public policies in Texas?

Building the Future: Public Policies for a Changing Texas

WHY PUBLIC POLICIES MATTER FOR THE FUTURE OF TEXAS

WThe Texas of the early twenty-first century is far different from the Texas of the nineteenth and twentieth centuries. One of the most significant changes is the fact that Texas has become a majority-minority state. That is, non-Hispanic whites now constitute a minority in the state. Latinos, African Americans, and Asian Americans combine to form a majority statewide, with Latinos now composing nearly 40 percent of the entire state population. This new reality has led to a wide variety of responses at the state level, as well as in many local communities. In particular, the issue of immigration has become more salient and will undoubtedly continue to dominate the headlines.

The issue of immigration has long affected Texas because it is a border state with Mexico. In recent years, because of national politics, state politicians have turned their attention to dealing with public policy issues related to the border. For example, in 2014 former governor Rick Perry sparred with the Obama administration by claiming that the federal government was not adequately protecting the border from illegal immigration and smuggling. He used his authority as governor to push for "Operation Strong Safety," a program aimed at investing $18 million per month of state funds to increase security along the border.[1] The people of Texas, despite the high numbers of Latinos in the state, seem to favor stricter controls on immigration and harsher punishments for undocumented immigrants. In a February 2016 poll of Texans conducted by the *Texas Tribune*, 53 percent of respondents agreed that undocumented immigrants should be deported, while 41 percent disagreed.

In the 2016 election, Donald J. Trump's campaign heavily emphasized immigration policy. With slightly over 11 million undocumented immigrants living in the United States (3.6 percent of the population), Trump called for efforts to remove and deport people living in the United States illegally. According to the Pew Research Center, Texas has 1,650,000 illegal immigrants living in the state (about 6.3 percent of the state population). Specifically, Trump also called for the construction of a border wall and the deportation of illegal immigrants. At the time of this writing, President Trump has been unable to secure funding from Congress to build the wall, which is estimated to cost up to $22 billion to construct.[2] During the campaign, Trump suggested that Mexico would pay for the construction for the wall, but Mexico has unequivocally said this will not ever happen.

Legal and illegal immigration continue to have an enormous impact on the state's politics, but the state is also changing in other profound ways. Texas has become more demographically, economically, and politically diverse. Population growth has strained the state's infrastructure, leading to proposals to make transportation more efficient. Higher education in the state also faces important challenges, given that state funding for higher education has not kept up with the state's booming population growth. Droughts have also challenged the ability of local governments to provide safe, clean, and reliable water to residents.

This chapter will explore the challenges Texas faces in transportation, demographic change (including immigration), education, and water. These are just some of the growing issues that Texas will face in the coming years, but they are the most critical. These challenges strain state and local bureaucracies and budgets and raise important questions of federalism. They are the issues that will continue to dominate Texas elections for the foreseeable future, and tackling them is likely to expose the deep divisions within and between the political parties that dominate Texas government today. In other words, we hope this chapter will answer the question, How will state and local politics shape, and be shaped by, a rapidly changing Texas?

CHAPTER GOALS

- Examine the major issues facing transportation policy in Texas (pp. 481–89)
- Analyze how immigration and border issues will change Texas in the coming years (pp. 489–99)
- Analyze the challenges facing Texas's system of higher education (pp. 499–509)
- Understand the challenges facing Texas's water supply (pp. 509–14)

Transportation Policy in Texas

Examine the major issues facing transportation policy in Texas

The growth of Texas, especially the growth of the state's cities, has led to major issues involving transportation. This section will describe the problems associated with transportation in the state. It will also examine proposed solutions, such as methods for paying for the costs of maintenance of existing roads and construction of new roads, the use of toll roads to fund roads, and alternative transportation systems. Additionally, this section will discuss the political problems associated with transportation in Texas—the desire for new and improved roads coupled with opposition to new taxes, public hostility to toll roads, and rural opposition to high-speed rail.

Texas Roads and Highways

Texas is a driving state. One recent survey found that 93 percent of Texans had a personal automobile or motorcycle as their primary means of transportation. Only 1 percent of Texans relied on public transportation, 1 percent on bicycling, and 2 percent on walking. On average, Texans drive their personal vehicles an astounding 17,321 miles a year, an increase of 3,970 miles per year since 2014. While 73 percent of Texans agree that there is a need to increase transportation funding in the state, there is not strong support for an increase—it's simply not a critical issue for most Texans.[3] Moreover, there is no agreement among Texans as to how an increase in transportation funding should be spent.

There are nearly 15.9 million licensed drivers in Texas. Only California, with nearly 26.2 licensed drivers, has more.[4] Texas has nearly 8.2 million registered automobiles on the road, nearly 12.9 million trucks, and over 374,000 motorcycles. Only California has more registered vehicles.[5]

The Texas highway network is the nation's largest, and Texas has a massive and expensive obligation to maintain a wide variety of roads and highways that people drive on approximately 455 million miles a day. Texas roads are usually measured in one of two ways: **centerline miles**, which is the total length of a road or a road segment, and **lane miles**, which are the centerline miles multiplied by the road's number of lanes. Another measure commonly used is **vehicle miles traveled**, which is an estimate of road usage. Vehicle miles traveled are calculated by multiplying average daily amount of traffic on a road by its length in centerline miles. Table 14.1 presents the types of roads maintained by the state, the centerline miles of the roads, the lane miles, and the daily vehicle miles traveled. The state highway network includes almost 73,000 centerline miles and more than 180,000 lane miles of interstate highways, U.S. highways, state highways, loops, spurs, business routes, farm and ranch-to-market roads, and park roads.[6]

centerline miles total length of a road or road segment

lane miles centerline miles multiplied by the number of lanes

vehicle miles traveled average daily amount of traffic on a road multiplied by length in centerline miles

TABLE 14.1

State-Maintained Roads and Highways in Texas

CLASSIFICATION	NUMBER OF CENTERLINE MILES	NUMBER OF LANE MILES	DAILY VEHICLE MILES TRAVELED
Interstate highways	3,417	16,376	167,083,705
U.S. highways	11,905	35,326	104,644,771
State highways, spurs, loops, business routes	16,390	42,726	112,992,589
Farm or ranch-to-market roads	40,910	84,925	69,154,237
Park roads	348	771	706,312
Total	72,970	180,124	454,581,615

SOURCE: Ginger Lowry and T.J. Costello, in "Texas Road Finance (Part 1) Paying for Highways and Byways," Texas Comptroller of Public Accounts Fiscal Notes, May 2016. Data is from Texas Department of Transportation.

The Problem with Texas Roads and Highways

Texas roads are showing their age. Many need maintenance and enhanced safety features. The American Society of Civil Engineering has determined that about 38 percent of Texas's major roads are only in poor or fair condition. In addition, Texas has about 53,000 bridges. The Federal Highway Administration has rated 19 percent as either "structurally deficient" or "functionally obsolete." A "structurally deficient" bridge is one with major components showing significant deterioration, and a "functionally obsolete" bridge is one that no longer meets modern highway design standards.[7]

Congestion of roadways has become a major problem in the state's urban areas. In 2015 the Texas Department of Transportation found that drivers in the largest metropolitan areas in the state averaged about 52 hours stuck in traffic, a situation that is only expected to get worse as the state's urban areas continue to grow.[8] The Texas A&M Transportation Institute compiled a list of the 100 most congested roads in the state, most of which were in Austin, the Dallas–Fort Worth area, Houston, and San Antonio. Six of the 10 most congested roadways in the state were in Harris County, three were in Dallas County, and one was in Travis County.[9] The American Transportation Research Institute listed the top 100 highway bottlenecks for commercial trucks in the United States. Table 14.2 shows that fourteen of those traffic bottlenecks were in Texas, of which ten were in Houston, two in Dallas, one in Austin, and one in Fort Worth. Needless to say, those traffic congestion points ranked high for professional truckers.

Road congestion is more than an irritant; it is expensive. A nationwide study of highway congestion estimated that the average automobile commuter in Houston was delayed about 61 hours a year as a result of traffic congestion and that the estimated cost of that congestion in time and fuel for the average Houston automobile commuter was $1,490. Other major cities in Texas also were estimated to have substantial costs associated with congestion. For example, the study estimated that average automobile commuters in Dallas–Fort Worth–Arlington had congestion costs of $1,185 per year, Austin automobile commuters had estimated costs of $1,159 per year, and San Antonio had estimated costs of $1,002 per year.[10] Overall, it was estimated that the total congestion costs for Texas metropolitan areas came to over $14 billion per year.[11]

The Costs of Texas Roads and Highways

Funding for roads and highways comes from federal and state sources, and most of that funding comes from taxes on motor fuels. Federal taxes for roads and highways are deposited in the federal Highway Trust Fund, which provides money for highways and mass transit programs. Funding for the Texas State Highway Fund was almost $21 billion in the 2016–17 biennium. The largest source of funding is the federal government. State motor fuel taxes and auto registration fees provide the bulk of Texas's funds for roads and highways. In recent years, however, those funding sources have been insufficient to meet needs. Part of the problem has been that the vast new production of oil and gas from shale in Texas has led to an increase in heavy trucks, which have damaged roads. Another problem has been that the costs of road construction and repair has vastly outpaced the rate of inflation, so tax dollars for roads do not purchase what they did even a few years ago. Finally, there have been significant increases in fuel efficiency of vehicles, so people are not buying as much gasoline as they once did. Because motor fuel taxes are based on amount of fuel sold on a cents-per-gallon basis, less fuel purchased means less tax revenue. Texas's gasoline tax is 20 cents per gallon, and the federal

Traffic in Texas has increased in recent years, causing commuters to experience significant delays and higher fuel expenses. The problem is expected to worsen as Texas's urban centers grow, posing problems for cities like Austin, which house some of the busiest stretches of highway in the state.

TABLE 14.2

Top Trucking Traffic Bottlenecks in Texas

NATIONAL RANK OF BOTTLENECK	CITY	BOTTLENECK LOCATION
#8	Houston	I-45 at US 59
#11	Houston	I-10 at I-45
#12	Dallas	I-45 at I-30
#13	Houston	I-10 at US 59
#22	Houston	I-610 at US 290
#25	Houston	I-45 at I-610 North
#28	Austin	I-35
#33	Houston	I-10 at I-610 West
#49	Fort Worth	I-35W at I-30
#59	Houston	I-610 at US 59 West
#60	Dallas	US 75 at I-635
#65	Houston	I-45 at Sam Houston Tollway North
#82	Houston	I-45 at I-610 South
#88	Houston	I-10 at I-610 East

SOURCE: American Transportation Research Institute, "The Nation's Top Truck Bottlenecks," (2017).

gasoline tax is 18.4 cents per gallon. The tax is not indexed to inflation, and the Texas tax has been the same since 1991, while the federal tax has been the same since 1993. When all fuel taxes on gasoline and diesel are considered, Texas's taxes are the lowest among the ten largest states. Combining state and federal taxes, Texans pay 38.4 cents in taxes for every gallon of gasoline and 44.4 cents per gallon for diesel. In contrast, Pennsylvanians pay 70 cents in taxes for every gallon of gasoline and 89.7 cents per gallon for diesel (the highest in the nation).[12]

In recognition of the fact that tax revenues dedicated to roads and highways were no longer sufficient, funding for transportation has been increased several times—by increased appropriations in 2013, an amendment to the Texas Constitution in 2014, reallocation of expenditures from the Economic Stabilization Fund, and another constitutional amendment in 2015. In the near future there will be more funds from the state motor vehicle tax placed in the highway fund, meaning more federal funding should be available. However, the demand for transportation expenditures is greater than the available supply of money even with these additional funds. And unless more money through taxation or tolls is spent on transportation, there will be greater congestion in the state.

Highways and the Future

The amount of money needed to fund Texas's roads, highways, and bridges is enormous. Yet more funding will be needed to fund Texas's future transportation needs. In 2040, Texas is expected to have 45 million people, and it is expected that Texans will drive 800 million daily vehicle miles. The Texas Department of Transportation estimates that to maintain current conditions on the state's highways, it needs an additional $5 billion annually. With current reasonably expected revenues, the only way that existing highways and bridges can be maintained in "good" condition—meaning roadways with minimal cracking and smooth rides with structurally sound bridges—is to move all highway expansion dollars to preventive maintenance and rehabilitation of existing highways. With $5 billion additional funding annually, the condition of highways and bridges would be "good" and congestion and mobility in urban area would be slightly worse than today while mobility in rural areas would be comparable to today.[13] The question is how to provide the funds for the necessary continued expansion of Texas's roads and highways.

Toll Roads Tax increases are politically unpalatable, and so for about 20 years politicians have turned to tolls as a way to fund, build, and maintain roads in the state. By 2016 there were twenty-five toll roads in Texas, providing new driving lanes in the rapidly growing urban areas. Toll roads solved a huge problem for the conservative political leadership of the state. Funding for the roads was off-budget. The money would be borrowed for the roads based on the planned tolls that would be collected, and the roads could be built without raising the gasoline tax, a move that was seen as overwhelmingly unpopular among voters.

The problem was that as more and more roads in urban areas became toll roads, tolls became more and more unpopular. The result was that political leaders such as Governor Greg Abbott and Lieutenant Governor Dan Patrick responded to that unpopularity of tolls by opposing additional toll roads. Regional transit leaders recently met to finalize their appeal to the Texas Transportation Commission to have tolled lanes be the best approach to deal with traffic congestion on I-635 East through the cities of Lake Highlands, Garland, and Mesquite. The plan called for two tolled managed lanes in each direction, with five lanes and the frontage roads in each direction being toll-free. It is universally agreed that I-635 East is the most needed highway project in the Dallas–Fort Worth area. Currently, the ten lanes of that highway handle more than 200,000 cars per day between US 75 and I-30. But that plan for tolled managed lanes and a tolled managed lane plan for I-35 in Austin (also a major traffic congestion area) were removed from the Texas Transportation Commission's ten-year funding plan because of opposition to tolls from Abbott and Patrick. Without tolls, by 2040 the DFW area can expect to see an 80 percent increase in travel time, a 44 percent decrease in average speeds, and a $50 billion annual increase in the cost of congestion.[14]

Stunned by the opposition to toll lanes, the Regional Transportation Council chair, Rob Franke, noted, "The RTC [Regional Transportation Council] has successfully utilized innovative finance tools such as tolled managed lanes to complete a dozen projects worth over $12 billion since 2005. These are projects that would still be waiting in line for pay-as-you-go funding to be available."[15] What Franke and the Regional Transportation Council had not understood, however, is that the very success of using tolls as a

Support for Revenue Increases for Transportation

Many people acknowledge that Texas faces major transportation challenges. Solutions, however, are hard to come by, and the public doesn't seem very supportive of raising revenue for transportation. Of all suggested revenue increases, the strongest support (and that support is very weak) is for small increases in vehicle registration fees and for increases in the gasoline tax. How would an urban, rural, or suburban Texas legislative candidate campaign for improvements in the state's transportation system?

SOURCE: Texas A&M Transportation Institute, "2016 Texas Transportation Poll" (a poll of 4,805 Texans taken between March 10, 2016, and July 28, 2016).

highway construction mechanism had led to the demise of tolls. There were so many tolls that the driving public had turned against them as a funding tool, and so Abbott and Patrick were now opposed to tolls. The problem for highway transportation policy is that without tolls, and with political opposition to tax increases, especially increases in the gasoline tax, there seems no funding mechanism to adequately meet the future needs for Texas roads and highways.

The Bullet Train At first glance, Texas might not seem an ideal place for a high-speed rail project: Texas's urban areas have a history of low public transportation use, Texans are very oriented toward the use of automobiles, and there is no significant intercity rail traffic in the state. Yet, a high-speed rail project between Dallas and Houston is only one of three such projects in the United States that is in advanced stages of development. There is a project between Los Angeles and San Francisco, which is considerably behind the Dallas-Houston project in development time, and there is a proposed train between Miami and West Palm Beach that will use a congested railway. In contrast to the California train, the Texas train will not be subsidized but will instead rely on private investment and federal loans. And the Texas train will travel at twice the speed of the Florida train.[16]

Relying on Japanese train technology, it is claimed the Texas train will travel at speeds as fast as 205 mph. It will make the 240-mile trip between Dallas and Houston in 90 minutes, and trains will run every 30 minutes. This massive project will take at least a $12 billion investment and possibly as much as $20 billion. It will require the purchase of thousands of parcels of land. Supporters of the train believe it will be an economic engine that will spur development in the Dallas-Houston corridor as well as generate jobs needed for the railway's construction and operation. It is also claimed the train will generate substantial tax revenues. Supporters argue that the dramatic growth of Houston and the Dallas–Fort Worth Metroplex provides justification for construction of the train. They point to air travel between Dallas and Houston being one of the most heavily traveled air routes in the United States, and they point to the flat and largely rural land between the cities as making construction of high-speed rail fairly easy and relatively inexpensive.

There is, however, major opposition to the high-speed rail proposal.[17] Opponents believe it cannot be profitable and that taxpayers will wind up paying its costs. Some opponents even oppose the reliance on Japanese train technology, believing the train will primarily benefit Japan. Most significantly, however, many landowners in the 240 miles between Dallas and Houston are opposed to the train. As Figure 14.1 shows, the train's path will run through miles of rural countryside, and many of those rural landowners do not want to sell their land in order to speed the travel of urban dwellers. For those who do not want to sell, their land will have to be seized under the governmental power of eminent domain, in which government may take property for a public purpose as long as just compensation is paid. Opponents of the train are claiming that the power of eminent domain does not extend to the Texas Central Railway (the corporate entity for the bullet train). Without that power of eminent domain, it is clear that the right of way for the bullet train cannot be obtained.[18]

Texas plans to use Japanese bullet train technology to construct a route between Houston and Dallas to both develop that corridor and ease transportation issues between the two cities. Debates continue over the cost of the project, as some worry taxpayers will shoulder the burden of the cost.

Public Transit in Texas

No part of Texas is known for its public transit or its use. Texas is a car-centered culture, and its sprawling cities are poorly designed for public transportation. Generally, larger cities in Texas have the best public transit, with the greatest availability of transit being at the city core and with less availability as the city spreads into the suburbs. In fact, many suburban cities see no advantage in participating in the public transit programs of central cities or in paying the taxes necessary to operate public transit programs. Houston is a special problem for the provision of public transit. The city was developed with cars in mind, and the city's territory extends over 1,285 square miles—an area so large that service is spread thin and that widespread transit coverage would be costly. Many public transit advocates believe bus and rail service is doomed in the city. For about 70 percent of the population in Harris and surrounding counties, transit access is poor, and more than half the population has no meaningful bus service.[19] Extreme as Houston's problems in providing public transit are, other cities in Texas face similar problems for similar reasons.

Table 14.3 offers a sense of how limited public transit and its use in Texas's major cities and metropolitan areas are compared to other major American cities and metropolitan areas. The Center for Neighborhood Technology has designed an overall transit score from 0–10, which considers the connectivity of public transit (the ease of reaching one's destination), access to land area, access to jobs, and the frequency of transit

FIGURE 14.1

Dallas to Houston Bullet Train

SOURCE: The Texas Bullet Train, "County Alignment Maps for Proposed Routes," Texas Central, www.texascentral
.com/project (accessed 9/20/18).

service. A score of 0 is the lowest possible score, and a score of 10 is the highest possible score. In terms of public transit, New York City is the highest rated city, with a score of 9.6 (a rating tied with San Francisco) and with 59 percent of the city's commuters using public transit. The New York City metropolitan area has a score of 6.8 with 32 percent of the area's commuters using public transit. Los Angeles, America's second largest city in terms of population, has a score of 7.7 with 11.26 percent of commuters using public transit. The Los Angeles metropolitan area has a score of 6.2 with 6.07 percent of the metropolitan area's commuters using public transit.[20]

The Texas cities and metropolitan areas shown in Table 14.3 have lower transit performance scores than New York City and Los Angeles (and their metropolitan areas) and also a lower percentage of commuters who use public transit. The very low use of public

TABLE 14.3

Public Transit in Major Texas Cities and Metropolitan Areas

CITY	OVERALL TRANSIT SCORE*	TOTAL COMMUTERS	COMMUTERS USING TRANSIT (%)
Houston	6.1	1,040,539	4.2%
Houston metro area	2.8	2,846,491	2.5
San Antonio	5.5	616,051	3.4
San Antonio metro area	3.8	988,708	2.3
Dallas	6.8	571,444	4.5
Dallas metro area	2.7	3,116,308	1.6
Austin	5.1	437,652	4.5
Austin metro area	2.7	887,952	2.6
El Paso	5.1	263,361	1.9
El Paso metro area	4.3	329,199	1.6

*An overall score ranging from 0–10 that looks at connectivity of transit, access to land area and jobs, and frequency of service.
SOURCE: Center for Neighborhood Technology 2016, AllTransit, alltransit.cnt.org.

transit, especially by those in the metropolitan areas, leads one to question the overall value of public transit as a solution to the increasing traffic congestion problems in Texas urban areas. Perhaps if there were more public transit available, more people would use it. And perhaps as congestion increases, there will be more use of public transit. For now, however, public transit seems to be having little effect on driving habits in Texas.

Demographic Change in Texas

Analyze how immigration and border issues will change Texas in the coming years

The Texas population continues to grow. This population boom is changing Texas socially and politically. These changes raise important questions that Texans are likely to be grappling with for generations: Are rates of immigration to Texas too high? Are immigrants enhancing Texas's economy and society, or are they taking away jobs and social services from American citizens? Should undocumented immigrants be prosecuted, deported, or provided a path to citizenship? Who is coming to Texas, and why?

Who Are Texas's Immigrants?

Americans from other parts of the country are flocking to Texas for economic opportunities. The state's oil and gas industry has largely recovered from the 2008 recession. Oil prices have gone up, and major companies have continued to expand and hire. This benefits the Houston region as well as other regions in the state with opportunities for natural gas exploration. In addition, migrants from all over the world continue to come to Texas, both legally and illegally. Indeed, as Figure 14.2 shows, Texas and New York are now tied in terms of total number of immigrants in the state. Only California has a larger immigrant population.

The state demographer estimated that in 2015, 16.4 percent of the state population was foreign born, as opposed to only 9 percent of the state population that was foreign born in 1990.[21] Foreign born individuals can go through the process of becoming **naturalized citizens**. This process can only happen if a person immigrated legally and has been a resident of the United States for at least five years. Individuals must also demonstrate good moral character, knowledge of American government, and a basic command of English.

naturalized citizen a foreign-born individual who becomes a citizen through a process involving examinations and demonstration of good moral character

---

FIGURE 14.2

Immigrant Population in Texas, California, and New York

SOURCE: Pew Research Center, "Texas Immigrant Population Now Rivals New York's in Size," April 20, 2016.

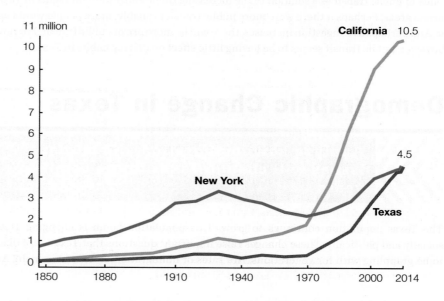

Immigrants have come to Texas from all over the world. According to the American Immigration Council, 55 percent of immigrants in Texas are from Mexico, 5 percent from India, 4 percent from El Salvador, 4 percent from Vietnam, and 2 percent from China. The rest of the immigrants in the state come from other countries. This diversity is most reflected in the state's major metropolitan areas. In fact, Fort Bend County, just southwest of Houston, is considered the most ethnically diverse county in the United States.[22] Native born Texans have deep connections to the immigrant experience. The American Immigration Council estimates that 15 percent of native born U.S. citizens in Texas have at least one immigrant parent. In the United States, even if someone is born to an immigrant parent, he or she will be a U.S. citizen.

Immigrants in Texas also come from all educational backgrounds. The American Immigration Council estimates that 25 percent of adult immigrants in the state have a college degree, while almost 40 percent have less than a high school diploma. As in every state, public education at the K–12 level is available to all Texans regardless of their immigration status. In terms of higher education, in 2001, Texas passed a law allowing undocumented immigrants the ability to pay in-state tuition at the state's public universities. This bill was known as the **Texas Dream Act**. When he ran for president in 2008, Governor Rick Perry received criticism for signing this legislation, but he defended his position during the presidential debates. In 2017 some Republican legislators attempted to repeal this law, but they were ultimately unsuccessful. Other bills addressing immigration, however, were successful, such as SB 4, the bill targeting sanctuary cities (see below).[23]

Texas Dream Act law passed in 2001 allowing undocumented immigrants living in Texas to pay in-state tuition rates at public universities

While most immigrants in Texas are legal residents, nearly 1.7 million of the total population is undocumented. This equates to 35 percent of the total immigrant population in the state, and 6 percent of the total state population. Many of the policy debates around immigration have to do with how to deal with this undocumented population. Because these individuals are not legally present in the United States, they are subject to deportation if caught by the Border Patrol or Immigration and Customs Enforcement (ICE). With the failure of Congress to pass immigration reform, states have filled the policy void by enacting policies aimed at border security.

The labor force in Texas largely depends on immigrants. The American Immigration Council estimates that nearly 3 million immigrant workers composed 22 percent of the state labor force in 2015, and The Pew Research Center estimates that 8.5 percent of the workforce in the state is composed of undocumented immigrants. Certain occupation groups have high immigrant shares in the state. Forty-five percent of all building and grounds cleaning and maintenance employees are immigrants. Forty-three percent of all construction and extraction employees are immigrants. Forty percent of farming, fishing, and forestry employees are immigrants, and nearly 30 percent of all food preparation and servers in the state are immigrants.

Studies show that immigrants in Texas have paid tens of billions of dollars in taxes. In Texas, most revenue the state collects is in the form of sales taxes. Everyone residing in the state has to pay these taxes when they purchase goods and services. In 2014 the Institute on Taxation and Economic Policy estimated that undocumented immigrants in Texas paid $1.6 billion in state and local taxes.[24] In addition,

SOCIAL RESPONSIBILITY: GET INVOLVED

- What benefits do undocumented workers bring to the state economy? What costs do they bring? All things considered, do you believe they are a net economic drain or gain for the state?

- What policies might be developed to better integrate undocumented workers and their families into the Texas economy?

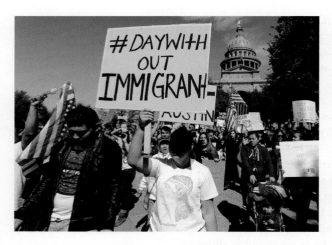

While debates over immigration policies continue in Texas and throughout the United States, it is clear that immigrants have a large impact on the business and economy of Texas. In 2017 many people in Texas and the nation held "A Day Without Immigrants" to underscore the importance of immigrants to businesses across the country.

many undocumented immigrants also indirectly pay taxes through rents that defray the cost of property taxes.

Immigrants contribute tens of billions of dollars to the Texas economy. One estimate reported by the American Immigration Council concluded that immigrant households had nearly $90 billion in after-tax income in 2014. This income is used to purchase goods and services, which improve the state's economy and provide work for many Texans.

Immigrants are also disproportionately business owners in the state, especially in the large cities. In the Houston metropolitan area, 42 percent of business owners are immigrants, in Dallas–Fort Worth 23 percent, and in the San Antonio area 19 percent, according to the American Immigration Council. Small business owners are the engine of today's economy, and they provide jobs for native born workers as well.

The large metropolises in the state have also seen explosive growth of immigration. Indeed, it is estimated that 24 percent of the population in the Houston metropolitan area is foreign born (including legal and undocumented immigrants).[25] Most immigrants are migrating to one of five counties: Harris County (Houston), Dallas County, Bexar County (San Antonio), Tarrant County (Fort Worth), and Travis County (Austin).[26]

Immigration Policy in Texas

With the growth of immigration in Texas and the United States, one key policy debate is how to deal with the undocumented population. In particular, conflict has emerged between local officials and state officials on whether to cooperate or not with federal immigration authorities when undocumented immigrants are arrested for violation of local ordinances or state laws.

Who Is Responsible for Immigration Policy?   The federal government is ultimately responsible for securing the borders of the United States and regulating entry of goods, services, and individuals. Land crossings between Texas and Mexico are monitored by the U.S. Border Patrol, an agency first created in 1924. The Border Patrol is now part of the U.S. Customs and Border Protection agency, which was created in 2003 following the terrorist attacks of September 11, 2001, to consolidate the functions of separate agencies into one department. Border Patrol agents engage in a practice known as *linewatch* to guard against illegal immigration and smuggling of narcotics. The Border Patrol also operates checkpoints well within U.S. territory. These checkpoints are another line of defense against undocumented immigrants who may have crossed the border illegally outside of a designated entry point.

Recent Texas governors have sought to address what they consider a crisis on the border by deploying members of the Texas National Guard to assist the Border Patrol in its mission. Members of the Texas National Guard patrolling the border cannot arrest or apprehend individuals, but they can notify the Border Patrol if they encounter situations requiring the attention of federal authorities. Sheriffs and local law enforcement along the border with Mexico also cannot enforce immigration laws, but they can communicate with federal immigration authorities regarding individuals they apprehend who are not legally present, as well as individuals smuggling contraband.

While the federal government is responsible for securing the border, cities and localities have attempted to deal with undocumented immigration by passing local ordinances aimed at addressing this issue. For example, the city of Farmers Branch, Texas, passed an ordinance in 2006 requiring property owners to verify that their tenants were legal residents.

Sanctuary Cities

In Texas, perhaps the most controversial issue dealing with immigration had to do with the extent to which local law enforcement cooperated with federal immigration authorities. Some city and county police departments, such as Austin, refused to cooperate with federal immigration authorities regarding apprehended individuals who were not legal residents. This led to a prolonged policy debate in the state legislature regarding how best to deal with these cities and counties, known as sanctuary cities. **Sanctuary cities** are localities where sheriffs have decided not to share information regarding the arrests of undocumented persons with federal immigration authorities. During the 2016 presidential campaign, Donald Trump declared that he would order his attorney general and secretary of homeland security to stop federal funding of sanctuary cities. In April 2017 the Trump administration followed through on this campaign promise when former Attorney General Jeff Sessions sent letters to nine cities warning them that if they did not cooperate with Immigrations and Customs Enforcement (ICE), they would lose funding from the Department of Justice. A few cities, including Seattle, have sued the federal government, and a federal court issued an injunction barring the removal of funding until a court could hear the dispute. In August 2018 the Ninth Circuit Court of Appeals agreed with challenges to the Trump administration's policy on withholding funds for sanctuary cities; however, this ruling currently only applies on the West Coast.

In the 2017 Texas state legislative session, state senator Charles Perry (R-Lubbock) introduced **Senate Bill 4 (SB 4)**, a bill that would end state funding of sanctuary cities. The bill would make it a crime for localities in Texas to refuse to cooperate with federal officials on immigration matters. Local sheriffs and law enforcement refusing to honor ICE holds would be subject to criminal prosecution. Local police departments of the major cities were largely opposed to this bill because they saw it as a way to deputize local law enforcement to enforce federal immigration laws in addition to city ordinances and state laws. In fact, Travis County sheriff Sally Hernandez was singled out by Governor Abbott for refusing to comply with ICE hold requests, and Abbott took executive action to prevent state funds from going to the Travis County sheriff's office. Houston police chief Art Acevedo opposed SB 4 by stating that it would go after "cooks and nannies, not hardened criminals."[27] However, Lieutenant Governor Patrick strongly pushed the bill through the state Senate, arguing that the bill was necessary to ensure that "no liberal local official can flaunt the law," by "allowing criminal aliens who have committed a crime to go free."[28] The state Senate acted first by passing SB 4 in February 2017 by a party line vote of 20–11.[29]

In late April 2017 the Texas House of Representatives took up SB 4. There it was met with more sustained opposition from the Democratic minority. Dallas state representative Rafael Anchía led a series of speeches against the measure in the chamber along with other members of the Mexican American Legislative Caucus (MALC). Of note were speeches by representatives Ana Hernandez (D-Houston) and Gene Wu (D-Houston).

sanctuary cities localities where sheriffs have decided not to share information regarding the arrests of undocumented persons with federal immigration authorities

Senate Bill 4 (SB 4) law passed in 2017 by the Texas legislature enacting penalties for sanctuary cities that refused to cooperate with federal immigration authorities

Hernandez spoke about her experience as an undocumented child and how the bill would instill fear in undocumented Texans. In particular, she and many local sheriffs opposing the bill argued that the new law would lead to an underreporting of crimes in the state as well as make it more difficult to solve crimes because of lack of cooperation with law enforcement. Undocumented immigrants would become less likely to cooperate with police or report crimes for fear of being reported to federal immigration authorities. Wu spoke about how the bill reminded him of the Chinese Exclusion Act of 1882, which he argued was inspired by fear and hatred of minorities.[30] Speaker Joe Straus, a moderate Republican from San Antonio, did not publicly support SB 4 yet allowed the bill to come to the floor given the support of both the lieutenant governor and governor. Despite fervent Democratic opposition, the bill passed the chamber on a party line vote of 93 in support and 54 against.

Abbott had signaled his support of SB 4, and once the measure passed the state House it was only a matter of time before the bill would become law. On a Sunday evening in early May, much to the consternation of opponents, Abbott broadcast his signature of the measure on Facebook Live. Critics accused Abbott of ignoring the bishops of his Catholic Church, who voiced opposition to the measure, and for signing the legislation on a day of worship for many Texans.

Before anyone had the opportunity to sue over SB 4, Texas attorney general Ken Paxton asked a federal court for a declaratory judgment the first week of May 2017. In other words, the state asked the U.S. District Court in Texas to rule that the law is not a violation of the Fourth or Fourteenth Amendment to the U.S. Constitution.[31] Nevertheless, the measure was immediately challenged in court by several border towns and the League of United Latin American Citizens (LULAC). They charged that the new law, which took effect September 1, 2018, should be struck down because it would lead to racial profiling and have a disparate impact on the state's Latino population.[32] Critics argue that the measure targets Latinos similar to how Arizona's unconstitutional SB 1070 "show me your papers" law targets Latinos. Defenders of the law claim that it will make communities safer by deterring illegal immigrants from committing crimes.

Civil rights groups have continued to protest the sanctuary cities law. On Mother's Day in 2017, hundreds gathered in Austin to protest the new law by marching from the state capitol building to the governor's mansion. Resistance to the law will also take place in the courts, where a long fight is inevitable. On May 21, 2017, El Paso County, along with the Texas Civil Rights Project, filed a lawsuit in federal court asking for the impending law to be ruled unconstitutional. The lawsuit alleges that SB 4 violates the Equal Protection Clause and Due Process Clause of the Fourteenth Amendment, as well as the Fourth Amendment's protection against unreasonable searches and seizures.[33] Other cities have joined El Paso in filing lawsuits against the state. In Houston, protesters interrupted Mayor Sylvester Turner at an event to demand that the city join a lawsuit against the legislation. In early June 2018, Turner asked the City Council to join other Texas cities' lawsuits against the new law.

In 2017 protesters gathered to demonstrate their opposition to SB 4, a bill that empowers police to question anyone's citizenship during routine stops. While the bill went into effect September 1, 2018, some expect it to increase instances of racial profiling and be eventually overturned by the courts.

The American Civil Liberties Union (ACLU) has also joined in litigation against the new law, created a "travel alert" for Texas, and developed a bilingual website to inform Texans about their constitutional rights.[34] The website includes information about how to respond if stopped by police or questioned by law enforcement offers with respect to immigration status.

Governor Abbott and Attorney General Ken Paxton have vowed to defend the law in court, claiming it is constitutional and necessary to ensure public safety. They point to the case of Kate Steinle, a woman who was killed by an undocumented immigrant in California. The argument is that this happened in a sanctuary city and that the person who committed this crime would have been off the streets had this happened in another city that fully cooperated with federal law enforcement.

The politically charged and controversial issue of sanctuary cities will likely continue to be debated nationally and in Texas. California became a sanctuary state in 2018, and some localities in that state wanting to cooperate with federal immigration authorities have filed lawsuits demanding that they should retain the ability to collaborate with the federal government. Conflicts among states, localities, and the federal government strike at the heart of federalism, and no doubt the courts will issue rulings further outlining the proper role of each in the realm of immigration policy.

Deferred Action for Childhood Arrivals (DACA)
Toward the end of his presidency, President Obama issued an executive order known as **Deferred Action for Childhood Arrivals (DACA)**, which shielded from deportation an estimated 800,000 young adults enrolled in college who were born abroad but brought to the United States as children by immigrant parents. With the decision of President Trump early in his presidency to rescind the program, the fate of these "dreamers" remains uncertain. After Trump's decision, many immigrant rights groups joined a lawsuit urging the federal courts to reinstate the program. While the lawsuit is pending, a federal judge allowed DACA permits to continue to be issued. In May 2018, Texas attorney general Ken Paxton joined six other states to sue the federal government, calling for an end to DACA.[35] Paxton and other opponents of DACA have argued that

Deferred Action for Childhood Arrivals (DACA) executive order implemented by President Obama, which shielded certain undocumented immigrants from deportation if they were enrolled in school, had no criminal records, and were making educational progress the program should be declared unconstitutional because President Obama effectively made a new law without congressional approval. In addition, they argue that the policy sets a bad precedent because individuals considering illegal entry to the United States might believe they will be granted amnesty in the future. They argue it is also unfair to those who have waited in line and immigrated legally to the United States.

According to the Migration Policy Institute, nearly 1.3 million undocumented immigrants were eligible for DACA in 2016, with the largest share of DACA-eligible recipients from California at 29 percent and Texas at 13.5 percent.[36] In Texas, nearly 125,000 residents were approved for DACA as of 2016. According to the American Immigration Council, 80 percent of DACA-eligible immigrants in Texas (about 140,000) had applied for DACA. In addition, more than 57,000 people living in Texas would be eligible for DACA but are not only because they do not meet the educational requirements. An additional 37,000 are estimated to become eligible as they grow older, according to the American Immigration Council.

An estimate by the Hobby School of Public Affairs at the University of Houston found that the DACA-eligible population in the state was 270,366 individuals, or 1 percent of the entire state population. Nearly 24 percent of the total DACA-eligible population (65,202 people) resides in Harris County. The "Who Are Texans?" feature on the facing page illustrates where DACA-eligible Texans have come from, where they live, their educational achievements, and language skills.

Border Security One of the most contentious areas of immigration policy is border security, and Texas is at the center of these controversies and debates. Because of its 1,254-mile border with Mexico, Texas is the first point of entry for many land crossings between Mexico and the United States.[37] While many land crossings involve Mexican nationals, a significant number of unaccompanied minors from Central America as well as other migrants fleeing gang violence in Central America are also crossing the border.

Governor Abbott deployed the Texas National Guard to the border in April 2018. His rationale for doing so was that illegal crossings had increased 200 percent in the prior year and that increased National Guard presence would help stem this increase.[38] Governor Abbott's plan called for 1,000 personnel to assist the Department of Homeland Security in securing the border. As members of the military, however, Texas National Guard troops do not have the authority to apprehend and arrest undocumented immigrants crossing the border, or smugglers attempting to traffic narcotics. They can, however, alert the proper authorities, such as the Border Patrol and the Drug Enforcement Agency, who in turn can apprehend and arrest individuals.

A vivid picture of the complexity of border security emerged in 2018 when reports arose of undocumented children being separated from their parents after being apprehended trying to cross the border into the United States. This resulted from the Trump administration's "zero tolerance" policy aimed at discouraging illegal immigration by demanding that anyone who attempts to cross the border illegally will be detained and prosecuted. Critics noted that the policy is inhumane because it separates children from their parents. The Border Patrol has detention centers in many states, including Texas, and although the normal holding period is 72 hours, children were being detained for much longer periods in facilities that lacked adequate medical care and bedding.[39]

Who Is Eligible for DACA?

DACA and DACA-eligible individuals were born abroad and arrived undocumented in the United States with their immigrant parents. These individuals were granted relief from deportation in 2012 under an executive order signed by President Obama, but their status is in limbo under the Trump administration and the failure of Congress to take action on the issue. But who are these individuals? Where are they from? How connected are they to the United States and Texas?

Regions of Birth for DACA Eligible Population in Texas*

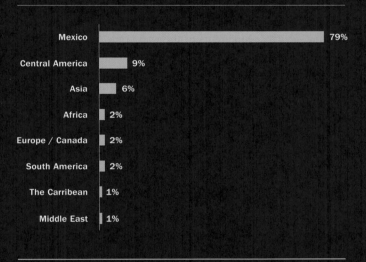

Mexico	79%
Central America	9%
Asia	6%
Africa	2%
Europe / Canada	2%
South America	2%
The Carribean	1%
Middle East	1%

DACA-Eligible Population by Regions in Texas

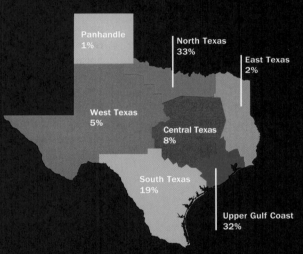

Panhandle 1%
North Texas 33%
East Texas 2%
West Texas 5%
Central Texas 8%
South Texas 19%
Upper Gulf Coast 32%

Note: There is no information about residential areas for 27,420 respondents. Therefore, the above figure is based on information for 242,946 respondents.

*Numbers may not add up to 100 percent due to rounding.

SOURCE: Hobby School of Public Policy, University of Houston.

Profile of DACA Eligible Population in Texas*

270,366 Total Population

Gender
46% Male
54% Female

Education
2%
2%
17%
34%
46%

- Graduate or professional school
- College undergraduate
- Grade 9 to grade 12
- Grade 5 to grade 8
- Grade 1 to grade 4

English Proficiency
5%
15%
80%

- Bilingual
- Speaks little or no English
- Speaks English only

QUANTITATIVE REASONING

- While all DACA recipients and DACA-eligible individuals are foreign born, what does their English proficiency and level of education say, if anything, about their connection to the United States?

- Based on the map, where are most DACA-eligible individuals residing in Texas? Why do you think most DACA-eligible people live in those areas?

Normally, the process calls for the Department of Health and Human Services to match unaccompanied children with foster families, but the backlog in the system prevented timely transfers. Although this is a national issue, many of the Border Patrol stations are located in South Texas.

In the 2018 gubernatorial election, Democratic candidate Lupe Valdez accused Abbott of being President Trump's "puppet," especially on issues relating to the border. Though Abbott deployed his Hispanic mother-in-law in his 2014 race for governor to appeal to the Latino vote, Valdez accused the Republican governor of enacting policies, such as SB 4, which she argued have been harmful to Latinos in the state.[40] The issue of border security remained a salient issue in the 2018 campaign largely because of President Trump's repeated efforts to keep the issue on the national agenda.

One of the major promises of President Trump in his 2016 election was the construction of a wall along the border with Mexico. Because of Texas's 1,254-mile-long border with Mexico, this policy is of obvious concern to Texans and has become an issue in statewide campaigns. Proponents of the wall argue that it is needed to keep smugglers, narcotics, and unauthorized individuals from entering the United States. Without a secure border, any other efforts at immigration reform are bound to fail, according to proponents of rigorous border security. Opponents of the wall argue that it would be expensive, disrupt commerce, and antagonize many immigrants. The wall would also not prevent a large source of entry of illegal immigrants: those who simply overstay a tourist visa. In April 2018, Congress approved $1.6 billion to build a border wall spanning 100 miles in parts of California, Texas, and New Mexico. Current plans are to build 33 miles of a wall in Texas, but it is still unclear precisely where the wall will be built.[41] Specific locations are being considered along the border with Mexico, as landowners reported receiving letters in July 2018 requesting consent to survey their land for possible construction.[42]

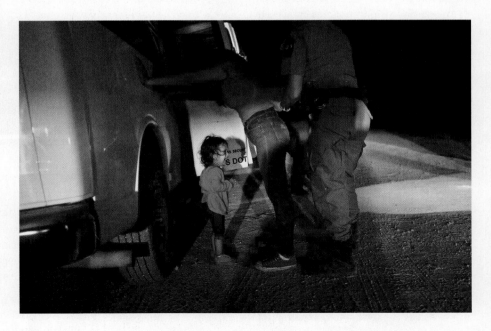

The Trump administration's "zero tolerance" policy on illegal immigration created controversy in 2018 when reports emerged that children were being separated from their families. This photo, taken in McAllen, was seen by millions around the world.

In July 2018, Mexico elected a new president, Andrés Manuel López Obrador, who has been an outspoken critic of President Trump and his policies on immigration. Bilateral relations between Mexico and the United States were already strained because of Mexican opposition to the border wall. Any significant policy changes regarding immigration are bound to have important effects on the Texas economy and will continue to impact the state in coming years.

Higher Education Policy in Texas

 Analyze the challenges facing Texas's system of higher education

One of the key goals of President Trump's administration is to build a wall along the U.S. border with Mexico to quell the flow of undocumented immigrants into the country.

A third challenge facing Texas in coming decades is in higher education. Higher education is an important link between an expanding and diversifying population and a rapidly transforming economy. Businesses in the modern world economy demand a highly skilled workforce. For Texas to compete nationally and internationally, the next generation of Texans must have the skills and training to thrive in an ever-changing high-tech economy. Earning a high school diploma is no longer enough to prepare oneself for the rigors of the job market in the twenty-first century. Associate degrees from community colleges and bachelor degrees from four-year colleges and universities are seen by employers as prerequisites for applying for good jobs. Increasing numbers of master's degrees in fields such as engineering, computer sciences, and business, as well as Ph.D.s. and other professional degrees in medicine, dentistry, and law, are seen by policymakers as the hallmark of an educated population.

A number of factors have structured the evolution of higher education policy in Texas and continue to define it today. First, there was the enormous expansion of higher education both in the number of schools and enrollments since the end of World War II. In 2017 almost 1.5 million students were enrolled in colleges or universities in Texas. Only California had more enrolled at 2.5 million. In a year when two-year and four-year enrollments were dropping in the United States, Texas added 34,400 students. The number of high school graduates in Texas is expected to grow, adding an additional 22.6 percent between the 2011–12 academic year and 2024–25.[43] The demand for college and university slots during this period is expected to grow correspondingly.

A second factor is that universities and colleges exist in a distinct geographic area. They are products of their local environment, and thus they address the educational needs of local as well as state workforces. They are also important local economic actors in their own right, being a source for jobs and personal income. Not surprisingly, local governments and state representatives have a strong interest in expanding the size and reach of universities and colleges located in their communities.

Third, higher education policy in Texas has long been defined by the University of Texas at Austin and Texas A&M University. Both have grown rapidly over the past fifty years to become nationally and internationally recognized institutions. The University of Texas at Austin enrollment increased to over 52,000 students in 2017. At the same time, Texas A&M enrolled a record 62,527 students at its flagship campus in College Station, a far cry from the 8,000 students enrolled there in 1963.[44] These institutions have been specially positioned to use their financial resources to expand their operations. Their large alumni bases enable both schools to mobilize much needed political support inside and outside the legislature. On the other hand, their prominent place in the state's educational hierarchy often has made it difficult for other higher education institutions in the state to attain national and international prominence.

The Texas university system has expanded rapidly as the number of high school graduates seeking higher education has increased in the last several decades. As that population increases and the working world demands a more skilled workforce, the two most prominent systems, Texas A&M University and the University of Texas at Austin, have become extremely crowded.

In Texas in the fall of 2017, 651,137 students were enrolled in 4-year public institutions and 124,748 were enrolled in private institutions (see Table 14.4). Another 726,699 were enrolled in 2-year public community and junior colleges and another 581 were enrolled in private community colleges. Public and private health-related institutions (including medical and osteopathy schools) enrolled another 28,078 students. In total, 1,531,243 students were enrolled in public and private institutions of higher education in the state in the fall of 2017.

TABLE 14.4

Public Higher Education in Texas, 2017

STATEWIDE FOUR-YEAR INSTITUTIONS

Total enrollment	651,137
Average tuition and fees	$8,875
Total degrees awarded	150,333
Bachelor's degrees awarded	104,933
Master's degrees awarded	39,701
Ph.D. research degrees awarded	3,848
Doctoral professional degrees awarded	1,918

STATEWIDE 2-YEAR COMMUNITY AND JUNIOR COLLEGES

Total enrollment	726,699
Average tuition and fees	$2,419
Part-time	76.3%
Full-time	23.7%
Academic program	73.7%
Technical program	26.3%

SOURCE: Texas Higher Education Coordinating Board, *2018 Texas Public Higher Education Almanac: A Profile of State and Institutional Performance and Characteristics.*

Higher education is big business in Texas. Public higher education comprises 37 general academic institutions, 3 lower division institutions, 6 technical college system schools, 50 community and junior college districts with multiple campuses, one technical college system, and 10 health-related institutions. In addition, there were 38 private colleges or universities, 1 private junior college, 1 private health-related institution, and 2 private chiropractic schools.[45]

Funding these institutions is a complicated affair. For the 2016–17 biennium, $17.3 billion was appropriated by the legislature to support public higher education in Texas, a $1.2 billion increase from 2014–15. An additional $2.0 billion was appropriated to support two-year public community and junior colleges, which were also funded by local property taxes in their respective communities. Aggregated appropriations by the state alone do not capture the policy issues facing higher education in the state. For that we must briefly understand how institutions of higher education were built and funded in the state.

Building a System of Higher Education in Texas

Public higher education was slow in coming to Texas. The Republic of Texas had set aside 50 acres of land for the establishment of a university, but little substantively was done. The Constitution of 1866 provided for the maintenance of a university fund and called upon the legislature to create a publicly supported university. Upon reentering the Union, Texas became eligible for a grant of federal land from the Morrill Land Grant Act of 1862. Because there was no federal land in Texas, federal monies came through the sale of public lands in another state in 1871. These monies became the first endowment of the agricultural and mechanical college that would become Texas A&M University in 1876. Another agricultural college that would become Prairie View A&M University was established for African-American youth in 1876.[46]

The Constitution of 1876 contained a number of important provisions for the future development of higher education in the state. A **Permanent University Fund (PUF)** was created out of the income from and sale of certain public lands. The Constitution of 1876 also called for the establishment of a University of Texas. Texas A&M was mandated to be part of the University of Texas. Prohibitions also were put into place forbidding the use of general revenue monies for the construction of buildings for the University of Texas. In 1881 a statewide popular vote chose Austin to be the site of the University of Texas. At the same time, the legislature created a governing board of eight regents who were empowered to oversee the affairs of the university. Galveston also was selected to be the site of the medical college for the University of Texas. The University of Texas formally opened in 1883.[47]

Permanent University Fund (PUF) a fund created by the state of Texas from the proceeds of public lands to finance public higher education in the state at selected institutions

Texas's two most prestigious public universities—The University of Texas and Texas A&M University—thus have their historical origins in the state constitution. Other state colleges and universities, however, emerged from the needs of local communities. Normal Colleges or Schools were established across the United States in the nineteenth century out of local and regional demands to increase the number of primary and secondary teachers. Normal Colleges were the predecessors to twentieth-century teachers colleges. Located in Huntsville, Sam Houston Normal Institute was the first state-supported teacher training institution in Texas in 1878. Initial control was given by the legislature to the State Board of Education subject to the appointment of three Huntsville citizens to a local board of directors. Normal Colleges were envisioned to be an adjunct to elementary and secondary education in the state.[48]

By 1923 eight Normal Schools had been established to train teachers throughout Texas. Normal Schools were renamed teachers colleges in 1923.

- Sam Houston Normal Institute, now Sam Houston State University (1879)
- North Texas Normal School, now University of North Texas (1901)
- Southwest Texas State Normal School, Now Southwest Texas State University (1899)
- West Texas State Normal School, now West Texas A&M University (1909)
- East Texas State Normal College, now Texas A&M University—Commerce (1889)
- Sul Ross State Normal School, now Sul Ross State University (1920)
- Stephen F. Austin Teachers College, now Stephen F. Austin State University (1922)
- South Texas Normal School, now Texas A&M University at Kingsville (1925)[49]

Paralleling the expansion of Normal Schools in Texas was the community college movement. Early community colleges were often church sponsored and offered first year and second year courses. In 1922 the first publicly supported junior college was established in Wichita Falls. As with normal schools, junior colleges were seen as an appendage to local school districts. In 1929 the legislature provided a process for establishing community colleges and supporting them with local tax dollars. In 1941 the state began providing direct funding to community and junior colleges and made the Texas Education Agency the supervising agency, confirming their close connections to the public-school system.

New institutions of higher learning were added across the state throughout the mid-twentieth century as the demand for higher education increased. Some universities grew out of what had been two-year community colleges. Others were initially private institutions that became state funded. In the 1960s and early 1970s a host of new institutions of higher education were established around the state in such places as San Antonio, Dallas, Midland-Odessa, Victoria, Texarkana, Corpus Christi, Brownsville, and Clear Lake. Along with the former Normal Schools and community and junior colleges, these schools began competing for the state resources once monopolized by the two flagship institutions.

Unlike other states, such as California, that had a comprehensive plan for expanding higher education in the second half of the twentieth century, Texas followed a more haphazard strategy. Decisions were made often on a case-by-case basis in the legislature, addressing the needs of local communities and institutions rather than those of the state as a whole. Ultimately, policymakers adopted two strategies to bring coordination and efficiency to higher education.

university systems
organizations in the state that coordinate the activities of various universities, medical schools, and special agencies involved in higher education and research

First, six **university systems** were created around the state. The general idea of a system was to have a chancellor who would administer colleges and agencies through a president or director. In 1911 a Board of Regents of State Colleges was created to oversee the operations of Normal Schools and teaching colleges. This became the Texas State University System. Today this system includes seven flagship institutions and 12 campuses and enrolls over 82,000 students. The Texas A&M System was created in 1948, bringing together the flagship school with other smaller agricultural schools around the state. Today Texas A&M University System schools enroll over 143,000 students. The University of Texas System was established in 1950, bringing together universities in Austin and El Paso along with medical branches in Galveston, Houston, and Dallas (see Figure 14.3). Today UT System Schools enroll over 216,000 students, the most in the state. The University of Houston System was established in 1977 and today enrolls over 70,000 students. The University of North Texas System was established in 1980 and today enrolls over 36,000 students. The Texas Tech University System was established in 1946 and today enrolls over 36,000 students.

A second strategy adopted by the legislature to bring cohesion to higher education policy in Texas was to create an administrative agency that could develop rules and regulations to coordinate the policies being developed at Texas's many state universities and community colleges. Before 1955 public colleges and universities (and existing systems) had to rely on their own efforts to secure funding from the legislature. Universities had to forge close connections with local state representatives and senators to make sure

FIGURE 14.3

Texas's University Systems

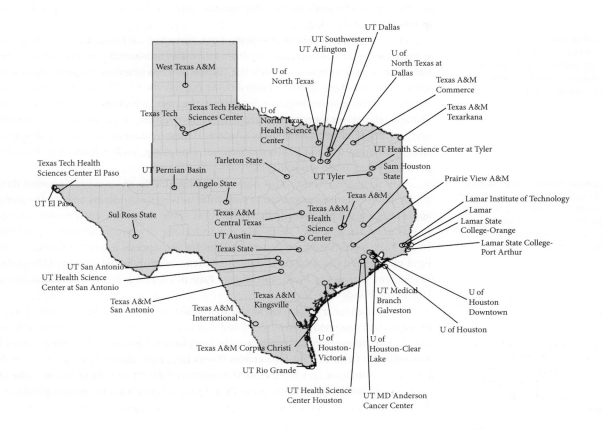

their financial interests were not lost in the state budgetary process. The Texas Commission on Higher Education was established by the legislature in 1955 to try to coordinate the development of new institutions of higher education. The commission had little regulatory or financial authority and was largely ignored by the legislature and higher education institutions. In 1965 a new regulatory body was created by the legislature—the Coordinating Board, Texas College and University System. This body was renamed the **Texas Higher Education Coordinating Board (THECB)** in 1987.

The THECB has guided the expansion of higher education in Texas into the second decade of the twenty-first century. Its functions are largely regulatory. Among its many activities are monitoring academic program development and reviews, establishing success goals across all universities, working on a standardized common core across all public institutions of higher learning, and providing for coordination across universities and community colleges. Significantly, however, it did not have the authority to coordinate or make authoritative decisions about how universities and colleges were to be financed. Financing higher education remained a highly decentralized affair decided elsewhere.

Financing Higher Education

Funding higher education in Texas is complicated. One source of funds is "formula funding" based upon enrollments and semester credit hours.[50] The THECB makes recommendations for formula funding for various state institutions, and the state legislature makes the final decision.

A second source is **tuition and fees**. These are set by the respective university system board of regents, based on requests from university presidents. The legislature reserves the right to stop or even roll back the tuition and fee schedule proposed by a university system board of regents. As noted in the introduction to Chapter 11, tuition and fees increases have become contentious affairs in the twenty-first century. As in other states, Texas is relying less on general revenue funding of higher education and more on tuition and fees. Students are having to spend more of their own money to attend public universities, and many are going into serious debt. One study in 2016 found that the average student debt in Texas was $26,292.[51]

A third source of funding for higher education has been so-called **"special items,"** which involve money designated to particular university programs outside the standard appropriation formulas for higher education. Over the years, universities have come to rely upon these special items as a way to initiate new programs and expand others. In 2015 the legislature provided $1.1 billion for 362 special items.[52] A fourth source of funding has been special funds established to promote higher education in the state: the Permanent University Fund, the Higher Education Fund, and the National Research University Fund.[53]

Financing higher education at the University of Texas and Texas A&M University through the Permanent University Fund was a constant source of contention throughout the late nineteenth and early twentieth centuries. Throughout the 1880s more land was added to the PUF, but for decades it was land rich and revenue poor. Texas A&M University sought to free itself from the control of the University of Texas in the latter part of the nineteenth century, preferring direct funding from the state legislature. But

The Future of Higher Education: The Political Parties Speak

TEXANS across the political spectrum recognize the importance of higher education to the state's future. But the two major political parties in the state—Republicans and Democrats—do not see eye to eye on the crucial issues confronting higher education or how they should be addressed. In 2018 the Republican and Democratic party platforms presented very different visions of the future of higher education in Texas. Party platforms are statements of each party's views on major policy issues. The platforms are discussed and voted upon at each party's state convention, and party platforms are the best indicators of the collective thinking of the political parties.

In recent years, conservative speakers discussing sensitive cultural topics such as race, ethnicity, and gender have sparked controversy on campuses across the country. Some schools have withdrawn invitations to speakers deemed too controversial for current campus life. In response, the Republican platform stressed the importance of maintaining a personal right to free speech and to practice one's faith. "We further urge that the legislature write legislation to protect the right of anyone who steps onto college campuses, to prohibit colleges campuses from stripping away their First Amendment rights of free speech and practicing their religions." Republicans called upon the state legislature to withdraw public funding from any university or college that actively or passively discriminates against speakers on campus. Republicans also stated that state universities should not make "special concessions based on religious practices that create undue burdens and costs on the institution."

Democrats saw the rights problems in higher education differently, calling upon universities to "offer culturally competent and culturally diverse curricula, student activities, and student recruitment policies that promote understanding, respect, and acceptance." Democrats wanted to enforce policies that prevented discrimination or harassment against any person due to "race, sex, color, religion, national origin, ancestry, age, marital status, disability, sexual orientation, gender identity/expression, citizenship, or military status."

The platforms also sharply disagreed on a number of financial problems facing higher education. While not addressing declining state support for higher education, Republicans called upon the legislature to take "reasonable measures to curtail tuition increases." Echoing concerns from the Texas Higher Education Coordinating Board, Republicans called for the setting of limits on cumulative loans to students based upon the average annual earnings in a particular degree. The Republican platform also called for eliminating in-state tuition for all illegal aliens.

The Democratic platform also called for rolling back tuition increases but replacing those lost funds with more state funding through a variety of programs. Democrats expressed concerns about the growing debt facing students attending universities and colleges in Texas. In contrast to the Republicans, they focused on increased funding in the form of state grants or a prepaid tuition program to

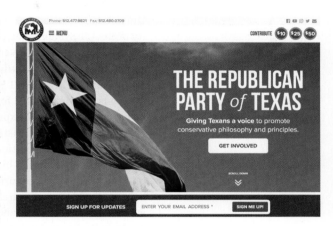

replace one that went bankrupt years earlier. The Democratic platform also focused attention on the role played by community colleges in educating the workforce, calling for more funding of current programs and the provision of tuition-free community colleges to all Texas high school graduates.

As long as Republicans dominate the three branches of state government in Texas, it is likely that the concerns of the Republican platform will play a larger role in shaping the policy agenda for higher education than those in the Democratic platform. Nevertheless, the ideas in the Democratic platform provide a sense of higher education policies if Democrats ever regain power in the state and a perspective on the alternative policies that will be offered in higher education policy debates.

COMMUNICATING EFFECTIVELY: YOUR VOICE

- What are the strengths and weaknesses of the Republican and Democrat approaches to higher education policy in the state? Which party platform do you believe is a better approach to confronting the complex issues facing higher education?

- How might you go about getting either party to modify its platform positions on higher education? What arguments might be made against denying in-state tuition to illegal aliens? What arguments could be made in favor of or against free community college tuition for all Texas high school graduates?

the discovery of oil on university lands changed the financial prospects of the PUF for both the University of Texas and Texas A&M University. Following years of negotiation between the University of Texas and Texas A&M University, higher education leaders agreed that the universities would be under the control of their own boards of regents and would split the proceeds of the PUF, with two-thirds going to the University of Texas and one-third going to Texas A&M.

Today the PUF consists of 2.1 million acres of lands dedicated to it and the return on the investment of revenues from those lands.[54] The PUF endowment is managed by the University of Texas Investment Management Company (UTIMCO) under the authority of the UT System Board of Regents, with the land itself being managed by the Land Office. The Available University Fund (AUF) consists of the revenue from the PUF and is used to guarantee bonds issued by the University of Texas System for various projects. Bonds can benefit all 14 UT System schools but only to finance capital expenditures. AUF money is also distributed to benefit A&M and UT System institutions. AUF money can be used for operational expenses of UT Austin and the UT System Administration, but not of other UT System institutions.

PUF and AUF operations have been complicated affairs and have influenced the growth and expansion of higher education in the state throughout the nineteenth and into the twenty-first centuries. The University of Texas and Texas A&M University have become world-class research universities because of the large amounts of monies made available to them above and beyond state appropriations or the tuition and fees paid by students. These funds have also been used to finance the building of a large number of capital construction projects across the UT and A&M System schools, although the flagship schools have been the primary beneficiaries of these construction projects. In 2018, $887 million was distributed from PUF through the AUF.

In an attempt to address the needs of non-PUF schools, constitutional amendments passed in 1984 and 1993 establishing a second fund for higher education for universities, health-related institutions, and the Texas State Technical College that were not included in PUF funding. The idea for the **Higher Education Fund (HEF)** mirrored that of the PUF. But instead of revenues from public lands, general revenue appropriation funds would be used to build a fund for backing and servicing bonds used for capital expenditures. By 2009 a decision was made by the legislature to repurpose the HEF permanent endowment to the newly established National Research University Fund (see Chapter 11). NRUF funds would be used to promote and encourage the emergence of new national research institutions among a small group of universities. The HEF would continue to be funded by general revenues.

The 2017 Texas legislative session was a watershed year for higher education. At the beginning of the session some policymakers projected a 6–10 percent cut in higher education funding. Early Senate drafts of the budget all but eliminated special item funding. In the end, special items remained in the budget. And although draconian cuts did not end up passing, there was enough pain to go around. Sixteen of the state's public universities and administrative offices saw decreases in state funding, while the funding of many others could not keep up with inflation or enrollment growth. A special Joint Interim Committee on Higher Education Formula Funding was established to report back to the legislature on overhauling the funding of higher education.[55] Finding a long-term solution to financing higher education in the future should be high on the 2019 legislative agenda.

Higher Education Fund (HEF) a fund supported by general revenue monies to finance public higher education for non-PUF institutions

Higher Education Spending and Outcomes

● United States   ● California   ● New York   ● Florida   ● Texas   ☐ Texas Ranking

Average Tuition and Fees

Annual State Spending*

Educational Attainment (24-34-year-olds)

High school diploma or less — 10th — 38%

Some college, no degree — 19th — 24%

Associate Degree or higher** — 38th — 38%

Bachelor degree or higher — 35th — 30%

6-year graduation rate — 32nd — 53%

Texas contains the full range of institutions of higher education, from community colleges to private universities and liberal arts colleges, to major public research universities. How does the experience of higher education in Texas compare to other states? What does the state spend on students and faculty, and how far do Texans progress in their education compared other states and the country?

*State spending on higher education, per full time enrolled student

** Includes bachelor and graduate degrees

SOURCE: 2018 Teas Higher Education Almanac: A Profile of State and Institutional Performance and Characteristics. Austin: Texas Higher Education Coordinating Board, 2018. Pp. 6-7.

CRITICAL THINKING

· What factors might explain the differences in tuition and fees at public 2-year and 4-year universities and colleges across the five states? If you were a state legislator would you increase funding for higher education by raising tuition and fees or by appropriating more general revenue funds? What are the costs and benefits of either strategy?

· Higher education is considered to be a key factor in preparing a workforce for the dynamic world of the twenty-first century. Given the above data, which state do you believe is doing the best job creating an educated workforce through higher education?

Setting Goals for the Future: 60x30TX

In 2000, the THECB drafted a 15-year plan called "Closing the Gaps by 2015." The plan identified a number of broad goals and benchmarks for the state's higher education system in regard to participation, success, excellence, and research. At the heart of the plan was finding ways to serve the higher education needs of all Texans, particularly those ethnic and racial minorities who were underrepresented in higher education.

In 2015 a new 15-year strategic plan called "60x30TX" was released by the THECB for higher education in Texas. Like "Closing the Gaps," the plan identified four targeted goals reflecting concerns about student success and the establishment of a globally competitive workforce in the state:

- The number of Texans between 25 and 34 with a certificate or degree will rise from 41 percent in 2015 to 60 percent in 2030.
- The number of individuals with a higher education degree or certificate will rise from 311,340 in 2015 to 550,000 in 2030.
- All graduates by 2030 will have completed programs with identified marketable skills.
- By 2030 undergraduate loan debt will not exceed 60 percent of first-year wages for graduates of public institutions.[56]

The goals of the report were laudable, calling upon universities to develop regional and statewide strategies to meet these goals and offering much needed data that would track out comparative institutional and statewide performance indicators. What 60x30TX didn't do (and really couldn't do), however, was spell out how public universities might manage the institutional and financial constraints in Texas that made it

The 60x30TX plan seeks to create a well-educated and highly skilled generation of Texas graduates but fails to outline how schools should accomplish this goal. The financial constraints on Texas colleges and universities pose considerable challenges.

difficult for other universities to become recognized as topflight universities in the image of the University of Texas at Austin or Texas A&M University. Nor did the report emphasize the significance of how much less Texas spends on higher education compared to states such as California and New York (see the "Texas and the Nation" graphic). It will be hard to meet the goals of 60x30TX without a significant rethinking of how to coordinate and fund higher education in the state. Without additional state funding (or significantly higher tuition) it likely will be difficult to compete with the educated workforces of other states.

When the THECB was established in 1965, Governor John Connally warned how mediocrity threatened higher education in Texas if resources were spread too thinly around the state and all universities and community colleges tried to be all things to all people. He hoped the Texas Higher Education Coordinating Board would bring some needed coordination to higher education policy in the state. The challenge today is less regulatory and more political. Reducing state funding and increasing tuition and fees may have worked in the past. Today, with growing student debt, Texas may be reaching a point where significant increases in tuition and fees are no longer politically acceptable either in the public's mind or in the state legislature. The legislature needs to find a better way to finance higher education than it has over the past 20 years.

Water Policy in Texas

 Understand the challenges facing Texas's water supply

Water is the lifeblood of Texas. Access to plentiful water supplies over the past 100 years has been a necessary precondition for a thriving economy and an expanding urban population in the state. Approximately 59 percent of the water used in Texas comes from aquifers (underground pools of water), and the vast majority of that water (60 percent) is used in irrigation, particularly in the arid Panhandle region (Figure 14.4). The remainder of the state's water supply comes from surface sources, including rivers and reservoirs. Twenty-seven percent of the state's water use is in metropolitan areas. Individual cities rely on various amounts of aquifer and surface water, but, overall, aquifers are the source for more than one-third of the water consumed by metropolitan areas.

Texas's water consumption is projected to increase from about 18 million acre-feet per year in 2010 to about 22 million acre-feet per year in 2060.[57] (An acre-foot is a volume measurement used by water planners, comprising an acre of land—43,560 square feet—one foot deep.)[58] At the same time, existing supplies under current systems of production and conservation are expected to decrease by 10 percent, largely as a result of the depletion of the Ogallala Aquifer in the Texas Panhandle and reduced reliance on the Gulf Coast Aquifer. By 2060 experts project that an additional 8.3 million acre-feet per year will be needed for the state to continue to thrive.

Formulating a coherent water policy in Texas to address these and other issues is difficult for many reasons. As noted in Chapter 1, Texas is a large state with a diverse climate. The water-related issues along the Gulf Coast in southeast Texas near Houston, which is subtropical and humid, are quite different from those in the high plains Panhandle, which is semiarid savanna, or in the El Paso desert. For example, along the

FIGURE 14.4

Water Usage by Sector

About 8.42 million acre-feet of water used in Texas (62 percent) came from groundwater sources. About 5.27 million acre-feet (38 percent) came from surface water sources. These two charts illustrate how these waters were used in various activities in Texas.

SOURCE: Texas Water Development Board.

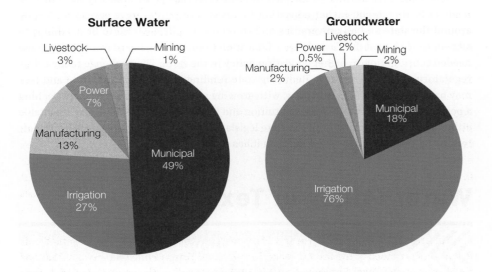

southeastern border with Louisiana, average annual rainfall is more than 80 inches per year, while near El Paso it is only 10 inches per year.[59] There are 15 major river basins and 8 coastal basins across the state, as well as 9 major and 21 minor aquifers.

Water policy is further complicated by the fact that various regions of the state have periodically experienced severe droughts and devastating floods. Throughout the twentieth century, reservoirs have been built to more effectively distribute water during times of shortage and to control flooding. In 1913, when the Texas Board of Water Engineers was established, there were only 8 major reservoirs in the state. By 1950 the number had grown to 53, and today there are 188.[60]

Water Law in Texas

Underlying water policy in Texas is a complicated system of private property rights derived from three sources: Spanish law, traditional English common law, and statutory law. Texas law recognizes several legal classes of water rights for surface water and groundwater, classes that are governed by different rules. Historically, these variations in the law have made the forging of water policy an arduous and at times a politically charged matter.

In 1967 the law covering surface water and relatively well-defined underground streams was clarified when the state legislature passed the Water Rights Adjudication Act. This legislation essentially merged the various water rights doctrines dating back to the nineteenth century into a unified water permit system. It requires individuals seeking water rights to file a claim with the Texas Commission on Environmental Quality (originally called the Texas Water Commission) before using the water. A complex administrative and judicial process was put into place that essentially grants to holders of water rights certificates demonstrating that the rights have been adjudicated. The 1967 act thus greatly expanded the state's ability to control and manage surface water use.[61]

Groundwater law—that is, law regarding water flowing, or "percolating," underground—differs significantly from surface water law.[62] In *Houston and Texas Central Railroad Company v. East* (1904), the Texas Supreme Court adopted a strict common-law notion of property law for percolating underground water, one called the **law of capture**. This standard, which is also found in Texas oil and gas law, essentially says that the first person to "capture" the water by pumping it out of the ground and using it owns it. Landowners have the right to capture as much groundwater lying under their property as they wish without regard to the interests of other owners whose land may also lie on top of the same pool of underground water. Because it encourages landowners to take as much water as possible from groundwater sources without considering the needs of other consumers, the law of capture can work against conservation efforts of private individuals who are trying to protect the water under their lands. It can also undercut efforts of planning authorities to develop a water plan for a particular area that takes into account the short-term and long-term availability of water as well as the competing uses for available water.

law of capture the idea that the first person to "capture" water or oil by pumping it out of the ground and using it owns that water or oil

Finding a balance between the law of capture and the need to plan has troubled policy makers for much of the last 60 years. *Houston and Texas Central Railroad v. East* was reaffirmed by the Texas Supreme Court in 1955. In its ruling, the court stated that "percolating waters are regarded as the property of the owner of the surface who may, in the absence of malice, intercept, impede and appropriate such waters while they are on their premises, and make whatever use of them they please, regardless of the fact that use cuts off the flow of such waters to adjoining land and deprives the adjoining owner of their use." Nevertheless, the court also accepted the state's authority to regulate groundwater. In 1949 the state legislature passed the Texas Groundwater Act, which created water districts to manage groundwater supply.

Today there are 99 groundwater districts in Texas, with varying powers. The smallest district is the Red Sands Groundwater Conservation District in Hidalgo County, covering 31 square miles. The largest is the High Plains Underground Water District, covering 12,000 square miles over the Ogallala Aquifer. Generally, the groundwater districts are able to develop regulations to protect the water supply provided by groundwater sources, including rules that may restrict pumping, require well permits, delineate well spacing, and establish rates of water use. The rules and regulations generated by these districts, however, can come into direct conflict with the law of capture, as we will see in the next section.[63]

Planning Authorities and Water Policy

The history of water planning in Texas stretches back to the early twentieth century. A constitutional amendment in 1904 paved the way for the development of various agencies and authorities concerned with water planning. Among the most important innovations put into place by the state legislature in the early 1900s were drainage districts (1905); conservation and reclamation districts, later referred to as "river authorities" (1917); and water control and improvement districts (1925).

From 1950 to 1956 Texas experienced its worst drought in history. Every major urban area experienced the effect of the drought, many turning to emergency supplies and to rationing. In 1957 the drought was ended by heavy rains that resulted in the massive flooding of every major river and tributary in the state. Two hundred fifty-three of Texas's counties were declared disaster areas. Estimates were that the drought had cost the state hundreds of millions of dollars, and damages from flooding another $120 million. Calls for a more permanent planning and policy agency to direct and coordinate water policy came from all over the state.[64]

In the 1960s the state established new agencies to address various water issues. In 1977 the three major state water agencies—the Texas Water Development Board (TWDB), the Texas Water Rights Commission, and the Water Quality Board—were combined into the Texas Department of Water Resources, whose job was to develop Texas's water resources, maintain the quality of water, and assure an equitable distribution of water rights. Sunset legislation in 1985 reorganized this single agency into two new agencies: a new Texas Water Commission and a new version of the TWDB. Today the TWDB is the state's primary water planning and financing agency. Enforcement of the state's environmental regulations regarding water is the job of the Texas Commission on Environmental Quality, an agency that resulted from the 1993 consolidation of the Texas Water Commission with the Texas Air Control Board.[65]

The TWDB is composed of a six-member board serving staggered six-year terms. Each member comes from a different part of the state. The board has had a number of important responsibilities, including:

- Supporting the development of 16 regional water plans
- Developing a state water plan every five years
- Providing financial assistance to local governments for (1) water supply and waste management projects, (2) flood protection and control projects, (3) agricultural water conservation projects, and (4) the creation of groundwater districts
- Administering the Texas Water Bank, which facilitates the transfer, sale, and lease of water and water rights throughout the state
- Administering the Texas Water Trust, which holds water rights for environmental flow maintenance purposes
- Collecting data for the state's freshwater needs[66]

A number of strategies for meeting the short- and long-term water needs in the state were articulated in the 2012 State Water Plan. Two elements of the plan stand out. First, there is a notable focus on the importance of conservation. One of the most important elements is a strategy throughout all regions that seeks a more efficient use of current water supplies. Second, there is an emphasis on the importance of expanding and developing available surface water throughout Texas. The plan calls for the building of 26 new major reservoirs by 2060 and new pipeline infrastructure from existing sources to new points of use. Such projects represent an important shift in existing water policy in some planning areas, as they shift the focus from flood control or hydroelectric power generation to the provision of water.

The plan's groundwater strategies include the expansion of production by drilling more wells or building treatment plants for water quality. Conservation efforts also play a major part in groundwater initiatives, as some of the aquifers are experiencing overuse. The TWDB estimates that total groundwater supplies available to Texans will decline by 30 percent between 2010 and 2060. The Ogallala Aquifer (which runs from the Texas High Plains up through western Kansas and into Nebraska) and the Edwards Aquifer (which runs along the Balcones fault line near San Antonio) are estimated to decline by 50 percent by 2060.

The total capital needs of these initiatives proposed by regional water planning groups were estimated to be $53 billion, along with annual operating and maintenance costs. But cost is not the only challenge facing water policy makers. Some environmental groups in the state are opposed to further expansion of the reservoir system, arguing that the costs to the ecosystem far outweigh the advantages provided by more water. On the other hand, some property owners, particularly in west Texas, are opposed to any new conservation restrictions put upon them by the state. Texas water law itself may be one of the most intractable problems that water planners may have to face in coming years.

In 2012 the Texas Supreme Court ruled on the case *The Edwards Aquifer Authority v. Burrell Day and Joel McDaniel,* which has important implications for future attempts to regulate water use in Texas, particularly in areas that rely heavily upon aquifers. The case involved two farmers who had applied to the Edwards Aquifer Authority for permission to pump 700 acre-feet per year of water to irrigate their 350-acre ranch in Van Ormy, a small town south of San Antonio. The farmers argued that they had rights to water from the aquifer based on their ownership of land above it. Maintaining that the farmers were unable to prove "historical use" of water from the aquifer, the authority granted them a permit for pumping only 14 acre-feet.

The Court sided with the farmers. Writing for the 9–0 court majority, Justice Hecht ruled that using "historical use" as a criterion for granting a permit to pump water was a departure from the Texas Water Code. "Unquestionably," Hecht wrote, "the state is empowered to regulate groundwater production . . . [but] groundwater in place is owned by the landowner on the basis of oil and gas law."[67] Texas regulatory authorities thus had the power to reasonably regulate in the public interest the use of water drawn from an aquifer, but they may have to pay property owners with a stake in that water any damages that are incurred by the regulation.

The ruling sparked a firestorm of controversy among interested parties. Landowners celebrated the decision as vindication of their ownership of water under their lands. In contrast, state planning authorities and environmentalists were aghast at the implications that the case could have for their attempts to efficiently allocate and conserve water in Texas. The court's ruling also raised an important question: Which policymaking body would dominate water policy in the foreseeable future in Texas? Would it be the courts, working through judicial interpretations of the applicability of water property law? Or would it be the regulatory bodies whose job was to plan and to allocate water based on their assessment of available water supplies and the competing needs for water? Developing regulatory rules for the use of aquifer water that both protect property rights and promote the public interest through reasonable and efficient regulations will be a challenge facing these policy makers in years to come.[68]

A major step toward planning for water in the future took place in 2013, when voters approved a constitutional amendment to create a $2 billion water fund. The bulk of the fund came from a onetime transfer of money from the Rainy Day Fund to the State

The Texas water supply faces many challenges. The drought of 2011–14 was the worst in the history of Texas. It damaged the state's prosperity, causing dust storms in the Texas Panhandle (top), and drying lake beds throughout the state. Many of the state's cities were put on various levels of water emergencies that restricted use.

Water Implementation Fund for Texas (SWIFT). Proponents claimed that the two accounts could fund over $25 billion in water development projects over the next 50 years.

The basic idea behind this water initiative is that SWIFT projects would generate revenue that would go into another account (the State Water Implementation Revenue Fund for Texas or SWIRFT) that could be used to fund more water projects. Proposals for projects to be funded by SWIFT and SWIRFT would come from regional water planning groups and could include such things as building new reservoirs, fixing pipes, and developing groundwater. A number of provisos were attached to the legislation that put forward the constitutional amendment, including requirements that 20 percent of the funds had to be directed to conservation and 10 percent had to serve rural areas. Interestingly, concerns were also raised about the fact that the agency managing the program, the TWDB, might be too close to the governor given that the board would be appointed by him or her. The authorizing legislation thus established a separate committee to oversee how SWIFT and SWIRFT funds are managed. The committee would be appointed by the Speaker of the House and the lieutenant governor and be composed of the comptroller, three state representatives, and three state senators. Planning for Texas's water future did not mean that traditional concerns over too much executive power in public policy matters would be ignored.[69]

★ ★

Facing Texas's Future

IN THIS CHAPTER, we have explored four of the most important challenges that are confronting Texas policy makers today. How Texas leaders address transportation problems, immigration and border issues, higher education policy, and water needs in the coming years will determine a large part of Texas's future.

Most policy makers and legislators recognize that each of these challenges is important in its own right. There is less agreement on the importance of these issues among the general public. In recent polls of registered voters in Texas, border control and immigration are believed to be the most important issues facing the state (see Table 14.5). The next greatest issue—a concern with political leadership and political corruption in the state—was not even close to border control and immigration as a perceived problem. Interestingly, transportation, higher education, and water were not perceived by voters as problems at all.

TABLE 14.5

What Is Important to Texas Voters Today?*

ISSUE	ALL VOTERS (%)	REPUBLICANS (%)	DEMOCRATS (%)	INDEPENDENTS (%)
Immigration	15%	24%	7%	14%
Border security	14	25	3	13
Political corruption/ leadership	9	2	18	10
Health care	7	4	10	4
Education	6	4	9	6

*Average of four polls. No other items were mentioned in all four polls. Items mentioned by more than 2 percent of the "All Voters" respondents in one poll were hurricane recovery with a 5 percent response in one poll; unemployment/jobs with a 6 percent response in one poll; the economy with a 5 percent response in one poll; crime and drugs with a 4 percent response in one poll; taxes with a 4 percent response in one poll; moral decline with a 3 percent response in one poll; and gun control/violence with a 6 percent response in one poll.
SOURCE: University of Texas/*Texas Tribune* polls of 1,200 registered voters in February 2017; October 2017; February 2018; and June 2018.

Texas Republican voters are especially concerned with immigration and border control, which seems to parallel the emphasis placed on such concerns by President Trump and other Republican leaders. Democrats place far less emphasis on immigration and border control and far more emphasis on political leadership and political corruption—no doubt because in a state with Republican leadership, Democrats are unhappy with their lack of influence.

The percentage of Texas voters who recognize issues such as health or education as being important problems for the state does not rise above single digits. And transportation, higher education, and water do not rate as concerns at all. Unless forward-thinking officials take the lead to highlight these problems and mobilize Texans to deal with them, the future of Texas will be a less educated citizenry facing gridlock in its urban areas and water shortages outside the Gulf Coast.

Use ᴜ IɴQᴜɪᴢɪᴛɪᴠᴇ to help you study and master this material.

Transportation Policy in Texas

- Examine the major issues facing transportation policy in Texas (pp. 481–89)

Texas transportation policy primarily involves maintaining and expanding Texas's roads and highways and designing a public transportation system that can lessen the state's reliance on automobiles. The major problems facing transportation in Texas are developing a politically acceptable funding system for roads and highways and developing a public transportation system that will be used by a reasonable proportion of commuters in Texas's major metropolitan areas.

Key Terms
centerline miles (p. 481)
lane miles (p. 481)
vehicle miles traveled (p. 481)

Practice Quiz
1. Opposition to the bullet train comes primarily from
   a) persons in rural areas.
   b) bus companies.
   c) the aviation industry.
   d) taxpayers.
   e) persons concerned with its safety.

2. Roads and bridges in Texas
   a) will need billions of dollars in new funding by 2040.
   b) can be maintained with funds from motor fuels taxes.
   c) will be paid for with tolls.
   d) will be maintained with the new federal infrastructure law.
   e) will be paid for with the new production of oil and gas from shale.

3. The solution to transportation congestion in Texas is
   a) more toll roads.
   b) the bullet train.
   c) public transportation.
   d) uncertain.
   e) raising motor fuel taxes.

4. Public transportation
   a) tends to be more available in central cities.
   b) is more available in wealthy suburbs.
   c) is more popular in small towns.
   d) has been most effective in Houston.
   e) is widely used in El Paso.

5. The most likely response to the need for transportation funding is to
   a) increase the gasoline tax.
   b) increase motor vehicle fees.
   c) impose a state income tax.
   d) delay dealing with the problem.
   e) build more toll roads.

6. Texas roads and bridges are *not* funded by
   a) tolls.
   b) gasoline taxes.
   c) vehicle registration fees.
   d) shale oil taxes.
   e) diesel taxes.

7. Texans pay this amount per gallon in gasoline taxes:
   a) 70 cents
   b) 20 cents
   c) 18.4 cents
   d) 6.25 percent of price per gallon
   e) 38.4 cents

Demographic Change in Texas

> • **Analyze how immigration and border issues will change Texas in the coming years (pp. 489–99)**

Because of its long border with Mexico, Texas has always been familiar with immigrants from Mexico and Central America. In recent years the issue of border security has taken center stage, as has the issue of how to respond to the state's large population of undocumented immigrants. Texas has passed laws taking aim at sanctuary cities, which have refused to cooperate with federal immigration authorities. In addition, Texas has a large population of DACA recipients, who are undocumented individuals brought to the United States at a very young age.

Key Terms
naturalized citizen (p. 490)
Texas Dream Act (p. 491)
sanctuary cities (p. 493)
Senate Bill 4 (SB 4) (p. 493)
Deferred Action for Childhood Arrivals (DACA) (p. 495)

Practice Quiz
8. The Texas economy is *most* affected by which industry?
a) the film industry
b) the high-tech industry
c) the oil and gas industry
d) the farming industry
e) the tourism industry

9. Which of the following industries is *most* reliant on immigrant labor in Texas?
a) construction
b) manufacturing
c) retail trade
d) health care
e) accommodation and food services

10. What percentage of immigrants in Texas are of Mexican origin?
a) 20 percent
b) 30 percent
c) 40 percent
d) 50 percent
e) 55 percent

11. Which state has the largest DACA population?
a) New Mexico
b) California
c) Texas
d) Wisconsin
e) New York

12. Senate Bill 4 addressed the issue of sanctuary cities by
a) mandating that every city in Texas cooperate with federal authorities.
b) enacting penalties for local police and sheriffs who refused to cooperate with federal authorities.
c) creating a commission to study the issue.
d) requiring that all cities create sanctuaries for undocumented immigrants.
e) providing additional state money for cities that did not cooperate with federal authorities.

13. To become a naturalized citizen, an individual must
a) have lived in the United States for ten years.
b) demonstrate a perfect command of English.
c) have arrived to the United States illegally.
d) demonstrate good moral character.
e) pay an additional tax on their income.

Higher Education Policy in Texas

> • Analyze the challenges facing Texas's system of higher education (pp. 499–509)

Higher education is an important link between an expanding and diversifying population and a rapidly transforming economy. Businesses in the modern world economy demand a highly skilled workforce. For Texas to compete nationally and internationally and thrive in an ever-changing high-tech economy, the next generation of Texans must have the necessary advanced skills and training. Finding new ways to finance higher education across the state's many universities and colleges will be difficult.

Key terms

Permanent University Fund (PUF) (p. 501)
university systems (p. 502)
Texas Higher Education Coordinating Board (THECB) (p. 504)
tuition and fees (p. 504)
special items (p. 504)
Higher Education Fund (HEF) (p. 506)

Practice Quiz

14. The Permanent University Fund
    a) is a major source of funding for community colleges.
    b) is open to all universities and colleges across the state.
    c) allocates revenue for selected University of Texas and Texas A&M University system schools.
    d) has recently been replaced by the Higher Education Fund.
    e) none of the above

15. Which of the following revenue sources do *not* play a role in funding 4-year colleges and universities in Texas?
    a) local property taxes
    b) tuition and fees
    c) special items legislation
    d) the Permanent University Fund
    e) none of the above (all play a role)

16. The Texas Higher Education Coordinating Board
    a) manages the affairs of elementary and secondary schools.
    b) is a subcommittee of the Texas House Committee on Education.
    c) controls the sales tax rates for money going to public higher education.
    d) watches over and coordinates higher education policy in the state.
    e) none of the above

Water Policy in Texas

> • Understand the challenges facing Texas's water supply (pp. 509–14)

A looming threat to Texas's further economic development is access to freshwater. Over the next 50 years, water consumption is expected to vastly increase, while existing supplies may decrease. Current water law in Texas adds complexity to the development of rational water policies for the state.

Key Term

law of capture (p. 511)

Practice Quiz

17. Which of the following is *true*?
    a) Texas water consumption will decrease as the population expands.
    b) The idea of planning for future water provision has been rejected by the Texas state legislature as being too socialistic.
    c) Water law in Texas distinguishes between surface water and groundwater.
    d) Providing water in Texas is primarily a federal responsibility.
    e) Current state water policies do not emphasize conservation.

18. The law of capture concerns
  a) property rights in underground percolating water.
  b) the right of the state to regulate rivers and estuaries.
  c) political control of the legislature by a particular policy interest.
  d) the Corps of Engineers' various attempts to direct the flow of the Rio Grande.
  e) the federal government's ability to override Texas water laws.

19. Which of the following is *true*?
  a) The Texas Supreme Court rejects the idea that the state can regulate *surface* water.
  b) Texas is empowered by the state constitution to seize without compensation an individual's right to use underground water.
  c) Aquifers provide a negligible supply of water to Texas.
  d) Attempts to regulate groundwater access frequently come into conflict with property rights.
  e) The Water Rights Adjudication Act of 1967 prohibits the state from regulating surface water permits.

Appendix

Here we include a series of documents that capture the nature of philosophical and practical problems the people of Texas confronted during their lengthy founding period. For each text we provide short introductions to guide the reader from the Texas Revolution, through statehood and the Civil War, to the Constitution of 1876. Copies of the various constitutions of Texas are available online at www.tarlton.law.utexas.edu/constitutions.

The Declaration of Independence (1836)

The Texas Declaration of Independence was the product of the Convention of 1836.[1] Drawing upon John Locke's Two Treatises of Government (1689) and Thomas Jefferson's Declaration of Independence (1776) for inspiration, it lays out an explanation of the nature of government, lists the grievances that Texas's people hold against the Mexican government, and declares independence and the establishment of a new "free, sovereign, and independent Republic." Note the appeals to "the first law of nature, the right to self-preservation," "the inherent and inalienable right of the People to appeal to first principles," and the "sacred obligation" that people have to their posterity to create a government that will "secure their future wealth and happiness." In addition to presenting the Texas Constitution of 1836, the Texas Declaration of Independence *lays down the republican principles that would define government and politics in Texas from 1836 to 1845, when Texas joined the United States of America.*

To the Public.
The undersigned, Plenipotentiaries from the Republic of Texas to the United States of America, respectfully present to the American People the unanimous DECLARATION OF INDEPENDENCE, made by the People of Texas in General Convention, on the 2d day of March, 1836; and, also, the CONSTITUTION framed by the same body.

Robert Hamilton,
GEO. C. CHILDRESS.
WASHINGTON CITY, May 22, 1836.

Unanimous Declaration of Independence, by the Delegates of the People of Texas.

In General Convention, at the town of Washington, on the 2d day of March, 1836.

When a Government has ceased to protect the lives, liberty, and property of the People from whom its legitimate powers are derived, and for the advancement of whose happiness it was instituted, and so far from being a guarantee for the enjoyment of their inestimable and inalienable rights, becomes an instrument in the hands of evil rules for their oppression: when the Federal Republican Constitution of their country, which they have sworn to support, no longer has a substantial existence, and the whole nature of their Government has been forcibly changed, without their consent, from a restricted Federative Republic, composed of sovereign States, to a consolidated central military despotism, in which every interest is disregarded but that of the army and the priesthood, both the eternal enemies of civil liberty, the ever-ready minions of power, and the usual instruments of tyrants: when, long after the spirit of the constitution

[1] "Unanimous Declaration of Independence, by the Delegates of the People of Texas," *Laws of the Republic of Texas, in Two Volumes* (Houston: Printed at the Office of the Telegraph, 1838), 1:3–4; Thomas W. Streeter, *Bibliography of Texas, 1795–1845* (5 vols.; Cambridge, MA: Harvard University Press, 1955–60). Errors in the original document are retained.

has departed, moderation is at length so far lost by those in power, that even the semblance of freedom is removed, and the forms themselves of the Constitution discontinued; and so far from their petitions and remonstrances being regarded, the agents who bear them are thrown into dungeons and mercenary armies sent forth to force a new Government upon them at the point of the bayonet.

When, in consequence of such acts of malfeasance and abdication on the part of the Government, anarchy prevails, and civil society is dissolved into its original elements: in such a crisis, the first law of nature, the right of self-preservation, the inherent and inalienable right of the People to appeal to first principles, and take their political affairs into their own hands in extreme cases enjoins it as a right towards themselves, and a sacred obligation to their posterity, to abolish such Government, and create another in its stead, calculated to rescue them from impending dangers, and to secure their future welfare and happiness.

Nations, as well as individuals, are amenable for their acts to the public opinion of mankind. A statement of a part of our grievances is therefore submitted to an impartial world, in justification of the hazardous but unavoidable step now taken, of severing our political connexion with the Mexican People, and assuming an independent attitude among the nations of the earth.

The Mexican Government, by its colonization laws, invited and induced the Anglo-American population of Texas to colonize its wilderness, under the pledged faith of a written constitution, that they should continue to enjoy that constitutional liberty and republican Government to which they had been habituated in the land of their birth, the United States of America.

In this expectation they have been cruelly disappointed, inasmuch as the Mexican nation has acquiesced in the late changes made in the Government by General Antonio Lopez de Santa Ana, who, having overturned the Constitution of his country, now offers us the cruel alternative, either to abandon our homes, acquired by so many privations, or submit to the most intolerable of all tyranny, the combined despotism of the sword and the priesthood.

It hath sacrificed our welfare to the State of Coahuila, by which our interests have been continually depressed, through a jealous and partial course of legislation, carried on at a far-distant seat of Government, by a hostile majority, in an unknown tongue; and this too notwithstanding we have petitioned in the humblest terms for the establishment of a separate State Government, and have, in accordance with the provisions of the National Constitution, presented to the General Congress a Republican Constitution, which was, without just cause, contemptuously rejected.

It incarcerated in a dungeon, for a long time, one of our citizens, for no other cause but a zealous endeavor to procure the acceptance of our Constitution and the establishment of a State Government.

It has failed and refused to secure, on a firm basis, the right of trial by jury, that palladium of civil liberty and only safe guarantee for the life, liberty, and property of the citizen.

It has failed to establish any public system of education, although possessed of almost boundless resources, (the public domain,) and although it is an axiom in political science that, unless a People are educated and enlightened, it is idle to expect the continuance of civil liberty, or the capacity for self-government.

It has suffered the military commandants stationed among us to exercise arbitrary acts of oppression and tyranny, thus trampling upon the most sacred rights of the citizen, and rendering the military superior to the civil power.

It has dissolved by force of arms the State Congress of Coahuila and Texas, and obliged our Representatives to fly for their lives from the seat of Government, thus depriving us of the fundamental political right of representation.

It has demanded the surrender of a number of our citizens, and ordered military detachments to seize and carry them into the interior for trial; in contempt of the civil authorities, and in defiance of the laws and the Constitution.

It has made piratical attacks upon our commerce by commissioning foreign desperadoes, and authorizing them to seize our vessels and convey the property of our citizens to far-distant ports for confiscation.

It denies us the right of worshipping the Almighty according to dictates of our own conscience, by the support of a national religion calculated to promote the temporal interests of its human functionaries rather than the glory of the true and living God.

It has demanded us to deliver up our arms, which are essential for our defence, the rightful property of freemen, and formidable only to tyrannical Governments.

It has invaded our country, both by sea and by land, with intent to lay waste our territory, and drive us from our homes; and has now a large mercenary army advancing, to carry on against us a war of extermination.

It has, through its emissaries, incited the merciless savage, with the tomahawk and scalping-knife, to massacre the inhabitants of our defenceless frontiers.

It has been, during the whole time of our connexion with it, the contemptible sport and victim of successive military revolutions, and hath continually exhibited every characteristic of a weak, corrupt, and tyrannical government.

These and other grievances were patiently borne by the People of Texas, until they reached that point at which forbearance ceases to be a virtue. They then took up arms in defence of the National Constitution. They appealed to their Mexican brethren for assistance. Their appeal has been made in vain: though months have elapsed, no sympathetic response has yet been heard from the interior. They are, therefore, forced to the melancholy conclusion that the Mexican People have acquiesced in the destruction of their liberty, and the substitution therefor of a military despotism; that they are unfit to be free, and incapable of self-government.

The necessity of self-preservation, therefore, now decrees our eternal political separation.

We, therefore, the Delegates, with plenary powers, of the People of Texas, in solemn Convention assembled, appealing to a candid world for the necessities of our condition, do hereby resolve and DECLARE that our political connexion with the Mexican nation has forever ended, and that the People of Texas do now constitute a FREE, SOVEREIGN, AND INDEPENDENT REPUBLIC, and are fully invested with all the rights and attributes which properly belong to independent States; and, conscious of the rectitude of our intentions, we fearlessly and confidently commit the issue to the decision of the Supreme Arbiter of the destinies of nations.

RICHARD ELLIS,
President.

C. B. Stewart,
Thomas Barnett, of Austin,
James Collinsworth,
Edwin Waller,
Asa Brigham
J. S. D. Byrom, of Brazoria,
Francisco Ruis,
Antonio Navaro,
Jesse B. Badgett, of Bexar,
Wm. D. Lacy,
Wm. Menifee, of Colorado,
James Gains,
M. B. Menard,
A. B. Hardin, of Liberty,
Baily Hardiman, of Matagorda,
J. W. Bunton,
Thos. J. Gazeley,

R. M. Coleman, of Mina,
Robert Potter,
Thos. J. Rusk,
Charles S. Taylor,
Jno. S. Roberts, of Nacogdoches
Robert Hamilton,
Collin McKinnee,
Alb. H. Lattimer, of Red River,
Martin Palmer,
W. Clark, jr., of Sabine,
John Fisher,
Matt. Caldwell, of Gonzales,
Wm. Motley, of Goliad,
L. de Zavala, of Harrisburg,
S. C. Robertson,
Geo. C. Childress, of Milam,
Steph. H. Everett,

Geo. W. Smith, of Jasper,
Elijah Stapp, of Jackson,
Claiborne West,
Wm. B. Scates, of Jefferson,
E. O. Legrand,
S. W. Blount, of San Augustine,
Syd. O. Bennington,
W. C. Crawford, of Shelby,
J. Power,
Sam. Houston,
David Thomas,
Edward Conrad, of Refugio,
John Turner, of San Patricio,
B. Briggs Goodrich,
G. W. Barnett,
James G. Swisher,
Jesse Grimes, of Washington.

Ordinance of Annexation Approved by the Texas Convention on July 4, 1845

The independent Republic of Texas ceased to exist in 1845 following the implementation of a new state constitution and Texas's formal admission into the Union as a state. Resolutions passed by the U.S. Congress stated the conditions under which Texas was to be admitted into the Union.[2] Note that the resolutions demand a republican form of government be adopted by the people through a constitutional convention (via a new constitution) and that the existing government consent to this action. Passage of this ordinance by the convention is an expression of the consent of the people of Texas to this new political configuration.

An Ordinance
Whereas,

the Congress of the United States of America has passed resolutions providing for the annexation of Texas to that Union, which resolutions were offered by the President of the United States on the first day of March, 1845; and

Whereas,

the President of the United States has submitted to Texas the first and second sections of said resolutions, as the basis upon which Texas may be admitted as one of the States of the said Union; and

Whereas,

the existing Government of the Republic of Texas, has assented to the proposals thus made,—the terms and conditions of which are as follows:

"Joint Resolutions for annexing Texas to the United States.
Resolved by the Senate and House of Representatives of the United States of America in Congress assembled, That Congress doth consent that the territory properly included within and rightfully belonging to the Republic of Texas, may be erected into a new State to be called the State of Texas, with a republican form of government adopted by the people of said Republic, by deputies in convention assembled, with the consent of the existing Government in order that the same may by admitted as one of the States of this Union.

2nd. And be it further resolved, That the foregoing consent of Congress is given upon the following conditions, to wit: First, said state to be formed, subject to the adjustment by this government of all questions of boundary that may arise with other governments,—and the Constitution thereof, with the proper evidence of its adoption by the people of said Republic of Texas, shall be transmitted to the President of the United States, to be laid before Congress for its final action on, or before the first day of January, one thousand eight hundred and forty-six. Second, said state when admitted into the Union, after ceding to the United States all public edifices, fortifications, barracks, ports and harbors, navy and navy yards, docks, magazines and armaments, and all other means pertaining to the public defense, belonging to the said Republic of Texas, shall retain funds, debts, taxes and dues of every kind which may belong to, or be due and owing to the said Republic; and shall also retain all the vacant and unappropriated lands lying within its limits, to be applied to the payment of the debts and liabilities of said Republic of Texas, and the residue of said lands, after discharging said debts and liabilities, to be disposed of as said State may direct; but in no event are said debts and liabilities to become a charge upon the Government of the United States. Third—New States of convenient size not exceeding four in number, in addition to said State of Texas and having sufficient population, may, hereafter by the consent of said State, be formed out of the territory thereof, which shall be entitled to admission under the provisions of the Federal Constitution; and such states as may be formed out of the territory lying south of thirty-six degrees thirty minutes north latitude, commonly known as the Missouri Compromise Line, shall be admitted into the Union, with or without slavery, as the people of each State, asking admission shall desire; and in such State or States as shall be formed out of said territory, north of said Missouri compromise Line, slavery, or involuntary servitude (except for crime) shall be prohibited."

Now in order to manifest the assent of the people of this Republic, as required in the above recited portions of said

[2] *Journals of the Constitution Convention of Texas, 1845* (Austin: Miner and Cruger, Printers to the Constitution, 1845), 367–70.

resolutions, we the deputies of the people of Texas, in convention assembled, in their name and by their authority, do ordain and declare, that we assent to and accept the proposals, conditions and guarantees, contained in the first and second sections of the Resolution of the Congress of the United States aforesaid.

In testimony whereof, we have hereunto subscribed our names.

THOMAS J. RUSK
President

followed by 61 signatures

Attest
JAMES H. RAYMOND
Secretary of the Convention

Sam Houston's Address on Secession (1860) and Declaration of Causes (1861)

Texas joined the Union in 1845 and left it in 1861. Following the lead of other southern states after the election of Lincoln, Texas called a Secession Convention that met in January 1861. Despite the efforts of Governor Sam Houston to keep Texas in the Union, the convention passed an Ordinance of Secession on February 1 and a Declaration of Causes on February 2, 1861.[3] Texas joined the Confederacy as a state on March 1, 1861. Following a four-year conflict, as a practical matter the war ended in April 1865 with the surrender of Lee's Army of Northern Virginia. The last battle of the war (the Battle of Palmito Ranch) was fought May 12–13, 1865, near Brownsville.

Sam Houston's address captures the minority pro-Union position in Texas. A disciple of Andrew Jackson who rigorously opposed the attempts of South Carolina to reject the dominance of the national government during the Nullification Debates of the 1830s, Houston argued that leaving the Union was a dangerous action for the South. Note that Houston does not reject slavery as an institution but argues that the best way to defend Texans and Texas's interests is within the existing constitutional structure.

The Declaration of Causes presents the pro-secession argument in Texas, the one that ultimately carried the day. Note this document expresses the fear that southern proslavery states will become a minority in the Union. It also rejects the northern abolitionist contention that there is a "higher law" operating above the U.S. Constitution.

From Sam Houston's Address on
Secession, Austin, Texas, 1860

. . . [I]n 1836, I volunteered to aid in transplanting American liberty to this soil, it was with the belief that the Constitution and the Union were to be perpetual blessings to the human race,—that the success of the experiment of our fathers was beyond dispute, and that whether under the banner of the Lone Star or that many-starred banner of the Union, I could point to the land of Washington, Jefferson, and Jackson, as the land blest beyond all other lands, where freedom would be eternal and Union unbroken. . . . Power, wealth, expansion, victory, have followed in its path, and yet the aegis of the Union has been broad enough to encompass all. Is not this worth perpetuating? Will you exchange this for all the

[3] Edwin Anderson Alderman, *Library of Southern History*, ed. Joel Chandler Harris (Atlanta: Martin and Hoyt, 1909).

hazards, the anarchy and carnage of civil war? Do you believe that it will be dissevered and no shock felt in society? You are asked to plunge into a revolution; but are you told how to get out of it? Not so; but it is to be a leap in the dark—a leap into an abyss, whose horrors would even fright the mad spirits of disunion who tempt you on.

. . . What is there that is free that we have not? Are our rights invaded and no Government ready to protect them? No! Are our institutions wrested from us and others foreign to our taste forced upon us? No! Is the right of free speech, a free press, or free suffrage taken from us? No! Has our property been taken from us and the Government failed to interpose when called upon? No, none of these! The rights of the States and the rights of individuals are still maintained. We have yet the Constitution, we have yet a judiciary, which has never been appealed to in vain—we have yet just laws and officers to administer them; and an army and navy, ready to maintain any and every constitutional right of the citizen. Whence then this clamor about disunion? Whence this cry of protection to property or disunion, when even the very loudest in the cry, declared under their Senatorial oaths, but a few months since, that no protection was necessary? Are we to sell reality for a phantom?

There is no longer a holy ground upon which the footsteps of the demagogue may not fall. One by one the sacred things placed by patriotic hands upon the altar of our liberties, have been torn down. The Declaration of our Independence is jeered at. The farewell counsels of Washington are derided. The charm of those historic names which make glorious our past has been broken, and now the Union is no longer held sacred, but made secondary to the success of party and the adoption of abstractions. We hear of secession— "peaceable secession." We are to believe that this people, whose progressive civilization has known no obstacles, but has already driven back one race and is fast Americanizing another, who have conquered armies and navies,—whose career has been onward and never has receded, be the step right or wrong, is at last quietly and calmly to be denationalized, to be rent into fragments, sanctioned by the Constitution, and there not only be none of the incidents of revolution, but amid peace and happiness we are to have freedom from abolition clamor, security to the institution of slavery, and a career of glory under a Southern Confederacy, which we can never attain in our present condition! When we deny the right of a State to secede, we are pointed to the resolves of chivalric

South Carolina and other States; and are told, "Let them go out and you can not whip them back." My friends, there will be no necessity of whipping them back. They will soon whip themselves, and will not be worth whipping back. Deprived of the protection of the Union, of the aegis of the Constitution, they would soon dwindle into petty States, to be again rent in twain by dissensions or through the ambition of selfish chieftains, and would become a prey to foreign powers. They gravely talk of holding treaties with Great Britain and other foreign powers, and the great advantages which would arise to the South from separation are discussed. Treaties with Great Britain! Alliance with foreign powers! Have these men forgotten history? Look at Spanish America! Look at the condition of every petty State, which by alliance with Great Britain is subject to continual aggression! And yet, after picturing the rise and progress of Abolitionism, tracing it to the Wilberforce movement in England, and British influence in the North, showing that British gold has sustained and encouraged Northern fanaticism, we are told to be heedless of the consequences of disunion, for the advantages of British alliance would far over-estimate the loss of the Union!

. . . It is but natural that we all should desire the defeat of the Black Republican candidates. As Southern men, the fact that their party is based upon the one idea of opposition to our institutions, is enough to demand our efforts against them; but we have a broader, a more national cause of opposition to them. Their party is sectional. It is at war with those principles of equality and nationality upon which the Government is formed, and as much the foe of the Northern as of the Southern man. Its mission is to engender strife, to foster hatred between brethren, and to encourage the formation here of Southern sectional parties equally dangerous to Southern and Northern rights. The conservative energies of the country are called upon to take a stand now against the Northern sectional party, because its strength betokens success. Defeat and overthrow it, and the defeat and overthrow of Southern sectionalism is easy.

I come not here to speak in behalf of a united South against Lincoln. I appeal to the nation. I ask not the defeat of sectionalism by sectionalism, but by nationality. These men who talk of a united South, know well that it begets a united North. Talk of frightening the North into measures by threats of dissolving the Union! It is child's play and folly. It is all the Black Republican leaders want. American blood, North nor South, has not yet become so ignoble as to be chilled by threats. Strife begets strife, threat begets threat, and taunt begets taunt, and these disunionists know it. American blood brooks no such restraints as these men would put upon it. I would blush with shame for America, if I could believe that one vast portion of my countrymen had sunk so low that childish threats would intimidate them. . . .

The error has been that the South has met sectionalism by sectionalism. We want a Union basis, one broad enough to comprehend the good and true friends of the Constitution at the North. To hear Southern disunionists talk, you would think the majority of the Northern people were in this Black Republican party; but it is not so. They are in a minority, and it but needs a patriotic movement like that supported by the conservatives of Texas, to unite the divided opposition to that party there and overthrow it. . . .

I came not here to vindicate candidates or denounce them. They stand upon their records. If they are national, approve them; if they are sectional, condemn. Judge them by the principles they announce. Let past differences be forgotten in the determination to unite against sectionalism. I have differed with all three of the candidates; but whenever I see a man at this crisis coming boldly up to the defense of the Constitution of the country, and ready to maintain the Union against its foes, I will not permit old scores to prejudice me against him. Hence I am ready to vote the Union ticket, and if all the candidates occupy this national ground, my vote may be transferred to either of them. This is the way to put Mr. Lincoln down. Put him down constitutionally, by rallying the conservative forces and sacrificing men for the sake of principles.

But if, through division in the ranks of those opposed to Mr. Lincoln, he should be elected, we have no excuse for dissolving the Union. The Union is worth more than Mr. Lincoln, and if the battle is to be fought for the Constitution, let us fight it in the Union and for the sake of the Union. With a majority of the people in favor of the Constitution, shall we desert the Government and leave it in the hands of the minority? A new obligation will be imposed upon us, to guard the Constitution and to see that no infraction of it is attempted or permitted. If Mr. Lincoln administers the Government in accordance with the Constitution, our rights must be respected. If he does not, the Constitution has provided a remedy.

No tyrant or usurper can ever invade our rights so long as we are united. Let Mr. Lincoln attempt it, and his party will scatter like chaff before the storm of popular indignation which will burst forth from one end of the country to the other. Secession or revolution will not be justified until legal and constitutional means of redress have been tried, and I can not believe that the time will ever come when these will prove inadequate. . . .

Declaration of Causes: February 2, 1861[4]
A declaration of the causes which impel the State
of Texas to secede from the Federal Union.

The government of the United States, by certain joint resolutions, bearing date the 1st day of March, in the year A.D. 1845, proposed to the Republic of Texas, then a free, sovereign and independent nation, the annexation of the latter to the former as one of the co-equal States thereof,

The people of Texas, by deputies in convention assembled, on the fourth day of July of the same year, assented to and accepted said proposals and formed a constitution for the proposed State, upon which on the 29th day of December in the same year, said State was formally admitted into the Confederated Union.

Texas abandoned her separate national existence and consented to become one of the Confederated States to promote her welfare, insure domestic tranquility [sic] and secure more substantially the blessings of peace and liberty to her people. She was received into the confederacy with her own constitution, under the guarantee of the federal constitution and the compact of annexation, that she should enjoy these blessings. She was received as a commonwealth holding, maintaining and protecting the institution known as negro slavery—the servitude of the African to the white race within her limits—a relation that had existed from the first settlement of her wilderness by the white race, and which her people intended should exist in all future time. Her institutions and geographical position established the strongest ties between her and other slave-holding States of the confederacy. Those ties have been strengthened by association. But what has been the course of the government of the United States, and of the people and authorities of the non-slave-holding States, since our connection with them?

The controlling majority of the Federal Government, under various pretences and disguises, has so administered the same as to exclude the citizens of the Southern States, unless under odious and unconstitutional restrictions, from all the immense territory owned in common by all the States on the Pacific Ocean, for the avowed purpose of acquiring sufficient power in the common government to use it as a means of destroying the institutions of Texas and her sister slave-holding States.

[4] Ernest William Winkler, ed., *Journal of the Secession Convention of Texas 1861, Edited from the Original in the Department of State by Ernest William Winkler, State Librarian* (Austin: Texas Library and Historical Commission, 1912), 61–65.

By the disloyalty of the Northern States and their citizens and the imbecility of the Federal Government, infamous combinations of incendiaries and outlaws have been permitted in those States and the common territory of Kansas to trample upon the federal laws, to war upon the lives and property of Southern citizens in that territory, and finally, by violence and mob law, to usurp the possession of the same as exclusively the property of the Northern States.

The Federal Government, while but partially under the control of these our unnatural and sectional enemies, has for years almost entirely failed to protect the lives and property of the people of Texas against the Indian savages on our border, and more recently against the murderous forays of banditti from the neighboring territory of Mexico; and when our State government has expended large amounts for such purpose, the Federal Government has refused reimbursement therefor, thus rendering our condition more insecure and harrassing [sic] than it was during the existence of the Republic of Texas.

These and other wrongs we have patiently borne in the vain hope that a returning sense of justice and humanity would induce a different course of administration.

When we advert to the course of individual non-slave-holding States, and that [of] a majority of their citizens, our grievances assume far greater magnitude.

The States of Maine, Vermont, New Hampshire, Connecticut, Rhode Island, Massachusetts, New York, Pennsylvania, Ohio, Wisconsin, Michigan and Iowa, by solemn legislative enactments, have deliberately, directly or indirectly violated the 3rd clause of the 2nd section of the 4th article of the federal constitution, and laws passed in pursuance thereof; thereby annulling a material provision of the compact, designed by its framers to perpetuate amity between the members of the confederacy and to secure the rights of the slaveholding States in their domestic institutions—a provision founded in justice and wisdom, and without the enforcement of which the compact fails to accomplish the object of its creation. Some of those States have imposed high fines and degrading penalties upon any of their citizens or officers who may carry out in good faith that provision of the compact, or the federal laws enacted in accordance therewith.

In all the non-slave-holding States, in violation of that good faith and comity which should exist between entirely distinct nations, the people have formed themselves into a great sectional party, now strong enough in numbers to control the affairs of each of those States, based upon the unnatural feeling of hostility to these Southern States and their beneficent and patriarchal system of African slavery, proclaiming the debasing doctrine of the equality of all men, irrespective of race or color—a doctrine at war with nature, in opposition to the experience of mankind, and in violation of the plainest revelations of the Divine Law. They demand the abolition of negro slavery throughout the confederacy, the recognition of political equality between the white and the negro races, and avow their determination to press on their crusade against us, so long as a negro slave remains in these States.

For years past this abolition organization has been actively sowing the seeds of discord through the Union, and has rendered the federal congress the arena for spreading firebrands and hatred between the slave-holding and non-slave-holding States.

By consolidating their strength, they have placed the slave-holding States in a hopeless minority in the federal congress, and rendered representation of no avail in protecting Southern rights against their exactions and encroachments.

They have proclaimed, and at the ballot box sustained, the revolutionary doctrine that there is a "higher law" than the constitution and laws of our Federal Union, and virtually that they will disregard their oaths and trample upon our rights.

They have for years past encouraged and sustained lawless organizations to steal our slaves and prevent their recapture, and have repeatedly murdered Southern citizens while lawfully seeking their rendition.

They have invaded Southern soil and murdered unoffending citizens, and through the press their leading men and a fanatical pulpit have bestowed praise upon the actors and assassins in these crimes, while the governors of several of their States have refused to deliver parties implicated and indicted for participation in such offences, upon the legal demands of the States aggrieved.

They have, through the mails and hired emissaries, sent seditious pamphlets and papers among us to stir up servile insurrection and bring blood and carnage to our firesides.

They have sent hired emissaries among us to burn our towns and distribute arms and poison to our slaves for the same purpose.

They have impoverished the slave-holding States by unequal and partial legislation, thereby enriching themselves by draining our substance.

They have refused to vote appropriations for protecting Texas against ruthless savages, for the sole reason that she is a slave-holding State.

And, finally, by the combined sectional vote of the seventeen non-slave-holding States, they have elected as president

and vice-president of the whole confederacy two men whose chief claims to such high positions are their approval of these long continued wrongs, and their pledges to continue them to the final consummation of these schemes for the ruin of the slave-holding States.

In view of these and many other facts, it is meet that our own views should be distinctly proclaimed.

We hold as undeniable truths that the governments of the various States, and of the confederacy itself, were established exclusively by the white race, for themselves and their posterity; that the African race had no agency in their establishment; that they were rightfully held and regarded as an inferior and dependent race, and in that condition only could their existence in this country be rendered beneficial or tolerable.

That in this free government all white men are and of right ought to be entitled to equal civil and political rights; that the servitude of the African race, as existing in these States, is mutually beneficial to both bond and free, and is abundantly authorized and justified by the experience of mankind, and the revealed will of the Almighty Creator, as recognized by all Christian nations; while the destruction of the existing relations between the two races, as advocated by our sectional enemies, would bring inevitable calamities upon both and desolation upon the fifteen slave-holding States.

By the secession of six of the slave-holding States, and the certainty that others will speedily do likewise, Texas has no alternative but to remain in an isolated connection with the North, or unite her destinies with the South.

For these and other reasons, solemnly asserting that the federal constitution has been violated and virtually abrogated by the several States named, seeing that the federal government is now passing under the control of our enemies to be diverted from the exalted objects of its creation to those of oppression and wrong, and realizing that our own State can no longer look for protection, but to God and her own sons—We the delegates of the people of Texas, in Convention assembled, have passed an ordinance dissolving all political connection with the government of the United States of America and the people thereof and confidently appeal to the intelligence and patriotism of the freemen of Texas to ratify the same at the ballot box, on the 23rd day of the present month.

Adopted in Convention on the 2nd day of Feby, in the year of our Lord one thousand eight hundred and sixty-one and of the independence of Texas the twenty-fifth.

Ordinance of Secession Null (1866) and Texas v. White et al. (1869)

Once the South and Texas had been defeated in the Civil War, the question arose as to the constitutional status of the secessionist states, including Texas. From the perspective of law and constitutional thought, had the southern states ever left the Union? Were the actions of state governments under the Confederacy legal or not? Two documents help clarify this issue.[5]

The ordinance declaring secession null and void answers these questions directly. By the expressed declaration of the Texas people in convention, the ordinance proclaims the 1861 act of secession to be null and void. Texas may have been in rebellion, but it never left the Union. Actions by the Confederate state of Texas thus were not legal.

The Texas v. White et al. *case answers this question further by exploring the legality of specific actions of the Confederate legislature in Texas. In 1850, Congress authorized $10 million in bonds to Texas. In 1862 the Confederate legislature authorized using the bonds for war supplies. In 1866, after the war, the Reconstruction government of Texas tried to reclaim the bonds on the grounds that the Confederate state government had illegally sold the bonds. Note the constitutional theory about the nature of the Union and the rebellion that is developed in the Chief Justice's opinion. The union established under the Articles of Convention and the U.S. Constitution is "perpetual" and "indissoluble." Once Texas joined the Union, Texas and Texans became part of this Union. Texas may have been in rebellion against the Union, but it had never left the Union. The actions of the Confederate government, like the act of secession, were thus null and void. The bonds thus had not been legally sold.*

An Ordinance, Declaring the Ordinance of
Secession Null and Void (*March 15, 1866*)

Be it ordained by the people of Texas in Convention assembled, That we acknowledge the supremacy of the Constitution of the United States, and the laws passed in pursuance thereof; and that an Ordinance adopted by a former Convention of the people of Texas on the 1st day of February, A.D. 1861, entitled "An Ordinance to Dissolve the Union between the State of Texas and the other States, united under the compact styled 'Constitution of the United States of America,'" be and the same is hereby declared null and void; and the right heretofore claimed by the State of Texas to secede from the Union, is hereby distinctly renounced. Passed 15th March, 1866.

From TEXAS v. WHITE ET AL. (*1869*)
Supreme Court of United States.

The CHIEF JUSTICE delivered the opinion of the court.

. . . If, therefore, it is true that the State of Texas was not at the time of filing this bill, or is not now, one of the United States, we have no jurisdiction of this suit, and it is our duty to dismiss it.

We are very sensible of the magnitude and importance of this question, of the interest it excites, and of the difficulty, not to say impossibility, of so disposing of it as to satisfy the conflicting judgments of men equally enlightened, equally upright, and equally patriotic. But we meet it in the case, and we must determine it in the exercise of our best judgment, under the guidance of the Constitution alone. . . .

. . . [T]he word . . . [*state* is] used in the clause which provides that the United States shall guarantee to every State in the Union a republican form of government, and shall protect each of them against invasion. . . .

The Republic of Texas was admitted into the Union, as a State, on the 27th of December, 1845. By this act the new State, and the people of the new State, were invested with all the rights, and became subject to all the responsibilities and duties of the original States under the Constitution.

From the date of admission, until 1861, the State was represented in the Congress of the United States by her senators and representatives, and her relations as a member of the Union remained unimpaired. In that year, acting upon the theory that the rights of a State under the Constitution might be renounced, and her obligations thrown off at pleasure, Texas undertook to sever the bond thus formed, and to break up her constitutional relations with the United States. . . .

The governor and secretary of state, refusing to comply, were summarily ejected from office.

The members of the legislature, which had also adjourned and reassembled on the 18th of March, were more compliant. They took the oath, and proceeded on the 8th of

---

[5] The Constitution of the State of Texas, as Amended by the Delegates in Convention Assembled, Austin, 1866 (Austin: Printed at the Southern Intelligencer Office, 1866), 32.

April to provide by law for the choice of electors of president and vice-president of the Confederate States.

The representatives of the State in the Congress of the United States were withdrawn, and as soon as the seceded States became organized under a constitution, Texas sent senators and representatives to the Confederate Congress.

In all respects, so far as the object could be accomplished by ordinances of the convention, by acts of the legislature, and by votes of the citizens, the relations of Texas to the Union were broken up, and new relations to a new government were established for them.

The position thus assumed could only be maintained by arms, and Texas accordingly took part, with the other Confederate States, in the war of the rebellion, which these events made inevitable. During the whole of that war there was no governor, or judge, or any other State officer in Texas, who recognized the National authority. Nor was any officer of the United States permitted to exercise any authority whatever under the National government within the limits of the State, except under the immediate protection of the National military forces.

Did Texas, in consequence of these acts, cease to be a State? Or, if not, did the State cease to be a member of the Union? . . .

The Union of the States never was a purely artificial and arbitrary relation. It began among the Colonies, and grew out of common origin, mutual sympathies, kindred principles, similar interests, and geographical relations. It was confirmed and strengthened by the necessities of war, and received definite form, and character, and sanction from the Articles of Confederation. By these the Union was solemnly declared to "be perpetual." And when these Articles were found to be inadequate to the exigencies of the country, the Constitution was ordained "to form a more perfect Union." It is difficult to convey the idea of indissoluble unity more clearly than by these words. What can be indissoluble if a perpetual Union, made more perfect, is not? . . .

When, therefore, Texas became one of the United States, she entered into an indissoluble relation. All the obligations of perpetual union, and all the guaranties of republican government in the Union, attached at once to the State. The act which consummated her admission into the Union was something more than a compact; it was the incorporation of a new member into the political body. And it was final. The union between Texas and the other States was as complete, as perpetual, and as indissoluble as the union between the original States. There was no place for reconsideration, or revocation, except through revolution, or through consent of the States.

Considered therefore as transactions under the Constitution, the ordinance of secession, adopted by the convention and ratified by a majority of the citizens of Texas, and all the acts of her legislature intended to give effect to that ordinance, were absolutely null. They were utterly without operation in law. The obligations of the State, as a member of the Union, and of every citizen of the State, as a citizen of the United States, remained perfect and unimpaired. It certainly follows that the State did not cease to be a State, nor her citizens to be citizens of the Union. If this were otherwise, the State must have become foreign, and her citizens foreigners. The war must have ceased to be a war for the suppression of rebellion, and must have become a war for conquest and subjugation.

Our conclusion therefore is, that Texas continued to be a State, and a State of the Union, notwithstanding the transactions to which we have referred. And this conclusion, in our judgment, is not in conflict with any act or declaration of any department of the National government, but entirely in accordance with the whole series of such acts and declarations since the first outbreak of the rebellion. . . .

These new relations imposed new duties upon the United States. The first was that of suppressing the rebellion. The next was that of re-establishing the broken relations of the State with the Union. The first of these duties having been performed, the next necessarily engaged the attention of the National government.

The authority for the performance of the first had been found in the power to suppress insurrection and carry on war; for the performance of the second, authority was derived from the obligation of the United States to guarantee to every State in the Union a republican form of government. . . . It follows that the title of the State was not divested by the act of the insurgent government in entering into this contract. . . .

From Governor Richard Coke's Second Inaugural Address (1876)

Following the Civil War, Texas operated under two constitutions (the Constitution of 1866 and 1869). The return to power of the Democratic Party in the elections of 1872 and 1873 effectively ended reconstruction in Texas. A Constitutional Convention dominated by the Democrats in 1875 drafted a new constitution for the state that took effect in 1876.

Governor Richard Coke's second inaugural address in 1876 captures how many people thought of the new constitution. For Coke the 1876 Constitution was not meant to be a reworking of the earlier state constitutions. The people of Texas had become dissatisfied with the power granted to governmental institution over the last decade and were seeking to limit the powers and reach of government. The new constitution was to be unabashedly conservative in design and intent.

After years of trial and struggle, the people of Texas have at length inaugurated a government made in all its parts by themselves. Its faults and errors, as well as its blessings, have no uncertain paternity. The highest exercise of sovereign power of which a State in the American Union is capable, is that through which the people of Texas have swept out of existence the old government and enacted in its stead that which today has been put in operation in all its departments. Thus has a great revolution been accomplished, without violence or disorder, and with no other conflict than the attrition of opposing opinions in the field of argument and discussion, preparatory to the grand arbitrament of the peaceful ballot.... This is the sixth time in the history of Texas that this sovereign right has been exercised....

In the more recently framed constitutions we plainly see a wide departure from the beaten track of constitutional structure, and in none of them is this more apparent than in the new Constitution of Texas.

The accepted theory of American constitutional government is that State constitutions are limitations upon, rather than grants of power; and, as a general rule, not without its exceptions, that powers not prohibited exist in State government. Hence, express prohibitions are necessary upon the powers the people would withhold from the State government, and as time and circumstances and experience suggest their wisdom, these restrictions upon the powers of govern-ment have multiplied in the more recently created instruments of fundamental law. Many causes have conspired to produce these great changes of constitutional theory, and prominent among them are the enormous amounts of capital concentrated in few hands, operating under charters which perpetuate its power; immense railroad systems, which drive off competition and monopolize the carrying trade of the country; the wonderful growth of towns and cities, whose immediate local governments are peculiarly subject to abuses and malign influences, general extravagance, and frequent corruptions of all departments of government, of late years becoming so alarming—all producing results which necessitate a clearer definition and closer guardianship of the rights of the people; and, for their protection, constitutional barriers not demanded by the conditions of society a quarter of a century ago.—

In this instrument we see mirrored the result of issues made in the politics of the State, in the halls of legislation, and in the primary assemblies of the people during the last decade; and we see faithfully reflected in its restrictions upon the power of government, as in its assertion of powers, the dangers of the past, a recurrence of which is so well guarded against in the future. The instrument presents in its fundamental and leading features a basis on which a government may be reared, eminently conservative of all the purposes for which government is instituted; adapted to a sound and healthy growth and development of the State. It may possibly be, in some respects too restrictive, but when such is the case, the error is on the safe side, and while temporary inconvenience may ensue, no permanent injury will result....

The country and people whose welfare depends upon our deliberations and action need and expect a government light in its burdens, effective in administration, and certain in its securities for person and property. Naught else is necessary to ensure prosperity and continued progress and advancement. With such government the elements of greatness so abundant in the noble State we represent, in the hands of our intelligent adventurous and enterprising people, will combine, and evolve from the womb of the future a destiny of grander proportions than the most gorgeous dream of the enthusiast now pictures....

The Texas Constitution's Bill of Rights (1876 plus amendments)

One of the distinguishing features of the Texas Constitution is a lengthy Bill of Rights. Here the Texas Constitution protects Texans from the actions of state government. Unlike the U.S. Constitution where the Bill of Rights comprising the first ten amendments is located at the end of the document, the Texas Bill of Rights is placed at the beginning as Article 1.

The Texas Bill of Rights articulates a distinctive governing philosophy about the "principles of liberty and free government" that underlies the Texas Constitution. Power comes from the people and Republican government is guaranteed. The people reserve "at all times the inalienable right to alter, reform or abolish their government in such a manner as they may think expedient." Texas is a free and independent state, "subject only to the Constitution of the United States." But the Texas Bill of Rights also declares that the "perpetuity of the Union" depends upon the preservation of unimpaired local self-government. Today such a statement might seem to be uncontroversial. Put in the proper historical context, however, this philosophy signals a rejection of the 1869 Constitution's explicit affirmation of the supremacy of the U.S. Constitution in matters of federalism. Such a philosophy reflects the return to power of traditional secessionist political elites in Texas. This philosophy would dominate (and haunt) Texas politics and government from 1876 until the 1960s when federal civil rights legislation would redefine what local self-government would mean, particularly in regard to the protections afforded minorities by the U.S. Constitution.

Some of the rights in Article 1 echo the protections provided by the U.S. Bill of Rights. Freedom of worship is guaranteed (Sec. 6), as is freedom of speech (Sec. 8), freedom of the press (Sec. 8), freedom of assembly and petition (Sec. 27), and freedom from the quartering of soldiers (Sec. 25). Texans are protected in the Bill of Rights from unreasonable searches and seizures (Sec. 9), and the accused has certain due process rights (for example, Secs. 10, 12, 13, 14, 15, and 19). The Texas Bill of Rights explicitly bans religious tests for public office or appropriations for sectarian purposes (Sec. 7).

Some protections provided by the Texas Bill of Rights seem strange to the modern ear. Monopolies are outlawed (Sec. 26). Primogeniture (limiting the inheritance of land to the first born) and entails (conditions put on the inheritance of land) are forbidden. No one can be found guilty due to corruption of blood (guilt by family association) or be punished in their inheritance by the suicide of a family member.

The Texas Bill of Rights most sharply diverges from the U.S. Bill of Rights in the amendments that have been added over the years. Many of these reflect the ebb and flow of political and cultural concerns in the state. In contrast to the federal government, Texas added an Equal Rights Amendment to the Bill of Rights in 1972, protecting people from discrimination because of sex, race, color, creed, or national origin (Sec. 31). Between 1956 and 2007, complicated provisions were added to the Bill of Rights allowing the denial of bail for multiple convictions (Secs. 11a, 11b, and 11c). Lengthy provisions were added to the Bill of Rights granting rights to crime victims in 1989 (Sec. 30) and providing for compensation for crime victims in 1997 (Sec. 31). Provisions protecting traditional marriage were added in 2005 in Section 32, although these are now inoperable due to a recent Supreme Court ruling. Access to public beaches is guaranteed to individuals in 2009 (Sec. 33) as is the right to hunt, fish, and harvest wildlife by traditional methods such a guns (Sec. 34). In 2009, an amendment was added to the Bill of Rights clarifying when property could be seized by the state under eminent domain. These protections were added to the Bill of Rights largely in response to the furor created by cities taking land from individuals and giving it to others for development projects, like the building of modern sports stadiums.

The extensive list of rights contained in Article 1 of the Texas Constitution shows the ongoing concerns of people and politicians in Texas to limit what government does through constitutional mandate. These rights will likely be expanded in the future.

ARTICLE 1. BILL OF RIGHTS

That the general, great and essential principles of liberty and free government may be recognized and established, we declare:

Sec. 1. FREEDOM AND SOVEREIGNTY OF STATE. Texas is a free and independent State, subject only to the Constitution of the United States, and the maintenance of our free institutions and the perpetuity of the Union depend upon the preservation of the right of local self-government, unimpaired to all the States.

Sec. 2. INHERENT POLITICAL POWER; REPUBLICAN FORM OF GOVERNMENT. All political power is inherent in the people, and all free governments are founded on their authority, and instituted for their benefit. The faith of the people of Texas stands pledged to the preservation of a republican form of government, and, subject to this limitation only, they have at all times the inalienable right to alter, reform or abolish their government in such manner as they may think expedient.

Sec. 3. EQUAL RIGHTS. All free men, when they form a social compact, have equal rights, and no man, or set of men, is entitled to exclusive separate public emoluments, or privileges, but in consideration of public services.

Sec. 3a. EQUALITY UNDER THE LAW. Equality under the law shall not be denied or abridged because of sex, race, color, creed, or national origin. This amendment is self-operative.

(Added Nov. 7, 1972.)

Sec. 4. RELIGIOUS TESTS. No religious test shall ever be required as a qualification to any office, or public trust, in this State; nor shall any one be excluded from holding office on account of his religious sentiments, provided he acknowledge the existence of a Supreme Being.

Sec. 5. WITNESSES NOT DISQUALIFIED BY RELIGIOUS BELIEFS; OATHS AND AFFIRMATIONS. No person shall be disqualified to give evidence in any of the Courts of this State on account of his religious opinions, or for the want of any religious belief, but all oaths or affirmations shall be administered in the mode most binding upon the conscience, and shall be taken subject to the pains and penalties of perjury.

Sec. 6. FREEDOM OF WORSHIP. All men have a natural and indefeasible right to worship Almighty God according to the dictates of their own consciences. No man shall be compelled to attend, erect or support any place of worship, or to maintain any ministry against his consent. No human authority ought, in any case whatever, to control or interfere with the rights of conscience in matters of religion, and no preference shall ever be given by law to any religious society or mode of worship. But it shall be the duty of the Legislature to pass such laws as may be necessary to protect equally every religious denomination in the peaceable enjoyment of its own mode of public worship.

Sec. 7. APPROPRIATIONS FOR SECTARIAN PURPOSES. No money shall be appropriated, or drawn from the Treasury for the benefit of any sect, or religious society, theological or religious seminary; nor shall property belonging to the State be appropriated for any such purposes.

Sec. 8. FREEDOM OF SPEECH AND PRESS; LIBEL. Every person shall be at liberty to speak, write or publish his opinions on any subject, being responsible for the abuse of that privilege; and no law shall ever be passed curtailing the liberty of speech or of the press. In prosecutions for the publication of papers, investigating the conduct of officers, or men in public capacity, or when the matter published is proper for public information, the truth thereof may be given in evidence. And in all indictments for libels, the jury shall have the right to determine the law and the facts, under the direction of the court, as in other cases.

Sec. 9. SEARCHES AND SEIZURES. The people shall be secure in their persons, houses, papers and possessions, from all unreasonable seizures or searches, and no warrant to search any place, or to seize any person or thing, shall issue without describing them as near as may be, nor without probable cause, supported by oath or affirmation.

Sec. 10. RIGHTS OF ACCUSED IN CRIMINAL PROSECUTIONS. In all criminal prosecutions the accused shall have a speedy public trial by an impartial jury. He shall have the right to demand the nature and cause of the accusation against him, and to have a copy thereof. He shall not be compelled to give evidence against himself, and shall have the right of being heard by himself or counsel, or both, shall be confronted by the witnesses against him and shall have compulsory process for obtaining witnesses in his favor, except that when the witness resides out of the State and the offense charged is a violation of any of the anti-trust laws of this State, the defendant and the State shall have the right to produce and have the evidence admitted by deposition, under such rules and laws as the Legislature may hereafter provide; and no person shall be held to answer for a criminal offense, unless on an indictment of a grand jury, except in cases in which the punishment is by fine or imprisonment, otherwise than in the penitentiary, in cases of impeachment, and in cases arising in the army or navy, or in the militia, when in actual service in time of war or public danger.

(Amended Nov. 5, 1918.)

Sec. 11. BAIL. All prisoners shall be bailable by sufficient sureties, unless for capital offenses, when the proof is evident; but this provision shall not be so construed as to prevent bail after indictment found upon examination of the evidence, in such manner as may be prescribed by law.

Sec. 11a. MULTIPLE CONVICTIONS; DENIAL OF BAIL. (a) Any person (1) accused of a felony less than capital in this State, who has been theretofore twice convicted of a felony, the second conviction being subsequent to the first, both in point of time of commission of the offense and conviction therefor, (2) accused of a felony less than capital in this State, committed while on bail for a prior felony for which he has been indicted, (3) accused of a felony less than capital in this State involving the use of a deadly weapon after being convicted of a prior felony, or (4) accused of a violent or sexual offense committed while under the supervision of a criminal justice agency of the State or a political subdivision of the State for a prior felony, after a hearing, and upon evidence substantially showing the guilt of the accused of the offense in (1) or (3) above, of the offense committed while on bail in (2) above, or of the offense in (4) above committed while under the supervision of a criminal justice agency of the State or a political subdivision of the State for a prior felony, may be denied bail pending trial, by a district judge in this State, if said order denying bail pending trial is issued within seven calendar days subsequent to the time of incarceration of the accused; provided, however, that if the accused is not accorded a trial upon the accusation under (1) or (3) above, the accusation and indictment used under (2) above, or the accusation or indictment used under (4) above within sixty (60) days from the time of his incarceration upon the accusation, the order denying bail shall be automatically set aside, unless a continuance is obtained upon the motion or request of the accused; provided, further, that the right of appeal to the Court of Criminal Appeals of this State is expressly accorded the accused for a review of any judgment or order made hereunder, and said appeal shall be given preference by the Court of Criminal Appeals.

(b) In this section:

(1) "Violent offense" means:
(A) murder;
(B) aggravated assault, if the accused used or exhibited a deadly weapon during the commission of the assault;
(C) aggravated kidnapping; or
(D) aggravated robbery.
(2) "Sexual offense" means:
(A) aggravated sexual assault;
(B) sexual assault; or
(C) indecency with a child.

(Added Nov. 6, 1956; amended Nov. 8, 1977; Subsec. (a) amended and (b) added Nov. 2, 1993.)

Sec. 11b. VIOLATION OF CONDITION OF RELEASE PENDING TRIAL; DENIAL OF BAIL. Any person who is accused in this state of a felony or an offense involving family violence, who is released on bail pending trial, and whose bail is subsequently revoked or forfeited for a violation of a condition of release may be denied bail pending trial if a judge or magistrate in this state determines by a preponderance of the evidence at a subsequent hearing that the person violated a condition of release related to the safety of a victim of the alleged offense or to the safety of the community.

(Added Nov. 8, 2005; amended Nov. 6, 2007.)

Sec. 11c. VIOLATION OF AN ORDER FOR EMERGENCY PROTECTION INVOLVING FAMILY VIOLENCE. The legislature by general law may provide that any person who violates an order for emergency protection issued by a judge or magistrate after an arrest for an offense involving family violence or who violates an active protective order rendered by a court in a family violence case, including a temporary ex parte order that has been served on the person, or who engages in conduct that constitutes an offense involving the violation of an order described by this section may be taken into custody and, pending trial or other court proceedings, denied release on bail if following a hearing a judge or magistrate in this state determines by a preponderance of the evidence that the person violated the order or engaged in the conduct constituting the offense.

Sec. 12. HABEAS CORPUS. The writ of habeas corpus is a writ of right, and shall never be suspended. The Legislature shall enact laws to render the remedy speedy and effectual.

Sec. 13. EXCESSIVE BAIL OR FINES; CRUEL AND UNUSUAL PUNISHMENT; REMEDY BY DUE COURSE OF LAW. Excessive bail shall not be required, nor excessive fines imposed, nor cruel or unusual punishment inflicted. All courts shall be open, and every person for an injury done him, in his lands, goods, person or reputation, shall have remedy by due course of law.

Sec. 14. DOUBLE JEOPARDY. No person, for the same offense, shall be twice put in jeopardy of life or liberty; nor shall a person be again put upon trial for the same offense after a verdict of not guilty in a court of competent jurisdiction.

Sec. 15. RIGHT OF TRIAL BY JURY. The right of trial by jury shall remain inviolate. The Legislature shall pass such laws as may be needed to regulate the same, and to maintain its purity and efficiency. Provided, that the Legislature may provide for the temporary commitment, for observation and/or treatment, of mentally ill persons not charged with a criminal offense, for a period of time not to exceed ninety (90) days, by order of the County Court without the necessity of a trial by jury.

(Amended Aug. 24, 1935.)

Sec. 15-a. COMMITMENT OF PERSONS OF UNSOUND MIND. No person shall be committed as a person of unsound mind except on competent medical or psychiatric testimony. The Legislature may enact all laws necessary to provide for the trial, adjudication of insanity and commitment of persons of unsound mind and to provide for a method of appeal from judgments rendered in such cases. Such laws may provide for a waiver of trial by jury, in cases where the person under inquiry has not been charged with the commission of a criminal offense, by the concurrence of the person under inquiry, or his next of kin, and an attorney ad litem appointed by a judge of either the County or Probate Court of the county where the trial is being held, and shall provide for a method of service of notice of such trial upon the person under inquiry and of his right to demand a trial by jury.

(Added Nov. 6, 1956.)

Sec. 16. BILLS OF ATTAINDER; EX POST FACTO OR RETROACTIVE LAWS; IMPAIRING OBLIGATION OF CONTRACTS. No bill of attainder, ex post facto law, retroactive law, or any law impairing the obligation of contracts, shall be made.

Sec. 17. TAKING, DAMAGING, OR DESTROYING PROPERTY FOR PUBLIC USE; SPECIAL PRIVILEGES AND IMMUNITIES; CONTROL OF PRIVILEGES AND FRANCHISES. (a) No person's property shall be taken, damaged, or destroyed for or applied to public use without adequate compensation being made, unless by the consent of such person, and only if the taking, damage, or destruction is for:

> (1) the ownership, use, and enjoyment of the property, notwithstanding an incidental use, by:
>> (A) the State, a political subdivision of the State, or the public at large; or
>> (B) an entity granted the power of eminent domain under law; or

> (2) the elimination of urban blight on a particular parcel of property.

(b) In this section, "public use" does not include the taking of property under Subsection (a) of this section for transfer to a private entity for the primary purpose of economic development or enhancement of tax revenues.

(c) On or after January 1, 2010, the legislature may enact a general, local, or special law granting the power of eminent domain to an entity only on a two-thirds vote of all the members elected to each house.

(d) When a person's property is taken under Subsection (a) of this section, except for the use of the State, compensation as described by Subsection (a) shall be first made, or secured by a deposit of money; and no irrevocable or uncontrollable grant of special privileges or immunities shall be made; but all privileges and franchises granted by the Legislature, or created under its authority, shall be subject to the control thereof.

(Amended Nov. 3, 2009.)

Sec. 18. IMPRISONMENT FOR DEBT. No person shall ever be imprisoned for debt.

Sec. 19. DEPRIVATION OF LIFE, LIBERTY, ETC.; DUE COURSE OF LAW. No citizen of this State shall be deprived of life, liberty, property, privileges or immunities, or in any manner disfranchised, except by the due course of the law of the land.

Sec. 20. OUTLAWRY OR TRANSPORTATION FOR OFFENSE. No citizen shall be outlawed. No person shall be transported out of the State for any offense committed within the same. This section does not prohibit an agreement with another state providing for the confinement of inmates of this State in the penal or correctional facilities of that state.

(Amended Nov. 5, 1985.)

Sec. 21. CORRUPTION OF BLOOD; FORFEITURE; SUICIDES. No conviction shall work corruption of blood, or forfeiture of estate, and the estates of those who destroy their own lives shall descend or vest as in case of natural death.

Sec. 22. TREASON. Treason against the State shall consist only in levying war against it, or adhering to its enemies, giving them aid and comfort; and no person shall be convicted of treason except on the testimony of two witnesses to the same overt act, or on confession in open court.

Sec. 23. RIGHT TO KEEP AND BEAR ARMS. Every citizen shall have the right to keep and bear arms in the lawful defense of himself or the State; but the Legislature shall have power, by law, to regulate the wearing of arms, with a view to prevent crime.

Sec. 24. MILITARY SUBORDINATE TO CIVIL AUTHORITY. The military shall at all times be subordinate to the civil authority.

Sec. 25. QUARTERING SOLDIERS IN HOUSES. No soldier shall in time of peace be quartered in the house of any citizen without the consent of the owner, nor in time of war but in a manner prescribed by law.

Sec. 26. PERPETUITIES AND MONOPOLIES; PRIMOGENITURE OR ENTAILMENTS. Perpetuities and monopolies are contrary to the genius of a free government, and shall never be allowed, nor shall the law of primogeniture or entailments ever be in force in this State.

Sec. 27. RIGHT OF ASSEMBLY; PETITION FOR REDRESS OF GRIEVANCES. The citizens shall have the right, in a peaceable manner, to assemble together for their common good; and apply to those invested with the powers of government for redress of grievances or other purposes, by petition, address or remonstrance.

Sec. 28. SUSPENSION OF LAWS. No power of suspending laws in this State shall be exercised except by the Legislature.

Sec. 29. PROVISIONS OF BILL OF RIGHTS EXCEPTED FROM POWERS OF GOVERNMENT; TO FOREVER REMAIN INVIOLATE. To guard against transgressions of the high powers herein delegated, we declare that everything in this "Bill of Rights" is excepted out of the general powers of government, and shall forever remain inviolate, and all laws contrary thereto, or to the following provisions, shall be void.

Sec. 30. RIGHTS OF CRIME VICTIMS. (a) A crime victim has the following rights:

> (1) the right to be treated with fairness and with
> respect for the victim's dignity and privacy

throughout the criminal justice process; and

> (2) the right to be reasonably protected from the accused throughout the criminal justice process.

(b) On the request of a crime victim, the crime victim has the following rights:

> (1) the right to notification of court proceedings;
> (2) the right to be present at all public court proceedings related to the offense, unless the victim is to testify and the court determines that the victim's testimony would be materially affected if the victim hears other testimony at the trial;
> (3) the right to confer with a representative of the prosecutor's office;
> (4) the right to restitution; and
> (5) the right to information about the conviction, sentence, imprisonment, and release of the accused.

(c) The legislature may enact laws to define the term "victim" and to enforce these and other rights of crime victims.

(d) The state, through its prosecuting attorney, has the right to enforce the rights of crime victims.

(e) The legislature may enact laws to provide that a judge, attorney for the state, peace officer, or law enforcement agency is not liable for a failure or inability to provide a right enumerated in this section. The failure or inability of any person to provide a right or service enumerated in this section may not be used by a defendant in a criminal case as a ground for appeal or post-conviction writ of habeas corpus. A victim or guardian or legal representative of a victim has standing to enforce the rights enumerated in this section but does not have standing to participate as a party in a criminal proceeding or to contest the disposition of any charge.

(Added Nov. 7, 1989.)

Sec. 31. COMPENSATION TO VICTIMS OF CRIME FUND; COMPENSATION TO VICTIMS OF CRIME AUXILIARY FUND; USE OF FUND MONEY. (a) The compensation to victims of crime fund created by general law and the compensation to victims of crime auxiliary fund created by general law are each a separate dedicated account in the general revenue fund.

(b) Except as provided by Subsection (c) of this section and subject to legislative appropriation, money deposited to the credit of the compensation to victims of crime fund or the compensation to victims of crime auxiliary fund from any source may be expended as provided by law only for delivering or funding victim-related compensation, services, or assistance.

(c) The legislature may provide by law that money in the compensation to victims of crime fund or in the compensation to victims of crime auxiliary fund may be expended for the purpose of assisting victims of episodes of mass violence if other money appropriated for emergency assistance is depleted.

(Added Nov. 4, 1997.)

Sec. 32. MARRIAGE. (a) Marriage in this state shall consist only of the union of one man and one woman.

(b) This state or a political subdivision of this state may not create or recognize any legal status identical or similar to marriage.

(Added Nov. 8, 2005.)

Sec. 33. ACCESS AND USE OF PUBLIC BEACHES. (a) In this section, "public beach" means a state-owned beach bordering on the seaward shore of the Gulf of Mexico, extending from mean low tide to the landward boundary of state-owned submerged land, and any larger area extending from the line of mean low tide to the line of vegetation bordering on the Gulf of Mexico to which the public has acquired a right of use or easement to or over the area by prescription or dedication or has established and retained a right by virtue of continuous right in the public under Texas common law.

(b) The public, individually and collectively, has an unrestricted right to use and a right of ingress to and egress from a public beach. The right granted by this subsection is dedicated as a permanent easement in favor of the public.

(c) The legislature may enact laws to protect the right of the public to access and use a public beach and to protect the public beach easement from interference and encroachments.

(d) This section does not create a private right of enforcement.

(Added Nov. 3, 2009.)

Sec. 34. RIGHT TO HUNT, FISH, AND HARVEST WILDLIFE. (a) The people have the right to hunt, fish, and harvest wildlife, including by the use of traditional methods, subject to laws or regulations to conserve and manage wildlife and preserve the future of hunting and fishing.

(b) Hunting and fishing are preferred methods of managing and controlling wildlife.

(c) This section does not affect any provision of law relating to trespass, property rights, or eminent domain.

(d) This section does not affect the power of the legislature to authorize a municipality to regulate the discharge of a weapon in a populated area in the interest of public safety.

(Added Nov. 3, 2015.)

Endnotes

CHAPTER 1

1. Alan Rosenthal, "On Analyzing States," in *The Political Life of the American States*, eds. Alan Rosenthal and Maureen Moakley (New York: Praeger, 1984), 11–12.

2. Political scientist Daniel Elazar has created a classification scheme for state political cultures that is used widely. He uses the concepts of *moralistic, individualistic*, and *traditionalistic* to describe such cultures. These three state political cultures are contemporary manifestations of the ethnic, socioreligious, and socioeconomic differences that existed among America's original thirteen colonies. Daniel Elazar, *American Federalism: A View from the States*, 2nd ed. (New York: Crowell, 1971), 84–126. See also John Kincaid, "Introduction," in *Political Culture, Public Policy and the American States*, ed. John Kincaid (Philadelphia: Center for the Study of Federalism, Institute for the Study of Human Issues, 1982), 1–24.

3. Rosenthal, "On Analyzing States," 13.

4. An excellent discussion of the problem of characterizing Texas political culture is found in Chandler Davidson, *Race and Class in Texas Politics* (Princeton, NJ: Princeton University Press, 1990), chap. 2.

5. Texas General Land Office, *History of Texas Public Lands* (Austin: Texas General Land Office, revised January 2015), 9–17.

6. The following is drawn from the *Texas Almanac 2014–2015* (Denton: Texas State Historical Association, 2014), 78–84.

7. See Joseph A. Schumpeter, *Capitalism, Socialism, and Democracy*, 3rd ed. (New York: Harper & Brothers, 1950), chap. 6. For a discussion of the relationship between long-term economic transformation and political change at the national level, see Brian J. L. Berry et al., *The Rhythms of American Politics* (Lanham, MD: University Press of America, 1998).

8. The following is drawn from *Handbook of Texas Online*, Karen Gerhardt Britton, Fred C. Elliott, and E. A. Miller, "Cotton Culture," www.tshaonline.org/handbook /online/articles/afc03 (accessed 5/2/18).

9. See *Handbook of Texas Online*, Cecil Harper, Jr., and E. Dale Odom, "Farm Tenancy," www.tshaonline.org /handbook/online/articles/aefmu (accessed 5/2/18).

10. *Texas Almanac 2014–2015* (Texas State Historical Association), 687; see *Handbook of Texas Online*, Cecil Harper, Jr., and E. Dale Odom, "Farm Tenancy," www .tshaonline.org/handbook/online/articles/aefmu (accessed 5/2/18).

11. *Handbook of Texas Online*, T. C. Richardson and Harwood P. Hinton, "Ranching," www.tshaonline.org /handbook/online/articles/azr02 (accessed 5/2/18).

12. "Principal Crops of Texas," *Texas Almanac Online* (Texas State Historical Association); *Texas Almanac 2014–2015* (Texas State Historical Association), 687–88; Southern Plains Regional Office, U.S. Department of Agriculture, National Agriculture Statistics Service, "Texas Cotton Production," Issue No. PR-123-14 (Austin: May 2014).

13. *Texas Almanac 2018–2019* (Texas State Historical Association), 693.

14. The following is drawn from Mary G. Ramos, "Oil and Texas: A Cultural History," *Texas Almanac 2000–2001* (Dallas Morning News), 29–35; Roger M. Olien, "Oil and Gas Industry," *Handbook of Texas Online* (Texas State Historical Association).

15. Olien, "Oil and Gas Industry."

16. See Texas Legislative Budget Board, *Fiscal Size-Up: 2018–19 Biennium* (September 2018), 31.

17. Permanent University Fund, "Report on Certain Specified Data as Required by Art. 4413 (34e) of the Civil Statutes" (June 30, 2017), 1.

18. Simone Sebastian, "New Data Show 'Meteoric' Rise of Texas Oil," fuelfix.com, December 3, 2013. See James Osborne, "Texas Oil Production Hits 2 Million Barrels a Day, the Most Since 1986," *Dallas Morning News*, April 25, 2014. See Texas Railroad Commission, "Texas

Permian Basin Oil Production 2008 through March 2016." For a more detailed discussion of the new technology of fracking and its impact on the oil boom in Texas and the United States, see Russell Gold, *The Boom: How Fracking Ignited the American Energy Revolution and Changed the World* (New York: Simon & Schuster, 2014).

19. "Petroleum Production and Income in Texas," *Texas Almanac Online* (Texas State Historical Association). See also BBC News, "Oil Hits $50 a Barrel for the First Time This Year" (May 26, 2016). See also www.macro trends.net/1369/crude-oil-price-history-chart.

20. See "Texas Manufacturing Facts" at www.nam.org /Data-and-Reports/State-Manufacturing-Data.

21. TechAmerica Foundation, *Tech Trade in the States: A State-by-State Overview of International Trade in Tech Goods* (TechAmerica Foundation, 2014); *Texas Almanac 2014–15* (Texas State Historical Association), 586.

22. Standard & Poor's, "Twenty Years into NAFTA, Mexico and Texas Have Been the Two Main Beneficiaries of Increased Trade" (January 17, 2014). https://comptroller .texas.gov/economy/economic-data/ports/laredo.php.

23. See Robert E. Scott, "NAFTA's Legacy: Growing U.S. Trade Deficits Cost 682,900 Jobs" (Economic Policy Institute, December 13, 2013). See also Anil Kumar, "Did NAFTA Spur Texas Exports?" *Southwest Economy* 2 (March–April 2006); U.S. Department of Labor Employment and Training Administration, "Trade Adjustment Assistance: Number of Certified Workers by State"; Robert E. Scott, "Heading South: U.S.-Mexico Trade and Job Displacement after NAFTA" (Economic Policy Institute, May 3, 2011).

24. U.S. Census Bureau, "State Exports for Texas 2013" and "State Imports for Texas 2013." See also Texas Economy Online Report from the Office of the Governor, "Overview of the Texas Economy" (June 2014).

25. Bruce Wright, "Military Installations Worth Billions for Texas," *Fiscal Notes* (Texas Comptroller Office, September 2016).

26. Daniel Gross, "Lone Star: Why Texas Is Doing So Much Better than the Rest of the Nation," *Slate.com*, April 19, 2010, www.slate.com/articles/business/moneybox /2010/04/lone_star.html.

27. Texas Comptroller of Public Accounts, "Comptroller's Weekly Economic Outlook," *The Texas Economy, Economic Outlook* (August 1, 2018).

28. See Erica Grieder, *Big, Hot, Cheap, and Right: What America Can Learn from the Strange Genius of Texas* (New York: Public Affairs, 2013). Some have argued that Texas's characteristics cannot be duplicated by other states. See, for example, Elizabeth McNichol and Nicholas Johnson, "The Texas Economic Model: Hard for Other States to Follow and Not All It Seems" (Center for Budget and Economic Priorities, April 3, 2012).

29. Bruce Wright, "Weathering the Storm," *Fiscal Notes* (Texas Comptroller Office, April 2009); D'Ann Petersen and Laila Assanie, "Texas Dodges Worst of Foreclosure Wars" (Federal Reserve of Dallas, Dallas, 2009).

30. Richard Parker, "The Grisly Death of the GOP," *Dallas Morning News*, October 29, 2017, Sunday edition, p. 4.

31. See Robert Plocheck, "American Indians in Texas," *Texas Almanac Online* (Texas State Historical Association), http://texasalmanac.com/topics/culture /american-indian/american-indian. The revival of the American Indian population in Texas was fostered by a federal government program between 1950 and 1980 that encouraged Indians to leave reservations (some in other states) and integrate themselves in post–WWII urban communities.

32. See Texas State Library and Archives Commission, "United States and Texas Populations 1850–2012."

33. See census data analysis on www.governing.com, Governing Data, "State Population Estimates: 2013 Births, Deaths, Migration Totals," www.governing.com/gov -data/census/census-state-population-estimates -births-deaths-migration-totals-2013.html.

34. See Alexa Ura and Ryan Murphy, "Texas Population Grew to 28.3 Million in 2017," *The Texas Tribune*, December 20, 2017.

35. How the U.S. Census counts individuals in certain demographic groups is a complicated affair and is getting more complicated. The U.S. Census did not provide data for non-Hispanic whites, Hispanics, or Latinos as separate groups prior to 1970. Beginning in the 2000 census the term *Hispanic* was included.

36. See Arnoldo De León, "Mexican Americans," *Handbook of Texas Online* (Texas State Historical Association).

37. See U.S. Census Bureau, "State & County QuickFacts"; U.S. Census Bureau, 2010 Census; Sharon R. Ennis, Merarys Rios-Vargas, and Nora G. Albert, "The Hispanic Population: 2010" (2010 Census Briefs, May 2011); *Texas Almanac 2014–2015* (Texas State Historical Association), 15.

38. See National Association of Latino Elected and Appointed Officials (NALEO), "2016 Latino Primary Profile: Texas" (NALEO Educational Fund, 2016).

39. See W. Marvin Dulaney, "African Americans," *Handbook of Texas Online* (Texas State Historical Association); Chandler Davidson, "African Americans and Politics," *Handbook of Texas Online* (Texas State Historical Association).

40. See John R. Ross, "Lynching," *Handbook of Texas Online* (Texas State Historical Association), www.tsha online.org/handbook/online/articles/jgl01 (accessed 10/31/17).

41. See U.S. Census Bureau QuickFacts, "The Asian Population in Texas," 2017.

42. See *Texas Almanac 2014–2015* (Texas State Historical Association), for county-by-county data. The Asian population of Texas counties can be found at www .indexmundi.com.

43. U.S. Census Bureau, "Texas."

44. Bruce H. Webster, Jr., and Alemayehu Bishaw, "Income, Earnings, and Poverty Data from the 2006 American Community Survey" (American Community Survey Reports, U.S. Census Bureau, August 2007); U.S. Census Bureau, "Poverty 2007 and 2008 American Community Surveys" (American Community Survey Reports, U.S. Census Bureau, September 2009); U.S. Census Bureau, *Texas QuickFacts: 2009*; Alemayehu Bishaw, "Poverty: 2000–2012" (American Community Survey Briefs, U.S. Census Bureau, September 2013).

45. The definition used to measure the urban/rural dichotomy has shifted over time. For a more detailed discussion, see U.S. Census Bureau, "2012 Census Urban Area FAQs."

46. The following is based on David G. McComb, "Urbanization," *Handbook of Texas Online* (Texas State Historical Association).

47. The following is drawn from David G. McComb, "Houston, Texas," *Handbook of Texas Online* (Texas State Historical Association).

48. Estimates are drawn from the U.S. Census Bureau, "State & County QuickFacts."

49. The following is drawn from Jackie McElhaney and Michael V. Hazel, "Dallas, Texas," *Handbook of Texas Online* (Texas State Historical Association).

50. The following is drawn from Janet Schmelzer, "Fort Worth, Texas," *Handbook of Texas Online* (Texas State Historical Association).

51. The following is drawn from T. R. Fehrenbach, "San Antonio, Texas," *Handbook of Texas Online* (Texas State Historical Association).

52. Estimates are drawn from the U.S. Census Bureau, "State & County QuickFacts."

53. See www.censusreporter.org/profiles/16000US480 5000-austin-tx/.

54. See www.utexas.edu/about/facts-and-figures.

55. The following paragraphs are largely drawn from David C. Humphrey, "Austin, TX (Travis County)," *Handbook of Texas Online* (Texas State Historical Association); and Anthony M. Orum, *Power, Money and the People: The Making of Modern Austin* (Austin: Texas Monthly Press, 1987), ch. 1.

56. Dorman H. Winfrey, "The Texas Archive War of 1842," *Southwestern Historical Quarterly*, Texas State Historical Association, 64 (2): 171–184.

57. See "City of Austin Population History, 1840–2016" at www.austintexas.gov.

58. See David C. Humphrey, "Austin, TX (Travis County)," *Handbook of Texas Online* (Texas State Historical Association); and Anthony M. Orum, *Power, Money and the People: The Making of Modern Austin* (Austin: Texas Monthly Press, 1987), 235–36, 312–16.

59. Austin has put in a competitive bid for Amazon's HQ2 location. See Kelly O'Halloran, "Meet Austin's Top 100 tech companies: Employee count up 11 percent in 2017," *BuiltinAustin.com*, October 31, 2017, www.built inaustin.com/2017/10/31/austin-top-100-tech -companies-2017.

60. "Austin economy in 2017: still strong but facing some challenges," *mystatesman.com*, January 6, 2017, www .mystatesman.com/business/austin-economy-2017 -still-strong-but-facing-some-challenges/IR4qyVW ATLQLDF5ZsXUfdI/.

CHAPTER 2

1. The following is drawn from Proposition 10, deleting constitutional references to county office of inspector of hides and animals; Eric Aasen, "Round 'Em Up: Hide Inspectors Abolished," *Dallas Morning News*, November 8, 2007; John Council, "Richmond Lawyer Has Personal Stake in Hide Inspector Position," *Texas Lawyer*, November 2, 2007; Mark Lisheron, "Prop. 10 Would Abolish Office That No One Holds," *Austin American-Statesman*, October 15, 2007.

2. See Dick Smith, "Inspector of Hides and Animals," *Handbook of Texas Online*, June 15, 2010, www.tsha online.org/handbook/online/articles/mbi01 (accessed 5/11/18).

3. Donald E. Chipman, "Spanish Texas," *Handbook of Texas Online*, modified on January 23, 2017, www.tsha online.org/handbook/online/articles/nps01 (accessed 5/11/18). Donald E. Chipman, *Spanish Texas, 1519–1821* (Austin: University of Texas Press, 1992).

4. S. S. McKay, "Constitution of 1824," *Handbook of Texas Online*, modified February 29, 2016, www.tshaonline.org /handbook/online/articles/ngc02 (accessed 5/11/18).

5. S. S. McKay, "Constitution of Coahuila and Texas," *Handbook of Texas Online*, June 12, 2010, www.tsha online.org/handbook/online/articles/ngc01 (accessed 5/11/8).

6. See Ralph W. Steen, "Convention of 1836," *Handbook of Texas Online* (Texas State Historical Association).

7. The following is drawn from Joe E. Ericson, "Constitution of the Republic of Texas," *Handbook of Texas Online*, June 12, 2010, www.tshaonline.org/handbook /online/articles/mhc01 (accessed 5/11/18).

8. Randolph B. Campbell, "Slavery," *Handbook of Texas Online*, modified October 30, 2017, www.tshaonline.org /handbook/online/articles/yps01 (accessed 5/11/18).

9. For a brief summary of the war, see Eugene C. Barker and James W. Pohl, "Texas Revolution," *Handbook of Texas Online*, modified March 30, 2017, www.tsha online.org/handbook/online/articles/qdt01 (accessed 5/11/18).

10. S. S. McKay, "Constitution of 1845," *Handbook of Texas Online*, June 12, 2010, www.tshaonline.org/handbook /online/articles/mhc03 (accessed 5/11/18).

11. The Texas Ordinance of Secession (February 2, 1861).

12. See Walter L. Buenger, "Secession Convention," *Handbook of Texas Online* (Texas State Historical Association); Walter L. Buenger, *Secession and the Union in Texas* (Austin: University of Texas Press, 1984).

13. See Claude Elliott, "Constitutional Convention of 1866," *Handbook of Texas Online* (Texas State Historical Association); S. S. McKay, "Constitution of 1866," *Handbook of Texas Online* (Texas State Historical Association); Charles W. Ramsdell, *Reconstruction in Texas* (New York: Columbia University Press, 1970).

14. See S. S. McKay, "Constitution of 1869," *Handbook of Texas Online* (Texas State Historical Association); Ramsdell, *Reconstruction in Texas*.

15. See John Walker Mauer, "Constitution Proposed in 1874," *Handbook of Texas Online* (Texas State Historical Association); John Walker Mauer, "State Constitutions in a Time of Crisis: The Case of the Texas Constitution of 1876," 68 *Texas Law Review* 1615–46 (June 1990).

16. Texas Legislative Council, "Amendments to the Texas Constitution since 1876" (Austin: March 1912).

17. For a further discussion, see George D. Braden et al., *The Constitution of the State of Texas: An Annotated and Comparative Analysis* (Austin: University of Texas Press, 1977), 707–10.

18. See Sam Kinch, Jr., "Sharpstown Stock-Fraud Scandal," *Handbook of Texas Online* (Texas State Historical Association); Charles Deaton, *The Year They Threw the Rascals Out* (Austin: Shoal Creek, 1973).

19. "Texas Voters Approve 7 Constitutional Amendments," CBSDFW.com, November 9, 2011, http://dfw .cbslocal.com/2017/11/07/texans-amendments-state -constitution/.

CHAPTER 3

1. Brandi Grissom, "Texas Gov. Greg Abbott calls for Convention of States to take back states' rights," reprinted in *Politician Review*, February 16, 2016.

2. Grissom, February 16, 2016.

3. Greg Abbott, "Restoring the Rule of Law with States Leading the Way," January 8, 2016, static.texastribune .org/media/documents/Restoring_The_Rule_Of_Law _01082016.pdf.

4. Edgar Walters, "Abbott Calls on States to Amend U.S. Constitution," *Texas Tribune*, January 8, 2016.

5. Greg Abbott, "Texas Gov. Greg Abbott: Why I called for a Constitutional Convention of States," *Dallas News*, May 3, 2017.

6. V. O. Key, Jr., *Southern Politics* (New York: Vintage Books, 1949), 255.

7. This discussion is taken from David Brian Robertson, *Federalism and the Making of America* (New York: Routledge, 2012), 1–3.

8. Robertson, *Federalism and the Making of America*, 20–21.

9. Robertson, *Federalism and the Making of America*, 20–22.

10. Robertson, *Federalism and the Making of America*, 27.

11. Robertson, *Federalism and the Making of America*, 29–30.

12. Robertson, *Federalism and the Making of America*, 31.

13. *McCulloch v. Maryland*, 17 U.S. 316 (1819).

14. *Gibbons v. Ogden*, 22 U.S. 1, 2 (1824).

15. *Gibbons v. Ogden*, 22 U.S. 1, 2 (1824).

16. Robert F. Nagel, *The Implosion of American Federalism* (New York: Oxford University Press, 2001), 5.

17. *Texas v. White*, 74 U.S. 700 (1869).

18. Morton Grodzins, *The American System*, ed. Daniel J. Elazar (Chicago: Rand McNally, 1966).

19. Equal Justice Initiative, "Lynching in America: Confronting the Legacy of Racial Terror," 2017, https://lynchinginamerica.eji.org/report/.

20. *Wickard v. Filburn*, 317 U.S. 111 (1942).

21. "Getting Stuck with the Check," *Bloomberg Businessweek*, www.businessweek.com/stories/1994-05-29/getting-stuck-with-the-check (accessed 3/24/14).

22. Clyde Wayne Crews Jr., "Unfunded Mandates on the States Rising Again," *Forbes*, July 28, 2016; Congressional Budget Office, "CBO's Activities under the Unfunded Mandates Reform Act," www.cbo.gov/publication/51335.

23. *Villas at Parkside Partners v. City of Framers Branch*, Texas, 726 F. ed 524 (2013).

24. "State officials warn White House against enforcing new gun regulations," FoxNews.com, January 15, 2013, accessed March 24, 2014, www.foxnews.com/politics/2013/01/15/ore-sheriff-says-wont-enforce-new-gun-laws/.

25. Greg Abbott, "Lawsuits against Obama Are Taxpayer Bargain," *dallasnews.com*, September 25, 2012, www.dallasnews.com/opinion/latest-columns/20120925-greg-abbott-lawsuits-against-obama-are-taxpayer-bargain.ece (accessed 3/24/14).

26. *McDonald v. Chicago*, 561 U.S. 742 (2010).

27. *Sweatt v. Painter*, 339 U.S. 629 (1950).

28. *Brown v. Board of Education of Topeka*, 347 U.S. 483 (1954).

29. *Shelby County, Ala. v. Holder*, Brief of the State of Texas as amicus curiae in support of Petitioner, Supreme Court of the United States (2013), p. 4.

30. *Shelby County, Ala. v. Holder*, Brief of the State of Texas, p. 2.

31. *Veasey v. Abbott*, 796 F.3d 487 (2015).

32. *Veasey v. Abbott*, 888 F.3d 792 (2018).

33. Jill D. Weinberg, "Remaking Lawrence," 98 *Virginia Law Review in Brief* 61, 66 (2012).

34. *San Antonio v. Rodriguez*, 411 U.S. 1 (1973).

35. *Edgewood Independent School District v. Kirby*, 777 S.W.2d 391, 398 (Tex., 1989).

36. Neena Satya, Ryan McCrimmon, and Becca Aaronson, "Texas v. the Feds: A Look at the Lawsuits," *Texas Tribune*, July 31, 2015; "About Attorney General Ken Paxton," The Attorney General of Texas, www.texasattorneygeneral.gov/agency/about-texas-attorney-general-ken-paxton (accessed 3/10/16).

37. *United States v. Texas*, 579 U.S. __ (2016).

38. Robert Barnes and Juliet Eilperin, "Clash on Immigration Heads to High Court," *Dallas Morning News*, January 20, 2016, pp. 1A, 6A; Amy Howe, "Court Will Review Obama Administration's Immigration Policy: In Plain English," SCOTUSblog, January 19, 2016, www.scotusblog.com/2016/01/court-will-review-obama-administrations-immigration-policy-in-plain-english/.

39. Tom Benning, "Eminent Domain for Trump's Border Wall Is Fine, Says Texas Attorney General Ken Paxton," *Dallas Morning News*, March 27, 2017.

40. "AG Paxton Leads 16-State Coalition in Amicus Brief Supporting President Trump's Travel Ban," The Attorney General of Texas, August 17, 2017, www.texasattorneygeneral.gov/news/releases/ag-paxton-leads-16-state-coalition-in-amicus-brief-supporting-presiden (accessed 5/21/18).

41. Benning, "Eminent Domain."

42. Jim Malewitz, "Texas Sues Feds—Including Rick Perry—for Failing to License Nuclear Waste Facility," *Texas Tribune*, March 15, 2017.

43. Ken Paxton to Jeff Sessions, June 29, 2017.

44. Tal Kopan, "Blue States Sue Trump over DACA," CNN, September 6, 2017.

YOU DECIDE: VOTING RIGHTS AND REDISTRICTING

a. *Perez v. Abbott*, 2017 WL 3495922 (2017); James Barragan, "Texas Map Ordered Redrawn," *Dallas Morning News*, August 16, 2017, pp. 1A, 8A.

b. Alexa Ura and Jim Malewitz, "Court: Texas House Map Intentionally Diluted Minority Votes," *Texas Tribune*, April 20, 2017.

CHAPTER 4

1. Jeffrey M. Jones, "Special Report: Many States Shift Democratic during 2005," Gallup, January 23, 2006, www.gallup.com.

2. Use of party affiliation as an ideological cue is discussed in Philip L. Dubois, *From Ballot to Bench* (Austin: University of Texas Press, 1980).

3. University of Texas, "Texas Statewide Survey," *Texas Tribune*, May 7–13, 2012.

4. University of Texas/*Texas Tribune*, "Texas Statewide Survey," 2016.

5. Quoted in Chandler Davidson, *Race and Class in Texas Politics* (Princeton, NJ: Princeton University Press, 1990), 198.

6. Davidson, *Race and Class in Texas Politics*, 24–25.

7. Jones, "Special Report: Many States Shift Democratic during 2005."

8. James R. Soukup, Clifton McClesky, and Harry Holloway, *Party and Factional Division in Texas* (Austin: University of Texas Press, 1964), 22.
9. Mark P. Jones, "Guest Column: The 2013 Texas House from Right to Left," *Texas Tribune*, October 15, 2013.
10. Robert T. Garrett, "2 Major GOP Donors Show Rift in Party," *Dallas Morning News*, February 3, 2006, p. 2A.
11. Robert T. Garrett, "PAC's Late Aid Altered Races," *Dallas Morning News*, March 10, 2006, pp. 1A, 16A.
12. Dante Chinni and James Gimpel, *Our Patchwork Nation: The Surprising Truth about the "Real" America* (New York: Gotham, 2011).
13. Anthony Champagne, "The Selection and Retention of Judges in Texas," 40 *Southwestern Law Journal* 80 (1986).
14. The lone Democratic survivor, Ron Chapman, became an appellate judge. Democratic judges who did not switch to the Republican Party were defeated.
15. Terri Langford, "District Judge Fends Off Democratic Rival's Challenge," *Dallas Morning News*, November 9, 2000, p. 36A.
16. Anthony Champagne and Greg Thielemann, "Awareness of Trial Court Judges," 75 *Judicature* 271–72 (1991).
17. Langford, "District Judge Fends Off Democratic Rival's Challenge."
18. David Koenig, "Democrats' Dream Team Falters," *Laredo Morning Times*, November 10, 2002, pp. 1A, 19A.
19. In 1994 it was estimated that there were between 420,000 and 460,000 illegal immigrants in Texas. Many of those illegal immigrants were Hispanic. See Leon F. Bouvier and John L. Martin, "Shaping Texas: The Effects of Immigration, 1970–2020," Center for Immigration Studies, April 1995. The Federation for American Immigration Reform cites the Immigration and Naturalization Service for a January 2000 estimate that there were 1,041,000 illegal immigrants then in Texas. See its report, "Texas: Illegal Aliens." An April 2006 study by the Pew Hispanic Center estimated that between 1.4 and 1.6 million unauthorized individuals were living in Texas: "Estimates of the Unauthorized Migrant Population for States Based on the March 2006 CPS, Fact Sheet: April 26, 2006," Pew Hispanic Center. Jeff Salamon reports 10.8 million undocumented immigrants in the United States and 1.68 million in Texas. Jeff Salamon, "Everything You Ever Wanted to Know about Illegal Immigration (But Didn't Know Who to Ask)," *Texas Monthly*, November 2010.
20. "Latinos in the 2012 Election: Texas," Pew Research Hispanic Trends Project, October 1, 2012. See also U.S. Census Bureau, "The Diversifying Electorate—Voting Rates by Race and Hispanic Origin in 2012 (and Other Recent Elections)," May 2013.

CHAPTER 5

1. Wayne Slater, "Strayhorn Gets Democratic Cash," *Dallas Morning News*, January 26, 2006, pp. 1A, 17A.
2. Pete Slover, "Independents' Day Is a Bid for the Ballot," *Dallas Morning News*, March 8, 2006, p. 14A.
3. Sam Acheson, *Joe Bailey: The Last Democrat* (New York: Macmillan, 1932), 354.
4. Joe Robert Baulch, "James B. Wells: State Economic and Political Leader" (PhD diss., Texas Tech University, 1974), 358–59.
5. Sue Tolleson-Rinehart and Jeanie R. Stanley, *Claytie and the Lady: Ann Richards, Gender, and Politics in Texas* (Austin: University of Texas Press, 1994), 18–19.
6. *United States v. Texas*, 384 U.S. 155 (1966).
7. *Beare v. Smith*, 321 F. Supp. 1100 (1971).
8. *Newberry v. United States*, 256 U.S. 232 (1921).
9. *Nixon v. Herndon*, 273 U.S. 536 (1927).
10. *Nixon v. Condon*, 286 U.S. 73 (1932).
11. *Grovey v. Townsend*, 295 U.S. 45 (1935).
12. *Smith v. Allwright*, 321 U.S. 649 (1944).
13. *Terry v. Adams*, 345 U.S. 461 (1953).
14. Gary Scharrer, "Holder Issues Challenge to Texas on Voter Rights," *Chron*, December 13, 2011, www.chron.com/news/article/Holder-issues-challenge-to-Texas-on-oter-rights-2401340.php (accessed 8/2/18).
15. National Conference of State Legislatures, "Voter Identification Requirements," April 30, 2014.
16. Texas Secretary of State, "Turnout and Voter Registration Figures, 1970–Current."
17. The motor voter law is a federal statute that requires states to allow voter registration when individuals apply for or renew their driver's licenses.
18. See U.S. Census Bureau, "Voting and Registration in the Election of November 2016—Detailed Tables," and Texas Secretary of State, "Turnout and Voter Registration Figures, 1970–Current." It is important to recognize how easily different studies can produce different registration rates or voting rates for different racial and ethnic groups. The Texas secretary of state's office uses hard data on the number of registered voters and divides by an agreed-upon number of people in the voting-age population given by state and federal demog-

raphers. But the secretary of state's office has no information on how people from different racial and ethnic groups actually voted. The statistics cited here were based upon a survey done after the election asking individuals to self-identify their race or ethnicity, whether or not they were registered to vote, and if they voted. Registration rates and voting rates were built up from the survey rather than being based on hard data provided by outside authorities. Different methodological approaches to the same question can lead to different numbers without any of the numbers being "wrong."

19. Jolie McCullough, "Gov. Abbott Signs Bill to Eliminate Straight-Ticket Voting Beginning in 2020," *The Texas Tribune*, June 1, 2017, www.texastribune.org/2017/06/01/texas-gov-greg-abbott-signs-bill-eliminate-straight-ticket-voting/ (accessed 8/2/18).

20. University of Texas, "Texas Statewide Survey," *Texas Tribune*, February 2013.

21. University of Texas, "Texas Statewide Survey," *Texas Tribune*, June 2013.

22. U.S. Elections Project, "2016 November General Election Turnout Rates," 2016, www.electproject.org/2016g (accessed 8/2/18).

23. Kevin Diaz, "Texas Latino Vote Splits," *Houston Chronicle*, November 6, 2014.

24. Ryan Murphy and Jay Root, "Texas Republicans Getting Almost 90 Percent of Money Flowing into State Elections," *The Texas Tribune*, February 19, 2018, www.texastribune.org/2018/02/19/texas-republicans-getting-almost-90-percent-money-flowing-state-electi/ (accessed 6/1/18).

25. Julian Aguilar, "Abbott Defends Corruption Remarks, Border Security Plan," *Texas Tribune*, February 10, 2014; Jens Manuel Krogstad and Mark Hugo Lopez, "Hispanic Voters in the 2014 Election," Pew Research Hispanic Trends Project, November 7, 2014.

26. Don Willett (@JusticeWillett), "When you're tired of cornbread shaped like Colorado and Wyoming," Twitter, March 22, 2016, 8:41 p.m., https://twitter.com/justicewillett/status/712484343298457600.

27. Jordan Rudner and Lauren McGaughy, "Texas Ag Commissioner Sid Miller Blames Staffer for Tweet That Called Hillary Clinton the C-Word," *Dallas News*, November 2016, www.dallasnews.com/news/texas-politics/2016/11/01/texas-ag-commissioner-sid-miller-calls-clinton-c-word-twitter.

28. Alexa Ura, "Davis Renews Equal Pay Attack on Abbott," *Texas Tribune*, March 24, 2014.

YOU DECIDE: VOTER IDENTIFICATION LAWS

a. Alexandra Jaffe, "GOP Hits Back at Hillary Clinton on Voting Rights," CNN.com, June 5, 2015, www.cnn.com/2015/06/05/politics/gop-responds-clinton-voting-rights/index.html.

b. Alyssa Dizon, "Passage of Voter ID Bill Stirs Strong Reaction, Pro and Con," *Lubbock Avalanche-Journal*, May 17, 2011.

CHAPTER 6

1. The above is drawn from Jeffrey Weiss, "How the Texas Testing Bubble Popped," *Dallas Morning News*, March 30, 2014; Jeffrey Weiss, "Looking into the 'Heart of the Vampire,'" *Dallas Morning News*, March 31, 2014; Jeffrey Weiss, "Testing System Shaken to Its Core," *Dallas Morning News*, April 1, 2014; Dax Gonzalez, "Finding the Funding," *Texas Lone Star*, August 2013; see also www.TAMSATX.org.

2. Mancur Olson, *The Logic of Collective Action: Public Goods and the Theory of Groups*, Harvard Economic Studies (Cambridge, MA: Harvard University Press, 1971).

3. James W. Lamare, *Texas Politics: Economics, Power and Policy*, 3rd ed. (St. Paul, MN: West, 1988), 82. See George Norris Green, *The Establishment in Texas Politics: The Primitive Years, 1938–1957* (Norman: University of Oklahoma Press, 1984).

4. Jon Herskovitz, "Texas Lawmakers Clear Way for Uber, Lyft Return to Major Cities," Reuters, May 21, 2017, www.reuters.com/article/us-texas-ridesharing/texas-lawmakers-clear-way-for-uber-lyft-return-to-major-cities-idUSKBN18H0IJ (accessed 8/2/18).

5. Morgan Smith, "Texas Advocacy Group Wields Charter Policy Power," *New York Times*, May 5, 2013.

6. Smith, "Texas Advocacy Group."

7. See Phillip Martin, "Progress Texas Releases ALEC Exposed in Texas," *Progress Texas*, January 17, 2012, http://progresstexas.org/blog/progress-texas-releases-alec-exposed-texas (accessed 8/2/18).

8. Texans for Public Justice, "Power Surge: TXU's Patronage Grid Plugs All but Seven Lawmakers," *Lobby Watch*, March 1, 2007.

9. Matt Stiles, "Lobbyist Gives 'Shocking' Gift to Lawmaker," *Texas Tribune*, February 15, 2010.

10. David Rauf, "Lavish Gifts a Perk for Attorney General Greg Abbott," *San Antonio Express News*, 2014.

11. R. G. Ratcliffe, "The Lobby: $1.8 Million Feeding the Legislature," *Texas Monthly*, May 20, 2015.

12. Johnny Kampis, "Senate Big Spender #4: John Whitmire," *The Texas Monitor*, June 14, 2017, https://texasmonitor.org/senate-big-spender-4-john-whitmire/.

13. 2017 Lobby Registration Lists, Texas Ethics Commission, http://www.ethics.state.tx.us/dfs/loblistsREG.htm#R2017 (accessed 8/6/18).

14. Summary of Lobby Expenditures Sorted By Government Recipient, Texas Ethics Commission, November 29, 2017, https://www.ethics.state.tx.us/dfs/LobbyExpendituresByGovernmentRecipient.pdf (accessed 8/6/18).

15. Andy Pierrotti, "Lobbyist's Lavish Party," Kvue.com, February 21, 2013.

16. 2017 Registered Lobbyists with Clients, Texas Ethics Commission, https://www.ethics.state.tx.us/dfs/loblistsREG.htm#R2017 (accessed 8/6/18).

17. Texas Monthly, Dave Mann, Eric Benson, and R.G. Ratcliffe, "Flush with Power," *Texas Monthly*, February 2017, https://www.texasmonthly.com/politics/flush-with-power/ (accessed 8/6/18).

18. Ross Ramsey, "Legislature Is a Training Ground for Lobbyists," *Texas Tribune*, June 10, 2010.

19. Ramsey, "Legislature Is a Training Ground."

20. Texans for Public Justice, "Is Joe Straus' House a Lobby Farm Club?" *Lobby Watch*, May 4, 2017.

21. Texans for Public Justice, "Ten New Lawmaker Retreads Merge into the 2009 Lobby," *Lobby Watch*, May 20, 2009.

22. "Rick Perry's Former Staffers Made Millions as Lobbyists," *Huffington Post*, December 19, 2011.

23. "Rick Perry's Former Staffers."

24. Ramsey, "Legislature Is a Training Ground."

25. Texans for Public Justice, "Texas Revolvers: Public Officials Recast as Hired Guns," *Lobby Watch*, February 5, 1999.

26. Tim Eaton, "Greg Abbott Looks to 2017 for Ethics Reform," *Austin American Statesman*, June 22, 2015; W. Gardner Selby, "Greg Abbott Strikes Out on His Ethics Campaign Promises," *Austin American Statesman* Politifact, July 5, 2015.

27. Texans for Public Justice, "Special-Interests Spend Up to $180 Million on Lobby Services in 1999 Legislative Session," May 24, 1999.

28. "Top Ten PACs of the 2018 Texas Election Cycle," Transparency Texas, February 5, 2018, https://www.transparencytexas.org/top-ten-pacs-of-the-2018-texas-election-cycle/ (accessed 8/6/18).

29. Anthony Champagne, 1992, "Campaign Contributions in Texas Supreme Court Races," *Crime, Law and Social Change* 17(2):91–106.

30. Texans for Public Justice, "Texans for Lawsuit Reform Sustains Pricey Primary Hits," *Lobby Watch*, March 5, 2010; Julian Aguilar, "Primary Color: HD-43," *Texas Tribune*, February 26, 2010.

31. Dick Weekley, "A Good Night for Lawsuit Reform in Texas," Texans for Lawsuit Reform PAC.

32. "Texans for Lawsuit Reform," Transparency Texas, May 17, 2017, https:www.transparencytexas.org/texans-for-lawsuit-reform/ (accessed 8/6/18).

33. Ryan Murphy and Jay Root, "Texas Republicans Getting Almost 90 Percent of Money Flowing into State Elections," *The Texas Tribune*, February 19, 2018, www.texastribune.org/2018/02/19/texas-republicans-getting-almost-90-percent-money-flowing-state-electi/ (accessed 6/1/18).

34. Patrick Svitek, "Latest Texas Fundraising Totals Shed Light on Key Races," *Texas Tribune*, July 18, 2017, www.texastribune.org/2017/07/18/tec-report-fundraising-roundup/ (accessed 8/6/18).

35. Kristen Mack, "New Lawmakers Learn to Juggle Hectic Lives; Everybody—Lobbyists, Family—Wants a Moment of Their Time," *Houston Chronicle*, February 6, 2005, p. 1B.

36. Texans for Public Justice, "Texans for Lawsuit Reform Sustains Pricey Primary Hits," *Lobby Watch*, March 5, 2010.

37. Jason Embry, "Most Powerful Group in Texas Politics Has Wentworth in Its Sights," *Austin American Statesman*, December 7, 2011; John W. Gonzalez, "Campbell Upsets Wentworth for Texas Senate," *San Antonio Express-News*, August 1, 2012.

38. Texans for Public Justice, "Operation Vouchsafe: Dr. Leininger Injects $5 Million into Election; Many Candidates Fail on His Life Support," *Lobby Watch*, n.d.

39. Jay Root and Ryan Murphy, "Does Business Group's Use of 'Dark Money' for Its Political Action Committee Follow State Ethics Rules?" *Texas Tribune*, January 29, 2018, www.texastribune.org/2018/01/29/does-texas-business-groups-use-dark-money-follow-state-ethics-rules/ (accessed 8/6/18).

40. Texans for Public Justice, "Texas PACs: 2012 Election Cycle Spending" (2013), p. 20.

41. Sunset Advisory Commission Staff Report, "Railroad Commission of Texas," November 2012, p. 12.

42. Public Citizen, "Drilling for Dollars: How Big Money Has a Big Influence at the Railroad Commission" (December 2010).

43. Public Citizen, "Drilling for Dollars," p. 4.

44. National Institute on Money in Politics data.

45. Jim Malewitz, "GOP Railroad Commission Hopefuls Split Donations," *Texas Tribune*, February 8, 2016.

46. Sunset Advisory Commission, "Railroad Commission of Texas," p. 2.

47. Brett Shipp, "Attempt to Overhaul Texas Railroad Commission Fails, Again," WFAA.com, May 31, 2013.

48. Ryan May Handy, "Gov. Abbott Signs Bill Reauthorizing the Railroad Commission," Chron, May 23, 2017, http://fuelfix.com/blog/2017/05/23/gov-abbott-signs-bill-reauthorizing-the-railroad-commission/.

49. Emily Ramshaw, "Fighting for Fair Warning—Man Who Lost Wife, Kids in Blaze Seeks Visual Smoke Alarms for Deaf," *Dallas Morning News*, April 17, 2009; "Tragedy Leads to Improved Fire Safety in Texas," National Association of the Deaf, July 1, 2009.

50. Regina Lawrence, Deborah Wise, and Emily Einsohn, *Texas Civic Health Index* (Austin: Annette Strauss Institute for Civic Life, 2013), 5–14.

51. Lawrence, Wise, and Einsohn, *Texas Civic Health Index*, 22.

YOU DECIDE: SHOULD FORMER LEGISLATORS BE LOBBYISTS?

a. Kelley Shannon, "Former Legislators Kicking Off New Careers as Texas Lobbyists," *Dallas Morning News*, March 7, 2013.

b. Ross Ramsey, "Legislature Is a Training Ground for Lobbyists," *Texas Tribune*, June 10, 2010.

c. Randy Lee Loftis, "State of Neglect: Revolving Door Lets Lawmakers Profit from Capitol Floor Time," *Dallas Morning News*, January 6, 2009.

CHAPTER 7

1. Andrea Zelinski and Bobby Cervantes, "After Reporting Protesters to ICE, Texas Lawmaker Threatens to Shoot Colleague," *Governing*, May 30, 2017, www.governing.com/topics/public-justice-safety/tns-texas-rinaldi.html.

2. "Senate Gives Tentative OK to Guns on Campuses," *Dallas Morning News*, May 20, 2009.

3. "Texas Bill to Allow Guns on Campus Rejected for Violating Constitutional Requirement," *Security Director News*, June 7, 2011.

4. "Texas Legislature Passes Record Number of Pro-Gun Bills but Key Items Remain as 'Unfinished Business,'" NRA-ILA, June 5, 2013.

5. Ann Marie Kilday, "Equal Measure," *Dallas Morning News*, May 24, 2001, p. 31A.

6. Texas Legislature, "Legislative Statistics," February 8, 2018.

7. Anthony Champagne and Rick Collis, "Texas," in *The Political Life of the American States*, eds. Alan Rosenthal and Maureen Moakley (New York: Praeger, 1984), 138.

8. Ross Ramsey, "Will Texas Lawmakers Cut Their Own Benefits?" *Texas Tribune*, March 11, 2011.

9. LegiScan, "Texas Legislature, 2017–2018, 85th Legislature, in Recess," legiscan.com, https://legiscan.com/TX.

10. Kelley Shannon, "Doctor Twice Honored by the Texas Legislature Registered as Sex Offender," *Sulphur Springs News-Telegram*, June 22, 2007, p. 1.

11. Frank M. Stewart, "Impeachment in Texas," *American Political Science Review* 24, no. 3 (August 1930): 652–58; George D. Braden et al., *The Constitution of the State of Texas: An Annotated and Comparative Analysis* (Austin: University of Texas Press, 1977), 707–18.

12. "Impeachment in Texas history," *Port Aransas South Jetty*, August 23, 2007.

13. Edgar Walters, "Texas Governor Signs $217 Billion Budget, Vetoes $120 Million," *Texas Tribune*, www.texastribune.org/2017/06/12/texas-governor-signs-217-billion-budget-vetoes-120-million/.

14. Terrence Stutz, "Texas Senate at Odds over Voter ID Legislation, Two-Thirds Rule," *Dallas Morning News*, January 14, 2009.

15. Joe Straus, letter to Sachi Dave, March 12, 2014.

16. Joe Straus, letter to Sachi Dave, March 12, 2014.

17. Paul Burka, "Partisanship Ranking: The Texas Tribune List," *Texas Monthly*, July 17, 2010.

18. Mark Jones, "Guest Column: The 2013 Texas House, from Right to Left," *Texas Tribune*, October 15, 2013.

19. Mark Jones, "Guest Column: The 2013 Texas Senate, from Left to Right," *Texas Tribune*, November 26, 2013.

20. Paul Starr, *Remedy and Reaction: The Peculiar American Struggle over Health Care Reform*, rev. ed. (New Haven, CT: Yale University Press, 2013), 162–63.

21. *Baker v. Carr*, 369 U.S. 186 (1962); *Reynolds v. Sims*, 377 U.S. 533 (1964).

22. *Wesberry v. Sanders*, 376 U.S. 1 (1964).

23. Sam Attlesey, "Panel OKs Map Favoring GOP," *Dallas Morning News*, December 7, 2001.

24. The preceding is drawn from Sam Attlesey, "Taking Stock of the Fallout from Redistricting," *Dallas Morning News*, December 11, 2001; Terrance Stutz, "GOP Expecting to Grab the House," *Dallas Morning News*, January 3, 2002; Sam Attlesey, "Before Election, House

Democrats Seeing Losses," *Dallas Morning News*, December 11, 2001.

25. Medill School of Journalism, "On the Docket," http://journalism/medill.northwestern.edu/docket.

26. *LULAC v. Perry*, Appellants' Brief.

27. See, generally, Steve Bickerstaff, *Lines in the Sand: Congressional Redistricting in Texas and the Downfall of Tom DeLay* (Austin: University of Texas Press, 2007).

28. "Texas Redistricting Battle Headed Back to Federal Courts," *Lubbock Avalanche-Journal*, June 21, 2013.

29. "Thus Spake Joe," *The Economist*, November 4, 2017.

YOU DECIDE: A FULL-TIME OR PART-TIME LEGISLATURE?

a. http://triblive.com/x/pittsburghtrib/news/regional/s_504876.html.

b. www.yourhoustonnews.com./archives/with-government-you-get-what-you-pay-for/article_ec96830b-897c-5952-b868-ca1894dd47e9.html.

CHAPTER 8

1. UT/*Texas Tribune* poll of 1,200 registered voters conducted June 8–18, 2018. The margin of error is =/-2.83%.

2. Brian McCall, *The Power of the Texas Governor: Connally to Bush* (Austin: University of Texas Press, 2009), 5.

3. McCall, *The Power of the Texas Governor*, 131–39.

4. McCall, *The Power of the Texas Governor*, 120.

5. Christy Hoppe and Robert T. Garrett, "How Deep Does Governor Dig into Issues?" *Dallas Morning News*, November 27, 2011, pp. 1, 30A.

6. "Abbott Calendar," *Austin-American-Statesman*, http://projects.statesman.com/news/abbott-calendar/.

7. Sam Kinch, in Government by Consent—Texas, A Telecourse (Dallas: Dallas County Community College District, 1990).

8. William P. Hobby, in Government by Consent—Texas, a Telecourse (Dallas: Dallas County Community College District, 1990).

9. Christy Hoppe, "Lt. Gov. Rick Perry, Honoring the Economic Generators of Texas Tourism," *Dallas Morning News*, February 28, 2000, p. 13A.

10. Office of the Texas Governor Greg Abbott, "Governor Abbott Announces Changes to Senior Staff," September 18, 2017.

11. Governor's Office, Texas State Directory.

12. Jamie Knodel, "Gov. Greg Abbott Gives Most of His Appointments to Whites," *Dallas Morning News*, April 17, 2016.

13. Jolie McCullough, "Dozens of Abbott Appointees Surpass Donor Threshold Targeted by Stalled 'Pay for Play' Bill," *Texas Tribune*, May 23, 2017.

14. Peggy Fikac, "Abbott Makes Scores of Political Appointments," *Houston Chronicle*, July 4, 2015.

15. Valerie Strauss, "Texas Governor Picks Home-Schooler to Lead State Board of Education," *Washington Post*, June 26, 2015.

16. Brandi Grissom, "Law enforcement group urges Gov. Abbott to rescind pension board appointment," *Dallas Morning News*, December 1, 2015; Texas Retired Teachers Association, "Membership Alert: Governor Abbott Appoints Controversial and Outspoken Public Pension Critic Chairman of State Pension Review Board," undated.

17. Tim Eaton, "Insurance Commissioner on Her Way Out," *Austin American-Statesman*, May 24, 2013; "Perry Names Rathgeber Insurance Commissioner," *Texas Tribune*, May 27, 2013; Terrance Stutz, "Exclusive: Texas Insurance Commissioner Withheld Annual Profit Numbers to Boost Confirmation Case, Sources Say," dallasnews.com, May 28, 2013.

18. Julian Aguilar, "Abbott Orders National Guard to Stay in Place on Border," *Texas Tribune*, December 15, 2015.

19. "Abbott Altered His Message on Jade Helm," *Houston Chronicle*, May 28, 2015; Cassandra Pollock and Alex Samuels, "Hysteria over Jade Helm Exercise in Texas Was Fueled by Russians, Former CIA Director Says," *Texas Tribune*, May 3, 2018.

20. Charlsy Panzino, Jeff Schogol, and Mark D. Faram, "Entire Texas National Guard activated in wake of Hurricane Harvey," *Army Times*, August 28, 2017.

21. Office of the Governor Greg Abbott, "Governor Abbott Delivers the State of the State Address," January 31, 2017.

22. Legislative Library of Texas, "Bill Statistics."

23. Madlin B. Makelburg, "What Actually Passed the Texas Legislature," *Chron*, June 2, 2015, www.chron.com/news/politics/article/What-actually-passed-the-Texas-legislature-6301754.php.

24. Legislative Library of Texas, "Bill Statistics."

25. Legislative Reference Library of Texas, "Vetoes Overridden, 1860–2013."

26. Office of Governor Rick Perry, "Governor Perry Signs State Budget That Reduces GR by $1.6 Billion," press release, June 19, 2009.

27. Legislative Reference Library of Texas, "84th Regular Session (2015)—Governor Greg Abbott."

28. Edgar Walters, "Texas Governor Signs $217 Billion Budget, Vetoes $120 Million," *Star-Telegram*, June 13, 2017.

29. Texas Legislative Library, Special Sessions of the Texas Legislature (2017).

30. Office of the Texas Governor Greg Abbott, "Governor Abbott Pardons Seven Texans," December 22, 2017.

31. Brandi Grissom, "Gov. Greg Abbott Pardons Four Texans Who Committed Minor Crimes," *Dallas Morning News*, December 22, 2015.

32. Jolie McCullough, "Gov. Greg Abbott commutes the sentence of Thomas Whitaker," *Texas Tribune*, February 22, 2018.

33. Andrea Valdez, "The Worst: Senator Dan Patrick," *Texas Monthly*, June 13, 2013.

34. Tim Eaton, "Joe Straus Avoids Hot Button Issues, in Contrast to Dan Patrick," *Austin American Statesman*, November 4, 2015.

35. With Straus's decision to not seek re-election in 2018, it seems likely that Patrick will be the dominant figure in state legislative policy making.

36. Office of the Attorney General of Texas, "About Texas Attorney General Ken Paxton."

37. Valerie Wigglesworth, "Judge OKs Amended Indictments in AG Ken Paxton's Criminal Case," *Dallas Morning News*, December 21, 2015; Terri Langford, "Investigation Targets Complaint against Paxton over Land Deal," *Texas Tribune*, January 15, 2016; Jordan Rudner, "State Bar Will Investigate Paxton for Conduct after Marriage Ruling," *Texas Tribune*, February 10, 2016.

38. Alex Arriaga, "Texas Lawmakers Battle with Land Office over Transparency in Alamo Restoration," *Texas Tribune*, December 5, 2017; Ross Ramsey, "Analysis: Why George P. Bush Is Jealous of Ken Paxton," *Texas Tribune*, December 12, 2017; Patrick Svitek, "Texas Land Office Reaches Settlement with Former Alamo Managers," *Texas Tribune*, June 20, 2016.

39. Lauren McGaughy, "Ag Chief Posts Cartoon Mocking Trump Foe," *Dallas Morning News*, October 25, 2017, p. 3B.

40. Dan Solomon, "Sid Miller Is Having Quite a Week," *Texas Monthly*, December 17, 2015; Liz Crampton, "Miller Defends Deep Fryers in Agriculture Address," *Texas Tribune*, July 8, 2015; Eva Hershaw, "Agriculture Commissioner Grants Amnesty to Cupcakes," *Texas Tribune*, January 12, 2015.

41. Texas State Auditor's Office, "A Summary Report on Full-Time Equivalent State Employees for Fiscal Year 2017."

42. Texas State Auditor's Office, "A Summary Report on Full-Time Equivalent State Employees for Fiscal Year 2007."

43. Christy Hoppe, "Perry's Appointees Give Him Unprecedented Hold on Texas—Longest-Serving Governor Spreads Pro-Business View," *Dallas Morning News*, December 19, 2008.

44. Will Weissert, "Texas Rejects Allowing Academics to Fact-Check Public School Textbooks," *Christian Science Monitor*, November 18, 2015.

45. Russell Shorto, "How Christian Were the Founders?" *New York Times Magazine*, February 14, 2010, p. MM32; Terrence Stutz, "Debate Continues over Social Studies," *Dallas Morning News*," March 11, 2010.

46. Texas Sunset Advisory Commission, "Frequently Asked Questions."

CHAPTER 9

1. The material on the Lewis case is from: State Commission on Judicial Conduct, "Notice of Formal Proceedings," October 11, 2016; State Commission on Judicial Conduct, "Voluntary Agreement to Resign from Judicial Office in Lieu of Disciplinary Action," October 11, 2016; Tanya Eiserer, "After an almost year of leave, Dallas judge resigns," WFAA.com, October 12, 2016; Naheed Rajwani and Jennifer Emily, "Dallas judge who resigned after battling depression, alcoholism found dead in his home," Dallas News, June 16, 2017; Jennifer Emily, "Dallas judge resigns before he can be removed from office after battling alcoholism, depression," *Dallas News*, October 12, 2016; Jennifer Emily, "Gov. Abbott appoints Austin lawyer to replace Dallas appellate judge," *Dallas News*, January 10, 2017; "Justice Jason Boatwright," www.txcourts.gov; John Council, "Officials Rule Former Texas Appellate Justice Died of Chronic Alcoholism," *Texas Lawyer*, October 19, 2017.

2. Legislative Budget Board Staff, "Specialty Courts," July 2016.

3. "Texas Department of Criminal Justice, Community Justice Assistance Division, "Texas Drug Courts," March 3, 2003.

4. Eric Dexheimer, "For Texas county judges, a $25,000 bonus with no questions asked," myStatesman, *Austin-American Statesman*, December 15, 2016.

5.	Texas Office of Court Administration, "2017 Statistical Report for the Texas Judiciary."

6.	Texas Office of Court Administration, "2017 Statistical Report for the Texas Judiciary."

7.	Barbara Kirby, "Neighborhood Justice: Non-Lawyer Judges, Repeat Players and Institutional Reform in Justice of the Peace Courts" (Ph.D. diss., University of Texas at Dallas, 2015), 70, 71, 74.

8.	Kirby, "Neighborhood Justice," 56.

9.	Ed Housewright, "Emotional Issues, Historical Pedigree," *Dallas Morning News*, April 9, 2001, p. 10A.

10.	Texas Office of Court Administration, "2016 Statistical Report for the Texas Judiciary."

11.	Thomas Petzinger, Jr., *Oil and Honor: The Texaco-Pennzoil Wars* (New York: Putnam, 1987).

12.	Task Force on Indigent Defense, "Evidence for the Feasibility of Public Defender Offices in Texas" (2006).

13.	Mary Alice Robbins, "West Texas Plans Public Defender Office for Capital Cases," *Texas Lawyer* 1, (August 20, 2007): 19; "New Public Defender for Capital Cases," *Tex Parte Blog*, October 16, 2007.

14.	Ken Anderson, *Crime in Texas* (Austin: University of Texas Press, 1997), 40.

15.	Anderson, *Crime in Texas*, 44; nationally, 95 percent of felonies are plea bargained.

16.	Of the 79 judicial appointments made by Governor William Clements, only 6 were either African American or Hispanic. In contrast, one-third of Governor Ann Richards's judicial appointees were minorities. See Michael Totty, "Is This Any Way to Choose a Judge?" *Wall Street Journal*, August 3, 1994, T1, T4.

17.	Texas Office of Court Administration, "Profile of Appellate and Trial Judges," September 1, 2017.

18.	Paul Burka, "Heads, We Win, Tails, You Lose," *Texas Monthly* (May 1987), 138, 139.

19.	Wallace B. Jefferson, "Reform the Partisan System," 79 *Texas Bar Journal* 90 (2016).

20.	"Here's Your 2014 Election Day Guide," abc 13 Eyewitness News.

21.	Mary Flood and Brian Rogers, "Why Some Harris County Judges Lost Not Entirely Clear," *Houston Chronicle*, November 6, 2008.

22.	Chuck Lindell, "Green vs. Green: State Supreme Court GOP Race a Study in Contrasts," *Austin American-Statesman*, February 14, 2016; Rick Carey, "Imperfect Paul Green Is a Better Choice than Rick Green," *mySA*, February 19, 2016; "Editorial: We Recommend Sid Harle in GOP Race for Texas Court of Criminal Appeals Place 5," *Dallas Morning News*, January 17, 2016; Bruce Davidson, "Bad Old Days Return to Criminal Appeals Court Races," *mySA*, December 10, 2015.

23.	Data are from the National Institute on Money in State Politics.

24.	Anthony Champagne, "The Cycle of Judicial Elections: Texas as a Case Study," 29 *Fordham Urban Law Journal* 907, 914 (2004).

25.	Data are from the National Institute on Money in State Politics.

26.	Texas Ethics Commission, "Campaign Finance Guide for Judicial Candidates and Officeholders," (2013).

27.	Professor Brest is quoted in Kevin R. Johnson and Luis Fuentes-Rohwer, "A Principled Approach to the Quest for Racial Diversity on the Judiciary," *Michigan Journal of Race and Law* 5 at 10 (2004).

28.	Professor Ifill is quoted in Kevin R. Johnson and Luis Fuentes-Rohwer, "A Principled Approach to the Quest for Racial Diversity on the Judiciary," *Michigan Journal of Race and Law* 5 at 10 (2004).

29.	Office of Court Administration, "Profile of Appellate and Trial Judges," September 1, 2017.

30.	State Bar of Texas, Annual Report 2016–2017.

31.	Citizens' Commission on the Texas Judicial System, "Report and Recommendations: Into the Twenty-First Century" (1993), p. 3.

32.	Executive Summary: Report of the Court Administration Task Force," 71 *Texas Bar Journal* 888, 889 (2008).

33.	Ray Blackwood, "Overlapping Jurisdiction in the Houston-Based Courts of Appeals—Could a Special En Banc Procedure Alleviate Problems?" 26 *Appellate Advocate* 277–81 (2013).

34.	David A. Anderson, "Judicial Tort Reform in Texas," 26 *Review of Litigation* 7 (2007).

35.	State Bar of Texas, Annual Report 2016–2017.

36.	John McCormack, "Barratry Suit Names Corpus Lawyers," *San Antonio Express News*, December 9, 2011.

37.	Isiah Carey, "Lawyer Filed Reynolds Barratry Complaint," myfoxhouston.com, April 25, 2012.

38.	Kari-Thomas Musselman, "Rep. Ron Reynolds Charged (again) with Barratry, Constituent Calls for Resignation," *Burnt Orange Report*, April 6, 2013.

39.	Ross Ramsey, "State Rep. Reynolds Guilty of Ambulance-Chasing," *Texas Tribune*, November 21, 2015; Kaitlin McCulley, "Rep. Ron Reynolds Out on

Bond While Appealing Barratry Conviction," abc 13 Eyewitness News, November 24, 2015.

40. Alana Rocha, "State Rep. Ron Reynolds: Sued, Convicted and Now Bankrupt," *Texas Tribune*, September 12, 2016.

41. State Bar of Texas website, "Find a Lawyer," www.texasbar.com; Brett Shipp, "Attorney Accused of Multiple Crimes, Still Working Courthouse Halls," wfaa.com, September 8, 2017.

42. State Bar of Texas.

43. State Commission on Judicial Conduct, "Annual Report for Fiscal Year 2017."

44. Commission on Judicial Conduct website, www.scjc.texas.gov; State Commission on Judicial Conduct, "Annual Report for Fiscal Year 2016."

45. State Commission on Judicial Conduct, "Public Admonition Honorable Nora Longoria Justice, Thirteenth Court of Appeals, Edinburg, Hidalgo County, Texas."

46. Ralph Blumenthal, "Texas Judge Draws Outcry for Allowing an Execution," *New York Times*, October 25, 2007; Christy Hoppe, "Criminal Appeals Court Creates Emergency Filing System," DallasNews.com, November 6, 2007; "Texas Judge Fosters Tough-on-Crime Reputation," MSNBC, October 23, 2007; State Commission on Judicial Conduct, "Special Master's Findings of Fact, In Re: Honorable Sharon Keller, Presiding Judge of the Texas Court of Criminal Appeals" (January 20, 2010); "Judge Who Refused Last-Minute Appeal Re-Elected," News 92 FM, November 6, 2012.

YOU DECIDE: ELECTED OR APPOINTED JUDGES?

a. Wallace B. Jefferson, "Reform the Partisan System," 79 *Texas Bar Journal* 90 (2016).

b. David Butts, "A Democratic Process Is the Best Choice," 79 *Texas Bar Journal* 91 (2016).

CHAPTER 10

1. February 2018 University of Texas/*Texas Tribune* poll.

2. The above material on Hurricane Harvey is from "Buffalo Bayou to remain at record level; Barker, Addicks reservoirs have peaked," KHOU.com, September 1, 2017; "Historic Hurricane Harvey's Recap," weather.com, September 2, 2017; Cindy George et al., "Storm deaths: Harvey claims lives of more than 75 in Texas," chron.com, October 9, 2017; J.J. Gallagher, "Hurricane Harvey wrecks historic devastation: By the numbers," abc news,
September 1, 2017; Justin Worland, "Why We Won't Be Ready for the Next Hurricane Harvey Either," *Time*, August 28, 2017; Camila Domonoske, "Why Didn't Officials Order the Evacuation of Houston?," NPR, August 28, 2017; "Release of reservoir water could affect thousands in Houston area," *USA Today*, August 28, 2017; Neena Satija et al., "Hell and High Water," *Pro Publica* and *Texas Tribune*, March 3, 2016; Vikas Bajaj, Jessica Ma, and Stuart A. Thompson, "How Houston's Growth Created the Perfect Flood Conditions," *New York Times*, September 5, 2017; Henry Graber, "Don't Blame Houston's Lax Zoning for Harvey's Destruction," Slate, August 31, 2017; Naomi Martin, "Flooded Houston-area homeowners might have been spared ruin—but only if they read the fine print," *Dallas Morning News*, September 20, 2017.

3. U.S. Census Bureau, 2012 Census of Governments. See http://www.governing.com/gov-data/number-of-governments-by-state.html.

4. The two states that don't use counties as units of local government are Connecticut and Rhode Island; Richard L. Cole and Delbert A. Taebel, *Texas: Politics and Public Policy* (Fort Worth: Harcourt Brace Jovanovich, 1987), 151.

5. Texas Association of Counties, "About Counties: County Government."

6. Cole and Taebel, *Texas: Politics and Public Policy*, 155.

7. Lawrence M. Crane, Nat Pinnoi, and Stephen W. Fuller, "Private Demand for Publicly Provided Goods: A Case Study of Rural Roads in Texas," *TAMRC Contemporary Market Issues Report No. CI-1-92* (1992).

8. Texas Association of Counties, "Debate Goes Back and Forth, Just like Overweight Trucks."

9. Texas Commission on Jail Standards, "Abbreviated Population Report," September 1, 2018.

10. Julie Wilson, "Montgomery County Drone Launch a Major Failure," *Liberty Beat*, May 15, 2013.

11. Texas Association of Counties, "About Counties."

12. Cole and Taebel, *Texas: Politics and Public Policy*, 152.

13. *Avery v. Midland County*, 390 U.S. 474 (1968).

14. Anthony Champagne and Rick Collis, "Texas," in *The Political Life of the American States*, ed. Alan Rosenthal and Maureen Moakley (Washington, DC: CQ Press, 1984), 140.

15. Bob Palmer, "AG Supports Commissioners in Courthouse Dog Dispute," *Daily Tribune*, August 29, 2013.

16. Harvey Rice and Emily Foxhall, "Fort Bend Leaders Weigh in on Galveston Co. Political Fight," Chron

.com, October 14, 2015; David Yates, "Texas SC sides with Galveston County judge in suit brought by district judge," *SE Texas Record*. May 22, 2017.

17. These are 2014 Census estimates. U.S. Census Bureau, "State and County Quick Facts."

18. Brenda Rodriguez, "Loving and Losing in West Texas," *Dallas Morning News*, March 14, 2001, p. 21A.

19. Roma Vivas, "Presidio County Officials Tackling Budget Problems," NewsWest9.com, undated.

20. Russell Gold, "Counties Struggle with High Cost of Prosecuting Death-Penalty Cases," *Wall Street Journal*, January 9, 2002, p. B1.

21. "Capital Trial Could Be Costly for Franklin Co.," *Sulphur Springs News-Telegram*, June 27, 2007, p. 4.

22. Andrew Becker and G. W. Schultz, "Drug Busts Strain County Budget," *Dallas Morning News*, July 28, 2013, p. 10A.

23. Jamie Thompson, "A Woman on the Verge," *D Magazine*, November 2015, pp. 46–51, 161–167; Sarah Mervosh, "Lawsuit to Remove Dallas DA Susan Hawk to Move Forward," *Dallas Morning News*, December 9, 2015; Ken Kalthoff, "Case to Remove Dallas DA Susan Hawk Dismissed," 5NBCDFW.com, January 8, 2016.

24. "Republican Appointed Dallas County DA Faith Johnson Loses," CBS Dallas/Fort Worth, November 7, 2018. https://dfw.cbslocal.com/2018/11/07/dallas-county -da-faith-johnson-john-creuzot/ (accessed 11/15/18).

25. Frank Heinz, "John Wiley Price Arrested, Accused of Taking $950,000 in Bribes," 5NBCDFW.com, January 25, 2014.

26. Jordan Smith, "What Happens Next? As D.A. Rosemary Lehmberg Serves Her Sentence, the County Attorney Takes on the Civil Lawsuit and the Next Steps," *Austin Chronicle*, May 3, 2013; Jason Trahan and Brett Shipp, "New questions surround John Wiley Price's secret art business," WFAA8abc. October 26, 2017.

27. Emily DeProng, "After Shady Campaign, Houston Community College Foe Becomes Trustee," *Texas Observer*, November 12, 2013.

28. There is some disagreement among scholars over why the population figure was lowered from 10,000 to 5,000 in 1909. John Keith argued that the changes enabled smaller cities to obtain special charters tailored to their needs. See John P. Keith, *City and County Home Rule in Texas*. Austin: Institute of Public Affairs, University of Texas, 1951. George D. Braden suggests that the reason may have been the desire of certain cities to escape a property tax provision in the existing constitution.

See George D. Braden et al., *The Constitution of the State of Texas: An Annotated and Comparative Analysis*. 1977, p. 681.

29. League of California Cities, "Charter Cities"; Ballotpedia, "Cities in Illinois"; "Cities in Texas."

30. Diane Lang, "Dillon's Rule . . . and the Birth of Home Rule," *The Municipal Reporter*, December, 1991.

31. Article 11, Section 5, of the Texas Constitution is concerned with home rule. For a further discussion of home rule in Texas, see Terrell Blodgett, *Texas Home Rule Charters* (Austin: Texas Municipal League, 1994); Terrell Blodgett, "Home Rule Charters," *Handbook of Texas Online* (Texas State Historical Association).

32. Correspondence with Terrell Blodgett, Wednesday, February 3, 2000; *Texas Almanac 2009–2010*, 500–510; League of California Cities, "Charter Cities"; Ballotpedia, "Cities in Illinois."

33. Jim Malewitz, "Dissecting Denton: How a Texas City Banned Fracking," *Texas Tribune*, December 15, 2014; Max B. Baker, "Denton City Council Repeals Fracking Ban," *Ft. Worth Star-Telegram*, June 16, 2015.

34. Patrick Svitek, "Abbott wants 'broad-based law' that pre-empts local regulations," *The Texas Tribune*, March 21, 2017; Patrick Svitek, "Gov. Abbott: This country isn't the 'United States of Municipalities,'" *The Texas Tribune*, March 27, 2017.

35. Jonathan Tilove, "With rejection of special session core agenda, is GOP civil war next?" My Statesman, *Austin American-Statesman*, August 19, 2017; Jonathan Tilove, "Abbott blames Straus for all that the special sessions didn't get done," My Statesman, *Austin American-Statesman*, August 17, 2017.

36. Colorado Municipal League, "Forms of Municipal Government."

37. *Texas Almanac 2018–2019*, Texas State Historical Association, Austin, Texas, 2018.

38. The following is drawn from Bradley R. Rice, "Commission Form of City Government," *Handbook of Texas Online* (Texas State Historical Association).

39. Dallas Morning News, *Texas Almanac 1996–97* (Dallas: *Dallas Morning News*, 1995), 513.

40. Correspondence with Terrell Blodgett, Wednesday, February 3, 2000.

41. Rice, "Commission Form of City Government."

42. Exactly what constitutes a municipality with a council-manager form of government is difficult to define. Local forms of governments are complex with many nuances in their power structures and positions. Here we are

referring to municipalities that have some form of professional manager or city manager or city administrator or town manager listed in the survey conducted by the *Texas Almanac* survey in 2017. See *Texas Almanac 2018–2019*, 531–540.

43. For a further discussion, see Terrell Blodgett, "Council-Manager Form of City Government," *Handbook of Texas Online* (Texas State Historical Association); Blodgett, *Texas Home Rule Charters*.

44. For a history of the Office of Controller in Houston, see the City of Houston Office of the City Controller, "Controller History."

45. PolitiFact Texas, "Austin Group Says Austin Is the Biggest U.S. City Lacking City Council Members Elected from Geographic Districts," August 17, 2012.

46. Sarah Coppola, "Grass-Roots Effort Drove Austin City Council District Plan to Victory, Observers Say," *Austin American-Statesman*, November 7, 2012.

47. The following paragraphs are drawn from Derek Okubo, "A Time for Change: El Paso Adopts the Council-Manager Form," *National Civic Review* 94, no. 3 (Fall 2005): pp. 3–9.

48. Jack C. Plano and Milton Greenberg, *The American Political Dictionary*, 10th ed. (Fort Worth: Harcourt, Brace, 1997).

49. See "Number of Special Districts," United States Census Bureau, www.census.gov/govs/go/number_of_special _districts_by_county.html; *Texas Almanac and State Industrial Guide, 2000–2001* (Dallas: *Dallas Morning News*, 1999), 533; see Local Governments in Individual County-Type Areas: 2012, 2012 Census of Governments; U.S. Census, "Number of Special Districts," Lists and Structure of Governments; Laura Langham, *Invisible Government: Special Purpose Districts in Texas* (Research Spotlight, Texas Senate Research Center, 2014); there is no centralized database that provides information regarding special purpose districts in Texas, although the Comptroller's Office reports information related to their taxing authority. A legislative study in 2014 concluded that there were approximately 3,350 special purpose districts in the state, of which 1,965 were reporting to the Comptroller's Office.

50. County Information Program, Texas Association of Counties. Data are for 2010.

51. County Information Program, Texas Association of Counties. Data are for 2010.

52. Brooks Egerton and Reese Dunklin, "Government by Developer," *Dallas Morning News*, June 10, 2001, p. 1A.

53. Richard Williamson, "Texas MUD Sinks toward Chap. 9; Others on Solid Ground," *The Bond Buyer*, May 18, 2009.

54. Sara C. Galvan, "Wrestling with MUDs to Pin Down the Truth about Special Districts," 75 *Fordham Law Review* 3041–80 (2007).

55. See Texas Association of Regional Councils, "About TARC."

56. Chuck DeVore, "On Prohibiting the Issuance of Capital Appreciation Bonds: Testimony to the Senate Committee on Intergovernmental Relations," Texas Public Policy Foundation, March 20, 2013.

57. Trey Bundy and Shane Shifflet, "Controversial School Bonds Create 'Debt for the Next Generation,'" Reveal, January 2013, https://www.revealnews.org/article /controversial-school-bonds-create-debt-for-the-next -generation/.

58. DeVore, "On Prohibiting the Issuance of Capital Appreciation Bonds."

59. Chuck DeVore, "CAB Rides Can Be Extremely Costly," *Austin American-Statesman*, September 11, 2012.

60. James Estes, "Capital Appreciation Bonds: The Creation of a Toxic Waste Dump in Our Schools," Alpha Wealth Management, April 2013.

61. DeVore, "CAB Rides Can Be Extremely Costly."

62. DeVore, "On Prohibiting the Issuance of Capital Appreciation Bonds."

63. Keeley Webster, "Lockyer Challenges California School's CAB Advisors," *The Bond Buyer*, 2012, https:// www.bondbuyer.com/news/lockyer-challenges -california-schools-cab-advisors.

64. Eva-Marie Ayala, "Anna ISD Used Costly Bonds to Cope," *Dallas Morning News*, June 16, 2013, p. 1; Aman Batheja, "Swelling School Districts Find a Costly Way to Grow Within State Debt Limits," *Texas Tribune*, August 29, 2014; Lisa Minton, "Capital Appreciation Bonds. Another Finance Option for Schools," *Fiscal Notes*, Comptroller.texas.gov.

65. Lisa Minton, "Capital Appreciation Bonds: Another Finance Option for Schools," Texas Comptroller of Public Accounts, March 2016.

66. Susan Combs, "Your Money and Pension Obligations," Texas Comptroller of Public Accounts, 2012, 4.

67. Brandon Formby, "Billions in pension shortfall threatening Texas cities' budgets," *Texas Tribune*, December 2, 2016.

68. Combs, "Your Money and Pension Obligations," 7.

69. Doug Miller, "Mayor Cuts Firefighter Pension Deal; Experts Call It Bad Bargain," KHOU 11 News, March 6, 2015.

70. Joe Martin, "If We Don't Fix Pension Problem, It's Game Over," *Houston Business Journal*, December 9, 2015.

71. Combs, "Your Money and Pension Obligations," 17.

72. This discussion of the Dallas pension crisis is from Tristan Hallman, "Retirees' Rich Perk Cut Off," *Dallas Morning News*, January 15, 2015, pp. 1B, 9B; Tristan Hallman, "Return of Only 2% Seen as Hole Deepens," *Dallas Morning News*, February 20, 2015, pp. 1B, 7B; Robert Wilonsky, "Moody's Lowers City's Bond Rating," *Dallas Morning News*, October 29, 2015, pp. 5A; Robert Wilonsky, "Police-Fire Fund Pursues Ex-Leaders," *Dallas Morning News*, December 3, 2015, pp. 1B, 4B.

73. Mary Williams Walsh, "In Texas Some Rare Good News About Cities with Pension Woes," *New York Times*, June 1, 2017.

74. Comparison of El Paso City Employees' Pension Fund, "Summary Plan Description First Tier for Persons Whose Participation Date Is before September 1, 2011," with "Summary Plan Description Second Tier for Persons Whose Participation Date Is after September 1, 2011."

YOU DECIDE: HOUSTON'S "BATHROOM ORDINANCE"

a. Alexa Ura, "Bathroom Fears Flush Houston Discrimination Ordinance," *Texas Tribune*, November 3, 2015.

b. Manny Fernandez and Mitch Smith, "Houston Voters Reject Broad Anti-Discrimination Ordinance," *New York Times*, November 3, 2015.

c. Justin William Meyer, "Why Houston's Gay Rights Ordinance Failed: Fear of Men in Women's Bathrooms," *Washington Post*, November 4, 2015.

d. Tierney McAfee, "Hillary Clinton, Sally Field, Matt Bomer and More Stars Rally to Fight Anti-Transgender Discrimination," *People*, October 30, 2015.

e. Lauren McGaughy, "The Texas bathroom bill is dead—for now," *Dallas Morning News*, August 15, 2017; Gromer Jeffers Jr., "House Speaker Joe Straus is Texas' last shield against the bathroom bill," *Dallas Morning News*, July 26, 2017.

CHAPTER 11

1. Jeannie Kever, "As Texas Public College Tuition Rises, Legislators Feel the Heat," *Houston Chronicle*, July 10, 2008; Texas Higher Education Coordinating Board, "Tuition Set-Aside-House Bill 3013, 78th Texas Legislature," *Overview* (February 2010).

2. Texas Legislative Budget Board Staff, *Financing Higher Education in Texas: Legislative Primer*, as submitted to the 82nd Texas Legislature (January 2011); Texas Higher Education Board, "Tuition Deregulation," *Overview* (March 2011). See also collegeforalltexans.com and trends.collegeboard.org.

3. See Ryan McCrimmon and Bobby Blanchard, "Deregulating Tuition Slowed Increase, Universities Say," *Texas Tribune*, March 17, 2016; Ross Ramsey, "Analysis: Raising College Tuition, Deflecting the Blame," *Texas Tribune*, February 12, 2016; Lauren McGaughy and J. David McSwane, "Rise in Costs Not as Steep after Legislature Gave Reins to Schools," *Dallas Morning News*. April 10, 2016; Matthew Watkins, "Lt. Gov. Patrick Slams Universities for Tuition Increases," *Texas Tribune*, April 26, 2016.

4. See "Tuition Cost Must Ease," *Dallas Morning News*, April 14, 2016. See also Minjae Park, "UT Regents Back Some Tuition Hikes, New Med Schools," *Texas Tribune*, May 3, 2012; Reeve Hamilton and Morgan Smith, "UT's Reform-Minded Chairman at the Center of Controversy," *Texas Tribune*, May 18, 2012; Reeve Hamilton, "For In-State Students, UT System Keeps Tuition Steady," *Texas Tribune*, May 20, 2014.

5. The following discussion is drawn from Texas Legislative Budget Board, *Fiscal Size-Up: 2018–19 Biennium* (September 2018), pp. 1–8.

6. See Henry Kaiser Family Foundation "Total State Expenditures per capita," www.kff.org.

7. Texas Legislative Budget Board, *Fiscal Size-Up: 2014–15 Biennium* (February 2014), p. 58.

8. Texas Legislative Budget Board, *Fiscal Size-Up: 2014–15 Biennium*, p. 59.

9. Texas Legislative Budget Board, *Fiscal Size-Up: 2018–19 Biennium*, p. 26.

10. Texas Legislative Budget Board, *Fiscal Size-Up: 2016–17 Biennium*, p. 26.

11. Tax Foundation, "Facts and Figures, How Does Your State Compare?" (2017). See also Texas Legislative Budget Board, *Fiscal Size-Up 2016–17 Biennium* (May 2016). See also data provided by the Federation of Tax Administrators at taxadmin.org and Texas Public Policy Foundation at http://tbs.lbb.state.tx.us/. See also tax burden rankings provided by the Tax Foundation at taxfoundation.org.

12. Tax Foundation, "Facts and Figures: How Does Your State Compare?" (2016).

13. Texas Legislative Budget Board, *Fiscal Size-Up: 2016–17 Biennium*, pp. 35–36.

14. Carl Davis et al., *Who Pays? A Distributional Analysis of the Tax Systems in All 50 States*, 3rd ed. (Washington, DC: Institute on Taxation and Economic Policy, January 2013), 4, 11–12.

15. Carl Davis et al., *Who Pays? A Distributional Analysis of the Tax Systems in All 50 States*, 5th ed. (Washington, DC: Institute on Taxation and Economic Policy, January 2015).

16. Clay Robinson, "Bullock Paints a Grim Picture/Says Income Tax Needed to Avert Financial Crisis," *Houston Chronicle*, March 12, 1991; Clay Robinson, "Bullock Plan May Open Door to Tax Battle," *Houston Chronicle*, March 2, 1993.

17. Texas Legislative Budget Board, *Fiscal Size-Up: 2018–19 Biennium*, pp. 9, 18, 20.

18. Texas Lottery Commission, "Demographic Survey of Texas Lottery Players 2015," University of Houston, Hobby Center for Public Policy (November 2015).

19. Texas Lottery Commission, "Demographic Survey of Texas Lottery Players 2015." See also James LeBas, "Who Wants to Be a Billionaire? Texas Spending Tobacco Money on Health Care, Endowments," *Fiscal Notes*, Texas Comptroller of Public Accounts (January 2000); Texas House of Representatives, House Research Organization, "State Finance Report No. 82-3" (March 11, 2011).

20. Texas Permanent School Fund, "Comprehensive Annual Financial Report for the Fiscal Year Ending August 31, 2017"; Texas Legislative Budget Board, *Fiscal Size-Up: 2018–19 Biennium*, p. 217.

21. See Texas Legislative Budget Board, *Fiscal Size-Up: 2018–19 Biennium*, September 2018, p. 39. These numbers do not take into account the complicated arrangements that were included in the final certification of the Budget by the Comptroller that delayed into the next fiscal year paying out some of the funds to the Highway Fund. See *Fiscal Size-Up 2018–19 Biennium*, September 2018, p. 61.

22. "Rainy Day Fund 101," *Fiscal Notes*, Susan Combs, Texas Comptroller of Public Accounts (February 2011); Texas Legislative Budget Board, *Fiscal Size-Up: 2018–19 Biennium*, pp. 21–22.

23. University of Texas System, "The Permanent University Fund and Available University Fund." PUF and UAF Issues Issue Brief_2018 Update.pdf; Texas Legislative Budget Board, *Fiscal Size-Up: 2016–17 Biennium*, pp. 295–96.

24. For the Higher Education Fund, see Texas Legislative Budget Board, *Fiscal Size-Up: 2018–19 Biennium*, pp. 286–87. For the National Research University Fund, see Texas Higher Education Coordinating Board, "National Research University Fund Eligibility: A Report to the Comptroller and the Texas Legislature" (March 2016).

25. Texas Legislative Budget Board, *Fiscal Size-Up: 2018–19 Biennium*, p. 28.

26. Texas Legislative Budget Board, *Fiscal Size-Up: 2018–19 Biennium*, p. 28.

27. The following is drawn from Senate Research Center, *Budget 101: A Guide to the Budget Process in Texas* (January 2011), p. 29.

28. Texas Legislative Budget Board, *Fiscal Size-Up: 2018–19 Biennium*, pp. 28–29.

29. Texas Legislative Budget Board, *Fiscal Size-Up: 2018–19 Biennium*, pp. 29–30.

30. Tax Foundation, "Facts & Figures: How Does Your State Compare?" (2015), table 36.

31. See Senate Research Center, *Budget 101*, pp. 24–25.

32. Senate Research Center, *Budget 101*, p. 28; "40 Years of Comptroller Revenue Estimates (1974–2013)," *Fiscal Notes*, Glenn Hegar, Texas Comptroller of Public Accounts; *Texas Transparency* (2015), window.texas.gov.

33. See the discussion in Senate Research Center, *Budget 101*, pp. 34–35.

34. Aman Batheja, "Hegar: Revenue Estimate 'Based on Expectation of Moderate Expansion,'" *Texas Tribune*, January 12, 2015.

35. These paragraphs are drawn from Texas Taxpayers and Research Association, "84th Legislative Session Wrap-Up," *Fiscal Notes*, June 2015; Michael Gibson, Elizabeth Barett, and Bruce Wright, "2015 Legislative Wrap-Up," *Fiscal Notes*, September 2015.

36. The material in this section is largely drawn from Brian Wellborn, "2017 Legislative Wrap-Up," *Fiscal Notes*, September 2017; Texas Taxpayers and Research Association, "Texas Budget Challenges are not over," Research Report, August 2017.

YOU DECIDE: WHAT TO DO WITH A BUDGET SURPLUS?

a. Aman Batheja, "Hegar: Revenue Estimate 'Based on Expectation of Moderate Expansion,'" *Texas Tribune*, January 12, 2015.

b. Aman Batheja and Julián Aguilar, "Legislature Sends $209.4 Billion Budget to Abbott," *Texas Tribune*, May 29, 2015.

CHAPTER 12

1. See www.dfps.state.tx.us. See also Edgar Walters and Emily Ramshaw, "Federal Judge: Texas Foster Care System Violates Children's Rights," *Texas Tribune*, December 17, 2015.

2. "M.D. vs. Greg Abbott," U.S. District Court. Southern District of Texas, Corpus Christie Division, December 17, 2015, p. 186.

3. M.D. vs. Greg Abbott," U.S. District Court. Southern District of Texas, Corpus Christie Division, December 17, 2015, p. 17.

4. Marissa Evans, "State Leaders order overhaul of Texas Child Protective Services," *The Texas Tribune*, October 12, 2016; Marissa Evans, "Report says Child Protective Service workers are overloaded, urges overhaul," *The Texas Tribune*, November 4, 2016.

5. Marissa Evans and Emma Platoff, "Federal judge says Texas still needs oversight to fix its "broken" foster care system," *The Texas Tribune*, January 19, 2018; Robert T. Garrett, "Appeals court temporarily halts federal judge's order that Texas make big improvements in foster care, *Dallasnews*, January 19, 2018.

6. Robert T. Garrett, "Texas pushes back on federal judge's foster care ruling, though children's lawyers say let it rip," *Dallasnews*, February 15, 2018.

7. See Benjamin Ginsberg et al., *We the People: Texas Edition*, 9th ed. (New York: W. W. Norton, 2012), 643.

8. B. Guy Peters, *American Public Policy: Promise and Performance*, 9th ed. (Washington, DC: CQ Press, 2012), chaps. 2 and 3; Charles O. Jones, *An Introduction to the Study of Public Policy*, 3rd ed. (Monterey, CA: Brooks, Cole, 1984).

9. Roger Cobb and Charles Elder, *Participation in American Politics* (Baltimore: Johns Hopkins University Press, 1983), 85.

10. See Herbert Simon, "Bounded Rationality and Organizational Learning," *Organizational Science* 2, no. 1: 125–34; Kristen Renwick Monroe, *The Economic Approach to Politics: A Critical Reassessment of the Theory of Rational Action* (New York: HarperCollins, 1991).

11. See Texas Legislative Budget Board, *Fiscal Size-Up: 2018–19 Biennium*, p. 205.

12. See Texas Legislative Budget Board, *Fiscal Size-Up: 2018–19 Biennium*, 197–212. See also schools.texastribune.org.

13. Data on public school enrollment is taken from Texas Education Agency, *Enrollment in Public Schools, 2017–18*, August 2018.

14. See www.niche.com.

15. See data from Texas Education Agency Graduation Rates, 2017.

16. See Texas Legislative Budget Board, *2018–19 Biennium*, Chapter 6. See also The Texas Tribune, https://schools.texastribune.org/states/tx/. Texas Education Agency. Pocket Edition 2016–17. Texas Public Schools Statistics.

17. Terrance Stutz, "Texas Moves up in Spending per Pupil, Still Ranks in Bottom Third," *Dallas Morning News*, March 18, 2015.

18. See Texas Education Agency, http://tea.texas.gov/Dropout_Information.html.

19. For a discussion of the history of public education in Texas from which the following is drawn, see Max Berger and Lee Wilborn, "Education," *Handbook of Texas Online*, (Texas State Historical Association); "Public Schools," *Texas Almanac 2000–2001*, Millennium Edition (Dallas: Dallas Morning News, 1999), 533–54. See also Lewis B. Cooper, *The Permanent School Fund of Texas* (Fort Worth: Texas State Teachers Association, 1934); Michael E. McClellan, "Permanent School Fund," *Handbook of Texas Online*, (Texas State Historical Association).

20. See Oscar Mauzy, "Gilmer-Aikin Laws," *Handbook of Texas Online*, (Texas State Historical Association); Dick Smith and Richard Allen Burns, "Texas Education Agency," *Handbook of Texas Online*, (Texas State Historical Association); Berger and Wilborn, "Education."

21. See Anna Victoria Wilson, "Education for African Americans," *Handbook of Texas Online*, (Texas State Historical Association).

22. Arnoldo De León and Robert A. Calvert, "Segregation," *Handbook of Texas Online*, (Texas State Historical Association).

23. The following discussion of the *Rodríguez* and *Edgewood* cases is drawn from Texas Legislative Budget Board Staff, "Financing Public Education in Texas: Kindergarten through Grade 12," *Legislative Handbook* (February 1999); Berger and Wilborn, "Education"; Cynthia E. Orozco, "Rodríguez v. San Antonio ISD," *Handbook of Texas Online*, (Texas State Historical Association); Teresa Palomo Acosta, "Edgewood ISD v. Kirby," *Handbook of Texas Online*, (Texas State Historical Association).

24. See Texas Legislative Budget Board Staff, "Financing Public Education in Texas: Kindergarten through Grade 12," 26–27.

25. Mark Wiggins, "Attorneys, Schools and 83rd Texas Legislature's Impact on Education," www.kvue.com; Morgan Smith, "Texas School Finance Trial Goes for Round Two," *Texas Tribune*, June 19, 2013; Terrance Stutz, "State Seeks to Remove School Finance Judge," *Dallas Morning News*, June 3, 2014, p. 3a.

26. See *Morath et al. v. The Taxpayer and Student Fairness Coalition et al*, Supreme Court of Texas (No. 14-0776). See also Kiah Collier, "Texas Supreme Court Upholds School Funding System," The Texas Tribune, May 13, 2016, www.texaxtribune.org.

27. Alex Samuels, "Local taxes in Texas have been rising to help pay for education. Who is to blame?" TEXplainer, The Texas Tribune, February 16, 2018, www.texastribune.org; Texas Taxpayers and Research Association, "Texas Budget Challenges are Not Over," Research Report, August 2017.

28. Aliyya Swaby, "Will Texas school finance panel tell schools to do more with less? Some members think it's predetermined," *The Texas Tribune*, March 16, 2018; Aliyya Swaby, "Texas panel set to discuss school finance fix. Can they iron out lawmakers' disagreements?" *The Texas Tribune*, January 22, 2018.

29. See Clark D. Thomas, "Education Reform in Texas," in *Texas Politics*, ed. Anthony Champagne and Edward J. Harpham (New York: W. W. Norton, 1998), 213–32.

30. National Commission on Excellence in Education, *A Nation at Risk: The Imperative for Educational Reform* (Washington, DC: Department of Education, 1983).

31. See Thomas, "Education Reform in Texas," 218.

32. See Thomas, "Education Reform in Texas," 221.

33. See Thomas, "Education Reform in Texas," 231; "Public Schools," *Texas Almanac 2000–2001*, Millennium Edition (Dallas: Dallas Morning News, 1999), 533. See also Terrence Stutz, "State's List Cites Sub-par Schools in Transfer Plan," *Dallas Morning News*, December 24, 1999, p. 1.

34. College Board, "Mean 2009 SAT Scores by State" (2009); College Board, "2009 College-Bound Seniors Total Group Profile Report" (2009), p. 3. See also Texas Education Agency, "College Admissions Testing of Graduating Seniors in Texas High Schools, Class of 2010" (October 2011) and Texas Education Agency, "2010 Comprehensive Annual Report on Texas Public Schools" (December, 2010). See also Joshua Benton, "Legislators Left Unanswered Questions on New State Tests," *Dallas Morning News*, June 11, 2007, p. B1. See also Terrence Stutz, "Failing Tests, Passing Grades," *Dallas Morning News*, March 8, 2012, p. A1.

35. See Kate McGee, "Two Big Education Bills Gain Approval from Texas Legislature," KUTnews.org, May 27, 2013.

36. See Aliyya Swaby, "Legislature unanimously approves last-minute overhaul of school A-F ratings," *The Texas Tribune*, May 28, 2017.

37. See College Board.

38. See Texas Legislative Budget Board, *Fiscal Note*, 83rd Legislative Regular Session (February 19, 2013). See also Texas Education Agency, "Initial STAAR Results Released," News, TEA (June 8, 2012); Jeffrey Weiss and Daniel Lathrop, "Low-Scoring Groups Slipping More," *Dallas Morning News*, June 9, 2014, pp. 1a and 8.

39. See Milton Friedman, *Capitalism and Freedom* (Chicago: University of Chicago Press, 1962).

40. See Tawnell D. Hobbs, "As Charter Schools Rise, Dallas ISD Rues Loss of Students—and Millions in Funding," *Dallas Morning News*, January 21, 2016. See also "Charters in Texas," Texas Charter Schools Association, http://www.txcharterschools.org/what-is-a-charter-school/charters-in-texas/.

41. See the respective websites of these organizations. See also Morgan Smith, "Education Reform Group Mobilizes for 2014 Elections," *Texas Tribune*, January 8, 2014.

42. See Jim Henson and Joshua Blank, "Polling Center: Threading the Needle on Education," *Texas Tribune*, April 10, 2014. See also University of Texas/*Texas Tribune*, "Texas Statewide Survey," February 2014 and earlier surveys.

43. www.census.gov/quickfacts/fact/table/TX/RHI125216. Alexa Ura, "Latest Data Shows Poverty Rate Highest at Border, Lowest in Suburbs," *Texas Tribune*, January 19, 2016. See also Texas Health and Human Services Commission, "Texas Medicaid Enrollment Statistics."

44. See data at Henry J. Kaiser Family Foundation, kff.org.

45. Texas Legislative Budget Board, *Fiscal Size-Up: 2016–17 Biennium*, p. 163.

46. The following is drawn from Edward J. Harpham, "Welfare Reform and the New Paternalism in Texas," in *Texas Politics*, ed. Anthony Champagne and Edward J. Harpham, 233–49.

47. See Vivian Elizabeth Smyrl, "Texas Department of Human Services," *Handbook of Texas Online*, (Texas State Historical Association).

48. Harpham, "Welfare Reform and the New Paternalism in Texas," 238.

49. See Charles Murray, *Losing Ground: American Social Policy, 1950–1980* (New York: Basic Books, 1984).

50. For a discussion of these programs, see Lawrence Mead, *The New Politics of Poverty: The Nonworking Poor in America* (New York: Basic Books, 1992).

51. The following paragraphs are drawn from Harpham, "Welfare Reform and the New Paternalism in Texas," 244–47.

52. See Texas Legislative Budget Board, *Fiscal Size-Up: 2014–15 Biennium*, 221–22; Texas Health and Human Services Commission, "Temporary Assistance for Needy Families (TANF): Frequently Asked Questions." See also Texas Health and Human Services Commission, "Presentation to the House Select Committee on Human Services: HHSC Overview" (February 12, 2013).

53. Texas Health and Human Services System, *Consolidated Budget, Fiscal Years 2016–17* (October 2014), p. 21. See also "Temporary Assistance for Needy Families (TANF) Statistics," January 2018, Texas Health and Human Services.

54. https://talkpoverty.org/state-year-report/texas-2017 -report/.

55. Center on Budget and Policy Priorities, "Texas' TANF Cash Assistance is Disappearing for Poor Families," www.cbpp.org/sites/default/files/atoms/files/tanf _trends_tx.pdf.

56. See Alexa Ura, "How Texas curtailed traditional welfare without ending poverty," *The Texas Tribune*, November 30, 2017.

57. Texas Health and Human Services Commission, *Texas Medicaid and CHIP in Perspective*, 9th ed. (December 2015). Medicaid and the Children's Health Insurance Program (CHIP) information and data for this section are taken from this document and from data for Texas on the Henry Kaiser Family Foundation website, www.statehealthfacts.org.

58. See Texas Legislative Budget Board, *Fiscal Size-Up: 2016–17 Biennium*, p. 165; Texas Health and Human Services, *Texas Medicaid in Perspective* (The "Pink Book"), February 13, 2015, chap. 5.

59. Texas Health and Human Services Commission, *Texas Medicaid and CHIP in Perspective* (The "Pink Book"), chap 1: "Texas Medicaid in Perspective."

60. See Henry J. Kaiser Foundation, "Federal Medical Assistance Percentage for Medicaid," kff.org.

61. See Henry J. Kaiser Family Foundation, "Total Medicaid Spending FY 2014," kff.org.

62. See Louis Radnofsky, "Texas Medicaid Funds Cut over Planned Parenthood," *Wall Street Journal*, March 15, 2012; Emily Ramshaw and Thanh Tan, "The Storm over Women's Health Care Had Been Brewing," *Texas Tribune*, March 23, 2012; Wade Goodwyn, "As Texas Cuts Funds, Planned Parenthood Fights Back," May 7, 2012, www.npr.com; Amanda Peterson Beadle, March 16, 2012, Thinkprogress.org; Sean Walsh, "Hutchison Backs Planned Parenthood in Funding Dispute," *Dallas Morning News*, March 22, 2012.

63. Moni Basu, "Court Rules Texas Can Ban Planned Parenthood from Health Program," CNN U.S., August 22, 2012, www.cnn.com; "Judge Says Texas Not Allowed to Cut Funds to Planned Parenthood," Fox News, May 4, 2012, www.foxnews.com.

64. See Nancy Flake, "Combs: Texas in Great Shape, but Watch out for Medicaid," *Cyprus Creek Mirror*, May 2, 2012. See also Kristie Avery, "Comptroller Warns of Medicaid Costs," *Texas Gazette*.

65. In the Senate, 58 Democrats and 2 independents voted for the Patient Protection and Affordable Care Act. All 39 Republicans in the Senate were opposed. In the House of Representatives, the final vote was 219 to 212. All supporters of the bill were Democrats, with 34 Democrats and 178 Republicans opposing the bill.

66. See Texas Health and Human Services Commission, *Texas Medicaid and CHIP in Perspective*, chap. 3, for a further discussion of the impact of federal health care reforms on Texas.

67. See Kaiser Family Foundation, "How Will the Uninsured in Texas Fare under the Affordable Care Act?" at kff.org/medicaid.

68. "Fewer Texas Doctors Taking Medicaid Patients," *Dallas Morning News*, July 9, 2012.

69. Robert T. Garrett, "State Slashes Health Law Estimate," *Dallas Morning News*, July 13, 2012.

70. See "Fewer Texans were uninsured in 2016, but state still has largest health coverage gap," *Texas Tribune*, September 12, 2017.

71. See Edgar Walters, "More Have Health Insurance but Texas Lags," *Texas Tribune*, December 18, 2016. See also Episcopal Health Foundation at www.episcopalhealth .org.

YOU DECIDE: ABORTION POLICY IN TEXAS

a. Emily Ramshaw, "For Abortion Providers, Sonogram Law Is a Complication," *Texas Tribune*, January 29, 2012.

b.   "Texas Sonogram Law Has Some Patients Unhappy," McClatchy DC, February 29, 2012, www.mcclatchydc .com/news/politics-government/article24725104.html.

CHAPTER 13

1.   Matt Pearce and Jaweed Kaleem, "12 officers shot, 5 fatally, by snipers in Dallas during protest over police shootings," *Los Angeles Times*, July 8, 2016; F. Brinley Bruton et al., "Dallas Police 'Ambush': 12 Officers Shot, 5 Killed During Protest," NBC News, July 8, 2016; Manny Fernandez, Richard Perez-Pena, and Jonah Engel Bromwich, "Five Dallas Officers Were Killed as Payback, Police Chief Says," *New York Times*, July 8, 2016; Rye Druzin, "Texas top state for law enforcement deaths in line of duty," *Politifact Texas*, September 19, 2016.

2.   Danielle Kaeble and Mary Cowhig, "Correctional Populations in the United States, 2015," Bureau of Justice Statistics, April 2018.

3.   Al Ortiz, "Different Views on Additional Staffing for the Houston Police Department," Houston Public Media, January 16, 2017, https://www.houstonpublicmedia.org /articles/news/2017/01/16/183687/different-views-on -additional-staffing-for-the-houston-police-department/.

4.   Sarah Rafique, "Rural Challenges: West Texas' smallest departments face difficulties policing rural towns," *Lubbock Avalanche-Journal*, December 5, 2016.

5.   "Number of Dallas Police Officers at Lowest Level in a Decade," AP, April 25, 2017.

6.   Texas Commission on Law Enforcement website, www .tcole.texas.gov.

7.   Rafique, "Rural Challenges."

8.   Material is from the Texas Commission on Law Enforcement website, www.tcole.texas.gov.

9.   Ayan Mittra, "T-Squared: The Launch of 'Unholstered,' a Look at Texas Police Shootings," *Texas Tribune*, August 30, 2016.

10. Tasha Tsiaperas, "No witnesses called for ex-cop in trial," *Dallas Morning News*, December 19, 2017.

11. John Sullivan et al., "Number of fatal shootings by police is nearly identical to last year," *Washington Post*, July 1, 2017.

12. Jolie McCullough, "Why the murder charge against the Texas police officer who killed Jordan Edwards is rare," *Texas Tribune*, July 18, 2017.

13. Eva Ruth Morasee, "Seven unarmed black men killed by officers in Texas in 2016," *San Antonio Express-News*, May 18, 2017.

14. Morasee, "Seven unarmed black men killed by officers in Texas in 2016."

15. The Sandra Bland case received widespread news coverage. See, for example, Dana Ford, "DA: Sandra Bland's Death Being Treated Like Murder Investigation," CNN, July 21, 2015; David Montgomery, "Sandra Bland Was Threatened with Taser, Police Video Shows," *New York Times*, July 21, 2015; "Texas Trooper Indicted over Sandra Bland Arrest Formally Fired," *Chicago Tribune*, March 2, 2016; St. John Berned-Smith, "DPS Director Affirms Firing of Trooper in Sandra Bland Case," Chron .com, March 2, 2016.

16. James Barragan, "Session's bills back the blue," *Dallas Morning News*, June 3, 2017.

17. Fred Dahr, "Crimes and Punishment in Texas State Court," texasdefenselaw.com; Texas Criminal Defense Lawyer, "Texas Criminal Laws and Penalties," mytexas defenselawyer.com.

18. Texas Board of Pardons and Paroles.

19. Texas Department of Criminal Justice, 2017 Statistical Report, August 31, 2017.

20. *O'Donnell v. Harris County*, 2017 WL 1735456 (2017).

21. Information is from the Texas Association of Counties. The term *district attorney* will be used to encompass district attorneys, county attorneys, and criminal district attorneys.

22. Texas Indigent Defense Commission, "Indigent Defense Data for Texas."

23. Dottie Carmichael, "Judgement and Justice," Public Policy Research Institute, Texas A&M University, June 2013, pp. vii–x.

24. Texas Department of Criminal Justice, "Fiscal Year 2017 Statistical Report."

25. Johnathan Silver, "Texas Prisons Ponder Cutting $250 Million," *Texas Tribune*, August 3, 2016.

26. Harry Mika and Lawrence J. Redlinger, "Crime and Correction," in *Texas at the Crossroads*, eds. Anthony Champagne and Edward J. Harpham (College Station: Texas A&M University Press, 1987), 245–46.

27. Mika and Redlinger, "Crime and Correction," 245–46.

28. *Ruiz v. Estelle*, 503 F. Supp. 1265 (1980).

29. Mika and Redlinger, "Crime and Correction," 247.

30. Texas Department of Criminal Justice, "Texas Board of Criminal Justice."

31. Texas Jail Project, "What is the difference between state jail and county jail in Texas?" December 21, 2010; John VanderWerff, "Texas state jails typically house

lower level classifications of criminals," *Kileen Daily Herald*, February 26, 2016.

32. Texas Department of Criminal Justice, "Rehabilitation Programs Division, Substance Abuse Treatment Program."

33. See Associated Texans against Crime, "Annual Report" (1998); Texas Department of Criminal Justice, "Fiscal Year 2011 Operating Budget and Fiscal Years 2010–2013 Legislative Appropriations Request" (August 16, 2010).

34. Brandi Grissom, "With crime, incarceration rates falling, Texas closes record number of prisons," *Dallas Morning News*, July 5, 2017.

35. See Associated Texans against Crime, "Annual Report" (1998).

36. Texas Department of Criminal Justice, "Fiscal Year 2017 Statistical Report."

37. Texas Department of Criminal Justice, "Fiscal Year 2017 Statistical Report."

38. Texas Department of Criminal Justice, "Fiscal Year 2006 Statistical Summary" (December 2006).

39. Texas Department of Criminal Justice, "Fiscal Year 2010 Statistical Reports."

40. Texas Department of Criminal Justice, "Fiscal Year 2017 Statistical Report."

41. *Texas Almanac 2010–2011*, Texas State Historical Association (2010), 482.

42. E. Ann Carson, "Prisoners in 2016," *Bureau of Justice Statistics Bulletin*, January 2018.

43. "Violent Crime Rate By State," *World Atlas*, August 25, 2017.

44. Texas Department of Criminal Justice, "Fiscal Year 2017 Statistical Report."

45. Texas Department of Criminal Justice, "Fiscal Year 2017 Statistical Report."

46. Death Penalty Information Center, "Facts about the Death Penalty," October 11, 2018, deathpenaltyinfo.org.

47. Death Penalty Information Center, "Facts about the Death Penalty."

48. Data comes from the National Registry of Exonerations at www.law.umich.edu.

49. Paul Brace and Brent D. Boyea, "State Public Opinion, the Death Penalty, and the Practice of Electing Judges," *American Journal of Political Science* 52, no. 2 (2008): 360–72.

50. UT/*Texas Tribune* poll of 1,200 registered Texas voters, June 8–18, 2018. Margin of error is +/−2.83 percentage points.

51. Texas Department of Criminal Justice, "Executed Offenders."

52. Texas Department of Criminal Justice, "Gender and Racial Statistics of Death Row Offenders," September 27, 2017.

53. Calculated from Texas Department of Criminal Justice, "Executed Offenders," July 27, 2017.

54. *McClesky v. Kemp*, 481 U.S. 279 (1987).

55. "Gov. Perry Commutes Sentences of Man Scheduled to Die Thursday," abc 13, August 30, 2007.

56. Larry Arnold, "The History of Concealed Carry, 1976–2011," Texas Concealed Handgun Association.

57. Eric Aasen, "Here's What You Should Know about Open Carry in Texas," KERA, January 5, 2016.

58. Ramsey, "UT/TT Poll."

59. Guns to Carry, "Active Concealed Carry Permits (2017)," www.gunstocarry.com/concealed-carry-statistics/.

60. Alex Samuels, "Lawmaker seeks to pass 'constitutional carry' gun bill in 2017," *Texas Tribune*, January 3, 2017.

61. National Registry of Exonerations, www.law.umich.edu.

62. Technically, an exoneration is an official finding of innocence from a court, whereas a wrongful conviction may not necessarily result in a formal determination of innocence by a court. All exonerations are wrongful convictions, but some wrongful convictions may not be exonerations.

63. National Registry of Exonerations.

64. National Registry of Exonerations.

65. Timothy Cole Advisory Panel on Wrongful Convictions, Final Report, December 2016.

66. Jordan Smith, "WilCo D.A.: Duty Upsets Bradley," *Austin Chronicle*, June 1, 2012.

67. Claire Osborn, "Ken Anderson Begins Serving Jail Sentence in Michael Morton Case," statesman.com, November 13, 2013.

68. Will Weissert, "Bill Named for Michael Morton Passes House," May 13, 2013, kxan.com; "Perry Set to Sign Michael Morton Act," May 16, 2013, kxan.com.

69. Maurice Chammah, "Bill Addresses Changing Science in Criminal Appeals," *Texas Tribune*, February 4, 2013.

70. Brian Rogers, "Harris County Officials Outline Plans to Curb Jail Population," *Houston Chronicle*, January 7, 2016.

YOU DECIDE: CITE AND RELEASE

a. Daily Texan Editorial Board, "High Time for Texas to Decriminalize Marijuana," January 31, 2014; Texas

Criminal Justice Coalition, "Findings Summary: Issues Facing County Jails."

b. Nathan Bernier, "In Austin, 1 in 4 Pot Busts Doesn't Lead to Arrest," KUT.ORG, November 9, 2012; Mikaela Cannizzo, "Cite and Release Policy in Austin to Soon Be Enacted in Other Texas Counties," *Daily Texan*, January 28, 2016.

c. "Marijuana: Despite Law Allowing Ticketing for Pot Possession, Most Texas Counties Still Arrest," StopThe DrugWar.org, January 8, 2008; "Marijuana Ticket Law Only Catching on Near Austin, Texas," *Dallas Morning News*, December 31, 2007.

d. Eric Nicholson, "Dallas County Will Experiment with Not Arresting People Caught with Marijuana," *Dallas Observer*, October 6, 2014.

CHAPTER 14

1. Antonio Olivo, "Deployed By Gov. Rick Perry, National Guard Adjusts to its New Role on the Texas Border," *Washington Post*, September 1, 2014, https://www.washingtonpost.com/national/deployed-by-gov-rick-perry-national-guard-adjusts-to-its-new-role-on-the-texas-border/2014/09/01/24968056-2f90-11e4-994d-202962a9150c_story.html?utm_term=.2d719ca54a1b (accessed 8/13/18).

2. Julia Edwards Insley, "Trump Border 'Wall' to Cost $21.6 Billion, Take 3.5 Years to Build; Internal Report," *Reuters*, February 9, 2017, https://www.reuters.com/article/us-usa-trump-immigration-wall-exclusive/exclusive-trump-border-wall-to-cost-21-6-billion-take-3-5-years-to-build-internal-report-idUSKBN15O2ZN (accessed 8/13/18).

3. Texas A&M Transportation Institute, 2016 Texas Transportation Poll.

4. "Licensed Total Drivers, by Age 1/2016," U.S. Dept. of Transportation, Office of Highway Policy Information, September, 2017.

5. "Number of private and commercial motor vehicle registrations in the U.S. in 2016, by state," statista: The Statistics Portal, www.statista.com/statistics/196010/total-number-of-registered-automobiles-in-the-us-by-state/.

6. Ginger Lowry and T. J. Costello, "Texas Road Finance (Part 1) Paying for Highways and Byways," *Fiscal Notes*, Texas Comptroller of Public Accounts (May, 2016).

7. Lowry and Costello.

8. Lowry and Costello.

9. "100 Most Congested Roadways in Texas," Texas A&M Transportation Institute, 2017.

10. David Schrank et al, "Urban Mobility Scorecard," College Station: Texas A&M Transportation Institute and INRIX, August 2015.

11. Jay Blazek Crossley, "How much do traffic crashes cost the people of Texas?," Farm and City, September 5, 2017, farmandcity.org.

12. John Heleman and Bruce Wright, "Texas' Motor Fuels Taxes," *Fiscal Notes*, Texas State Comptroller of Accounts (February, 2016).

13. Texas Department of Transportation, "Texas Transportation Plan 2040" (2014).

14. Ray Leszcynski, "Officials back toll lanes to fix LBJ East," *Dallas Morning News*, January 16, 2018.

15. Leszynski, January 16, 2018.

16. Aman Batheja and Stephen J. Smith, "The Bullet Train that Could Change Everything," *Texas Tribune*, August 18, 2014.

17. Batheja and Smith.

18. Brandon Formby, "Some Texans dodge bullet train, others are square in its path," *Texas Tribune*, December 15, 2017; "Starts and stops: A history of the Texas bullet train project," abc13 Eyewitness News, December 18, 2017, abc13.com; Madeleine Rivera, "Texas bullet train proposal pits rural landowners against urbanites," Fox News, January 4, 2018, foxnews.com.

19. Dug Begley, "Houston's public transit challenges highlighted in U.S. analysis of bus, rail networks," *Houston Chronicle*, June 10, 2016.

20. Center for Neighborhood Technology 2016, All Transit, alltransit.cnt.org.

21. "The Foreign-Born Population in Texas: Sources of Growth," Office of the State Demographer, http://demographics.texas.gov/Resources/Publications/2015/2015_10_07_ForeignBorn.pdf.

22. Corrie Maclaggan, "Fort Bend County, the Picture of Ethnic Diversity," *Texas Tribune*, November 25, 2013, www.texastribune.org.

23. Elena Mejia Lutz and Peggy Fikac, "All bills targeting the Texas dream died, but DACA students feel like they didn't dodge the bullet," *San Antonio Express-News*, June 3, 2017, www.expressnews.com.

24. Institute on Taxation and Economic Policy, "Undocumented Immigrants' State and Local Tax Contributions," March 2, 2017, https://itep.org/immigration/.

25. Greater Houston Partnership, "Foreign-Born Population," September 14, 2017, http://www.houston.org.

26. Office of the State Demographer, "The Foreign-Born Population in Texas: Sources of Growth," http://demographics.texas.gov.

27. Amanda O'Donnell, "Houston Police Chief Art Acevedo: 'Sanctuary Cities' Bill Targets 'Cooks and Nannies,' Not Criminals," *Statesman*, September 22, 2018, http://www.statesman.com/news/local/houston-police-chief-art-acevedo-sanctuary-cities-bill-targets-cooks-nannies-not-criminals/CmdOjFrzxU9Hy6SuOzHoMM/ (accessed 10/10/18).

28. Lt. Governor Dan Patrick: Statement on SB4 Concurrence, "Sanctuary Cities Legislation is On Its Way to the Governor's Desk," The State of Texas, Lt. Governor, May 3, 2017, https://www.ltgov.state.tx.us/2017/05/03/lt-governor-dan-patrick-statement-on-sb-4-concurrence/ (accessed 10/10/18).

29. Ashley Goudeau, "Texas Lawmakers Vote on 'Sanctuary Cities' Bill," KVUE, April 26, 2017, http://www.kvue.com/news/politics/texas-lawmakers-vote-on-sanctuary-cities-bill/434441733 (accessed 10/10/18).

30. Lyanne A. Guarecuco, "'Sanctuary Cities' Debate Brings Tears, Protests, Feuds to Texas House," *Texas Observer*, April 27, 2017, https://www.texasobserver.org/sanctuary-cities-tears-protests-feuds-texas-house/ (accessed 10/10/18).

31. Patrick Svitek, "Paxton Looks to Get Ahead of Legal Challenges to 'Sanctuary Cities' Ban," *Texas Tribune*, May 8, 2017, https://www.texastribune.org/2017/05/08/paxton-looks-get-ahead-legal-challenges-sb4/ (accessed 10/10/18).

32. Kelsey Jukam, "Border City & County Declare Legal War on Texas," *Courthouse News Service*, May 9, 2017, https://www.courthousenews.com/border-city-county-declare-legal-war-texas/ (accessed 10/10/18).

33. Julian Aguilar, "El Paso County Files Lawsuit Seeking to Halt Texas 'sanctuary' Law," *Texas Tribune*, May 22, 2017, https://www.texastribune.org/2017/05/22/el-paso-county-files-lawsuit-seeking-halt-states-immigration-law/ (accessed 10/10/18).

34. "Know Your Rights Under SB4," ACLU of Texas, March 13, 2018, https://www.aclutx.org/en/sb4 (accessed 10/10/18).

35. Madlin Mekelburg, "Texas Attorney General Ken Paxton files 7-state lawsuit seeking to end DACA," *El Paso Times*, May 1, 2018, www.elpasotimes.com.

36. Maria Sacchetti, "Federal judge gives respite to 'dreamers,' says DACA can't end while lawsuit is pending," January 10, 2018, www.washingtonpost.com.

37. Texas Department of Transportation, "Texas-Mexico Border Crossings," www.txdot.gov.

38. Texas Military Department, "Texas National Guard deploys to Texas-Mexico border to enhance border security," April 10, 2018, https://tmd.texas.gov.

39. Julia Ainsley and Courtney Kube, "Hundreds of migrant kids separated from parents are stuck at border stations," NBC News, January 5, 2018, www.nbcnews.com.

40. Patrick Svitek, "Lupe Valdez sees Texas Gov. Gregg Abbott as President Donald Trump's 'puppet,'" *Texas Tribune*, May 29, 2018, www.texastribune.org.

41. Molly Hennessy-Fiske, "The great test for Trump's border wall: Texas' Rio Grande Valley," *Los Angeles Times*, April 30, 2018, www.latimes.com.

42. "More South Texas Land Owners Getting Letters on Border Wall," U.S. News, July 8, 2018, www.usnews.com.

43. Lindsay Ellis, "Texas leads nation in university enrollment growth," *Houston Chronicle*, December 20, 2017.

44. Steve Kuhann, "Texas A&M hits record-high enrollment with fall 2017 semester," *The Eagle*, October 5, 2017.

45. The education data used in this section are drawn from two sources: Texas Higher Education Coordinating Board, *2018 Texas Public Higher Education Almanac: A Profile of State and Institutional Performance and Characteristics* and Texas State Historical Association, *Texas Almanac 2018-2019* (Austin: Texas, 2018). Community college data generally included information on the Lamar State Colleges and the Texas State Technical Colleges. See also http://www.txhighereddata.org/.

46. See Cardozier; see also Matthews (2018) Chapter 5.

47. See Matthews (2018), Chapter 5 for a more detailed discussion.

48. See Matthews (2018) for a discussion of the normal school movement in Texas.

49. Much of the following discussion draws upon Matthews (2018); *Handbook of Texas Online*, V. R. Cardozier, "Higher Education," accessed July 23, 2018, http://www.tshaonline.org/handbook/online/articles/khhxr; *Handbook of Texas Online*, H. Stanton Tuttle, "Junior-College Movement," accessed July 23, 2018, http://www.tshaonline.org/handbook/online/articles/kdj02.

50. See Cardozier, "Higher Education." See also Texas Higher Education Coordinating Board, "Formula Fund-

ing Recommendations for the 2020-21 Biennium," April 2018, www.thecb.state.tx.us.

51. Institute for College Access & Success, *Student Debt and the Class of 2016*, September 2017, Table 3.

52. Matthew Watkins, "Texas Colleges fret about $1 billion in expected funding missing from budget plan," *Texas Tribune*, January 24, 2017.

53. See Legislative Budget Board, "Agencies of higher education; Higher Education," May 2016, in *Fiscal Size-Up 2016–17 Biennium*, pp. 220–4.

54. The following is drawn from "Understanding PUF: What is the Permanent University Fund?," University of Texas System, August 22, 2016, https://www.utsystem .edu/offices/chancellor/blog/what-is-the-permanent -university-fund. See also "Permanent University Fund (PUF) Quick Facts," University of Texas System, https://www.utsystem.edu/puf.

55. See Matthew Watkins, "Texas Universities forced to trim their budgets, even with big state cuts averted." *Texas Tribune*, July 27, 2017.

56. See Texas Higher Education Coordinating Board, *2018 Texas Public Higher Education Almanac*, 2018.

57. Peter G. George, Robert E. Mace, and Rima Petrossian, "Aquifers of Texas," Texas Development Board, Report 380 (July 2011).

58. An acre-foot is equal to 325,851.43 U.S. gallons. Planners typically assume that a suburban family will consume an acre-foot of water a year.

59. Texas Water Development Board, "Water for Texas 2012 State Water Plan" (January 2012), p. xii.

60. See Texas Water Development Board, "Water for Texas 2012," pp. 17–18.

61. See Otis W. Templer, "Water Law," *Handbook of Texas Online*; Otis W. Templer, "Water Rights Issues: Texas Water Rights Law; East Meets West," *Journal of Contemporary Water Research and Education* 85 (Spring 1991).

62. The following is drawn largely from Templer, "Water Law" and "Texas Water Rights." See also Terry L. Hadley, "Texas Water Commission," *Handbook of Texas Online*; Laurie E. Jasinski, "Texas Water Development Board," *Handbook of Texas Online*; Texas Water Development Board, "Water for Texas 2012," Executive Summary and chap. 1. See also Texas Water Development Board, "A Texan's Guide to Water and Water Rights Marketing"; Ronald Kaiser, *Handbook of Texas Water Law: Problems and Need Water Monograph No. 87–1* (College Station: Texas Water Resources Institute, Texas A&M University, 1987). We also thank Benedict Voit for his useful summary of water policy issues. See Benedict Voit, "Texas Water Policy for the 21st Century" (unpublished paper, University of Texas at Dallas, April 10, 2008).

63. See Texas Water Development Board, "A Texan's Guide to Water."

64. Texas Water Development Board, "Water for Texas 2012," pp. 15–16.

65. See the historical timeline regarding environmental policy, Texas Commission on Environmental Quality, www.tceq.texas.gov.

66. See Texas Water Development Board, "About the Texas Water Development Board," www.txdb.texas.gov.

67. See Kate Galbraith, "Texas Supreme Court Rules for Landowners in Water Case," *Texas Tribune*, February 24, 2012. See also Forrest Wilder, "The Texas Supreme Court Turns Water into a Landmark Groundwater Decision," *Texas Observer*, February 24, 2012; Chuck Lindell, "Supreme Court Delivers Major Water Ruling on Water Regulation," *Austin American Statesman*, February 24, 2012.

68. For a good discussion of some of these issues, see a five-part series published by the *Texas Tribune*: Neena Satija, "Beneath the Surface," *Texas Tribune*, November 19, 2013–January 19, 2014.

69. Michael Marks and Terence Henry, "Everything You Need to Know about Proposition 6, Texas' Water Fund," *State Impact: A Reporting Project of NPR Member Stations*, November 4, 2013.

AnswerKey

CHAPTER 1
1. B
2. A
3. C
4. D
5. B
6. D
7. E
8. A
9. E
10. C
11. B
12. C
13. A
14. A

CHAPTER 2
1. A
2. E
3. D
4. C
5. E
6. D
7. A
8. D
9. D
10. B
11. C
12. B
13. A
14. A
15. B

CHAPTER 3
1. C
2. C
3. A
4. B
5. B
6. A
7. A
8. C
9. A
10. C
11. B
12. A
13. B
14. C
15. E

CHAPTER 4
1. B
2. B
3. A
4. B
5. A
6. A
7. A
8. D
9. C
10. B
11. B
12. A

CHAPTER 5
1. C
2. C
3. D
4. E
5. C
6. C
7. A
8. C
9. A
10. A
11. D
12. A
13. C
14. B

CHAPTER 6
1. B
2. E
3. E
4. E
5. A
6. E
7. A
8. D
9. C
10. C
11. E
12. B
13. D
14. B
15. A
16. B

CHAPTER 7
1. A
2. A
3. D
4. B
5. E
6. B
7. C
8. B
9. D
10. D
11. C
12. A
13. D
14. A
15. A
16. D
17. B

CHAPTER 8
1. D
2. E
3. E
4. B
5. D
6. A
7. A
8. B
9. B
10. B
11. E
12. A
13. C
14. A
15. E

CHAPTER 9

1. C
2. C
3. C
4. B
5. B
6. A
7. E
8. D
9. E
10. A
11. E
12. A
13. A
14. C

CHAPTER 10

1. B
2. D
3. D
4. D
5. C
6. A
7. B
8. B
9. D
10. E
11. A
12. A
13. A
14. C
15. A
16. A
17. D
18. A

CHAPTER 11

1. A
2. B
3. A
4. C
5. B
6. B
7. C
8. A
9. B
10. D
11. D
12. B
13. A

CHAPTER 12

1. B
2. E
3. A
4. B
5. C
6. A
7. B
8. E
9. A
10. C
11. B
12. C

CHAPTER 13

1. C
2. A
3. A
4. A
5. B
6. C
7. C
8. D
9. C
10. D
11. A
12. A
13. E
14. E
15. C
16. E
17. C

CHAPTER 14

1. A
2. A
3. D
4. A
5. E
6. A
7. B
8. C
9. A
10. E
11. B
12. B
13. A
14. C
15. A
16. D
17. C
18. A
19. D

Credits

Glossary/Index

selected as state capital, 37
traffic in, 482
Austin, Moses, 24, 32
Austin, Stephen F., 3, 24, 32, 51
Austin American-Statesman, *174*, 298, 307, 358

Available School Fund (ASF), **369**, **381**, **383**, **506** dedicated fund established by the constitution for the support of public education in the state

Avery v. Midland County, 332
ayuntamientos, 329

B
Bahorich, Donna, 264

bail, **451–52**, *452* payment of money to the state as an assurance that an accused person who is released from jail pending trial will appear for trial; if the accused does not appear, the bail is forfeited

bail bonds, *452*
Bailey, Joseph Weldon, 155
Baker v. *Carr*, 240
Balch Springs Police Department, 445
Bandera County River Authority, 281
banking industry, 21, 22
barratry, 317–18, 319
Basin and Range Province, 10
Bastrop County, 314
"Bathroom Bill," 345, *345*
Battleground Texas, 199
Battle of San Jacinto, 3, 54–55
Baum, Elmer, 74
Baylor University, 319
Beaumont, 14
Beaver, Jenni, 433
Begala, Paul, 127
Bell, Cecil, 256
Bell, Chris, 126

bench trial, **302** a trial held without a jury and before only a judge

Bentsen, Lloyd Jr., 132
Bentsen, Lloyd Sr., 130
Bettencourt, Paul, 221
Bexar County, 36–37
    assigned counsel in, 457
    immigration in, 492
    marijuana possession citations and, 450
    public defenders in, 302
Beyle, Thad, 253

beyond a reasonable doubt, **303** the legal standard in criminal cases that requires the prosecution to prove guilt beyond a reasonable doubt

bicameral, **52**, **55**, **215–16** having a legislative assembly composed of two chambers or houses

biennial, **216** occurring every two years

Biennial Revenue Estimate (BRE), 390
Big Bend country, 10, 335
Bilingual Education Act, 121

bill, **220**, **223–33**, ***224–25*** a proposed law that has been sponsored by a member of the legislature and submitted to the clerk of the House or Senate
    committee action, 226
    conference committee, 228, 230
    floor action, 226–27, 228
    governor's action, 230
    introduction in the House, 223, 226
    referral, 226

Bill of Rights (Texas), 66–67
Bill of Rights (U.S.), 48, 49, 66, 67, 92, 93, 101
bipartisanship, 118
birth control, 430–31
Black Codes, 27, 59
Blackland Belt, 8
Black Lives Matter movement, *440*, 441–42
Bland, Sandra, 446–47, *447*

block grants, **98** federal grants that allow states considerable discretion on how funds are spent

Blue Dog Democrats, **136** another name for conservative Democrats, mostly from the South

Board of Regents of State Colleges, 502
Boatwright, Jason, 294
boll weevils, 12
Bond Review Board, 274
Bonnen, Dennis, 128, 205, *232*, 234
boom-and-bust mentality, 14
boomtowns, 14
border security, 6, 18, 39, 107–8, *108*, 176, 492–93, 496–98
border wall, proposed by Trump, 107–8, *108*
boundaries, 8

bounded rationality, **407–8** the idea that in policy making decision makers may seek solutions to problems that are satisfactory to them but not necessarily optimal or efficient

Boyea, Brent, 466
Brace, Paul, 466
Bradley, John, 469, 470
Brest, Paul, 312
Brewster County, 334

Briscoe, Dolph, 74–75, 125, 252, *257*, 272
Brooks County, *335*
Brown, David, 441
Brown, George R., 187–88
Brown, Lee, 142
Brown, Michael, shooting of, 441
Brownsville, 10, 32
Brown v. Board of Education of Topeka, 28, 102, 410–11
Bruner, Mary Lou, 286
budgets, 368, 369–71
    balancing, 367, 368, 392
    budgetary process, 388–96, *389*
    budget deficits, 392, 393, 395
    budget-execution authority, 388
    budget process today, 395–96
    budget shortfalls, 367
    budget surpluses, 393, 394
    challenge of budgeting in Texas, 392–95
    constitutional spending limit and, *387*
    "dual-budget system," 388
    estimation and planning, 390, 392–93
    key players in budgetary process, *389*
    legislative process, 390–92, *391*
    spending limits and, 386, 387, *387*
    summary of All Funds state budget allocation, *370*
    Texas biennial budget cycle, *385*
    Texas Constitutions and, 384–88, 392
    welfare spending limit, 387
bullet train, 486–87, *487*, *488*
Bullock, Bob, 243, 251, 283, 376

bundling, **189** the interest-group practice of combining campaign contributions from several sources into one larger contribution from the group, so as to increase the group's impact on the candidate

bureaucracy, 281 the complex structure of offices, tasks, rules, and principles of organization that are employed by all large-scale institutions to coordinate the work of their personnel

Burks, Tyrus, *206*
Burleson County, 314, 472
Burnam, Lon, 191
Bush, George H. W., 17, *18*, 132–33, 134, 277
Bush, George P., *172*, 194
    campaign contributions to, *273*
    as candidate for land commissioner, *172*, 272
    as land commissioner, *272*, 277, 287
Bush, George W., 115, 252, *254*, 272, 283
    2004 election campaign of, 140
    budgetary power and, 266
    concealed carry legislation signed by, 467
    criticizes welfare system in race for governor, 423
    election as President, 260
    as governor, *231*, 254, 256–57, 261, 415, 467
    immigration policy when Governor, 176
    "No Child Left Behind," 184
Bush, Jeb, 272, 277
business, *21*
    business dominance, 24
    business interests, 198
    interest groups and, 188
Butt, Charles, 189
Butts, David, 307

C

CAB. *See* Capital appreciation bond (CAB)
Caddo Lake Compact Commission, 281
Cain, Darrell, 445
Calhoun, John C., 92
California
    gubernatorial power in, 255
    Latino population of, 127
    lobbyists in, 193
    as sanctuary state, 495
    voting in election of 2016, 171
California Watch, 358
Cameron County, poverty in, 420
campaign contributions and spending
    contributions and spending for statewide offices (2018), *172*
    to incumbents and challengers for the Texas Legislature (2018), 202
    interest groups and, 201
    for statewide offices (2018), *273*
campaigns, 149–81
    candidates, 168
    elections and the future of Texas, 177–78
    importance of, 149–50
    important issues in recent, 175–77
    media and, 174–75
    money and, 168–70
    political parties and, 172–73
    public opinion and, 173–74
    social media and, 174–75
    strategy in, 173
Campbell, Donna, 200, 203
Camp Bowie, 36
Canada, 17–18
Canon, Mike, 202

capital appreciation bond (CAB), 357–58 a long-term,

high-interest-paying bond that pays off both principal and interest in one lump sum when the bond reaches maturity

capital case, 302 a criminal case in which the death penalty is a possible punishment

capitation payments, 427
Carrollton, 35
Carter, Jimmy, 122
caseworkers, *402*, 403–4
Cash Management Committee, 274
Castro, Joaquín, *140*, 144, 149
Castro, Julián, 39, 121, *140*, 144, 149

categorical grants, 96 congressionally appropriated grants to states and localities on the condition that expenditures be limited to a problem or group specified by law

cattle ranching, 11, 12–13, *13*, 36
Cedar Bayou, 327
Center for Neighborhood Technology, 487–88
Center for Public Policy Priorities, 394

centerline miles, 481 total length of a road or road segment

Centers for Medicare and Medicaid in the Department of Health and Human Services, 428–29
Central Unit prison, closure of, 461
change, 4, 5, 6, 64
Chapman, Ron, 139
charter schools, 408
Chase, Salmon, 93–94

checks and balances, 47, 55, 65 the constitutional idea that overlapping power is given to different branches of government to limit the concentration of power in any one branch

Cherokee County, 314
Chevalier, Joi, *172*, *273*
chief justice, 59
Child Nutrition Grants, 408
Child Protective Services (CPS), 268, *402*, 403–4, 425
Children's Health Insurance Program (CHIP), 369, 428–29, 432
Childress, George C., 52
child support collection, 276
child welfare, reform of, 403–4
Chinese Exclusion Act, 494
Chinni, Dante, 138
CHIP. *See* Children's Health Insurance Program (CHIP)
chubbing, 227
cite and release, 450
cities, 6, 338
citizenship, Latinos and, 142
Citizens United v. Federal Election Commission, 203
City Charter's Citizen Advisory Committee, 347
city councils, 342–43, 349
city government, 337–50, 349
    in Austin, 347
    in Dallas, 346–47
    in El Paso, 347–48, 349
    forms of, 341–43
    general-law vs. home-rule cities, 338–41
    in Houston, 343–44
    in San Antonio, 344, 346
city managers, 342–43, 344–45, 346, 347
Ciudad Juarez, Mexico, 39, *478*
civil cases, 301–2

civil law, 300–301 a branch of law that deals with disputes, usually between private individuals over relationships, obligations, and responsibility

closed primary, 152, a primary election in which only registered members of a particular political party can vote

coercive federalism, 98, 100–109 federal policies that force states to change their policies to achieve national goals

commissioner form of government, 341–42 a form of city government in which the city is run by a small group of elected commissioners who act in both legislative and executive capacities

complaint, 300 the presentation of a grievance by the plaintiff in a civil case

comptroller, 46, 55, 68, 231–32, 279, *372*, 378, 386, *389*, 390, 393, 394, 423, 431 elected state official who directs the collection of taxes and other revenues and estimates revenues for the budgeting process

concurrent resolution, 220 a resolution that is of interest to both chambers of the legislature and must pass both the House and Senate and generally be signed by the governor

Confederacy, 19, 56–58, 60, 93, 94, 165 the Confederate States of America, those southern states that seceded from the United States in late 1860 and 1861 and argued that the power of the states was more important than the power of the central government

conference committee, 223 a joint committee created to work out a compromise on House and Senate versions of a piece of legislation

Congressional Reconstruction, 59 the reconstruction program put forward by radical Republicans in Congress in 1866 that disenfranchised former Confederates and granted former slaves American citizenship and the right to vote

consideration by standing committee, 223 the third step in the legislative process, during which a bill is killed, amended, or heard by a standing committee

precinct-level county official involved with serving legal papers and, in some counties, enforcing the law

constituent, 217 a person who is represented by an elected official

constituent service, 218 nonlegislative activities legislators perform to assist people living in their districts, including writing letters of recommendation, giving speeches to civic groups, or working to solve a problem for someone in their community

constitution, 47 the legal structure of a government, which establishes its power and authority as well as the limits on that power

contingent fee, 300 a fee paid to the lawyer in a civil case that is contingent on winning the case

cooperative federalism, 96 a type of federalism existing since the New Deal era in which grants-in-aid have been used to encourage states and localities (without requiring them) to pursue nationally defined goals; also known as intergovernmental cooperation

corn pone, 6
Cornyn, John, *38*, 142, 175, 252
corporations, private, 72
Corpus Christi, 32, 103, 104
corrections, 441–77
corruption, 64
corruption and scandals, 197
cosmopolitanism, 6
cotton production, 10, 11, 12, *12*, 13, 34, 36

council-manager form of government, 342–43, 344, 346–47, 348 a form of city government in which public policies are developed by the city council and executive and administrative functions are assigned to a professional city manager

council of government (COGs) *356*, **356–57** a regional planning board composed of local elected officials and some private citizens from the region

counties, 333–36. *See also* county government; *specific counties*

county attorney, 330, 455–56 county official who prosecutes lesser criminal cases in the county court; an elected official in some counties who prosecutes misdemeanor cases

county auditor, 331 public official, appointed by the district judges, who receives and disburses county funds; in large counties, this official also prepares the county budget

county chair, 123 the county party official who heads the county executive committee

county clerk, 330 public official who is the main record-keeper of the county

county commissioner, 331–32 government official (four per county) on the county commissioners' court whose main duty is the construction and maintenance of roads and bridges

county commissioners' court, 329–30, 331, *332*, *334* the main governing body of each county; has the authority to set the county tax rate and budget

county convention, 124 a meeting held by a political party following its precinct conventions, for the purpose of electing delegates to its state convention

county-court-at-law judges, 333

county courts, 297, 313, 316 the courts that exist in some counties and that are presided over by county judges

county executive committee, 123 the party group, made up of a party's county chair and pre-

cinct chairs, that is responsible for running a county's primary elections and planning county conventions

county government, 329–37, *334*
    accountability of county officials, 336–37
    challenges of, 333–37
    construction and maintenance responsibilities of, 330–31, 332
    countywide and precinct-level elected officials, *333*
    dispute resolution and, 331
    functions of, 329–31
    large number of, 331–33
    law enforcement and, 330
    law-enforcement budgets and, 330
    record-keeping and, 330–31
    social services and, 331
    taxing and budgeting powers of, 332
county jails, 330, 332

county judge, 297, 331 the person in each of Texas's 254 counties who presides over the county commissioners' court, with responsibility for the administration of county government; some county judges carry out judicial responsibilities

county tax assessor-collector, 330 public official who maintains the county tax records and collects the taxes owed to the county

county treasurers, 333
countywide and precinct-level elected officials, *333*
courts, legislative process and, 233 (*see also specific courts*)

courts of appeal, 70, 295, 314 the 14 intermediate-level appellate courts that hear appeals from district and county courts to determine whether the decisions of these lower courts followed legal principles and court procedures correctly

Cox, Lonnie, 332–33
CPS. *See* Child Protective Services (CPS)
Craddick, Christi, *172, 273*
Craddick, Tom, 168, 242
Crawford, 136
Creager, R. B., 130
"creative destruction," 11
credit markets, 21
Creuzot, John, 336
crime, 441–77
    categorizing of, 448–51, *449*
    cite and release, 450
    felonies, 448–51, *449*
    misdemeanors, 448–51, *449*
    punishing, 448–49
criminal defense, 457
criminal justice process, 451–57
    arraignment, 451–52
    assigned counsel, 457
    bail, 451–52, *452*
    county attorneys, 455–56
    criminal defense, 457
    district attorneys, 455–56
    grand jury indictment, 453
    indigent defense, *457*
    plea bargains, 453–54
    pretrial hearings, 453
    public defenders, 457
    sentencing, 454
    trial, 454
criminal justice system
    compared with other states, 465
    DNA testing and, 469–71

does it create criminals, 454–55

drug treatment and, 461, 462, 464, 471

exonerations in, 468–71

fairness of, 468–71

favorability toward by race/ethnicity, 314, *314*

integrity of, 468–71

jailhouse informants, 472

reforms of, 471–72

wrongful convictions, 469–72

criminal law, **300**, **302–3** the branch of law that regulates the conduct of individuals, defines crimes, and specifies punishment for criminal acts

"crop lien" system, 12

Cruz, Ted, 28, *101*, 115, 116, 120, 122, 135, *148*, 149, 150, 175

Crystal City, 125

Cuellar, Henry, *136*

Culberson, Charles A., *257*

Culberson, John, 177

cultural conservatives, vs. pro-business Republicans, 6–7

Cypress-Fairbanks, 408

D

DACA. *See* Deferred Action for Childhood Arrivals (DACA)

Dallas, 5, 17, 35–36, 116
   African American population of, 30, 140, 141
   Asian American population of, 30
   bullet train and, 486–87, *487*
   city government in, 346–47, 349
   commissioner form of government and, 342

cotton production and, 36

council-manager form of government in, 346–47

Democratic stronghold of, 138

economy of, 35–36

high-tech industry in, 36

at-large council in, 343

Latino population of, 26, 140

liberals in, 121

manufacturing in, 36

oil booms and, 15

oil industry in, 36

pensions and, 359–60

petroleum financing in, 36

population growth and, 34, 36

railroad system and, 35–36

school district in, 408

shooting of five police officers in, 441, 468

special purpose districts in, 355

Dallas County, 35, 132, 138–40, 336, 492

Dallas–Fort Worth metropolitan area, 8–9, 35–36
   American Indians in, 23
   poverty in, 420
   suburban growth around, 138–40
   traffic in, 482, 483, 485

Dallas Independent School District (DISD), 417

Dallas Morning News, 132, 139, 174, *174*, 196

Dallas Police and Fire Pension System, 359–60

Dallas Police Department, *440*, 443, 471

Daniel, David E., 367–68

Daniel, Price, 256, *257*

Daniel, Price, Sr., 411

DAPA. *See* Deferred Action for Parents of Americans and Lawful Permanent Residents (DAPA)

dark money, **203** political contributions whose donors are not legally required to be disclosed

Daughters of the Republic of Texas, 277

Davis, Edmund J., 61, *62*, 64, 129

Davis, Greg, 450

Davis, Sarah, *114*, 115, 116, 200

Davis, Wendy, 143–44, *407*
   2014 gubernatorial campaign and, 122, 260
   campaign contributions to, *273*
   campaign of, 258, 260
   filibuster and, *227*
   interest groups and, 188

death penalty, 302, 459, 464–67, *464*, 465

debt service, **388** money spent by the state to pay off debt; includes interest and principal payments

Deep Water Committee, 341–42

Deferred Action for Childhood Arrivals (DACA), **495–96**, **497** executive order implemented by President Obama, which shielded certain undocumented immigrants from deportation if they were enrolled in school, had no criminal records, and were making educational progress

Deferred Action for Parents of Americans and Lawful Permanent Residents (DAPA), 107, 108–9

deferred retirement option plan (DROP), **359–60** retirement plan in which local

government employees who are eligible to retire have their retirement benefits deposited in an account in which the benefits draw interest until actual retirement. Some of these plans pay high interest and cost-of-living adjustments and may be coupled with very early retirement ages

DeLay, Tom, 136, 242

Dell Computers, 17, 38

DeLuna Castro, Eva, 394

Democratic Party, 4, 5–6, 9, 74, 78, 115, 140, 287
   2018 convention in Fort Worth, *117*
   2018 election and, 177
   African Americans and, 119, 121, 132, 140, 141
   conservatism and, 132–33, 136, *136*, 137
   contemporary, 121–22
   decline of, 134, 136
   disappearance of conservative Democrats, 136
   division within, 116
   Dixiecrats and, 125
   dominance of after Civil War, 129–30, 132
   early voting impact on, *160*
   era of conservative Democrats, 132–33
   factions within, 137–38
   federalism and, 109
   gains in 2018 elections, 288
   gains since 2014, 134, 288
   higher education and, 505
   Latinos and, 116, 137, 140
   need to adopt moderate policies in order to make inroads, 143–44
   party organization, 123–25
   party politics, 137–38
   redistricting and, 103
   regains control of legislature, 61

increased funding and, 419
  in a new era, 416–18
  public policy, 408–19
  roots of, 409–10
Edwards, Chet, 136
Edwards Aquifer, 513
Edwards Aquifer Authority, 513
Edwards Aquifer Authority v.
    Burrell Day and Joel
    McDaniel, 513
Eisenhower, Dwight, 130, *132*,
    137
El Capitán, 10
El Centro Community Col-
    lege, 441
Elder, Charles, 405
elections, 149–81. *See also*
    electoral cycle
  features of, 150–55
  general, 153
  importance of, 149–50
  independents in, 153–54
  interest groups and, 170
  participation in, 155–61
  primary (*see* primary
    elections)
  special, 153
  turnout in, 77, 81, 141, *141*, 142,
    153, 164–65, *165*, 166, 171

electoral cycle, **151** the process in which candidates run
for office beginning with campaigns for the party primary
and ending with the general
election, usually in November

electoral power, **221** the
legislature's mandated role
in counting returns in the
elections for governor and
lieutenant governor

electricity, 11
electronics industry, 17
elementary education, 7, 70, 416
Elkins, James, 188
Ellis, Mark Kent, 308

El Paso, 10, 20, 39, *478*
  city government in,
    347–48, 349
  commissioner form of
    government and, 342
  council-manager form of
    government in, 348
  Democratic stronghold
    of, 138
  downtown development, *348*
  Latinos in, 26
  pensions and, 360–61
  population growth and, 34
  Proposition 7 and, 75–76
El Paso desert, water supply
    and, 509
El Paso Times, 174
emancipation, 27
Emergency Assistance Pro-
    gram, 424
emergency services districts, 353
EMILY's List (Early Money Is
    Like Yeast), 202
Empower Texans political ac-
    tion committee, 194–95,
    203

empresario, **24**, **32**, **51** Spanish word for an individual
who promotes, organizes, or
helps to finance a particular
endeavor

entrepreneurs, 11, 22
environment, oil industry
    and, 16
environmental legislation,
    federalism and, 88
Episcopal Health Foundation,
    434
Equality Texas, 345
Equal Justice Initiative, 95

equal protection clause, **60**,
410–11 provision in the Fourteenth Amendment of the U.S.
Constitution guaranteeing
citizens the "equal protection

of the laws"; this clause has
been the basis for the civil
rights of African Americans,
women, and other groups
  African Americans and,
    102, 410–11
  coercive federalism and,
    101–2
  SB 4, ban on sanctuary cit-
    ies and, 495

Equal Rights Amendment,
    105–6
Escobar, Veronica, *27*
ESF. *See* Economic Stabiliza-
    tion Fund (ESF)
Estelle, W. J., Jr., 458
ethnic minorities, 3–4
Evenwel v. Abbott, 164, 240
evolution, teaching of, 137

executive budget, **266** the
state budget prepared and
submitted by the governor to the
legislature, which indicates the
governor's spending priorities.
The executive budget is overshadowed in terms of importance by the legislative budget

executive powers, 56, 68
exurbs, 5, 6
Exxon Mobil, 188

F
Family Support Act, 423
Farenthold, Blake, 103
Farmers Branch, 100, 493
Farmers Branch Police De-
    partment, 445
farmers' movements, 125

Federal Funds, **97**, **369**, **371**,
372, **378**, **424** includes all
grants, payments, and reimbursements received from the
federal government by state
agencies and institutions

Federal Highway Administra-
    tion, 482

federalism, **48**, **87–113**, **89**,
109, **480**, **495** a system of
government in which power
is divided, by a constitution,
between a central government
and regional governments
  ACA and, 432
  coercive, 98, 100
  constitutional roots of,
    90–92
  cooperative, 94–96, *95*
  dual, 94–95, *95*
  dual vs. cooperative,
    94–95, *95*
  in Early America, 92–94
  future of Texas and, 109
  interstate commerce and,
    93, *93*, 94, 96
  layer-cake, 94–95
  litigation concerning,
    88
  marble-cake, 95–98
  roots of, 89–94
  Texas and the nation over
    time, 94–98

Federalist Papers (Madison),
    47, 186
Federal Reserve System, 21
federal system, 87–113

felony, **302**, **448**, *449* a serious criminal offense, punish-
able by a prison sentence or
a fine; a capital felony is possibly punishable by death

FEMA (Federal Emergency
    Management Agency),
    327–28
Ferdinand VII, King of Spain,
    50
Ferguson, James E., 156, *257*,
    260
Ferguson, Margaret, 253

plural executive and, 271–80
power of position, 255
power sharing, 255
powers of, 255
power to reorganize state government, 255
qualifications for office, 256
staff, 261
succession line in, 260–61
term limits, 255
women and, 256
Governor's Office of Budget, Planning, and Policy (GOBPP), 388, *389*, 390

grand jury, **302**, **453** jury that determines whether sufficient evidence is available to justify a trial; grand juries do not rule on the accused's guilt or innocence

grand jury indictment, 453
Grand Prairie, 35

Grange, **12**, **61**, **61–62**, **125** a militant farmers' movement of the late nineteenth century that fought for improved conditions for farmers

Grant, Ulysses, 93
Great Depression, 12, 96, *96*
Great Plains, 10
Great Recession, 21–22, 31, 359, 368, 372, 375, 376, 429, 490
Great Society, 96
Green, Al, 141
Green, Paul, 308
Green, Rick, 308
Grimes County, 355
Grodzins, Morton, 94–95
groundwater disticts, 511, 512
Grovey v. Townsend, 157
Guadalupe Peak, 10
Guadalupe Range, 10

Guanajuato, Mexico, 50
gubernatorial power, limitations on, 61–62
Gulf Coast, 30, 32, 509
Gulf Coastal Plains, 8–9, 14
Gulf Oil, 14
gun control, 176
gun laws, 100
gun rights, 143–44, 176
gun safety, 176
gun safety laws, 215
Gutiérrez, José Ángel, 125
Guzman, Eva, *313*

H
Halback, Joseph, 308
halfway homes, 461
Hall, Ralph, 136
Halliburton Company, 188
Hamilton, Andrew Jackson, 58
Hammond, Bill, 233
handguns, concealed/open carry of, 467–68
Harle, Sid, 308
Harris County, 14, 34–35, 140
assigned counsel in, 457
bail system in, 452, 455
DACA and, 496
district attorney in, 456, 471
immigration in, 492
marijuana possession citations and, 450, 455
population of, 334
public transit in, 487
Republicans defeated by Democrats countywide in 2018 midterms, 140, 306
size of, 334
special purpose districts in, 355
straight-ticket voting in, 306
unprecedented turnout in 2018 midterm elections, 153
Hawk, Susan, 336
Hayden, Michael, 268

Hays County, 450
HB 40, 340
Health and Human Services Commission, 262
Health Care and Education Reconciliation Act, 431
health care policy, 107, 426–35
health insurance, 96, 98, 413, *434*
percentage of people without, 435
private, 429–30
uninsured population, *427*, 434
HEB Grocery store chain, 189
Hecht, Nathan, 310, 513
Hegar, Glenn, *172*, *272*, *273*, 280, 287, *372*, 393
Henderson County, 314
Henry J. Kaiser Foundation, 420
Heritage Foundation, 261.
Hernandez, Ana, 493–94
Hernandez, Sally, 493
Herrero, Abel, 189, 220
HHS. *See* Texas Health and Human Services Commission (HHS)
Hidalgo, *108*
Hidalgo County, 420, 511

hidden government, **354** a term that refers to special purpose districts of which many citizens are unaware

higher education, 7, 37, 70, 371, 501–4, *503*
budget shortfalls and, 367–71
building a system of, 501–4
Democratic Party and, 505
financing of, 367–68, 383–84, 393, 395, 480, 501, 504, 506
future of, 505
mineral rights and, 53
oil and gas industry and, 15

oil industry and, 38
political parties and, 505
Republican Party and, 505
setting goals for the future, 508–9
spending and outcomes, 507
tuition and fees and, 367–68
Higher Education Coordinating Board, 262

Higher Education Fund (HEF), **383**, **504**, **506** state higher education fund for universities not having access to PUF monies

higher education policy, 499–509
High Plains Underground Water District, 511
High-Quality Prekindergarten Grant Program, 393
high-speed rail, 486–87, *487*
high-tech digital economy, 11
high-tech industry, 17, 36, 37, 38
highway system. *See* Interstate Highway System
Highway Trust Fund, 483
Hill, John, 75, 257, 272
Hinojosa, Michael, 417–18
Hispanics. *See* Latinos
Hobby, William P., 75, *257*, 261, 376
Hockley County Sheriff's Office, 443
Hogg, James S., *257*

home-rule charter, **338**, **339** the rules under which a city operates; local governments have considerable independent governing power under these charters

Home-Rule Charter Amendment, 338
home-rule cities, 338–41, *338*

hospital districts, 353
hotel and motel tax, 376
House Bill 1863, 424
housing market, 21, 22
Houston, 5, 9, 37, 38, 115, 116,
      344
   African American popula-
      tion of, 30, 34, 141
   Asian American popula-
      tion of, 30
   "bathroom ordinance"
      in, 345
   bullet train and, 486–87, *487*
   as center of medical re-
      search, 17, *17*
   city government in,
      343–44, 349
   commerce in, 34
   commissioner form of
      government and, 342
   cotton production and, 34
   court system in, 314
   Democratic influence in,
      122, 138
   economy of, 34–35
   Hurricane Harvey and,
      327
   industrialization of, 14
   Latinos in, 26
   liberals in, 121
   mayor-council form of
      government in, 343
   oil industry in, 15, 35
   pensions and, 359, 360
   percentage of white stu-
      dents in, 414
   political life in, 34–35
   population of, 34, 35, 338
   public education in, 414
   public transit in, 487
   railroad system and, 34–35
   school district in, 408
   segregation in, 34
   suburban growth around,
      138
   traffic in, 482–83
   urbanization and, 32
Houston, Sam, 3, 34, 37

   Battle of San Jacinto and,
      54–55
   refuses to convene special
      session to discuss
      secession, 57
Houston and Texas Central
   Railroad Company v.
   East, 511
Houston Astros, 192
Houston Chronicle, 174, *174*
Houston Community College,
   337
Houston County, 314
Houston Firefighters' Relief
   and Retirement Fund, 359
Houston Methodist Research
   Institute, *17*
Houston Municipal Employ-
   ees Pension System, 359
Houston Police Department,
   443
Houston Police Officers Pen-
   sion System, 359
Houston Ship Channel, 35
Howard, Donna, 196
Hubbard, Richard B., *257*
Hudspeth County, 335, *335*
Huey, Mary Ann, 139–40
Hughes, Sarah, 312
Human Rights Campaign, 345
Humble Oil, 14
Humphrey, Hubert, 125
Hunter, Todd, 194
Huntsville, 458, 501–2
Hurd, Will, 141
Hurricane Harvey, 267–68,
   326, 327–28
Hurricane Rita, 327–28
Hutchison, Kay Bailey, 115,
   122, 258, 430

I
IBM, 38
Ifill, Sherrilyn, 312
Illinois, 255
immigration and immigrants,
   6, 12, 39, 107, 137, 177,
   479, 490–99

"A Day Without Immi-
   grants," *492*
detention of children
   separated from their
   parents, 496
domestic, 23–24
federalism and, 88
German, 36–37, 132
illegal, 18, 39, 40, 107, 120,
   176, 392, 434, 479, 480,
   491–92, 495–96, 498–99
immigration policy, 88,
   107, 176, 479, 492–99
impact on business and
   economy, 490–92, *492*
international, 23–24
land grants and, 51
Latin American, 25, 36,
   108–9, *478*
legal, 480
Mexican, 25, 36, 108–9, *478*
population size in Texas,
   California, and New
   York, *490*
Trump adminstration and,
   39, 479
who is responsible for,
   492–93

impeachment, **72–73, 223,**
227, 260 according to the
Texas Constitution, the
formal charge by the House
of Representatives that leads
to a trial in the Senate and
possibly to the removal of a
state official

income tax, 372, 376, 377, 378
independents, 119, 137, 153–54

independent state grounds,
105 allow states, usually under
the state constitution, to expand
rights beyond those provided by
the U.S. Constitution

Indian Wars, 22

indictment, **302** a written
statement issued by a grand
jury that charges a suspect
with a crime and states that a
trial is warranted

indigent defense, *457*
industrialization, 14
Institute on Taxation and
   Economic Policy, 376, 491
Instructional Materials Fund,
   381
insurance commissioner, 265
insurance occupation taxes,
   375
interest, 372

interest group, **185, 186–88,**
198, 201 an organization
established to influence the
government's programs and
policies
   civil rights and, 190
   contributions to Texas
      Legislature candidates
      (2016), 201, *202*
   democratic politics and,
      186–88
   free rider problem and,
      186–87
   future of Texas and, 208
   get out the vote, 199
   importance of, 183–84
   interests represented by,
      187–88
   legislative process and, 233
   lobbying and, 183–211
   policy makers and, 188–89
   political process and,
      185–98
   resources and strategies
      of, 185–86
   types of, 190–91

interest-group capture,
204–5 process by which a
government agency comes
to serve the objectives of the

interests that the agency is supposed to regulate

Interior Lowlands, 9–10
interstate commerce, regulation of, 93, *93*, 94, 96
Interstate Highway System, 14, 138, 481–84
    costs of, 483–84
    the future and, 485–86
    state-maintained, *482*
    toll roads, 485–86

introduction, **223** the first step in the legislative process, during which a member of the legislature drafts a bill and files a copy of it with the clerk of the House or secretary of the Senate

investigative power, **221** the power, exercised by the House, the Senate, or both chambers jointly, to investigate problems facing the state

Ireland, John, *257*
irrigation, 10
Irving, 35

issue advocacy, **199** independent spending by individuals or interest groups on a campaign issue but not directly tied to a particular candidate

J
Jack, Janis, 403–4
Jack County, 457
Jackson, Andrew, 92
Jade Helm 15 conspiracy theory, 267–68

Jaybird Party, **157** after the white primary was ruled unconstitutional, this offshoot

Democratic Party preselected candidates for the Democratic primary and prohibited African Americans from participating

Jefferson, Thomas, 52
Jefferson, Wallace, 142, 307
Jester, Beauford H., *257*, 260
Jim Crow segregation, 8
Johnson, Andrew, 58
Johnson, Ann, 115
Johnson, Cliff, 196
Johnson, Eddie Bernice, 141
Johnson, Faith, 336
Johnson, Ken, *445*
Johnson, Lyndon B., 28, 137, 150, 158
    adds to new programs to Social Security Act, 96
    in Congress, 19
    progressive views of, 132
    as schoolteacher in Cotulla, Texas, 3
    signs Voting Rights Act, 103
    sworn in as president, 312
    "War on Poverty," 422
Joint Committee on Prison Reform, 458
Joint Interim Committee on Higher Education Formula Funding, 506

joint resolution, **221** a resolution, commonly a proposed amendment to the Texas Constitution or ratification of an amendment to the U.S. Constitution, that must pass both the House and Senate but that does not require the governor's signature

Jones, Anson, 55
Jones, Elizabeth Ames, 203
Jones, Jesse, 188
Jones, Mark, 136, 240
Jordan, Barbara, 28, 141

judicial branch. *See* Texas judiciary

Judicial Campaign Fairness Act, **310** a judicial reform that places limits on judicial campaign contributions

judicial discipline, 294
judicial elections, 303–4, 307
    money in campaigns, 303, 304, 308
    partisanship and, 304–5
    special interests and, 303
    voter confusion and, 306, 308, 309

judicial power, **223** the power of the House to impeach and of the Senate to convict members of the executive and judicial branches of state government

judicial selection, 294
    compared to other states, 310, 311
    election or appointment, 307
    merit selection, 306, 307
    proposed reforms of, 305–12
"Juneteenth Day," 27

justice of the peace courts, **70**, **298–300**, **313** local trial courts with limited jurisdiction over small claims and very minor criminal misdemeanors

K
Kaiser Family Foundation, 432
Kaiser Foundation Study, 371
Kansas, 8
Keller, Sharon, 320
Kenedy County, *335*
Kennedy, Anthony, 79
Kennedy, John F., 28, 312
Kent County Sheriff's Department, 443

Kerrigan, Patricia, 308
Key, V.O., 88
Kinch, Sam, 256
King, Bill, 359
King, Ken, 189
King Ranch, *13*
Kirby, Barbara, 299
Kirby, William, 412
Kirk, Ron, 142
Kitzman, Eleanor, 265–66

L
Lake Highlands, 485
Lamar, Mirabeau, 37
land, 7–10, 12–13

land commissioner, **276** elected state official who is the manager of most publicly owned lands

land grants, 8, 32, 51, 53
land rights, 55
land titles, 72

lane miles, **481** centerline miles multiplied by the number of lanes

Laney, Pete, 241
Lang, Katie, 79
Lanham, S. W., *257*
LAR. *See* Legislative Appropriation Request (LAR) instructions

La Raza Unida Party, **26–27**, **125** former political party created in 1970 in Texas in order to bring attention to the concerns of Mexican Americans

Laredo, 17–18
Latinos, 4, 10, 24, 25–27, *26*, 29, 33, 40, 109
    anti-immigrant rhetoric and, 39
    citizenship and, 142

2006 gubernatorial election and, 126
as acting governor, 261.
appointment power and, 264, 281, 307, *313*
budgetary power and, 266
campaign of, 258
"citizen congress" and, 222
commutes sentence of Kenneth Foster, *467*
deployment of National Guard troops to border in 2014, 392
elects not to expand Medicaid, 432, *432*, 434
as governor, 251, 254, 256, *256*, *257*, 260–62, 479, 491
judicial branch and, 307, *313*, 316
lobbyists and, 194
Medicaid Women's Health Program and, 430–31
Obama administration and, 479
redistricting and, 215, 241
signs Texas Dream Act, 491
Texas-Mexico border, 266–67
veto power and, *231*, 268
Personal Responsibility and Work Opportunity Reconciliation Act, 424
petrochemical industry, 8, 14
petroleum equipment manufacturing, 35
petroleum financing, 36
petroleum industry, 340
petroleum production, 10
Pew Research Center, 479, 491
Physician Education Loan Repayment program, 375
Pierre, Goodwille, 308

pigeonholing, **226** a step in the legislative process during which a bill is killed by the chair of the standing commit-

tee to which it was referred, as a result of his or her setting the bill aside and not bringing it before the committee

Pitts, James, 194
Planned Parenthood, 233, 430–31
planning authorities, water policy and, 511–14
Plano, 35
plantation slavery, 8
plantation system, 30

plea bargain, **302, 453–54** negotiated agreement in a criminal case in which a defendant agrees to plead guilty in return for the state's agreement to reduce the severity of the criminal charge or prison sentence the defendant is facing

Plessy v. Ferguson, 102, 410

plural executive, **68, 271–80,** **272** an executive branch in which power is fragmented because the election of statewide officeholders is independent of the election of the governor
accountability of, 286–87
agriculture commissioner, 278–79
attorney general, 275–76
commissioner of the general land office, 276–77
comptroller of public accounts, 279–80
the governor and, 280–81
lieutenant governor, 274–75
secretary of state, 280
single executive compared with, 283

"pocket veto," 230
Pojman, Joe, 233

police and policing, *440*, 441–48, 471
controversies surrounding, 444–48
favorability toward, *446*
marijuana possession citations and, 450
police officers charged with murder, 445
police powers, 266–68
racial bias and, 445, 446–47
use of force and, 444, 445, 446
use of video cameras and, 445
police shootings, 441, 444, 445, 446
policy legitimation, 406
policy makers, access to, 191–92, 198, 201
policy-making process, 405–8, *407*
evaluation, 406, *407*
implementation, 406, *407*
policy formation, 405–6, *407*
problem identification, 405, *407*
rationality in policy making, 406–8

political action committee (PAC), **199** a private group that raises and distributes funds for use in election campaigns
to defeat opponent, 200–203
to get out the vote, 199–200
interest-group capture and, 204–5

political culture, **5–7, 24,** **26, 28, 40** broadly shared values, beliefs, and attitudes about how the government should function and politics

should operate; American political culture emphasizes the values of liberty, equality, and democracy

political elites, 5
political participation, by race and ethnicity, 166
political parties, 115–47
African Americans in, 119, 121, 122, 132, 140, 141–42
campaigns and, 172–73
digital media and, 129
factions within, 143
future of Texas and, 143–44
higher education and, 505
Latinos in, 142–43
party organization, 123–25, *123*
public attitudes about, 119–20
role and structure of, 117
third parties, 125–26, 128

political socialization, **119** the introduction of individuals into the political culture; learning the underlying beliefs and values on which the political system is based

Polk, James K., *56*
Polk County, 334
polling places, times and locations of, 102

poll tax, **26, 28, 156** a state-imposed tax on voters as a prerequisite for voting; poll taxes were rendered unconstitutional in national elections by the Twenty-Fourth Amendment, and in state elections by the U.S. Supreme Court in 1966

population growth, 22–24, 32, 33, 34, 480, 489–90
Populist movement, 12, 14, 125

Populist or People's Party, 130
Port Arthur, 14

**post-adjournment veto,
230, 269** a veto of a bill that
occurs after the legislature
adjourns, thus preventing the
legislature from overriding it

poverty, 31, 419–21, *420*
Powell, David Lee, 466
powers
 directive and supervisory,
 221
 electoral, 221
 investigative, 221
 judicial, 223
 legislative, 220–21
 military and police, 266–68
Prairie View A&M University,
 501
prayer in schools, 137

precinct, 123 the most basic
level of political organization
at the local level

precinct chair, 123 the
local party official, elected in
the party's primary elec-
tion, who heads the precinct
convention and serves on
the party's county executive
committee

precinct convention, 124
a meeting held by a political
party to select delegates for
the county convention and
to submit resolutions to the
party's state platform; precinct
conventions are held on the day
of the party's primary election
and are open to anyone who
voted in that election

preclearance, 102, 103, 162
provision under Section 5 of

the Voting Rights Act of 1965
that required any changes to
election procedures or district lines to be approved by
the U.S. Department of Justice or the U.S. District Court
for the District of Columbia

**preemption, 98, 100, 340,
340–41** the legislature's power
to overrule ordinances or actions of local home-rule cities;
powers to act in a particular
area are exclusively granted
by the Constitution to the national government and cannot
be interfered with by the states

**preponderance of the
evidence, 301** the standard
of proof in a civil jury case, by
which the plaintiff must show
that the defendant is more
likely than not the cause of the
harm suffered by the plaintiff

**Presidential Reconstruction,
58** a reconstruction plan for reintegrating former confederate
states back into the Union and
freeing the slaves that placed
mild demands upon the existing white power structure

**presidential Republican-
ism, 130, *132*** a voting pattern
in which conservatives vote
Democratic for state offices
but Republican for president

Presidio County, 334–35
presidios, 31
pretrial hearings, 453
Price, John Wiley, 336

**primary election, 120,
151–52, 166, *418*** a ballot
vote in which citizens select

a party's nominee for the
general election

prison system, 458
 African Americans in, 459
 alternatives to imprisonment, 461
 Anglo Americans in, 459
 death row population by
 race, 459
 decline in prison construction, 471
 executions, 465
 expansion of, 461
 history of, 458, 460
 incarceration rate, 465
 inmate population,
 1980–2016, *463*
 Latinos in, 459
 percentage of prison
 sentence served by
 inmates, *462*
 population by race, 459
 prison closings, 471
 prison population by of-
 fense, *463*
 today, 460–64
 who is in prison, 459

**privatization of public
property, 7–8** the act(s) by
which Texas gave public land
owned by the state over to private individuals for cultivation and development

probate judges, 333

probation, 448, 451 punishment where an offender is
not imprisoned but remains
in the community under
specified rules and under the
supervision of a probation
officer

progressive tax, 376 type of
tax wherein the tax burden

falls more heavily on upper-
income individuals

Progress Texas, 191
property rights, 510–11

**property tax, 177, 354,
411–14** a tax based on an
assessment of the value of
one's property, which is used
to fund the services provided
by local governments, such as
education

Property Tax Relief Fund,
 369, 375

**proportional representa-
tion, 128** a multimember district system that allows each
political party representation
in proportion to its percentage of the total vote

Proposition 2, 78, 79
Proposition 4, 75
Proposition 7, 75–76
Proposition 8, 76
Proposition 12, 78

provincialism, 6–7, 24 a
narrow, limited, and self-
interested view of the world
often associated with rural
values and notions of limited
government

PSF. *See* Permanent School
 Fund (PSF)
Public Citizen, 190, 204

**public defender, 302,
457** salaried lawyer who is
funded by the government
or by grants who represents
indigents in Texas in some
counties or for some types of
cases

religious freedom, 78

religious right, 137

ration a special exemption from state law

special election, 153 an election that is not held on a regularly scheduled basis; in Texas, a special election is called to fill a vacancy in office, to give approval for the state government to borrow money, or to ratify or reject amendments to the Texas Constitution

special interests, 65, 303

special items, 504 special pieces of legislation passed to support particular programs or building projects at state universities outside normal funding mechanisms

special purpose district, 350–57 a unit of local government that performs a single service, such as education or sanitation, within a limited geographic area
  abuses of power and, 354–56
  community college districts, 353
  councils of government (COGs), 356–57
  creating, governing, and paying for, 353–54
  emergency services districts, 353
  flood control districts, 353
  hospital districts, 353
  municipal utility districts, 352–53
  nonschool special purpose districts, 352–53
  problems with, 354–56, *355*
  reputation as hidden governments, 354
  school districts, 352
  types of, 350–52

special session, 216–17, 269 a legislative session called by the governor that addresses an agenda set by him or her and that lasts no longer than 30 days

specialty courts, 297 usually part of district courts and focusing on trying to resolve the underlying problems such as mental health, alcohol and drug abuse, and prostitution that lead to recurring criminal behavior

spending, 371
  spending limits, 386
  trends in state government expenditures, *370*
  trends in state spending, 371–72
Spindletop, 14
SSI. *See* Supplemental Security Income (SSI)
STAAR. *See* State of Texas Assessments of Academic Readiness (STAAR), 417
standardized testing, 415–16, 417

standing committee, 226, 227 a permanent committee with the power to propose and write legislation that covers a particular subject, such as finance or agriculture

STAR. *See* State of Texas Access Reform program (STAR)
Starr, Paul, 240
Starr County, poverty in, 420

state auditor's office, 392 develops independent audits of state agencies, including institutions of higher education. These audits are used to evaluate agencies

state bar commission, 313
State Bar of Texas, 276, 316–19, *318*
State Board of Education (SBOE), 70, 264, *272*, 282, 284–86, 410, 502

state chair, 124 one of the top two state-level leaders in the party

state commissioner of education, 410, 412
State Commission on Judicial Conduct, 262, 293–94, 308, 319–20
state constitutions, 105
  length of, 71
  main functions of, 47–49
  role of, 47–49

state convention, 124 a party meeting held every two years for the purpose of nominating candidates for statewide office, adopting a platform, electing the party's leadership, and in presidential election years selecting delegates for the national convention and choosing presidential electors

State Department of Education, 410
State Depository Board, 280

state executive committee, 124 the committee responsible for governing a party's activities throughout the state

state funds, 380–84
state governments
  vs. federal government, 87–113
  popular control of, 61–62

State Highway Fund, 369, 381, 393, 483 fund that supports the construction, maintenance, and policing of roadways and acquires rights of way; funded through a variety of taxes such as motor vehicle registration fees, the federal highway fund, and the sales tax on motor lubricants

State Instructional Materials Fund, 369
state interests, protection of, 91
state lottery, 378
State Medical and Education Board, 46
State Medical Education Fund, 46
state officials
  impeachment of appointed, 73
  salaries of, 59, 60, 62
State of Texas Access Reform program (STAR), 427
State of Texas Assessments of Academic Readiness (STAAR), 416
State Pension Review Board, 265
State Preservation Board, 262
State Seed and Plant Board, 281
States' Rights Party, 125. *See also* Dixiecrats
state taxes, top state marginal income tax rates, 377
state treasurer, 55
State Water Implementation Fund for Texas (SWIFT), 513–14
State Water Implementation Revenue Fund for Texas (SWIRFT), 514
state water plans, 512

statutory county courts at law, **298** courts that tend to hear less serious criminal cases than those heard by district courts; they usually hear civil cases that involve smaller economic claims than are heard by district courts

statutory probate courts, **298, 313** specialized courts whose jurisdiction is limited to probate and guardianship matters

Steinbeck, John, 3
Steinle, Kate, 495
Stenholm, Charles, 136
Stephen F. Austin State University, 502
Stephen F. Austin Teachers College, 502
Sterling, Ross, *257*
Stevenson, Adlai, 130, 137
Stevenson, Coke, 256, *257*
St. Mary's University, 319
stockholders, 72

straight-ticket voting, **160, 306** a method of voting where a voter checks a box by one of the political parties on the ballot, which casts his/her vote for every candidate on the ballot with that political party affiliation

Straus, Joe, 22, 115, 118, 129, 243, 340–41, 345, *345*, 403–4, 494
 contributions to, 200
 house committee chair appointments, 237
 retirement from the House in 2018, 129
 as Speaker of the House, 234, *235*, 275
Strayhorn, Carole Keeton, 126, 154, 261.

strong mayor-council form of government, 341, 343, 347, 348
student debt, 367
Suazo, Miguel, *172, 273*
subcultures, 5
substance abuse, 297, 461, 462, 464, 471
Substance Abuse Felony Punishment Facilities (SAFPF), 461
suburbanization, 9
suburbs, 5, 6, 9
 Democratic gains in 2018 elections, 177, 203
 as hybrid areas, 138
 partisanship and, 138–40, 177, 203
Suehs, Tom, 434

suffrage, **70, 155** the right to vote. *See also* voting rights

Sullivan, Michael Quinn, 170
Sul Ross State Normal School, 502
Sul Ross State University, 502
Sun Oil, 14
Sunset Act, 220

Sunset Advisory Commission (SAC), **205, 286** a commission created in 1977 for the purpose of reviewing the effectiveness of state agencies

Sunset process, 407
Sunset Review Act, 286
Supplemental Nutritional Assistance Program (SNAP), 420, *423*

Supplemental Security Income (SSI), **422, 428** a national welfare program passed in 1972 that provides assistance to low-income

elderly or disabled individuals; replaced the federal-state programs that had offered assistance to the blind, the permanently and totally disabled, and the aged

supremacy clause, **48, 98, 100** Article VI of the U.S. Constitution, which states that the Constitution and laws passed by the national government and all treaties are the supreme law of the land and superior to all laws adopted by any state or any subdivision

Sweatt, Heman, 102, *102*
Sweatt v. Painter, 28
SWIFT. *See* State Water Implementation Fund for Texas (SWIFT)
"swing" voters, 120
SWIRFT. *See* State Water Implementation Revenue Fund for Texas (SWIRFT)
"systemic agenda," 405

T

TAAS. *See* Texas Assessment of Academic Skills (TAAS) test
TAKS. *See* Texas Assessment of Knowledge and Skills (TAKS)
TAMSA. *See* Texans Advocating for Meaningful Student Assessment (TAMSA)
TANF. *See* Temporary Assistance for Needy Families program (TANF)
Tarrant County, 35, 103, 320, 492
TASER International, 191
tax cuts, 395
taxes, 5, 70, 72, 135, 372–76, *374, 386. See also specific taxes*

alcoholic beverage taxes, 372, 375
exemptions for spouses of first responders killed in action, *78*
franchise tax, 375
gasoline tax, 483–84
hotel and motel tax, 376
income tax, 372, 376, 377, 378, 379
insurance occupation taxes, 375
low, 22
motor fuels tax, 372, 374, *375*, 483–84
motor vehicle and home sales tax, 375
oil production and regulation taxes, 372
as percentage of income, 379
progressive tax, 376
property taxes, 177, 411–14
proposed amendments concerning, 75–76
regressive tax, 376
restrictions on, 62
sales tax, 372, 491
tax collections biennial comparison by source, *380*
tax policy, 176
tobacco taxes, 372, 375
top state marginal income tax rates, 377
trade-offs in public policy and, 435
undocumented workers and, 491–92
utility taxes, 375–76
Tax Foundation Study, 372, 388
Taylor, 343
Taylor, Ivy, 142, *344*
TEA. *See* Texas Education Agency (TEA)
teacher pay, 408–9
teachers, race and ethnicity of, 408–9

TEAMS, Texas Educational Assessment of Minimal Skills (TEAMS)

Tea Party movement, 75–76, 78, **115–16**, **120**, **128–29**, **135**, **137**, *139*, **199**, **203**, **243**, **275–76** reaching prominence after Barack Obama's election, a political movement that advocates lower government spending, lower taxes, and limited government
    co-opted by Republican Party, 129
    education policy and, 417, 419

Tech-America Foundation, 17
technological innovation, 11, 32, 34
technology companies, 36
Tejanos, 119

Temporary Assistance for Needy Families program (TANF), **420**, **424**, **425**, **428** a welfare program passed in 1996 to provide temporary assistance to families with needy children; replacing the AFDC program, TANF sought to make poor families self-sufficient and to give states greater flexibility in setting benefit levels, eligibility requirements, and other program details

tenant farmers, 12
terrorism, 18, 39
Terry v. Adams, 157
Texans Advocating for Meaningful Student Assessment (TAMSA), 183–84
Texans Deserve Great Schools, 419
Texans for Educational Reform, 419

Texans for Lawsuit Reform, 200, 203
Texans for Public Justice, 203
Texas
    demographics in (*see* demographics)
    direction of, *106*
    economy of (*see* economy)
    "low service, low tax" reputation of, 371, 372
    as majority-minority state, 143, 479
    myths of, 3, 4, 49
    size of, 3, 8
    "travel alert" for, 495
    and the Union, 56–58
Texas A&M University System, 15, 70, 194, 383, 501, 503, 504, 506
    establishment of, 501
    higher education policy and, 499–500
    law school, 319
    Texas A&M Transportation Institute, 482
    Texas A&M University at Kingsville, 502
    Texas A&M University at Texarkana, 367
    Texas A&M University—Commerce, 502
Texas Alcoholic Beverage Commission, 281
Texas Alliance for Life, 233
Texas and Pacific Railroad, 35
Texas Apartment Association, 206
Texas Assessment of Academic Skills (TAAS) test, 415, 417
Texas Assessment of Knowledge and Skills (TAKS), 415–16
Texas Association of Business, *21*, 172, 184, 203, 233
Texas Association of Realtors, 198
Texas Association of School Administrators, 183

Texas Bar Association, 185
Texas Bill of Rights, 66
Texas Board of Pardons and Paroles, 271, 451, 461, 466
Texas Board of Water Engineers, 510
Texas Central Railroad, 35, 38
Texas civic health, measures of, 207
Texas Civil Rights Project, 495
Texas Commerce Bank and Tenneco, 188
Texas Commission on Environmental Quality (originally called the Texas Water Commission), 269, 511, 512
Texas Commission on Higher Education, 504
Texas Commission on Law Enforcement, 444
Texas Company, 14
Texas Comptroller's Office, 20, 46, 378. *See also* comptroller
Texas Constitutions, 45–85, *63*, *65*, 230, 274
    1836–1876, 49–64
    of 1836, 51–55
    of 1845, 53, 55–56, 58, 59
    of 1861, 53, 56–58, 59, 60
    of 1866, 53, 58–60, 63, 501
    of 1868, 59
    of 1869, 27, 53, 59–61, 66
    of 1876, 53, 61–64, *62*, 75, 253, 410, 411, 501
    amendments to, 45–46, 56, 64, 73, *74*, 75–76, *76*, 77, 78, 79, 80, *80*, 81
    Anglo-American model of jurisprudence in, 53
    Article 1: Bill of Rights, 45, 66–67, 467
    Article 2: Powers of Government, 67
    Article 3: Legislative Department, 67–68
    Article 4: Executive Department, 68

    Article 5: Judicial Department, 68, 70
    Article 6: Suffrage, 70
    Article 7: Education, 70–71
    Article 8: Taxation and Revenue, 70, 72
    Article 16: General Provisions, 22, 73
    Article 17: Amending the Constitution, 73
    Articles 9 and 11: Local Government, 72
    bail in, 67
    bicameral legislature in, 55
    Bill of Rights, 45, 66–67, 467
    budgets and, 230, 384–88, 392
    checks and balances in, 47, 52, 55, 65
    of Coahulla y Tejas, 1827, 50–51, 54
    community property in, 52
    compared to U.S. Constitution, 47–49, 64, 65
    constitutional spending limit and, *387*
    Constitution of the Republic of Texas, 409
    current version of, 64–73
    debtor relief in, 52
    education in, 70
    English Common Law rules in, 53
    Equal Rights Amendment in, 106
    equal rights in, 66
    executive power in, 56, 68
    failed reforms of 1974, 74–75
    federalism in, 48
    freedom of assembly in, 48
    freedom of religion in, 48, 66
    freedom of speech in, 48, 66
    freedom of the press, 66
    home-rule cities and, 339
    homestead protections in, 52, 63

use of force, **444**, **445**, **446** peace officers may use reasonable force to effect an arrest or to protect themselves or others

user fee, **354** a fee paid for public goods and services, such as water or sewage service

V

vehicle miles traveled, **481** average daily amount of traffic on a road multiplied by length in centerline miles

veto, **230**, *231*, **268** according to the Texas Constitution, the governor's power to turn down legislation; can be overridden by a two-thirds vote of both the House and Senate

vice chair, **124** one of the top two state-level leaders in the party

Voting Rights Act of 1965, **28**, **102**, **103**, **104–5**, **158**, **218**, **241** important legislation passed in order to ensure that African Americans would be guaranteed the right to vote. Renewed several times since 1965, the act also prevents the dilution of minority voting strength